A Gentle Introduction to Effective Computing in Quantitative Research

A GENTLE INTRODUCTION TO EFFECTIVE COMPUTING IN QUANTITATIVE RESEARCH:

WHAT EVERY RESEARCH ASSISTANT SHOULD KNOW

HARRY J. PAARSCH

AND

KONSTANTIN GOLYAEV

The MIT Press
Cambridge, Massachusetts
London, England

This book was set using LATEX.

Printed and bound in the United States.

The MIT Press has no responsibility for the persistency or accuracy of URLs for external or third-party Internet websites referred to in this publication, and does not guarantee that any content on such websites is, or will remain, accurate or appropriate.

Trademarked names appear in this book. Rather than use a trademark symbol with every occurrence of a trademarked name, we use the names only in an editorial fashion and to the benefit of the trademark owner, with no intention of infringement of the trademark.

Library of Congress Cataloging-in-Publication data

Names: Paarsch, Harry J. | Golyaev, Konstantin.
Title: A gentle introduction to effective computing in quantitative research
    : what every research assistant should know / Harry J. Paarsch and
    Konstantin Golyaev.
Description: Cambridge, MA : The MIT Press, [2015] | Includes bibliographical
    references and index.
Identifiers: LCCN 2015039694 | ISBN 9780262034111 (hardcover : alk. paper)
Subjects: LCSH: Quantitative research–Computer programs. | Electronic data
    processing. | Research–Data processing. | Statistics–Data processing.
Classification: LCC Q180.55.E4 P37 2015 | DDC 001.4/20285–dc23 LC record available
at http://lccn.loc.gov/2015039694

10 9 8 7 6 5 4 3 2 1

Dedicated to Ken Judd

De Manu In Manum

Contents

Prologue

THIS BOOK IS a practical guide to using modern software effectively in quantitative research. As the subtitle suggests, we hope to inform research assistants, typically graduate students paid to complete basic (but important) tasks to defray the costs of their education and to provide them with hands-on research experience. Having had jobs like this, we know what they often entail: you are thrown into the middle of an ongoing project, usually with little or no documentation or guidance, and expected to complete a task—by the end of the summer, the end of the term, or even the end of next week.

In the olden days, computing usually involved working in a terminal room where many other research assistants also accessed a mainframe computer using computer terminals.[1] Some of these students may have had a year of extra experience, and they passed along useful knowledge, typically garnered during the hard-fought battles won by those who came before them. In short, word of mouth was how you learned the tricks of the trade that increased productivity.

---

[1] A computer terminal looked something like an old cathode ray tube television, but it had a keyboard attached. The terminal had a circuit board which permitted limited interaction with the mainframe computer. Sometimes, the computer terminal had a direct connection to the mainframe computer, but more often than not you needed to use a modem in conjunction with a telephone to access the mainframe. In the 1980s the speed of that communication was a baud rate of 1200, if you were lucky, but 300 if you were not. The baud rate is measured in signals or symbols per second, and was named in honor of Jean-Maurice-Émile Baudot, who invented the Baudot telegraph code. The baud rate is sometimes confused with the bit rate, which is often quoted in bits per second, or bps. In converting a baud rate to a bit rate, you must know the number of bits in a signal or symbol; most modems had just two bits per signal, but other combinations were possible. Currently, communication on the Internet via an ethernet connection occurs in gigabits per second, in other words, at modem baud rates that are millions of times faster than in the 1980s. Tables 6.1 and 6.2 define *giga* and other prefixes.

Over time, with the advent of personal (desktop) computers, and then especially laptop computers and Wi-Fi, being a research assistant has become a somewhat solitary occupation: the terminal room is no more. Consequently, word of mouth is less important in the spread of knowledge. Instead, the Internet is the main way that research assistants acquire information today. The Internet is a powerful substitute for word of mouth because the information on it often represents the collective insights and knowledge of many people. James Surowiecki (2004) coined the phrase "wisdom of crowds" to describe this amazing phenomenon of information aggregation.

On the Internet, you can always search to find information, or submit questions to the family of `StackExchange` websites at the uniform resource locator (URL) `http://stackoverflow.com`.[2] In addition, YouTube and Software Carpentry as well as Coursera, the massive open online course platform, provide helpful videos on a variety of computing topics. However useful these resources may be, information on the Internet specifically concerned with computing is spread over potentially hundreds of thousands of web pages, so it takes both time and effort to collect and organize. In addition, contrary to popular belief, not everything on the Internet is either true or useful. By collecting valid and useful information in one place as well as organizing it in a coherent way, we hope both to save the reader time and to continue the oral tradition of the terminal room, albeit in print.

Intended Audience

In general, the students for whom this text will have the most value are upper-year undergraduate and master's level students in the natural and social sciences and business, who think they want to enter Ph.D. programs or to work in quantitative jobs in industry but who have had little or no experience with modern scientific computing. Similarly disadvantaged first- and second-year

---

[2]Useful `StackExchange` websites include: `Computational Science`—for scientists using computers to solve scientific problems; `Computer Science`—for students, researchers, and practitioners of computer science; `Cross Validated`—for people interested in statistics, machine learning, data analysis, data mining, and data visualization; `Mathematics`—for people studying math at any level and professionals in related fields; and `TeX-LaTeX`—for users of TeX, LaTeX, ConTeXt, and related typesetting systems.

doctoral students in those disciplines who are about to accept or have already accepted positions as research assistants really need to read this book.

In addition to increasing the productivity of those new to computing, regardless of their field of research, we also hope this book will be a helpful resource for seasoned researchers who may not have had the privilege of working in a terminal room. In short, we are convinced that the material organized here will be useful to anyone seeking to improve her or his computing skills—be they undergraduate or graduate students, or those whose formal education is complete. That said, the bulk of the material presented in this book has really only been tested on students in accounting, economics, finance, and marketing; in other words, the applications and the examples have a particular slant.

The book can also be used to supplement textbooks for courses devoted to computational methods in various disciplines. For example, Judd (1998) and Stachurski (2009) wrote two important books on using computational methods in economics, but for many graduate students and professional economists with limited computational experience those texts are difficult to use. In addition, such texts provide no guidance in the new field of *data science*, which draws on techniques from mathematics and statistics as well as computer programming, data mining, information technology, machine learning, and numerical analysis.

Based on anecdotal evidence, we believe that learners inexperienced in computing face this problem in other disciplines, such as biology, as well. In fact, after a draft of this book was written, we encountered *Practical Computing for Biologists* by Haddock and Dunn (2011), which is clearly a well-thought-out response to the problem. Unfortunately, that book is directed mainly at biologists, so the material may not be as useful to social scientists, other natural scientists, or business students.

Because instructors of courses in data science and numerical methods find that they do not have enough time to focus on the main techniques, let alone teach basic facts about computing, learners are left to their own devices, which means that productivity suffers. Thomas J. Sargent and John Stachurski have sought to reduce the barriers to entry in economics by creating the valuable website `http://quant-econ.net` on which free lectures concerning quantitative modeling are available; the primary programming language used is Python. In their book *Doing Data Science*, Schutt and O'Neil (2013) provided a number of interesting and useful examples that pertain to data science, also in Python.

Unfortunately, the main problem remains, namely, many researchers and students simply do not have enough basic knowledge of computing to be effective in their work. We hope the material presented here can partly fill this void. In particular, we believe that the material presented in this book is a prequel to the website of Sargent and Stachurski as well as to Schutt and O'Neil's book.

Preparation and Expectations

In organizing the material, we presumed very little on the part of a learner. Specifically, we assumed no background in computer science beyond that taught in most grade and high schools: a learner will only require access to a computer linked to the Internet. The best way to read this book is at the keyboard of your computer, mimicking as you read.

Although this is not a book you can read in an evening and then expect to do world-class research the next morning, with time as well as a good dose of stubborn perseverance almost anyone can become reasonably proficient at computing. To master the material presented here will take considerable practice, but for most people computing is like arithmetic or reading—initially daunting, then natural.

Structure of Book and the Software Used

This book has eleven chapters. In Chapter 1, a brief introduction, we describe some important developments and problems in all fields of science during the Information Revolution, the Age of Computing, when faced with Big Data (that takes care of the buzz words). In Chapters 2–4, we introduce a minimal set of skills that a research assistant must know in order to be at all productive: first, how to use the operating system; second, how to organize data; and third, how to complete simple programming tasks.

Our demonstrations are conducted assuming a UNIX-based (UNIX-like) operating system. An operating system is the software that allows you to interact with your computer, running in the background; the operating system also keeps your computer in sync with the Internet around it. Currently, two main operating systems exist—UNIX and Windows. Windows is more popular than UNIX; UNIX is better than Windows.

Here's why: UNIX is more flexible than Windows; for example, UNIX can be installed on many different types of computers. UNIX is also more stable than Windows; Windows will often crash your computer. We have never had a computer failure due to UNIX. This does not mean that a computer using the UNIX operating system cannot crash, just that in our experience UNIX was not the cause of any crashes we have encountered. UNIX has a richer system of file permissions than Windows and a better history with respect to security threats, so it is safer to use on the Internet. In fact, a major portion of the Internet is run using UNIX-like computers. In sum, we chose UNIX because it is a mature, stable operating system.

If UNIX is so good, then why isn't it popular? When International Business Machines (IBM) first developed the desktop personal computer in the early 1980s, the firm chose Microsoft to provide the operating system, DOS, which is an acronym for disk operating system. Although DOS was really no easier to learn than UNIX, its choice for the personal computer created a huge user base. Subsequently, when Microsoft developed the Windows operating system, a good portion of that user base converted to Windows. In addition, at the time, Windows was much easier to use than UNIX. Today, however, the differences between UNIX and Windows are really not that great.

Some may suggest Cygwin as an alternative to UNIX because it allows you to continue to use Windows. Although Cygwin is a useful collection of free software tools similar to those available on UNIX-like operating systems as well as a command-line user interface for Windows, Cygwin is not an operating system. Moreover, Cygwin cannot magically enable Windows to be a better operating system. Therefore, we have chosen not to discuss Cygwin. If you know UNIX, however, then picking up Cygwin is a snap.

Different versions of UNIX exist. For example, on an Apple Macintosh, UNIX is named OS X. A UNIX-like operating system (for non-Apple computers) is Linux, which comes in several distributions as well. Strictly speaking, Linux is not UNIX: OS X has been certified as UNIX, but the various distributions of Linux have not. Even though UNIX and OS X as well as the distributions of Linux are all slightly different, the commonalities are striking. As with American, British, and Canadian English, differences exist, but they are largely unimportant. From a practical perspective, the three are basically the same. In fact, we make no distinction between UNIX-based and UNIX-like.

We believe that working in a UNIX-like environment is central to effective computing, particularly high-performance scientific computing, but also large-scale distributed computing in the cloud. For example, data science at such firms as Amazon and Google is conducted almost exclusively within Linux environments because Linux is an efficient, flexible, and stable environment that scales well and within which complex tasks can be automated effectively.[3] By being able to work effectively in a UNIX-like environment, you increase your chances of being employed in data science at any firm.

We recognize that learning UNIX may be too high an entry barrier for some, but such is the nature of computing in the era of Big Data. Thus, rather than avoiding the potentially unpleasant, we have simply plunged right in, hoping others will follow us into the twenty-first century.

In the first instance, the material presented here was developed on an Apple MacBook Pro under the OS X operating system. As mentioned, for those having access to a computer on which some variant of the Linux operating system has been installed, no substantive differences will exist. For those using Microsoft Windows-based computers, we have created a virtual machine that will mimic the OS X environment (albeit in the Linux environment). On the virtual machine, we have chosen the Linux Ubuntu system, which is based on the Debian/GNU distribution, because it is free and because a large community supports this operating system.[4] The instructions for installing this virtual machine are contained in Appendix A.

To complete programming tasks, we have chosen the scripting language Python because it is relatively easy to learn and use, and free. In fact, all the software we have chosen is not only free but also available for the three major operating systems—Linux, OS X, and Windows.

That we have chosen the interpreted language Python rather than a compiled language like C may cause some to question our claim of effectiveness; this

---

[3]In this context, to scale well means that you can use code written for a medium-size problem on a large one without a significant loss in performance.

[4]In 1983, Richard M. Stallman of MIT began the GNU Project, a mass collaboration to develop free software. GNU is a recursive acronym meaning *GNU's not UNIX*. Through the project, Stallman sought to give computer users control over their computers by developing and providing software based on the "freedom rights": users should be free to run the software, to share it (to copy it, to distribute it), to study it, and to modify it. In fact, the GNU Project has established legally binding agreements that guarantee these freedom rights. You can learn more about the GNU project at http://en.wikipedia.org/wiki/GNU.

choice warrants some explanation.[5] We recognize that an interpreted language can never yield the performance of a compiled language. Typically, however, the fruit of compiled code is harvested during repeated use in production, not when implementing the one-off projects often encountered in research. Moreover, writing computer code in a compiled language like C is much more demanding than writing it in a scripting language like Python. Therefore, we believe that the trade-off between developer time and cycle time is better served using Python.

Developer time is the amount of time that a human requires to design, write, and test the computer code, whereas *cycle time* is the amount of time a particular piece of computer code uses to run once. Cycle time is different from *run time*, which is the total elapsed time that a computer program takes to complete once it has been submitted. Run time can be affected by the number and the type of tasks running on a computer at the time when a particular program is submitted for execution.

If, however, a particular part of a Python script is used many times, and speed really becomes an issue, there are ways in which to extend Python by incorporating C code and even legacy FORTRAN code. We discuss those methods, sometimes referred to as extensions, separately.

Because we have assumed that the reader has no background in computer science, we believe our choice of Python is the best one, from a pedagogical perspective, at this time. Campbell, Gries, Montojo, and Wilson (2009) reported that their students made fewer syntax errors when learning Python than with C-like languages. Python is not only easier to learn than C but also a language in which it is much easier to implement code, in part because of Python's dynamic typing capabilities. In short, Python reduces the initial frustration that many novices encounter when first learning to code. Nevertheless, Python can scale relatively effectively; that is, you can begin with small scripts but count on the fact that larger problems can be solved using the language. Moreover, in addition to the imperative and procedural programming paradigms, Python supports elements of both object-oriented programming and functional

---

[5]Two things to note: First, for parsimony, throughout this book, we make no distinction between C and C++ but recognize that there are differences both large and small; thus, when you read C, simply map that to C and (or) C++. Second, some programmers believe that the distinction between interpreted and compiled makes no sense because any programming language can be made either interpreted or compiled, or both; we refuse to engage in such pedantry.

programming. Although such features are largely irrelevant to novice programmers, this flexibility and richness means that you can grow as a programmer as you learn Python.

Some serious programmers wax fondly about the virtues (particularly the elegance of syntax) of another scripting language, Ruby. We do not dispute the elegance of Ruby's syntax, and acknowledge the simplicity and productiveness of the language. Unfortunately, the community supporting Ruby today is a small fraction of that supporting Python. Currently, hundreds of thousands of scientists around the world use Python, so the network externalities associated with Python dwarf the benefits that derive from Ruby's elegance.[6] Python is both simple to learn and productive to use.

Others may note that the scripting language Perl has a large community of users and an extensive collection of scripts in the repository of the Comprehensive Perl Archive Network. We do not dispute the popularity of Perl and acknowledge its usefulness for completing many computing tasks, especially in system administration. For tasks involving regular expressions, Perl is probably without peer. Unfortunately, we have found that Perl is difficult for novices to learn because the syntax is quite cryptic: to a novice, Perl code is almost unreadable. On the other hand, Python's creator, Guido van Rossum, designed the language to be easy to read. In addition, based on our experiences, we believe it is much easier to implement numerical methods in Python than in Perl.

We have sacrificed additional effectiveness and efficiency in other software choices as well. Consider Chapter 3, Organizing Data. There, we have chosen to use the SQLite database management system (DBMS), which we believe is a perfectly reasonable implementation of Codd's relational algebra as a structured query language for a single user. Although SQLite is a useful tool, it is obviously not Oracle Database, which is a sophisticated, industrial-strength DBMS used by many major corporations. In fact, SQLite is not even as powerful as MySQL or PostgreSQL, two other free DBMSs which, like Oracle Database, allow multiple users. Oracle Database is extremely expensive, and installing either MySQL or PostgreSQL requires considerable knowledge of the operating system. The SQLite executable can just be placed in a pathed subdirectory and then invoked from the command line with a minimum of fuss or bother.

---

[6]In *Learning Python*, Lutz (2009) reported that roughly a million people are actively using Python around the world.

Moreover, SQLite databases are files that can be transferred from one computer to another easily.

The use of "Lite" in the name suggests that SQLite is only useful for small applications, which is false. Despite some of its limitations, SQLite is a powerful DBMS. For instance, SQLite has been used to organize a variety of different types of data on the Apple iPhone. Also, as with Database, MySQL and PostgreSQL (which can manage geospatial data) you can use SpatiaLite in conjunction with SQLite to organize and analyze geospatial data, a fast-developing part of science. Unless a data set is absurdly large (for example, more than 100 terabytes), SQLite is reported to work without too many problems.[7] In addition, SQLite commands can be invoked from Python by importing the `sqlite3` module as an application programming interface (API). In short, Python and SQLite are highly compatible.

Similarly, although both SAS and Stata are certainly fine products to use when conducting econometric and statistical analyses of data, we have chosen instead the freely available R system, a programming language and software environment for statistical computing and graphics. R is the lingua franca of statistics, so a large community supports it, providing network externalities. Because R has no licensing requirements, it is extremely easy to install and update: simply go to the Comprehensive R Archive Network and download packages. R also plays well with Python. In fact, RPy is a simple and robust interface between R and Python that allows you to manage R objects as well as to execute arbitrary R functions from within Python.

One drawback of R is that it appears to have no memory management capabilities: the software simply gobbles up memory until either the task is completed or your computer crashes. For serious practitioners of data science, this is an unattractive feature, but it really only matters when data sets are larger than, say, one-half of the main memory of your computer. As computer memory increases over time, this restriction may become relatively unimportant. Nevertheless, one strategy for dealing with large data sets is to query databases maintained under SQLite using R; others exist as well.

Because R has some problems dealing with relatively large data sets, we have introduced the Python `pandas` library, which we found to be useful for not crashing your computer while analyzing large data sets.

---

[7] At `http://www.sqlite.org/limits.html` "a maximum SQLite database size of about 140 terabytes" is reported.

In lieu of the commercial product MATLAB (an acronym formed from the words matrix and laboratory), a sophisticated environment in which to conduct numerical analysis that one of the authors chose as the teaching tool for a previous book—Paarsch and Hong (2006)—we suggest that learners initially try invoking IPython (that is, `ipython` on the command line) in conjunction with the `-pylab` flag. Under this flag, Fernando Pérez, the creator of IPython, attempted to create a MATLAB-like environment by importing by default the `matplotlib` module and the `numpy` package as well as packages from the SciPy ecosystem. In short, IPython provides many important features similar to those contained in MATLAB. For those wedded to using an environment like MATLAB, both Octave and Scilab are free alternatives to consider.

In the same vein, although Mathematica is an extremely powerful environment within which to undertake symbolic mathematics, using the Python library `sympy` in conjunction with the Notebook feature of IPython, is a cost-effective alternative. Another alternative is Sage (see `http://www.sagemath.org`).

As you can see, we have collected and organized information concerning a small set of free software tools that run on each of the three major platforms and that are widely used around the world. Because these tools are very compatible with one another, we believe economies of scope exist in their application in concert. We also believe that our choices increase the chances that a learner will develop a skill set compatible with those of other researchers around the world.

In Chapters 5–9, we describe particular ways in which to complete tasks frequently assigned to research assistants: first, analyzing data using R and the Python library `pandas`; second, learning how to implement commonly used numerical methods and graphics using Python; third, creating C or FORTRAN extensions to Python to reduce cycle time.

Finally, in Chapter 10, we provide advice concerning how to write up research in a clean, crisp way using LaTeX, a document markup language and preparation system for the TeX typesetting program. We also illustrate how to use BIBTeX, a tool for formatting and managing bibliographic references, and `Beamer`, a LaTeX class to create slides for presentations.

Even though we believe distributed and parallel computing will be incredibly important in the future, at this time we have chosen not to describe either because the tools in these areas are changing fast. In Chapter 11 we present some final thoughts on these topics as well as suggestions concerning where a learner might next look for new quarry.

Caveats

After completing a first draft of this book, we circulated it among colleagues, friends, students, and other researchers. What struck us was how strongly some people felt about specific computer programs. One representative email said, "you simply cannot think that this book will have ANY value unless [a particular program] is included."

We do have strong opinions about how to proceed effectively in research, that is, regarding the process. We are not, however, wedded to specific software tools. Unlike some software development engineers, we do not sit around after work debating the virtues of one scripting language over another, nor do we denigrate other researchers because, for instance, they prefer the old functional programming language Lisp over the newer one Haskell. It is important to realize that opinions are neither right nor wrong—they just are. That is, opinions are like tastes. Recall the Latin maxim *De gustibus non est disputandum* (in matters of taste there can be no disputes).[8]

In the main, we chose software tools that are free as well as available across the three major platforms; also, when possible, we favored mature tools. Most young scholars really do not know whether they will continue in the business, so why invest in some very expensive software that turns out to be a passing fad? In addition, if you are going to learn a programming language or a particular application, then it should at least be portable across platforms so that you can work with others with a minimum of disruption. By focusing on mature tools, we have chosen those that have survived the test of time.

That said, should you want to use some particular software because you like it or because you are familiar with it, then use it. This book is intended for people who have had very little experience with computing, people who have not yet made a choice but who would really like some advice.

By the same token, if you are one of those people who likes to figure out everything by yourself, then this book is not for you: you will simply get too much advice, and that will annoy you. Life is too short to become annoyed.

---

[8]From http://en.wikipedia.org/wiki/De_gustibus_non_est_disputandum.

On a related point, some research assistants may not have the option to use the software we recommend. For legacy reasons, perhaps, their employers may want them to use other software. We still believe that learning Python, R, and SQLite is useful. For in learning the new software on the job, the already-known Python, R, or SQLite can be used to double-check that you actually understand what the new software is doing.

Using Our Code

You can use and redistribute the examples of computer code provided here, either as is or with modifications. We want you to learn from these examples, and we hope that you can use them productively in your research. That said, we provide these examples *WITHOUT ANY WARRANTY*, without even the implied warranty of *MERCHANTABILITY* or *FITNESS FOR A PARTICULAR PURPOSE*. (The lawyers asked us to put in this notice.)

If you do use the code or other material from the book, the appropriate bibliographic reference would be

> Paarsch, Harry J. and Konstantin Golyaev. *A Gentle Introduction to Effective Computing in Quantitative Research: What Every Research Assistant Should Know*. Cambridge, Massachusetts: MIT Press, 2016.

When TEX is used in conjunction with LaTEX and BIBTEX (see Chapter 10), the BIBTEX entry would look something like the following:

```
@book{paargoly:2016,
author    = "Harry J.~Paarsch and Konstantin Golyaev",
title     = "A Gentle Introduction to Effective Computing in
             Quantitative Research: What Every Research
             Assistant Should Know",
publisher = "MIT Press",
address   = "Cambridge, Massachusetts",
year      = {2016}
}
```

Style of Presentation

To those with some experience in computing, our presentation may seem scattered, even incomplete: ours is not intended to be a definitive or an exhaustive tome containing all that is available. In fact, it would be impossible to write such a book in this era because no sooner had the ink dried than it would be out-of-date. Instead, we have chosen to describe a small set of relatively mature tools that we know can enhance productivity. Like the advice proffered by senior graduate students in the terminal room, our book with its references to important books and papers as well as useful web pages provides a direction in which to proceed rather than a complete road map. Although some seasoned researchers may claim that most of what we present is well known, our experiences teaching graduate students as well as interacting with junior faculty suggest that much of what we describe will be new to *many* learners. Even when some of the information sounds familiar, the learner has probably never really used it.

Comments and Suggestions

Many pairs of eyes have proofread earlier drafts of this book, but we recognize that some errors will remain and apologize for those. We would appreciate reports via email of any errors, typographical or otherwise, so they may be eliminated in future printings. You are also encouraged to send us email should you have questions or comments concerning any part of the book. We will endeavor to answer such questions as quickly as we can. Because people move around a lot, perhaps the easiest way to find a current email address would be to search on the Internet for the authors' names.

Acknowledgments

WE HAVE GATHERED the material in this book over the past 35 years, mostly from experience. Although Paarsch's knowledge of punch cards is surely of no use today, our combined UNIX experience over the past 25 years definitely is. By taking courses as well as attending conference and seminar presentations, we have benefited immensely from the collective wisdom of our colleagues, students, and teachers. In addition, we have read widely—articles, books, and web pages. Where possible, we have made explicit citations to these sources, but in many cases, as occurs with word-of-mouth communications, we are simply unaware of the original sources. If we have not cited your work, or have done so improperly, then please alert us to this fact, and we will endeavor to correct this problem—first, on the web page for this book and then in any subsequent printings of the book.

Paarsch thanks Richard J. Arnott, James G. MacKinnon, and John G. Rowse for encouraging his interest in computation when he was an undergraduate at Queen's University. Subsequently, as a graduate student at Stanford University, Paarsch benefited from the experience and wisdom of his friends R. Mark Gritz and Stephen A. Langlois, but he learned the most about using numerical methods in resource-constrained computing environments from Thomas A. Mroz; he thanks each.

Paarsch is also grateful to a sequence of departmental administrators (first at the University of British Columbia, next at the University of Western Ontario, then at the University of Iowa, and finally at the University of Melbourne) who indulged him for more than 20 years while he thought through the challenges of teaching computing to nonspecialists; without this support, the project would surely have stalled. For providing him the time to work on this material and a venue (the classroom) to test it, he thanks James B. Davies, John F. Helliwell, Nilss Olekalns, Charles H. Whiteman, and Stephen D. Williamson.

We have both taught material from parts of the book to a variety of different audiences over the past 25 years. In fact, the idea for this book came to Paarsch when he held a workshop each week for his Ph.D. students in the economics department at the University of Melbourne. For humoring him as he tried out different ideas, Paarsch thanks Colette Marais, Ingrid E. Burfurd, and Andrea La Nauze; he is especially grateful to Andrea for presenting some introductory lectures on Python, which forced him to think carefully about how to proceed. In all cases, we are extremely grateful to these audiences for enduring our initial efforts.

For the past decade or so, Paarsch has had the good fortune to have participated in initiatives spearheaded by Kenneth L. Judd to improve the use of numerical methods in economics.[9] Of course, implementing all but trivial numerical methods requires using a computer and, thus, developing software. Ken's attempts to drag the seemingly recalcitrant economics profession into the modern computing era have been sources of inspiration, and sometimes amusement as well. In appreciation of the effort and time Ken has spent with many cohorts of graduate students trying to help them learn about numerical methods, we dedicate this book to him.

Several other people have helped us with this book, but two in particular stand out: Paarsch's close friend and former colleague Alberto M. Segre, and our colleague and friend Jack H. S. Chua. Alberto provided much helpful advice and many useful suggestions throughout the project, and read most of the manuscript just before it was sent to the publisher; Jack answered many practical questions during the writing of the book. We thank both, and remain aware of our debts.

Two anonymous referees vetted most of the manuscript midway in its writing. We thank them for the generous gift of their time and for their helpful prodding. Because we did not follow all of their advice, they cannot be held responsible for any remaining errors of omission or commission.

---

[9]Some of these efforts were administered through the Initiative on Computational Economics, which is located on the campus of the University of Chicago, whereas others are now part of the Zürich Initiative on Computational Economics, which is administered by the Zürich Center for Computational Financial Economics at the Universität Zürich.

Many friends, colleagues, and researchers provided concrete feedback concerning previous drafts of this book in the form of useful comments, important information, and helpful suggestions as well as reporting typographical errors. Specifically, we thank Johan Brannlund, Colette Marais, Dimitriy V. Masterov, David A. Prentice, Devesh R. Raval, Charles Elkan, Kenneth L. Judd, Vathy M. Kamulete, Clinton J. Levitt, Todd S. Munson, Houssam Nassif, Denis Nekipelov, Megan Payne, Walt Pohl, Jeffrey S. Racine, Andrey A. Shabalin, Che-Lin Su, Stefan M. Wild, Robert E. Bixby, Martin Grötschel, and Gregor P. Reich.

Benjamin S. Skrainka helped us create the first virtual machine that makes it easier for novices to get started quickly; we thank him for providing us a path to follow when constructing the final virtual machine.

We also thank Professor Douglas W. Jones of the Department of Computer Science at the University of Iowa for permission to use his photograph of the punch card, which is presented as Figure 9.1.

In May 2014, Ali Hortaçsu invited Paarsch to spend a week of his vacation at the Gary Becker Milton Friedman Institute for Research in Economics at the University of Chicago. Paarsch thanks Ali for the invitation; he is grateful to the BFI for the hospitality and for providing a stimulating environment within which to hone the manuscript.

In November 2014, Kim P. Huynh and Nathalie Swift arranged for Paarsch to visit the Bank of Canada for a week. Paarsch thanks Kim and Nathalie for the invitation; he is grateful to the Bank for the hospitality and for providing a quiet place in which to edit the manuscript.

Just before the manuscript went to print, Karl Schmedders arranged for Paarsch to test the material in this book on live students in the field at Universität Zürich, thus allowing us to eliminate some overlooked typographical errors. Paarsch thanks Karl as well as Vanessa Kummer, who provided excellent teaching assistance, and Megan Payne, who provided outstanding computer support.

At the MIT Press, Jane Macdonald efficiently arranged a contract for us and gently managed the project from start to finish; we thank her for her expertise and professionalism. We also thank Emily Taber, who provided invaluable editorial advice, Alice Cheyer, who copyedited the penultimate draft with evident care, and Marcy Ross, who guided the manuscript through the production process.

We are both grateful to Amazon.com for providing a stimulating workplace. Although none of the work presented here was completed during work time at Amazon, from our first-hand experiences at work we have learned to appreciate what is important and what can be safely ignored, at least when it comes to using modern scientific computing in our research. Working at Amazon has also allowed us to see clearly which parts of our years of toil in academic environments apply to real-world situations, which parts were pure pedantry, and which parts were simply entertainment.

Finally, each of us thanks his family as well as his co-author for tolerating the impositions that a project like this imposes on their lives. We are grateful to all for providing us the time to complete this book. Golyaev is particularly grateful to his wife, Nadia Golyaeva, for love and support.

Notation

MOST OF THE notation in this book is devoted to distinguishing between the text and computer code. The text of the book is set in Palatino, whereas computer commands in the text are set in fixed-width font, for instance, `grep theta results.out`. Also rendered in fixed-width font are uniform resource identifiers (URIs), for example, the main web page address of our former employer `http://www.amazon.com` and particular tools within computer programs, like `vi`, which is a programmer's text editor available in UNIX.

To simulate how the terminal window might appear, we use a box containing fixed-width computer code comprising commands as typed or output as it would appear. For example, the command to move a file from one location on a computer to another would appear in the text as `mv OldFile.nam NewFile.nam` and in the terminal window as

```
$ mv OldFile.nam NewFile.nam
```

The source code, as in the case of Python, is set nonitalic, and the comments, which begin with #, are italicized. This convention is illustrated by the following short Python function:

```
def InchesToCentimetres(inches):
  """ This function converts inches to centimetres. """
  # This function converts inches to centimetres.
  return 2.54 * inches
```

The words `def` and `return` are keywords of the Python language; the very long word `InchesToCentimetres` is a function name; `inches` is a variable name. The second line is a coder-supplied comment, referred to as a a docstring (see Chapter 4, page 151). To distinguish docstring comments from actual comments, like the one in the third line, we do not italicize the former.

In some parts of the book, mathematics is used—especially in Chapters 5–8. There, we adopt a readable notation consistent with the current literature in the field, be it computer science, linear algebra, numerical optimization, or statistical simulation. Because we are drawing from several different fields, inevitably the same symbol is used more than once, and can mean different things in different contexts. You should be aware of this, and adjust accordingly.

We denote vectors by boldface, lowercase letters (either Greek or Roman) and matrices by boldface, uppercase Roman letters. The elements of the vectors and matrices are denoted by the lowercase math versions of the letters with the appropriate subscripting. For example, the (1×3) vector of variables (v_1, v_2, v_3) is denoted by $\mathbf{v}$ and a representative (i, j) element of the matrix $\mathbf{H}$ by h_{ij}.

The transpose operator used in linear algebra is denoted by superscripted $\top$. Thus, an $(N \times 1)$ vector of parameters $(\mu_1, \mu_2, \ldots, \mu_N)^\top$ is denoted $\boldsymbol{\mu}$. The matrix $\mathbf{I}_M$ denotes the $(M \times M)$ identity matrix, while the vector $\mathbf{0}_K$ denotes an $(K \times 1)$ vector of zeros, and the vector $\boldsymbol{\iota}_J$ denotes a $(J \times 1)$ vector of 1s. $(I \times 1)$ vectors of zeros except for a 1 in the ith row, *unit vectors*, are denoted by $\mathbf{e}_i$ for $i = 1, 2, \ldots, I$.

The letter i is usually used as the first subscript index, followed by j and k and then m and n if necessary, but sometimes p, r, and t as well. Unless the subscript indexing is defined elsewhere, the range of, say, index i is from $1, 2, \ldots, I$; the range of j is from $1, 2, \ldots, J$; and so on.

Computer scientists employ notation that is somewhat different from what natural and social scientists typically use. The most important notation used by computer scientists is the *Big O notation*, which is employed in the asymptotic analysis of algorithms in Chapter 6.[1] There, for example, the statement that $f(n)$ is $\mathcal{O}(g(n))$ means that the absolute value of $f(n)$ is no more than a constant multiplied by the absolute value of the function $g(n)$, where n is the size of the input and is allowed to approach infinity. That is,

$$|f(n)| \leq k|g(n)| \quad \text{for some number } k > 0.$$

---

[1]Big O notation is part of a larger notation, sometimes referred to as Landau notation or Bachmann-Landau notation in honor of Edmund Landau and Paul Bachmann, two German mathematicians.

In some places, the ceiling and floor functions are also used. The ceiling of real number x, denoted $\lceil x \rceil$, is the least integer greater than or equal to x, and the floor of x, denoted $\lfloor x \rfloor$, is the greatest integer less than or equal to x.

Some of our descriptions concern random variables from probability and statistics, in Chapters 5, 7, and 8. We denote random variables by uppercase Roman math-font letters, for example, U. Realizations of random variables are then denoted by lowercase Roman math-font letters: u is a realization of U. Vectors of random variables are denoted by boldface uppercase Roman math-font letters and realizations of those random variables are denoted by boldface lowercase Roman math-font letters: $\boldsymbol{u}$ is a realization of $\boldsymbol{U}$. Under this convention, we have no way of representing matrices of random variables. Fortunately, those did not arise.

Whenever possible the uppercase math-font letter F is used to denote a cumulative distribution function, and the lowercase f to denote a probability density function. The uppercase subscript following F and f indicates the corresponding random variable and the lowercase version of that letter as an argument refers to a particular realization. Hence, $F_V(v)$ denotes the cumulative distribution function of the random variable V evaluated at the realization v and $f_U(u)$ denotes the probability density function of the random variable U evaluated at the realization u. In Chapter 8 the associated survivor function of the random variable T is introduced as $S_T(t)$, and the related hazard function (rate) is denoted $h_T(t)$.

In discussing probability and statistics we use the blackboard letters $\mathbb{E}$ and $\mathbb{V}$ to denote the expectation and the variance operators, respectively. In general, we reserve the math calligraphic letters to denote special functions, for example, $\mathcal{L}$ for the likelihood function, or special families of random variables, such as $\mathcal{N}$ for the normal (Gaussian) family. In contrast, the regular calligraphic letter $\mathcal{L}$ denotes the Lagrangian function in a constrained optimization problem, while $\mathcal{G}$, $\mathcal{V}$, and $\mathcal{E}$ are used in graph theory to denote the graph as well as the sets of vertices (nodes) and edges (arcs), respectively.

We use the symbol "plim" to denote convergence in probability, which is sometimes also denoted by "$\xrightarrow{\text{p}}$", and the symbol "$\xrightarrow{\text{d}}$" to denote convergence in distribution.

Throughout the book, we introduce additional notation, which is made clear as it occurs.

1

Introduction

THE INFORMATION REVOLUTION has changed how scientists conduct research. When we use the phrase Information Revolution, we refer not only to the rapid increase in computing power over the past half century, sometimes called the Age of Computing, particularly by Barrett (2006), but also to the explosion in the variety and volume of data available as a consequence of that computing power, often called Big Data, at least recently. Encouraged by the enthusiasm of Halevy, Norvig, and Pereira (2009) in their paper entitled, "The Unreasonable Effectiveness of Data," many people have high expectations. In his book *On Computing*, Rosenbloom (2013) argued that the creation of what he calls computing science has changed the intellectual landscape fundamentally. In fact, he claimed (somewhat controversially) that computing science now joins the physical, life, and social sciences as the fourth scientific domain. Similarly, *The Fourth Paradigm*, a collection of essays, honors the vision of the pioneering computer scientist Jim Gray (2009), who foresaw a fourth paradigm of discovery based on data-intensive science, the first three being experimental, theoretical, and computational science. Less controversially, Brynjolfsson and McAfee (2014), in *The Second Machine Age*, predicted that harnessing computing power will be one of the most important tasks of humankind during the second part of the Information Revolution. In all cases, to participate in this revolution, you will need to be able to use a computer effectively. To borrow from Wing (2006), you will need to think computationally.

During the Age of Computing, people's ability to calculate has improved immensely. This rapid growth has expanded the set of problems that scientists can feasibly investigate. For example, calculations that took months of computer time to complete in 1985 now only take a few minutes. Although devices designed to help people compute more accurately and quickly have been invented since the times of Blaise Pascal and Gottfried Wilhelm von Leibniz, Ceruzzi (2003) argued that modern computing is characterized by five factors: (1) electricity; (2) storage; (3) control; (4) calculation; and (5) communication.

The confluence of these factors really only occurred during the Second World War, when engineers struggled desperately to develop fire control mechanisms, such as those used in anti-aircraft weapons. Others, including John von Neumann, were interested in electronic computers to solve pressing scientific problems, like how to complete the multitude of calculations necessary when investigating a nuclear reaction. Closed-form mathematical methods could not provide sufficiently accurate solutions to the problems faced by physicists on the Manhattan project, but numerical methods could. At that time, however, computing was done by humans, sometimes with the assistance of mechanical calculators. In short, existing computing methods were slow as well as error prone. That all changed after von Neumann created the computer architecture that now bears his name, the *von Neumann machine*, which Ceruzzi (2012) argued convincingly should really bear the names of J. Presper Eckert and John Mauchly as well, and perhaps Konrad Zuse, who developed working electronic computers along these lines in Germany during the Second World War. Smiley (2010) argued convincingly that John V. Atanasoff should be included in this august group as well.

Even though several different computing devices were developed during the latter half of the 1940s and early 1950s, most of them based on the Atanasoff-Zuse-Eckert-Mauchly-von Neumann research, it was not until the late 1950s that using a computer to solve scientific problems became relatively common. The first academic department devoted solely to the science of computing was founded at Purdue University in 1962.[1] Other departments followed.

The Age of Computing predated the availability of Big Data, but Big Data is a direct result of improved computing. Without computers, how can Big Data be processed? At this point, we should probably note that the term Big Data

---

[1]In 1953, at the University of Cambridge in the United Kingdom, the Computer Laboratory established the Diploma in Numerical Analysis and Automatic Computing, which later became the Cambridge Diploma in Computer Science, but that is something quite different from an academic department.

currently appears to have at least two somewhat different meanings: One is just that more data exist than can be physically brought into the memory of the computer. Under this definition, Big Data have existed since at least the time of Babbage.[2] When, however, most people speak of Big Data, they typically have another meaning in mind, namely, the easy accessibility and sheer volume of data in a variety of different formats previously unknown. In this sense, Big Data is changing not only what questions we ask but also how we answer them. For example, remote sensors permit us to measure phenomena at such fine granularity that the deluge of data is almost overwhelming. Moreover, the scale of problems that can be investigated is expanding almost daily.

In short, the Information Revolution has enriched both theory and data.

1.1 Theory

In the words of Scott (2011, xi), "numerical analysis provides the foundations for a major paradigm shift in what we understand as an 'answer' to a scientific or technical question." An early example of how computing expanded theory involves solving differential equations. Prior to electronic computers, only certain kinds of models could be entertained in physics and engineering because the theory then led to differential equations that had closed-form solutions. Once electronic computing became readily available, however, finite element methods could be applied, and a whole new set of richer models could be considered. In their book *Finite Elements and Approximation*, Zienkiewicz and Morgan (2006) provided some excellent examples.

The use of computers in physics, chemistry, and biology is by now well known and, for the most part, considered natural. Although a long tradition exists in the social sciences of using computers in empirical research, resistance to using them in theoretical research (for instance, in economics) has been strong. Leading a research program to use computers in theoretical research in economics is Kenneth L. Judd. For example, in Judd (1997), he proposed a "computational approach to economic theory," arguing that economic theory need not be confined to proving theorems. Judd also predicted that computers

---

[2]Charles Babbage was an English mathematician and philosopher who invented the concept of a programmable computer, a contribution for which he is sometimes called the father of the computer. For having constructed such a device Babbage is also famous among both mechanical engineers and computer scientists.

would create new possibilities for theoretical analysis. During the past 15 years, this movement has attracted many converts, but considerable work remains to bring the remaining heathens into the fold.

One of the reasons why young economic theorists may not adopt computational methods is that relatively high entry barriers exist. For although most students are provided some training in mathematical methods in graduate school, little formal training exists in computational methods, except perhaps in econometrics. In this book we provide some helpful advice and useful guidance in developing effective computing habits. We hope this will help junior scholars to expand on Judd's vision of computation augmenting theory in all disciplines.

1.2   Data

In much of science, computing and data go hand in hand. The efforts in the nineteenth century of such people as Florence Nightingale, who used statistics derived from data gathered in the field to convince the British Army to reform how it cared for its wounded, influenced firms and governments alike: gathering and organizing information could be useful in both decision making and policy analysis.

During the first half of the twentieth century, however, most data were still collected and organized in much the same way they had been in the nineteenth century, just on a larger scale. Because the costs of collecting and organizing data during this period were high, only really important data were collected. For example, in the tradition of Lambert Adolphe Jacques Quetelet (a Belgian astronomer, mathematician, statistician and sociologist), birth and death records as well as marriage and tax data were collected. Two kinds of constraints existed: first, data were typically recorded on paper; second, computing was done by humans, although sometimes assisted by mechanical devices—calculators. For example, the great English biologist and statistician Sir Ronald A. Fisher, collected a good portion of his data from old log books and used only a mechanical calculator (fabulously named the Millionaire) to perform all his early calculations at the Rothamsted Experimental Station during the 1920s.

With the development of electronic computing devices during and after the Second World War, the second constraint was relaxed somewhat. Instead of using mechanical calculators, analysts could now use electronic ones. The electronic computers were faster than the mechanical calculators but not always reliable: a moth once crashed the entire system, hence the term *computer bug*. Electronic computers were also very expensive. In fact, only the military could really afford them, although the first computers were situated on the campuses of prestigious universities, such as the University of Pennsylvania and Harvard University. Typically, national security was the primary justification, as in the case of research involving nuclear weapons.

Throughout the 1950s, 1960s, and 1970s, however, the real prices of electronic computing fell, and alternative media for storing data (such as magnetic tapes) were developed. With regard to computing devices, the invention of the transistor and then the microprocessor represented significant technological advances. Together, these developments reduced the costs of both computing time and data storage.

Although magnetic storage media were certainly more convenient than paper, and relatively large, the physical size of a hard disk drive (permanent storage) in the 1970s was a constraint, at least by today's standards, as was the volatile main memory (not permanent storage) of a computer. For example, the best IBM System/360 series mainframe computer available in 1978 had about 8 megabytes of internal main memory that could be augmented by another 8 megabytes of large core storage, a slower kind of storage, that is, about 16 megabytes of memory.[3] Punch cards and magnetic tapes were the two most common ways to store data permanently. Today, by contrast, the Apple iPhone 6 has $1,024$ megabytes of volatile (random access memory), and up to 128 gigabytes of nonvolatile, (permanent) storage. (See Tables 6.1 and 6.2 for definitions of these units.) Consequently, during the quarter century after the Second World War, only important data were collected and organized.

In the final decades of the twentieth century, however, the prices of both computing hardware and storage media fell dramatically. For example, a gigabyte of hard disk drive storage in the 1980s cost approximately one million dollars, whereas today it probably costs less than ten cents. Berndt, Griliches, and Rappaport (1995) estimated average decreases in the prices of personal computers to be 25 percent per year during the 1980s and 1990s.

---

[3]From `http://en.wikipedia.org/wiki/IBM_System/360`.

As prices for both memory and storage fell in real terms, alternative data formats could be entertained. In the 1980s, video terminals were supplanted by graphics terminals, especially ones with color. The ability to create and store computer graphics ushered in a different way of conducting data analysis. Today, data represent names and dates, quantities and prices, and images and music. In short, the variety and volume of data have exploded because storage has become relatively cheap, and computers appear to increase in capacity and power more or less continuously—some apparently feel without bound.

Changes in the relative prices of computing and storage have been reflected in developments in statistics and subsequently econometrics. Initially, statistics involved just counting, then summarizing (for example, reporting the mean), then regression (controlling for confounding factors), then nonlinear models (relaxing the assumption of a single index), then nonparametric models (relaxing the constraint of a known family of functional forms), then simulation-based models (what to do when the model is so complicated that you cannot calculate its predictions exactly but can simulate it), and so forth.

Efron (2010, ix) suggested that the history of statistics can be divided into three eras:

1. The age of Quetelet and his successors in which huge census-level data sets were brought to bear on simple but important questions: Are there more male than female births? Is the rate of insanity rising?

2. The classical period of Pearson, Fisher, Neyman, Hotelling, and their successors, intellectual giants who developed a theory of optimal inference capable of wringing every drop of information out of a scientific experiment. The questions dealt with still tended to be simple — Is treatment A better than treatment B? — but the new methods were suited to the kinds of small data sets individual scientists might collect.

3. The era of scientific mass production, in which new technologies typified by the microarray allow a single team of scientists to produce data sets of a size Quetelet would envy. But now the flood of data is accompanied by a deluge of questions, perhaps thousands of estimates or hypothesis tests that the statistician is charged with answering together; not at all what the classical masters had in mind.

The field of data science was, in fact, born of this recent data-wealthy environment.

1.3 At the End of the Day

Despite all the advances in hardware and software as well as the increasing availability of data, most of the tasks faced by a research assistant today remain the same as they were 30 years ago. A research assistant must know how to organize and to analyze data as well as how to perform basic calculations and then to present findings derived from this research in a clear, crisp way. In the natural sciences, research assistants often need to conduct field or laboratory work as well. True, more and better data exist, computers are faster, software is easier to use and can do more things. But, seriously, the basics remain unchanged. In this book we present a guide to computing effectively using modern software.

2

Productivity Tools

E ARLY COMPUTERS RELIED on very awkward forms of input. For example, Paarsch first learned to compute using punch cards; he remembers vividly his first experience with a VT-100 terminal. With the advent of the graphical user interface (GUI), the mouse has become perhaps the most important piece of hardware when interacting with a computer through the operating system. The mouse has made computing relatively easy for almost everyone because you need only identify the appropriate icon and then click. That some small children are reported to have learned how to use a mouse well before they could speak, let alone type meaningfully on a keyboard, illustrates the mouse's power.[1] However useful a mouse may be, effective computing typically requires input from a keyboard, on the command line, in a terminal window, that is, using a command-line user interface (CLUI), alternatively, a command-line interface (CLI). Therefore, we begin our presentation at a basic level—the UNIX operating system.

2.1 Opening a Terminal Window

Specifically, in order to make use of the rich set of commands available on a UNIX operating system, you must first open a terminal window. Typically, on an Apple Mac, this will require your going to the `Applications` folder and

---

[1]In the future, the touch screen icon will probably supplant the mouse. In fact, some infants have demonstrated the ability to identify favorite icons on their parents' tablet computers.

there finding the `Utilities` folder.[2] Because you will be using the terminal window a lot, drag the `Terminal` icon to the `Dock`. On the virtual machine, the `Terminal` icon appears on the dock on the left: click on the `Terminal` icon. A terminal window will then appear, which you can resize if you want.

2.2   Working on the Command Line

Once you have opened a terminal window, you will typically be presented with the UNIX command prompt. The command prompt can vary from computer to computer as well as user account to user account, depending on the system configuration. In fact, you can control how the prompt will appear when you log in by specifying relevant features in a particular system file; we discuss how to do this later. For the time being, we assume that your system has not been changed from its default settings. Thus, you will be presented with the following prompt:

```
$
```

In Linux, depending on the distribution, the default prompt is typically the following:

```
username@computername:~$
```

where `username` is the login name you have on the computer whose name is `computername`. On the virtual machine, the prompt will look like this

```
pgbook@pgbookvm:~$
```

Later, we discuss what the ~ means.

2.3   Some UNIX Commands

Having opened a terminal window and been prompted by the operating system, you are now in a position to exploit the incredible flexibility and power of UNIX. In order to do this, however, you need to know some commands. Fortunately, although the UNIX vocabulary is quite rich, it is also fairly small.

---

[2]On a computer using the Linux operating system, a terminal icon may appear on the desktop but can also be found by searching "`terminal`" using the appropriate GUI tool.

However small the UNIX vocabulary may be, these commands will simplify immensely your interactions with the computer via the operating system. Also, by stringing the commands together, you have the potential to complete some extremely complicated tasks with only a few, judiciously employed key strokes. It is this parsimony that makes UNIX so powerful.

2.3.1   Getting Your Bearings

When you initially log in to any operating system, you are assigned a default location within that system; at any time you are logged in, you have a specific location. Thus, the first thing to do in UNIX is to find out exactly where you are. To find out where you are on the system, simply type the following:

```
$ pwd
```

which is the command to "print the working directory." Typically, on a Mac, the system will respond with

```
/Users/username
```

where `username` is the name you gave your laptop. In general, however, `username` is the name of your account on the UNIX system. For example, for Paarsch, who has named his Mac `hjp`, the system would respond with

```
/Users/hjp
```

whereas in Linux on a computer that Golyaev uses, the system would respond with

```
/home/kgolyaev
```

On the virtual machine, the system will respond with

```
/home/pgbook
```

By default, when you open a terminal window, you are placed in the home directory for that user. In the following sections, we refer to movements from this home directory. The home directory is important because in it reside many important files.

2.3.2   Learning about Commands

In UNIX you can learn how to use a command effectively (and about its relevant flags) by invoking the `man` command, which is short for *manual*. Thus,

```
$ man pwd
```

will send output from the manual pages for the `pwd` command to the terminal window. If more information exists than can be depicted on one terminal screen, then the command will pause; you can use the space bar to continue further one page at a time or the down arrow to go through the output line by line. Using the up arrow and B, an abbreviation of *back*, allows you to go backward. To get out of the `man` page, just type Q, an abbreviation of *quit*.

Of course, for the `man` command to be at all useful, you need to know the name of the UNIX command in the first place; we have collected the most common UNIX commands in an index at the end of the book under the heading "UNIX commands." Why don't you learn about some of these commands now?

2.3.3   Seeing What's There

To discover what is in the current working directory, simply type the following:

```
$ ls
```

where `ls` is an abbreviation of "list directory contents." The `ls` command returns as output to the terminal window all the visible files in the current working directory. Depending on how your system is configured, you may notice that some of the files are in different colors: for now, do not worry about this. Also, some "files" may not be files in the sense you think; we explain this later when we discuss directories and subdirectories (see Sections 2.3.10 and 2.3.12).

Most UNIX commands have flags that you can use to complete more complicated tasks. Flags typically follow the command, separated by a space, and preceded by a - sign, the hyphen or dash. Thus,

```
$ ls -l
```

is a command to list the contents of the current working directory, where the flag -l indicates the long format. Under the long format, a variety of useful information concerning each file (such as how large each file is, who owns the file, what its protections are) is returned. Much of this information will mean nothing to you now, but you will find it useful later.

In UNIX certain files are hidden from you by having the filenames begin with a dot, such as `.bash_aliases`. In short, such files are hidden when the `ls` is invoked without flags, but can be made visible if the flag `-a` is included, as in

```
$ ls -a
```

Often, you will be interested to know whether files having certain patterns in their names reside in the current working directory. Rather than wading through all the files that will be produced if the command `ls` is invoked, you can just look for filenames that contain specific patterns. To do this effectively, use wildcard characters (specifically, the *) from regular expressions, which are discussed later (see Sections 2.3.20 and 2.7). Thus, the command

```
$ ls paper*
```

finds all files with the letters `paper` at the beginning, including "`paper`"; that is, one that has no additional letters. On the other hand,

```
$ ls *.out
```

finds files with the extension `.out`, except those with a leading dot—the hidden files. We often refer to the extension `.out` as the *suffix* because the word *extension* has another meaning in Chapter 9.

Because the wildcard * is quite inclusive, you might want to look for just those files that have everything in common except one character. Thus,

```
$ ls file?.out
```

will find all files beginning with `file` and ending with `.out`, where the ? can be any letter from `a-z`, `A-Z`, and `0-9` as well as some other symbols that are not reserved by the UNIX system. To find those files that have everything in common except two consecutive characters, try

```
$ ls exp??.out
```

By now, you probably have inferred the pattern: use one ? for every wildcard character, and * for an unspecified number of characters.

The following is a favorite variant of `ls` of some users:

```
$ ls -lrt
```

which is the long format, in reverse order (`r`), with respect to the last time (`t`) at which the file was first created or last modified. (Notice that you can stack several flags in series after the − sign.) Thus, when you invoke this command, the last files are the ones you have most recently modified.

2.3.4 Filenames

Unlike other operating systems used in the past (such as Microsoft DOS), UNIX has no practical limitations concerning the length of filenames: in UNIX filenames can have up to 255 characters. Although this is clearly an advantage, Paarsch is old-school and only uses filenames that are up to 12 characters in total, three for the suffix (such as `tex`), one for the dot `.`, and up to eight for the prefix (as in `paper`). But even he will admit that this is a bit constraining. The main point to note here is the following: do not make filenames into novels; keep them relatively short but informative.

One ubiquitous principle used in computer science is self-description: the names of your files should tell the reader something about their contents. For example, the filenames `file1`, `file2`, and `file3` are devoid of content, other than having `file` in the name, which would be patently obvious to anyone examining the contents of the current working directory.

`FirmCounts.dat`, `PoissonMLE.py`, and `PoissonMLE.out` are referred to as *self-describing* filenames. `FirmCounts.dat` certainly hints to the reader that the file probably contains data and that those data probably concern counts of the number of firms. The suffix (extension) `py` of `PoissonMLE.py` suggests that this is a Python script, whereas the first part of the filename suggests that this script implements the maximum likelihood estimator of a Poisson model. Similarly, the suffix `out` in the filename `PoissonMLE.out` suggests that this file contains the output for a Poisson model estimated using the method of maximum likelihood.

The structure of the prefixes (the part before the dot) of filenames also warrants comment: `FirmCounts` is an example of what some refer to as the Camel-Case (or camel case) naming convention; others refer to this as Pascal case because the convention was advocated by users of the Pascal programming language. Under this naming convention, a compound word or an abbreviation begins each element with a capital (uppercase) letter. CamelCase names may begin with a capital or, especially for variables in the scripting language Python, with a lowercase letter; Pascal case always begins with a capital letter. Thus, `firstEntrant` would be CamelCase, while `ConvertValue` would be Pascal case, or it could also be called CamelCase. As you can see, some ambiguity exists under these conventions.

Learners who have only worked in the Windows environment should note that filenames must *never* include blank spaces, known as whitespaces. Newer versions of the Windows operating system permit spaces in filenames, but such spaces can wreak havoc when you work with other researchers who do not use Windows. You need to use escape characters if you want to introduce spaces into a filenames (see the next section).

2.3.5 Reserved Characters

Although UNIX is very flexible and general, some of the characters available on your keyboard are reserved—treated as special. In particular, the following all have special meanings or uses in UNIX:

$$* \ ? \ [\ ] \ - \ \{ \ \} \ ! \ | \ \sim \ . \ \# \ \hat{} \ \$ \ < \ > \ ; \ ' \ " \ / \ \backslash \ \& \ (\ ) \ @$$

We have already introduced the wildcard characters `*` and `?`; brackets `[ ]` and braces `{ }` are metacharacters used in pattern matching and regular expressions. You are advised not to use these characters for anything but pattern matching or regular expressions, specifically not in filenames. If, for some reason, you *really* need to use them, then the escape character `\` (backslash) must precede them, as in `\[`. The character `-` is used in pattern matching (between `[` and `]`) and to signify flags to UNIX commands. Because the `-` is so useful, it is difficult to avoid using it.

The characters `!` and `|` as well as `~` and `.` have special meanings in UNIX. The exclamation point `!` is referred to as the bang operator, and the character `|` is used as a UNIX "pipe." The characters `~` and `.` are shorthand notations for the home directory and the current working directory, respectively.

We discuss regular expressions and shell scripts in Sections 2.7 and 2.8. In a shell script, everything after the `#` is ignored because that character signifies that the line that follows is a comment. In regular expressions, the character `^`

is used to signify the start of a line, and the character $ is used to signify the end of a line. In addition to denoting *bang*, the exclamation mark character ! also means "not" as in negation, so using it except for those two purposes is wrong two ways to Sunday.

Both ' and " are used as quotation marks; the single quote ' is sometimes called the strong quotation mark, and the double quote " the weak quotation mark. These characters should only be used to specify exact expressions.

The forward slash / is used in UNIX path names, and the backslash \ is an escape character. In short, the escape character removes any special meaning from the character that follows it.

The ampersand & as well as the parentheses ( ) are used to control processes; do not use them for anything but that. The characters < and > are used by UNIX to direct standard input (`stdin`) and standard output (`stdout`) from programs, and the semicolon ; is used by UNIX to separate different commands listed on the same command line. The character @ has legacy uses that can vary across implementations, so avoid using it except in email addresses.

2.3.6   Case Sensitivity

UNIX is case sensitive. This means that the filenames `paper.tex` and `Paper.tex` are considered different by the operating system. In the past, other operating systems, such as Microsoft DOS, did not make this distinction. The flexibility of UNIX admits a wider variety of naming conventions than many other previous operating systems.

Now for the bad news. The default file system used on the Apple Mac is not case sensitive because OS X runs on the Hierarchical File System Plus (HFS+). By default, HFS+ is case insensitive, but is case preserving. This means that you can create a file named `Paper.tex`, but it will appear in the directory if you type `ls paper*`. Most disturbing is the following: If you introduce a file named `paper.tex`, then OS X will treat it as if it were `Paper.tex`. In other words, under OS X HFS+, `paper.tex` and `Paper.tex` point to the same location in the index of the file system. Practically speaking, when you introduce `paper.tex`, the contents of `Paper.tex` are lost.

No other UNIX system uses HFS+. For OS X Version 10.6 and later, you can reformat HFS+ as HFSX, which is the case-sensitive version of HFS+. After a reinstallation, however, some applications may no longer work because they have problems with case sensitivity; a commonly reported example is Adobe Reader.

In this book we make use of filenames that have both lowercase and uppercase letters, but we do not make use of UNIX's case-sensitive features. If you are using the Linux operating system, you can make use of UNIX's case-sensitive features. Note, however, that if some researchers on a project are using the Linux operating system while others are using OS X, then a potential for confusion exists, for example, if the Linux researchers have made use of the case-sensitive features of UNIX and used, say, both `paper.tex` and `Paper.tex` at the same time.

2.3.7 Redirecting Output

Sometimes, you may want to direct the output of a command that normally appears in the terminal window elsewhere, perhaps to a file. UNIX allows you to perform this task using the redirect command >, as in the following:

```
$ ls -alh > Directory.out
```

In this case, the output is sent to the file `Directory.out`, which resides in the current working directory. The information in this file can then be used for some other purpose. By the way, the flag `h` asks that UNIX report file sizes in units that a human can readily understand, rather than in bytes, which is standard but requires conversion. In other words, `h` signifies human readable output.

If you were to repeat the command, it would overwrite the previous version of `Directory.out`. Thus, it would be useful to have a command that appends information to the end of an existing file. To append information to the end of an existing file, you use the append command >> , as in

```
$ ls -alh >> Directory.out
```

which adds the contents to the end of the file `Directory.out`. If the file `Directory.out` does not exist, then the >> command will just create that file in the current working directory and put the output of the `ls -alh` command in it.

2.3.8   Examining the Contents of a File

As you might expect, UNIX has a variety of ways in which to examine the contents of a file. The main command for this purpose is `cat`, which lists the entire contents of the file. Thus,

```
$ cat Directory.out
```

would list the contents of the previously created file `Directory.out`; `cat` does not pause, so if the file is incredibly long, most of the file will pass you by.

You can also use `cat` to redirect output to a file. In fact, the terminal window is a file of sorts, having the name `/dev/tty` on an Apple Mac, and `/dev/tty0` on a Linux operating system. (As some old-timers would say, "In UNIX, everything is a file.") For example, if you type `cat > TestFile.out` and then hit **return**, you can enter text into the file named `TestFile.out` in the current working directory. When you are done typing, hit **return**, and then enter the control sequence **control**-D, which will get you out of `cat` (for more on keyboard control sequences, see Section 2.4.5). In the following, we enter eleven lines and at the end of each line hit **return**, denoted <cr> for "carriage return"—a vestige of the era when typewriters ruled. On the final line <ctrl-D> is an abbreviation of **control**-D.

```
$ cat > TestFile.out
The quick brown fox jumped over the lazy dogs.<cr>
1<cr>
2<cr>
3<cr>
4<cr>
5<cr>
6<cr>
7<cr>
8<cr>
9<cr>
10<cr>
<ctrl-D>
$
```

If you just want to see the first ten lines of the file `TestFile.out`, then simply type

```
$ head TestFile.out
```

which would yield

```
The quick brown fox jumped over the lazy dogs.
1
2
3
4
5
6
7
8
9
```

To see the last ten lines of the file `TestFile.out`, type

```
$ tail TestFile.out
```

which would yield

```
1
2
3
4
5
6
7
8
9
10
```

If you want to scroll through the file `Paper.tex`, then type either

```
$ more Paper.tex
```

or

```
$ less Paper.tex
```

Although the `less` and `more` commands each complete the same task, some UNIX gurus prefer the `less` command because, in their words, "`less` is `more`." (If you program long enough, you will get used to this kind of humor.)

The `head` and `tail` commands have flags that allow you to see more than ten lines. For example,

```
$ head -20 MLEResults.out
```

will output the first 20 lines of the file `MLEResults.out` to the terminal window. You should use the `man` command to look up these details concerning `head` and `tail`, namely, practice using `man`.

2.3.9 Comparing Files

Because comparing the contents of two files (for example, `Old.out` and `New.out`) is a commonly needed task, UNIX has a command to do this. Thus,

```
$ diff Old.out New.out
```

will return the lines where the two files differ.

2.3.10 Pathing

Although much work can be completed in your current working directory, you may want to access files from other parts of your computer—its file system. Thus, knowing how to reference the location of these files is important.

The root of every UNIX file system is the directory /. In the directory / on a Mac are the subdirectories `Applications/`, `Library/`, `Users/`, `bin/`, `dev/`, `etc/`, `opt/`, `sbin/`, and `usr/`, just to name a few.[3] The trailing / is the way UNIX differentiates between a file and a subdirectory. We mention these directories because many important files reside in them. That said, a subdirectory is just a file: specifically, you could not have a subdirectory named `/Parts/` and a file named `/Parts` living in the same root directory.

For example, on Paarsch's Mac, in the subdirectory `Users/` resides the subdirectory `hjp/`, which is the home directory for that author. In `/Users/hjp/` resides the subdirectory `PGBook/`, which is the main subdirectory for this book.

The character `~` is the UNIX shorthand for the home directory of your account; that is, `~` is the equivalent of, say, `/Users/hjp/` on Paarsch's Mac. You can use `~` to navigate the system: if you are in `/Users/hjp/Projects/Auctions/Docs/`, but would like to examine the contents of `/Users/hjp/`

---

[3]Notice that the subdirectory `Applications/` is just the `Applications` folder (see Section 2.1). In other words, *folder* and *subdirectory* are synonyms.

Letters/ using the ls command, then one way to do this would be to invoke the following command:

```
$ ls ~/Letters
```

Notice that we have omitted the trailing / because UNIX understands that Letters/ is a subdirectory. In this book, we include the trailing / in our descriptions to distinguish between a subdirectory and a file.

To refer to a subdirectory above the current working directory, the shorthand is ../, so another way to implement ls ~/Letters would involve

```
$ ls ../../../Letters
```

Clearly, when using ../ you must know where you are in the file system, whereas when using ~ you only need to know where the subdirectory is relative to the home directory, which is much easier to remember.

A third shorthand to use is ./, which denotes the current working directory. Usually, you do not have to use ./ because it is implicit. By default, however, you must use ./ before certain executable programs.[4]

2.3.11 Changing Locations

To change from one directory to another involves the "change directory" command, abbreviated cd. To move to the subdirectory SubDir/ of the current working directory, simply type the following:

```
$ cd SubDir
```

Returning to your home directory just involves

```
$ cd
```

whereas moving to the directory directly above involves

```
$ cd ..
```

---

[4]You can include the current working directory in the path for your account, but many experienced users counsel against this practice because it is a security problem. For example, suppose some nefarious individual leaves a malicious program falsely named, say, ls in a subdirectory: You would run it without realizing what that program was doing. Therefore, do not put the current working directory in the path.

You can also use the complete path when changing directories. For example, on a Mac, one common subdirectory that you may need to visit is `/opt/local/bin`, which would involve the following:

```
$ cd /opt/local/bin
```

whereas on a Linux system that subdirectory is `/usr/local/bin`, which would involve

```
$ cd /usr/local/bin
```

In these subdirectories, by default, reside the binary (machine-readable) files local to that computer. Local binary files are often the compiled programs that you have installed on your computer to perform specific tasks beyond what the operating system does. For example, the executable of SQLite can be found in `/opt/local/bin`; it is the file `sqlite3`. To see this, type

```
$ cd /opt/local/bin
$ ls sql*
```

which would yield the following:

```
sqlite3
```

On the Linux virtual machine, the location would be `/usr/local/bin`.

2.3.12   Creating Directories and Subdirectories

An organized computer account is central to effective computing. Keeping different projects in different folders or subdirectories accomplishes this goal. Keep all your projects in the subdirectory `Projects/` of your home directory `/Users/username/`. Again, the trailing / is the way UNIX differentiates between a file, and a directory or subdirectory. Each subdirectory of `Projects/` must have its own unique name. Suppose `Auctions/` is such a subdirectory. Within `Auctions/` could reside other subdirectories, such as `Code/`, `Data/`, `Docs/`, and `Papers/`. Finally, within `Docs/`, you may want a subdirectory containing `Figures/`.

As you can see, this naming convention is self-describing, a practice we encouraged you to follow during our discussion of filenames. Imagine how confusing `Stuff/Other/Mine/` would be to understand. On the other hand, `Auctions/Docs/Figures/` is quite easy to recall and to understand. Also, if all subdirectories of, say, `Projects/` have an identical structure for their subdirectories (for example, `Code/`, `Data/`, `Docs/`, and `Papers/`), then you won't have to guess about where you put something in a new project's subdirectories: by habit all project subdirectories in `Projects/` will have the same structure. Having a regularized structure also means that you can reuse code designed for one project for another without having to make many, if any, changes. We illustrate this in Section 8.8 with the example `Makefile`.

To create a subdirectory (say, `Docs/`) in the current working directory, invoke the following command:

```
$ mkdir Docs
```

To create a subdirectory elsewhere (say, `Papers/` in the home directory `/Users/hjp/`), use

```
$ mkdir /Users/hjp/Papers
```

2.3.13 Deleting Files

The command to delete (or remove) files is abbreviated `rm`. Thus,

```
$ rm Test.out
```

will remove the file `Test.out` from the current working directory, but

```
$ rm /Users/hjp/Projects/Code/*.txt
```

will remove all files having the suffix `*.txt` residing in the subdirectory `/Users/hjp/Projects/Code/`. Like other UNIX commands, the `rm` command has flags as well. One of those flags is `-r`, which involves deleting files recursively in subdirectories below the current one. Thus,

```
$ rm -r *.*
```

removes all files in the current working directory as well as any subdirectories below the current working directory. Clearly, the `rm -r` command is a potentially dangerous command to invoke, so use it with the care it warrants. In Section 2.4.6, Aliases, we illustrate how you might protect yourself.

Those familiar only with Windows should take note of another important caution. Deleting a file in Windows does not actually delete the file. Instead, Windows just moves the deleted file to another subdirectory; the file can be retrieved if it was deleted by mistake. But in UNIX, when the `rm` is invoked, the file is gone forever. Moreover, you will *not* be prompted for confirmation that you really want to delete the file, so be careful when you use this command. If you want to be prompted, then use `rm -i` instead.

2.3.14   Deleting Subdirectories

A separate command exists to remove a subdirectory. For example, to remove `Docs/` subdirectory from the current working directory, you would type the following:

```
$ rmdir Docs
```

Once again, notice that we have not included the trailing / in the UNIX command because it is unnecessary. If, however, files exist in `Docs/`, then this command will fail, and the following output will appear in your terminal window:

```
rmdir: Docs/: Directory not empty
```

One way to circumvent this problem involves invoking the following:

```
$ rm -rf Docs
```

which will delete everything in `Docs/` and anything in subdirectories within `Docs/`. If you are in your home directory when you invoke the command `rm -rf`, then you will delete *everything* in your account. By the way, the flag `f` forces the issue. Because of its ability to destroy lots of files, you should probably use this command sparingly, if at all.

2.3.15   Copying Files

Copying one file (say, `OldFile.nam`) to another (say, `NewFile.nam`) is a common task, and UNIX has an easy way to complete it:

```
$ cp OldFile.nam NewFile.nam
```

If you want to keep the same filename but have the file reside in another subdirectory, you can just use the `.` to signify this

```
$ cp OldFile.nam /Users/hjp/Papers/Auctions/Docs/.
```

Here, `OldFile.nam` is copied from the current working directory to a new subdirectory `/Users/hjp/Papers/Auctions/Docs/` using the same filename. If you attempt to copy a file onto itself, as with the following command:

```
$ cp OldFile.nam .
```

UNIX is smart enough to stop you. It will return the following:

```
cp: ./OldFile.nam and OldFile.nam are identical (not copied).
```

Such consideration is uncharacteristic of UNIX. The designers of UNIX seem to have assumed that users know what they were doing (even if that is patently false) and so allowed the operating system to do whatever users have told it to do. This flexibility creates power. With power, however, comes responsibility.[5]

2.3.16 File Protections

Because you may have files that you would prefer not to delete, how can you protect yourself? All UNIX files have certain levels of protection. These protections exist across types of users on the computer. Each file has three levels of usage: read (`r`), write (`w`), and execute (`x`). Three types of file access exist as well: those for the user who created the file (`u`), those for the group (`g`) in which that user resided at the time of file creation, and those for the world (`w`). For example, if (in the current working directory) the file `test` exists, then it might have the following protections:

```
-rw-r--r--  1 hjp  staff  6  8 Jun 17:12 test
```

which you could discover using the command

```
$ ls -l test
```

Consider the sequence `-rw-r--r--`. Here, the first `-` indicates that this is a file; were it a directory that leftmost character would have been a `d`. The next three characters indicate the protections for the user: in this case, read and write privileges exist, but no execute privileges have been granted. We can see by the next three characters that all users in the current user's group have read (`r`) access, but neither write (`w`) nor execute (`x`) access has been granted, whereas

---

[5]The dot in the `cp` command is, in fact, optional, but we include it to reinforce what is being done here.

the last three characters indicate that the world has read access, but neither write nor execute access has been granted.

To change the permissions on the file, you must use the `chmod` command, an abbreviation of "change file modes." For example, to grant the user execute permission, use the following:

```
$ chmod 744 test
```

so `ls -l test` would yield

```
-rwxr--r--  1 hjp  staff  6  8 Jun 17:13 test
```

To make the file `IncomeTax.dat` read-only for you and invisible to your group and the world, simply type

```
$ chmod 400 IncomeTax.dat
```

so `ls -l IncomeTax.dat` would yield

```
-r--------  1 hjp  staff  6  8 Jun 17:14 IncomeTax.dat
```

What do the numbers 744 and 400 mean? In UNIX the file protections are done using base 8, also referred to as octal. A 4 means read access, a 2 means write access, and a 1 means execute access. Thus, in 744 you note that the user has $4 + 2 + 1$ or `rwx` access. In words, the user has read, write, and execute access. But the group and the world have $4 + 0 + 0$ or `r--` access. Similarly, in 400 you note that the user has $4 + 0 + 0$ or `r--` access (read access), while the group and the world have $0 + 0 + 0$ or `---` access, that is, no access.

2.3.17   Moving Files

Moving (or renaming) one file (for example, `OldFile.nam`) to another (for example, `NewFile.nam`) is another common task, and UNIX has an easy way to complete this task:

```
$ mv OldFile.nam NewFile.nam
```

The `mv` command is similar to the `cp` command, except with `mv` the original is "lost" because it has been *moved* elsewhere.

Because subdirectories are just files in which the locations of other files are indexed, you can move subdirectories using the same command. For example, to move the subdirectory `OldSubDir/` in the current working directory to `NewSubDir/` in the home directory, use

```
$ mv OldSubDir /Users/username/NewSubDir
```

You can use the `mv` command to rename files as well.

2.3.18 Accounting

Sometimes, you need to know the exact character count, word count, or line count in a file. For example, some journals require that the abstract be no more than 100 words, or less than 600 characters. For tasks like this, you can use the UNIX command `wc`, which is an abbreviation of "word count."

Consider the following contents of the file `Final.dat`, which you can find using `cat Final.dat`:

```
123     83
234     75
456     97
```

If you invoke

```
$ wc Final.dat
```

then the following will be sent to the terminal window:

```
       3       6       21 Final.dat
```

The number 3 in the first column returns the number of lines, whereas the number 6 in the second column returns the number of words. Here, each of the numbers is interpreted as a separate word. What about the number 21? It is the number of characters. How does this work? The six numbers $(123, \ldots, 97)$ have a total of fifteen characters, and the spaces between the numbers on each line account for three characters, for a total of eighteen. The remaining three characters are the line feeds at the end of each line. These characters do not appear when the `cat` command has been invoked, but they are there nonetheless and therefore counted.

In some text editors, a line feed will appear as `\n`, which is an abbreviation of "new line." Had the preceding file included tab-separated values, then those same editors would have depicted the tabbed spaces as `\t`.

Another useful command is `df`, which is an abbreviation of "disk free." By invoking

```
$ df
```

you will be able to see something like the following:

```
Filesystem      512-blocks        Used Available Capacity  Mounted on
/dev/disk0s2    976101344 302457200 673132144       32%    /
devfs                 356        356          0      100%   /dev
map -hosts              0          0          0      100%   /net
map auto_home           0          0          0      100%   /home
/dev/disk1s1     31326160   18838160   12488000      61%    /Volumes/
    KINGSTON2
```

On this Mac, about one-third of the file system /dev/disk0s2/, where the root directory / resides, is currently being used. The next three lines are not very interesting, but the last one (/dev/disk1s1, which is mapped to /Volumes/ KINGSTON2) refers to a flash disk that has about 60 percent of its capacity used. In general, you would not know that /Volumes/KINGSTON2 is a flash disk unless you had installed it. (Note, too, that many people find the -h flag helpful when using the df command.) You can go to that file system using the command cd /Volumes/KINGSTON2 and then create subdirectories as well as cp files from other file systems to those subdirectories.

2.3.19 Discovering Processes

To see all the processes running on your computer, type top at the command line prompt:

```
$ top
```

We would like to show you a screenshot of the output of this command, but it is updated continually as the computer works, so that is impossible.

To view just those processes related to your account use ps, which is an abbreviation of "process status":

```
$ ps
```

which might give rise to

```
  PID TTY           TIME CMD
 1015 ttys000    0:00.01 -bash
```

If you would like to see information concerning other processes, type

```
$ ps aux
```

What does aux mean? The `a`, `u`, and `x` are the flags for `ps` command, but in this case the lead `-` is omitted. Note that `ps -aux` is different from `ps aux`: the former prints all processes owned by a user named `x` as well as all processes that would be selected by the `-a` option. If the user named `x` does not exist, then this command will not work and a warning will be printed. Thus, don't use the dash in front of the flag.

Again, we would like to show you a screenshot of the output of this command, but there is too much output. Suppose you want to find just certain processes. How could you do that?

2.3.20 Searching for Regular Expressions

To find certain strings in a file, use the command `grep`, which is an abbreviation of "get regular expressions and print." For example,

```
$ grep 123 Final.dat
```

would yield

```
123 83
```

Notice that the 123 is not typed within quotation marks; using delimiters such as `' '` or `" "` is unnecessary in this case, but you may need to do this in other applications, for example, if you want to include blank spaces or dashes. Dashes would clearly confuse `grep` because they could mean flags as in `grep -i all ProdTools.tex`. Hence, in general, you would use the following:

```
$ grep -flags 'string' file.nam
```

2.3.21 Linking Commands—Piping

Perhaps one of the most powerful UNIX commands is the pipe, which is signified by `|`. Piping allows you to take the output from one UNIX command and use it as the input to another program. An example may make this clear. Consider the previous command `ps aux`, which allowed you to see all the processes associated with your account. Suppose you want to use `grep` to print out certain regular expressions. With this in mind, consider the following:

```
$ ps aux | grep octave
```

which allows you to examine information concerning processes having the term octave in the `ps` output.

2.3.22   Sorting the Contents of Files

Sorting the lines of a file based on the contents of a column is a task you may need to complete. The UNIX command `sort` allows you to do this. Consider using the `cat` command to view the contents of the file `Names.dat`, so

```
$ cat Names.dat
```

might yield

```
Taylor
Jones
Smith
```

The names in this file are not in alphabetical order. If, however, you invoke

```
$ sort Names.dat > SortedNames.out
```

and then invoke

```
$ cat SortedNames.out
```

you will get

```
Jones
Smith
Taylor
```

By using the `man` command, you can discover how to sort on, say, the second column of a file that is six columns wide; for example, check out "`sort -k 2`".

2.3.23   Cutting, Pasting, and Joining

The UNIX commands `cut`, `paste`, and `join` allow you to take parts of different files and merge them together. For example, suppose file `A.dat` looks like this:

```
a b
c d
e f
```

where a space is used to separate the two columns. Introduce file B.dat, which looks like this:

```
1 2 3 4
5 6 7 8
```

where, again, a space is used to separate each of the columns. Now,

```
$ paste A.dat B.dat
```

will look like this:

```
a b 1 2 3 4
c d 5 6 7 8
e f
```

which you could redirect to a third file, C.dat, using

```
$ paste A.dat B.dat > C.dat
```

The two files do not have to have the same number of rows; paste will simply put in null spaces for the third line that does not exist in B.dat in this case. Note that the columns from A.dat are separated from those in B.dat by a tab separator.

To cut, say, the middle two columns from B.dat, you would do the following:

```
$ cut -d ' ' -f 2-3 B.dat > D.dat
```

Here, -d ' ' would use the space ' ' as the delimiter, which is what the flag -d means, and then extract fields (columns) 2 and 3, hence the flag -f 2-3. The output has been redirected to D.dat, which can then be merged with, say, A.dat, using the paste command, as in

```
$ paste D.dat A.dat
```

to get the following:

```
2 3 a b
6 7 c d
    e f
```

Of course, you could also use piping to do all this in one command. Why not give it a try?

Consider now two files of grades, `Midterm.dat` and `Final.dat`, that have a common column, sometimes referred to as a *key*, which is assumed by default to be in the first column. Now,

```
$ cat Midterm.dat
```

yields

```
123 23
234 25
456 33
```

and

```
$ cat Final.dat
```

yields

```
123 83
234 75
456 97
```

with

```
$ join Midterm.dat Final.dat > AllGrades.dat
```

so

```
$ cat AllGrades.dat
```

yields

```
123 23 83
234 25 75
456 33 97
```

For this to work, the keys must be in the same order in both files, but you already know how to use `sort` to make that happen.

2.3.24 Superuser Powers

In UNIX a special account used for system administration has the name `root`; the owner of that account is the *superuser*. The superuser's account `root` has privileges to do things that the accounts of normal users do not. Clearly, protecting normal users from themselves is a good thing. In fact, even if you are allowed to use it, you are not encouraged to use the account `root` unless you need to perform some chore of system administration that really requires that privilege. That said, to log in to the `root` account, you need to use the `su` command (an abbreviation of superuser), as in

```
$ su
Password:
```

which requires you to know the superuser's password.

Often, on multiuser systems, the superuser is the system administrator, so you won't know the password to the account `root`. What if you need superuser privileges, for example, to install software? Because the system administrator is typically busy with other things, you do not want to pester that person with such mundane tasks as software installation, which you can probably do yourself. The `sudo` command allows a permitted user to execute commands as if that person were the superuser, without actually logging into the account `root`. For example, on an Apple Mac, with `xcode` installed, you can install software using MacPorts. Suppose someone installed some software for you, but you want to update that software; then

```
$ sudo port -v selfupdate
Password:
```

would achieve that goal, where you would use the password to your account.

2.3.25 Standard Input, Output, and Error

Sometimes, software development engineers will use default file specifications to input and to output data. Thus, knowing what these default standards are can be useful. When a UNIX program begins execution, connections exist between that program's input and output, and the terminal window. Three input/output (I/O) streams exist: *standard input* (`stdin`), *standard output* (`stdout`), and *standard error* (`stderr`). As mentioned, the terminal window is `/dev/tty`, while `stdin` is 0, `stdout` is 1, and `stderr` is 2.

2.4 Shortcuts

Because entering commands at the keyboard is time consuming and error prone, UNIX has many ways to reduce typing through shortcuts. Here, we describe six ways in which you can reduce the amount of typing you do.

2.4.1   Autocomplete

Autocomplete is simple to use. Suppose you are using the UNIX tool `wc` to calculate the number of lines in a file that you think starts with `Adjust`, but you are uncertain about the remaining characters. In this case, simply type `wc Adjust` followed by the **tab** key. If `Adjust` identifies the file uniquely in the current working directory, then UNIX will autocomplete the line, whereas if `Adjust` does not uniquely identify the file in the current working directory, then UNIX will prompt you with relevant choices. On the other hand, if the characters `Adjust` do not exist in any of the files in the current working directory, then UNIX will alert you.

2.4.2   Reusing Past Commands

If you have (or someone else has) been working within a terminal window on the current UNIX account in the past, then a history of what has been typed at the command line will be kept in a file whose name will depend on the shell you are using.

What's a shell? A *shell* is a command-line interpreter (program) that provides access to the operating system through the terminal window. UNIX has several different shells. The two most influential shells are the Bourne shell `sh`, which was written by Stephen Bourne, and the C shell `csh`, which was written by William N. Joy. Yet another shell is the Bourne again shell `bash`, which was written by Brian Fox for the GNU project. The Bourne again shell is a superset of `sh`; `bash` is the default shell on the Linux and OS X operating systems, so most of the discussion in this chapter refers to that shell. Each shell is, however, slightly different from the others, particularly in the way environment and shell variables are defined and manipulated (see Section 2.10).

Thus, for example, if you are using the `bash` shell, then the history file will be named `.bash_history`; it lives in the home directory of the account.

Because viewing the history is a common task, UNIX has a command to do this, `history`, which outputs to the terminal window up to the last 500 commands typed. Because most terminal windows are only about 24 lines long, you will just see the last 20 or so when you invoke

```
$ history
```

For example, here are the last ten commands

```
491 ls -al intro.tex
492 grep 'labour' intro.tex
493 sed s/labour/labor/ intro.tex
494 latex book
495 latex book
496 bibtex book
497 latex book
498 dvips book
499 ps2pdf book.ps
500 cp book.pdf /Users/hjp/Drafts/.
```

but you can always pipe history through more or less, or through grep, if you know what command you want to reuse.

Two other ways exist to reuse information from the history: one involves scrolling through past commands using the up arrow that appears on the right-hand side of the keyboard and the other uses the bang feature in UNIX.

2.4.3 Up Arrow

The up arrow key can be used to scroll through past commands until you find what you want. Try it, you'll like it. If you keep going, then you will eventually run out of recorded history. Yikes!

2.4.4 Bang

Another way to proceed is to use the bang feature, which is represented by the character !. Thus, to reuse the last command, do the following:

```
$ !!
```

Given the .bash_history listed in Section 2.4.2, this would result in

```
$ cp book.pdf /Users/hjp/Drafts/.
```

That is, the current version of paper.pdf would be copied atop of the previous one that lives in /Users/hjp/Drafts/.

Another way to invoke bang would be to use a line number derived from .bash_history, for example,

```
$ !491
```

which would result in

```
$ ls -al intro.tex
```

Here, again, the number comes from the history in Section 2.4.2.

A third way to use the bang feature is in conjunction with the UNIX facility to pattern-match concerning commands in `.bash_history`. For example, if you were to type `!lat`, then the most recent command from the `.bash_history` having the first three letters as `lat`, in this case, line 497, would be executed, and the file `book.tex` would be recompiled using the typesetting program TEX in conjunction with the LATEX markup language. To be clear, you only need to use as many letters as is necessary to identify uniquely the first part of the command in the `.bash_history`. In other words, one character could be sufficient.

2.4.5 Keyboard Control Sequences

When working in a terminal window, the **control** key on a Mac keyboard (the **Ctrl** key on a Windows keyboard) allows you to control the outcome of an executing program. Remember, the terminal window is an executing program. Here, we indicate this by **control**-ℓ, where ℓ is from the set $\{\,\backslash, C, D, H, Q, S, U, W, Z\,\}$.

For example, if you have directed the output of a program to the terminal window, then **control**-S freezes the terminal window, preventing any display in the terminal window from continuing. (Note: You do not have to use the uppercase letter S—an s will do; we use the uppercase letters because that is how they appear on the keyboard.) On the other hand, **control**-Q releases control of the terminal window, allowing display to the terminal to continue. **control**-D is used to exit from many programs, for example, Python as well as the UNIX tool `cat`, which we demonstrated previously. The control sequence **control**-C terminates a program that is executing, making it seem the most draconian sequence, but **control**-\ is even more powerful than **control**-C because you can use it when the terminal window just refuses to cooperate. The sequence **control**-Z is used to suspend (to background, to make it sleep, hence the Z) an executing program; to get a suspended program to continue, use `fg`, which is an abbreviation of "foreground." Sometimes, for some unknown reason, your terminal window can become unusable, in which case the `reset` command is useful.

To see how this might work in practice, type the following (exactly) into a file named `InfiniteLoop.py`:

```
n = 0
while (True):
  n += 1
  print n
```

Listing 2.1: An Infinite Loop

If you do not know how to use an editor yet, then try

```
$ cat > InfiniteLoop.py
```

This will direct whatever you type to the file `InfiniteLoop.py`; everything from the keyboard will go to that file. Carefully type the following five lines, including **return**s at the end of lines. Two important things to note: first, the `n += 1` and the `print n` instructions after the `while(True):` need to be indented (try two spaces); second, the "control-D" is **control** and the letter D together (this gets you out of `cat`); we mentioned the control sequence **control**-D in the previous paragraph of this section. Once you get out of `cat`, you will see the $ prompt.

```
n = 0
while (True):
  n += 1
  print n
control-D
$
```

After you have successfully saved the file, checked to see that it is in the current working directory using `ls InfiniteLoop.py`, and then viewed its contents using `more InfiniteLoop.py`, you can now execute the script and then view using the following:

```
$ python InfiniteLoop.py
```

A whole mess of integers will appear in the terminal window. You can stop them from streaming through the terminal window temporarily by typing **control**-S; to resume the deluge of integers, simply type **control**-Q. To halt the process temporarily, type **control**-Z; to resume it, type `fg`. You can

terminate the process using **control**-C, which will result in the following
error message:

```
Traceback (most recent call last):
File "./InfiniteLoop.py", line 5, in <module>
  print n
KeyboardInterrupt
close failed in file object destructor:
sys.excepthook is missing
lost sys.stderr
```

whereas if you use **control**-\, you will get something like

```
Quit: 3
```

Keyboard control sequences **control**-H, **control**-W, **control**-U, and
control-D are useful in a terminal window: **control**-H deletes last character typed; **control**-W deletes last word typed; **control**-U deletes last line
typed; and **control**-D ends text input.[6]

2.4.6   Aliases

Often, you will need to execute certain combinations of UNIX commands repeatedly, which can be tedious and invites typing errors. For example, Paarsch
invokes cd /Users/hjp/PGBook a lot when going to the subdirectory containing this book. One way to reduce errors would involve his typing

```
$ alias book='cd /Users/hjp/PGBook'
```

each time he opened a terminal window to work on the book. This is referred to
as *aliasing*. Aliasing means that book is now a UNIX command that executes cd /
Users/hjp/PGBook. Another example of aliasing involves the command rm.
The following,

```
$ alias rm='rm -i'
```

redefines rm to include the flag -i, which will then ask you whether you want
to delete the file; that is, the new command provides a safeguard. However, as

---

[6]Here, we introduce material that foreshadows what is to follow, namely, the programming
language Python, specifically, Version 2. We use this device here and elsewhere to maintain your
attention and to encourage you to think ahead about upcoming material.

this example illustrates, you should use caution when choosing the name of an alias: do not remap important UNIX commands.

Another thing to realize about aliasing is that it only exists while the terminal window in which you defined it is open; should you close that terminal window, then the aliasing disappears. In short, if you open another terminal window, then you will have to redefine the alias. Because creating an alias every time you log on to your account could be tedious, UNIX has a shortcut, which involves collecting all the alias commands into a file named .bash_aliases. How do you create this file? Using a text editor.

2.5 Text Editors

When teaching courses in applied econometrics or computational economics, Paarsch is wont to begin the software tools section of those courses with the following advice:

> Choose your editor with more care than you would your spouse because you will continue to use the editor long after the spouse is gone.

Paarsch chose a text editor (the UNIX tool vi) in 1990 and has used it ever since. Now, we are certainly not advocating that everyone run out and learn to use vi, or its improved relative vim. If he had to choose an editor today, Paarsch would probably choose either Emacs or jEdit. He chose vi at the time because it was the standard editor shipped with Sun Microsystems computers. In fact, in the documentation of some system tools, examples describing how to make changes to certain files were illustrated using the vi editor. In short, it was the best choice at the time. Why not switch to a different editor now? Over time, editing with vi has become part of his muscle memory. The costs of switching to a new editor would be high, such as when after five years Paarsch switched from the Norton editor ne to vi. By the way, Golyaev uses Emacs.

Some well-known researchers we know use the Microsoft Windows tool Notepad, apparently without recognizing the loss in productivity. Others even use the word processor Word, saving the files as ASCII. Using a tool like Notepad instead of an editor optimized for programming is akin to a right-handed scratch golfer playing with left-handed clubs: he can probably break

90, but getting to par is all but ruled out. In short, using a programmer's editor whose features you have mastered is central to effective computing. We suggest that you choose Emacs or jEdit or `vim`. Although we do not present any instructions concerning how to use any of these tools, good books are available: for Emacs, consider the book by Cameron, Elliott, Loy, Raymond, and Rosenblatt (2005) and for `vim`, the book by Neil (2012). For jEdit, go to the useful website `http://www.jedit.org`.

We implore you to take the time and make the effort to become proficient using a programmer's editor; it will yield immense dividends later.[7]

2.6 Other Tools for Text Processing

In some research endeavors, such as natural language processing, large amounts of text need to be searched and then perhaps transformed. Experienced computer programmers will often recommend `sed` or `awk` for such tasks. In the prologue, we suggested that the scripting language Perl is probably without peer when it comes to text processing, but we also noted that Perl is a cryptic language that is difficult for novices to learn. Because Python is easier to learn than Perl, we suggest that you use the Python `re` module if you need to process text or to parse regular expressions (see Section 2.7). We describe `sed` and `awk` briefly, just so you can understand what old-timers are telling you when they suggest that you use either of these languages. Who knows? You may find them well suited to your task.

2.6.1 sed

The stream editor `sed` is a UNIX tool that you can use to parse and transform text, either from files or from other input streams. Depending on your perspective, `sed` is either a compact programming language or a very primitive one. Lee E. McMahon developed `sed` around 1973 at AT&T Bell Labs as a successor to the UNIX command `grep`. Like many other editors of its time, `sed`

---

[7]Several text editors for programmers are available for purchase as well. Because we have limited ourselves to free software, we do not discuss them, other than to mention that several very productive friends have recommended the Sublime Text editor (see `http://www.sublimetext.com`).

is *line-oriented*, which means that when `sed` takes in data from, say, a file (or some other input stream) it does so line by line. What determines the end of a line? The end-of-line control character (see Section 4.3.4). The line is placed in the computer's memory, referred to as a *word buffer* or *pattern space*, and then `sed` uses whatever pattern you have provided, for example, in the form of a `sed` program, or *script*, to complete whatever task you requested. What many old-school computer programmers like about `sed` is that you can execute it from the command line as well as from inside a UNIX tool, say, the programmer's editor `vi`. In short, `sed` is a very flexible tool. If you know the grammar of `sed`, then using it is a snap. For example, suppose you want to change all occurrences of the English word *labour* to the American word *labor* in the file `InputFile.txt`,

```
labour
labor
labour
labor
labour
labor
```

and then place the output in the file `OutputFile.txt`. Then `sed` would require your executing the following on the command line in a terminal window:

```
$ sed 's/labour/labor/g' InputFile.txt > OutputFile.txt
```

Note: You must provide an output file. If you do not, the output will be directed to the terminal window, whereas if you use the input file `InputFile.txt` as the output file, you will overwrite the input file—an empty file will result. To be clear, you will lose the contents of all that you were trying to change. Not good. Successful use of the command will yield the following:

```
labor
labor
labor
labor
labor
labor
```

Listing 2.2: `sed` Output—`OutputFile.txt`

2.6.2 `awk`

Many seasoned computer programmers wax fondly about the text processing capabilities of `awk`, which is an interpreted programming language named for its three creators, Alfred V. Aho, Peter J. Weinberger, and Brian W. Kernighan. `awk` was designed to improve on both `grep` and `sed`. Historically, `awk` was used to extract data and to create reports. Although `awk` has been historically very important, it was supplanted by Perl in the 1990s. Why bring up this language then? We advocate that you learn to use the Python module `re` to process text instead of either `awk` or Perl, but many old-time UNIX programmers may suggest you use, say, either `awk` or Perl, and you want to have a good answer. The short answer is, I don't know `awk`; the long one is, I am using the `re` module in Python.

2.7   Regular Expressions

In computing, the term *regular expression*, sometimes referred to as regex or regexp, is used to describe a sequence of characters that are typically used to form a search pattern. For example, in Section 2.8, we introduce the shell script `sub`, which uses the stream editor `sed` to find regular expressions and match strings and replace them with other strings. As mentioned, the UNIX tool `grep` as well as the streaming editor `sed` and the programming language `awk` were all created to deal with regular expressions. As we also described, `sed` works with streams of characters on a per-line basis, using a primitive programming language where only two variables exist—pattern space and hold space. `awk` is much more sophisticated, but it is still oriented toward delimited fields on a per-line basis. Both use regular expressions to select and process text.

In a regular expression, any character is either a regular character or a special character, sometimes called a *metacharacter*. For example, the following text line,

```
<line>The quick brown fox jumped\t over the lazy dogs.\n</line>
```

has some metacharacters, such as `\t` and `\n`, as well as some tags `<line>` and `</line>`, which are not regular characters but are written in combinations of regular and special characters. On the Internet, many files and web pages are generated by computers. (Hereafter, we refer to web pages as files since that is what web pages are on the host computers.) The structure of these files is often extremely regular. The presence of metacharacters or tags in the files can, however, prevent (or at least impede) further analysis. Consequently, you often need to clean up the raw data; tools that allow you to process regular expressions exploit the specific structure of a file and thus speed up the cleaning process, sometimes called *munging* or *wrangling*.

For example, you could use a regular expression to locate the same word spelled two different ways in a collection of documents, like the English word *labour* and its American cousin *labor*. A regular expression language, like `awk`, processes regular-expression statements using particular rules (a grammar). Over time, the rules of regular expressions have become standardized.

Our intent in this section is to make you aware of the Python module `re`, which can be used to process regular expressions, and to mention some situations in which regular expressions can be used. An example of how you would use regular expressions is given in Section 4.8.9.

Because regular expressions are used so frequently, many good books have been written describing how they work in many different languages (see, for example, Fitzgerald 2012).

2.8   Shell Scripts

Computers are extremely useful for automating mundane tasks. One such task might be adding up billions of numbers, but many other tasks not involving arithmetic exist as well. For example, instructing a computer to perform a sequence of monitoring tasks (such as verifying that a host is up and running) at fixed intervals (say, every hour) can be automated. One easy way to save time executing repeated tasks on a computer involves a *shell script*, which was sometimes called a *batch file* on the Microsoft DOS operating system.

A shell script is a file that contains UNIX shell commands. The following are the contents of a shell script whose name is `Conversion.sh`; this shell script was used by the authors to convert hundreds of files from one graphics format to another.

```
for f in *.eps;
do
  x=$(echo $f | sed 's/.eps//g')
  epstopdf $f --outfile=$x-eps-converted-to.pdf
done
```

Without really knowing too much about programming, you can probably infer what is happening. For every file that has the suffix .eps, use sed to strip the suffix of the filename, assigning the prefix of the filename to the variable x. Then use the software tool `epstopdf` to convert each file's input from the encapsulated PostScript (EPS) format (hence, the `.eps` suffix) to the Portable Document Format (PDF) (hence, the `.pdf` suffix) but include the self-describing term `-eps-converted-to` in the new filename.

A shell script can be executed by typing its name at the command prompt or by placing its name in another shell script. To be executable, a shell script file must meet some conditions. The file must have a special first line that names an appropriate command processor; although the preceding example is clearly an exception, in most cases, this line should be `#!/bin/bash`. To be sure, go to `/bin/` using the `cd` command, and then type `ls -l bash`. If the `bash` executable is not there, then type the following:

```
$ which bash
```

which should return its location. That new location should be used after the `#!` in the first line of the shell script. By the way, when `bash` is in its default location, `which bash` will return

```
/bin/bash
```

Note, too, that in order to use a shell script, it must be executable. Earlier, we saw that the `chmod` command could be used to do this. For example, if the file is `Script.sh`, then

```
$ chmod 744 Script.sh
```

will make it executable to you, the user, but read only to your group as well as to the world.

Whether a shell script has a suffix like `.sh` is unimportant: the name `Script` would work as well. In fact, Paarsch, out of a habit developed while working on a VAX–11/780 using the VMS operating system, uses the suffix `.com`, which is short for "command file," instead of the standard UNIX shell script suffix `.sh`; most UNIX gurus, however, consider this heresy. Using the suffixes `.com` and `.sh` is just an example of the self-describing principle.

To execute the shell script `Script.sh`, invoke the following:

```
$ ./Script.sh
```

Here, the notation `./` tells the operating system that `Script.sh` lives in the current working directory. Recall that we described several different shortcuts

involving the user's home directory ~, the subdirectory above the current working directory ../, and the current working directory ./ as well.

When should you use a shell script? One rule of thumb is that you should
create a shell script when you notice that you do something more than once
a day. Clearly, once a day is arbitrary, but the key notion is that you are doing something repeatedly, and that this act takes time and can be error prone.
Often, novices balk at creating shell scripts because the first one can take a bit
of time to create. This is of course true, but the more shell scripts you create, the
faster later ones will be to create, and the more time you will save. In short, the
learning curve of creating shell scripts is very steep.

Example of a Shell Script

In the course of your research, you will frequently need to change all occurrences of one sequence of letters in a file (or several files) to another sequence
of letters. The second sequence could, of course, be no letters; that is, you might
want to delete all occurrences of the first sequence. For example, you might
want to change the word increase to the word decrease in all files having the
suffix *.tex. The following shell script sub, which was created by Alberto
M. Segre, a close friend and former colleague of Paarsch, is a great example of
a powerful shell script.

```
#!/bin/bash

# Replace one string for another inside a (set of) filename(s).
# Usage: sub "foo" "bar" foo??

a="$1"
shift
b="$1"
shift

for file in $*;
  do
    echo $file: $a "->" $b
    sed -e"s%$a%$b%g" < $file > $file.$$
    mv $file.$$ $file
  done
```

Listing 2.3: Shell Script to Implement Global Substitution

Paarsch keeps this shell script in a pathed subdirectory with other important, frequently used tools so that he can use it whenever and wherever he must make global changes. (You will need to learn a bit more about pathing in order to do this; try looking it up on the Internet.)

After you have learned how to use a text editor, type the preceding material into a file called `sub`, make that file executable using the `chmod` command, and then create a file named `test`, which lives in that subdirectory and in which the word `labour` is typed. Now execute

```
$ ./sub 'labour' 'labor' test
test: labour -> labor
```

The line `test: labour -> labor` should appear if you typed in the file correctly, and the following should occur when you type `more test`:

```
$ more test
labor
```

Beware: Trying to substitute UNIX reserved characters (in or out) using `sub` can result in unexpected outcomes because the shell script is based on the UNIX `sed` tool, which does not deal well with reserved characters. For example, when Paarsch once tried to make a global change in the final draft of a book manuscript, he discovered that `sub` had deleted the entire text of the book. Needless to say, this was disconcerting. Fortunately, he had another copy of the manuscript stored elsewhere.

Although this story was intended to assure you that everyone makes mistakes, the point you should take from it is to maintain backups of your work. Then, even if you make a large error, you can recover. For this reason, you should pay special attention to the material on archiving files and version control in Sections 2.14 and 2.15.

2.9   Dealing with Dependencies

The shell script is a clear, simple, useful tool to execute a sequence of tasks that are independent of one another, or at least can be broken into a linear sequence of instructions. Often, however, files can depend on other files, which may have changed since the last time the sequence of tasks was executed. In short, dependencies can exist. One solution to this problem would be to rerun everything and then to proceed as before, but this could be really wasteful. What you would like is for the computer to check whether all necessary files are current, rerun the ones that are not, and then proceed to execute the task at hand. The UNIX `make` tool is extremely effective at doing this.

By computing standards, the `make` tool is very old, having been created in 1977 by Stuart Feldman as a summer project at AT&T Bell Labs. One of the drawbacks with `make` is that it is from a different era in computing, so it is particularly sparse concerning documentation, and it contains a variety of flags that are far from obvious, even to those with considerable experience in UNIX. That this old piece of software is still used speaks to its usefulness. Like the shark in biology, `make` is extremely fit, having survived many changes in computing over time. Thus, even though other contending tools exist, we recommend using `make`.

As mentioned, the `make` tool is both subtle and sophisticated. We do not expect you to become an expert with this tool. In fact, we continue to learn about `make`. What we hope to do in this section is to show you how to automate a few common tasks. We hope this experience will help you to understand the contents of any `Makefile` that you may encounter, often when installing software on your computer.

A basic `Makefile` has the following structure:

```
target: dependencies
<tab> system command
```

where the `<tab>` is the **tab** character on the Mac keyboard. In other words, blank spaces cannot be used; it must be a tab. As an example, suppose you have entered the following four lines into the file `MyPaper` in the current working directory:

```
paper:
    pdflatex Paper.tex
clean:
    rm Paper.pdf
```

which processes the TeX/LaTeX code in the file `Paper.tex` to create a file `Paper.pdf`—a file in the Portable Document Format.

To run this `Makefile`, you would type the following in a terminal window of the current working directory:

```
make -f MyPaper
```

The `clean:` label allows you to input that term, and have the `Makefile` remove old copies of the file `Paper.pdf`. It would be invoked as follows:

```
make -f MyPaper clean
```

For more on `make`, read the useful book by Mecklenburg (2005). An example of how you would develop a `Makefile` for use in your research is given in Section 8.8, at which point we hope you will know enough to appreciate the power of the tool.

Sometimes, particularly when developing and testing a `Makefile`, nothing has changed. In such cases, you could open all the files with an editor and then save them, to update the time stamps, but for binary files this would be a major disaster. In UNIX, the command `touch` can be used to change file access as well as modification times. For example,

```
$ touch MyPaper.tex
```

would not modify the contents of `MyPaper.tex`, but it would update the time stamp of the file to the computer's current date and time. If `MyPaper.tex` does not exist, then `touch` will create a zero-length file having that name.

2.10   Environment and Shell Variables

The UNIX operating system has two types of variables, environment variables and shell variables. Shell variables typically only apply to the current shell (that is, the terminal window), whereas environment variables are determined when you log in to your account and are valid for the duration of the session. By convention, environment variables have uppercase names and shell variables have lowercase names. We focus on environment variables because their values often have an important impact on how your terminal window appears as well as how other programs behave.

To see the values current environment variables have been assigned, type

```
$ printenv
```

To find the specific value for a particular environment variable, use `echo` `$VARIABLE_NAME`. For example, the following could be used to find out about `PS1`:

```
$ echo $PS1
```

Variable	Description
EDITOR	user's preferred text editor
HISTFILE	file in which command history is saved
HISTFILESIZE	maximum number of lines contained in history file
HOME	user's home directory to store files
HOSTNAME	system's host name
PATH	lists directories the shell searches, for the commands
PS1	shell prompt in the Bourne shell and variants
PWD	path to the current directory
SHELL	current shell
TEMP	path to where processes can store temporary files
TERM	set terminal emulator being used by UNIX
TZ	timezone settings
USER	current logged-in user's name

Table 2.1: Commonly Used UNIX Environment Variables

Note that the `$` prior to the `VARIABLE_NAME` is important. If you typed

```
$ echo PS1
```

the system would just respond with

```
$ PS1
```

Table 2.1 presents descriptions of some commonly used environment variables in the UNIX operating system.

Some Tricks with Environment Variables

Earlier, we mentioned that you could control what information the UNIX prompt conveys to the user. Controlling the UNIX prompt is achieved using the environment variable `PS1`. In order to change the default value of `PS1`, you must edit the `.bashrc` file, which lives in your home directory. (Note: It is important to use uppercase letters for this variable.) Because the `.bashrc` file begins with a `.` you cannot see it, unless you use `ls -a`. On the other hand, the `.bashrc` may not even exist in your home directory, in which case you must create it using a text editor such as Emacs or jEdit.

On his Mac, Paarsch has a UNIX prompt that looked like

```
[hjp 13:54:05 PGBook]
```

one day at 13:54:05 (so 1:54 p.m.) while he was in the current working directory `PGBook/`. In other words, the prompt appears in `[ ]` with the account name first, then the time (according to a 24-hour clock), and finally the current working directory, with a space after the trailing `]`. To set up this sort of prompt, put the following into the `.bashrc` file:

```
PS1='[\u \t \w] '
```

of your home directory. Here, `\u` indicates the username, `\t` the current time, and `\w` the current working directory. You can find other ways to customize the prompt as well.

Another environment variable you may want to change is the `$PATH`. Suppose you want to add the subdirectory `/directory/path` to the existing path; then the following would work:

```
$ PATH=$PATH\\:/directory/path ; export PATH
```

2.11   Using Other Computers Remotely

Often, you need to use a computer at a remote site, somewhere on a network, or you need to transfer information to that remote computer. Prior to the Internet, this was impossible or difficult to do. Now these tasks are a part of everyday research. Several different programs exist that use GUIs to link computers and to transfer information. Because such programs can be awkward to use when working from the CLUI, we discuss alternatives.

2.11.1   Secure Shell

The command `ssh`, an abbreviation of "secure shell client," allows you to access a remote computer and then to execute commands on it. Suppose you have an account `username` on a computer named `remote` which is at the `university` in the United States, so the last three letters of the URL will be `edu`. If you type the following at the command line:

```
$ ssh username@remote.university.edu
```

then (provided you have an account on this computer) the remote computer
will respond with

```
username@remote.university.edu's password:
```

Enter your password, and you will then be in the home directory on the
remote computer. Note that when you type in the password the terminal window will give no indication that typing has occurred, which some users find
disconcerting.

By default, ssh uses port 22. If that port is blocked (for example, for security
reasons), then you must obviously use another one. Suppose, say, port 40 is
available, then invoke the following:

```
$ ssh -p 40 username@remote.university.edu
```

Internet Protocol Address

An Internet Protocol (IP) address is a numerical label assigned to each device
on a computer network (for example, a computer or a printer) that uses the
Internet Protocol for communication; 128.255.44.253 is an example of such
an IP address. IP addresses serve two main functions: first, to identify the interface for a device; second, to find the address of a device:[8] Because remembering
long strings of digits is difficult for some, IP addresses are typically mapped to
real names (an example of indirection); for instance, at the time of this writing
the preceding IP address was mapped to vinci.cs.uiowa.edu. You can find
the name associated with an IP address using the following command:

```
$ nslookup 128.255.44.253
```

which will query a name server on the Internet and return a name, provided
one has been registered. You can also find the name from the IP address using
the command

```
$ nslookup vinci.cs.uiowa.edu
```

What does this have to do with ssh? You can ssh into an IP address if you
don't know the name of the server, for example,

```
$ ssh username@128.255.44.253
```

---

[8]From http://en.wikipedia.org/wiki/IP_address.

2.11.2   Secure Copy

Suppose that while working on a remote computer you have some work (say, a paper) you would like to copy to your local computer.[9] Use the command `scp`, an abbreviation of "secure copy"; this command copies files between hosts on a network. The `scp` command uses the `ssh` command for data transfer, in other words, the same authentication process, which provides the same security as `ssh`.

To see how `scp` works, assume that the home directory on the remote computer is `/home/username/`, and the file you want on that computer is named `Paper.tex`, but that file lives in the subdirectory `Docs/` of the home directory. To copy this file to `Remote.tex` in the current working directory, invoke the following:

```
$ scp username@remote.university.edu:Docs/Paper.tex Remote.tex
```

Provided you have an account on the remote computer, that computer will respond with

```
username@remote.university.edu's password:
```

Enter your password; if your password is correct, then the task will be completed, and the following will appear in the terminal window:

```
Paper.tex                               100%   61KB    61.2KB/s   00:01
```

Because `ssh` uses port 22 by default, so does `scp`. If that port is blocked, but 40 is open, then

```
$ scp -P 40 username@remote.university.edu:Docs/Paper.tex Remote.tex
```

will work. Note that the flag has an uppercase `P`, unlike `ssh`, which had a lowercase `p`. As mentioned, the terminal window will provide no indication that typing has occurred when you input the password.

You can also do this file transfer in reverse. Suppose `Local.txt` is a file that you would like to place under the filename `Home.copy` in the subdirectory

---

[9]We say "local" here, but both computers could be remote relative to your geographic location. *Local* in this context means the computer on which your shell is running, whereas *remote* means another computer.

`Doc/Backups/` of the home directory on the account `username` on the computer named `remote.university.edu`. Type

```
$ scp Local.txt username@remote.university.edu:Docs/Backup/Home.copy
```

(In this example, port 22 is assumed to be working.)

2.12 Running Long Jobs Remotely

A hallmark of scientific computing is that jobs can take hours or days, even months, to complete. On a desktop computer, you can just leave a terminal window and go about your business using other terminal windows; on a laptop, complications can arise, particularly if you run out of power, but such issues are surmountable by alert planning. When you are working remotely on another server, however, logging out of your user account kills the process unless you do something to prevent that. Because this is a relatively common problem, UNIX has more than one solution.

2.12.1 nohup

The `nohup` command forces the operating system to ignore the hangup signal that is issued when you log out of your user account. For example, suppose you have a program `MLEstimation` that you know will take a long time to complete. You would like to start the program on a remote server using, say, the desktop computer at your office, but then go on vacation. During your vacation, you want to examine interim output using your laptop. What to do?

Initially, assume that within this program you only get input from and direct output to specified files; that is, `stdin`, `stdout`, and `stderr` are not used for either input or output. The following invokes the program so that you can then `exit` the user account:

```
1 $ nohup MLEstimation &
2 $ exit
```

The command in line 1 must always end in the ampersand `&`, which signals to UNIX to *spawn* the process, that is, to create a process separate from the one in the command window. With the command in line 2, you exit the user account. Now, the spawned process runs `MLEstimation` while the original process continues in the terminal window. So far, so good.

Although the `nohup` prevents the process from being halted on logout, if either input or output are received from or directed to `stdin`, `stdout`, or `stderr`, then the spawned process will just hang there because you logged out: no terminal window exists to receive or to direct the input or output. Now what? Formal redirection can solve the problem. For example,

```
$ nohup MLEstimation > MLEstimation.out 2> MLE.err < /dev/null &
$ exit
```

In this case, the output to `stdout` is redirected to `MLEstimation.out`; the file descriptor for `stderr` is 2. Thus, 2 is redirected to `MLE.err`. Input from `stdin` is to be taken from `/dev/null`, which is a *null* device (file) that exists for completeness. Nothing is in `/dev/null`, but it is a formal device that will prevent `MLEstimation` from hanging.

2.12.2 screen

The `nohup` command permits you to run a program persistently, but what if you want to begin a command-line session in a terminal window on one computer, but then go home to resume that session on another computer? The `screen` command is the answer.[10]

To begin, you must first create a named session. For example, by invoking

```
$ screen -S hjp
```

in a terminal window, Paarsch ensures that he will remember the name of that session on the remote computer, so that when he resumes on another computer, he can reattach to the session. First, he would `ssh` into the remote computer, and then he would use

```
$ screen -d -R hjp
```

to resume session `hjp`. Two separate commands are being invoked at this step: with the flag `-d`, the terminal from the initial location is detached, and with the flag `-R`, the current terminal window is reattached to session `hjp`.

The `screen` command permits you to have ten (numbered consecutively from 0 to 9) terminal windows (often called shells) open at the same time, but having too many terminal windows open is really just an invitation to make

---

[10]An alternative to `screen` is `tmux`.

mistakes. Thus, we recommend you have only one or two but never more than three open.

When you begin a new session, you will be in shell 0. To create a new shell, hold down the **control**-A and then type the letter C. That will be shell 1. If you execute the **control**-A C sequence again, you will be in shell 2. To get to a particular shell number (for example, shell 0 when you are in shell 2), simply invoke **control**-A 0.

To get out of the screen command, exit all of the terminal windows (shells) that you started within the command.

What are the virtues of screen over nohup? The command nohup pertains to a process, whereas screen pertains to a terminal window session. In short, screeen is more sophisticated than nohup. One problem you may encounter when using screen is that by default it will not use any aliases you may have defined in, say, .bash_aliases or in .bashrc. The quick solution is to exec bash right after you have invoked screen; the long-run solution is to create a .screenrc file that lives in the home directory in which you make all the relevant definitions.

2.12.3 Being Polite

Often, on remote servers, you may not be the only person using the computer. By default, UNIX provides the highest priority to processes that are spawned from the command line. This means that very long jobs get the same priority as small ones. Common courtesy dictates that you reduce the priority of long jobs. To do this, use the command nice. Thus, when used in conjunction with nohup, you would invoke the following:

```
$ nohup nice MLEstimation &
$ exit
```

You can also use the nice command without nohup. For example,

```
$ nice MLEstimation &
```

In this case, however, if you did exit the user account, the program MLEstimation would be terminated.

2.13   Saving Space

Many computer files that are saved on your hard disk drive are in formats that are wasteful in terms of space. Given the sizes of new hard disk drives, this may not seem like an important problem, but as the sizes of data sets increase, it will become one. Thus, it is useful to know how to save hard disk space.The command `gzip`, invoked as follows,

```
$ gzip BigFile.txt
```

takes `BigFile.txt` as an input and replaces it with `BigFile.txt.gz`, which can be much smaller. For example, the compressed file could be one-tenth the size of the original file. By the way, don't try to look at `BigFile.txt.gz`; it will be unreadable in a terminal window.

The mate of `gzip` is `gunzip`. When this command is invoked as

```
$ gunzip BigFile.txt.gz
```

it will return `BigFile.txt` in its orginal format.

2.14   Archiving Files

At times, you may want to collect files from a particular subdirectory, either to send to a co-worker or to copy to another computer, perhaps using `scp`, or just to maintain a backup of your work. Many tools exist to archive files. We suggest using `zip`, but `tar` or `gzip` are alternatives as well. The `zip` command is portable across a variety of platforms, whereas `tar` may not be. That said, some distributions of Linux have trouble with `.zip` files created on Windows-based computers.

The command `zip` packages and compresses a collection of files. For example, suppose you want to create a backup of all the files in the current working directory, invoking

```
$ zip Backup.zip *
```

will do just that, whereas

```
$ zip -r Backup.zip *
```

will include all files in subdirectories below the current working directory as well: the flag `-r` is an abbreviation of "recursive."

Suppose you have used `scp` to transfer this file to another computer. On that computer, you can `unzip` the files in the current working directory by invoking

```
$ unzip Backup.zip
```

2.15 Version Control

Inevitably, in any research project, you will have to interact with others. Some of those researchers may have good habits; others may not. Although the archiving software `zip` and `tar` permit you to make backups of your work, in projects where several people are working on the same code more or less at the same time, such backups are at best imperfect. Moreover, what do you do when a co-worker has really messed up the most recent program you have been working on, but he has not made backups? In the software industry, such problems surfaced almost immediately, so solutions had to be developed. During the past half century, several procedures were developed to undertake what is collectively referred to as *version control*.

During the past three decades, at least five programs have been popular: the Concurrent Versions System (CVS), also known as the Concurrent Versioning System, a free centralized version control program; Apache Subversion, a free successor to CVS; Perforce, a proprietary centralized version control system; BitKeeper a proprietary distributed version control system; and Git, a free distributed version control system.

Four keywords appear to distinguish the different programs: free versus proprietary and centralized versus distributed. Since we limit our discussion in this book to free software that runs on the three major platforms, that rules out two of the programs. Also, we believe that distributed version control is better than centralized version control because not all eggs are in one basket when distributed version control is used. That leaves us with Git.

Git was initially designed and developed in 2005 by Linus Torvalds, the man who created the Linux kernel.[11] To appreciate the power of Git, you need

---

[11] The kernel contains the core components of the operating system used to manage devices, files, and processes as well as interactions with the network.

to have a context within which to place the tool, so we delay discussing its use until Section 8.9.

2.16   Package Managers

For this book we created a Linux virtual machine on which all the software you will need to undertake the demonstrated code has been installed. The instructions to install the virtual machine are contained in Appendix A. At some point, however, you will need to install software that is not already on your computer or on the virtual machine. At that time, you should learn about package managers, such as MacPorts for Apple computers and `apt-get` for the Ubuntu dialect of Linux.[12]

2.17   UNIX File Systems

Sometimes, it is helpful to know a bit about the UNIX file systems, say, because you need to know where a file or program resides. As mentioned in Section 2.3.10, the root of the UNIX file systems is in the directory `/`. In that directory reside the major subdirectories of the UNIX filesystem, specifically, those documented in Table 2.2. On an Apple Mac, the subdirectory (folder) `Users/` replaces `home/`, and the subdirectories (folders) listed in Table 2.3 also exist.

Back to Filenames

In UNIX a filename uniquely identifies a computer file in a file system. Up to this point, we have used filenames that have a base name, or prefix, such as `paper`, and a suffix, such as `.tex`, as in `paper.tex`. In addition to "extension," sometimes the suffix is known as the "type," or the "format." A filename can include other parts as well. For example, a directory (or path), such as `/Users/hjp/Projects/Auctions/` (see Section 2.3.10) or a hardware device (or drive), such as `/dev/disksda1/` or `/dev/disks1/`, can be part of the filename. In addition, a filename can have a reference to a *host* or a *node* or a *server*, such as the server maintained by Alberto Segre `http://vinci.cs.uiowa.edu`.

---

[12]Another dialect of Linux goes by the name Red Hat; the package manager for Red Hat Linux is `rpm`, which is usually used in conjuction with the front-end `yum`, an acronym for Yellowdog Updater Modified. `yum` is the analog of `apt-get`.

Subdirectory	Description
bin/	abbreviation of *binaries*; contains the important UNIX commands, such as ls
boot/	contains files and programs for booting up your computer
dev/	abbreviations of *devices*; contains files for the definition of peripheral devices, e.g., the terminal, which is /dev/tty
etc/	contains configuration files and system databases
home/	contains the home directories of users
lib/	contains system libraries
media/	default mount point for removable devices, such as a USB stick
mnt/	abbreviation of *mount*; contains the mount points for the filesystems
opt/	contains locally installed software, e.g., R
proc/	virtual filesystem that has information concerning all the UNIX processes in the form of files
root/	home directory of the superuser root
sbin/	abbreviation of *system binaries*
tmp/	abbreviation of *temporary*;place to put temporary files
usr/	originally the directory for containing the home directories of *users*; now contains binary executables, e.g., in /usr/bin/
var/	abbreviation of *variable*; contains files subdirectories related to system logs (log/), mail (mail/), printing (spool/), and temporary files (tmp/)

Table 2.2: Subdirectories of the UNIX Filesystem

Subdirectory (Folder)	Descriptions
`Applications/`	contains application programs, typically those having a graphical user interface
`Developer/`	contains developer tools, if installed
`Library/`	contains primarily user-installed programs
`System/`	contains system programs and parts of the operating system itself
`Volumes/`	contains mounted devices, such as the hard drive

Table 2.3: Additional System Subdirectories—Apple Mac

2.18 Uniform Resource Identifiers

A URI is a very general naming convention. URIs are formed with two parts. The first is the *scheme name*, for example, `http`, followed by a colon `:`, and the remainder is the *scheme-specific part*; this latter part can vary considerably. Sometimes URIs are referred to as protocols, but this is incorrect; *scheme* is the preferred term. For example, the `http` scheme is generally used for interacting with web resources using HyperText Transfer Protocol, hence the `http`, but the scheme can be used with others as well, for instance, the Resource Description Framework (RDF) is a family of World Wide Web Consortium (W3C) specifications currently used.

Perhaps the best-known URI is the uniform resource locator (URL); the URL appears in the navigation window of your browser. Often, people use URI and URL interchangeably, but the latter is a special case of the former. In addition to web pages (`http`), URIs are used for file transfer (`ftp`), email (`mailto`), and many other purposes. In fact, the list has several dozen elements. A common scheme used in the 1990s was `telnet`, but it was replaced by `ssh` because of security issues.

One common but unofficial URI is `doi`, which stands for "digital object identifier." A digital identifier is used for any object of intellectual property, such as a published journal article.

Another unofficial URI is `javascript`, which is used to execute a JavaScript on a website. JavaScript is an interpreted computer programming language, often used in web browsers. In that sense, JavaScript is like Perl, Python, or Ruby. Note that JavaScript is not the programming language Java.[13]

---

[13]From `http://en.wikipedia.org/wiki/Uniform_resource_locator`.

3

Organizing Data

THE MOST COMMON task assigned a research assistant involves organizing information so that it can subsequently be analyzed. Much of the current literature concerning Big Data describes how extant mature methods of organizing information are poorly suited to the new formats and types of data that are arising naturally with increasing frequency and volume in both business and science. We begin this chapter, however, by recommending the spreadsheet as a tried-and-true, mature tool for organizing moderate-size data sets. Then, as the next step up from the spreadsheet, we describe the relational model: data modeling; Codd's relational algebra; SQLite, a dialect of a structured query language; and solving a prototypical research problem using SQLite. In this way, we believe you will learn enough about relational databases (RDBs) to solve other research problems. We also discuss briefly alternative data models that have been used to process the tsunami of new information that is Big Data, specifically, aggregate stores and graph databases.

3.1 Spreadsheet

Currently, perhaps the best-known and most commonly used tool to organize data is the spreadsheet. Microsoft Excel is one implementation of this tool. For moderate-size data sets, that are relatively flat, Excel is the perfect tool. What *flat* means in this context is that the data can be represented in a table, where the columns are typically variables (for example, units sold and sales revenue), and the rows typically represent the observations concerning those variables (for example, week of year). Under this model, when i indexes rows and j indexes columns, cell (i, j) represents the value of variable j for observation i.

Many different operations can be completed using a spreadsheet, so it is impossible to minimize its utility. Without question, since its invention in the 1960s, the spreadsheet has become the main tool of business because it is intuitive as well as easy to use and provides results quickly. The spreadsheet has been adopted as the standard across the world. In short, network externalities exist: if you do not know how to use a spreadsheet program like Excel, then you should learn, soon. The book *Excel 2013 Bible* by Walkenbach (2013) is an excellent manual to use.

For quick one-off analyses of, say, fewer than 1 million observations, you cannot go wrong with a spreadsheet, particularly if the original data have been provided in a comma-separated values file, that is, a file in which each value on each line is separated by a comma; such files usually have the suffix `.csv` on the filename. You simply import the contents of the file into, say, Excel, and it is ready to use.

Often, however, representing data in a flat data file is awkward or impossible. In other cases, you can represent the data easily in a spreadsheet but only with considerable redundancy: the spreadsheet can become large and unwieldy. In such cases, it is often possible to represent the data succinctly as a number of tables, sometimes referred to as *relations*, that are linked by identification numbers, or *keys*. Like the spreadsheet, each row of a table corresponds to an observation, often called a *tuple*, and each column of a table corresponds to a variable, or an *attribute*. As you can see, this collection of tables is a natural extension of the spreadsheet.

Considerable care must be taken when constructing the tables; otherwise you won't be able to manipulate the data contained in the tables efficiently. Also, some sort of logical system is required to structure the process of manipulation. Fortunately, Edgar F. Codd (1972) invented what is now referred to as *Codd's relational algebra* for this exact purpose.[1] How the logical system is constructed is inextricably intertwined with the organization of the tables.

---

[1] For this and other contributions, in 1981, Codd won the A. M. Turing Award, which is presented by the Association for Computing Machinery (ACM) in honor of Alan Turing, a pioneering British mathematician and computer scientist. The Turing award is the ACM's most prestigious technical award; it is given for major contributions of lasting importance to computing. Prior to Codd, in 1973, Charles Bachmann won the Turing Award for his contributions to databases. After Codd, in 1999, Jim Gray won a Turing Award for databases. Clearly, having garnered so much attention, databases are an important part of computer science.

3.2 Data Modeling

A common pedagogical device in teaching is the example. In medicine, when describing how medical students learn a procedure, the mantra is "see one, do one, teach one." We embrace that mantra. Therefore, in this section, we illustrate how to organize data using an example based on a research project that Paarsch began nearly 30 years ago, an empirical analysis of auctions.

Specifically, we imagine a situation in which a government agency sells timber at auction to loggers (harvesters). Beside standing in different locations, the timber is of different species and volumes. The bidders who participate at the auctions differ, too, in where they live, and in, say, a feature determined by the government: some bidders are members of a preferred class.

From this brief description, depending on your experience, you may realize that trying to collect the data for auctions and bidders as well as bids at auctions into a single spreadsheet would involve needless duplication of information. For instance, for each bidder who participated at a given auction, all the features of that auction need to be recorded; in addition, the relevant personal information of that particular bidder must be included. In the example presented here, only a small amount of data is used, so the redundancies are unimportant, but in larger real-world applications redundancies can be crippling.

What you really want to do in this example is to collect the data concerning the auctions in one location. With an eye to future developments, let's refer to that location as a *table*. The data concerning the bidders should be collected in another table, and the data concerning the bids made by bidders at auctions should be collected in yet a third table. Thus, even before contemplating using an RDB to organize these hypothetical data, we have divided them into three different tables. This is quite convenient because the principal organizing device of an RDB is the table, also known as the relation. Our structuring the data in this way was no accident: considerable malice aforethought took place. With time and practice, you will be able to develop this forethought, too.

Analysts often break the task of modeling data into three parts: the conceptual model, the logical model, and the physical model. Let's focus on the conceptual and logical models first. Over time, researchers have developed high-level tools that can be used in modeling data well before an RDB is constructed.

3.2.1 Entity-Relationship Model

One commonly used, high-level approach to modeling data involves using the *entity-relationship* model, or ER model. First proposed by Peter P. S. Chen (1976), this way of modeling data is often described as a top-down approach because you begin with broad divisions among the sorts of information and then become more and more specific as you proceed. Sanders (1995) provided an excellent introduction to data modeling in general and the ER model in particular; many other references exist as well, for example, the book by Garcia-Molina, Ullman, and Widom (2009).

When using the ER model, tables collect data that are related. Diagrammatically, such relationships are depicted by rectangles, perhaps a visual cue that the objects are tables. Variables within a table (for example, the name of a bidder) are depicted as circles, whereas relationships among tables are depicted as diamonds. Lines between the circles, rectangles, and diamonds depict important connections. For example, a line between a circle and a rectangle means that the variable should belong to that table, whereas a line connecting rectangles through a diamond means that the two tables are related in some fashion. Within the circles, rectangles, and diamonds are descriptions.

Thus, in Figure 3.1, which is an *entity-relationship diagram*, or ER diagram, three table rectangles are depicted: one named `Auctions`, another named `Bidders`, and a third named `Bids`—truly a self-describing notation. These three tables are linked together by the diamond marked `Attended`, another example of self-describing notation.

Around each table rectangle are variable circles with names in them. For example, the circles with names `Address`, `Name`, `Preferred`, and `BidderID` are linked to the `Bidders` table. Similarly, linked to the `Auctions` table are the circles with names `Date`, `Location`, `Volume`, and `AuctionID`. Finally, linked to the `Bids` table are the circles with names `Bid`, `BidID`, *AuctionID*, and *BidderID*.

In Figure 3.1, the variable circles `AuctionID`, `BidderID`, and `BidID` are underlined in the tables `Auctions`, `Bidders`, and `Bids`, respectively. Why? In these tables, these `ID` variables identify the data for different auctions, bidders, and bids.

Associated with the `Bids` table are the circled variables *AuctionId* and *BidderId*, which are in a slanted font. Again, why? Because the information

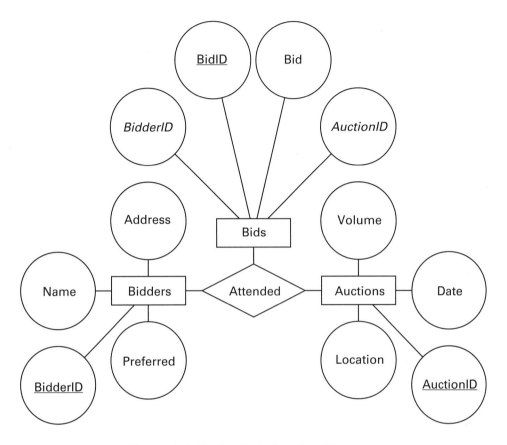

Figure 3.1: Entity-Relationship Diagram

in the `Auctions` and `Bidders` tables needs to be linked to the `Bids` table. The only way to do that is to import the `AuctionID` and `BidderID` variables into that table. You may think that importing the `AuctionID` and `BidderID` variables into the `Bids` table involves considerable redundancy relative to, say, a spreadsheet. In fact, by doing this, we reduce redundancies considerably.

Whereas `AuctionID`, `BidderID`, and `BidID` are the *primary keys* in their respective tables `Auctions`, `Bidders`, and `Bids` because these ID keys are the primary way in which the variables and records are manipulated, in the `Bids` table the variables *AuctionId* and *BidderId* are *foreign keys* because these ID variables are the keys from other tables.

3.2.2 Database Normalization

In contrast to the top-down approach of the ER model is the bottom-up approach of database normalization. Normalization involves organizing the variables and tables of an RDB to minimize redundancies and dependencies.

Usually, under database normalization, you try to divide large tables into smaller ones that have fewer redundant data and then to define relationships among the new tables. Although redundancies are perhaps by now obvious, dependencies may not be.

Another goal of database normalization is to make it easy to add, delete, and modify a variable in just one table, and have that change propagate throughout the remainder of the database using the relationships defined. One of the worst fears of a database administrator is that a change in one table is not propagated throughout. You may have encountered this problem in your own interactions with firms or organizations that maintain databases. For example, you inform the firm or organization of some change, such as a new address, only to find that this change does not appear to have been made. Yet, a representative claims the change has been made. One reason for this could be that your address information exists in two tables, but the information in only one table has been changed. A dependency occurs when information in one table depends on information in other tables. Therefore, data should exist in only one place and then be linked to other tables, for example, by foreign keys. Under this strategy, you only need to make a change in one place.

The inventor of the relational model, Edgar F. Codd, introduced the concept of normalization to eliminate dependencies (see Codd 1970). Normalization has many forms, but the most basic is Codd's *First Normal Form* (1NF). At a minimum, the 1NF requires that each table have a unique key and that no column have a null value (see Date 2012b). A null value is a missing value for a particular record of a column. Also, no duplicate values may occur. In addition, neither a top-to-bottom ordering of the rows nor a left-to-right ordering of the columns may exist under 1NF: the particular order of rows or columns should not matter to the organization of the table. Clearly, it is sometimes impossible to satisfy Codd's requirements; for example, null values arise all the time in business and probably in science, too. Because not satisfying the 1NF can make things a bit more difficult, you just have to be vigilant.

Codd (1972) also defined the *Second Normal Form* (2NF) and *Third Normal Form* (3NF). For a table to satisfy the 2NF, it must first satisfy the 1NF. In addition, each non-key column must depend on the primary key of the table. For a table to satisfy the 3NF, it must first satisfy the 2NF, which means that it also satisfies the 1NF. Also, each non-key column may only depend on the primary key.

Other versions of normalization exist, for example, the *Fourth* and *Fifth* versions, due to Ronald Fagin, and the *Sixth* version, due to Christopher J. Date, Hugh Darwen, and Nikos Lorentzos. Codd and Raymond F. Boyce developed another one, the *Boyce-Codd Normal Form* (BCNF). We do not discuss these because most 3NF tables are typically free of anomalies that can occur when a variable is added, deleted, or modified.

3.3 Relational Algebra

Having described data modeling at a high level, we now outline the elements of the relational algebra (RA) developed by Codd (1970). Although this material concerning Codd's RA may appear a bit abstract, we believe that understanding the theory behind an RDB makes using it easier. Not everyone concurs with this notion. In fact, in many textbooks on RDBs, the RA is not discussed. Thus, depending on how you learn, you may want to skip this section at your first reading of this chapter.

Codd's RA is an abstraction that cannot be used directly on a computer. It has been implemented in a declarative programming language, *Structured Query Language*, or SQL, pronounced "sequel." To read more about this, consider the outstanding book by Garcia-Molina et al. (2009).

Many dialects of SQL exist; two popular free ones are MySQL and PostgreSQL. We have chosen SQLite, another free dialect, to illustrate our examples because SQLite is easy to install and is also included as a module of Python, the modern programming language introduced in Chapter 4. In addition, SQLite plays well with R, a programming language and software environment for statistical computing and graphics introduced in Chapter 5.

In Section 3.4 we demonstrate various concepts from Codd's RA using commands from SQLite. To cement the concepts of Codd's RA and the commands from SQLite, we then illustrate how to use an RDB to organize data from a real-world research project, the example discussed in Section 3.2. Finally, in the last section of this chapter, we discuss alternatives to the relational model that are broadly collected under the term *NoSQL*.

Codd's RA is built on sound mathematical foundations: set theory and predicate logic. At the heart of Codd's RA are two fundamental concepts, relation and tuple. Formally, a tuple is a set of (attribute, value) pairs, where each attribute has a known predefined data type, and corresponding values that respect the constraints of that data type.

What is a data type? In computer science different types of information exist. The most primitive data type is the *logical* data type, sometimes referred to as a *Boolean*, which can take on either the value 0 (for false) or the value 1 (for true), except in SQL, where it can take the value "unknown" as well. The next most complicated data type is the *integer*, followed by the *real* data type (sometimes called *floating point*), and the *character* data type (sometimes called *string*).

Thus, (Name, "John") is an example of an (attribute, value) pair where Name is the attribute, having data type CHAR, an abbreviation of CHARACTER, and "John" is the value. On a computer, "John" is a character (string) variable. Such a distinction is important because RDBs use the data type of a variable to conduct a variety of consistency checks when performing operations. In general, tuples may contain many such pairs that are stored in no particular order.

A relation is a set of tuples that share the same attributes and the same number of pairs of each tuple. For instance, the pair of tuples [(Name, "John"); (Name, "Jane")] is a relation, whereas a pair such as [(Name, "John"); (Gender, "Male")] is not—it is an example of a single tuple with two (attribute, value) pairs. On the other hand, this is a relation:

$$[((Name, "John"), (Gender, "Male"));$$
$$((Name, "Jane"), (Gender, "Female"))]$$

In the previous section, we suggested that you think of tables as relations in a database and tuples as records in those tables. Strictly speaking, this is inaccurate because database tables can contain duplicate rows, whereas within Codd's RA a relation does not admit identical tuples: duplicates in a set are ignored, essentially dropped. Similarly, whereas tuples are really *sets*, in the mathematical sense, that is, collections of unordered elements, the columns of most RDBs are ordered. Consequently, an important practical difference exists between Codd's RA and how that RA is implemented on a computer. Bear these facts in mind as we proceed.

Having introduced the core objects of Codd's RA, the next step, as in mathematics, is to define operations that can be used to manipulate those objects to achieve a particular purpose. The first key property, central to all subsequent operations, is referred to as *closure*. In mathematics a set is said to have closure under a particular operation defined on the members of the set when that operation always produces a member of the same set. For instance, the set of integers is closed under addition, multiplication, and subtraction because any of these three operations when applied to two integers in the set yields another integer in the set. Integers are not closed under division: 5 divided by 3 is not in the set of integers.

All primitive operations in Codd's RA have closure over relations. It is precisely this fact that makes Codd's RA so useful in practice. SQLs are internally consistent because Codd's RA is mathematically sound.

Although some disagreement exists concerning the number of operations defined under Codd's RA, we consider the following primitive operations:[2]

- Restriction, commonly denoted σ

- Projection, commonly denoted π

- Join, which has several distinct subtypes, and is commonly denoted $\bowtie$

- Cartesian product, commonly denoted $\times$

- Union, intersection, and difference, commonly denoted $\cup$, $\cap$, and $-$, respectively

In some books concerning relational algebra, restriction is also referred to as *selection*, which is indeed unfortunate because in SQL the keyword SELECT is actually synonymous with projection. In any case, borrowing from Date (2012b, 9), we depict restriction and projection in Figure 3.2.

When the restriction operator σ is applied to a relation, another relation is returned, one in which all tuples satisfy a particular condition. For example, consider a list of your contacts, denoted by R. In the relation R, every tuple corresponds to a single person. To see how restriction works, apply the operator

---

[2]Many of the differences in definitions are of little relevance to the novice user. For those interested in a deeper understanding of Codd's RA, consider reading Garcia-Molina et al. (2009) and the books by Date (2012a,b).

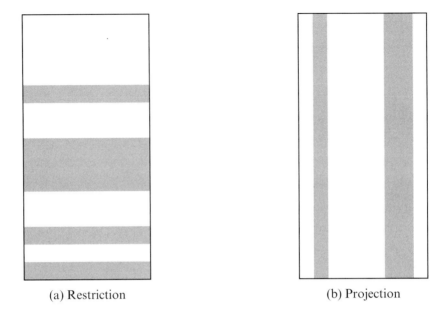

(a) Restriction   (b) Projection

Figure 3.2: Restriction and Projection

to choose only the males from your list of contacts, which would be written formally as

$$\sigma_{\texttt{Gender=Male}} \left(\texttt{R} \right).$$

Thus, in Panel (a) of Figure 3.2, only the rows having `Gender=Male` are chosen.

When the projection operator π is applied to a relation, another relation is returned, one in which every tuple contains only a particular set of attributes. For example, if you only wanted the names and personal email addresses of your contacts, instead of all the other information, this would be written formally as

$$\pi_{\texttt{Name,Personal Email}} \left(\texttt{R} \right).$$

Thus, in Panel (b) of Figure 3.2, only the columns for `Name` and `Person Email` are chosen.

When the join operator $\bowtie$ is applied to two relations, another relation is returned, one in which tuples are combined according to a set of criteria. The exact criteria applied are usually determined by the type of join, of which three exist: the *natural join*, the *Cartesian product* and the *theta join*. The natural join is depicted in Figure 3.3, and the Cartesian product is depicted in Figure 3.4.

a1	b1
a2	b1
a3	b3

(a) Left table

b1	c1
b2	c2
b3	c3

(b) Right table

a1	b1	c1
a2	b1	c1
a3	b3	c3

(c) Join

Figure 3.3: Natural Join of Two Tables

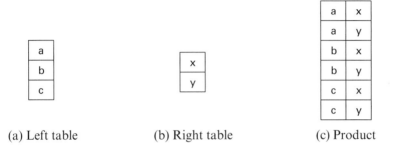

a
b
c

(a) Left table

x
y

(b) Right table

a	x
a	y
b	x
b	y
c	x
c	y

(c) Product

Figure 3.4: Cartesian Product of Two Tables

Because the theta join has four possibilities, it is illustrated later in the chapter. Despite this abundance of choice among joins, only one is widely used in practice—the theta join.

To understand why the theta join is such an important operation, you must understand what the alternatives do. To this end, consider the natural join between the relations R_1 and R_2, which is a relation R_3 having the following properties:

- Each tuple in R_3 contains all the attributes from tuples in both R_1 and R_2.

- Tuples with different values of the attributes that are common to both R_1 and R_2 are eliminated.

At this point, an example may be helpful. Suppose R_1 is your list of personal contacts, and R_2 is your list of business contacts. For simplicity, assume that both R_1 and R_2 have two tuples each, where each tuple has only two attributes:

```
R₁ ≡ [ (Name, "John Smith"), (Home Phone, 555-1234);
       (Name, "Jane Brown"), (Home Phone, 555-7890) ]
```

and

```
R₂ ≡ [ (Name, "John Smith"), (Work Phone, 888-4321);
       (Name, "Roger White"), (Work Phone, 888-0987) ].
```

Then

```
R₃ ≡ R₁ ⋈ R₂
   = [ (Name, "John Smith"), (Home Phone, 555-1234),
       (Work Phone, 888-4321) ].
```

The natural join operation automatically identifies common attributes across tuples that are to be joined and also eliminates tuples from either R_1 or R_2 for which corresponding tuples in R_2 or R_1, respectively, do not exist. In this example, R_3 has no tuples with Name equal to "Jane Brown" or "Roger White". Only some dialects of SQL support natural joins. In our experience, the natural join is not an operation that is used often in practice, mostly because the theta join can do all that the natural join does, and more.

$R_1 \times R_2$, the Cartesian product between relations R_1 and R_2, is a relation R_3 that contains every possible pairwise combination of tuples from R_1 and R_2. This is depicted in Figure 3.4.

The Cartesian product is the most primitive form of a join in the sense that you can express the other types of joins using a sequence of restrictions and projections applied to a Cartesian product. For instance, you could obtain the output of a natural join by first performing a Cartesian product, then restricting the output to include only those tuples having identical values of common attributes, and last, projecting only nonduplicate attributes of the final output.

In practice, experienced SQL users counsel against using Cartesian products. Why? Suppose that R_1 contains n_1 tuples, each with k_1 attributes, whereas R_2 contains n_2 tuples with k_2 attributes in each: R_3 will contain $(n_1 \times n_2)$ tuples with $(k_1 + k_2)$ attributes in each tuple. If both n_1 and n_2 are sufficiently large, then $(n_1 \times n_2)$ will be too large for all practical purposes. That said, Cartesian products are unavoidable in some applications.

$R_1 \bowtie_\theta R_2$, the theta join between relations R_1 and R_2, is a relation R_3 that results from the restriction θ having been applied to the output of a Cartesian product $R_1 \times R_2$. The logic behind a theta join can be expressed formally in two ways—first, using restriction on the Cartesian product

$$R_3 \equiv R_1 \bowtie_\theta R_2 \equiv \sigma_\theta \left(R_1 \times R_2 \right).$$

Given what we said about Cartesian products, why is the theta join the most commonly used join operation?

Let's revisit the simple example where R_1 and R_2 are lists of personal and business contacts. Consider a second way in which to represent a theta join. Combining these two relations involved a natural join. The same result obtains under a theta join:

$$R_3 \equiv \sigma_{R_1.\texttt{Name}=R_2.\texttt{Name}} \left(R_1 \times R_2 \right).$$

In this notation, $R_1.\texttt{Name}$ and $R_2.\texttt{Name}$ denote that `Name` is a variable in both relation R_1 and relation R_2. This example of a theta join is commonly referred to as an *equi-join* because the restriction θ requires values of certain attributes to be equal in joined relations.

In practice, four different types of theta joins exist; each operates in exactly the same fashion but differs in its treatment of tuples with nonmatching values of common attributes. Because these theta joins involve `NULL` values, a concept not defined within Codd's RA, we postpone discussing theta joins to Section 3.5.

The *union, intersection*, and *difference* operations are only well-defined for a pair of relations R_1 and R_2 that have identical sets of attributes in each tuple. These operations are shown in Figures 3.5, 3.6, and 3.7. If you are familiar with basic set operations from mathematics, and Venn diagrams in particular, these relational algebraic operations perform as you would expect. Specifically,

- $R_3 \equiv R_1 \cup R_2$ will yield all tuples present in either R_1 or R_2 (recall that in Codd's RA, relations are not permitted to have duplicates);

- $R_3 \equiv R_1 \cap R_2$ will yield all tuples present in both R_1 and R_2;

- $R_3 \equiv R_1 - R_2$ will yield all tuples present in R_1, but absent in R_2.

Clearly, $R_1 \cup R_2 = R_2 \cup R_1$ and $R_1 \cap R_2 = R_2 \cap R_1$, but $R_1 - R_2 \neq R_2 - R_1$.

A *rename* operation also exists, commonly denoted ρ. Sources disagree as to whether rename is a primitive RA operation. The rename operation replaces the name of an attribute for all tuples in a relation. We mention it because relations are closed under this operation as well.

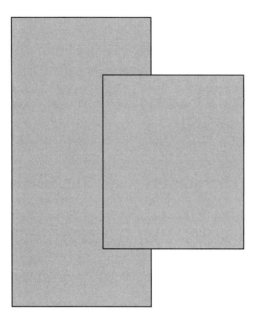

Figure 3.5: Union

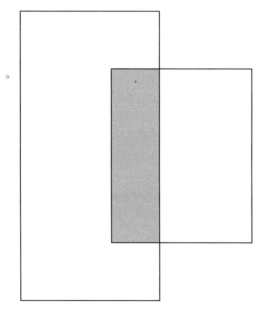

Figure 3.6: Intersection

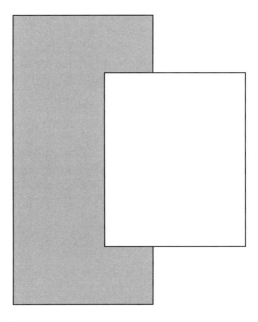

Figure 3.7: Difference

This description of Codd's RA is incomplete. In fact, you could take entire courses at the undergraduate and graduate level concerning the topic. We have introduced some of its operations to indicate that dialects of SQL based on Codd's RA have an internal logic that is incredibly powerful. Thus, you can use SQLite as a tool to implement very complex expressions and have faith that the results will be logically valid.

3.4 Basic SQL

In this section, we demonstrate how to implement some of the operations defined under Codd's RA using SQL. The difference between Codd's RA and a dialect of SQL is similar to the difference between linear algebra and a computer language in which you can do linear algebra, such as MATLAB. In fact, Codd's RA is to a dialect of SQL what linear algebra is to MATLAB. Octave and Scilab are other implementations of languages in which to perform linear algebra. Thus, you can think of different dialects of SQL in the same way as you think of MATLAB, Octave, and Scilab.

We have chosen the SQLite dialect of SQL for several reasons: first, it is free; second, unlike MySQL and PostgreSQL, SQLite requires little or no knowledge of system administration to install—simply place the executable in a pathed subdirectory, and you are done; and third, SQLite commands can be invoked from within Python scripts by importing the `sqlite3` module as an application programming interface (API), and you can query SQLite databases from R.

Committees have attempted to impose standards on SQL, but most vendors deviate in small ways from those standards. Also, not all implementations of Codd's RA do everything. For example, SQLite has omitted some common features of SQLs, most notably the `FULL OUTER JOIN` and the `RIGHT OUTER JOIN`.[3] By changing the table order, the `RIGHT OUTER JOIN` can be implemented as a `LEFT OUTER JOIN`, so that is not a real limitation.

SQLite has two types of commands: native SQL commands and those specific to SQLite. The commands specific to SQLite begin with a dot, which is why they are sometimes referred to as *dot-command*s. Dot-commands must begin in the first space of a line and be entirely contained on that single input line. In addition, dot-commands may not be included in an ordinary SQL command.

To illustrate how you might use a dot-command, suppose that the database `SampleDataBase.db` lives in the current working directory and you have invoked the following:

```
$ sqlite3 SampleDataBase.db
```

Something like the following will result:

```
SQLite version 3.8.1 2013-10-17 12:57:35
Enter ".help" for instructions
Enter SQL statements terminated with a ";"
sqlite>
```

The exact output will depend on your installation of `sqlite3`. If you type `.tables` at the SQLite prompt `sqlite>`, then you will see

```
sqlite> .tables
sqlite>
sqlite> .exit
$
```

---

[3]In the past, the `FULL OUTER JOIN` was uncommon. In the Big Data era, however, it is becoming more and more common, so the absence of this feature may be a problem.

namely, nothing. No tables exist yet in the `SampleDataBase.db`. We are going to populate the `SampleDataBase.db` with data concerning two tables we have named `FirstTable` and `SecondTable`. Either `.quit` or `.exit` will allow you to quit or exit SQLite and return to the terminal window with the command-line prompt `$`, as is illustrated by the preceding `.exit` dot-command.

If you type `.help` at the SQLite prompt `sqlite>`, you will see all the SQLite dot-commands, some 28 of them. Table 3.1 shows all the dot-commands.

The names of the commands are relatively self-describing. Abstracting from `.help` as well as `.quit` and `.exit`, in order of importance, we find the following to be useful:

`.tables`—what tables are available

`.schema`—what is the structure of the tables

`.read FILENAME`—read in commands from a file

`.import FILE TABLE`—import raw data into a table

`.mode MODE ?TABLE?`—what mode should output take

`.separator STRING`—symbol to separate variables in output

`.output FILENAME`—where to direct data to an output file

`.backup ?DB? FILENAME`—backup a database to a file

We illustrate some of the other commands in Section 3.5.

Because dozens of SQL keywords exist, and many other commands as well, we do not have a similar table for them. Instead, we recommend you consult the SQLite web page (which you can find by searching for `sqlite commands`) or read a book on SQLite, such as the one by Kreibich (2010).

As a stylistic convention, we represent the SQL commands in uppercase letters and SQLite dot-commands in lowercase letters preceded by a dot.

You can work on a SQLite database interactively or using command files. We recommend that you use command files. To illustrate why, we first work interactively.

We create two tables (`FirstTable` and `SecondTable`) in the SQLite database `SampleDataBase`. The first table has three variables—`KeyID` (the

sqlite3 Command	What It Does
.backup ?DB? FILE	backup DB (default "main") to FILE
.bail ON|OFF	stop after hitting an error (default OFF)
.databases	list names and files of attached databases
.dump ?TABLE? ...	dump the database in an SQL text format
.echo ON|OFF	turn command echo on or off
.exit	exit this program
.explain ON|OFF	turn output mode suitable for EXPLAIN on or off
.genfkey ?OPTIONS?	options are
	-no-drop—do not drop old fkey triggers
	-ignore-errors—ignore tables with fkey errors
	-exec—execute generated SQL immediately
.header(s) ON|OFF	turn display of headers on or off
.help	show this message
.import FILE TABLE	import data from FILE into TABLE
.indices TABLE	show names of all indices in TABLE
.iotrace FILE	Enable I/O diagnostic logging to FILE
.load FILE ?ENTRY?	Load an extension library
.mode MODE ?TABLE?	Set output mode where MODE is one of
	csv—comma-separated values
	column—left-aligned columns, see .width
	html—HTML \<table> code
	insert—SQL insert statements for TABLE
	line—one value per line
	list—values delimited by .separator string
	tabs—tab-separated values
	tcl—TCL list elements
.nullvalue STRING	print STRING in place of NULL values
.output FILENAME	send output to FILENAME
.output stdout	send output to the screen
.prompt MAIN CONTINUE	replace the standard prompts
.quit	exit this program
.read FILENAME	execute SQL in FILENAME
.restore ?DB? FILE	restore content of DB (default "main") from FILE
.schema ?TABLE?	show the CREATE statements
.separator STRING	change separator used by output mode and .import
.show	show the current values for various settings
.tables ?PATTERN?	list names of tables matching a LIKE pattern
.timeout MS	try opening locked tables for MS milliseconds
.timer ON|OFF	turn the CPU timer measurement on or off
.width NUM NUM ...	set column widths for "column" mode

Table 3.1: SQLite Commands

primary key), Date, and Name—and the second table has three variables—KeyID (the primary key), OtherID (the foreign key), Name. We use the CREATE TABLE command to create the tables and then the INSERT INTO command to put the relevant data into each table. Subsequently, we use the trio of keywords SELECT ... FROM ... WHERE ... to implement a theta join.

```
$ sqlite3 SampleDataBase.db
SQLite version 3.8.1 2013-10-17 12:57:35
Enter ".help" for instructions
Enter SQL statements terminated with a ";"
sqlite> CREATE TABLE FirstTable (
   ...> KeyID         INTEGER NOT NULL ,
   ...> Date          TEXT NOT NULL ,
   ...> Name          TEXT NOT NULL ,
   ...> PRIMARY KEY (KeyID)
   ...> );
sqlite> .schema
CREATE TABLE FirstTable (
KeyID         INTEGER PRIMARY KEY ,
Date          TEXT NOT NULL ,
Name          TEXT NOT NULL ,
PRIMARY KEY      (KeyID)
);
sqlite> INSERT INTO FirstTable(KeyID, Date, Name)
   ...> VALUES(1, "20131204", "Harry J. Paarsch");
sqlite> INSERT INTO FirstTable(KeyID, Date, Name)
   ...> VALUES(2, "20131204", "Konstantin Golyaev");
sqlite> INSERT INTO FirstTable(KeyID, Date, Name)
   ...> VALUES(3, "20131204", "Alberto M. Segre");
sqlite> CREATE TABLE SecondTable (
   ...> KeyID         INTEGER PRIMARY KEY ,
   ...> OtherID       INTEGER PRIMARY KEY ,
   ...> Name          TEXT NOT NULL ,
   ...> FOREIGN KEY (OtherID) REFERENCES FirstTable (KeyID) ,
   ...> PRIMARY KEY (KeyID)
   ...> );
sqlite> INSERT INTO SecondTable(KeyID, OtherID, Name)
   ...> VALUES(101, 1, "Harry J. Paarsch");
sqlite> INSERT INTO SecondTable(KeyID, OtherID, Name)
   ...> VALUES(102, 2, "Konstantin Golyaev");
sqlite> .tables
FirstTable    SecondTable
sqlite> .schema
CREATE TABLE FirstTable (
```

```
KeyID         INTEGER NOT NULL ,
Date          TEXT NOT NULL ,
Name          TEXT NOT NULL ,
PRIMARY KEY   (KeyID)
);
CREATE TABLE SecondTable (
KeyID         INTEGER NOT NULL ,
Name          TEXT NOT NULL ,
FOREIGN KEY   (OtherID) REFERENCES FirstTable (KeyID) ,
PRIMARY KEY   (KeyID)

);
sqlite> SELECT * FROM FirstTable;
1|20131204|Harry J. Paarsch
2|20131204|Konstantin Golyaev
3|20131204|Alberto M. Segre
sqlite> SELECT * FROM SecondTable;
101|1|Harry J. Paarsch
102|2|Konstantin Golyaev
sqlite> SELECT FirstTable.KeyID ,
   ...>         SecondTable.KeyID ,
   ...>         FirstTable.Name
   ...> FROM   FirstTable, SecondTable
   ...> WHERE (FirstTable.Name  = SecondTable.Name)
   ...> AND   (FirstTable.KeyID = SecondTable.OtherID);
1|101|Harry J. Paarsch
2|102|Konstantin Golyaev
sqlite>
```

By illustrating how painful it is to build a SQLite database interactively, we hope to have convinced you to use the command-file approach. Another virtue of using a command file to create and use a SQLite database is that a lasting record of your work exists, which you can subsequently check to ensure that you did what you had intended. A command file also provides those who follow you with a blueprint of what has been done. To this end, we list three SQL scripts that would carry out the preceding tasks.

```
CREATE TABLE FirstTable (
KeyID         INTEGER NOT NULL ,
Date          TEXT NOT NULL ,
Name          TEXT NOT NULL ,
PRIMARY KEY   (KeyID)
);
```

```
INSERT INTO FirstTable(KeyID, Date, Name)
        VALUES(1, "20131204", "Harry J. Paarsch");
INSERT INTO FirstTable(KeyID, Date, Name)
        VALUES(2, "20131204", "Konstantin Golyaev");
INSERT INTO FirstTable(KeyID, Date, Name)
        VALUES(3, "20131204", "Alberto M. Segre");
```

Listing 3.1: SQL Commands to Construct `FirstTable`

```
CREATE TABLE SecondTable (
KeyID        INTEGER NOT NULL ,
OtherID      INTEGER NOT NULL ,
Name         TEXT NOT NULL ,
FOREIGN KEY  (OtherID) REFERENCES FirstTable (KeyID) ,
PRIMARY KEY  (KeyID)
);
INSERT INTO SecondTable(KeyID, OtherID, Name)
        VALUES(101, 1, "Harry J. Paarsch");
INSERT INTO SecondTable(KeyID, OtherID, Name)
        VALUES(102, 2, "Konstantin Golyaev");
```

Listing 3.2: SQL Commands to Construct `SecondTable`

```
.separator ,
.mode csv
.output ExampleThetaJoin.csv
SELECT FirstTable.KeyID ,
       SecondTable.KeyID ,
       FirstTable.Name
FROM   FirstTable,
       SecondTable
WHERE  (FirstTable.Name  = SecondTable.Name)
AND    (FirstTable.KeyID = SecondTable.OtherID);
```

Listing 3.3: SQL and SQLite Commands to Execute Theta Join

Within the interactive window of SQLite, at the `sqlite>` prompt, type the following:

```
sqlite> .read FirstTable.sql
sqlite> .read SecondTable.sql
sqlite> .tables
FirstTable    SecondTable
sqlite> .schema
```

```
CREATE TABLE FirstTable(
KeyID        INTEGER NOT NULL ,
Date         TEXT NOT NULL ,
Name         TEXT NOT NULL,
PRIMARY KEY  (KeyID)
);
CREATE TABLE SecondTable(
KeyID        INTEGER NOT NULL ,
OtherID      INTEGER NOT NULL ,
Name         TEXT NOT NULL ,
FOREIGN KEY  (OtherID) REFERENCES FirstTable (KeyID) ,
PRIMARY KEY  (KeyID)
);
sqlite> .read ExampleThetaJoin.sql

sqlite>
```

Now, if you simply type `more ExampleThetaJoin.csv` in a terminal window, you will see the following:

```
1,101,"Harry J. Paarsch"
2,102,"Konstantin Golyaev"
```

Listing 3.4: Example csv Output of Theta Join

As you can see, no more typing is really involved in the command-file approach than in the interactive approach. In fact, if you are not an accurate or a fast typist, the command-file approach is the most efficient way to proceed. In Section 4.8.7, we present a short Python script to import the `sqlite3` module and do a similar task, the example from Sections 3.2 and 3.5.

3.5 Solved Example

We now return to the example introduced in Section 3.2. Here, we assume that you have access to the Microsoft spreadsheet Excel or a similar tool and that you know how to use it.

In this example, we imagine that you are trying to decide whether a particular auction format in conjunction with a specific pricing rule is working well. Suppose the data concern first-price, sealed-bid auctions of timber, so the auction format is *sealed-bid*, and the pricing rule is *pay-your-bid*, that is, the highest bidder is the winner, and he pays what he bid.

Here, we are deliberately vague concerning what *well* means, choosing instead to focus on the set of tasks you would need to complete in order to get to that point. McMillan (2002) described issues of market design in general, while Timothy Hubbard and Paarsch (2015) provided a brief introduction to auctions for laypeople specifically. At a high level, this example will guide you through the steps necessary to create the data required to make a nontrivial business decision. In short, the data set created will allow you to answer such questions as, What are the average revenues garnered? How do average revenues vary with actual competition, species composition, and scalable volume? Of course, at this scale, you could do this with a spreadsheet. The difference is that the RDB allows you to scale up relatively easily. In addition, an RDB allows you to slice and dice the data in ways that would be awkward or impossible with a spreadsheet.

3.5.1 Designing Databases and Tables

Before constructing the RDB, thinking a bit about how that database will be employed can be helpful. In fact, we introduced the ER diagram and discussed database normalization in Section 3.2 because we hoped that you would start plotting how to proceed: strategic forethought can make a world of difference in the performance of an RDB once it is in use. Because the present example is just a toy, the benefits of forethought will not be as apparent, but we assure you that in larger applications, such forethought can deliver considerable efficiency.

Before continuing, let's recap from Section 3.2. We imagine that the standing timber is sold at auction in different locations and that the bidders also live in different places. The timber on each tract for sale is of different volumes but may also have different species compositions and reserve prices. Thus, you would like to leave the door open to add new data should that become possible.

In this example, three kinds of information are important. The first kind of information concerns the auctions. Such information includes when the auction was held (`Date` in Figure 3.1), how much timber was sold (`Volume`), and where that timber is being sold (`Location`) but could also include the species composition and the reserve price, the minimum price that must be bid. A second kind of information concerns the bidders: name, address, telephone number, email address, but also other properties, for example, whether the bidder was a preferred participant. The third kind of information concerns the bids tendered by the participants at each auction: auction identifier, bidder name, bid tendered, and so forth. In order to reduce redundancies of information when constructing an RDB, we organized each type of information in its own table (see Section 3.2).

We use `AuctionsDataBase` a self-describing name for the database. Under the self-describing convention, the table concerning the auctions is named `Auctions`, the table concerning the bidders `Bidders`, and the table concerning the bids `Bids`.

In the `Auctions` table, the primary key will be some sort of auction identifier, such as `AuctionID`, whereas in the `Bidders` table, the primary key will be a bidder identifier, such as `BidderID`. How should `AuctionID` and `BidderID` be determined? You might think it natural to start at 1 and then increment by 1, but if the database is large, this could be inefficient. Some data engineers assign primary keys at random, without replacement, from a set of integers: randomization can reduce average access time. In our toy example, and in most applications with under, say, 1 million records, the obvious approach (starting at 1) will not seriously degrade performance.

What about the `Bids` table? What should the primary key be? Because the `Bids` table will likely be linked to both the `Auctions` and the `Bidders` tables, neither of those keys can be used. In short, an alternative key, say `BidID`, needs to be created for the primary key, even though this primary key will likely never be used. Thus, even before a database is created, the layout of each table is quite clear, having the structure depicted in Table 3.2.

3.5.2   Using Excel to Create Tables for SQLite

We imagine that you have created spreadsheets of data using a tool like Microsoft Excel. Thus, the first spreadsheet, which has the filename `Auction-sTable.xlsx`, has four columns. The first row of each column includes the names `AuctionID`, `Volume`, `District`, and `Date`. The `A2` cell then contains the auction identifier for the first auction, the `B2` cell contains the volume of timber for sale at that auction, the `C2` cell contains the district code for the location of the first auction, and the `D2` cell contains the date of the first auction. The rows of the spreadsheet will look like those depicted in Table 3.3.

Similar spreadsheets having names like `BiddersTable.xlsx` and `Bid-sTable.xlsx` can be created in a straightforward way. The data concerning this example as well as the others in this book can be found on the `.ova` of the virtual machine; the link to the `.ova` is provided in Appendix A. We do

Auctions	Bidders	Bids
AuctionID	BidderID	BidID
Volume	FirstName	AuctionID
District	LastName	BidderID
Date	Address1	Bid
	Address2	
	Town	
	Province	
	PostalCode	
	Telephone	
	Email	
	Preferred	

Table 3.2: Tables and Variables in `AuctionsDataBase`

	A	B	C	D
1	AuctionID	Volume	District	Date
2	1	1234	1	20111003
3	2	345	3	20111107
4	3	2346	2	20111205
5	4	1278	4	20120109
6	5	789	7	20120206
7	6	934	6	20120305
8	7	269	9	20120402
9	8	357	8	20120507
10	9	1503	4	20120604
11	10	239	7	20120709

Table 3.3: Excel Spreadsheet `AuctionsTable.xlsx`

not provide the programs because we believe that it is an important part of the learning process for you to type those in yourself, encountering errors and making corrections to those errors.

Now, the Excel format is not always seamlessly readable by other programs, so researchers often export the contents of Excel spreadsheets into other formats. The most common format is the csv format, which is a file with entries separated by commas; the suffix `.csv` on a filename is an abbreviation of "comma-separated values." To create csv data files, do the following. While in Excel, go to the `File` tab and then to the `Save As` option. Then scroll down through the options until you see `Windows Comma Separated Values (.csv)`, and click on `Save`. The file `AuctionsTable.csv` should appear in that subdirectory. You can view the first ten lines by invoking `more AuctionsTable.csv`, which will yield the following:[4]

```
1,1234,1,20111003
2,345,3,20111107
3,2346,2,20111205
4,1278,4,20120109
5,789,7,20120206
6,934,6,20120305
7,269,9,20120402
8,357,8,20120507
9,1503,4,20120604
10,239,7,20120709
```

Listing 3.5: Sample `AuctionsTable.csv`

3.5.3 Creating a SQLite Database and Its Tables

Three steps are required: creating database `AuctionsDataBase`; creating tables `Auctions`, `Bidders`, and `Bids` as well as defining the variables within those tables; and reading in the data from the `.csv` files that were created using Excel.

Collecting all the commands for these three steps into a file having a self-describing name like `CreateAuctionsDataBase.sql` is our recommended approach. Loading data from a file into a SQLite database programmatically can, however, be somewhat tedious: you must insert each observation into the database one record at a time. This can become prohibitively time-consuming if the data set is large; even if the data set is small, the process can be error prone. In Chapter 4 we demonstrate how to automate such tasks using Python. Here, we demonstrate how to accomplish this using the built-in SQLite dot-commands. As mentioned, we believe it is good programming practice to

---

[4]Careful readers may notice that we have deleted the header row from the csv file. This can be accomplished either via Excel, or, in UNIX via the command `sed -i "" '1d' AuctionsTable.csv`. The `-i ""` flag means "edit current file and do not back up the original, and the '1d' command instructs `sed` to remove the first line in the file.

create command files rather than working interactively because command files represent lasting records of your work. You can share command files with others, for example, co-authors, and you can also double-check a command file to ensure that you did what you wanted to do. Also, we recommend that you introduce comments, which will be helpful should you ever need to revisit the project. If you are a research assistant, these comments will be extremely valuable to those who succeed you on a project.

To create a SQLite database, invoke the following command:

```
$ sqlite3 AuctionsDataBase.db
```

where the database `AuctionsDataBase.db` is an input to SQLite. By invoking this command, you are asking the SQLite database engine to create the `AuctionsDataBase` database and make it available. Any changes you make to the database will automatically be saved to the file `Auctions-DataBase.db`, which lives in the subdirectory you were in when you invoked SQLite on the command line.

Note again the self-describing name `AuctionsDataBase`: Inexperienced SQLite programmers often use uninformative names or ones that do not admit distinction; for example, `MyRDB` is really not helpful unless you just have one database.

Unlike most other modern programming languages, SQLs in general and SQLite in particular are case insensitive. Depending on the settings, the `AuctionsDataBase` name may be represented internally either as `auctions-database` or as `AUCTIONSDATABASE`.

Having created the database `AuctionsDataBase`, we may now populate it with tables. The first table we create and for which we define variables is `Auctions`. The following SQLite code does this. Note that the text between /* and */ represents comments and is not executed.

```
 1  /*
 2      Create Auctions table with variables:  AuctionID, Volume,
 3      District, and Date.  The Primary Key is AuctionID.
 4  */
 5
 6  CREATE TABLE Auctions
 7  (
 8  AuctionID    INTEGER ,
 9  Volume       INTEGER NOT NULL ,
10  District     INTEGER NOT NULL ,
```

```
11 | Date            TEXT NOT NULL ,
12 | PRIMARY KEY (AuctionID)
13 | );
```

In the first executable statement, line 6, the `Auctions` table is created, and in line 7 an open parenthesis signals to SQLite that the variable definitions will begin; this is referred to as the *schema*. You do not need to put the lead parenthesis (on a separate line; that is a stylistic convention. In line 8 the variable `AuctionID` is defined to be an integer. It is used to save space and to increase the absolute value of the number.

Defining a variable's type as well as its domain may appear excessively pedantic, but it is always better to be more specific about what the variables will be than to use the default definition SQLite imposes. In fact, the more structure you impose at this stage, the more likely that the computer will be able to check for the logical consistency of the data you enter into the RDB; that is the virtue of a SQL schema. SQLite is generally very forgiving to poorly specified variable types, but most SQL implementations are not, and thus we encourage you to develop proper habits early on. The term `NOT NULL` means a value is required; when a value is required, it is better to let SQLite enforce this constraint. The constraint becomes increasingly difficult to enforce, however, when dealing with large data sets. If a data set is large, it is often better to relax the `NOT NULL` restriction so that you can then load and inspect the data. A primary key designation, however, implies `NOT NULL`.

Lines 9 and 10 define the variables `Volume` and `District`, which are also integers, that cannot be empty, `NULL`. Line 11 defines the `Date` variable, which contains date information, but we elect to store it as text instead. This is because SQLite does not have a built-in storage type for dates. We will have to transform its contents under the hood into a date object to use the SQLite date routines. In line 12 `AuctionID` is defined formally as the primary key of the table. The last line, line 13, contains a closing parenthesis followed by a semicolon; the closing parenthesis ends the definition of variables in the table, and the semicolon ends the command. Note that we have left a space before the commas at the end of lines; this, too, is a stylistic convention that helps the reader ascertain quickly that the commas are where they must be.

Some SQL programmers have strong feelings about where to place commas in the code. Because missing commas will cause SQLite code to fail to execute, these programmers insist that commas should come at the beginning of lines, followed by a space, as in the following:

```
/*
    Create Auctions table with variables: AuctionID, Volume,
    District, and Date.  The Primary Key is AuctionID.

    Author:      Harry J. Paarsch
    Modified by: Konstantin Golyaev
    Date:        December 1, 2014

  Stored im Code/CreateAuctionsTable.sql

*/;

CREATE TABLE Auctions
(
    AuctionID      INTEGER
  , Volume         INTEGER NOT NULL
  , District       INTEGER NOT NULL
  , Date           TEXT NOT NULL
  , PRIMARY KEY (AuctionID)
)
;
```

Listing 3.6: SQL to Create Auctions Table

That we did not put our names on the previous snippet of code indicates to you how we feel about those who put commas at the ends of lines. In short, put the commas at the beginnings of lines. Some other programmers have strong preferences concerning where to put the parentheses. That we put the parentheses on separate lines indicates to you that this is the appropriate way in which to proceed. Yet still others insist on having the commands defining the variables types lining up—that is, having spaces after the defined variables, which are presumably of different lengths. Even though this may be interpreted as the manifestations of obsessive compulsive disorder, we recommend it as well.

The reason for this ritual is to create an environment within which you can spot errors quickly. Also, by always using the same convention, you will be able to spot small changes to your baseline code easily, which will in turn increase your productivity.

Assuming the code has been saved in a file (for instance, we have used the self-describing name CreateAuctionsTable.sql), the SQL code can be executed inside SQLite in two ways. The first is to pass the file as an input into the SQLite executable using the standard UNIX syntax:

```
$ sqlite3 AuctionsDataBase.db < CreateAuctionsTable.sql
```

The second is to invoke SQLite, and then to use internal SQLite commands interactively:

```
$ sqlite3
SQLite version 3.8.1 2013-10-17 12:57:35
Enter ".help" for instructions
Enter SQL statements terminated with a ";"
sqlite>.read CreateAuctionsTable.sql
```

With the latter method, three things are worth noting: First, the command *must* begin with the dot symbol as the first symbol of the line; no spaces can precede the dot. If you do not heed this advice, then you will get an error message something like this:

```
sqlite> .read CreateAuctionsTable.sql
   ...> ;
Error: near ".": syntax error
```

Second, the end of the command *must not* include a semicolon because .read is not a standard SQL command. (In the preceding simulation of an error, we needed to include a semicolon because a space was introduced before .read, which then created a whole other set of issues.) Third, ensure that the path to the file CreateAuctionsTable.sql is specified correctly.

Next, we create the Bidders table. The SQLite code necessary to create this table has a similar format. First, the Bidders table is created, then it is populated with variables whose types have been defined. The variable BidderID is defined like the primary key variable AuctionID of the Auctions table. Most of the remaining variables are defined as characters TEXT.

None of these definitions is extremely surprising because variables like FirstName and LastName as well as Address1, Address2, Town, Province, and Email are predominantly characters. Because most of these variables will have inputs, NOT NULL is imposed, except for the variable Address2, where it is assumed to be NULL by DEFAULT: not everyone has an address that requires two lines. In this case, the variable Preferred has been coded as Y or N (and thuse defined as text), but it could also have been coded as 1 or 0, in which case INTEGER NOT NULL could have been used. Experienced database architects discourage the use of numeric values when coding binary categorical variables. Once a categorical variable is numerically encoded, you must keep track of the mapping from numbers to category descriptions and vice versa. Inevitably, something will be forgotten. A variable named `Preferred` that takes values `Y` or `N` is much more self-explanatory than the same variable with values 1 or 0, or should it be 0 and 1? You could even go wild with self-description and use `Yes` or `No`.

The only two somewhat odd definitions are those for `PostalCode` and `Telephone` number. `PostalCode` is defined as `TEXT` because in Canada postal codes are *"letter number letter space number letter number"* as in "V9K 1P6" for some address in Qualicum Beach, British Columbia. In the United States a five digit number would be used for a variable named, say, `ZipCode`.

Why is the variable `Telephone` defined as `TEXT`? Isn't a Canadian telephone number like an American one, having a format like "(604) 459-2437"? Clearly, the parentheses and dash are assumed absent, and no spaces are allowed, so "6044592437" is expected. Why then not read this in as an integer? First, a straight `INTEGER` is too small to hold this number. Also, you might want to perform string manipulations on the variable, for example, to find all bidders in a particular area code. One can perform string matches with characters easily, but that is more complicated with integers.

```
/*
    Create Bidders table with variables:  BidderID, FirstName,
    LastName, Address1, Address2, Town, Province, PostalCode,
    Telephone, Email, and Preferred (whether the bidder is
    preferred).  The Primary Key is BidderID.

    Author:      Harry J. Paarsch
    Modified by: Konstantin Golyaev
    Date:        December 1, 2014

    Stored in Code/CreateBiddersTable.sql

*/;

CREATE TABLE Bidders
(
    BidderID    INTEGER
  , FirstName   TEXT NOT NULL
  , LastName    TEXT NOT NULL
```

```
  , Address1    TEXT NOT NULL
  , Address2    TEXT DEFAULT NULL
  , Town        TEXT NOT NULL
  , Province    TEXT NOT NULL
  , PostalCode  TEXT NOT NULL
  , Telephone   TEXT NOT NULL
  , Email       TEXT DEFAULT NULL
  , Preferred   TEXT
  , PRIMARY KEY (BidderID)
)
;
```

Listing 3.7: SQL to Create Bidders Table

The `Bids` table is the final table to create; this table involves the most complications. Note that `AuctionID` cannot be the primary key because it will not be unique unless each auction received only one bid. Similarly, `BidderID` isn't useful. Here, the primary key should really be a composite of `AuctionID`, `BidderID`, and `Bid` because all three determine an entry uniquely. One way to deal with this problem is to have an alternative internal `BidID` that will never be used for anything but indexing, and to make that variable the primary key. When, however, a variable is imported from another table, it should be declared as a `FOREIGN KEY` so that an index is built internal to the database to make eventual operations on that variable (such as joins) much faster. With this in mind, examine the following code:

```
/*
   Create Bids table with variables: BidID, AuctionID, BidderID,
   and Bid.   The Primary Key is BidID.

   Author:      Harry J. Paarsch
   Modified by: Konstantin Golyaev
   Date:        December 1, 2014

   Stored in Code/CreateBidsTable.sql
*/;

CREATE TABLE Bids
(
    BidID       INTEGER
  , AuctionID   INTEGER NOT NULL
  , BidderID    INTEGER NOT NULL
  , Bid         REAL
```

```
 , FOREIGN KEY (AuctionID) REFERENCES Auctions (AuctionID)
 , FOREIGN KEY (BidderID) REFERENCES Bidders (BidderID)
 , PRIMARY KEY (BidID)
)
;
```

Listing 3.8: SQL to Create Bids Table

Note that by defining `Bid` as `REAL` we are using the computer to double-check data input for features we know should exist.

3.5.4   Importing csv Files into SQLite

Having created the database `AuctionsDataBase` as well as the tables `Auctions`, `Bidders`, and `Bids`, we now want to populate the variables of those tables with data from the spreadsheets that have been saved as the following csv files:

`AuctionsTable.xlsx` as `AuctionsTable.csv`

`BiddersTable.xlsx` as `BiddersTable.csv`

`BidsTable.xlsx` as `BidsTable.csv`

Loading data into a table from a file is one example where different SQL dialects do not work the same way. Certain commands that can be executed within, say, MySQL are not supported by SQLite. There exists a way to write SQL code that would work for any platform, but this comes at the expense of readability. To be specific, the following SQL code reads in the first two observations from the `AuctionsTable.csv` file into the `Auctions` table:

```
INSERT INTO Auctions (AuctionID, Volume, District, Date)
VALUES (1, 1234, 1, 20111003)
;
INSERT INTO Auctions (AuctionID, Volume, District, Date)
VALUES (2, 345, 3, 20111107)
;
```

Rather than going down this clearly tedious path, we demonstrate how you can load the data using the built-in SQLite `.import` command. Note that under the hood the `.import` command reads in the input file line by line, creates the

INSERT SQL statements along the lines of the preceding example, and then loads in each row individually. The following set of SQLite commands loads data into the `Auctions`, `Bidders`, and `Bids` tables, assuming the SQL code for creating them has already been executed:

```
.separator ,
.import AuctionsTable.csv Auctions
.import BiddersTable.csv Bidders
.import BidsTable.csv Bids
```

The code is relatively self-describing, but it is useful to review what is there because later we make changes to the database. The first command tells SQLite to treat commas in input files as column separators. The next three commands load tables `Auctions`, `Bidders`, and `Bids` from the corresponding `.csv` files.

3.5.5   Querying the RDB

Once you have created an RDB, you can use it repeatedly for many different tasks. To invoke SQLite, type the following into a terminal window at the prompt:

```
$ sqlite3 AuctionsDataBase.db
```

You will then face the following prompt within SQLite:

```
sqlite>
```

At this prompt, you could type the following:

```
sqlite>.schema
```

This command will yield the source SQL code for all tables that have been defined within `AuctionsDataBase`. It should have the entries for the three tables `Auctions`, `Bidders`, and `Bids`.

Several other useful built-in SQLite dot-commands exist. We suggest invoking them at this point because they will make subsequent interactive work a lot easier.

```
sqlite>.mode column
sqlite>.headers on
sqlite>.output stdout
```

The first command ensures that SQLite will display query output in a way that is easy for humans to read. Although the command is unnecessary, we recommend invoking it prior to interactive work. The second command will add column headers to every query output. The last command guarantees that SQLite prints output to the screen, and not into an output file.

Now start by typing the following:

```
sqlite> SELECT * FROM Auctions;
```

This will yield a table of data where the first column is the `AuctionID`, the second is the `Volume`, the third is the `District`, and the fourth is the `Date`. The table has ten rows of data because that is how many auctions exist in the data set.

The real power of SQL lies in its ability to manipulate data very efficiently. The first, and perhaps the most important, concept to learn is how to filter the query output to a subset of interest. Although the preceding query returned only ten rows of data, and thus you could visually inspect the output in its entirety, visual inspection becomes prohibitively difficult for larger tables. Indeed, even the `Bids` table already has 37 records; simply returning all of them as the query output is unhelpful.

Suppose you are interested in understanding the bidding patterns for the bidder whose `BidderID` is 1. You can accomplish this easily using the following SQL code:

```
/*
    This query returns all bids made by bidder 1.

    Author:        Konstantin Golyaev
    Last modified: November 30, 2014
*/;

.mode column
.headers on
.output Data/SelectBidsForBidder.out

SELECT
    bids.BidderID  AS BidderID
  , bids.AuctionID AS AuctionID
  , bids.Bid       AS Bid
```

```
FROM Bids bids

WHERE bids.BidderID = 1
;

.output stdout
```

Listing 3.9: SQL to Select Bids for Bidders

Assuming you executed the .mode column command, this SQL code should yield the following output:

```
BidderID    AuctionID   Bid
----------  ----------  ----------
1           1           12.1
1           4           12.27
1           5           19.21
1           8           12.59
1           9           14.16
1           10          10.86
```

Listing 3.10: SQL Output of Select Bids for Bidders

The first column is the BidderID, the second column is the AuctionID, and the last column is the Bid. We have explicitly requested that these three columns be in this particular order in the SQL query because we are not interested in seeing the BidID column.

Two things to note about this query: first, the WHERE clause was used to limit the query output. (Remember "SELECT ... FROM ... WHERE ... ".) SQLite does not display any records from the Bids table that have values of BidderID different from 1, as was requested. Second, an *alias* bids for the Bids table was used. Aliases are used for column disambiguation in case we use more than one table in the query and some of the column names are the same across tables. If both Bids and Bidders tables had been queried, then SQLite would have had to be told explicitly from which table to fetch the BidderID column.

SQL also makes it extremely easy to aggregate and to summarize data. Suppose you are interested in the bidding patterns by bidder across all auctions in which they participated. Specifically, consider the minimum, the average, and the maximum bid for each bidder. To accomplish this, consider the following query:

```
/*
    This query calculates the smallest, the average, and the
    largest bids for every bidder.

    Author:         Konstantin Golyaev
    Last modified: November 30, 2014

    Stored in Code/ComputeBidSummariesByBidder.sql
*/;

.mode column
.headers on
.output Data/ComputeBidSummariesByBidder.out

SELECT
    bids.BidderID AS BidderID
  , MIN(bids.Bid) AS SmallestBid
  , AVG(bids.Bid) AS AverageBid
  , MAX(bids.Bid) AS LargestBid

FROM Bids bids

GROUP BY
    bids.BidderID
;

.output stdout
```

Listing 3.11: SQL to Compute Summary Statistics

This SQL code generates the following output:

BidderID	SmallestBid	AverageBid	LargestBid
1	10.86	13.5316666666667	19.21
2	8.81	11.3842857142857	13.09
3	7.39	10.5825	15.62
4	7.93	12.2675	15.67
5	7.35	10.09	14.28
6	7.14	9.89833333333333	13.03
7	7.99	10.128	12.34

Listing 3.12: SQL Output of Compute Summary Statistics

The first column is `BidderID`, the second column shows the smallest bid, the third column returns the average bid, and the fourth column displays the maximum bid placed by the corresponding bidder. These calculations were performed by the built-in *aggregation functions* MIN, AVG, and MAX. Other built-in functions include the SUM and COUNT functions, which are self-describing.

The critical thing to note about this query is the addition of the GROUP BY clause whose purpose it is to inform the aggregation functions of the granularity at which the data must be aggregated. Many SQL novices tend to forget the GROUP BY clause, assuming that the SELECT clause provides sufficient information concerning of the granularity of the desired query output. Unfortunately, this is not the case. It would perhaps be useful for you to think of the GROUP BY clause as an input to the aggregation function(s). The code

```
SELECT
 <...>
 , AVG(bids.Bid) AS AverageBid
 <...>
GROUP BY
    bids.BidderID
<...>
```

should be read as "select average bid size *for each bidder.*" In our experience, even intermediate users tend to forget to adjust the GROUP BY clause of the query with the aggregation function after deciding to add an extra column in the SELECT clause. This is such a common mistake that most SQL engines detect the error and provide informative error messages that make it easy to fix the problem.

Once you understand how to manipulate data in a single table, the next logical step is to explore how to combine data from several tables into a single query. We build on the preceding query by replacing `BidderID` with the first and last names of bidders, to make the output more readable. The following SQL code accomplishes that:

```
/*
    This query calculates the smallest, the average, and the
    largest bids for every bidder.  It also joins bidder
    names from the Bidders table.

    Author:        Konstantin Golyaev
    Last modified: December 1, 2014
```

```
    Stored in Code/ComputeBidSummariesAndJoinNames.sql

*/;

.mode column
.headers on
.output Data/ComputeBidSummariesAndJoinNames.out

SELECT
    bidders.FirstName AS FirstName
  , bidders.LastName  AS LastName
  , MIN(bids.Bid)     AS SmallestBid
  , AVG(bids.Bid)     AS AverageBid
  , MAX(bids.Bid)     AS LargestBid

FROM Bids bids

INNER JOIN Bidders bidders
  ON  bids.BidderID = bidders.BidderID

GROUP BY
    bidders.FirstName
  , bidders.LastName
;

.output stdout
```

Listing 3.13: SQL to Compute Bid Summaries and Join Names

The following output will be generated:

```
FirstName   LastName    SmallestBid  AverageBid        LargestBid
----------  ----------  -----------  ----------------  ----------
Adam        Cooper      10.86        13.5316666666667  19.21
Bryan       Dykstra     8.81         11.3842857142857  13.09
Charles     Elan        7.39         10.5825           15.62
David       Forester    7.93         12.2675           15.67
Edward      Gulden      7.35         10.09             14.28
Frank       Hollister   7.14         9.89833333333333  13.03
George      Ivanov      7.99         10.128            12.34
```

Listing 3.14: SQL Output of Compute Summaries and Join Names

It is easy to verify that columns three through five are identical to columns two through four in the previous output. This time, however, instead of meaningless `BidderID`s, you are returned first and last names of bidders, as expected.

The INNER JOIN clause is responsible for combining information from multiple tables. You must explicitly tell SQLite on which columns to join the tables; in our example, BidderID was used.

In addition to INNER, several types of OUTER JOINs exist—namely, the LEFT OUTER JOIN, the RIGHT OUTER JOIN, and the FULL OUTER JOIN. This simple example illustrates the difference. Consider two tables A and B:

ID	X
1	X1
2	X2

(a) Table A

ID	Y
2	Y2
3	Y3

(b) Table B

Figure 3.8: Two Tables

Now consider the following SQL code:

```
SELECT
      a.ID
    , a.X
    , b.Y

FROM A a

JOIN_TYPE B b
   ON  a.ID = b.ID
;
```

Depending on whether JOIN_TYPE equals INNER JOIN or LEFT OUTER JOIN or RIGHT OUTER JOIN or FULL OUTER JOIN, you will see the following outputs:

For INNER JOIN,

```
ID X   Y
2  X2 Y2
```

For LEFT OUTER JOIN,

```
ID X   Y
1  X1
2  X2 Y2
```

For `RIGHT OUTER JOIN`,

```
ID X   Y
2  X2  Y2
3      Y3
```

For `FULL OUTER JOIN`,

```
ID X   Y
1  X1
2  X2  Y2
3      Y3
```

In short, an `OUTER JOIN` preserves some of the rows that do not have a corresponding match in the other table that is joined. Clearly, you can turn a `LEFT JOIN` into a `RIGHT JOIN` simply by switching the order of tables; for this reason, the `RIGHT JOIN` is rarely used in practice.

Similarly, more than two tables can be joined. For example, you might be interested in the first and last dates of auction participation for each bidder, which would require you to combine all three tables to get this information. To accomplish this, we need to perform some data wrangling on the `Date` column in the `Auctions` table. SQLite is able to transform text information correctly into date objects if the text conforms to the "YYYY-MM-DD" format only. Since our `Date` information is in the "YYYYMMDD" format instead, we need to do the following: first, split the string into the year, month, and date components, and second, concatenate them back into a string of the appropriate format using "-" as delimiter. The following SQL code accomplishes the task:

```
/*
   This query calculates the date of first and last bid for
   every bidder.  For this, it combines all three tables from
   the AuctionsDataBase.

   Author:        Konstantin Golyaev
   Last modified: December 1, 2014

   Stored in Code/ComputeFirstAndLastBidDates.sql
*/;

.mode column
.headers on
.output Data/ComputeFirstAndLastBidDates.out
```

```
SELECT
    bidders.FirstName  AS FirstName
  , bidders.LastName   AS LastName
  , MIN(auctions.Date) AS FirstBidDate
  , MAX(auctions.Date) AS LastBidDate

FROM Bids bids

INNER JOIN Bidders bidders
  ON  bids.BidderID = bidders.BidderID

INNER JOIN
(
  SELECT
      AuctionID
    , DATE(Year || '-' || Month || '-' || Day) AS Date

  FROM
  (
    SELECT
        a.AuctionID
      , SUBSTR(a.Date, 1, 4) AS Year
      , SUBSTR(a.Date, 5, 2) AS Month
      , SUBSTR(a.Date, 7, 2) AS Day

    FROM Auctions a
  )

) auctions
  ON  bids.AuctionID = auctions.AuctionID

GROUP BY
    bidders.FirstName
  , bidders.LastName
;

.output stdout
```

Listing 3.15: SQL to Compute First and Last Bid Dates

This query will produce the following output:

```
FirstName    LastName    FirstBidDate  LastBidDate
----------   ----------  ------------  ----------
Adam         Cooper      2011-10-03    2012-07-09
Bryan        Dykstra     2011-10-03    2012-07-09
```

```
Charles      Elan          2011-10-03    2012-04-02
David        Forester      2011-12-05    2012-07-09
Edward       Gulden        2011-10-03    2012-05-07
Frank        Hollister     2011-10-03    2012-06-04
George       Ivanov        2011-10-03    2012-06-04
```

Listing 3.16: SQL Output of Compute First and Last Bid Dates

Note that the double pipe operator || is used to concatenate (glue together) strings in SQL. We could of course have avoided the two-layered subquery at the expense of code readbility; we chose not to do so. Note also how we use joins in this example. The INNER JOIN statements are used sequentially: no columns are returned from the Bids table at all; the Bids table is used to stitch together the Auctions and Bidders tables.

The beauty of SQL and Codd's RA is that you can perform sophisticated manipulations of the data while remaining within the confines of the database.

Next, we build on the previous example in which summary statistics by bidder were computed, but now we restrict attention to those bidders who, on average, bid at least $12. This is not as simple as it may initially sound because you cannot directly filter the rows of the Bids table within the WHERE clause. You need all these rows to compute the averages properly; only then can you filter the resulting output in the second step. The following query accomplishes the task:

```
/*
    This query calculates the average bid for every bidder.
    It then returns only bidders with average bids exceeding
    twelve dollars.  It also joins bidder names from the
    Bidders table.

    Author:       Konstantin Golyaev
    Last modified: December 1, 2014

    Stored in Code/ComputeBidSummariesAndFilter.sql

*/;

.mode column
.headers on
.output Data/ComputeBidSummariesAndFilter.out

SELECT
    all_data.FirstName    AS FirstName
```

```
  , all_data.LastName    AS LastName
  , all_data.SmallestBid AS SmallestBid
  , all_data.AverageBid  AS AverageBid
  , all_data.LargestBid  AS LargestBid

FROM (

  SELECT
      bidders.FirstName
    , bidders.LastName
    , MIN(bids.Bid) AS SmallestBid
    , AVG(bids.Bid) AS AverageBid
    , MAX(bids.Bid) AS LargestBid

  FROM Bids bids

  INNER JOIN Bidders bidders
    ON  bids.BidderID = bidders.BidderID

  GROUP BY
      bidders.FirstName
    , bidders.LastName

) all_data

WHERE all_data.AverageBid >= 12
;

.output stdout
```

Listing 3.17: SQL to Compute Bid Summaries and Filter

The following output is produced:

```
FirstName    LastName    SmallestBid  AverageBid         LargestBid
----------   ----------  -----------  ----------------   ----------
Adam         Cooper      10.86        13.5316666666667   19.21
David        Forester    7.93         12.2675            15.67
```

Listing 3.18: SQL Output of Compute Bid Summaries and Filter

When you compare these results with the previous ones, you realize that only bidders whose average bid is at least \$12 are included. Some SQL developers might insist that structuring the query in this way is inefficient and superfluous. Indeed, a better way exists to filter down query results based on the values returned by aggregation functions. The HAVING clause was introduced into SQL for precisely this reason.

```
/*
    This query calculates the average bid for every bidder.
    It uses the HAVING clause to narrow down results
    to bidders with average bid of at least twelve dollars.
    It also joins bidder names from the Bidders table.

    Author:         Konstantin Golyaev
    Last modified: December 1, 2014

    Stored in Code/ComputeBidSummariesAndFilterWithHaving.sql

*/;

.mode column
.headers on
.output Data/ComputeBidSummariesAndFilterWithHaving.out

SELECT
    bidders.FirstName AS FirstName
  , bidders.LastName  AS LastName
  , MIN(bids.Bid)     AS SmallestBid
  , AVG(bids.Bid)     AS AverageBid
  , MAX(bids.Bid)     AS LargestBid

FROM Bids bids

INNER JOIN Bidders bidders
  ON  bids.BidderID = bidders.BidderID

GROUP BY
    bidders.FirstName
  , bidders.LastName

HAVING AVG(bids.Bid) >= 12
;

.output stdout
```

Listing 3.19: SQL to Compute Bid Summaries with Having Filter

This query produces identical results but is much easier to understand. The main difference between the WHERE and the HAVING clauses is that the former gets executed before aggregation functions, whereas the latter is performed after them. Put differently, WHERE is concerned with individual table rows, while HAVING operates on the *output* rows.

To this point we have considered fairly simple data manipulations that could be implemented using Microsoft Excel. Consider now the situation where for every bidder we would like to compute his average bid in every auction and contrast that average to the average bid of all competitors. We can accomplish this using the following SQL. The code makes use of the following fact: at an auction, with $i = 1, \ldots, I$ bidders, each of whom bids b_i, the average bid of bidder i's competitors is given by

$$\left(\sum_{j=1}^{I} b_j - b_i \right) / (I - 1).$$

```
/*
    This query calculates the average bid for every bidder,
    as well as the average bid of all competitors across
    every auction.  It then returns these two averages
    side-by-side for comparison.

    Author:         Konstantin Golyaev
    Last modified: December 1, 2014

    Stored in Code/ComputeAverageForBidderAndCompetitors.sql

*/;

.mode column
.headers on
.output Data/ComputeAverageForBidderAndCompetitors.out

SELECT
      bidders.FirstName                       AS FirstName
    , bidders.LastName                        AS LastName
    , AVG(all_bids.Bid)                       AS AverageBid
    , MAX(all_bids.average_competitor_bid) AS AverageCompetitorBid

FROM
(

  SELECT
      bids.AuctionID
```

```
    , bids.BidderID
    , ( (temp.auction_total_bids - bids.Bid) / (
        temp.auction_count_bidders - 1) ) AS average_competitor_bid
    , bids.Bid

  FROM Bids bids

  INNER JOIN
  (
    SELECT
        bids.AuctionID
      , SUM(bids.Bid)                   AS auction_total_bids
      , COUNT(DISTINCT bids.BidderID)   AS auction_count_bidders

    FROM Bids bids

    GROUP BY
        bids.AuctionID

  ) temp
    ON  bids.AuctionID = temp.AuctionID

) all_bids

INNER JOIN Bidders bidders
  ON  all_bids.BidderID = bidders.BidderID

GROUP BY
    bidders.FirstName
  , bidders.LastName
;

.output stdout
```

Listing 3.20: SQL to Compute Average Bids for Competitors

The output should look like this:

```
FirstName    LastName    AverageBid          AverageCompetitorBid
----------   ----------  ----------------    --------------------
Adam         Cooper      13.5316666666667    12.0175
Bryan        Dykstra     11.3842857142857    13.7266666666667
Charles      Elan        10.5825             14.4733333333333
David        Forester    12.2675             15.62
```

Edward	Gulden	10.09	12.2766666666667
Frank	Hollister	9.89833333333333	12.1166666666667
George	Ivanov	10.128	12.0225

Listing 3.21: SQL Output of Compute Average Bids for Competitors

Let's analyze this query, line by line. First, it is critical to understand that the desired result cannot be achieved without scanning the `Bids` table more than once. You need to compute an average bid by auction, and an average bid by bidder—two entirely different objects. The `temp` subquery computes the auction-level averages and bidder counts. Its results are joined back to the main `Bids` table, which then gets averaged at the bidder level. It might be helpful to visualize the `AllBids` subquery, particularly what columns it has before you limit the set of returned columns in the SELECT clause. First, there are four native columns from the `Bids` table:

    BidID

    AuctionID

    BidderID

    Bid

Next, three more columns are brought in from the `temp` subquery:

    AuctionID

    auction_total_bids

    auction_count_bidders

Values of the last two columns are constant across different `BidderID`s within the same value of `AuctionID`. Therefore, it is irrelevant which aggregation function you use when you roll up the query to the level of `BidderID`. Here, MAX was used, but AVG or MIN would have worked just as well.

Although we did a bit of this in Section 3.4, the last thing we demonstrate concerning SQLite is how to redirect query output into a file instead of the screen. Two ways exist to accomplish this, depending on whether you operate in interactive mode or from the command line. In interactive mode, the following SQLite commands will get the job done:

```
sqlite>.mode csv
sqlite>.output PATH/TO/OUTPUT/FILE
sqlite>.read PATH/TO/QUERY/SQL/FILE
sqlite>.output stdout
```

The first line switches output mode to comma-separated values because this format is usually much easier to consume within other applications. The second command tells SQLite to redirect all subsequent query output to a specified file `PATH/TO/OUTPUT/FILE`; for example, the file might be `/Users/hjp/ PGBook/Output/SQLOutput.out`. If the file does not exist, then it will be created; if the file already exists, then the query output will be appended to the end of the existing file. We have already encountered the third command: it simply executes SQL code from an existing file on disk. The last command switches back from writing output to file to printing output into the terminal window. Having an output file with results from more than one query is rarely a good idea because it could be quite difficult to understand its contents. For this reason, we suggest manually switching output mode back to `stdout` after every file write operation.

The second way to direct output to a file is to use the standard UNIX input-output redirection syntax. Recall that < tells UNIX that it should find the input to SQLite in the path to the query file, whereas > leads to the output file. Note that the output file will be overwritten if it exists; to avoid this, simply append the output as described in Chapter 2.

```
$ sqlite3 PATH/TO/Auctions_DataBase.db < PATH/TO/QUERY/SQL/FILE > PATH
    /TO/OUTPUT/FILE
```

This command loads `AuctionsDataBase.db` into SQLite, executes the source SQL query from a file against this database, and writes the output to the output file. All this can be done from a command line, which means it can be automated using a shell script should that be necessary.

3.6 NoSQL

In this chapter, we focused on the relational model, which was introduced over 40 years ago. That this data model has survived and is widely used today is a testament to its usefulness and versatility. RDBs are unparalleled when it comes to storing, accessing, and manipulating large amounts of structured data; RDBs are invaluable when those data need to be shared across multiple users, particularly when it is critical that the stored data be the same for all users—consistent. In business, having two financial analysts execute identical queries against a database only to obtain different answers would be unsettling, to say the least.

Over the past decade, however, the growth rate of available data has outpaced the rate of innovation in hardware storage. Consequently, in many applications, the data sets are too large for any DBMS to handle on a single computer. To circumvent this problem, RDBs have become distributed systems. In other words, the data are distributed across several computers. One problem with distributed systems is that the four pillars on which DBMS are built—availability, consistency, independence, and durability—cannot be guaranteed.

This fact was recognized in the CAP theorem, first conjectured by Eric A. Brewer at a conference in 2000 but proven formally by Gilbert and Lynch (2002). The CAP theorem claims that a distributed computer system is unable to satisfy the following three reasonable requirements:

1. Consistency—all computers in the system see exactly the same data at any point in time.

2. Availability—if some of the computers in the system fail, then the remaining ones operate normally.

3. Partitioning—if two computers cannot communicate, each should be able to operate independently.

In a distributed system that must handle petabytes of data and serve thousands of users, availability and partitioning are generally considered to be nonnegotiable. You would not be willing to wait for, say, Google to refresh its search cache before accepting another query from a user, so availability is a must. Partition tolerance is unavoidable once the number of users exceeds a threshold: no single computer can survive millions of simultaneous requests. In fact, this is the reason that denial-of-service attacks work.[5] Therefore, some users are all

---

[5]In computing, a conscious attempt to force a computer to attempt to exceed its resources by repeated requests is referred to as a denial-of-service attack.

but guaranteed to receive varying responses from such a service were they to query it at the same time. In other words, full consistency is impossible. Thus, a relaxed condition of *eventual consistency* is used: users must be able to receive the same set of results at some point in the future.

In general, consistency is a non-negotiable property of the system in the relational model. Compromises can be made concerning availability (whenever database nodes become out of sync, the whole system has to go down for synchronization) or partition tolerance (in the preceding example, SQLite solves this problem by storing the entire database within a single file, and whoever can access this file will get the latest data).

Another situation in which an RDB may be inappropriate is when the data do not fit easily into the format of a table. For instance, consider a data set for which many records are only sparsely populated. An RDB would create and maintain many columns populated mainly by NULL values, which is inefficient.

Thus, with the advent of the three Vs of Big Data (volume, velocity, and variety), RDBs are with increasing frequency becoming infeasible as data stores because the data sets are simply too large. When you use the SELECT ... FROM ... WHERE mantra to perform a join in an SQL, at least two (potentially) large tables are part of any operation. When a JOIN is performed, the number of operations required involves a polynomial in the number of rows N, where the highest order is 2 (that is, the number of operations is a quadratic function $\alpha N^2 + \beta N + \gamma$) of the number of rows N; this takes place *before* any filtering is done. When N is in the millions, so 10^6, N^2 is in the 10^{12} (trillions), which is surmountable. But if N is in the hundreds of millions, so 10^8, then N^2 is in the 10^{16} (tens of quadrillions). At least on current computers, such large numbers of operations are insurmountable. As data sets in Big Data increase in size, this problem will only get worse. In response to the computational burden accompanying three-V growth, computer scientists have sought alternative data models.

As mentioned, the relational model is organized around the following four basic concepts, often referred to as ACID, an acronym for

- atomicity—the entire sequence of actions must be either completed or aborted, that is, no transaction is partially successful;

- consistency—a transaction takes the resources from one consistent state to another;

- isolation—a transaction's effect is invisible to other transactions until the transaction is committed;

- durability—changes made by the committed transaction are permanent and can survive system failure.

What is a state? At any point in time, you can think of the database as a large collection of, say, N pigeonholes, each containing some information. Suppose you can represent the contents of those pigeonholes using a huge vector $\mathbf{x}_t = (x_{1,t}, x_{2,t}, \ldots, x_{N,t})$. In period t, a transaction, which is a collection of, say, M instructions, $\mathbf{u}_t = (u_{1,t}, u_{2,t}, \ldots, u_{M,t})$ alters the state variable $\mathbf{x}_t$ to produce a new one $\mathbf{x}_{t+1}$ in the next period $(t+1)$.

Creating alternative models of data stores is challenging unless you relax the ACID requirements that provide the foundation on which RDBs are built. One alternative to ACID is referred to as BASE (we kid you not), which is an acronym for

- basic availability—the data store is available even if multiple failures have occurred, something achieved by distributing data across the Internet;

- soft state—the consistency requirement of the ACID model is abandoned;

- eventual consistency—the data store need only converge to consistency, like a statistical estimator, so no guarantees of consistency exist at any point in time.

Relaxing ACID while requiring BASE has resulted in several alternatives.

In 1998, Carlo Strozzi created a UNIX command-line tool designed to organize data using various UNIX tools; he named it NoSQL, as in "not an SQL" database, because it did not have a standard SQL interface. You can learn about this tool at `http://www.strozzi.it/` where a link to NoSQL exists; that link will lead you to a variety of interesting information. This is the first way in which the term *NoSQL* was used.

During the past decade, however, many researchers have explored alternatives to the relational model, sometimes referred to as the NoSQL movement, where the term *NoSQL* is now used for "not only SQL." Essentially, within the NoSQL movement, several related data models have been proposed and implemented as alternatives to the relational model. Because the notion of *key-value* pairs is central to these data structures, we begin with that.

Key-value stores allow you to store data without formally defining the schema required for an RDB. In a key-value store, each record has two parts: first, some sort of datum that uniquely identifies the record, known as the *key*; second, associated with the key are the actual data, referred to as the *value*.

In principle, the key can be any combination of variable types, provided a key uniquely identifies its corresponding record. For example, until recently, in many states of the United States, the social security number was used as a key for a person because it is unique; for security reasons, that practice has been systematically replaced. In practice, a key is typically a string, one that is often generated by a *hash fuction*.

A hash function is a computer algorithm that accepts an input of variable length (for instance, a name) and then maps the input to an output of fixed length (for instance, a key). The values returned by a hash function are referred to by a variety of names, including *hash values*, *hash codes*, *hash sums*, *checksums*, and just *hashes*. As an example, consider using the string `HarryJ.Paarsch` as an input to the `md5` hash function available on most computers including the Apple Mac; `md5` would return the following hexadecimal (base 16) representation of the index:

`5e38905749bce500fc79088560df9345.`

For the string `KonstantinGolyaev`, the same hash function would return

`113e0097a6b13ae3895e5288e88a0af1.`

Although each string is a different length, the hash function returns hash values of the same length. One drawback of the hash function is that two men named `JohnSmith` will get the same hash value. Consequently, the name can be augmented with date and place of birth and other related information. For example, if you lived in Italy, then your *codice fiscale* (fiscal code) would be a 16 character key where the first three letters are the first three consonants of your surname; the next three are selected consonants from your first name; the next five involve the last two digits of your birth year, a letter for your birth month, and two digits from your birth day; the next four letters concern your birth place; and the last one is a parity, either even or odd, depending on the sum of the first 15 characters made into digits.[6] Although the keys produced in

---

[6]From `http://en.wikipedia.org/wiki/Italian_fiscal_code_card`.

this manner are unique, they are hardly secure because anyone could reverse-engineer your *codice fiscale* from your first and last name as well as birth date and place.

Constructing a hashing algorithm can be quite complicated to do well. Well-constructed hash functions avoid collisions, mapping two different strings to the same key. Hashing algorithms provide the foundations of cryptography, the analysis and implementation of techniques for secure communication. For a well designed hash function in cryptography, it should be difficult (ideally impossible) to reverse-engineer quickly the inputs from the hash value.

Hash functions are often used to create the indices of unordered lists because they can provide average-case improvements in the number of operations required to find a randomly selected record in those lists. An *unordered list* of elements is a list for which the elements have no natural ordering. For example, the list $[1, 2, 3]$ has natural order, whereas $[\texttt{cat}, \texttt{dog}, \texttt{snake}]$ does not. Specifically, $1 < 2 < 3$, but what ordered relations exists among $\texttt{cat}$, $\texttt{dog}$, and $\texttt{snake}$?

What about the value—the data? First, note that the value need not be just a number or a string. In fact, the value could be a *blob*, a binary large object containing a variety of different variables of different data types and having almost arbitrary size. Constraints on the computer will limit the blob to a finite size, but this is often left to the user or perhaps the system administrator—in general, the creator of the software.

Although the key-value data model may appear quite restrictive, this type of data store is, in fact, considerably more flexible than tables within an RDB. The flexibility derives from the ability to store composite objects as values in the key-value pair. In most cases, a value is usually a list or an array that in turn contains several pieces of information, some of which can also be other lists or other arrays. Nesting data in this way is well-suited to handling sparse data storage, that is, data sets that may have many missing or NULL values, which are problematic in the relational model.

For example, consider a list of contacts for a person. Any particular contact can have different amounts of information—multiple phone numbers, physical and email addresses, user accounts within various online services. Storing such information within RDBs would require maintaining a single table with a column for each possible item of contact information. In short, a database table would involve many empty cells. In a key-value store, you would only need to store the relevant information for each contact.

Within the Python programming language a data type referred to as a *dictionary* is a key-value store. One example of commercial software for manipulating key-value stores is Amazon's Dynamo.

Another data model is referred to as the *column store*, and sometimes a *transposed store*, which is related to both the relational and the key-value store models.[7] Transposed stores are reportedly quite old, dating from the 1960s. Whereas RDBs are designed to scale vertically—that is, adding more rows of information concerning a fixed number of columns—column stores are designed to scale horizontally—that is, adding more columns of information concerning a potentially fixed number of rows. Nevertheless, information is still accessed using a key; it is just that entire columns, indexed by keys, may live on a particular computer. For example, with a column data store, you can distribute data across computers by the columns of a database. In essence, under a column data store, each column becomes a table of an RDB. Thus, one way to think about a column store is that each column is a table of an RDB that can live on a separate computer. In this way, distributed computing—computing on separate computers—is facilitated. One example of commercial software for manipulating column stores is Google's BigTable.

A third data model is the document store.[8] As you might expect from the name, the main object of interest in a document store is a document, for example, a paper, or a file, or some similar object. Document stores are less rigid than RDBs. In an RDB, every record contains the same number of variables (entries for columns), with unused fields being left empty; empty fields do not exist in a document store. In short, a document store has a variable number of columns for each record. Once again, however, each record is identified by a unique key. Therefore, like column and key-value stores, document stores are indexed by a key. That key may just be the path and filename of a file, but it could be a string transformed using a hash function. Programs like MongoDB implement this notion.

Together, these three models of data stores are often referred to as *aggregate data stores*. A common way to manipulate this data model in a distributed

---

[7]From `http://en.wikipedia.org/wiki/Column-oriented_DBMS`.
[8]From `http://en.wikipedia.org/wiki/Document-oriented_database`.

computing paradigm involves using the MapReduce model (see Section 11.2), a common implementation of which is the program Hadoop.

A final alternative to the RDB is a graph database, where information is stored according to the nodes of a graph.[9] In a graph database, mathematical techniques from graph theory are used to access and manipulate the data. As you might expect, data from social networks are probably best stored and analyzed using graph databases. An example of a graph database program is Neo4j. Unlike the aggregate data stores, graph databases like Neo4j do respect ACID.

The primary disadvantage of storing data as a collection of key-value pairs is the added complexity of information retrieval. Although most RDBs can be accessed using SQL, which is relatively simple to use, accessing data from key-value records generally requires the user to develop an explicit set of instructions in a programming language such as Python. Tools have been developed to make it easier to manipulate such data with a relatively high-level programming language, most notably Pig and Hive.

Each of these alternative data models has virtues as well as drawbacks. Graph databases are grounded in graph theory, but key-value and column and document store models really have no logical foundation, unlike the relational model, which is grounded in set theory and predicate logic. On the other hand, key-value and column and document store models all perform very well when data sets are extremely large; that is, they all scale well. In addition, the key-value and column or the document store data models are not that complex to learn; each is flexible. According to some, this could not be said of graph database models. You can decide whether you agree with this claim by going to `http://http://www.neo4j.org/download` and downloading a free version of Neo4j. Beware: This is not simple to do because you also require the Oracle Java SE (Software Engineer) Development Kit, Oracle JDK.

Because key-value models and the related column and document store models are not bound by the same consistency requirements that govern RDB models, these NoSQL databases are typically very fast. This speed comes at a price—consistency, however you want to define it. Consistency is central to large commercial enterprises, be they financial (like banks) or e-commerce (like Amazon). In research, however, often only one person accesses a data set at a

---

[9]From `http://en.wikipedia.org/wiki/Graph_database`.

time. Thus, consistency may be an irrelevant requirement because two people will probably never access the database at the same time. In short, for many research projects, NoSQL data models and related implementations could be extremely helpful.

Because NoSQL data models are in their infancy, no established corpus of mature material exists that can be taught. In short, you are on your own with these. We knew you would have to leave the nest eventually; we just did not think it would be in Chapter 3. Don't worry, you'll be fine.

Although the current literature concerning NoSQL databases is evolving as we write, it is worth investigating two commonly used data formats for key-value data stores (XML and JSON) and mentioning two others (YAML and BSON).

Because the JSON and XML formats are commonly encountered when you access, for example, an `http` API (that is, when you go to a web page, and try to download data), we spend some time discussing the virtues and drawbacks of those formats, particularly as they relate to Python, the scripting language introduced in Chapter 4.

3.6.1 XML

XML is an acronym for eXtensible Markup Language, which is is related to Hypertext Markup Language (HTML), the language used to create web pages.[10] In fact, both HTML and XML are dialects of a richer language, SGML, Standard General Markup Language.[11] Unlike HTML, however, which is designed to display data, XML is a data format. In short, XML is another way to store data. As mentioned, the term *NoSQL* has become associated with data formats other than those used in RDBs. Within NoSQL, XML is one alternative data format.

Like HTML, XML makes extensive use of tags in the formatting of data. Unlike HTML, however, where tags are predefined (for example, `<h1>` defines the first level of a header), you can invent your own tags in XML. If the tags are chosen in a meaningful way, then XML can be self-describing. In order to

---

[10]From `http://en.wikipedia.org/wiki/XML`.
[11]From `http://en.wikipedia.org/wiki/SGML`.

impose some discipline on XML, a schema for the tags is defined in a file having the suffix, `xsd`, which is an abbreviation for "XML schema definition."

Because XML is flexible and readable, this format is a useful complement to HTML. Consider, for example, the following XML record:

```
<studentInfo studentNo="1234567">
  <name>
    <firstName>Harry</firstName>
    <middleInitial>J.</middleInitial>
    <lastName>Paarsch</lastName>
  </name>
  <address>
    <residence>Brockington House</residence>
    <room>210</room>
  </address>
</studentInfo>
```

This information about Paarsch when he was a freshman in college is encoded in XML, that is, his name as well as a (fictitious) student number and where he lived on campus.

As you can see, XML is verbose: each opened tag requires a closing tag: `<studentInfo>` must be balanced with `</studentInfo>`, and so forth. Often, the tags take up more space than the data! The point of XML is self-description, not parsimony.

The primary way to store data using XML is using key-value pairs. In this example, the key is the `studentNo="1234567"`, whereas the value includes everything between `<studentInfo>` and `</studentInfo>`.

3.6.2   JSON

Another way to store data in key-value pairs is the JSON format. JSON (pronounced "jay-son") is an acronym for JavaScript Object Notation.[12] Whereas XML has many tags, JSON is more like a dictionary data type in Python, so this format is highly compatible. In fact, the JSON format conforms to the native data types in Python. If JSON is so good, then why did we introduce

---

[12]From `http://en.wikipedia.org/wiki/Json`.

XML above? XML is by far the most common key-value format. Consider the following JSON record of the same data:

```
{"studentNo": "123457", "name": {"lastName": "Paarsch",
"middleInitial": "J.", "firstName": "Harry"}, "address":
{"residence": "Brockington House", "room": 210}}
```

Section 4.4.11 explains how this was created using Python.

3.6.3   YAML and BSON

YAML is another human-readable data format that combines concepts from C, Perl, and Python with ideas from XML. YAML is a recursive acronym for "YAML Ain't Markup Language." The syntax of YAML is designed to be easily mapped into data types common to most high-level languages, for example, dictionaries, lists, and scalars.[13]

BSON is another data format used mainly to store large amounts of data as well as to transfer data over the Internet, particularly in conjunction with the MongoDB database. The name is based on the term JSON and stands for "binary JSON." Because BSON is a binary representation of data structures and associative arrays, files in BSON are not readable by humans. The BSON format is, however, extremely efficient at storing large amounts of data.[14]

---

[13]From http://en.wikipedia.org/wiki/YAML.

[14]From http://en.wikipedia.org/wiki/BSON.

4

Simple Programming

MUCH OF THE work assigned a research assistant involves completing sequences of simple tasks, such as transforming some data in a file, or finding certain files and merging their contents, or reformatting a data set, or creating a table for a paper using the output of some other computer program. The list can seem endless. Often, the tasks are not particularly difficult to describe, but trying to complete them without the aid of a computer can be time consuming and error prone. Knowing a common, simple, flexible, and powerful programming language can make completing such tasks relatively painless.

4.1 Python

Python is a commonly used, general-purpose, high-level interpreted programming language, sometimes referred to as a *scripting language* because its instructions are executed, more or less, as they are interpreted, with little or no optimization.[1] Because Python is not a compiled language, when completing identical tasks, code written in Python is slower than code written in a compiled language, such as C.

---

[1] For many computer languages, such as C, the computer code you have written is passed as input to another program, referred to as the *compiler*, which does not just translate the written code into the binary instructions that are then executed by the computer. Instead, the compiler reorganizes the binary instructions to make them run faster, a process known as *optimization*.

If Python has these limitations, then why learn it? One reason that compiled code runs faster than interpreted code is that it takes more effort and skill to write code in, say, C—in short, more developer time. The economics of software creation suggest that a large up-front investment in developer time is warranted for production code because this fixed cost can be amortized over potentially billions of uses of the code as in, say, a procurement system for a large firm. Research, however, often involves implementing one-off projects or prototyping examples whose lifetimes are relatively short. In fact, the computer code developed in research may be used just once or twice to demonstrate a point or to satisfy someone's curiosity. Therefore, the economics suggest that a large up-front investment in development is not really warranted in the research case. In short, the trade-off between developer time and cycle time is better served using an interpreted language such as Python. But because Python can also scale reasonably effectively, you can use the language to solve fairly large problems as well.

In the design of Python, its creator, Guido van Rossum, emphasized the readability of code; that is, the syntax of Python allows programmers to express concepts in fewer lines of code than would be possible in languages such as C. Writing code in C is time consuming because the language is not particularly forgiving. Even experienced software development engineers (SDEs) make errors when using C; novice coders make even more errors. But unlike experienced SDEs, novice coders often do not know how to correct their errors quickly. Because novice coders can read Python code more easily, and it is less prone to syntax errors, the language reduces the frustration that inevitably accompanies any software development project.

Van Rossum also emphasized *extensibility*, that is, using code created by others in the past or in the future should be easy.[2] Whereas including C libraries can often be complicated and tedious, importing Python modules and packages is easy, almost trivial.

Although these are relatively unimportant to a novice programmer, Python also supports several different programming paradigms, such as object-oriented programming and functional programming. What this means is that you can grow into Python as a programmer.

---

[2]Extensibility is a design principle of software engineering where implementation takes into consideration future growth. From `http://en.wikipedia.org/wiki/Extensibility`.

Python also has many specific features that make it particularly attractive to use. For example, one attractive feature of Python is dynamic typing, which means that you as the programmer do not have to define each and every variable you introduce. That said, some SDEs view this feature of Python as a failing; they believe that a programming language should force you to be clear concerning your intent for a variable when you introduce it. Python also has automatic memory management, which means that it cleans up after itself. Thus, although still possible, memory leaks are less likely in Python than in C. Finally, Python has a large community that supports the language, particularly by creating and maintaining a large and comprehensive standard library as well as a collection of modules and packages for almost any application.

4.1.1 IDE or Not?

Often, using an integrated development environment or interactive development environment (IDE) can speed up implementing ideas in a programming language. An IDE is a software application that brings together in an interactive GUI many tools that computer programmers use in software development, typically an editor and a debugger as well as tools to automate building the executable image. Of course, in Python no executable image is created, so that feature of an IDE is irrelevant.

Paarsch feels that an IDE represents just another layer of complexity that does not necessarily speed up implementation. He simply opens two terminal windows: in one, he edits the source code, while in the other he runs the code using Python on the command line. Shaw (2014), the author of *Learn Python the Hard Way*, maintains this position as well.

Many different IDEs exist. Eclipse is the standard IDE used by SDEs at Amazon because it is particularly well-suited to coding in Java. In the Python world, perhaps the best-known free IDE is IDLE. Yet another is Wing IDE 101. Unfortunately, at this time, one cannot call IPython from within Wing IDE 101. Thus, in an effort to avoid creating dependencies, we propose not to use an IDE because later we want you to be comfortable in switching to IPython.

If you do use IPython, you will probably want to use Notebook, a web-based interactive computational environment inside IPython. You can use it to combine executing computer code, writing text, doing mathematics, creating figures and graphs, and exporting rich media into a single document, much like the software environment of Mathematica.

4.1.2 Useful Website

Although we hope what we describe in this chapter will teach you enough Python to get started coding, we are realistic: different people learn in different ways. A website that is useful for learning Python is Software Carpentry at `http://software-carpentry.org/v4/python/`.

4.2 Important Concepts in Computer Science

Before proceeding with a description of the basic grammar of Python, we first discuss five guiding concepts in computer science.

One very important concept in computer science that we have emphasized is *self-description*. In short, the naming convention that you adopt should provide the reader with a good idea of what you are doing.

That said, perhaps the most important concept in computer science involves *encoding* and *decoding*. As you know, computers do not deal directly with numbers, text, images, or music. Instead, these objects are encoded into sequences of zeros and ones (binary representations), which are then manipulated. Subsequently, when you require some output, computers decode the objects and render them in a suitable way.

Another important concept is *modularity*. In order to avoid having everything depend on everything else, large tasks are divided into several smaller tasks; each smaller task is then solved. The main way the concept of modularity is illustrated here involves a construct referred to as the *function*.

A commonly used concept in computer science is *indirection*. Giving an object a name and operating on the named object instead of manipulating specific numbers or characters themselves is an example of indirection, but indirection is more general than that. Indirection is the ability to reference some object using a name, reference, or container instead of the value itself.

Last, a guiding concept in computer science is *abstraction*, which involves the process of separating ideas from specific applications of those ideas. For example, you may want to sort a particular list of numbers, but the principles that allow sorting of *any* set of objects (that is, numbers or names, even pictures) are general. Abstraction requires you solve the general problem rather than a particular application. Moreover, in abstraction, you would gloss over the specifics of implementation and focus on the general strategy to solve a problem. In other fields, the process of abstraction is sometimes referred to as *modeling*, that is, developing a model of the phenomenon at hand.

These five concepts provide a useful high-level framework within which to think about computing. As you proceed through this book, you should be thinking about how the five concepts appear in various guises throughout the presentation.

4.3 Basic Grammar

We now introduce the basic grammar of the Python language, but first a slight hiccup.

4.3.1 Version 2 or 3?

At this time, two versions of Python exist, the most recent of each being Version 2.7.6 and Version 3.4.1. The bad news: Version 3.4.1 is not backwardly compatible with Version 2.7.6. Because much of the current software has been written in Version 2.x of Python, we have chosen to use Version 2. It has proved impossible to ensure that all our examples will run in Version 3.

4.3.2 Classic Exercise

Because many people just want to accomplish something, we dive right into a classic exercise in programming, one devised by Dennis M. Ritchie, the creator of the C programming language (see Kernighan and Ritchie 1988).[3] In a terminal window, at the prompt $, type python followed by a **return** key on an Apple Mac (also labeled as **enter**, and **Enter** on a standard keyboard).

```
$ python<cr>
```

Here, <cr> denotes typing the **return** key. On an Apple Mac, something like the following will appear:

---

[3]With Kenneth L. Thompson, Ritchie also created the UNIX operating system. For this, in 1983, the two won the A.M. Turing Award, a well-deserved honor.

```
Python 2.6.1 (r261:67515, Jun 24 2010, 21:47:49)
[GCC 4.2.1 (Apple Inc. build 5646)] on darwin
Type "help", "copyright", "credits" or "license" for more information.
>>>
```

whereas on a computer using the Linux operating system you will see something like

```
Python 2.7.3 (default, Sep 26 2013, 20:08:41)
[GCC 4.6.3] on linux2
Type "help", "copyright", "credits" or "license" for more information.
>>>
```

We write "something like" because small differences can exist depending on your installation. For example, neither of the preceding code demonstrations is version Python 2.7.6.

Right after the three > characters (the Python prompt) type the following: print "Hello World", exactly followed by a **return**. (Do *not* type <cr>; just hit the **return** key.) The following will appear:

```
>>> print "Hello World"<cr>
Hello World
>>>
```

You have two options to exit Python: you can type quit() (be sure to include the pair of parentheses) or the sequence **control**-D. (For more on control sequences, see Section 2.4.5.) When you have successfully quit Python, you should be back in the terminal window, being prompted by the $.

Okay, that just about wraps up our discussion of Python: you are now certified to claim that you have written Python code. Go forth and pilfer in the Silicon Valley. (Just kidding.)

4.3.3 Data Types

The basic building blocks of the Python language are the data types. Data types are just different ways of storing information. The nine most important data types in the Python language are

- numbers (in three flavors—integer, floating point, and complex);

- Booleans (true/false);

- strings;

- lists;

- dictionaries;

- tuples;

- files.

Numbers—Integers, Floats, Complex

Let's begin with the numbers, and use Python as you would a calculator. Having invoked Python from the command line and having seen the Python prompt, type 3+4 followed by **return**.

```
>>> 3+4<cr>
7
>>>
```

Okay, so far so good. Recall that

$$x^{1/2} = x^{0.5} = \sqrt{x}.$$

In Python, an exponent is written as x**0.5, so

```
>>>2.**0.5<cr>
1.4142135623730951
>>>
```

which is approximately true, since

```
>>> 1.4142135623730951**2
2.0000000000000004
```

Notice that in the last code segment we did not include <cr> at the end of the first line; from now on, we assume that you know enough to type **return** (or **Enter**) at the end of a Python command.

The difference between 2.0000000000000004 and 2. arises because of the finite precision of a computer, that is, a computer only has so much room in which to store a number. When the constraint on size is reached, the remaining part of the number is lost. We discuss the effects and importance of this error further in Chapter 7. For now, just ignore it.

Let's try something else.

```
>>>2**(1/2)
1
>>>
```

Whoah! Seattle, we have a problem.

Previously, we wrote two as 2. and one half as 0.5, whereas here we wrote them as 2 and $(1/2)$. The absence of a decimal place is important to Python. Python interprets both 1 and 2 as integers. In integer arithmetic, $(1/2)$ is 0, and 2^0 is 1.[4] The moral is that you need to use a decimal when writing real numbers (floating-point numbers) in Python.[5]

What about complex numbers? As you know, complex numbers were invented in 1545 by the Italian mathematician Gerolamo Cardano to get around the problem that $\sqrt{-1}$ did not exist at the time. Specifically, the equation $x^2 = -1$ did not have a root that was a real number, which was causing considerable consternation within the community of mathematicians.

A complex number z can be represented in two ways: the first involves decomposing it into two parts x and y, where x is the real part and y is the imaginary part; the second involves transforming (x, y) into the polar coordinates (r, θ). For now, we focus on the first way to write a complex number z as

$$z = x + \mathbf{i}y,$$

where $\mathbf{i} = \sqrt{-1}$. In Python you represent a complex number as a function of two arguments, x, the real part, and y, the imaginary part, in short, `complex(x, y)`. Suppose $(x, y) = (1., -1.)$, then

```
>>> complex(1., -1.)
(1-1j)
>>>
```

---

[4]Integer arithmetic involves a function referred to as the *floor*, which for the value x is denoted $\lfloor x \rfloor$. The floor of x is the greatest integer less than or equal to x. Perhaps some examples will help. Specifically, when dividing two integers, say, i and j, keep only the part before the decimal place of the result. Thus, $(1/2)$ is 0.5, so drop the .5 to get 0. Similarly, $(4/3)$ is 1.3, so drop the .3 to get 1. Finally, $(6/2)$ is 3.0, so drop the .0 to get 3.

[5]In Chapter 7, page 361, we explain why not all real numbers can be represented as floating-point numbers, but for now let's just assume that the real and the floating-point numbers are the same.

Representing **i** as j is a bit unusual, but we are sure that the creators of Python had a good reason.[6] Consider now the representation of **i**:

```
>>> z = complex(0., -1.)
>>> z*z
(-1-0j)
>>>
```

In words, **i**, when squared, does not equal -1 but rather another complex number complex(-1., 0.).

Although Python is perfectly fine to use as a calculator, one of the virtues of computers is that you can store a large expression at a specific location in memory, referred to as an *address*, and then later access the contents of that address for other computations. Thus, we need a way to refer to such addresses. Variables are central to this pursuit. Consider the following:

```
>>> x = 3
>>> y = 4
>>> x + y
7
>>> y % x
1
>>> x % y
3
>>>
```

What is this y % x operation? It is an implementation of the modulus function, often denoted $\text{mod}(y, x)$, which returns the remainder after you have divided y by x. For example, $\text{mod}(4,3)$ is 1 because after dividing 4 by 3 there is 1 remaining. Similarly, $\text{mod}(3,4)$ is 3 because after dividing 3 by 4 you have 3 remaining.

Also, consider

```
>>> f = 2.
>>> e = 0.5
>>> f ** e
1.4142135623730951
>>>
```

---

[6]Johan Brannlund and Colette Marais have pointed out that this convention is most common in electrical engineering, probably because *i* is used for current in that field.

Instructions like x = 3 are referred to as *assignment statements*. You should not interpret the instruction to mean that x equals 3. If you do, then you will be confused by the following:

```
>>> x = 3
>>> x = x + 3
>>> x
6
>>>
```

In the preceding code segment, the contents of the address where x resides are added to the number 3. Now, 6 lives at the address referenced by x. Using a variable instead of a number is an example of indirection; in what follows you will see other examples of indirection.

Note in the preceding example that if you want to know what resides at the address of a variable, simply type the variable's name. In any case, for a complex number, you would do the following:

```
>>> x = 1.
>>> y = -1.
>>> zxy = complex(x, y)
>>> (x, y, zxy)
(1.0, -1.0, (1-1j))
>>> u = 2.
>>> v = 2.
>>> zuv = complex(u, v)
>>> zxy + zuv
(3+1j)
>>> zxy * zuv
(4+0j)
>>> zxy / zuv
-0.5j
```

If you are ever unsure about a variable's type, then do the following:

```
>>> type(x)
<type 'float'>
>>> type(y)
<type 'float'>
>>> type(zxy)
<type 'complex'>
>>>
```

Similarly,

```
>>> i = 1
>>> type(i)
<type 'int'>
>>> r = 2.345
>>> type(r)
<type 'float'>
>>> type(i*r)
<type 'float'>
>>>
```

Python is clever enough to determine the best type for the resulting operation, which we referred to as *dynamic typing*. In other languages, such as C, you would have to decide which data type to use, declare the variable to have that type, and then make the assignment. For example, in C, when introducing the character `letter` as well as the integers `i` and `j`, you would have to do the following:

```
char letter;
int i, j;
letter = 'A';
i = 2;
j = 3;
```

If you did not define the types for `letter` as well as `i` and `j` before the assignment, then C would return an error. This clever feature of Python allows the computer/interpreter to do some of the work for you, but only if the conversion of type is in fact permitted by the language. The following is an example where even Python balks:

```
>>> string = "Golden"
>>> number = 1.0
>>> type(string + number)
Traceback (most recent call last):
  File "<stdin>", line 1, in <module>
TypeError: cannot concatenate 'str' and 'float' objects
>>>
```

Of course, in order to be much use in science, you must be able to calculate mathematical functions, such as sine, cosine, and logarithm. Python maintains many of these functions in a separate module, which is a collection of functions, appropriately named the `math` module. This module provides access to the mathematical functions defined by the C standard, which is important to many SDEs. To make use of the `math` module, you must `import` it into Python, as in the following:

```
>>> import math
>>>
```

To find out what functions are available, you can invoke the command `dir(math)`, which will provide you with a very long list. For the time being, we ignore the ones that begin and end with __, and collect the other functions in Table 4.1. By the way, among Python users, __ is often referred to as *dunder*, an acronym derived from "double underscore."

Having imported the `math` module, you can use these functions without much bother, provided you prefix them by `math.` as demonstrated below:

```
>>> math.e
2.718281828459045
>>> math.pi
3.141592653589793
>>> math.sqrt(2.)
1.4142135623730951
>>> math.degrees(math.pi/2)
90.0
>>> math.log(math.e)
1.0
>>>
```

Booleans

Perhaps the most primitive data type is the Boolean. Booleans can only take one of two values, either `True` or `False`. In what follows, we demonstrate how to create a Boolean variable and then how the rules of logic can be used when manipulating Boolean variables.

```
>>> x = 1.
>>> a = x > 2.
>>> a
False
>>> b = True
>>> a and b
False
>>> a or b
```

Function	Description/Use
`acos(x)`	arc cosine of x, in radians
`acosh(x)`	hyperbolic arc cosine of x, in radians
`asin(x)`	arc sine of x, in radians
`asinh(x)`	hyperbolic arc sine of x, in radians
`atan(x)`	arc tangent of x, in radians
`atan2(x, y)`	arc tangent of (x/y) where sign of x and y observed, unlike for `atan(x)`
`atanh(x)`	hyperbolic arc tangent of x, in radians
`ceil(x)`	$\lceil x \rceil$, ceiling of x, least integer greater than or equal to x
`copysign(x, y)`	returns x with the sign of y
`cos(x)`	cosine of x, in radians
`cosh(x)`	hyperbolic cosine of x, in radians
`degrees(x)`	convert angle x from radians to degrees
`e`	$e = 2.718281828459045$
`erf(x)`	$\frac{2}{\sqrt{\pi}} \int_0^x e^{-t^2/2}\, dt$
`erfc(x)`	the complement of `erf(x)`, that is, $1 - \text{erf}(x)$
`exp(x)`	e^x
`expm1(x)`	$1 - e^x$
`fabs(x)`	absolute value of x, $|x|$
`factorial(x)`	$x!$ for integer x
`floor(x)`	$\lfloor x \rfloor$, floor of x, greatest integer less than or equal to x
`fmod(x, y)`	C implementation of $\text{mod}(x, y)$, which could be different from `x % y`
`frexp(x)`	returns mantissa m and exponent p of x as (m, p), where $x = m \times 2^p$
`gamma(x)`	$\Gamma(x) = \int_0^\infty u^{x-1} e^{-u}\, du$
`hypot(x,y)`	hypotenuse of x and y, that is, $\sqrt{x^2 + y^2}$
`isinf(x)`	a Boolean variable which is true if x is infinite
`isnan(x)`	a Boolean variable which is true if x is not a number, `NaN`
`ldexp(x, n)`	$x \times 2^n$, where n is an integer
`lgamma(x)`	$\log_e [\Gamma(x)]$
`log(x[, b])`	logarithm of x in base b, $\log_b(x)$, where default b is e
`log10(x)`	logarithm of x in base 10
`log1p(x)`	natural logarithm of $(1 + x)$, $\log_e(1 + x)$
`modf(x)`	returns fraction and integer part of x, e.g., `modf(1.2)` is $(0.2, 1)$
`pi`	$\pi = 3.141592653589793$
`pow(x, y)`	x to the y power, that is, x^y
`radians(x)`	convert angle x from degrees to radians
`sin(x)`	sin of x, in radians
`sinh(x)`	hyperbolic sine of x, in radians
`sqrt(x)`	square root of x, that is, $\sqrt{x}$
`tan(x)`	tangent of x, in radians
`tanh(x)`	hyperbolic tangent of x, in radians
`trunc(x)`	truncates x to the nearest integer toward zero

Table 4.1: Python `math` Module Constants and Functions

```
True
>>> type(a)
<type 'bool'>
>>> x + a
1.0
>>>type(x + a)
<type 'float'>
>>> x + b
2.0
>>>type(x + b)
<type 'float'>
>>>
```

In this example, x = 1. is an event, and x > 2. assigns the value False to the variable a because x is, in fact, less than 2. The variable b is assigned the value True. The event a and b is then false because the first variable is False but the second is True, so the intersection is False. On the other hand, the event a or b is then true: even though the first variable is False, because the second is True the union of the two is True.

What about x + a? How do you add False to 1.0 to get 1.0? False is represented internally as 0, whereas x + b is 2.0 because b, which is True, is represented internally as 1; both x + a and x + b are floats because Python uses dynamic typing to select the type it thinks is best for the resulting variable, and x was initially a float.

Some SDEs would claim that this example illustrates everything that is wrong with Python. To us, it just illustrates that Python has some quirks, like all languages, computer or natural. The most important thing to remember is that intersection ∩ is and, whereas union ∪ is or.

Strings

A string is a collection of characters in a particular order. In Python a character is any of the letters, numbers, or symbols that you can type in one keystroke on a keyboard; strings can contain blank spaces, also referred to as *whitespaces*. A string cannot include some control sequences, such as **control**-C. If a string has no characters, then it is referred to as an *empty string*. You might need an empty string to initialize some method; that is, the empty string allows you to start with nothing.

To define a string in Python, you must place the characters within either single quotes (strong quotation marks) or double quotes (weak quotation marks). Perhaps the most famous string in all of computing is

```
>>> ritchie = "Hello World"
>>> ritchie
'Hello World'
>>> type(ritchie)
<type 'str'>
>>>
```

Did you notice that the string `ritchie` was defined using double quotes, but when `ritchie` was typed alone, Python returned the contents in single quotes? In Python, you can use either single or double quotes, provided they balance. For example, if you typed `knuth = 'TeX"`, then Python would throw a syntax error

```
>>> knuth = 'TeX"
  File "<stdin>", line 1
    knuth = 'TeX"
               ^
SyntaxError: EOL while scanning string literal
>>>
```

In Python a string is referred to as *immutable*, which means that it cannot be modified after it has been assigned. Once you have assigned a string, you cannot change it. However, this is not as restrictive as it sounds.

A string of a particular length is stored like a vector, with the indexing beginning at zero. The index value of the string is contained within `[` and `]`. Thus, `ritchie[0]` would equal `'H'`. You can find the length of a string using the function `len()`, for example,

```
>>> n = len(ritchie)
>>> n
11
>>>
```

Although `ritchie` has length 11, if you type

```
>>> ritchie[len(ritchie)]
Traceback (most recent call last):
  File "<stdin>", line 1, in <module>
IndexError: string index out of range
>>>
```

Python will throw an `IndexError: string index out of range`. Even though the string is 11 characters long, the index begins at zero, making the largest index value `10`. Because this is a common mistake, Python allows you to index the last value as follows:

```
>>> ritchie[-1]
'd'
>>> ritchie[-2]
'l'
>>>
```

That is, you can use negative indices to count back from the end when the length of the string is unknown. You can access parts of the string, which is referred to as *slicing* in Python, using the following:

```
>>> ritchie[0:5]
'Hello'
>>>
```

Notice that the value of index 5 is not included; that is, `[0:5]` includes only 0 to 4, inclusive. Under these definitions, you would think that `ritchie[6:-1]` should give you `'World'`, but

```
>>> ritchie[6:-1]
'Worl'
>>>
```

To select from the first index value up to and including the index value n-1, use `ritchie[:n]` (or `ritchie[0:n]`), whereas to select from index value n to the end of the string, use `ritchie[n:]`. Hence,

```
>>> ritchie[:5]
'Hello'
>>> ritchie[6:]
'World'
>>>
```

To see the exact contents of a string, without the quotes, use the `print` function, as in

```
>>> print ritchie
Hello World
>>>
```

You can do this with numbers as well, for instance,

```
>>> x = 3.
>>> print x
3.0
>>>
```

In Python some characters are special; for example, the backslash character \ as well as single ' and double " quotes have a functional meaning; others do, too (see Section 4.3.4). Since special characters are sometimes awkward to accommodate because they involve *escape characters*, Python allows you to express strings in the *raw*; this means including an r before the open quote that defines the string. As a case in point, consider the TeX language, in which most control sequences begin with the backslash character \.[7] For example, in TeX, the Greek lowercase letter α is written as \alpha. In Python you could let the variable alpha be defined as follows:

```
>>> alpha = r"\alpha"
>>> alpha
'\\alpha'
>>> print alpha
\alpha
```

This suggests that the escape sequence for \ is, in fact, \\ (see Section 4.3.4). When we invoked print alpha, only the raw string \alpha was shown.

Even though strings are immutable, you can combine them—add them, so to speak. In computer science, combining strings is referred to as *concatenation*. For example,

```
>>> firstWord = "Hello"
>>> secondWord = "World"
>>> space = " "
>>> firstWord + space + secondWord
'Hello World'
>>>
```

Thus, concatenation + combines two (or more) strings into a new string. Python also allows you to concatenate using whitespaces, for example,

---

[7]TeX is a typesetting program that is particularly well-suited for creating technical documents, such as those that include mathematical equations. We discuss TeX and its offspring LaTeX and BibTeX in Chapter 10.

```
>>> ritchie = "Hello" " " "World"
>>> ritchie
'Hello World'
>>>
```

We do not recommend that you concatenate this way because it is too difficult to understand.

Any string, for example ritchie, can be manipulated using functions created especially for string data types. Examples include

```
>>> ritchie.lower()
'hello world'
>>> ritchie.upper()
'HELLO WORLD'
>>>
```

The functions are different from functions like type() or len() in that they follow the variable, preceded by a dot. In some languages, such functions are referred to as *decorator functions*. Although this is not a formal name in Python, you may hear people refer to these functions in this way. You can also replace parts of strings to create new strings, for example,

```
>>> australian = ritchie.replace("Hello", "G'day")
>>> australian
"G'day World"
>>>
```

Did you notice that the presence of a single quote inside a double quote induced Python to change how it wrote out the variable australian?

You can also multiply strings.

```
>>> Nah = "Nah, "
>>> na = "na "
>>> print 3 * (Nah + 10 * na + '\n')
Nah, na na na na na na na na na na
Nah, na na na na na na na na na na
Nah, na na na na na na na na na na
>>>
```

By the way, what is that character \n? See Section 4.3.4.

You can also break up strings into smaller strings in Python, but you need to specify a character that determines when to split. If you do not specify that character, then Python uses the whitespace. For example,

```
>>> med17 = "Ask not for whom the bell tolls, it tolls for thee."
>>> med17.split()
['Ask', 'not', 'for', 'whom', 'the', 'bell', 'tolls,', 'it', 'tolls',
    'for', 'thee.']
```

As you can see, Python deals very effectively with strings. This may be one reason that the researchers who developed the Natural Language Toolkit NLTK chose Python (see Bird, Klein, and Loper 2009).

Lists

In terms of sophistication, the next most complicated data type in Python is a *list*, also called a *data structure*.[8] (A string is a data structure as well.) A list is a collection of items; the items can be Booleans, integers, floats, complex numbers, or text strings. In fact, a list can contain other lists. Lists are enclosed in [and], and each element in the list must be separated by a comma. For example,

```
>>> scores = [20, 18, 19]
>>> names = ["Golyaev", "Paarsch", "Segre"]
>>> grades = [names, scores]
>>>
```

Each element in a list has an assigned index value; the index always begins at 0. If a list is of length N, then the last element in the list has index value N-1. You can find the length of a list by using

```
>>> len(scores)
3
>>> len(grades)
2
>>> scores[0]
20
>>> names[1]
'Paarsch'
>>> grades[0][2]
'Segre'
>>> grades[0][2][3]
'r'
```

---

[8]In computer science, a data structure is a particular way of organizing data and then storing them in a computer. Data structures are used so that information can be accessed efficiently.

As you can see, indexing a list of lists involves at least two sets of indices; in this case, the first corresponds to the first list, while the second corresponds to the second list. Why does grades[0][2][3] return 'r'? Because grades[0][2] is 'Segre' and the fourth character of that string is the letter r. Remember: In Python, the initial index of a list and a string is 0.

A list can be empty, too, for example,

```
>>> empty = []
>>> len(empty)
0
>>>
```

in which case its length is zero.

As mentioned, strings are immutable, which means that you cannot change them. Of course, you can reassign a value to a string, and you can "add" (concatenate) strings, but changing a specific element is forbidden in Python. Lists, on the other hand, are *mutable*, that is, you can change them. For example, you can replace an element in the list using the following:

```
>>> grades[1][1]
18
>>> grades[1][1] = 25
>>> grades[1][1]
25
>>>
```

```
>>> favorites = ["Python"]
>>> favorites.append("R")
>>> favorites
['Python', 'R']
>>>
```

An element can be inserted into a list—see the .insert(1,"SQLite") command, an element can be removed from a list—see the .remove("R") command, or the entire list can be deleted—see the del favorites command.

```
>>> favorites.insert(1, "SQLite")
>>> favorites
['Python', 'SQLite', 'R']
>>> favorites.remove("R")
>>> favorites
['Python', 'SQLite']
>>> del favorites
```

```
>>> favorites
Traceback (most recent call last):
  File "<stdin>", line 1, in <module>
NameError: name 'favorites' is not defined
>>>
```

One of the most useful commands creates a list from a range of numbers, as in

```
>>> counter = range(0, 10)
>>> counter
[0, 1, 2, 3, 4, 5, 6, 7, 8, 9]
>>>
```

where the upper bound of the range, in this case 10, is not included. You can just create the even numbers, or the odd numbers, using

```
>>> evens = range(0, 10, 2)
>>> evens
[0, 2, 4, 6, 8]
>>> odds = range(1, 10, 2)
>>> odds
[1, 3, 5, 7, 9]
>>>
```

Of course, you can sort a list as well.

```
>>> numbers = [5, 2, 3, 1, 4]
>>> numbers.sort()
>>> numbers
[1, 2, 3, 4, 5]
>>> scientists = ["Galileo", "Newton", "Einstein"]
>>> scientists.sort()
>>> scientists
['Einstein', 'Galileo', 'Newton']
>>>
```

If you do not want the list to be changed by the sort operation, then use the following:

```
>>> numbers = [5, 2, 3, 1, 4]
>>> sorted(numbers)
[1, 2, 3, 4, 5]
>>> numbers
[5, 2, 3, 1, 4]
>>>
```

which returns a new copy of the list, but sorted. Other, less commonly used commands exist as well. You can learn about them using the `pydoc` command, which is invoked on the command line of a terminal window, as in

```
$ pydoc list
```

but you can invoke `pydoc` for just about anything within Python: `pydoc file` or `pydoc open` or `pydoc os` or `pydoc raw_input` or `pydoc sys`. Just to be clear, you cannot execute `pydoc` from within the Python interactive window; you have to exit Python and use the command within a terminal window.

For help within the Python interactive window use `help`, as in

```
>>> emptyList = list()
>>> help(emptyList)
Help on list object:

...
```

and

```
>>> import gzip
>>> help(gzip)
Help on module gzip:

...
```

You might want to explore a bit with the Python functions and modules that we listed.

The following exercise illustrates an important feature of lists:

```
>>> x = 3
>>> y = x
>>> x, y
(3, 3)
>>> y = 4
>>> x, y
(3, 4)
>>> xList = [1, 2]
>>> yList = xList
>>> xList, yList
([1, 2], [1, 2])
>>> yList[1] = 3
>>> xList, yList
```

```
([1, 3], [1, 3])
>>> yList.append(4)
>>> xList, yList
([1, 3, 4], [1, 3, 4])
>>>
```

Something curious has happened: when an element of yList is changed, or an element is appended to yList, xList changes, too. What's going on here?

In Python an assignment statement does *not* copy the contents of the source location to a new location for the target. Instead, the assignment links the target to the source; that is, in memory xList and yList point to the same location.

For collections of objects that are mutable, such as lists, a copy may be required, so you can change one version without changing the other. To do this, you will need the copy module. Thus, to copy the elements of one list into another, you must do the following:

```
>>> import copy
>>> xList = [1, 2]
>>> yList = copy.copy(xList)
>>> xList, yList
([1, 2], [1, 2])
>>> yList[1] = 3
>>> xList, yList
([1, 2], [1, 3])
>>> yList.append(4)
>>> xList, yList
([1, 2], [1, 3, 4])
>>>
```

In addition to the copy.copy() function, a copy.deepcopy() function exists. The output of copy.copy() is sometimes referred to as a *shallow copy* to distinguish it from the output of copy.deepcopy(). We don't pursue this here but mention the issue to avoid surprises and to encourage you to learn about the two functions on your own.

Tuples

Tuples are a curious data type in Python. Like strings, tuples are immutable, but like lists, tuples are sequences of objects. Python distinguishes between lists, which are enclosed in [and], and tuples, which are enclosed in (and). Thus,

```
>>> scores = [20, 18, 19]
>>>
```

is a list, whereas

```
>>> weekDays = ("Su", "M", "Tu", "W", "Th", "F", "Sa")
>>>
```

is a tuple. A tuple with just one item is referred to as a *singleton*. One curious fact about a singleton is that the element must be followed by a comma; otherwise, it will not be typed as a tuple. For example, consider

```
>>> unique = ("Paarsch")
>>> type(unique)
<type 'str'>
>>> unique
'Paarsch'
>>>
```

whereas

```
>>> unique = ("Paarsch",)
>>> type(unique)
<type 'tuple'>
>>> unique
('Paarsch',)
>>>
```

Tuples can be sliced, just like strings, and it is possible to exceed the range of a tuple, as with strings, for example,

```
>>> unique[0]
('Paarsch')
>>> unique[3]
Traceback (most recent call last):
  File "<stdin>", line 1, in <module>
IndexError: tuple index out of range
>>>
```

Like strings, tuples can be concatenated.

```
>>> first = ("Harry",)
>>> type(first)
<type 'tuple'>
>>> last = ("Paarsch",)
```

```
>>> type(last)
<type 'tuple'>
>>> name = first + last
>>> name
('Harry', 'Paarsch')
>> len(name)
2
>>> type(name)
<type 'tuple'>
>>> name[0]
'Harry'
>>> type(name[0])
<type 'str'>
>>>
```

In short, the elements of a tuple are not tuples but rather the type of the data, for instance, integer, float, string, and so forth.

Dictionaries

Perhaps the most sophisticated of the basic data types in Python is the *dictionary*. Elsewhere in computer science, this data structure is referred to as a *map* as well as an *associative array*, a *hash table*, and a *symbol table*. Elements in a dictionary are referenced by a *key* which is connected to a *value*. Together, these are referred to as *key-value pairs*. In Python the key and the value are connected by :, a colon. Key-value pairs are separated by commas. Whereas the list is contained within [and] and the tuple is contained within (and), the dictionary is contained within { and }. Like lists and tuples, the elements of a dictionary can be referenced, but the index is not a number. In fact, you can decide what the index should be. Some rules exist: the most important rule is that each key must be unique. In other words, a key can be used only once in the dictionary. Because the index of a dictionary need not have a natural ordering, some refer to dictionaries as *unordered*.

An example may make things clearer.

```
>>> hashTable = {"hjp": "Paarsch, Harry J.",
                 "kg":  "Golyaev, Konstantin",
                 "ams": "Segre, Alberto M."}
>>> type(hashTable)
<type 'dict'>
>>> len(hashTable)
```

```
3
>>> hashTable['kg']
'Golyaev, Konstantin'
>>> type(hashTable['kg'])
<type 'str'>
>>> len(hashTable['kg'])
19
>>> hashTable
{'ams': 'Segre, Alberto M.', 'kg': 'Golyaev, Konstantin', 'hjp': '
    Paarsch, Harry J.'}
>>>
```

Even though the elements of the dictionary were entered in a particular order, they come back in another order when hashTable is typed. In short, dictionaries are unordered.

Python has some functions that allow you to manipulate the keys and values of a dictionary. For example,

```
>>> hashTable.keys()
['ams', 'kg', 'hjp']
>>> hashTable.values()
['Segre, Alberto M.', 'Golyaev, Konstantin', 'Paarsch, Harry J.']
>>>
```

To update an element of a dictionary or to add a new element or to delete an element, you would proceed as you would with a list, except now you would use the key:

```
>>> hashTable['kg'] = "Golyaev, Konstantin"
>>> hashTable['kg']
'Golyaev, Konstantin'
>>> hashTable['klj'] = "Judd, Kenneth L."
>>> hashTable['klj']
'Judd, Kenneth L.'
>>> del hashTable['klj']
>>>
```

Variable Names

In the olden days, when computer memory was scarce, programming languages such as FORTRAN were forced to use short variable names of at most six characters. Consequently, it was difficult to use self-describing variables names. Today, memory is cheap, so self-describing names are encouraged.

One common naming convention is CamelCase (see Section 2.3.4). Under this convention, the first word of a variable name is in all lowercase letters, whereas later words are mixed, that is, the first letter is uppercase, and the rest are lowercase. Thus, `tempInCelsius` represents the variable name for temperature in Celsius and `tempInFahrenheit` the variable name for temperature in Fahrenheit. Although this is a stylistic convention, not a rule, we encourage you to adopt this naming convention because it is commonly used by others.

4.3.4 Python Backslash Characters

Python has several control (escape) characters that you should know in order to work effectively within the language. These characters begin with the \ and are thus called *backslash characters*. Because the backslash character \ has special meaning in Python, you need to be able to express it. To do this, use two backslash characters, \\. Other such characters appear in Table 4.2. We include several of these characters for completeness and to make you aware that they exist. In practice, the most commonly used ones are \\, \', \", \n, \r, and \t; sometimes, you may have to use \N but rarely the others. Fine, but what is a Unicode value?

4.3.5 A Digression on Character Sets

The American National Standards Institute (ANSI, pronounced "ann-see") is a private nonprofit organization created to oversee the development of standards for products, services, processes, systems, and personnel in the United States. The organization also coordinates American standards with international ones so that American products can be sold and used worldwide.[9]

In the 1950s the American Standards Association (ASA), a predecessor of ANSI, sought to define a system under which computer characters would be consistently mapped across different computers. In 1963 the ASA (which became ANSI in 1969) released the first version of the American Standard

---

[9]From http://en.wikipedia.org/wiki/American_National_Standards_Institute.

Character	Description
\\	backslash
\'	single quote, strong quotation mark
\"	double quote, weak quotation mark
\a	bell
\b	backspace
\f	form feed
\n	line feed
\N	character having `name` in the Unicode database
\r	carriage return
\t	horizontal tab
\uxxxx	16-bit hexadecimal Unicode value xxxx
\uxxxxxxxx	32-bit hexadecimal Unicode value xxxxxxxx
\v	vertical tab

Table 4.2: Backslash Characters in Python

Code for Information Interchange (ASCII, pronounced "ask-key").[10] Under the ASCII encoding system, the numbers 0–9, the letters a–z and A–Z as well as some basic punctuation symbols and control codes were represented uniquely by a seven-bit binary integer for each. For example, the letter "A" has the ASCII representation "1000001", whereas "a" has the ASCII representation "1100010".

The ASCII system was adopted quickly by the majority of American computer manufacturers and was eventually turned into an international standard. Although ASCII became the de facto international standard, the system could not admit some special characters, such á, ê, and ü, which are common in non-English, Latin-based alphabets. To get around this problem, ANSI extended ASCII to include additional codes.

Despite these accommodations, the International Organization for Standardization (ISO) in Geneva, Switzerland, adapted the ASCII code to accommodate other languages by substituting some characters.[11] Because ISO 646 did not satisfy all requirements, the ISO 8859-1 standard was subsequently created and then the Universal Character Set (UCS, or Unicode).

---

[10]From http://en.wikipedia.org/wiki/ASCII.

[11]From http://en.wikipedia.org/wiki/International_Organization_for_Standardization.

By the way, IBM, the dominant mainframe computer manufacturer in the 1960s and 1970s, created its own six-bit Binary Coded Decimal Interchange Code (BCDIC), which it then developed into a proprietary eight-bit Extended Binary Coded Decimal Interchange Code (EBCDIC).[12] You may see reference to this format in software documentation, but it is unlikely that it will affect you today.

You are more likely to encounter references to ANSI on a Microsoft Windows system where the term refers to the Windows ANSI code pages, which are not ANSI standards.

4.3.6 Single or Double or Triple Quotes?

As mentioned in Section 2.3.5, two types of quotation marks exist in UNIX: the single quote ′ (the strong quotation mark) and the double quote " (the weak quotation mark). UNIX has no use for triple quotes, but Python does.

In Python you can use single or double quotation marks interchangeably, but we suggest that you decide when you are going to use the singles and when the doubles.

One convention is to use the double quotation marks in string interpolation or for natural language messages. What is string interpolation? Consider the following:

```
numberDogs = 10
print "The quick brown fox jumped over %d lazy dogs." % numberDogs
```

The interspersing of strings (in this case, %d) within strings is referred to as *interpolation*. In this case, the integer contents of numberDogs is brought into the text being printed.

What are natural languages? Language spoken by people; for instance, English, French, German. Proceeding further under this convention, single quotation marks are then used for small symbol-like strings. Obviously, if you have quotations inside of quotations, you will need to break from tradition. For example,

```
print "The quick brown fox jumped o'er the lazy dogs."
```

---

[12]From http://en.wikipedia.org/wiki/EBCDIC.

produces

```
The quick brown fox jumped o'er the lazy dogs.
```

whereas

```
print "He\'s \"crazy,\" you know."
```

produces

```
He's "crazy," you know.
```

For more on escape characters, see Section 4.3.4 and Table 4.2.

Sometimes, for whatever reason, you may need to include long strings of alphanumeric data, such as a poem. You could include both continuation and escape characters, but that would not be very elegant and could become tedious. Python allows you to create strings using triple quotation marks, that is, either three single quotes in a row, without spaces between them or three double quotes in a row, without spaces between them, for instance, """. Although either will work, we suggest you stick to """ exclusively. Note that when you use triple quotes, whitespace(s) at the beginning of a line will be included in the string. Thus,

```
rhyme = """
Mary had a little lamb whose fleece was white as snow.
And everywhere that Mary went that lamb was sure to go.
"""
print rhyme

Mary had a little lamb whose fleece was white as snow.
And everywhere that Mary went that lamb was sure to go.
```

The blank line above `Mary had ...` is induced by the linefeed after `rhyme = """`, whereas

```
rhyme = """Mary had a little lamb whose fleece was white as snow.
And everywhere that Mary went that lamb was sure to go.
"""
print rhyme
Mary had a little lamb whose fleece was white as snow.
And everywhere that Mary went that lamb was sure to go.
>>>
```

results in no blank line above.

Docstrings

A *docstring* is a string literal that occurs as the first statement of a function (see Section 4.3.7).[13] Docstrings are contained within two sets of triple weak quotes. A docstring becomes the __doc__ special attribute of that object. An example might be the following:

```
def FeetToMetres(feet):
    """ This function converts feet into metres. """
    centi  = 2.54
    inches = 12.0
    return feet * inches * centi / 100.
```

Beware: The indentation in the preceding example is critical. If you were to type help(FeetToMetres) at the three >s within the Python interpreter window, then you would see the following:

```
Help on function FeetToMetres in module __main__:

FeetToMetres(feet)
    This function converts feet into metres.
(END)
```

4.3.7 Functions

After data types, the next most important construct in Python is the *function*. Up to now, the Python code you have written has been imperative: do this, then do that, then do this. Early in the history of programming on digital computers, Maurice Wilkes, David Wheeler, and Stanley Gill proposed the notion of a purpose-built collection of computer instructions, bundled as a logical unit, that could be reused. They referred to this as a *subroutine*, but the terms *method*, *procedure*, *routine*, and *subprogram* have been used elsewhere in computer science as well. Thus, another idea in computer science is referred to as *modularity*. In order to avoid having everything depend on everything else, completing tasks is divided into smaller tasks, where each task takes an input (or inputs) and returns an output (or outputs).

---

[13]The docstring should also be the first statement of a module, a class, or a function definition. This is discussed later.

In Python *function* is the term used, where each function has the following structure:

```
def FunctionName(argumentList):
  """ Docstring description. """
  instruction1
  instruction2
  and_so_forth
  return someOutput
```

That is, the first line always begins with `def`, followed by the name of the function, with arguments of the function always in parentheses; the first line always ends with `:`, a colon. It is considered good programming practice in Python for the next few lines to be a docstring in which the purpose of the function is described. Following the docstring are the instructions that do the work. At the end of the function, control is passed from the function back to whatever program called the function. This is done using the instruction that begins with the keyword `return`, and typically some information is sent back to the calling program. The main thing to note is that every line after the first line defining the function has to be indented; indentation is a logical feature of the Python language. By how much? In many textbooks on Python, four spaces is the convention. In Section 4.3.12 we discuss indentation in some detail. In these examples, we just use two spaces, which is sometimes referred to as *Google style*.

The following is a working example of a function:

```
def InchesToCentimetres(inches):
  """ This function converts inches to centimetres. """
  return 2.54 * inches
```

In this function, the user must supply an input, a dimension in inches, and the function converts this to centimetres.

Suppose you have saved this function in the file `Functions.py`. To use it, invoke `python` at the command line prompt `$`. At the Python prompt, type the following:

```
>>> import Functions
>>> Functions.InchesToCentimetres(12)
30.48
>>>
```

Had you typed the following instead,

```
>>> import Functions
>>> InchesToCentimetres(12)
Traceback (most recent call last):
  File "<stdin>", line 1, in <module>
NameError: name 'InchesToCentimetres' is not defined
>>>
```

you would have received an error message. Why didn't a direct call to the function `InchesToCentimetres(12)` work?

The function `InchesToCentimetres` lives in `Functions.py`. If you just want to refer to `InchesToCentimetres` without `Functions.`, then you need to use the following:

```
>>> from Functions import InchesToCentimetres
>>> InchesToCentimetres(12)
30.48
>>>
```

Function Names

For functions, we modify the self-describing CamelCase naming convention slightly: all functions must begin with a capital letter. Thus, if you were to encounter the name `Celsius2Fahrenheit`, you would know that this is a function because the first letter is capitalized. As we mentioned in Chapter 2, this is sometimes referred to as Pascal case because the convention was advocated by users of the Pascal programming language. Because the name `tempInCelsius` begins with a lowercase letter, it clearly refers to a variable that is passed to the function; the function would return the variable `tempInFahrenheit`. Under this convention, you can distinguish clearly between functions and variables.

Should you use the cutie-pie convention of converting the preposition "to" into the integer "2" or "for" into "4" as some coders do? You can probably tell from the way the previous question is worded how we feel about that.

Golyaev advocates a naming convention where the first word in all functions is a verb, which is also part of Google style. You may want to follow this convention, but in the following we did not.

Another question is whether you should use underscores _ in either function or variable names. We counsel against using underscores in either function or variable names because it is sometimes difficult to see them.

Of course, in Chapter 3, we did use the underscore when writing SQL code. We deviated from our convention because dialects of SQL are case insensitive; for example, `AuctionsTable` can appear either as `auctionstable` or as `AUCTIONSTABLE`, depending on how your preferences are set. Here, the underscore makes `AUCTIONS_TABLE` easier to read. In short, the convention that you choose may be language-specific; within a language, however, you should be consistent.

4.3.8   Input/Output

Raw computing and data processing are typically the two main functions of a Python script. Without getting data into the script and then being able to see the output, however, all efforts are for naught. Until now, we have used hardcoded assignment statements to input data. When we wanted to see what a variable's address contained, we simply typed the name of the variable at the Python prompt; in some cases, we used `print` statements. At least two other options exist to get data into a Python script: input from the keyboard or input from a file. Similarly, other ways exist to output data.

Perhaps the simplest way to input data into a Python script involves typing in the information at the keyboard. Clearly, this is both time consuming and error prone, but in some cases this alternative really is best. For example, suppose you want to write a script that calculates the body-mass index (BMI) for a person. You want the script to take in user-specific information, such as height and weight, and then to return a BMI and perhaps a recommendation like "Maybe you should lose some weight!"

The `raw_input` function is your friend. The `raw_input` function accepts information that has been typed in at the keyboard; this function also allows you to include a text string that will prompt the user. A slight problem exists: `raw_input` stores the user-supplied information as a string. Therefore, if you want this information to be Boolean, integer, float or complex, then you need to convert the user-supplied information into a data type of your choice, which can be processed further. Fortunately, this conversion is relatively straightforward to execute.

Consider the following example where the user supplied the inputs `69` and `198.5` is typed into a Python interpreter window:

```
height = raw_input("What is your height, in inches?  ")
What is your height, in inches?  69
```

```
>>> height
'69'
>>> type(height)
<type 'str'>
weight = float(raw_input("How much do you weigh, in pounds?   "))
How much do you weigh, in pounds?   198.5
>>> weight
198.5
>>> type(weight)
<type 'float'>
>>> height = int(height)
>>> type(height)
<type 'int'>
>>> height
69
>>>
```

You could accept the input, and then convert it to a different data type, as in the case of `height`, or just do it all at once using a conversion function, as in the case of `weight`.

Clearly, the scope for major data processing or statistical analysis is extremely limited when the `raw_input` function is used. The most efficient alternative is to read in data from a computer file. This is not as straightforward as you might like it to be. Consider `InputFile.dat`, which has the following contents viewed using `more`.

```
The first line.
The second line.
The third line.
```

Listing 4.1: Sample `InputFile.dat`

You require two steps: First, you must identify the relevant file to the Python interpreter; second, you must read in the data. To execute the first step, do the following:

```
>>> inputFile = open('InputFile.dat', 'r')
>>> type(inputFile)
<type 'file'>
>>> inputFile
<open file 'InputFile.dat', mode 'r' at 0x2b5180>
>>>
```

The first instruction assigns the variable name `inputFile` to the object `open('InputFile.dat', 'r')`. From the self-describing name, it seems obvious that 'InputFile.dat' is an input file containing data, but what about 'r'? The 'r' means that you want to 'r'ead from that file. Other modes include 'w'rite and 'a'ppend; on a Windows machine, you also have the option of 'b'inary, that is, either reading in binary data or writing them out. If, however, you try the 'b' mode on UNIX-like machines, you will get an error message.

The second step involves reading in the data from the file. Try the following:

```
>>> fileData = inputFile.read()
>>> type(fileData)
<type 'str'>
>>> fileData
'The first line.\nThe second line.\nThe third line.\n'
>>>
```

The entire contents of the file has been read into one long string, where the end-of-line characters are the \n. For some problems, such as text processing using regular expressions, this may be acceptable; for other problems, it is downright awkward. Is there a way in which we could just go through the file line by line? Of course, there is: this is Python. A clunky way would be the following:

```
>>> inputFile = open('InputFile.dat', 'r')
>>> firstLine = inputFile.readline()
>>> secondLine = inputFile.readline()
>>> thirdLine = inputFile.readline()
>>> [firstLine, secondLine, thirdLine]
['The first line.\n', 'The second line.\n', 'The third line.\n']`
>>>
```

whereas a streamlined way would be

```
>>> lines = []
>>> for line in open('InputFile.dat', 'r'): lines.append(line)
...
>>> lines
['The first line.\n', 'The second line.\n', 'The third line.\n']
>>>
```

That is, the lines of the file now reside in a list named lines. You could now loop through this list (see Section 4.3.9) and process the information as you see fit. Now send the output to the file OutputFile.out.

```
>>> outputFile = open('OutputFile.out', 'w')
>>> for n in range(0, len(lines)): outputFile.write(lines[n])
...
>>> outputFile.close()
>>>
```

What is this `.close()` feature?

If you do not formally close the file, you will be unable to see the contents when you then type `more OutputFile.out` in another terminal window. Having closed the file, you will see the following:

```
The first line.
The second line.
The third line.
```

Listing 4.2: Sample `OutputFile.out`

Sometimes, however, you do not want to have each line as an element of a list; for example, you may want to split a line at certain points, perhaps at the end-of-line characters or at whitespaces. What to do? Use the `split()` function. For example, consider `InputNumbers.dat`, which has the following structure:

```
1 2 3
4 5 6
7 8 9
```

Listing 4.3: Sample `InputNumbers.dat`

The following Python script brings in the file, splits the file into lines, and then splits the lines into lists of integers.

```
inputFile = open('InputNumbers.dat', 'r').read()
lines = inputFile.split('\n')
x = []
y = []
z = []
N = len(lines)
for n in range(0, N-1):
  row = lines[n].split()
  x.append(int(row[0]))
  y.append(int(row[1]))
  z.append(int(row[2]))
```

Listing 4.4: Python Example `Split.py`

In the preceding code examples, we used the native Python functions `int` and `float` to convert strings into integers and floats, and then collected them in lists. This is certainly an acceptable way to proceed. Although lists look like vectors or arrays, they really aren't. In particular, the kind of algebra that you are used to using on vectors does not work with lists. For example, having imported the script `Split.py`, you could do the following:

```
>>> import Split
>>> Split.x
[1, 4, 7]
>>> Split.y
[2, 5, 8]
>>> Split.z
[3, 6, 9]
>>> Split.x + Split.y + Split.z
[1, 4, 7, 2, 5, 8, 3, 6, 9]
>>>
```

What to do now? You could write a whole mess of Python code to perform scientific calculations, or you could just import the package `numpy`, or other modules and packages like it, to make your work easier (see Section 4.4).

4.3.9 Loops

In Python the `for` statement allows you to execute a block of code repeatedly. Python is different from programming languages like C and FORTRAN in that you can iterate over members of a list, or elements of a string. The `for` statement has the following structure:

```
for element in list:
  instruction1
  instruction2
  and_so_forth
```

An example of this would be the following:

```
# Print out centimetres for each integer inch from 1 to 6.
for inch in range(1, 7):
  print "%d inches equals %4.2f centimetres." % (inch, 2.54*inch)
```

Notice three features: first, the loop begins with `for`; second, the `for` line ends with a colon; and third, the code block to be executed repeatedly is indented.

Each of these features is required; without them, the code will not work. The output of this loop looks like this:

```
1 inches equals 2.54 centimetres.
2 inches equals 5.08 centimetres.
3 inches equals 7.62 centimetres.
4 inches equals 10.16 centimetres.
5 inches equals 12.70 centimetres.
6 inches equals 15.24 centimetres.
```

We looped over integers in a range of numbers, but you could loop over the names in a list, as in

```
for author in ["Paarsch", "Golyaev"]:
  print author
```

which would yield

```
Paarsch
Golyaev
```

or

```
word = "elk"
for letter in word:
  print letter
```

which would yield

```
e
l
k
```

4.3.10   Conditional Statements

Sometimes you would like to perform one set of instructions if one condition is met, but another set of instructions if a second condition is met. In Python you can use *conditional statements* to do this. Specifically, the keywords of the Python language that allow you to implement conditional logic are if, elif, and else. The basic structure can have one of the following forms:

```
if (logical expression):
  perform a task
```

when you want to perform the task only if the logical expression is true. On the other hand, you would use the following code,

```
if (logical expression):
  perform True task
else:
  perform False task
```

to perform the "True" task if the logical expression is `True`, or the "False" task if the logical expression is `False`. The instructions are evaluated sequentially: specifically, the second branch (the "False" task) will never be reached if the logical expression is `True`.

The following code can be used when more than two alternatives exist:

```
if (first expression):
  perform a task
elif (second expression):
  perform a second task
elif (third expression):
  perform a third task
else:
  perform the last task
```

By now the basic structure is clear: the first keyword is an `if` or an `elif` or an `else`. (You have probably guessed that `elif` is an abbreviation of "else if.") The last character of each statement must be a colon. Both the `if` and the `elif` statements must have a logical condition. Finally, the text after the `if`, `elif`, and `else` statements must be indented; this is a logical feature of the Python language.

4.3.11   While

Although the `for` loop is a very powerful construct in Python, it is really only suited for iterating through a list of fixed, known length. What to do in cases where the number of iterations depends on some criterion that evolves as the instructions within the loop are being executed?

For example, in optimization, one strategy used to maximize (or to minimize) a continuous and differentiable function f having argument x is to continue to try to improve the function until the derivative function g, often referred to as the *gradient function*, evaluated at a candidate solution $\hat{x}$, is near zero, that is, $g(\hat{x}) \approx 0$, or $|g(\hat{x})| < \delta$, where δ is some prescribed tolerance.

Abstracting from the specifics concerning how the function is optimized and how the gradient is calculated, the Python pseudocode for this case would be something like the following:[14]

```
maxIter = 100
noIter = 0
tolerance = 1.e-6
x = initialX
converged = False
while ( (not converged) and (noIter < maxIter) ):
  improve objective function
  calculate gradient
  noIter += 1
  if (abs(gradient) < tolerance):
    converged = True

if ( (noIter >= maxIter) and (not converged) ):
  print "No convergence after %d iterations." % noIter
```

In this pseudocode, we first assign a parameter `maxIter` (short for maximum iterations) to 100, and a counter `noIter` to zero, while a `tolerance` is prescribed to be 0.000001, which can be written in scientific notation as `1.e-6`. The variable of interest `x` is then assigned an initial value `initialX`. As the function is not yet optimized, the Boolean variable `converged` is assigned the value `False`. While convergence has not obtained and the number of iterations is less than `maxIter`, we continue to try to improve the objective function and measure our progress using the gradient. When the absolute value of the gradient falls below the tolerance level `tolerance`, `converged` is assigned the value `True`. If convergence has not been attained after `maxIter` iterations, the user is notified.

4.3.12 Indentation, Whitespaces, and Tabs

To some SDEs, one serious design problem with the Python language is the use of blank spaces, or whitespaces, as part of the language. In short, if you write the following two lines of Python code,

---

[14]Pseudocode is a high-level outline of the instructions, one without the specific details; that is, pseudocode is an abstraction of the actual code. Pseudocode is often written using the conventions of a programming language (for example, here we use the conventions of Python), but it is intended only to help the reader understand, not to be executed on a computer. In short, pseudocode won't work as written.

```
n = 12345
  print "n = %d" % n
```

where two spaces have been included (for whatever reason) before the `print`
statement in the second line, you will get the following error message:

```
File "Error.py", line 2
    print "n = %d" % n
    ^
IndentationError: unexpected indent
```

Some SDEs believe that this is simply *wrong* (their emphasis, not ours). We
do not feel this way. In fact, to us, all the debate concerning whitespacing is
really misplaced. Whitespaces are not the issue in Python: indentation is. And
indentation is really not an issue because the style of indentation is up to you.
Namely, the exact number of spaces or tabs used does not matter at all; only
relative indentation, which determines nested blocks, matters. Thus, the use of
two whitespaces to indent

```
for n in range(0, 10):
  print "n = %d" % n
  if (n % 2 == 0):
    print "n is even."
  else:
    print "n is odd."
```

Listing 4.5: Two-Whitespace Style of Indentation in Python

is one feasible implementation, but so is

```
for n in range(0, 10):
    print "n = %d" % n
    if (n % 2 == 0):
      print "n is even."
    else:
      print "n is odd."
```

Listing 4.6: Another Style of Indentation Using Tabs

where a tab has been used. You can see the problems with tabs right away:
tabs look like a collection of whitespaces, at least to the naked eye.[15] Moreover,
although we do not agree with the following formatting:

---

[15]Good text editors can automatically replace tabs with spaces and automatically insert spaces
instead of tabs, useful in creating Python scripts—in fact, in creating any file except `Makefiles`,

```
for n in range(0, 10):
  print "n = %d" % n
  if (n % 2 == 0):
    print "n is even."
  else:
      print "n is odd."
```

Listing 4.7: A Style We Don't Like

it would work as well. We do not like the last implementation because the instruction after `else:` has an extra tab and thus does not balance with the instruction after `if (n % 2 == 0):`. Balance makes the logic easy to see, thus helping the reader understand the code.

In short, in Python you can insert arbitrary numbers of whitespaces anywhere, except at the beginning of lines. Moreover, the limit point of whitespaces—blank lines—can be inserted virtually anywhere. See, for example,

```
for n in range(0, 10):

  print "n = %d" % n

  if (n % 2 == 0):

    print "n is even."

  else:

    print "n is odd."
```

Listing 4.8: A Ridiculous but Acceptable Style

which, in our opinion, is ridiculous but acceptable to Python.

At the beginning of lines, however, relative indentation changes the language's logic. The issue that concerns some SDEs is that an inadvertent stray indentation could change the logic of a Python script. Note, too, that if you use explicit or implicit continuation lines, the indentation level is ignored. For example, in the following:

---

which require tabs. For example, in the case of the `vim` text editor, you can use the `retab` command, and in your `.vimrc` you can set `expandtab`, set `smarttab`, set `shiftwidth=4`, and so forth.

```
Names = ["Paarsch, Harry",
         "Golyaev, Konstantin"]
```

a list has been split across two lines, and the indentation is ignored.

One thing you really need to be careful with in Python is mixing spaces and tabs. To be clear, spaces and tabs are processed without any problems by the Python interpreter; human beings are the problem. Here's why: If you borrow code that has tabs in it, say from another project, then the indentation induced by tabs may not be obvious to the naked eye, but the existence of potentially multiple tabs could change the logic of your code. You will eventually figure out the problem, particularly if you have a good programming editor, such as jEdit, but it could take some extra time. Thus, the moral is, do not use tabs when writing Python code; just use spaces. Moreover, only use a couple of spaces, not five or ten; two spaces will make the logical point, are visually perceptible, and make parsimonious use of space. (We know that disk space is cheap, but why waste space?)

4.3.13   Exceptions

Inevitably, in programming, despite your best intentions, something will happen that causes your script to fail. Python will throw an exception, which is usually accompanied by an error message that may look something like the following:

```
>>> N = 10
>>> numbers = range(0, 10)
>>> numbers[N]
Traceback (most recent call last):
  File "<stdin>", line 1, in <module>
IndexError: list index out of range
>>> x = 0.
>>> y = 1. / x
Traceback (most recent call last):
  File "<stdin>", line 1, in <module>
ZeroDivisionError: float division by zero
>>>
```

Most of the time, these error messages are somewhat informative, but sometimes you really cannot tell what happened just from the information provided by Python. Now, you could just stand by or perhaps try to repair the problem after the failure. One drawback with this is that the script may have been running for several days, so the failure could result in your losing considerable output. Even if you exercise care and attention, some information is inevitably lost when a script crashes. Moreover, to the extent that you can, you would like the computer to take care of these events on its own—to be automated to address errors, so to speak. The keywords `try` and `except` and `finally` allow you to do this. In Section 4.8.7 we demonstrate how to use this trio of instructions when creating a SQLite database.

4.3.14 Recursion

Recursion is not a keyword of the Python language, nor is it a function. Instead, it is a particular way of implementing an algorithmic strategy referred to as *divide-and-conquer* (see Section 6.2.7, page 344). Under the divide-and-conquer strategy, the solution to a problem depends on solutions to smaller instances of the same problem. An example will help make this clear. Consider the expression $n!$, the factorial of n, where n is an integer. The factorial of n is defined as

$$n! = n \times (n-1) \times \cdots \times 3 \times 2 \times 1 = \prod_{i=1}^{n} i = n \prod_{i=1}^{n-1} i = n \times (n-1)!.$$

Specifically, $n!$ can be broken into the product of n and $(n-1)!$, the factorial of $(n-1)$. Thus, you need a function that calculates the factorial of $(n-1)$. But $(n-1)!$ can be broken down further into the product of $(n-1)$ and $(n-2)!$. You can see this will eventually end when 0 is reached; by convention $0!$ is 1.

Like many modern programming languages, Python supports a function's calling itself, which is referred to as *recursion*. The following function implements the idea of recursion, which is central to the elegant calculation of $n!$:

```
def Factorial(n):
    """ A function to calculate n! for some integer n.
        Divide-and-conquer strategy is exploited as well
        as Python's ability for a function to call itself,
        also known as recursion.
    """
    if (type(n) != int):
```

```
    print "The input variable is not an integer."
    return n
  if (n < 0):
    print "The input is negative."
    return n
  if (n == 0):
    return 1
  else:
    return n * Factorial(n-1)
```

Listing 4.9: Using Recursion within a Python Function

The first two sets of `if` statements check to see whether the input is, in fact, an integer, and whether it is then positive. If one of these conditions fails, then the function returns a flag as well as the offending input. Only when a valid input is given does the function do any work.

4.3.15 Keywords Not Yet Introduced

In the Python language, the vocabulary has only 34 keywords, listed in Table 4.3. Up to this point, we have used 19 of them: `and`, `as`, `def`, `del`, `elif`, `else`, `except`, `finally`, `for`, `from`, `if`, `import`, `in`, `not`, `or`, `print`, `return`, `try`, and `while`. Most of the others are introduced later. In the meantime, you should research what the remaining ones do.

and	as	assert	break	class
continue	def	del	elif	else
except	exec	filter	finally	for
from	global	if	import	in
is	lambda	map	not	or
pass	print	raise	reduce	return
try	while	with	yield	

Table 4.3: Keywords in the Python Language

4.3.16 Modules

Although the Python interpreter is a handy calculator, the main strength of any computer language is that you can reuse code created previously, perhaps for other tasks, with only minor or no modification. We introduced the function as a way to modularize computer code. However convenient the function may be, having dozens or hundreds of purpose-built functions that must be placed at the top of each program so they will be defined before being used is a pretty clunky way of reusing code. Thus, Python provides the *module*, in which any number of function definitions can be collected and then brought in all together using the keyword `import`.

Another guiding principle in computer science is *abstraction*. Abstraction is the process of separating ideas from specific applications of those ideas. For example, you may want to sort a list of numbers, but the principles that allow sorting of any set of objects are general. Abstraction requires solving the general problem rather than the particular application.

Suppose the module `Misc` lives in `Misc.py` and contains the following two functions:

```
def Factorial(n):
  """ A function to calculate n! for some integer n.
      Divide-and-conquer strategy is exploited as well
      as Python's ability for a function to call itself,
      also known as recursion.
  """
  if (type(n) != int):
    print "The input variable is not an integer."
    return n
  if (n < 0):
    print "The input is negative."
    return n
  if (n == 0):
    return 1
  else:
    return n * Factorial(n-1)

def PartialSum(x):
  """ This function returns the partial sum of the elements
      of a list of integers or floats.
  """
  for n in range(0, len(x)):
    if ( (type(x[n]) != int) and (type(x[n]) != float) ):
      print "Invalid input:  neither int nor float."
      return type(x[n]), 'Element', n

  partialSum = [x[0]]
```

```
  for n in range(1, len(x)):
    partialSum.append(partialSum[n-1]+x[n])

  return partialSum
```

Listing 4.10: Example Module `Misc`

To use these functions within the Python interpreter, do the following:

```
>>> import Misc
>>> x = range(1, 6)
>>> n = 10
>>> Misc.Factorial(n)
3628800
>>> Misc.PartialSum(x)
[1, 3, 6, 10, 15]
>>>
```

Another way to use the functions in the module `Misc` would be

```
>>> from Misc import Factorial, PartialSum
>>> x = range(1, 6)
>>> n = 10
>>> Factorial(n)
3628800
>>> PartialSum(x)
[1, 3, 6, 10, 15]
>>>
```

The general consensus among those skilled in Python is that this latter alternative is poor programming practice. Previous programmers may have introduced functions like `Factorial` and `PartialSum`. By importing those names, you could be overwriting those functions, which may be needed for other operations. So avoid that.

If you are using a Python script, for example `TestOfMisc.py`, then it could have the following form:

```
import Misc
x = range(1, 6)
N = 10
print "%d! = %d." % (N, Misc.Factorial(N))
print "The partial sum of: %s." % x
print "is:              %s." % Misc.PartialSum(x)
```

Listing 4.11: Test of `Misc` Module

The next code segment illustrates executing the script from the command line:

```
$ python TestOfMisc.py
10! = 3628800.
The partial sum of: [1, 2, 3, 4, 5].
is:                 [1, 3, 6, 10, 15].
$
```

Built-in dir() Function

Sometimes, when you are within the Python interpreter, you might want to know what is available and what is not. In such cases, the built-in function dir() can be helpful. For example, when you first invoke Python, before any module has been imported, using dir() yields the following:

```
>>> dir()
['__builtins__', '__doc__', '__name__', '__package__']
>>> import Misc
>>> dir()
['Misc', '__builtins__', '__doc__', '__name__', '__package__']
>>> dir(Misc)
['Factorial', 'PartialSum', '__builtins__', '__doc__', '__file__', '
    __name__', '__package__']
>>>
```

4.3.17 Packages

One of the reasons to use the Python language is that other researchers are doing so too. In short, network externalities exist. Inevitably, with many people working in Python, duplicate names are going to arise. How to get around the fact that a name like Factorial used by one person in one context could mean something else to another in another context? The creators of Python developed a device, referred to as a *package*, that admits a particular naming convention for the module namespace, sometimes called *dotted module names*.

For example, the module name numpy.random designates the dotted module random in the package numpy. Modules prevent the creators of different modules from having to worry about global variable names used by others. The use of dotted module names means that the creators of multimodule packages (such as numpy) do not need to worry about module names.

Modules versus Packages

A module is a single file that is imported under one `import` instruction, as in `import Misc`, whereas a package is a collection of modules in directories with a hierarchy, for example, `from numpy.random import uniform` brings in a `uniform` pseudo-random number generator from the `random` dotted module of the `numpy` package.

Technically, any Python file is a module, its name being the file's base name without the `.py` extension, whereas a package is a collection of Python modules. Although a module is a single Python file, a package is a directory of Python modules containing an additional `__init__.py` file, to distinguish a package from a directory that just happens to contain a bunch of Python scripts. Packages can be nested at any depth, providing the corresponding directories contain their own `__init__.py` file. At this point, you do not need to worry about the fine details; just remember that modules are different from packages.

4.3.18 Different Ways to Execute Python Scripts

In the preceding examples, we typically executed Python commands within the interpreter window because most of the commands were simple and the interpreter gives quick feedback. Also, unlike, say, IPython, the basic Python interpreter window is not very forgiving, so you must be precise (or type fast). In any case, for most important projects, you need to collect Python commands in a file, or *script*, and then execute them together. This can be done in three ways. In all cases, the commands are entered into a file; the key differences are in how the file is executed.

Consider the first example, where the Python script is actually named `ScriptName.py`. The contents of `ScriptName.py` are displayed here, perhaps by invoking `more ScriptName.py`.

```
#!/usr/bin/python
# Script:  ScriptName.py
# Author:  Harry J. Paarsch
# Date:    29 October 2013
def Factorial(n):
  """This is an example of a Python function.
     Notice that the docstring must be indented.
  """
  if n == 0:
```

```
      return 1
  else:
      return n * Factorial(n-1)

def main():
  """This is an example of a Python script.
      Here the docstring needs to be indented, too.
  """
  # Capture a user-supplied number and make it an integer.
  number = int(raw_input("Enter an integer:   "))
  # Print out the user-supplied number and its factorial.
  print "%d! = %d" % (number, Factorial(number))

if __name__ == '__main__':
  main()
```

Listing 4.12: Sample Python Script

```
$ python ScriptName.py
Enter an integer:   10
10! = 3628800
```

Another way involves making the Python script executable. To use this method, you must first make your script (again, `ScriptName.py`) executable using the following command:

```
$ chmod 744 ScriptName.py
```

The second condition is that the first line of `ScriptName.py` must look something like

```
#!/usr/bin/python
```

Whether this is the correct default path depends on the Python interpreter you are using. On an Apple Mac, it is the correct default path name. Paarsch uses a different version of Python from the default installed on an Apple Mac. In that case, the first line would be

```
#!/Library/Frameworks/Python.framework/Versions/Current/bin/python
```

To find out which version of Python is used by default, type the following in a terminal window:

```
$ which python
```

If you are using the default installation of Python, then the response will be as stated, namely,

```
$ /usr/bin/python
```

Having made `ScriptName.py` executable, you can then invoke the following:

```
$ ./ScriptName.py
Enter an integer:   10
10! = 3628800
```

Yet a third way to execute this code involves the following: first, get into the Python interpreter window; next, `import ScriptName`; and, finally, invoke the `main()` program using `ScriptName.main()`.

```
$ python
Python 2.6.1 (r261:67515, Jun 24 2010, 21:47:49)
[GCC 4.2.1 (Apple Inc. build 5646)] on darwin
Type "help", "copyright", "credits" or "license" for more information.
>>> import ScriptName
>>> ScriptName.main()
Enter an integer:   10
10! = 3628800
>>>
```

Of course, if you did the following,

```
$ python
Python 2.6.1 (r261:67515, Jun 24 2010, 21:47:49)
[GCC 4.2.1 (Apple Inc. build 5646)] on darwin
Type "help", "copyright", "credits" or "license" for more information.
>>> from ScriptName import main
>>> main()
Enter an integer:   10
10! = 3628800
>>>
```

you would not have to include `ScriptName.` in the call to `main()`.

4.4   Useful Modules and Packages

In this section, we describe briefly some Python modules and packages that will make your work easier.

4.4.1 `copy`

By default, Python does not make deep copies of objects like lists, which may give unexpected results, if you do not know what, say, list assignment actually does. For this reason, the `copy` module is useful.

4.4.2 `math`

This module is useful because it provides access to the mathematical functions defined by the C standard. The functions are listed in the Table 4.1.

4.4.3 `numpy`

The website `http://www.numpy.org` reports that `numpy` is the fundamental package for scientific computing with Python. Among other things, it contains

- a powerful *N*-dimensional array object,

- sophisticated (broadcasting) functions,

- tools for integrating C/C++ and FORTRAN code,

- useful linear algebra, Fourier transform, and random number capabilities.

4.4.4 `matplotlib`

Creating figures and graphs is a common task assigned to research assistants. Fortunately, these are straighforward to accomplish in Python using the `matplotlib` module.

Typically, the figures and graphs you create are used with other inputs to prepare a final document or presentation. Therefore, controlling the font size and style is important. `matplotlib` has the option to use LaTeX to manage text layout (see Chapter 10). This option has the following choices: Anti-Grain Geometry (AGG); Portable Document Format (PDF); and Postscript (PS). At this time, AGG is relatively uncommon, whereas PDF and PS are quite common and very mature, so we focus on those two. The LaTeX option is turned on using `usetex=True` in the `rc` settings. The `rc` setting is just a name for formatting.

You can control all the `rc` settings in the `matplotlibrc` file, but for many novices simply changing certain `rc` settings within a Python script is the easiest way to get the job done. For example, this book is typeset in Palatino fonts, so we wanted the text in the figures to match that font. Hence, we used

```
import matplotlib
#for Palatino and other serif fonts use:
matplotlib.rc('font',**{'family':'serif','serif':['Palatino']})
#for Helvetica and other sans serif fonts use:
#rc('font',**{'family':'sans-serif','sans-serif':['Helvetica']})
matplotlib.rc('text', usetex=True)
```

4.4.5 pandas

A library for data manipulation and analysis, `pandas` offers data structures and operations for manipulating numerical tables and time series. Fernando Pérez wrote the following about the book by Wes McKinney (2013) in which using the `pandas` package for data analysis is described:

> The scientific and data analysis communities have been waiting for this book for years: loaded with concrete practical advice, yet full of insight about how all the pieces fit together. It should become the canonical reference for technical computing in Python for years to come.

Among many machine learners in industry, McKinney's book has become the bible, and the `pandas` library an important tool.

4.4.6 scipy

As the website `http://www.scipy.org` reports, SciPy (pronounced "sigh pie") is a Python-based ecosystem of open-source software for mathematics, science, and engineering. In particular, the core modules and packages are:

- `numpy`,

- `matplotlib`,

- `ipython`,

- `pandas`,

- `scipy`.

The `scipy` library is a core package of SciPy that provides many user-friendly and efficient numerical routines, for example, routines to carry out numerical integration and optimization.

4.4.7 `ipython`

Fernando Pérez, the creator of IPython, has attempted to create a MATLAB-like environment by importing by default the `matplotlib`, `numpy`, and `scipy` modules and packages that provide many of the important features similar to those contained in MATLAB. You can import the module `ipython` (either interactively or from within a Python script) or invoke IPython at the command-line prompt. If you invoke IPython on the command line with the flag `-pylab`, then you have something like the MATLAB environment; `pylab` is meant to mimic MATLAB.

As mentioned, IPython also has Notebook, a web-based interactive computational environment inside IPython. Using Notebook, you can combine executing computer code, writing text, doing mathematics, creating figures and graphs, and exporting rich media into a single document, much like the software environment of Mathematica.

4.4.8 `sys`

The module `sys` provides access to some variables used or maintained by the interpreter and to functions that interact with the Python interpreter. For example, `sys.argv` is perhaps the most commonly used command; it provides a list of command-line arguments passed to a Python script, where `argv[0]` is the script name. Another commonly used command is `sys.exit([arg])`, which is used to exit from Python in a graceful way when an exception (error) is thrown.

4.4.9 `os`

The module `os` provides a way to interact with the operating system. For example, `os.path` allows you to manipulate paths of the UNIX operating system.

Using the `os` module requires considerable knowledge of the operating system on your computer. Although this module is incredibly powerful and useful, we suggest you wait until you are more experienced before using it extensively.

4.4.10   csv

The csv format is the most common import and export format for spreadsheets and databases. The module `csv` allows you to read and to write tabular data in csv format; writing data in formats that Excel can read effortlessly is clearly important (see Section 3.1).

4.4.11   json

A common format on the Internet is JSON. Python has a module that allows you to deal with JSON format efficiently and painlessly.

Consider the following Python code,

```
>>> hashTable = {
"studentNo": "123457",
"name":{"firstName":"Harry","middleInitial":"J.",
"lastName":"Paarsch"},
"address": {"residence": "Brockington House", "room": 210} }
>>>
```

which creates a dictionary containing the information shown in Section 3.6.2. Were you to import the `json` module into Python, you could write out the `hashTable` in JSON format using the following:

```
>>> import json
>>> with open('outFile.json', 'w') as outputFile:
...    outputFile.write(json.dumps(hashTable))
>>> hashTable
{'address': {'residence': 'Brockington House', 'room': 210},
 'name': {'firstName': 'Harry', 'lastName': 'Paarsch',
 'middleInitial': 'J.'}, 'studentNo': '123457'}
>>>
```

If you now invoke `more  outFile.json`, you will see something like this:

```
{"studentNo": "123457", "name": {"lastName": "Paarsch",
"middleInitial": "J.", "firstName": "Harry"}, "address":
{"residence": "Brockington House", "room": 210}}
```

Although XML is more commonly used than JSON, you may prefer JSON because the format supports the main data types in Python, for example, Booleans, integers, floats, strings, and dictionaries.

4.4.12 `sqlite3`

SQLite is a DBMS written in the C programming language (see Section 3.4). In contrast to, say, MySQL, SQLite is a free-standing program. Because it is incredibly compact (fewer than 700 kilobytes in size) and free-standing (easy to call from other languages), SQLite has been used extensively in situations where an RDB is required, but where size and portability are important. Thus, being able to use a compact, powerful DBMS from within Python is a boon.

4.4.13 `re`

As mentioned in Chapter 2, regular expressions are used to describe sequences of characters that are typically used to form a search pattern. The Python module `re` is a suite of tools that allows you to process text for regular expressions.

4.4.14 `nltk`

As the website `http://nltk.org` outlines, NLTK, the Natural Language Toolkit is a leading platform for building Python programs to work with human language data. NLTK provides easy-to-use interfaces to over 50 corpora and lexical resources, and a suite of text-processing libraries for classification, tokenization, stemming, tagging, parsing, and semantic reasoning. In *Natural Language Processing with Python*, Bird, Klein, and Loper (2009) provide a complete guide to `nltk`.

4.4.15 `urllib` and `urllib2`; `requests`

The `urllib` and `urllib2` modules provide functions to download data from the Internet. For example, the `urllib.urlopen()` function works like the built-in function `open()`, but instead of a filename, the function accepts a URL. A URL is, in fact, a file, just one on another computer. For example, consider the following:

```
>>> import urllib
>>> uniRecLoc = 'http://vinci.cs.uiowa.edu/~hjp/PGBookTest.html'
>>> bookWebPage = urllib.urlopen(uniRecLoc)
>>> bookWebPage
<addinfourl at 7839616 whose fp = <socket._fileobject object at 0
    x492f70>>
>>>
```

Because the functions in the `urllib2` module are more general than those in the `urllib` module, some users may find them easier to use. Other users recommend the `requests` module. Often, practical requirements determine which module to use. In other words, you need to examine the functions in each to decide which is better for the problem you are trying to solve.

4.4.16 `distutils`

The `distutils` package provides support for building and installing additional modules into a Python installation. The new modules may be either pure Python or extension modules written in C. In Chapter 9 we demonstrate how to incorporate code written in C to improve the performance of Python. For that task, the `distutils` package is important and useful.

4.4.17 `f2py`

Also in Chapter 9 we demonstrate how to incorporate code written in FOR-TRAN, again to improve the performance of Python. For that task, the `f2py` module of the `numpy` package is invaluable.

4.4.18 `numba`

The `numba` package is an essential part of any effort to speed up Python (see Chapter 9).

4.4.19 `xml`

Tools for processing XML are collected in the `xml` package. You may want to wait to use this package until you are more experienced, as using it requires some sophistication.

4.4.20 **`Tkinter`**

Although the main focus of this book is working on the command line, in a terminal window, you may be required to interact through a GUI. The module `Tkinter` allows you to create GUIs in Python. In this book, we do not review these tools. For an introduction, consider the final chapter of Campbell et al. (2009).

4.4.21 **Abbreviating Module and Package Names**

Some SDEs find typing out the complete name of a module or package very tedious and time consuming but do not recommend using the `from` option. You can abbreviate the module name as follows:

```
>>> import numpy as np
>>> A = np.array([[1.,2.],[3.,4.]])
>>> b = np.array([1.,1.])
>>> soln = np.linalg.solve(A, b)
>>> soln
array([-1.,   1.])
>>>
```

Because of this practice, some standard abbreviations have evolved, for example, as illustrated, `numpy` is imported as `np`, and it is common to import `matplotlib.pylab` as `plt`, and `pandas` as `pd`. Some also import `sqlite3` as `API`, but that is not as common.

4.5 Python Template

To reduce the amount of boilerplate typing that you do, we suggest that you create a Python template that has all the necessary structure already done. For example, in Listing 4.13 we provide an example of the form such a Python template might take. Thus, when beginning a new project, use the template as the foundation for the Python script you create.

```
#!/usr/bin/python
# The location of Python that you use.
# Script:   Template.py
# Author:   Harry J. Paarsch
# Date:     22 June 2014
```

```python
"""
Template of Python script format.
"""
# Bring in the necessary module and packages,
# using whatever abbreviations you would like.
import numpy as np

# Define the relevant functions.
def Function1(inputArgs):
  """ Docstring description of Function1.
  """
  # Some instructions would take place here
  # where inputArgs would create outputArgs.
  print "Inside Function1"
  print "Inputs: %1i and %s" % (inputArgs[0], inputArgs[1])
  outputArgs = (1, True)
  return outputArgs

def Function2(inputArgs):
  """ Docstring description of Function2.
  """
  # Some instructions would take place here
  # where inputArgs would create outputArgs.
  print "Inside Function2"
  print "Inputs: %1i and %s" % (inputArgs[0], inputArgs[1])
  outputArgs = (2, True)
  return outputArgs

# Begin the Python script that will do the work.
def main():
  """ Docstring description of the main function.
  """
  # Here is where the work would be done.
  inputArgs = (0, False)
  outputArgs = Function1(inputArgs)
  print "Exiting Function%1i: %s" % (outputArgs[0], outputArgs[1])
  outputArgs = Function2(inputArgs)
  print "Exiting Function%1i: %s" % (outputArgs[0], outputArgs[1])

if __name__ == '__main__':
  main()
```

Listing 4.13: Python Template

4.6   Design Documents, Flowcharts, and Unit Testing

Although writing and documenting your computer code would appear to be the most important part of solving a computing problem, successful programming involves a stage before that, and two after as well.

Whenever you develop computer code, you should follow a deliberate protocol. First, write a *design document* in which you describe the problem you want to solve. The design document need not be long, but it should contain enough details so that another person could understand what you are trying to accomplish. In particular, a good design document should spell out what problem you are trying to solve and how you propose to solve it, in broad algorithmic terms. In the design document, the input data should also be described—where you will get them, in what format they will be delivered, and so forth; the design document should describe how the output will be delivered and in what format.

The mere act of writing a good design document will require you to think clearly about what you are trying to accomplish. In addition, the design document can then form part of a technical appendix that accompanies your research.

Often, you will find it helpful to use a *flowchart* to depict pictorially what you are trying to accomplish. A flowchart is a type of diagram that represents how a computer program proceeds. In a flowchart, certain geometric shapes have particular meanings. For example, circles (or ovals) represent either the start or the end of a program, while arrows describe the flow of control. A rectangle presents a processing step (a collection of instructions), a diamond symbolizes that a decision must be made, and a parallelogram signifies either input or output. (Other symbols are used, too, but these five are the most common.)

In Figure 4.1, as an illustration, we depict a simple example of the flowchart for optimizing a function using a particular algorithmic strategy, quasi-Newton in this case. Typically, in such a simple example, a flowchart is unnecessary. In complex programs, however, a flowchart is invaluable; it is an important and useful tool that helps you visualize the flow of control in your computer code.

In order to know whether your code actually does what you had intended, you will need to test it. In fact, the process of testing the code has a name, *unit testing*. Unit testing involves developing several problems and accompanying

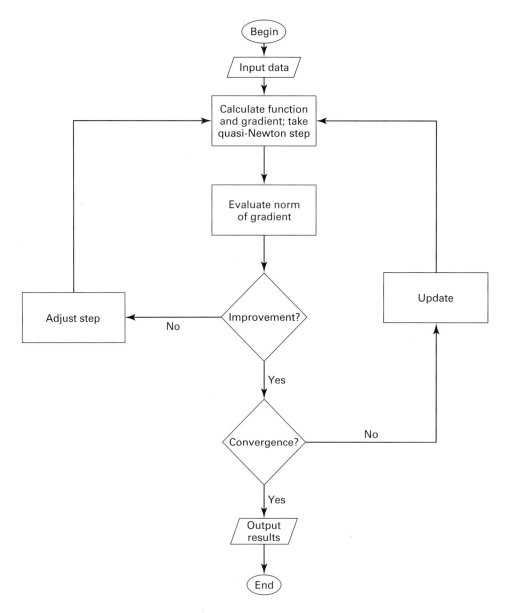

Figure 4.1: Example of a Flowchart

known solutions; the data from these problems are then used to demonstrate that your computer code does what you intended. Unit testing should be applied to the smallest testable part of the code. For example, in Python, a unit would typically be an individual function, but could be an entire module as well. Ideally, you should develop the unit test problems *before* you begin the coding, as part of the design document. Moreover, each test case should be independent of the others. Good test cases are designed to ensure that pathologies, often referred to as *edge cases* or *corner cases*, are handled by your code.

Having developed the design document, the flowchart, and the test cases, you are then in a position to write the code, documenting it as you go. Having completed writing and documenting the code, you are then in a position to unit test the code.

So, now you are done, right? Not exactly. At this point, you may want to optimize your code—improve it. At the very least, you should examine how the various parts of the code perform. To examine the code's behavior, you need to employ a software tool referred to as a *profiler*. We illustrate how profiling is done in the case of the R programming language in Section 5.5.5 and in the case of Python scripts in Section 9.1.

The following summarizes the steps involved in successful programming:

1. Create design document with flowchart and unit test problems.

2. Write code.

3. Document code.

4. Test code.

5. Profile and perhaps optimize code.

We hope that this brief description provides a useful direction for you to follow when developing code. But there is much more to learn about writing good software than we can provide. A helpful place to start is the book *Code Complete: A Practical Handbook of Software Construction* by McConnell (2004).

4.7 Miscellaneous Topics

As mentioned in Chapter 2, by convention standard Python scripts have the suffix .py. If you look in your current working directory, you may see files having the suffix .pyc. What are these files? Where do they come from? After a user-created module is imported, Python will generate another file with the same prefix, but the suffix `.pyc`. The code in a `.pyc` file is compiled bytecode; such code does not run any faster, but it is read in faster than standard Python source code.

You may also encounter files with the suffix `.pyo`, particularly if someone has sent you an archive of work done by another researcher. If the Python interpreter is invoked with the `-O` flag, then optimized code is generated and stored in `.pyo` files. Currently, the optimizer in Python does not do much; for example, it will remove assert statements, but it is not an optimizing compiler in the way some programmers feel an optimizer should work. When `-O` is used, all bytecode is optimized, that is, preexisting `.pyc` files relevant to the script are ignored and `.py` files are used to create optimized bytecode.

You may also encounter the suffix `.pyd`, which is basically a Windows `dll` file. To be clear, these are files that you would have taken an active role in creating, a role you would most likely remember; if these files appear in one of your subdirectories, then you probably did not create them. Put another way, if they are in your subdirectory, and you did not create them, they are either *really* important (so don't delete them) or *potentially* evil (so you should find out how they got there). We discuss what `dll` files do in Chapter 9.

4.8   Bringing It All Together

In this section, we present several solved examples that will allow you to bring together all the tools described so far. You can find many other examples on the Internet or in books like *Automate the Boring Stuff with Python* by Sweigart (2015). Each of our examples represents a task that a research assistant can be expected to complete. In fact, we have completed all of the tasks during our research lives, often many times. In many cases, other software tools exist that could be used to complete these tasks—tools that are perhaps faster, tools that may produce output of a higher quality than what is presented here.

At this point, a story may be instructive. The family of a former colleague of Paarsch, the Whitemans, had a homestead near the town of Biggsville, Illinois. When that colleague's father was about ten years old, he accompanied his father on a wagon trip to Burlington, Iowa, a town on the Mississippi River some 15 miles away. There, at the Sears, Roebuck & Company store, the colleague's grandfather purchased a thresher. When the salesman asked the colleague's grandfather whether he would like the machine assembled, he simply replied

"No, Dale [his son] and I 'll put 'er together." This last piece of information came as something of a surprise to the young boy and resulted in his enduring considerable anxiety during the wagon ride home.

When the pair arrived back at the homestead, they assembled the thresher together, with the boy carefully following each step. Soon, the boy was put to work harvesting with the thresher.

One day, he was in the fields harvesting with a cousin; the cousin found a snake, which he threw into the thresher, causing the machine to seize up and become totally useless. Although the boy was frustrated with his cousin's actions, because it meant several unproductive hours cleaning the machine in the hot sun, he simply got out his toolbox, disassembled the thresher, cleaned out the snake parts, and then reassembled it. Then the two continued with the harvest.

In short, the colleague's grandfather had been quite forward thinking when he accepted the thresher unassembled: by having his son help assemble it, he had a working machine and a mechanic who knew how it worked and who could repair it if necessary.

The moral of this story is that, in many cases, you do not save time by using software produced by others. Although a greedy approach to solving problems may yield short-run gains, the act of learning increases productivity and can yield even greater long-run gains, especially early in a career. Feed a man fish, feed him for a day; teach a man to fish, feed him for a lifetime.

4.8.1 Reading and Writing Numeric Data

One of the most common tasks faced by a research assistant involves reading in some data from a file, processing those data, and then writing some or all of the resulting data to another file, perhaps for further processing. As might be expected, Python's flexibility offers several different ways in which to complete such tasks, some straightforward, others not. In fact, the website `stackover-flow.com` has many ingenious suggestions concerning how to complete tasks like this, some of them needlessly complicated.

Here, we demonstrate how to use the `loadtxt` and `savetxt` functions from the `numpy` package. Based on our experience, we have found those functions easy to understand and straightforward to implement as well as versatile. We should mention, however, that Wes McKinney (2013), the developer of the

Python library `pandas`, recommends against using these two functions. However, we simply state our opinions when making these suggestions; you are free to use whatever tools make you effective when computing.

We begin by considering the file `Input.dat`, whose first ten rows are listed by invoking the command `head Input.dat`. In this example, the columns of data are separated by whitespaces.

```
# The variables (x, y, h) are (x,y) coordinates in the plane  of
# height h.   The data were created on <<date>> using <<source>>.
# x        y            h
  0.100   0.100       0.0019
  0.200   0.100       0.0038
  0.300   0.100       0.0075
  0.400   0.100       0.0145
  0.500   0.100       0.0276
  0.600   0.100       0.0516
  0.700   0.100       0.0944
```

Listing 4.14: First Ten Lines of `Input.dat`

The first three rows of `Input.dat` begin with the character #, which represents a comment in Python. The presence of the #s implies that these rows will be ignored by the interpreter. Each comment line is used to describe the variables that follow. Documenting data by describing when and where you got them as well as labeling the data are good habits to develop; when you return to a project in the future, you won't have to guess. If you are a graduate student, it is essential that you document data in this way; you may have graduated before the project is finished, and such documentation will often be the only information available to your successors to help them understand what you did.

The following code can be used to read in these data, to perform a transformation, to repackage the data as a new object, and then to write out the new data to another file in a particular format.

```
1  # Script:  ReadWrite.py
2  # Author:  Harry J. Paarsch
3  # Date:    29 October 2013
4  """ Read in a text file, process data, and output a new text
5      file in another format.
6  """
7  import numpy
8  x, y, h = numpy.loadtxt('Input.dat', unpack=True)
```

```
 9  d = numpy.sqrt(x*x + y*y)
10  dataOut = numpy.column_stack((d,h))
11  numpy.savetxt('Output.dat', dataOut, fmt=('%15.10f %10.4f'),
12      header='Created by ReadWrite.py on 29-Oct-2013:\n (d,h)')
```

Listing 4.15: Sample Python Script to Read and Write

The first executable line of the script, line 7, imports the `numpy` package, while in line 8 the contents of the file `Input.dat` are assigned to the `numpy` arrays x, y, and h using the `unpack` option which assigns each column to a particular array. If you do not provide enough arrays, Python will throw an error like this:

```
Traceback (most recent call last):
  File "<stdin>", line 8, in <module>
ValueError: too many values to unpack
```

In line 9 a transformation of the two vectors x and y is created, in this case, the Euclidean distance between each element in each of the two vectors, which is collected in the `numpy` array d. That is,

$$ d[i] = \sqrt{x[i]^2 + y[i]^2}. $$

The element-by-element multiplication of the vectors is possible because these are `numpy` arrays. Thus, the `numpy` array d is the same length as the `numpy` arrays x and y. If the vectors were `numpy` (or `scipy`) matrices, then a different operation would be required in order to complete element-by-element multiplication within the matrices. We believe that `numpy` arrays are more flexible than `numpy`/`scipy` matrices, so we use them almost exclusively and encourage you to do this as well.

In line 10 the object `dataOut` is created from the two vectors d and h, and in line 11 the output is saved to the file `Output.dat` with the two variables being written in the special floating-point formats `%15.10f` and `%10.4f`. These are fixed-format writes, where the first is fifteen columns wide with ten places after the decimal place, and the second is ten columns wide with four places after the decimal place. In line 12, which is a continuation of line 11, the argument

```
    header='Created by ReadWrite.py on 29-Oct-2013: \n (d,h)'
```

puts two comment lines at the top; the default first character is #.[16] Having

---

[16]Notice that the indentation does not matter here.

executed `ReadWrite.py`, you can invoke `head Output.dat` to see the following:

```
# Created by ReadWrite.py on 29-Oct-2013:
#   (d,h)
   0.1414213562        0.0019
   0.2236067977        0.0038
   0.3162277660        0.0075
   0.4123105626        0.0145
   0.5099019514        0.0276
   0.6082762530        0.0516
   0.7071067812        0.0944
   0.8062257748        0.1688
```

Listing 4.16: First Ten Lines of `Output.dat`

Two other useful formats exist as well: first, `%wi`, which is for a signed integer of width `w`, where `i` denotes the variable type integer; second, `%w.de`, which is a scientific format, where the field has width `w`, with precision `d`, and `e` is mnemonic for the exponential notation used in scientific format. For example,

```
n = 12345
print "n = %5i" % n
```

would yield

```
n = 12345
```

whereas

```
from numpy import pi
pi = (10**3) * pi
print "1000pi = %20.10e" % pi
```

would yield

```
1000pi =        3.1415926536e+03
```

Unlike in some other programming languages, such as FORTRAN, these formats are quite forgiving in the following sense: If you don't provide enough space to accommodate the width, then Python will adjust; if you provide more space than the width, then whitespaces will be added.[17] In short, the field will

---

[17]In FORTRAN, if you do not provide enough space for the values in a fixed-format write, then the field is returned full of asterisks.

be right-justified. Later, we demonstrate how you would proceed if you need to left-justify fields having variable lengths.

We should note that in general "unpacking" is not a great idea because the command splits the data columns into separate variables; subsequently, when using those columns, you must ensure that all observations align correctly. This is particularly important when analyzing data, which is described in Chapter 5. In that chapter, we introduce the Python library pandas, which is better suited to loading large blocks of data that can then be analyzed.

Reading Files That Have Comma-Separated Values

As mentioned, comma-separated values (csv format) is a commonly encountered format.[18] We discussed this format in Chapter 3 when we converted the contents of Excel spreadsheets to text files that could be brought into SQLite to create tables of a database. You can use the loadtxt function to read in the data, but need to add delimiter=',' as in the following,

```
import numpy
i, j, k = numpy.loadtxt('Input.csv', unpack=True, delimiter=',')
```

Listing 4.17: Python Script to Read csv File

where head -5 Input.csv would yield

```
# A csv file, for example, some integers separated by commas.
# i, j, k
1,2,3
4,5,6
7,8,9
```

Listing 4.18: First Five Lines of Input.csv

4.8.2 Reading in Mixed Numeric and String Data

Consider the contents of the file Grades.dat, which contains both numeric and textual data, namely, midterm and final examination scores as well as the first and last names of students.

---

[18]In fact, characters other than commas can be used to separate fields.

```
# Lastname, Firstname Mid1(max 25) Mid2(max 25) Final(max 50)
Golyaev,  Konstantin 22  18   40
Paarsch,  Harry J.  12  18   45
Segre,    Alberto M.  24  16   40
```

Listing 4.19: Input File `Grades.dat`

The `numpy` function `loadtxt` is ill-suited to reading in a mixture of variable types, but the `genfromtxt` function works just fine. To see how you can use this command, consider this script:

```
 1 | # Script:  Grades.py
 2 | # Author:  Harry J. Paarsch
 3 | # Date:    29 October 2013
 4 | """ Script to read in a text file of mixed data, process
 5 |     those data, and then write the output left-justified.
 6 | """
 7 | import numpy
 8 | import sys
 9 | grades = numpy.genfromtxt('Grades.dat', dtype=None,\
10 |                         delimiter='\t')
11 | N = len(grades)
12 | score = numpy.zeros([N,1])
13 | print "Grades"
14 | sys.stdout.write("{:<10}{:<10}{:<6}{:<6}{:<6}\n".format\
15 | ('Lastname,', 'Firstname', ' Mid1 ', ' Mid2 ', ' Final'))
16 | for n in range(0, N):
17 |   #print "%9s %10s %4i %4i %4i" % \`
18 |   #(grades[n][0], grades[n][1], grades[n][2], grades[n][3],\
19 |   # grades[n][4])
20 |   sys.stdout.write("{:<10}{:<10}{:=4}{:=6}{:=7}\n".format\
21 |   (grades[n][0], grades[n][1], grades[n][2], grades[n][3],\
22 |    grades[n][4]))
23 |   score[n] = grades[n][2] + grades[n][3] + grades[n][4]
24 |
25 | smin = numpy.min(score)
26 | sbar = numpy.mean(score)
27 | smax = numpy.max(score)
28 | sds  = numpy.sqrt(numpy.var(score))
29 |
30 | print "\nSummary Statistics of Final Scores\n"
31 | print "Students: %2i\n"  % N
32 | print "Mean:     %4.2f"  % sbar
33 | print "St.Dev.:   %4.2f" % sds
```

```
34 │ print "Minimum:   %2i"    % smin
35 │ print "Maximum   %2i\n"   % smax
```

Listing 4.20: Python Script `Grades.py`

Executing by `python Grades.py > Grades.out` yields the following,

```
Grades
Lastname,  Firstname  Mid1  Mid2  Final
Golyaev,   Konstantin  22    18    40
Paarsch,   Harry J.    12    18    45
Segre,     Alberto M.  24    16    40


Summary Statistics of Final Scores

Students:   3

Mean:       78.33
St.Dev.:     2.36
Minimum:    75
Maximum     80
```

Listing 4.21: Output File `Grades.out`

that is, the file `Grades.out`.

The first two executable instructions, lines 7 and 8, import the `numpy` package and `sys` module. The `sys` module is used to left-justify data, specifically, the first and last names of the students. In lines 9 and 10, the `numpy` function `genfromtxt` is used to take the data in the file `Grades.dat` and read them into the object `grades`. The length of `grades` is determined in line 11, and then the `numpy` array `score` is initialized to be zeros in line 12. In Python initialization is unnecessary; in a previous era, however, in other programming languages, initialization was taught as good practice, so we continue it here. The file is identified with the `print` statement in line 13, and then the function `sys.stdout.write` is used to print out a header identifying the data in `grades` in lines 14 and 15. The loop that begins in line 16 then outputs information concerning each student in lines 21–23. The format

$$\texttt{"\{:<10\}\{:<10\}\{:=4\}\{:=6\}\{:=7\}"}$$

ensures that the values corresponding to `grades[n][0]`, which is the last name, and `grades[n][1]`, which is the first name, are left-justified, whereas the values corresponding to `grades[n][2]`, `grades[n][3]`, and `grades[n][4]` are right-justified. Specifically, the `:<10` sequences mean that the last and first names are at most ten characters wide, whereas the `:=4`, `:=6`, and `:=7` mean that space of four, six, and seven should be used exactly. The remainder of the script simply processes the midterm and final examination grades into a final `score`, the summary statistics for which are calculated and then written out in a nice format.

The formatting statement in the writing case is much more complicated than that for printing cases, at the bottom of the script. That said, you can examine whether the effort was worth it by removing # for the `print` instruction and commenting out the lines that refer to the `sys.stdout.write` instruction, which would yield

```
Grades
Lastname, Firstname  Mid1  Mid2  Final
 Golyaev, Konstantin   22    18    40
 Paarsch,   Harry J.   12    18    45
   Segre, Alberto M.   24    16    40

Summary Statistics of Final Scores

Students:  3

Mean:      78.33
St.Dev.:    2.36
Minimum:   75
Maximum    80
```

Listing 4.22: Unattractive Output File for `Grades.py`

4.8.3 Creating a Histogram and an edf

Surowiecki (2004) began his book *The Wisdom of Crowds* with a fascinating anecdote involving the famous English polymath, Sir Francis Galton. In the story, Galton, then in his eighties, travels from his home in Plymouth to the West County Fat Stock and Poultry Exhibition. While attending this fair, Galton observes a competition of sorts in which participants, for a price, are encouraged to guess the dressed weight of a live ox, that is, after all the guesses have been gathered, the ox is slaughtered, dressed for meat, and weighed. The person who guessed closest to the dressed weight of the ox won a prize.

Although Galton was able to procure all 800 pieces of paper on which estimates were written, only 787 proved readable. As might be reasonably expected, some guesses were off by a lot. Nevertheless, even though not one person guessed the dressed weight of the ox exactly, three people did get within less than 2 pounds on either side, and sixteen within less than 5 pounds on either side. Moreover, about two-thirds of the guesses were within 5 percent on either side of the dressed weight.

Galton had an inherent distrust of allowing the general population to vote. In fact, his motivation for collecting the data was to demonstrate that the masses could not predict even the outcome of a straightforward contest. What astounded Galton, however, was that the sample median of the guesses ($1,207$ pounds) differed from the actual dressed weight ($1,198$ pounds) by only 9 pounds; in modern parlance, the median voter was out by a minuscule 0.8 percent. Galton reported these findings in the paper entitled "Vox Populi," which was published in the journal *Nature* (see Galton 1907).

Subsequently, Paarsch visited the Special Collections at University College London, where Galton's papers are archived, and obtained copies of the original 787 guesses. The sample mean of these guesses is $1,196.7$ pounds, which differed from the dressed weight by only 0.1 percent.

In this anecdote, you can view each guess as a realization of an unbiased estimator of the dressed weight. Presumably, the sample mean of 787 guesses (estimates) was so close to the true unknown weight because of the *law of large numbers*, which states that the sample mean converges to the population mean with probability 1 as the sample size gets large (787 is pretty large).

What does this have to do with Python? After some data have been read in, a frequent task involves describing those data using a histogram or perhaps the empirical distribution function (edf). Following are two scripts used to complete these tasks.

```
1  # Script:   GaltonHistogram.py
2  # Author:   Harry J. Paarsch
3  # Date:     29 October 2013
4  """ This script creates a histogram, labels it nicely, and then
5      saves it in two different formats for later processing.
6  """
7  import numpy
8  import matplotlib.pyplot
9  # Load the UCL File 179 data.
10 guess = numpy.loadtxt('../Data/Galton179.dat', unpack=True)
```

```
11 # Create a grid on which to evaluate the normal probability
12 # density function, in order to create a contrast.
13 g = numpy.array(range(801, 1600, 1))
14 # Calculate the mean and standard deviation of guess as
15 # well as the normal pdf under those parameters.
16 meanGuess = numpy.mean(guess)
17 stdGuess  = numpy.std(guess)
18 pdfGuess  = numpy.exp(-(g-meanGuess)**2/2./stdGuess/stdGuess)
19 pdfGuess  = pdfGuess / stdGuess / numpy.sqrt(2.*numpy.pi)
20 # Define the color gray.
21 gray = (0.7, 0.7, 0.7)
22 # Create the histogram.
23 matplotlib.pyplot.hist(guess, 50, normed=1, facecolor=gray,
24                        alpha=0.75)
25 # Plot the normal pdf.
26 matplotlib.pyplot.plot(g, pdfGuess, color='k')
27 # Put in some labels and a title as well as a grid.
28 matplotlib.pyplot.xlabel("Guess of Weight")
29 matplotlib.pyplot.ylabel("Relative Frequency")
30 matplotlib.pyplot.title("Histogram of Weight Guesses")
31 matplotlib.pyplot.axis([800, 1600, 0, 0.01])
32 matplotlib.pyplot.grid(True)
33 # Save the resulting figure in eps and pdf formats.
34 matplotlib.pyplot.savefig('../Figures/GaltonHistogram.eps')
35 matplotlib.pyplot.savefig('../Figures/GaltonHistogram.pdf')
36 matplotlib.pyplot.show()
```

Listing 4.23: Python Script to Create Histogram

After reading in the data and creating a grid on which to evaluate a normal probability density function, some descriptive statistics used in creating an estimate of the normal pdf are calculated; you have seen something like this before.

The first really interesting instruction begins at line 21, where we have defined the variable `gray`. What does $(0.7, 0.7, 0.7)$ mean? It is the representation of the color light gray in the R(ed)/G(reen)/B(lue) color model that is used throughout computing. In this model, any color can be formed by adding different amounts of the three colors red, green, and blue. If the RGB values are all the same, for example $(0, 0, 0)$, then the color is black; if the RGB values are

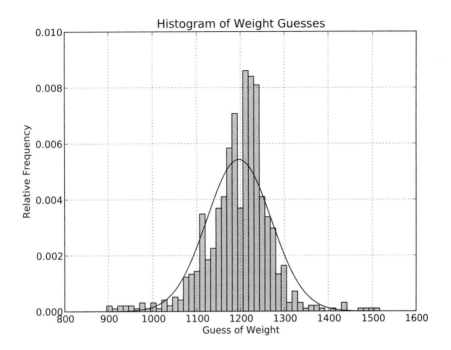

Figure 4.2: Histogram of Weight Guesses. Figure Created by `GaltonHistogram.py`

$(1, 1, 1)$, then the color is white. Thus, under this system, $(0.7, 0.7, 0.7)$ is light gray.[19]

Subsequently, the histogram as well as the approximate normal pdf are plotted, the labels and axes are rendered, a title is provided, a grid is laid down, and then the graphs are saved in two formats (EPS and PDF). Finally, the graph is shown in an interactive window, so you can decide whether this is what you want. Figure 4.2 shows such a histogram.

Following is a similar exercise for the edf. Recall that, for $\{y_n\}_{n=1}^{N}$, a sample of N observations, the edf at point y is defined by

$$\hat{F}_Y(y) = \frac{1}{N} \sum_{n=1}^{N} \mathbb{1}(y_n \leq y),$$

---

[19]In fact, the three values of RGB usually take on values between 0 and 255, that is, from the binary representation of zero 00000000 to the binary representation of 255, which is 11111111. Under this scheme, this shade of gray would be $(204, 204, 204)$.

where $\mathbb{1}(A)$ is an indicator function of the event A; that is, it equals 1 if the event is true, and 0 otherwise. In words, the edf is the proportion of the sample below the value y. Most of the code is the same as for the histogram, except for the instruction

```
edf = 1.*(1+numpy.arange(0,len(guess)))/len(guess),
```

which creates a vector of length `len(guess)`, which characterizes the proportion of the sample, and the instruction

```
matplotlib.pyplot.step(numpy.sort(guess), edf, 'k'),
```

which creates the step function that characterizes the edf and plots it with the sorted `guess` data. Figure 4.3 shows the output.

```
# Script:   GaltonEDF.py
# Author:   Harry J. Paarsch
# Date:     29 October 2013
""" This script creates the empirical distribution function (EDF),
    labels it nicely, and then saves it in two different formats
    for later processing.
"""
import matplotlib.pyplot
import numpy
from   scipy.stats import norm
# Load the UCL File 179 data.
guess = numpy.loadtxt('../Data/Galton179.dat', unpack=True)
# Calculate the mean and standard deviation of guess as
# well as the normal cdf under those parameters.
meanGuess = numpy.mean(guess)
stdGuess  = numpy.std(guess)
cdfGuess  = norm.cdf((guess-meanGuess)/stdGuess)
# Define the color gray.
gray = (0.7, 0.7, 0.7)
# Create the edf and then plot using the step function.
edf = 1. * (1+numpy.arange(0, len(guess))) / len(guess)
matplotlib.pyplot.step(numpy.sort(guess), edf, 'k')
# Plot the normal pdf.
matplotlib.pyplot.plot(numpy.sort(guess), cdfGuess, 'k--')
# Put in some labels as well as text.
matplotlib.pyplot.xlabel("Guess of Weight")
matplotlib.pyplot.ylabel("Empirical Distribution Function")
matplotlib.pyplot.axis([800, 1600, 0, 1.])
matplotlib.pyplot.grid(True)
matplotlib.pyplot.text(1220., 0.90, 'EDF')
matplotlib.pyplot.text(1305., 0.89, 'Normal')
matplotlib.pyplot.text(1305., 0.85, 'CDF')
```

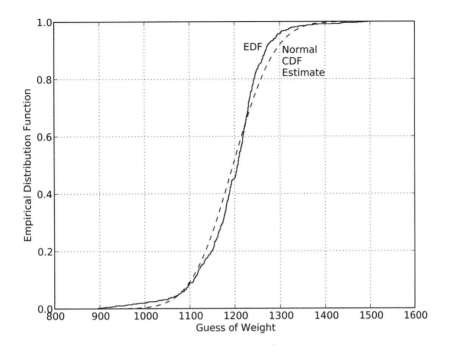

Figure 4.3: Figure Created by `GaltonEDF.py`

```
matplotlib.pyplot.text(1305., 0.81, 'Estimate')
# Save the resulting figure in eps and pdf formats.
matplotlib.pyplot.savefig('../Figures/GaltonEDF.eps')
matplotlib.pyplot.savefig('../Figures/GaltonEDF-eps-converted-to.pdf')
matplotlib.pyplot.show()
```

Listing 4.24: Python Script to Create an edf

4.8.4 Creating a Figure with TeX Characters

One common task given to a research assistant is to create figures for a paper or presentation. The figures often need to be integrated into the style of the paper or presentation. We have demonstrated creating such a figure, a histogram, using data. Here, we provide an example of Python code to generate a figure, with TeX fonts and symbols, that is then exported to EPS, which can then be used in later processing.

In the listing of `TeXFigure.py`, the first seven lines are really just boiler-plate, that is, the setup of the script that does not vary too much from script to script. In fact, you could have a template for this part to speed up your coding. At line 8, however, the real work begins. For the next six lines, we set up the fonts and the look of the figure. In line 14 we create axes, the abscissa of the function x, and the ordinate `g(x) = np.log(x)`. The self-describing naming convention of the creators of the `matplotlib` module and the `numpy` package, in conjunction with the comments introduced, make reading the remainder of the script straightforward.

```
1  # Script:   TeXFigure.py
2  # Author:   Harry J. Paarsch
3  # Date:     30 July 2013
4  """ Using TeX fonts and symbols in figures and graphs.
5  """
6  import matplotlib as plt
7  import numpy as np
8  # Use the TeX fonts.
9  plt.rc('text', usetex=True)
10 # Use fonts with serifs.
11 plt.rc('font', family='serif')
12 # Make a figure with x-dimension of 6 and y-dimension of 4.
13 plt.pyplot.figure(1, figsize=(6,4))
14 # Introduce the axes in fractions between 0 and 1.
15 ax = plt.pyplot.axes([0.1, 0.1, 0.8, 0.7])
16 x  = np.arange(0.01, 2.0-0.01, 0.01)
17 g  = np.log(x)
18 # Control line width and color, dynamically.
19 plt.rcParams['lines.linewidth'] = 2
20 plt.rcParams['lines.color'] = 'k'
21 # Create plot and then add x and y labels as well as title
22 # and grid.  Save the file to an eps file that can be
23 # brought into LaTeX using includegraphics.  Show the
24 # figure, too.
25 plt.pyplot.plot(x, g, color='k')
26 plt.pyplot.xlabel(r'$x$',fontsize=12)
27 plt.pyplot.ylabel(r'$g(x)=\log(x)$',fontsize=12)
28 plt.pyplot.title(r'Using \TeX\ Fonts', fontsize=16, color='k')
29 plt.pyplot.grid(True)
30 plt.pyplot.savefig('TeXFigure.eps')
31 plt.pyplot.show()
```

Listing 4.25: Python Script to Create Figure with TeX Annotation

The output is presented in Figure 4.4.

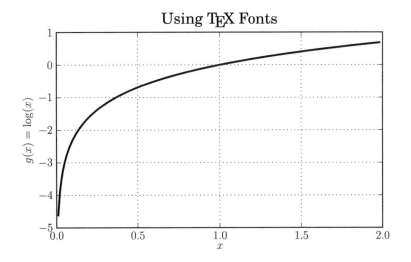

Figure 4.4: `matplotlib` Figure Using TEX Fonts and Symbols

4.8.5 Creating a Scatterplot

Sir Francis Galton, who was a half-cousin of the famous biologist Charles Darwin, was one of the most creative scholars of the latter part of the nineteenth century. When his father died, Galton inherited a considerable sum of money, which he used to indulge his wide intellectual interests. At various points in his life, Galton conducted research in anthropology, criminology, eugenics, genetics, geography, and meteorology as well as statistics and its application to psychology—psychometrics. In short, as mentioned, Galton was a polymath.

Although some of Galton's views have subsequently become controversial (for example, eugenics, the selective breeding of human beings), he was a prolific academic. His lasting contributions are in criminology (fingerprinting) and meteorology (the weather map) as well as statistics, where he introduced the concepts of *standard deviation* as well as *correlation*. In addition, Galton invented and made popular the technique of *regression analysis*, which is used to describe the expectation of one random variable (for example, the height of a son) conditional on another random variable (for example, the height of his father), a now ubiquitous technique in science. In fact, Galton's work concerning the heights of father and sons is perhaps his best-known and most lasting contribution to knowledge.

Galton noticed that fathers whose heights were above average had sons whose heights were, on average, less than theirs, whereas fathers whose heights were below average had sons whose heights were, on average, greater than theirs. He coined the term *regression towards mediocrity in hereditary stature*, which is today referred to as *regression towards the mean*, to describe this phenomenon.

In this example, we examine the original father/son height data that Galton gathered and tabulated. Colin Hanley and Louise Koo (under the direction of Professor James A. Hanley of McGill University) photographed the original pages of Galton's notebooks (see Hanley 2004). Paarsch keypunched the data into the file `GaltonFatherSon.dat`; the file has five columns and 934 rows. In fact, if you were to type `head -20 GaltonFatherSon.dat`, you would see the following:

```
# GaltonFatherSon.dat key-punched by Harry J. Paarsch in June
# 2005 from the jpgs of these photographs that live at the
# following URL:
#
# http://www.med.mcgill.ca/epidemiology/hanley/galton/
#
# The data are in five columns and 934 rows:  The first column is a
# family identification number, while the second column contains the
# height of the father in inches minus 60 inches (so a 9.0 means
# the father was five foot nine inches tall), the third column
# contains the height of the mother in inches, again minus 60 inches,
# while the fourth column is an indicator variable that equals one if
# this is a son and zero if this is a daughter.  The fifth, and final,
# column contains the height of an offspring, in inches minus 60.
#
   1 18.5   7.0 1 13.2
   1 18.5   7.0 0  9.2
   1 18.5   7.0 0  9.0
   1 18.5   7.0 0  9.0
   2 16.5   6.5 1 13.5
```

Listing 4.26: First Twenty Lines of `GaltonFatherSon.dat`

The following Python script creates a scatterplot with the height of the son on the ordinate and the height of the father on the abscissa.

```
1  # Script:   GaltonScatterplot.py
2  # Author:   Harry J. Paarsch
3  # Date:     18 December 2013
```

```
4  """ Script to create scatterplot using original data from Galton's
5      1885 research; data are annotated in first fifteen lines of
6      input file.
7  """
8  import matplotlib.pyplot as plt
9  import numpy as np
10 # Read in data from GaltonFatherSon.dat
11 familyID, heightFather, heightMother, isSon, heightOffspring = \
12 np.loadtxt("../Data/GaltonFatherSon.dat", unpack=True)
13 # Use the TeX fonts.
14 plt.rc('text', usetex=True)
15 # Use fonts with serifs.
16 plt.rc('font', family='serif')
17 # Select only the sons, and then plot son's height versus
18 # father's, adding in the 60 inches that Galton subtracted.
19 plt.scatter(60.+heightFather[isSon==1],\
20             60.+heightOffspring[isSon==1], color='k')
21 # Put in some labels and a title as well as a grid.
22 plt.xlabel("Height of Father, in Inches", fontsize=12)
23 plt.ylabel("Height of Son, in Inches", fontsize=12)
24 plt.title("Scatterplot of Heights:  Galton 1885 Data",\
25           fontsize=16)
26 plt.axis([56., 80, 56., 80.])
27 plt.grid(True)
28 # Save the resulting figure in eps and pdf formats.
29 plt.savefig('../Figures/GaltonScatterplot.eps')
30 plt.savefig('../Figures/GaltonScatterplot-eps-converted-to.pdf')
31 plt.show()
```

Listing 4.27: Python Script to Create Scatterplot

The script `GaltonScatterplot.py` has a very similar structure to two of our previous scripts. First, like `ReadWrite.py`, the data are read in using the numpy function `loadtxt`. Second, like `TeXFigure.py`, the TEX style for text is introduced. Third, the last part of the script, from lines 21–31, has a structure like the other scripts that created figures, with variation for content. The interesting instruction straddles lines 19 and 20 where the heights of fathers and offspring are plotted, for sons: notice the elegant way in which Python can select from the numpy array only those records for which the index has `[isSon==1]`. Very cool!

Figure 4.5 presents the scatterplot created by this Python script.

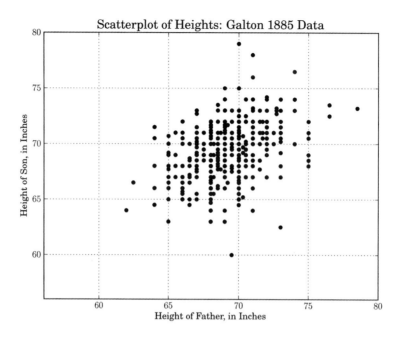

Figure 4.5: Scatterplot of Heights: Galton 1885 Data. Figure Created by `GaltonScatterplot.py`

4.8.6 Creating a LaTeX Table

Creating a table for a paper or presentation is a mundane yet important task. Accuracy is central to the success of the endeavor. In the distant past, such tables were generated by hand on a typewriter, but today they are often generated using a word processor, such as Microsoft Word. But typing each element of a table by hand using a word processor is fraught with potential error. Of course, you can always double- or triple-check your work, but humans are fallible. What you really want to do is use a computer program to read in all the data, to calculate the necessary descriptive statistics, and then to write out the table in a format that can be easily incorporated into a document or the slides of a presentation.

When writing up our research, we use LaTeX, a document markup language and preparation system for the TeX typesetting program. We recommend you do this too. Chapter 10 describes how to get started using LaTeX as well as other tools that accompany it. For example, for presentations, we use `Beamer`, a LaTeX class, to create slides.[20] Therefore, we want the output to be in the table format used by LATEX.

A LATEX table has the following basic structure,

```
1  \begin{table}
2  \centering
3  \begin{tabular}{|l|r|r|r|}
4  \hline
5  columnName1& columnName2& columnName3& columnName4\\
6  value11&value12&value13&value14\\
7  .
8  .
9  .
10 valueN1&valueN2&valueN3&valueN4\\
11 \hline
12 \end{tabular}
13 \caption{tableTitle}
14 \label{tab:labelName}
15 \end{table}
```

Listing 4.28: Example of Format of LATEX Table

where lines 1 and 15 begin and end the table, and line 2 centers the main part of the table. Lines 3 and 12 begin and end the tabular structure of the table, where the arguments {|l|r|r|r|} in line 3 indicate that the table is four columns wide, with the values in the first column left-justified (l), and the values in the next three columns right-justified (r). (If you want the values centered, the parameter would be c.) The vertical bars | tell LATEX to put vertical lines between columns of the table; these are added to make the table easier to read. Line 13 provides a caption for the table, while line 14 provides a label name that can be used to refer to the table elsewhere in the document or presentation. Line 5 introduces names for each of the four columns; the & (ampersand) characters define the columns, whereas \\ forces a new line. Lines 6 and 10 are representative lines where valueij denotes the (i, j) element of the table. Lines 4 and 11 simply place horizontal lines to bound the table. In lines 7–9 the dots represent ellipsis; in other words, they represent other data that might potentially appear in the table.

---

[20]The name Beamer derives from the German word *Beamer*, a pseudo-Anglicism for video projector.

Using these tools, you can automate this process. For example, suppose that Monte Carlo methods have been used to examine the small-sample performance of several different estimators of a key parameter θ. Denote the different estimators by $\hat{\theta}$, $\tilde{\theta}$, and $\check{\theta}$. Although the outcomes of the experiments could be in many different files, we assumed that the realized values from the Monte Carlo experiments are collected in the file `InputTable.dat`, which has three columns, one for each of the estimators $\hat{\theta}$, $\tilde{\theta}$ and $\check{\theta}$, respectively. In this example, the file is quite small, as `more InputTable.dat` reveals,

```
0.0 1.1 0.1
2.0 1.9 0.2
4.0 3.2 0.1
6.0 4.0 0.3
8.0 5.9 0.3
```

Listing 4.29: Contents of `InputTable.dat`

We have written a short program to load all these data and to create a LaTeX table of the summary statistics concerning the input data. The Python code is presented in Listing 4.30, the LaTeX code is presented in Listing 4.31, and the compiled table as Table 4.4. The key thing to note is that the backslash character in TeX needs special treatment in Python. Hence, in defining the character-string variables `begtable`, `centering`, `caption`, `label`, `begtabul`, `header`, `blank`, `cr`, `vskip`, `endtable`, and `endtabul`, an `r` precedes the string definition. The `r` means that the string is to be treated as a raw string, so all escape codes (such as the backslash \) are ignored. That is, the escape character \ is included in the variable name.

```python
# Script:   LaTeXTable.py
# Author:   Harry J. Paarsch
# Date:     10 July 2013
""" This script creates a LaTeX table using data from a structured
    input file of Monte Carlo data.
"""
import numpy as np
#
# Hard code the input file as well as the format of the inputs.
# In principle, this could be made more general.
#
inputFile = '/home/hjp/PGBook/Code/InputTable.dat'
x1, x2, x3 = np.loadtxt(inputFile, unpack=True, usecols=[0,1,2])
#
```

```
# Some example code to illustrate calculating descriptive statistics.
#
x1min  = min(x1)
x2min  = min(x2)
x3min  = min(x3)
x1max  = max(x1)
x2max  = max(x2)
x3max  = max(x3)
x1ran  = (x1max - x1min)
x2ran  = (x2max - x2min)
x3ran  = (x3max - x3min)
x1bar  = sum(x1)/len(x1)
x2bar  = sum(x2)/len(x2)
x3bar  = sum(x3)/len(x3)
sortx1 = np.sort(x1)
sortx2 = np.sort(x2)
sortx3 = np.sort(x3)
x1med  = sortx1[np.floor(len(x1)/2)]
x2med  = sortx2[np.floor(len(x2)/2)]
x3med  = sortx3[np.floor(len(x3)/2)]
#
# Now create the TeX characters:
# Note the r, which is mnemonic for 'raw'.
# r is used so Python won't trap the escape character \ .
#
that = r'$\hat\theta$'
ttil = r'$\tilde\theta$'
tchk = r'$\check\theta$'


begtable  = r'\begin{table}'
centering = r'\centering'
caption   = r'\caption{\Latex\ Table Created by \Python\ Script}'
label     = r'\label{tab:pytab}'
begtabul  = r'\begin{tabular}{|c|r|r|r|r|r|}'
header    = r'Estimator& Mean& Min.& Med.& Max.& Range\\'
hline     = r'\hline'
blank     = r' & & & & & \\'
amp       = '&'
cr        = r'\\'
vskip     = r'\vskip 2pt'
endtabul  = r'\end{tabular}'
endtable  = r'\end{table}'
#
# Now start to build the table in a brute-force way.
```

```
#
print begtable
print centering
print vskip
print begtabul
print hline
print header
print hline
print that,amp,'%.2f'%x1bar,amp,'%.2f'%x1min,amp,'%.2f'%x1med,amp,'%.2
    f'%x1max,amp,'%.2f'%x1ran,cr
print hline
print ttil,amp,'%.2f'%x2bar,amp,'%.2f'%x2min,amp,'%.2f'%x2med,amp,'%.2
    f'%x2max,amp,'%.2f'%x2ran,cr
print hline
print tchk,amp,'%.2f'%x3bar,amp,'%.2f'%x3min,amp,'%.2f'%x3med,amp,'%.2
    f'%x3max,amp,'%.2f'%x3ran,cr
print hline
print endtabul
print caption
print label
print endtable
```

Listing 4.30: Python Script to Create LATEX Table

Estimator	Mean	Min.	Med.	Max.	Range
$\hat{\theta}$	4.00	0.00	4.00	8.00	8.00
$\tilde{\theta}$	3.22	1.10	3.20	5.90	4.80
$\breve{\theta}$	0.20	0.10	0.20	0.30	0.20

Table 4.4: LATEX Table Created by Python Script

```
\begin{table}[!h]
\centering
\vskip 2pt
\begin{tabular}{|c|r|r|r|r|r|}
\hline
Estimator& Mean& Min.& Med.& Max.& Range\\
\hline
$\hat\theta$ & 4.00 & 0.00 & 4.00 & 8.00 & 8.00 \\
\hline
$\tilde\theta$ & 3.22 & 1.10 & 3.20 & 5.90 & 4.80 \\
\hline
```

```
$\check\theta$ & 0.20 & 0.10 & 0.20 & 0.30 & 0.20 \\
\hline
\end{tabular}
\caption{\Latex\ Table Created by \Python\ Script}
\label{tab:pytab}
\end{table}
```

Listing 4.31: LaTeX Output Table

In short, the output can then be inserted directly into a LaTeX document.

4.8.7 Creating a SQLite Database

In Chapter 3 we extolled the virtues of SQLite, a dialect of SQL. First, it is free; second, unlike MySQL and PostgreSQL, SQLite requires little or no knowledge of system administration to install—simply, place the executable in a pathed subdirectory, and you are done; and third, SQLite commands can be invoked from within Python scripts by importing the `sqlite3` module as an API. In short, SQLite is highly compatible with Python. In this section, we use the `sqlite3` module of Python to see whether SQLite really does play nicely with Python.

In particular, we want to demonstrate how to create a SQLite database using Python. First, to use SQLite within Python, you need to import the `sqlite3` module. Second, you need an input file that has the data. Let's use data concerning auctions that exist in `AuctionsTable.csv`, a file we `.import`ed into SQLite (see Section 3.5.4). Because this file has comma-separated values, we also import the `csv` module. Finally, we want to interact with the system, so we import `sys` as well.

To create the table `Auctions` in `AuctionsDataBase`, use the following Python script:

```
# Script:  SQLiteAuctionsDB.py
# Author:  Harry J. Paarsch
# Date:   12 December 2013
""" Script to read in a csv file of (potentially mixed) data,
    and create the table of a SQLite database, which is assumed
    to exist; in this case, its name is AuctionsDataBase.db.
    You need to change this if it is not.
"""
import csv
import sqlite3
```

```python
import sys

connection = None

try:
  connection = sqlite3.connect("AuctionsDataBase.db")
  with connection:
    current = connection.cursor()
#   Drop the old table, if there is one; create a new one.
    current.execute("DROP TABLE IF EXISTS Auctions;")
    current.execute("""CREATE TABLE Auctions (
        AuctionID     INTEGER
      , Volume        INTEGER NOT NULL
      , District      INTEGER NOT NULL
      , Date          TEXT NOT NULL
      , PRIMARY KEY   (AuctionID) );""")
#   Now populate the columns of the table.
    reader = csv.reader(open('AuctionsTable.csv', 'r'),\
                        delimiter=',')
    for row in reader:
      toDB = [unicode(row[0], 'utf8'), unicode(row[1], 'utf8'),
              unicode(row[2], 'utf8'), unicode(row[3], 'utf8')]
      current.execute("""INSERT INTO Auctions
                          (
                              AuctionID
                            , Volume
                            , District
                            , Date
                          )
                          VALUES(?, ?, ?, ?);""", toDB)

    connection.commit()

except sqlite3.Error, errorOutput:
  print "Error %s:" % errorOutput.args[0]
  sys.exit(1)

finally:
  if connection:
    connection.close()
```

Listing 4.32: Python Script to Create Table in SQLite Database

This Python script is relatively self-describing. What is perhaps most interesting about the script is the use of try, except, and finally, not discussed yet. Basically, having imported the appropriate modules, we establish a connection to the database through `sqlite3`. If no connection is made, then control is passed to `except`, and the error message is printed. With a good connection, we drop the old `Auctions` table, if it already exists, and then create the `Auctions` table, introducing four variables: `AuctionsID`, the primary key, as well `Volume`, `District`, and `Date`.

The complicated part is reading the data from `AuctionsTable.csv`. We chose to use a dictionary and process the input file line by line. Having read in all the lines of the file, and inserted each line into the table `Auctions` of the database, we then commit our changes. And `finally`, we close the connection; this last part is really overkill in the sense that by using `with` we guarantee the connection will be closed, but we consider this good programming practice.

4.8.8 Downloading Data from the Internet

Consider the following contents of a web page:

```
<html>
<head>
<title>What Every Research Assistant Should Know: Web Page</title>
</head>
<center><h1>Harry J. Paarsch and Konstantin Golyaev</h1></center>
<h2>This is a test web page designed so you can see how the
    function urllib2.urlopen() works.</h2>
</body>
</html>
```

Listing 4.33: Contents of Sample `html` Web Page

which lives at the following URL:

`http://vinci.cs.uiowa.edu/~hjp/PGBookTest.html`

The following Python script:

```
# Script:   DownloadWebPage.py
# Author:  Harry J. Paarsch
# Date:    22 December 2013
""" Read an html file from a web page on the Internet.
"""
import urllib2

uniRecLoc   = 'http://vinci.cs.uiowa.edu/~hjp/PGBookTest.html'
```

```
dataWebPage = urllib2.urlopen(uniRecLoc)

for line in dataWebPage.readlines():
  print line
```

Listing 4.34: `DownloadWebPage.py` Script

will yield

```
<html>
<head>
<title>What Every Research Assistant Should Know: WebPage</title>
</head>
<center><h1>Harry J. Paarsch and Konstantin Golyaev</h1></center>
<h2>This is a test web page designed so you can see how the function
    urllib2.open() works.</h2>
</body>
</html>
```

when the following is invoked on the command line of a terminal window:

```
$python DownloadWebPage.py
```

In short, you can read the lines of a web page and then use regular expressions to find and process relevant material. This is not always as difficult as it sounds because many web pages are computer generated and therefore have very regular structures, which are amenable to parsing using regular expressions.

4.8.9   Manipulating Text Using Regular Expressions

In any empirical project, on average, around 80 percent of your time will be spent cleaning data, a task often referred to as munging or wrangling. That is, more often than not, the raw data encountered in the wild are anything but clean. Here, *clean* means in a format that can be easily imported into other software with a minimum of bother. What complicates matters is that, unlike in the past, when only small amounts of data existed, today the volumes of data available are almost overwhelming.

For example, on the Internet, web pages contain a bewildering variety of data in many different formats, updated so frequently that cleaning these data in real time is impossible to do manually. Nevertheless, because web pages are just long text files, typically written in HTML, you can retrieve their source contents. With sufficient perseverance, you can then use a computer to reformat their contents into formats suitable for analysis.

In fact, both Python and R have packages that simplify such tasks. For example, the `elementtree` package in Python helps parse documents in HTML and XML formats; the `XML` package in R helps import files in the XML format. Once the data are in a clean format (see Section 5.3), existing software (for example, Python, R, and SQLite) can be used to process them easily and efficiently.

In other cases, however, data in the wild exist in not so tidy plain text formats, such as software execution logs: whenever you go to a website, a record is made each time you access a web page (a file) on that server. Such log files typically contain the date and time of the visit, the file touched as well as the operating system and the Internet address of the visitor. Ready-made packages are often of little use when analyzing the information in such files. Nevertheless, because information technology firms generate petabytes of raw data in log files, countless hours of computer time are spent converting the contents of these log files into clean data that can be analyzed. Even though such log files can be huge, they usually have a special structure. Because they are written by computer programs, the contents of such files possess a regular structure, although that structure may be complex. This regularity can be exploited using the tools associated with regular expressions (see Section 2.7).

Here, we demonstrate how you can use the Python regular expressions module `re` to clean data. Our example is based on real-world research. In graduate school, Golyaev was asked to clean some extremely messy data concerning the cable television industry in the United States. Covering the majority of all cable networks, the data were incredibly rich, providing information concerning channel bundle compositions as well as pricing, and subscriber counts. Unfortunately, the data were only available in printed form—a snapshot for each year.

In order to create a usable data set, Golyaev performed the following tasks: first, he scanned the paper copies to PDF files; next, he applied optical character recognition (OCR) on the scanned files to create ASCII formatted text files; finally, he used regular expression software to clean the plain text files and then to format the data into usable tables.

In this example, we demonstrate only the last task. In fact, to simplify matters, we pretend that the scanning and OCR parts were completed perfectly. Although perfection is usually a safe assumption when parsing log files that are computer generated, the OCR technology can make mistakes. Of course, imperfect recognition can be accommodated using sophisticated regular expressions, but that would make this example less instructive. In addition, we modified the source data, imposing additional regularity, mostly to simplify exposition; otherwise, the parsing code becomes unwieldy.

We provide the first few lines of the raw data file, those that concern one observation, namely, Albany.

```
ALBANY---Time Warner Entertainment Company LP. 130 Washington Avenue
    Ext,
Albany, NY 1220 3-5336.

Basic Service
Subscribers: 66,819.
Programming (received off-air): WEWB-TV (WBN) Albany-Schenectady; WMHT
(PBS) Schenectady-Albany-Troy; WNYT (NBC) Albany-Troy-Schenectady;
WRGB (CBS) Albany-Schenectady-Troy; WTEN (ABC) Albany; WXXA-TV (FOX)
Albany; WYPX (PAX) Amsterdam, Comedy Central; C-SPAN; TBS Superstation
    ;
TV Guide Channel.
Fee: $56.44 installation; $10.77 monthly.

Expanded Basic Service 1
Subscribers: N.A.
Programming (via satellite): ABC Family Channel; American Movie
Classics; Animal Planet; Arts & Entertainment; BET; Bravo!; Cartoon
Network; CNBC; CNN; Country Music TV; Court TV; C-SPAN 2; Discovery
Channel; Disney Channel; E! Entertainment Television; ESPN; ESPN 2;
ESPN Classic Sports; Eternal Word TV Network; Food Network; Fox News
Channel; Fox Sports Net New York; FX; Golf Channel; Headline News;
HGTV; History Channel; Home Shopping Network; Jewelry Television;
Learning Channel; Lifetime; Lifetime Movie Network; Madison Square
Garden Network; MSNBC; MTV; National Geographic Channel; Nickelodeon;
oh! Oxygen; QVC; Sci-Fi Channel; Shop at Home; ShopNBC; SoapNet; Spike
TV; Style Network; Travel Channel; Turner Classic Movies; Turner
Network TV; TV Land; Univision; USA Cable; VH1; Weather Channel;
Women's Entertainment; Yankees Entertainment & Sports (YES).
Fee: $10.00 installation; $31.18 monthly.

Digital Basic Service
Subscribers: 21,323.
Programming (via satellite): America's Store; BBC America; BET On
Jazz; Bloomberg Information TV; CNBC World; CNNfn; C-SPAN 3; Direct to
You; Discovery Digital Networks; DMX Music; Do-It-Yourself; ESPNews;
```

Fine Living; Fox Sports World; FSN Digital Atlantic; FSN Digital
Central; FSN Digital Pacific; G4; Great American Country (GAC); GSN;
Hallmark Channel; History Channel; Lifetime Real Women; National
Geographic Channel; New York 1 News; Newsworld International; Noggin;
Outdoor Channel; Outdoor Life Network; Ovation; Speed Channel; Suite
from MTV & VH1; TechTV; Toon Disney; Trinity Broadcasting Network; TV
Asia; Zee TV.
Fee: $4.95 monthly.

Pay Service 1
Pay Units: 33,000.
Programming (via satellite): Cinemax; HBO (multiplexed); Showtime.
Fee: $10.00 installation; $9.95 monthly.

Digital Pay Service 1
Pay Units: N.A.
Programming (via satellite): Cinemax (multiplexed); Flix; Fox Movie
Channel; HBO (multiplexed); Independent Film Channel; Showtime
(multiplexed); STARZ! (multiplexed); Sundance Channel; The Movie
Channel (multiplexed); The New Encore (multiplexed). Fee: N.A.

Pay-Per-View
Addressable Homes: 21,323.
Programming (via satellite): iN Demand; Playboy TV; NBA/WNBA League
Pass (delivered digitally); NHL
Center Ice/MLB Extra Innings (delivered digitally); ESPN Full Court
(delivered digitally); ESPN Gameplan (delivered digitally); Spice; iN
Demand (delivered digitally); Playboy TV (delivered digitally); Spice
(delivered digitally); Spice 2 (delivered digitally); Hot Choice
(delivered digitally); Pleasure (delivered digitally); Adult PPV
(delivered digitally). Fee: N.A.

Telephone Service
Operational: No.

Listing 4.35: One Observation of Parsing Data File

Except in the simplest of applications, we advise you to spend considerable
time thinking about the structure of the problem at hand. For example, you
want to create a clean data set, but what does that mean in this case? Note that
the text has five major components: (1) city name (here, ALBANY); (2) cable
network name (here, Time Warner); (3) address; (4) list of channel bundles offered along with data concerning subscriber counts and all channels; (5) details
of the telephone service offered.

Suppose your primary interest is in the fourth component. Here, too, a well-defined structure exists: (1) name; (2) number of subscribers; (3) list of channels; (4) fees.

List Comprehension

Although you could solve this problem without this construct, one appealing feature of Python is *list comprehension*. Even though this technique can be applied to dictionaries, too, it is best explained using lists as well as a simple example:

```
>>> lowercaseList = ['a', 'b', 'c', 'd', 'e']
>>> uppercaseList = list()
>>> for element in lowercaseList :
...     uppercaseList.append(element.upper())
...
>>> uppercaseList
['A', 'B', 'C', 'D', 'E']
>>> # Here is the same logic done with list comprehension.
...
>>> anotherUppercaseList = [element.upper() for element in \
... lowercaseList]
>>> anotherUppercaseList
['A', 'B', 'C', 'D', 'E']
>>>
```

From this example, you can see immediately that list comprehension is ideal when you need to manipulate every element of a list in a particular way. Clearly, list comprehension will not be that helpful if you need to access more than one element of the list at every iteration of the loop.

List comprehension also supports conditional statements. Continuing with the example, suppose you would like to get a list of uppercase vowels only. You can do this using list comprehension:

```
>>> lowercaseList = ['a', 'b', 'c', 'd', 'e']
>>> listOfVowels  = ['a', 'e', 'i', 'o', 'u']
>>> uppercaseVowelsList = [element.upper() for element in \
... lowercaseList if element in listOfVowels]
>>> uppercaseVowelsList
['A', 'E']
>>>
# Compare this to an implementation using if and for.
```

```
...
>>> uppercaseVowels = list()
>>> for element in uppercaseVowels:
...     if element in listOfVowels:
...         uppercaseVowels.append(element.upper())
...
>>> uppercaseVowels
['A', 'E']
>>>
```

You can also implement nested loops as list comprehension. In practice, such constructs tend to lose their primary appeal—readability. We, therefore, discourage you from using them.

As another example, consider a list of countries that in turn consists of two lists—countries in North America and some in Europe. Imagine that you are interested in retrieving only countries whose names end in an "a":

```
>>> allCountries = [['USA', 'Canada', 'Mexico'], \
                    ['Germany', 'France', 'Italy', 'Russia']]
>>> result = [country for countries in allCountries \
              for country in countries \
              if country.lower()[-1] == 'a']
>>> result
['USA', 'Canada', 'Russia']
# Compare this to an implementation using if and for.
...
>>>
>>> countriesEndingWithA = list()
>>> for countries in allCountries:
...     for country in countries:
...         if country.lower()[-1] == 'a':
...             countriesEndingWithA.append(country)

>>> countriesEndingWithA
['USA', 'Canada', 'Russia']
>>>
```

The expression `country.lower()[-1]` serves the purpose: take the string stored in `country`, convert it to lowercase, and extract the last symbol in it. Despite the fact that nested list comprehension is often difficult to read, some avid users of Python swear by it.

Solution Using Divide-and-Conquer

To solve this parsing problem, the algorithmic strategy of divide-and-conquer is employed; that is, the data are split into the five mutually exclusive components, and then each component is processed separately. This can be done here because the solution to one of the components does not determine the solutions to the others.

To this end, two auxiliary functions are developed to parse the data. First, the general function FindAndReplace() is created, which takes all remaining data as input, identifies the substring that corresponds to the particular component, and returns this substring together with the remaining data. Second, a function ParseBundle is created to parse the contents of individual bundles. Even though several bundles exist, they all have the same structure.

The following Python script completes these tasks:

```
1  # Script:   ParseExampleData.py
2  # Author:   Konstantin Golyaev
3  # Date:     29 October 2014
4  """ This script takes dirty data and wrangles them to create
5      a tidy data set for later processing.
6  """
7  import re
8  dropboxPath = "/Users/hjp/"
9  inputDataPath = dropboxPath + "Data/"
10 inputFileName = inputDataPath + "ParsingExampleData.txt"
11
12 ####################################################################
13 ##### Configuration Part: Where Regular Expressions Are Defined #####
14 ####################################################################
15
16 tvBundleNames    = ['Basic Service', 'Expanded Basic Service 1', \
17                     'Digital Basic Service', 'Pay Service 1', \
18                     'Digital Pay Service 1', 'Pay-Per-View']
19 cityRegexp       = "[A-Z ]+"
20 phoneRegexp      = "Telephone Service"
21 numberRegexp     = "((-?[0-9,.]+)|(N.A.))"
22 subscriberLabels = ['Subscribers', 'Addressable Homes', 'Pay Units']
23 subscriberLabels = ["(" + s + ": " + numberRegexp + ")" \
24                     for s in subscriberLabels]
25 subscriberRegexp = "|".join(subscriberLabels)
26 channelsRegexp   = "Programming.*?:"
27 feesLabels       = ['installation', 'monthly']
```

```
28  feesRegexp       = ["[$]" + numberRegexp + " " + s \
29                     for s in feesLabels]
30
31  ###################################################################
32  #####            Configuration Part Ends Here            #####
33  ###################################################################
34
35  def FindAndReplace(data,regexpEnd,regexpStart="^",regexpBody=".*?"):
36    '''Use regexpStart, regexpBody, and regexpEnd to define a regular
37       expression, find it in data and extract the match, return matched
38       pattern and leftover data string.'''
39    regexp = regexpStart + regexpBody + regexpEnd
40    regexpObject = re.search(regexp, data)
41    if regexpObject :
42      result = regexpObject.group(0)
43      data   = data.replace(result, regexpEnd)
44      result = result.replace(regexpEnd, "")
45    else :
46      result = ""
47    return([result, data])
48
49  def ParseBundle(data,subscrRegexp,channelsRegexp,feeRegexp):
50    '''Parses individual bundles by slicing information into four parts:
51       name, number of subscribers, list of channels, and fees. Uses
52       regular expressions to match the last three from data.'''
53    # Get name and user counts.
54    subscrCount = re.search(subscrRegexp, data)
55    bundleName = data[0:subscrCount.start()]
56    bundle = {'name' : bundleName}
57    userCount = subscrCount.group(0).split(':')[1].strip(',. ')
58    userCount = int(userCount.replace(',', '').replace('.', '').replace(
          'NA', '-1'))
59    users = {"users" : userCount}
60    bundle.update(users)
61    data = data.replace(bundleName, '').replace(subscrCount.group(0), ''
          ).strip()
62
63    # Get channels.
64    [channels, data] = FindAndReplace(data, regexpEnd = "Fee:", \
65                                      regexpStart = channelsRegexp)
66    channels = re.sub(channelsRegexp, '',  channels).strip(',. ')
67    channelsArray = [s.strip() for s in channels.split(";")]
68    channels = {"channels" : channelsArray}
69    bundle.update(channels)
```

```
70
71    # Get fees.
72    fees = dict()
73    for s in feeRegexp:
74      feeSearch = re.search(s, data)
75      if feeSearch :
76        entry = feeSearch.group(0).replace('$', '').strip(',. ').split(
                    ' ')
77        fees[entry[1]] = float(entry[0])
78
79    # Organize resuls.
80    bundle.update({'fees' : fees})
81    return(bundle)
82
83 ######################################################################
84 #####   Main code starts below and makes use of functions above  #####
85 ######################################################################
86
87 # Load data and turn it into one string, clean up whitespace.
88 data = open(inputFileName, "r").read()
89 data = data.replace("\n", " ").replace("  ", " ")
90
91 # Extract city name.
92 [city, data] = FindAndReplace(data, regexpBody = cityRegexp, regexpEnd
       = "---")
93 city = city.title()
94
95 # Extract cable network name and address.
96 [cableInfo, data] = FindAndReplace(data, regexpStart = "---", \
97                                      regexpEnd = tvBundleNames[0])
98 cableInfo = cableInfo.strip('. ').replace('---', '')
99 [companyName, companyAddress] = cableInfo.split('. ')
100
101 # Extract information on all tv bundles.
102 [channelsData, data] = FindAndReplace(data, \
103                         regexpStart = tvBundleNames[0], \
104                         regexpEnd = phoneRegexp)
105 channelsArray = []
106 bundles = tvBundleNames[:]
107 bundles.append("$")
108
109 # Slice up bundles into a list.
110 for i in range(len(bundles) - 1) :
111   reStart = bundles[i]
```

```
112    reEnd    = bundles[i + 1]
113    [channel, channelsData] = FindAndReplace(channelsData,\
114                          regexpStart = reStart,regexpEnd=reEnd)
115    channelsArray.append(channel)
116
117 # Given a list of bundles, parse each bundle with a function.
118 bundles = [ParseBundle(channel, subscriberRegexp, channelsRegexp, \
119                      feesRegexp) for channel in channelsArray]
120
121 # Creating final output dictionary.
122 output = {'city'    : city,  \
123           'company'  : companyName.strip(), \
124           'address'  : companyAddress.strip(), \
125           'bundles'  : bundles
126          }
127 print output
```

Listing 4.36: `ParseExampleData.py` Script

To explain what was done, it is useful to break this script into three parts: first, define the main, major regular expressions that will be used throughout the subsequent code; second, develop the two auxiliary functions that slice up the data into chunks; third, do the actual parsing work using the previously developed two parts. In a real project, the third part would itself be a function as well because you would need to apply it to many observations; we chose not to do this for pedagogical reasons.

Consider now the first part of the code: however short that part may appear, understanding it is critical to understanding the remainder of the script. Thus, lines 16–18 define a list of names for bundles of channels that are offered by cable companies.

In line 19 you encounter the first regular expression: "[A-Z]+". How do you interpret it? In general, the majority of regular expressions are straightforward: an expression "a" will simply match the lowercase Roman letter "a", as one would expect. The power of regular expressions comes from their flexibility—being able to define abstract patterns of characters. For example, "[A-Z]" means "any of the 26 uppercase Roman letters, from A to Z." In addition, a space symbol was added, yielding "[A-Z]". The plus sign "+" at the end means "repeat the pattern in brackets one or more times", so the overall expression is interpreted as "any combination of uppercase letters and spaces." This way you can match strings like "ALBANY" and "BATON ROUGE", but you won't be able to match "Grand Forks" because the latter contains lower-case letters. The choice is a deliberate one: in these data, all city names are in uppercase. When parsing data, you typically want to be as specific as you can and to use the computer to find data that are imperfect or incomplete.

Of course, it would be trivial to modify the regular expression to match the "Grand Forks" string: you would just need to write "`[A-Za-z]+`" instead. This expression is so popular that many implementations of regular expressions have shortcuts for it. Unfortunately, implementations of these shortcuts differ across languages and applications. Therefore, we avoid them, sticking to first principles.

In line 21 you encounter a slightly more complicated regular expression that is intended to match a number, such as price. So "`[0-9.,]+`" means "at least one digit, dot, or comma," where the latter two symbols allow for thousands separators and decimal separators. The extra "`-?`" before the square brackets is read as "a minus symbol that can appear zero times or once," namely, an optional minus before the number. This enables the pattern to match negative numbers should they be encountered; for example, it is not uncommon to see missing values encoded with negative numbers in some applications. The parentheses in regular expressions define groups, and the symbol "`|`" is the logical operator OR. Hence, the entire expression "`((-?[0-9.,]+)|(N.A.))`" is read as "either a number, possibly negative, or an exact string N.A." The latter piece is necessary because sometimes in the data missing numeric values are represented by the "`N.A.`" string.

In lines 23 and 24, list comprehensions are used to put together a building block of a rather long regular expression, and in line 25 the `join()` function is used to concatenate elements of a list with the pipe string. All this results in a rather convoluted regular expression intended to match the number of subscribers for a bundle:

```
(Subscribers: ((-?[0-9,.]+)|(N.A.)))|
(Addressable Homes: ((-?[0-9,.]+)|(N.A.)))|
(Pay Units: ((-?[0-9,.]+)|(N.A.))).
```

As you can see, it can become difficult to read quickly, but the essence is very straightforward: the number of subscribers follows one of the three patterns: "Subscribers: Number" or "Addressable Homes: Number" or "Pay Units: Number" and the recurring expression will match any of these patterns, allowing for `N.A.` in numbers.

Note, however, that when groups are concerned, most regular expression evaluators are lazy in the software sense: as soon as one of the groups is matched, the search returns a success. This can create subtle issues. Consider the regular expression "`(Sam)|(Samuel)`". You would think that this should match either "Sam" or "Samuel". In fact, the longer name will never be matched. Since "Samuel" contains "Sam", the search will always return "Sam". The solution to this edge case is straightforward: use "`(Samuel)|(Sam)`" instead. That way, the matching engine is forced to search for "Samuel" first, and it only falls back to "Sam" when the former is not returned as a match.

In line 26 a simple, but very useful, regular expression is presented. Its first part is the word "Programming", which will have to be matched exactly; its second part is "`.*?`", and its last part is the colon symbol "`:`" which again will be matched exactly. The "`.*?`" snippet is deceptively simple. In it, the dot means "any symbol", and the asterisk modifier "*" reads "repeat the previous symbol zero or more times". Thus, the combination "`.*`" literally matches any string, including an empty one.

The question mark symbol "?" after "*" forces the match not to be *greedy*, which is best explained by example. Consider the following two strings:

`Programming:` and `Programming: Educational:`

A greedy regular expression "`Programming.*:`" will match the entire first string and the entire second string. In other words, a greedy expression will return the longest string that matches the pattern. Because, in the second example, the substring "`: Educational`" clearly conforms to the "any symbol zero or more times" pattern, the end of the expression will be at the second "`:`" sign. By contrast, a *minimal* (nongreedy) match will return the shortest possible string; that is, in both cases, it will return the same text, "`Programming:`". To summarize, the expression "`Programming.*?:`" reads as "the shortest string that starts with the word Programming and ends with :". Notice that "?" has a slightly different meaning here: it is modifying the "`*`" and not a pattern as in the previous case "`-?`". Pattern matching is both complex and subtle; to do it well requires both education and experience.

Finally, in line 28, you see a new expression, "`[$]`". Normally, in regular expressions, the dollar sign has a special meaning: end of string (and the caret sign ˆ means the beginning of a string). To match the dollar sign explicitly, you must put the square brackets around it, creating a character class that consists of a dollar sign only. Given the previous discussion of Python, the remainder of this section should be straightforward to understand.

Note that regular expressions are terrific for parsing texts that may contain typographical errors. For example, consider the phrase "Telephone Service." Because in real applications, the input text might be generated by, say, OCR software, you cannot expect a perfect success rate for that process. For example, depending on the font, the OCR software can mistake l (lowercase L) and I (uppercase i) as well as i for 1 (digit one). Forewarned is forearmed. You can make a regular expression relatively immune to these typographical errors using the following: "Te[l1Ii]ephone Serv[iI1l]ce". As before, the square brackets define a class of admissible symbols, so this expression will match any incorrectly spelled "Telephone Service" provided the typographical errors conform to the defined class.

Of course, such flexibility comes at a cost: a sufficiently flexible regular expression can be tricky to understand. For this reason, in the current example, this extra layer of complexity was eschewed.

Getting back to the parsing code, in lines 35–47, the main parsing function `FindAndReplace()` is defined. `FindAndReplace()` is used to process chunks of the data incrementally. In its simplest representation, `FindAndReplace()` accepts a string like "A<...>BC<...>D" and returns two strings: "A<...>B" and "C<...>D". The function uses a regular expression to identify the "A<...>B" piece; if no match is found, then it returns an empty string as the first argument and the entire input data as the second argument. The function relies on the Python module `re`, in particular, the `re.search()` function. At least two arguments are required: the regular expression to be searched, and the string in which the search should be conducted. An object `regexpObject` that contains information on search results is returned; `None` is returned when the search is unsuccessful. If successful, then the object will have one or more *groups* that contain matched strings. Because Python starts counting at zero, `group(0)` will contain the first matched string. Applying the function `FindAndReplace()` recursively, the entire input string will eventually be parsed.

At first, the second function `ParseBundle()` may appear more convoluted than the first function. To understand this function's logic, recall that there are four major pieces of data available for each bundle: title, number of subscribers, list of channels, and usage fees.

The title is the easiest to obtain; using the (rather long) regular expression for subscriber counts that we defined earlier, you can locate the relevant substring, and everything to the left of it will be the bundle title. The `start()` function of the object returned by `re.search()` returns the string position of the first symbol of the matched string.

Lines 57 and 58 perform clean up of the subscriber count data, converting them to numbers. That `subscrCount.group(0)` will return the entire matched string has been established. The `split(":")` function breaks the string into a list, using the colon symbol as delimiter, and the `[1]` means "return the second element of the list." (Remember that the first element has index zero.)

Finally, the `strip(",. ")` function purges all dots, commas, and whitespaces from the beginning and the end of the string to which it gets applied. In short, line 57 turns the string "Subscribers: 21,456." into "21,456"; line 58 turns the string into a number. To this end, all commas and dots are `replace()`d; the "NA" string is also replaced with a negative one: after all, negative subscriber counts should not occur naturally. The processed data are stored in a dictionary; the `update()` method of a `dict` object is used to add key-value pairs to it.

Most of the work in processing the list of channels can be accomplished using the `FindAndReplace()` function. The `re.sub()` function is used in line 66. As the name suggests, the function exists to find and replace a substring that conforms to a regular expression pattern within a larger string. Because the list of channels is preceded by a string that conforms to the `Programming.*?:` pattern, the `re.sub()` must be used to eliminate this uninformative piece.

Line 67 should now be clear: split by the semicolon the string of channel names into a list, strip the whitespace from the name of each channel, and save the results as a list.

A similar process is also used to parse the fee data. For every potentially available fee type, `re.search()` is used to extract the relevant substring, where dollar signs are replaced, unnecessary whitespace and punctuation are stripped, and splits are performed on spaces. Capturing fee types is achieved in line 77. For the string "$9.95 installation", the contents of `entry` will be `'9.95'`, `'installation'`; the second entry is used as the dictionary key, the first one as its value.

Finally, in lines 83–127, everything we have defined is used to perform the actual parsing. If you understood the previous discussion, these instructions should be clear; otherwise, go back to the beginning of the section and start again.

You should note a couple of things, however. In lines 106 and 107, a copy of the `tvBundleNames` list is created, and then another element is appended to it—the dollar sign $. As mentioned previously, in regular expressions $ means "end of string." This enables the `for` loop construct in lines 111–115.

In lines 118 and 119, the `ParseBundle()` function is used in a list comprehension construct to process each bundle separately. The final output of this script is a Python dictionary, which you can write to disk as a JSON object or, in general, use for whatever purpose you see fit. Regardless of how it is used, this dictionary object now adheres to a transparent and predictable structure, which can be easily manipulated. Moreover, it is trivial to combine several such dictionaries into a larger dictionary that can store the entire data set for analysis.

We do not list the entire dictionary output of the script because it is simply too large, but here are the first 200 or so characters

```
{'city': 'Albany', 'company': 'Time Warner Entertainment Company LP',
    'bundles': [{'channels': ['WEWB-TV (WBN) Albany-Schenectady', '
    WMHT (PBS) Schenectady-Albany-Troy', 'WNYT (NBC) Albany-Troy-
    Schenectady', ...
```

5

Analyzing Data

A NALYZING DATA IS perhaps the second most common task undertaken by a research assistant. In this chapter, we describe how you can use the R system in conjunction with the RDBMS SQLite as well as the Python library `pandas` to conduct empirical analyses of data like those organized in Chapter 3. We also introduce an approach to conducting empirical analysis that involves the triad of training, validation, and testing—an approach that distinguishes data miners and machine learners from social scientists. At the conclusion of the chapter, we describe a computational problem—linear regression with many fixed-effect regression coefficients—that illustrates the limits to intuitive discussions, at least when it comes to investigating mathematical concepts.[1]

We first describe an approach to deciding whether your ultimate answers are reasonable, one that should ideally precede your empirical work; we then discuss methods of sampling data; and, finally, we describe some convenient data formats.

5.1   Is Your Answer Right?

Douglas W. Hubbard (2010) recounted an anecdote involving the Nobel Prize–winning physicist Enrico Fermi when he taught at the University of Chicago. Apparently, Fermi would routinely ask his graduate students in physics to find

---

[1]That intuition has limitations is perhaps unsurprising: had intuition been sufficient, people would never have invented logic and mathematics.

approximate answers to questions like, How many piano tuners are there in Chicago? Such questions became known as *Fermi questions*.

Why would Fermi ask physics students to answer such odd, mundane questions? He was trying to get his students to develop a way of thinking that would allow them to decide whether the answers derived in their research, which often involved pages of complicated mathematics, were reasonable. In particular, Fermi wanted the students to develop the habit of calculating an alternative answer, derived by other means and preferably before the research was conducted, to help them decide later whether a mistake had inadvertently crept into their work.

Given all the transformations and calculations that you will complete when conducting empirical work, making a mistake seems almost inevitable. How will you know whether your answer is correct? You won't. What to do? Obviously, being careful in your research is important, but let's assume that you are doing that anyway. What you want is to be able to spot answers that are obviously wrong. Prior to conducting any analysis, you are encouraged to use facts known about the question at hand to decide what the correct order of magnitude of the answer should be: will it be of the order 10^{-2} (that is, in percent) or 10^2 (in the hundreds) or 10^6 (in the millions)?

Calculate what Weinstein and Adam (2008) called a *guesstimate* before you actually go on to do the main calculations. Having done so, you can then compare your calculated answer to the guesstimate. If the two are of very different magnitudes, then chances are you have made a mistake somewhere, perhaps in forming the guesstimate but more likely in your calculations. A guesstimate, done properly, should be fairly robust, at least in terms of its order of magnitude. On the other hand, when the guesstimate and the answer are of the same magnitude, you should not assume that the answer is correct, just that it is not obviously wrong. You still want to double- and triple-check your work.

How does guesstimation work? Weinstein and Adam (2008) and Weinstein (2012) demonstrated the approach by deriving guesstimates for a number of examples from different fields. Hubbard (2010) also provided several detailed examples from business, including the Fermi question about piano tuners.

Clearly, the practice of guesstimation will depend on the problem at hand, but as an example of how it works, consider obtaining a guesstimate to the piano tuner Fermi question.

In the following, we describe the approach presented by Hubbard (2010, 11–12). Specifically, first find the population of Chicago, then estimate the number of people in each household, the fraction of households that will have a piano tuned, the number of tunings per year, the number of tunings a tuner can complete in a day, and the number of days a tuner will work in a year. With these data, an estimate of the number of piano tuners can be formed using the following equation:

Tuners in Chicago =

        Population / people per household

        × percentage of households with tuned pianos

        × tunings per year /

        (tunings per tuner per day × workdays per year).

Hubbard also provided data and estimates concerning Chicago for the period between 1930–1950, when Fermi was teaching there: population, around 3 million people; people per household, about two or three; percentage of households with tuned pianos, not more than one in ten but probably not less than one in thirty; tunings per year, about one; tunings per day, about four or five; workdays per year, about 250.

Based on these data, you can derive a lower-bound guesstimate (assuming the upper bound on the average number of people in a household, the lower bound on the percentage of households getting tunings, and the upper bound on the number of tunings that a tuner can complete in a day) and an upper-bound guesstimate (assuming the lower bound on the average number of people in a household, the upper bound on the percentage of households getting tunings, and the lower bound on the number of tunings that a tuner can complete in a day), or

$$20 \approx (3 \times 10^6 / 3) \times (1/30) \times (1/(5 \times 250)) < \text{Tuners in Chicago}$$
$$< (3 \times 10^6 / 2) \times (1/10) \times (1/(4 \times 25)) = 150.$$

Following the counsel of Weinstein (2012, 5–6), who advised using the geometric mean instead of the arithmetic mean when the orders of the lower-bound and upper-bound guesstimates are quite different (for example,

20 versus 150), you can calculate the following guesstimate:

$$20^{\frac{1}{2}} \times 150^{\frac{1}{2}} \approx 50.$$

That is, where the arithmetic mean of two numbers a and b is

$$\frac{a+b}{2},$$

the geometric mean of those numbers is the square root of their product

$$\sqrt{a \times b}.$$

Based on these calculations, Hubbard concluded that there were probably around 50 piano tuners in Chicago at the time Fermi taught there.[2]

The moral is that you should always look for ways to triangulate your answers, that is, find ways to ensure that the numbers you have calculated are consistent with other known, established facts.

5.2   Methods of Sampling Data

Where do data come from? Surveying every member (such as a person) of a population (that is, taking a census), although exhaustive and representative, is clearly costly in terms of both time and money. To reduce such costs, samples are usually taken from populations. Those samples are proper subsets of

---

[2]In general, for $\{a_1, a_2, \ldots, a_N\}$, the arithmetic mean is

$$\frac{1}{N}\sum_{n=1}^{N} a_n,$$

whereas the geometric mean of those same N numbers is

$$\prod_{n=1}^{N} a_n^{\frac{1}{N}}.$$

The economists among you will recognize that the following Cobb-Douglas production function:

$$q = \ell^{\alpha} k^{\beta}$$

where q is output, ℓ and k are inputs, and α and β are technological coefficients, is a more general version of the geometric mean.

the populations, so some information is lost, but often useful statements (estimates) can still be made concerning the populations.

Under what conditions is sampling useful? First and foremost, for the sampled data to be useful, the numbers of observations must be large enough to be representative of the population: a sample of one really isn't very useful. As the economics Nobel Prize winner George J. Stigler is reported to have quipped, "The plural of anecdote is data." From a practical perspective, however, the data samples must be small enough to be manageable. Samples sizes have historically been manageable. The Information Revolution, however, has made gathering large samples of data—Big Data—almost trivial. Abstracting from the engineering problems that arise when managing huge amounts of data, we ask, Are such large samples of data, in fact, useful? It depends on how the samples of data were gathered.

Several different sampling methods exist; some are cheaper and easier to implement than others. Naturally, everyone gravitates toward the cheap, easy methods. But you should not ignore the fact that understanding how the collected data were sampled is as important as analyzing those data. In fact, if the sample of data is unrepresentative of the population to be studied, then any analysis of these data would be for naught.

5.2.1 Opportunity Sampling

The most commonly used method of sampling, particularly in archival research but also on the Internet, is *opportunity sampling*, also known as *convenience sampling*. Under this method, a sample is formed from the units available at the time of data collection. For example, these units could simply be the first $1,000$ files discovered in an old trunk, or the first 1 million records in a log file on a server.

Opportunity sampling is popular because it is cheap to implement in terms of time and money. Some believe that opportunity sampling is an adequate method to investigate phenomena that are presumed to work in similar ways for most individuals.

Sometimes, particularly in the natural sciences, opportunity sampling is the only method available to a researcher. For example, when sampling animals in the field to estimate the incidence of a parasite, the weakest (maybe because of the parasite) are more likely to be caught than those who are healthy and strong. Thus, the parasite may be overrepresented in a sample of those animals who were caught. In short, sampling bias is a limiting weakness of opportunity sampling.

Another example of why opportunity sampling can produce biased samples involves the following: a researcher might oversample people from his own cultural, ethnic, or social group because such subjects are easier for him to interview than those from other groups; this can be a problem on the Internet, when using groups from social networks.

Another problem with opportunity sampling is that chosen subjects may subsequently decline to participate, for example, fail to click on a link. Those who choose to participate may yield an even more biased sample than those selected in the first instance.

Many SDEs at Internet firms believe that large samples can overcome non-random sampling—sampling bias—arguing that the law of large numbers will eventually prevail. Even though it is true that when the numbers of observations are large, the sampling variability of estimates will be small (eventually going to zero as the sample goes to infinity), it does *not* follow that those estimates converge to the truth, however defined. In short, having petabytes of nonrepresentative data really is not very useful. In data science, the *quality* of the data sampled is typically much more important than the *quantity* of those data.

5.2.2 Prospective Sampling

Under *prospective sampling*, eligible subjects are selected over time as they appear to the researcher, for example, those people who shopped last Tuesday morning on a particular website. An important consideration in designing a prospective sample is how to minimize the variation in the sampling weights—which parts of the population to sample—and still achieve a prescribed sample size at the end of data collection. On the one hand, a predetermined sample size is typically required to achieve certain goals, such as estimator accuracy; on the other hand, operational requirements, such as the number of interviews that can be completed within each time period, dictate what can be accomplished given the resources available. One problem with prospective sampling is that the population being sampled can change over time, a factor often beyond the sampler's control. Clearly, prospective sampling is similar in spirit to opportunity sampling and therefore suffers from similar weaknesses.

5.2.3 Random Sampling

Only *random sampling*, where each unit in the population has some chance (that is, positive probability) of being selected, is considered respectable among scientists. At least five different methods of random sampling exist: (1) simple random sampling; (2) systematic sampling; (3) stratified sampling; (4) cluster sampling; (5) multistage sampling. In much of statistics, however, researchers constrain themselves to *simple random sampling*.

Under simple random sampling, each unit in a population has an *equal* chance of being included in the sample. For example, suppose you would like to learn about the members in a large club. In this case, each name on the club roster would be assigned a number sequentially. If the sample were to contain 100 members, then 100 numbers would be selected at random from an urn containing all the numbers. These numbers would then be matched to names on the club roster, thereby providing a randomly sampled list of 100 members to interview.

The primary advantage of simple random sampling is that it is easy to implement, particularly when populations are relatively small. Because every unit in a population has to be listed before the corresponding numbers can be chosen randomly, this method is very cumbersome to use for large populations. That said, the social security numbers of workers in the United States or the customer numbers of an online firm already provide such numbers, so firms and governments find simple random sampling relatively easy to implement.

5.2.4 Choice-Based Sampling

For some statistical problems, particularly in economics and marketing but also in medicine, simple random sampling will yield on average too few observations for certain choices that subjects typically make. Under *choice-based sampling*, a researcher selects random samples of particular sizes for each of the choices subjects have made or outcomes that have obtained.[3] For example,

---

[3]This approach is also referred to as *biased sampling*, *oversampling*, and *retrospective sampling*. Medical studies of this kind are often referred to as *case-control studies*.

suppose you are interested in studying a relatively rare disease. In a choice-based sample, those with and without disease might have the same sample size. By allowing the sampling rate to depend on the category, certain outcomes can be sampled at higher (or lower) rates than those occurring on average in the population. Thus, you can ensure sufficient numbers of observations to conduct reliable empirical analyses.

Under certain conditions, consistent estimates of the population can be constructed from choice-based samples (for example, in logistic regression), but in general the sampling variabilities of such estimates are different from what would obtain under simple random sampling, so testing hypotheses and constructing confidence intervals are more complicated than under random sampling.

We have introduced this brief discussion of sampling to make you aware that how data were sampled influences what they can tell you. Too often in the analysis of Big Data researchers place undue faith in the law of large numbers, ignoring the biases that certain sampling methods introduce. In the following, we assume no sampling biases.

5.3   Useful Data Formats

Before you can conduct an analysis of data using any statistical software (for example, R), you must first organize those data; that is, you must put them in a format that statistical programs can access easily and quickly. As mentioned, data scientists refer to the process of casting data into useful formats as cleaning or munging or wrangling. Often, in econometrics or statistics courses, the data are already in a nice format; all the necessary cleaning has been done.

It is useful when teaching courses in the techniques of data science to provide clean data, but it can be misleading to learners. Cleaning often takes 80 percent of the time involved in any data analysis, and the programming of estimators can take 15 percent of the time; the analysis itself often requires just 5 percent of the time.

What is a useful format to represent data? To address this question, let's introduce some vocabulary. In data science, it is common to refer to the data for each observation (each *example*, in machine learning) as the *record*, and the variables for the records as the *fields*. The records can be thought of as lines (rows) and the variables as fields (columns). In short, the file containing the data is like a table.

We mentioned comma-separated values, the csv format, as one choice to represent records and fields in a table. Another common format is *tab-delimited values*. These two formats are, in fact, just special cases of a most general format where the comma ", " and the tab character "\t" are used to separate values of variables in a data record. In principle, you could use any character as a separator, but the convention is to use either the comma or the tab. Because csv is the most common format used to export data from Excel, many data scientists use that format. A third format, referred to as *fixed format*, is sometimes used as well. Under this format, each field has a fixed width, where numbers in a specific field are right-justified within the fixed width, and the format of the data concerning the field has a fixed structure.[4] We believe it safe to say that most human-readable data files have one of these three formats.

Another format, which is not readable by humans without software, is the *binary format*. Data in binary format can be read by computers much more quickly than those in human-readable formats; in addition, binary-formatted data take up less space than human-readable formats. Statistical software (like SAS and Stata) uses the binary format or some variant based on it.

What to do when the format of the data has been determined by someone else? R can import data from such programs as SAS and Stata, but other more esoteric formats can cause complications. In such cases, you may want to consider purchasing proprietary software, such as StatTransfer, which makes it easier to get data written using proprietary software into your open-source tools.[5]

5.4 R System

The R system is a powerful programming language and software environment for statistical computing and graphics. R is a free version of the popular statistical programming language S-PLUS, which grew out of the program S, developed at AT&T Bell Labs. Becker, Chambers, and Wilks (1988) provided

---

[4]Note that strings are treated differently.

[5]The URL http://www.stattransfer.com has useful information if you need to go this route.

a complete discussion of S; Chambers (2009) provided a useful description of the relation between the R system and the S language.

As mentioned, R is the lingua franca among statisticians. We believe that the main reason R is so popular is that it is both powerful and useful. Even though we hope to provide you with enough information to get started in R, we can only present a finite number of examples. Thus, we suggest that you also consider reading Kabacoff's (2013) introduction to R. If you want to become really proficient in R, then you will need to read and understand the material developed by Matloff (2011), who is trained as a statistician but who teaches in a computer science department, and that presented by Chambers (2009), the creator of the S programming language and a core member of the R development project. The book by Wickham (2014) is also strongly recommended, and the introduction to statistical learning using R by James, Witten, Hastie, and Tibshirani (2013) provides important perspectives on the problems the language is suitable for in practice.

5.4.1 Getting R and Its Packages

R and its packages as well as easily understood instructions to install the precompiled binary distributions of the base system and contributed packages for Windows-based computers as well as the Apple Mac are available at `http://cran.us.r-project.org` in the United States. R is typically part of most Linux distributions; you can verify this by typing into a terminal window:

```
$ whereis R
```

Outside of the United States, mirror sites exist, which can speed up downloading; see `http://cran.r-project.org/mirrors.html`.

5.4.2 RStudio IDE

Most novice users of R will be well served by using RStudio, a front-end application for developing R code—an IDE. Even though we counseled against using an IDE in the case of Python, several advantages exist for using RStudio. First, RStudio combines several windows through which R users typically interact during work sessions. Next, RStudio provides the user with background help that can improve code and reduce the chance of making simple typographical errors; for example, RStudio automatically closes matching braces and parentheses. Third, RStudio makes plotting figures and graphs much easier; the user can browse an entire history of plots created during the session and then export the desired ones into various formats. Fourth, RStudio provides ample support for more advanced work, for example, integrating with version control systems such as Git. Finally, RStudio is free to academic as well as individual users and works well on the three major platforms—Windows, OS X, and Linux. In short, if you are new to R, we encourage you to use RStudio, or at least try it. In either case, you will need to know the basic grammar of R.

5.4.3 Basic R Grammar

Like Python, R is an interpreted language, primarily designed for performing matrix algebra and analyzing data sets of modest sizes. To invoke R on a UNIX host, open a terminal window and type R; this will bring up the default R prompt >:

```
$ R

R version 3.1.2 (2014-10-31) -- "Pumpkin Helmet"
Copyright (C) 2014 The R Foundation for Statistical Computing
Platform: x86_64-apple-darwin10.8.0 (64-bit)

R is free software and comes with ABSOLUTELY NO WARRANTY.
You are welcome to redistribute it under certain conditions.
Type 'license()' or 'licence()' for distribution details.

Natural language support but running in an English locale

R is a collaborative project with many contributors.
Type 'contributors()' for more information and
'citation()' on how to cite R or R packages in publications.

Type 'demo()' for some demos, 'help()' for on-line help, or
'help.start()' for an HTML browser interface to help.
Type 'q()' to quit R.

>
```

As the preamble to the program's interactive window states, you can use the `demo()` and `help()` functions to learn about R, and `q()` to exit (quit) the program. When you type `q()` in the interactive window, which is referred to as the *console*, you will be asked the following skill-testing question:

```
> q()
Save workspace image? [y/n/c]:
```

Because you have not yet done anything, type n, which will then bring you back to the command line. Sometimes, if you have completed a lot of work interactively, you will want R to save a copy of that work. If you want to save an R object (for example, `my.object`) for later use, use the following command:

```
> save(my.object, file="my.object.rda")
>
```

The file `my.object.rda` will be placed in the current working directory; it is an example of a binary file. Typing `more my.object.rda` into a terminal window will yield the following:

```
$ more my.object.rda
"my.object.rda" may be a binary file.  See it anyway?
```

You should type n since the contents of the file are not readable by humans. What will happen if you type y? Your terminal window could freeze, in which case you will have to start afresh.

In a new R session, you can then attach the file using the following:

```
> load("my.object.rda")
>
```

Having invoked R again, after your successful exit, you can use R interactively by submitting commands at the prompt >. For example, you can use R as a calculator:

```
> 2 + 3
[1] 5
```

To understand the subtle details behind this admittedly simple example, you need to be aware of the two basic objects within R: the *function* and the *vector*. In this example, 2 and 3 are both interpreted as vectors of length 1, and the plus sign "+" is a function that performs vector addition. Remember: When you add two conformable vectors, the corresponding elements in each of the vectors are summed.

In the next line, R renders the output of the addition operation. The notation [1] should be read as "what follows immediately after is the first element of the output vector." A major difference between the indexing of vectors in R, and their indexing in, say, Python manifests itself here: R's indexing begins at 1, whereas Python's begins at 0.

In this example, the output is a vector of length 1, and its value is 5. Therefore, the correct way to read the R output is, "The result of adding a vector of length 1 having value 2 in it to another vector of length 1 having value 3 in it is yet another vector of length 1 having the value 5 in it."

The entire sequence 2 + 3 is referred to as an *expression*. Because the result of this expression was not assigned to another object, R has simply printed the result to the console. But the result of the latest interactively executed expression is stored in R under the variable named .Last.value. Therefore, you can recover that value, if needed, for example,

```
> 2 + 3
[1] 5
> .Last.value
[1] 5
```

In most cases, however, you will execute expressions to obtain results that will be used in subsequent calculations. To this end, you must *assign* the result to a new object. For example,

```
> two.plus.three <- 2 + 3
> two.plus.three
[1] 5
>
```

The left arrow symbol <– is the assignment operator: it should be read as "evaluate the expression on the right-hand side of the operator and write the result of this evaluation into the object on the left-hand side of the operator." Note that the same expression generated no output when the result was assigned to the variable two.plus.three. When this variable was called in the next line, R printed its contents to the console.

You can also use the equal sign = as an assignment operator, but you need to be careful when you use the = operator because some older versions of R treat = differently from <–. For example, in some older versions of R, if = is used in a function, then odd things can happen. To see this, consider the following snippet of code:

```
1  > x <- 1:10
2  > x
3   [1]  1  2  3  4  5  6  7  8  9 10
4  > y = 1:10
5  > y
6   [1]  1  2  3  4  5  6  7  8  9 10
7  > median(x)
8  [1] 5.5
9  > median(y)
10 [1] 5.5
11 > median(z = 1:10)
12 Error: object 'z' not found
13 >
```

The first line creates the vector x having the values 1 to 10, and the fourth line creates the vector y, also having the values 1 to 10. In lines 7 and 9, the built-in function median is used to find the medians of x and y. Ideally, because z is defined like y, line 11 should not return an error.

Most of the time, either <- or = can be used, but the two are not identical; the differences are subtle. In short, the operator <- can be used anywhere, whereas the operator = is only allowed at the top level. Thus, to avoid subtle complications, use the <- assignment operator consistently.

Does this mean that = is superfluous? No, you still need to use = when calling functions to avoid assigning them globally.

Why is the operator <- used? The <- operator existed in S and then in S-PLUS (predecessors to R), so presumably consistency with extant S code was an important factor. Although the = operator is used in other modern programming languages (such as MATLAB or Python) as the assigment operator, some purists insist that using = is confusing; users might mistakingly interpret the symbol for the logical operator that tests for equality of two objects. However, as is the case in many other languages, the double-equal operator == performs the logical operator function of equality in R. Other users insist that the <- operator can inadvertently cause unexpected program behavior, particularly if you are used to writing code with as few spaces between objects as possible. Indeed, in this case, most languages interpret the line x<-3 as "x is less than −3," whereas R will interpret it as "assign value 3 to variable x." Such issues can be easily avoided by employing good coding habits. This edge case cannot occur when proper spacing is used and the expressions x <- 3 and x < -3, properly spaced, are easier to read as well as completely unambiguous. In the remainder of this book, we use the <- operator for assignments.

Because computers cannot represent all numbers, complications can arise— some in cases that may be frequent. For example, the arithmetic expressions $(1/0)$ and $[(1/0) - (2/0)]$ are not defined. Nevertheless, in the course of per- forming calculations in R, arithmetic expressions like these can arise. What to do? In R two special numbers exist: Inf and NaN. The value Inf is a shorthand for *infinity*, ∞, the limit to which $(1/x)$ goes as x goes to zero, whereas the value NaN is shorthand for *not a number*. Here, we illustrate how both Inf and NaN can arise in R:

```
> (1/0)
[1] Inf
> (1/0) - (2/0)
[1] NaN
>
```

Object names in R are case sensitive and can consist of the letters a to z as well as A to Z, the digits 0 to 9, the underscore symbol _ , and the dot symbol . which may be called the period. Object names may *not* begin with either a digit or an underscore. It is relatively easy to make the mistake of creating an internally inconsistent named object within R. Therefore, we believe it is very important to adopt a consistent style and to maintain it; the costs are relatively low, but the benefits are potentially great and long-lasting. Moreover, over time, it becomes easier to study and follow R code written in a consistent notation than in an inconsistent one.

Golyaev suggests using the following stylistic conventions used at Google. (Paarsch is not convinced of all this newfangled stuff but is willing to give it a decade before dismissing the notation as absurd.) First, whenever possible, do not abbreviate object names. Thus, x <- 2 + 3 is a poor naming conven- tion, whereas two.plus.three <- 2 + 3 is a good one. Second, use dots instead of underscores to separate words: two_plus_three is a poor nam- ing convention, whereas using two.plus.three is a good one. Why are dots better than underscores? They are easier to read. Third, use lowercase, dot- separated words, preferably nouns, for variable names and Pascal case as well as verbs for function names; for constants, use CamelCase with the prefix k. Hence, two.plus.three is a good variable name, AddTwoAndThree is a good function name, and `kNumberOfElements` is a good name for a constant, even though it is quite long.

Like Python, R is a dynamically typed programming language. Recall from Chapter 4 that this means an object's type can change as the program executes. To illustrate the concept, consider the following R code:

```
> x <- 2 + 3
> x
[1] 5
> class(x)
[1] "numeric"
> x <- "abc"
> x
[1] "abc"
> class(x)
[1] "character"
>
```

Initially, the result of adding 2 and 3 is assigned to x, making it a numeric vector of length 1 whose value is 5. We use the `class()` function to be sure that x is of type "numeric". The string abc is then assigned to x, turning x into a character vector of length 1 whose value is `"abc"`. Now the `class()` function tells us that x is of type "character", which in R means string. Some other programming languages (such as C and FORTRAN) do not permit these sorts of changes. As discussed in Chapter 9, those languages are statically typed. As an aside, whether you use single or double quotes does not matter in R:

```
> x <- "abc"
> x
[1] "abc"
> y <- 'def'
> y
[1] "def"
>
```

However, we recommend that you use double quotes consistently. According to folklore, single quotes are normally used only to delimit character constants containing double quotes.

Another type of quote also exists in R—the backtick `. The backtick is used *to escape* names of functions that are otherwise illegal. For instance, as a trivial

example, suppose you want to compute a + b. You can also write this as
`'+'(a, b)`: the two are identical.

```
> a <- 1
> b <- 2
> a + b
[1] 3
> `+`(a, b)
[1] 3
>
```

R is also a strongly typed language, which means that R does not permit
implicit type conversion of expression operands. For example,

```
> x <- "2" + 3
Error in "2" + 3 : non-numeric argument to binary operator
>
```

results in an error because when R is told to add a character vector that takes
value "2" to a numeric vector that takes value 3, the addition operator refuses to proceed because the language can only operate on numeric inputs. In a
weakly typed programming language, such as Perl, the numeric value 3 would
have been converted to a string, and the plus operator would have performed
string concatenation, resulting in x taking on the value "23". To perform that
operation in R, you would need to use the built-in `paste` function:

```
> x <- paste("2", 3, sep = "")
> x
[1] "23"
>
```

As mentioned, R, like Python, is an interpreted language, in contrast to compiled languages like C or FORTRAN. Briefly, in a compiled language, once a
program has been written, the user must then compile the code to build a binary file that can be executed (sometimes referred to as an *executable image*).
An interpreted language is effectively, interpreted on the fly, at run time, line
by line. In general, it is much easier to develop interpreted code because you
can iterate, spotting errors quickly, without having to recompile each time. Of
course, the downside is that programs written in interpreted languages are
inherently slower, particularly when it comes to executing nested loops. In
short, by using an interpreted language, you trade off developer time for cycle

time. For many research-related tasks, where production-quality code is rarely necessary, initial prototyping in an interpreted language is almost always a good idea.

A subtle drawback of some interpreted languages, including R, is a feature referred to as *lazy evaluation*. Consider the following example of an R function:

```
 1  > DemonstrateLazyEvaluation <- function(input) {
 2  +   if (input == 1) {
 3  +     input <- input + "a"
 4  +   }
 5  +   print(input)
 6  + }
 7  > DemonstrateLazyEvaluation(2)
 8  [1] 2
 9  > DemonstrateLazyEvaluation(1)
10  Error in input + "a" : non-numeric argument to binary operator
11  >
```

Note how braces { and } are used to define when a function begins and ends (lines 1 and 6) as well as to define the `if` statement (lines 2 and 4). That structure is non-negotiable; like indentation in Python, it is part of R's syntax.

What does this function do? If the value of its only input argument `input` equals 1, then the function attempts to add a character "a" to the value; otherwise the function simply prints the input and concludes without returning anything.

Note that R does not return an error until the internal condition `if (input == 1)` is found to be `TRUE`. When we call the function with an input other than 1, the line `input <- input + "a"` never gets executed, so no error is thrown. The function is lazy in the sense that it does not evaluate what will happen with all feasible inputs before it is used; it only evaluates arguments on a case-by-case basis. This means that testing R code is sometimes more challenging than testing code written in other computer languages.

5.4.4 Types of R Objects

In R the basic unit is referred to as an *object*. For example, the most basic object type in R is the vector. Although it is not recommended for large amounts of data, you can manually create a vector of arbitrary length using the `c()` function, for example,

```
> x <- c(1, 2, 5, 7)
> x
[1] 1 2 5 7
>
```

To anyone who knows even a little bit of linear algebra, R has a potentially confusing feature: no distinction is made between row and column vectors. The following illustrates a number of important facts concerning vectors and matrices in R:

```
# First, let x be a vector
> x <- 1:4
> x
[1] 1 2 3 4
> length(x)
[1] 4
> dim(x)
NULL
# Now let x be a matrix
> x <- matrix(1:4, nrow = 2)
> x
     [,1] [,2]
[1,]    1    3
[2,]    2    4
> length(x)
[1] 4
> dim(x)
[1] 2 2
>
```

First, as in Python, introducing the character # at the beginning of a line signifies a comment in R. Second, the length() function returns the length of a vector, much like the len() function in Python. The length function computes and returns the length of an object, which is usually the number of elements in this object. Third, the dim() function returns the dimension of an array. Specifically, the dim function returns a vector whose length equals the number of dimensions in an object and whose values represent the number of elements in each dimension. The dim() function returns a NULL value for one-dimensional objects, such as vectors.

In this example, the vector x, which has length 4, is first assigned and then redefined as a two-by-two matrix. Note that `length(x)` equals 4, regardless of whether x is a vector or a matrix.

Now, let's examine the format in which the matrix x is presented, because this brings up the topic of accessing the contents of objects in R, namely, *indexing*. As mentioned, unlike Python, R indices begin at 1. The square brackets "[]" are used to refer to elements of an object. For example, x[3] should be read as "third element of object x." This is why, by default, R prints [1] at the beginning of an output string. Consider the following example in which a long vector is printed to the console:

```
> # fix the output width
> options(width = 60)
> x <- 1:100
> x
  [1]    1    2    3    4    5    6    7    8    9   10   11   12   13
 [14]   14   15   16   17   18   19   20   21   22   23   24   25   26
 [27]   27   28   29   30   31   32   33   34   35   36   37   38   39
 [40]   40   41   42   43   44   45   46   47   48   49   50   51   52
 [53]   53   54   55   56   57   58   59   60   61   62   63   64   65
 [66]   66   67   68   69   70   71   72   73   74   75   76   77   78
 [79]   79   80   81   82   83   84   85   86   87   88   89   90   91
 [92]   92   93   94   95   96   97   98   99  100
>
```

The exact output will differ depending on the width of your R console window, but the principle is the same. The first output line begins with [1] and contains thirteen elements of the vector x, whereas the second line begins with [14] where the first element in that line is the fourteenth element—that is, x[14]—and so forth.

You can access the contents of matrices and other multidimensional objects in exactly the same way because matrices are stored internally as column-major vectors. What does that mean? R stores matrices by column, like FORTRAN (see Chapter 9). For example, consider the following:

```
> x <- matrix(1:4, nrow = 2)
> x
     [,1] [,2]
[1,]    1    3
[2,]    2    4
> x[3]
[1] 3
```

```
> # Let us now override the column-major default matrix behavior:
> x <- matrix(1:4, nrow = 2, byrow = TRUE)
> x
     [,1] [,2]
[1,]    1    2
[2,]    3    4
> x[3]
[1] 2
>
```

The first part of this example, presents something you have already seen. The `matrix` function takes a numeric vector as an input and reshapes it into a two-dimensional array (that is, a matrix) by column. Once the first column is filled up, the second column is populated, and so on. This can also be seen from the output of x[3], which equals 3. You can partly override the column-major behavior of the `matrix` function by supplying the byrow = TRUE argument. Even though this command populated the matrix by rows first, the internal vector-based representation of the matrix is still column-major; the third element of x is now 2, not 3.

You can also reference elements of a matrix in the more traditional [row, column] way. Because all linear algebra textbooks adhere to this notation, this will seem natural.

Consider the following latest definition of x:

```
> x
     [,1] [,2]
[1,]    1    2
[2,]    3    4
> x[1, ]
[1] 1 2
> x[2, ]
[1] 3 4
> x[ ,1]
[1] 1 3
> x[ ,2]
[1] 2 4
>
```

The notation x[i, j] refers to the element of x that is in the ith row and the jth column. For example, x[1, 1] = 1 and x[2, 1] = 3. As can be seen in the example, to select an entire row of a matrix, you must omit the column index but retain the comma; to select a column, the row index must be left out but

the comma retained. The notation [,1] should be read as "first column," and
[2,] should be read as "second row."

When you select a single row or a single column of a matrix in R, a subtle issue presents itself: when possible, R's default behavior is to simplify the object's type. Hence, the result of selecting a column from an n-by-k matrix will not be an n-by-1 matrix, as you would expect (especially given experience with `numpy` arrays) but rather a vector of length n, which is not always what is wanted. This is referred to as *type coercion*, a sinister term if there ever was one. The following example illustrates how to override type coercion:

```
> x.matrix <- matrix(1:4, nrow = 2)
> x.matrix
     [,1] [,2]
[1,]   1    3
[2,]   2    4
> class(x.matrix)
[1] "matrix"
> x.column.vector <- x.matrix[, 1]
> x.column.vector
[1] 1 2
> class(x.column.vector)
[1] "integer"
> x.column.matrix <- x.matrix[, 1, drop = FALSE]
> x.column.matrix
     [,1]
[1,]   1
[2,]   2
> class(x.column.matrix)
[1] "matrix"
>
```

To select all but some elements of a vector or an array, negative indices are used, which is obviously different from anything you have probably seen before. Don't be scared! For example, x[-1,] will return all rows from array x except the first one, whereas x[,-2] will return all columns from array x except the second one. To omit several rows, just provide a vector of negative numbers, as in x[c(-1, -4),], which will return all rows of x except the first and fourth.

In addition to vectors and matrices, several other data structures deserve mention. First, R supports *arrays*, which are best thought of as matrices that can potentially have more than two dimensions. This is a compact way to store data, and handy in certain applications.

Second, R supports *lists*, which are essentially collections of key-value pairs of arbitrary R objects, not quite like Python lists—in fact, more like the Python dictionary type. A list is the most flexible data structure available in R, particularly because lists can be nested. With flexibility, however, comes the potential for errors. In short, additional care is required to retrieve list components and their contents. The rules are best illustrated using examples.

Consider the following snippet of R code:

```
> string.vector <- "a"
> numeric.vector <- 1
> example.list <- list(string.vector, numeric.vector)
> example.list
[[1]]
[1] "a"

[[2]]
[1] 1

>
```

At first, the representation of the raw output of the list may be confusing. The notation `[[1]]` should be read as "first element of the list." Unlike with vectors, referencing `example.list[1]` will *not* return the first element of `example.list`. In fact, the following will obtain:

```
> example.list[1]
[[1]]
[1] "a"

> example.list[[1]]
[1] "a"
>
```

When single rather than double square brackets are used, R returns a list with a single element rather than the corresponding element of the master list; the double square brackets are used to retrieve the actual element of the master list.

Wickham (2014) provided an interesting analogy that may help you understand better the difference. Suppose the list `example.list` is a train with two cars, indexed 1 and 2. In this case, `example.list[1]` returns the first car of this train, which can be thought of as a train with a single car, but `example.list[[1]]` returns the contents of the first car rather than the car itself.

In many applications, accessing the elements of a list by name (instead of referring to the indices) is much more convenient. Therefore, you can name the elements using the `names()` function, which is illustrated in the following:

```
> names(example.list) <- c("string", "number")
> example.list
$string
[1] "a"

$number
[1] 1

> str(example.list)
List of 2
 $ string: chr "a"
 $ number: num 1
>
```

This example introduces the `str()` function, which is an abbreviation of the word structure. By printing a concise description of the object to which it is applied, the `str()` function earns a place among the most useful diagnostic tools in R, in this case, returning the names and values of the contents of `example.list`.

Returning to lists, note that each element of `example.list` has a name, courtesy of the `names()` function used. Although you can retrieve list elements using `[[1]]` and `[[2]]`, it is now easier to use the element names, an example of indirection.

```
> example.list[["string"]]
[1] "a"
> example.list["number"]
$number
[1] 1
> example.list$string
[1] "a"
>
```

Again, the single square brackets return a list, whereas the double square brackets return an element of the list. Note, too, the introduction of the $ operator, which can only be used with names. The $ operator is useful when working interactively in R; we discourage you from using the operator in batch scripts, where readability is important.

Interactively, the $ operator is useful because you can abbreviate names, so `example.list$string` and `example.list[["string", exact = FALSE]]` are equivalent internally; provided the name abbreviation is unambiguous, R will not throw an error.

By the way, in case you haven't already noticed, you can use the up arrow to retrieve a previously used command that you typed into the console. In addition, you can use the **tab** key to autocomplete to reduce the amount of typing. A number of keyboard shortcuts common to most UNIX shells are also supported by the R console, for example, `Ctrl+L` will clean the screen.

The final data structure worth mentioning is the *data frame*. For all practical purposes, a data frame is a list of vectors where each vector is restricted to have the same length as the others in the data frame. Data frames are more flexible than matrices because matrices require all columns to be of the same data type. Recall from Chapter 3 that data are most commonly stored in a tabular format, where rows represent observations and columns represent variables, but the variables can be of different types. For example, one might be an integer, another a real, and yet a third some unordered type, such as the gender. R data frames were designed with precisely this kind of structure in mind. In fact, all basic R functions that read data into memory from disk create data frame objects as output.

Everything described so far about accessing list elements translates directly to data frames. Once you understand how to use the single and double square bracket notation, you can also use the $ operator, provided the data frame columns have been named.

Before dealing with data in R, let's consider how the `help()` function works. For the novice, the `help()` function is not particularly user-friendly; occasionally, even intermediate users struggle with `help()`. To invoke a help page for, say, *command*, type either `help(`*command*`)` or `?`*command*. Typically, what results is a listing of pages of information, most of which is overwhelming. If you really needed help, the minutiae presented are too detailed. Thus, just scroll through the help page to the most useful part—the very bottom, where examples of code are provided. It appears that users are encouraged either to copy/paste said code into the console window (or a batch script) or to enter it manually, thus facilitating learning by doing. For many commands, the same result can be achieved using the built-in `example()` function. Although somewhat laborious, this process can yield satisfactory results. Another useful option is to search the Internet for "how to [do something] in R," which will usually return a link to a discussion forum such as `stackoverflow.com`, where the exact problem has often already been solved.

5.4.5 Reading in Data

In the next several sections, we refer periodically to the auction example of Chapter 3. If you skipped that chapter, you are encouraged to revisit Section 3.5, to become familiar with the basic problem.

Reading data into R from a flat file that resides on disk is usually the first step in any empirical analysis. Use the following `read.table()` function to complete the task:

```
> example.data.frame <- read.table(file = "/Users/hjp/PGBook/Data/
    Input.dat")
>
```

In this example, the data from the file `Input.dat`, which reside in the subdirectory `/Users/hjp/PGBook/Data/`, are read into a data frame named `example.data.frame`. The string that is passed to the `file` argument of `read.table()` can be a URL, that is, the source file can reside on a remote host.

The `read.table()` function has several parameters. For this function (unlike most other R functions) choosing these parameters intelligently can make a world of difference. The choices are especially important when reading large data files because R is particularly inefficient at managing memory. We strongly recommend that you adopt these parameters.

- Handling the data file header. `header = FALSE` is the default, and there is almost never a good reason to change it unless the data file really has a header, but even then it is possible to use the combination of `col.names` and `skip` to bypass the data header and supply your own.

- Handling column separators. `sep = ""` is the default and should be read as "any kind of whitespace such as spaces, tabs, or carriage return, or line feed symbols." It is usually a good idea to be explicit about separators because R is not always good at guessing; for example, if you know the data are tab-delimited, then `sep = "\t"` is appropriate.

- Handling variable names. A vector of variable names can be passed to the `col.names` argument.

- Handling variable types. A vector of variable types can, and usually should, be passed to the `colClasses` parameter; othewise R has to guess, which results in longer read times and excessive memory consumption. Supplying this argument can have a noticeable impact on `read.table()`'s performance; at a minimum, using high-level variable types such as `numeric`, `character`, or `Date` is encouraged.

- Handling number of observations. `nrows` tells R how many rows from the data file should be read, which is another parameter that we strongly encourage you to use so that R does not have to guess.[6]

- Handling comments in the data file. `comment.char = "#"` is the default choice which can be surprisingly unhelpful, so we recommend using `comment.char = ""` to turn this option completely off, provided you are certain no comments exist in the data file, because this option will improve performance on large files.

- Handling categorical variables. `stringsAsFactors = FALSE` is almost always a good idea, particularly if the data are split across files. Generally, we advise against using `factor` variables in R unless you know why you need them.

We recommend reading in the file `AuctionsTable.csv` using the following command:

```
> auctions <- read.table(file = "Data/AuctionsTable.csv",
                          header = FALSE,
                          sep = ",",
                          col.names = c("AuctionID", "Volume",
                                        "District", "Date"),
```

---

[6]In UNIX you can discover the number of records in a file using the command `wc -l file-name` where `wc` is an abbreviation of "word count" and the flag `-l` makes it count the number of lines instead of words. You can read more about this command in Chapter 2, page 27. Note that even an overestimate will be helpful in improving performance.

```
                            colClasses = c(rep("numeric", 3),
                                           "character"),
                     nrows = 10,
                     comment.char = "")
> auctions[["Date"]] <- as.Date(auctions[["Date"]], format = "%Y%m%d")
>
```

R has two convenient functions, `read.csv()` and `read.delim()`, which internally call the `read.table()` function with appropriately chosen defaults. For obvious reasons, these two functions do not have any defaults for the `colClasses` and `nrows` arguments, which we recommend using whenever possible for performance reasons.

Even when you are diligent in instructing `read.table()` about data set details, it can still take R minutes if not hours to read large data sets from a text file. In our context, large usually means between 5 and 20 gigabytes. You can expect R to handle smaller data sets somewhat gracefully, whereas working with larger data sets in R alone becomes quite time consuming. Section 5.5 discusses the `data.table` R package, to handle R's memory management quirks. Here, we only mention the `fread()` function from this package; in our experience, this function works a lot better than native R functions for reading raw data from disk. The differences in performance become dramatic on data sets that are measured in gigabytes—not uncommon these days when some files are terabytes or petabytes in size (see Table 6.2).

In general, you can use the `Date` type for the column of the same name, but the default implementation of `read.table()` can only recognize two date masks (formats): `YYYY-MM-DD` and `YYYY/MM/DD`. For all other date masks, the date should be read in as a `character` type, and the `as.Date()` function then used to convert it to `Date`.

As you may know, every software product stores date information internally as a numeric variable. Some date is chosen by an SDE to represent the *date origin*, and then every date is represented as the number of days, seconds, or other calendar units elapsed since the origin date. On the one hand, this is convenient for calculating relative differences between two points in time, for example, the number of days that have elapsed between 1 January 1983 and 15 March 2014. On the other hand, this strategy makes work difficult when data need to be ported across applications because the origin date typically differs across programs. Therefore, we *strongly* encourage you to represent dates as character strings for the purposes of importing and exporting data. Of course, this strategy requires you to know how every application handles data conversion from strings to dates, and vice versa.

Although the `as.Date()` function is frequently more than adequate, the `lubridate` package is an even better alternative. The `lubridate` package provides several advantages.

First, `lubridate` is sufficiently smart to handle minor perturbations in string formats. The `ymd()` function accepts the date masks YYYYMMDD, YYYY-MM-DD, YYYY/MM/DD, and virtually anything else. Both `mdy()` and `dmy()` functions work equally well, as does `ymd_hms()` for time-stamped data. In contrast, `as.Date()` must be supplied with a specific date mask, which can be a bit tedious.

Second, `lubridate` provides several convenient helper functions to extract information from a date variable. These include not only the self-describing `year()`, `quarter()`, `month()`, `day()`, `hour()`, `minute()`, and `second()` but also the less obvious but very useful `yday()` and `mday()` for day of year and day of month as well as `wday()` for day of week, with a useful option `label` for explicit naming.

Third, `lubridate` has the ability to manage information concerning time zones, date interval objects, and set operations over several such intervals.

Fourth, `lubridate` handles leap years correctly.

Fifth, `lubridate` handles vector inputs correctly, so performance is not degraded relative to base R functions.

In short, we highly recommend using the functions in the `lubridate` package. Although installing this package may take some effort and time, part of what makes a successful R user is a familiarity with several key packages that make data manipulation and analysis less tedious and faster.

5.4.6 Descriptive Statistics

Having loaded the data into R, you then want to explore them. As is typical in R, several methods are available to complete this task. Here, we consider first the simple case of summarizing the bids data from auctions—first summarizing the entire data set and then demonstrating how to calculate summaries on subsets of data. To ensure that the data have been loaded and are available for analysis, do the following:

```
> bids <- read.csv(file = "Data/BidsTable.csv", header = FALSE,
                   col.names = c("bid.id", "auction.id", "bidder.id",
                      "bid"),
                   colClasses = "numeric", nrows = 100)
>
```

Note that even though several columns exist in the file, we only supplied one value to the `colClasses` argument because R will *recycle* the argument until its dimensions agree with the rest of the inputs. Here, under the hood, `colClasses = "numeric"` becomes `colClasses = rep("numeric", 4)`.

To get some idea concerning the overall structure of the data, use the `summary()` function. Its output will depend on variable types, so we override some of them and also introduce a missing value:

```
> bids.copy <- bids
> bids.copy[["auction.id"]] <- as.factor(bids.copy[["auction.id"]])
> bids.copy[["bid.id"]] <- as.character(bids.copy[["bid.id"]])
> bids.copy[["bidder.id"]][1] <- NA
> summary(bids.copy)
    bid.id            auction.id    bidder.id            bid
 Length:37          1      : 6    Min.   :1.000    Min.   : 7.14
 Class :character   4      : 5    1st Qu.:2.000    1st Qu.: 8.84
 Mode  :character   8      : 5    Median :4.000    Median :10.88
                    5      : 4    Mean   :3.972    Mean   :11.16
                    9      : 4    3rd Qu.:6.000    3rd Qu.:12.76
                    2      : 3    Max.   :7.000    Max.   :19.21
                    (Other):10    NA's   :1
>
```

As you can see, almost no summary information is provided for the character columns of the data frame; frequency tabulations are reported for categorical variables (which are referred to as *factors* in R); several summary statistics are computed for the numeric columns. Numbers of missing values are also reported.

Similar information can be obtained using the `describe()` function, which resides in the `Hmisc` package.

```
> install.packages("Hmisc")
> library(Hmisc)
> describe(bids.copy)
bids.copy
```

```
 4  Variables      37  Observations
--------------------------------------------------------------------
bid.id
      n missing  unique
     37        0      37

lowest : 1  10 11 12 13, highest: 5  6  7  8  9
--------------------------------------------------------------------
auction.id
      n missing  unique
     37        0      10

           1 2 3  4  5 6 7  8  9 10
Frequency  6 3 3  5  4 2 2  5  4  3
%         16 8 8 14 11 5 5 14 11  8
--------------------------------------------------------------------
bidder.id
      n missing  unique    Mean
     36        1       7   3.972

           1  2  3  4  5  6  7
Frequency  5  7  4  4  5  6  5
%         14 19 11 11 14 17 14
--------------------------------------------------------------------
bid
      n missing  unique    Mean     .05     .10      .25      .50
          .75     .90
     37        0      37   11.16   7.382   7.834    8.840   10.880
         12.760  14.404
    .95
 15.630

lowest :  7.14  7.35  7.39  7.69  7.93, highest: 14.28 14.59 15.62
    15.67 19.21
--------------------------------------------------------------------

>
```

This function computes several extra percentiles and also reports the largest and smallest values for numeric variables. Together, the two functions `summary()` and `describe()` provide good insights into the overall structure of the data. We can think of no instance where you would want to begin an analysis of data without examining the output of one of these functions first.

In many applications, however, calculating summary statistics for nonoverlapping subsets of data is important. For example, you may be interested in the average bid for every auction. The best way to tackle this problem is using the so-called *split-apply-combine* technique, which was made popular by Wickham (2011). In this case, you first split the entire data set into nonoverlapping pieces; the sizes of pieces are chosen so that performing the calculations of interest on each piece is all but trivial. Here, you would allocate all records pertaining to a given auction into a piece. Next, perform the calculations desired for each piece, and then store the results as intermediate inputs. Finally, assemble the intermediate inputs, possibly transforming them in a way that mimics the original input data structure, should that be required.

As mentioned, many ways exist in R to accomplish the same task. We suggest using the `plyr` package because it is very flexible, has a transparent structure, and reduces the amount of bookkeeping code that you need to develop.

```
> install.packages("plyr")
> library(plyr)
> ComputeAverage <- function(data, variable = "bid") {
    average <- mean(data[[variable]])
    names(average) <- paste("average", variable, sep = ".")
    return(average)
  }
> average.bid <- ddply(.data = bids, .variables = .(auction.id),
                       .fun = ComputeAverage, variable = "bid")
> average.bid
   auction.id average.bid
1           1    10.21833
2           2     9.76000
3           3    12.25000
4           4    12.06800
5           5    12.77750
6           6    10.46000
7           7    11.77500
8           8    10.16800
9           9    11.10000
10         10    11.42000
>
```

The function `ComputeAverage()` is relatively straightforward. In fact, the built-in `mean()` function could have been used. We did not because we wanted to illustrate a few other features of R using this example. First, the construct `variable = "bid"` passes a default value to a function input argument; in case the second input argument is not provided, the value `"bid"` will be used. Second, we use the `names()` function to take care of the name of the new variable created by our function. Third, we use the `paste()` function for string concatenation so that the function can be used to compute any kind of average, not just an average bid, and the output name would automatically reflect this.

Let's now focus on the call to `ddply()` function. The `plyr` package has a collection of `ABply()` functions where A captures input type and B reflects output type. Therefore, `ddply()` takes a data frame as an input and returns a data frame, whereas `alply()` would expect an array as an input and return a list. Four inputs are necessary for `ddply()` and its variants to work. First, `.data` instructs the function to which input it will be applied. Second, `.variables` is a vector of variable names that defines the pieces into which the data must be split. In our example, we split the data into pieces that correspond to every distinct value of `auction.id`. Third, the input is the name of the function that we would like to apply to each piece. Finally, additional parameters can be passed to this function by name, which is how we pass the `variable = "bid"` parameter in the example. The output is a data frame with the number of rows equal to the number of distinct values in `.variables`.

How do you combine the average bid information with the original bids data? One way to accomplish this is to use the `merge()` function, which performs an operation akin to `JOIN` in relational algebra. The syntax is actually quite straightforward:

```
> bids.with.averages <- merge(x = bids, y = average.bid)
> head(bids.with.averages, n = 10)

  auction.id bid.id bidder.id   bid average.bid
1          1      1         1 12.10    10.21833
2          1      2         2 12.38    10.21833
3          1      3         3 11.63    10.21833
4          1      4         5  8.84    10.21833
5          1      5         6  8.37    10.21833
6          1      6         7  7.99    10.21833
7          2      7         5  9.80     9.76000
8          2      8         6  7.14     9.76000
```

```
9                2        9          7 12.34       9.76000
10               3       10          2 12.84      12.25000
>
```

By default, `merge()` finds all columns in both data frames that have identical names and uses them as join keys. Here, the `by.x` and `by.y` parameters can be used to override this behavior. Also, by default an inner join is returned, and parameters `all.x` and `all.y` can be set to `TRUE` for a left, right, or full outer join instead.

As an alternative to `merge()`, you can use `ddply()`, which is useful when you want to compute results for a part of the original data frame. Suppose you want to add the fifth column to the `bids` data frame with the value of average bid per auction. Clearly, it would take the same value for every bidder in each auction, but there are many reasons we might want to have this kind of data structure, at least temporarily. The following achieves this:

```
> bids <- ddply(bids, .variables = "auction.id", transform,
                average.bid = mean(bid))
> head(bids, n = 10)
   bid.id auction.id bidder.id   bid  average.bid
1       1          1         1   1 12.10    10.21833
2       2          2         1   2 12.38    10.21833
3       3          3         1   3 11.63    10.21833
4       4          4         1   5  8.84    10.21833
5       5          5         1   6  8.37    10.21833
6       6          6         1   7  7.99    10.21833
7       7          7         2   5  9.80     9.76000
8       8          8         2   6  7.14     9.76000
9       9          9         2   7 12.34     9.76000
10     10         10         3   2 12.84    12.25000
>
```

A few other things are worth noting. First, it is unnecessary to name explicitly each function input; instead, we rely on the order in which inputs are supplied. Second, variable names for splitting data into pieces can be passed as strings. The important difference is the `transform` argument, which instructs `ddply()` to modify the original data frame. The final argument should be read as "new variable name = expression that defines its values". The `head()` function prints the top n rows of a data frame, where the default value for n is six, which would not have been as informative in terms of illustrating the output. The output is identical to the one where we performed the merge manually, with the exception of the column order in the resulting data frame.

5.4.7   Flow Control and Loops

As demonstrated at the end of Section 5.4.3, like other programming languages, R supports conditional logic using the `if` statement, which has the following syntax:

```
> if (condition.to.evaluate) {
    # code to execute when condition.to.evaluate == TRUE
  } else {
    # code to execute when condition.to.evaluate == FALSE
  }
```

We have learned the hard way that the syntax of the `if` statement should be *exactly* the same as shown here. For `condition.to.evaluate`, the parentheses are mandatory. R will throw a somewhat cryptic error message if they are omitted. Also, the `else` keyword should be on the same line with the closing curly brace `}` for the block of code that must be evaluated when `condition.to.evaluate` is TRUE. To evaluate multiple conditions, the `&` and `|` symbols can be used for logical AND and OR, respectively. When just one expression needs to be executed conditionally, wrapping it in curly braces is unnecessary. Also, in this case, the following expression can be used:

```
> result <- ifelse(condition.to.evaluate, result.if.true,
                    result.if.false)
```

When `condition.to.evaluate` is a vector, it is evaluated element by element. For example, consider the following:

```
> ascending.vector   <- 1:3
> ascending.vector
[1] 1 2 3

> descending.vector <- 4:2
> descending.vector
[1] 4 3 2

> result <- ifelse(ascending.vector > descending.vector,
                    ascending.vector, descending.vector)
> result
[1] 4 3 3
```

The first two elements of `result` are taken from `descending.vector`, and the last value is taken from the `ascending.vector`.

R also supports several loop constructs. The most popular one is the following `for` loop:

```
> for (iteration.counter in container) {
    # code to execute at every iteration of the loop
  }
```

Such constructs are available in virtually every language; they all work in much the same way. A subtle R-specific issue exists with `for` loops, however. Consider the following code:

```
> n <- 3
> for (i in 1:n-1) {
    print(i)
  }
[1] 0
[1] 1
[1] 2
```

Most people would expect to see i take values 1 and 2, but in R the colon : operator is executed before the minus – operator. So the 1:n creates the sequence from 1 to 3, and then 1 gets subtracted from every element of this sequence. To fix this, you should write `for (i in 1:(n-1))` instead.

If the number of loop iterations is unknown in advance, then we advise you to use the `while` loop:

```
> while (expression.to.evaluate) {
    # code to execute at every iteration
    # this code should modify expression.to.evaluate
    # otherwise the loop will run forever
  }
```

The `break` keyword can be used to terminate the loop, and the `next` keyword can be used to skip to the next loop iteration.

Because R is an interpreted language, loops are slow; nested loops are particularly slow. As we suggested in Chapter 4, to maximize performance, wherever possible, your R code should be vectorized.

Finally, with regard to looping, you frequently need to perform the same operation on every element of an object, for example, every column in the data frame or every element in a list. The proper way of doing this in R is to define a function that performs the operation first, and then to use one of the many *functionals* such as the `ddply()` to apply the function to each element. Many subtle differences exist between the functionals, but you can usually accomplish most of the common tasks with the help of the `plyr` package.

5.4.8 Figures and Graphs

Plotting figures and graphs is where R really shines. Base R is very flexible, but it can take some time to master because learning how the many auxiliary functions modify different aspects of a figure or graph can take both time and patience. If, however, you have a clear idea concerning how a figure or graph should appear, and are willing to spend some time fine-tuning every little detail to perfection, then these functions are outstanding. An excellent source on doing this is the book by Murrell (2006).

For exploratory data analysis, employing the various functions is both laborious and superflous; what matters is the ability to plot many graphs quickly, thus uncovering important patterns in the data. The quality of each graph is relatively unimportant. In such circumstances, the R package `ggplot2` is extremely helpful.

To introduce `ggplot2`, we have simulated some data using the following code:

```
> rm(list = ls())
> set.seed(123457)
> library(ggplot2)
> n <- 1000
> # make up some data
> x1 <- rnorm(n, mean = 10, sd = 1)
> x2 <- rnorm(n, mean =  3, sd = 1)
> mode <- (runif(n) <= 0.5)
> x <- x1 * mode + x2 * (1 - mode)
> error <- rnorm(n, sd = 2)
> y <- x + error
> d <- data.frame(x, y, mode)
>
```

Most of the instructions should be easy to follow. In particular, the first line clears all objects that currently reside in R's memory, ensuring you begin with a clean slate every time the script is executed. The second line fixes the seed of the pseudo-random number generator, ensuring that results can be replicated, no matter how many times the code is run. (For more on pseudo-random number generation, see Chapter 7.) The library `ggplot2` is then loaded, and the sample size n is assigned to the value 1, 000. Samples concerning two normally distributed random vectors x1 and x2 are generated using the rnorm() function; x1 has a mean of 10 and a variance of 1, whereas x2 has a mean of 3 and a variance of 1. A hidden Bernoulli random variable mode is defined, which equals 1 for half the time and 0 the other half of the time. The variable x is a mixture of the two normals, and y is simply the sum of x and an error. The variables of interest are then collected in a data frame, because this is how ggplot2 works.

Wickham (2009) provided a complete guide to ggplot2, but the general idea behind ggplot2 is both simple and elegant. Every plot is thought of as a collection of configurable layers. A data frame is passed to each layer as an input, together with an aesthetic mapping such as "put variable v1 on the x-axis and variable v2 on the y-axis." This concept is best illustrated using a sequence of examples. To begin, we consider the simplest plot of all—the histogram.

```
> ggplot(data = d, aes(x = y, y = ..count..)) +
+        layer(geom = "bar", stat = "bin")
stat_bin: binwidth defaulted to range/30. Use 'binwidth = x' to adjust
     this.
>
```

Although this may appear like a lot of code, we have been deliberately verbose: the extra words make understanding the command easier. First we create a ggplot object using the function of that name. The function takes the data frame d and the aesthetic mapping aes(x = y, y = ..count..)) as inputs. At this point, ggplot has not been told how to visualize the data, which is why the separate layer(geom = "bar", stat = "bin") is then added. At least one of the two parameters passed is mandatory: the geom parameter controls how the data are plotted. Histograms are almost always plotted using vertical bars, but you could use geom = "point" instead. The stat parameter controls the transformation that is applied to the data before plotting; without stat = "bin" the built-in variable ..count.. does not exist. A critical parameter that determines the histogram's appearance is the bin width; ggplot2 will warn you if one is not provided. Figure 5.1 shows the output.

In reality, ggplot2 is a lot less verbose, for there exists the qplot() function, an abbreviation of "quickplot." Depending on inputs, qplot() guesses

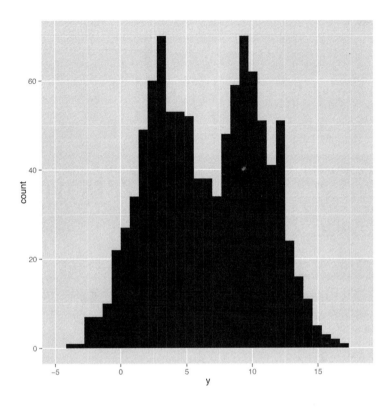

Figure 5.1: First Histogram

what kind of graph to use. Here is how you can reproduce Figure 5.1 with
qplot():

```
> bin.width.value <- (max(d[["y"]]) - min(d[["y"]])) / 30
> qplot(y, data = d, binwidth = bin.width.value)
>
```

The last argument is again unnecessary, but we use it to illustrate how ggplot
picks default bin width. Figure 5.2 shows the result.

For continuous data, an alternative to the histogram is a plot of the
kernel-smoothed density function. In this next example, we illustrate the
kernel-smoothed density function (see Figure 5.3) and demonstrate the over-
laying of layers:

```
> ggplot(data = d, aes(x = y, y = ..density..)) +
+    geom_histogram() +
```

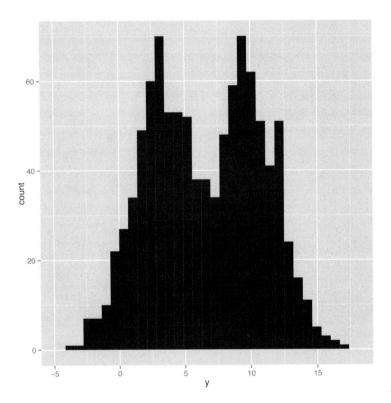

Figure 5.2: Second Histogram

```
+    geom_density(size = 1.5, linetype = 2, color = "gray")
>
```

Instead of the `layer()` function, we used the `geom_histogram()` and the `geom_density()` shortcut functions. Plenty of other `geom`s exist in `ggplot2`; see `http://docs.ggplot2.org` for the online documentation. The auxiliary variable `..density..` is computed by function `geom_histogram()`.

One powerful feature of `ggplot2`, perhaps the hallmark of R, is the ability to plot subsets of data side by side. Because `y` is a mixture of two normal variables, you can use this facility to visualize the mixture:

```
> qplot(y, data = d, facets = mode ~ .)
stat_bin: binwidth defaulted to range/30. Use 'binwidth = x' to adjust
    this.
```

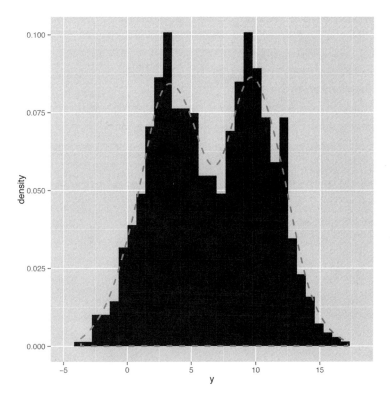

Figure 5.3: Kernel-Smoothed Density Function

```
stat_bin: binwidth defaulted to range/30. Use 'binwidth = x' to adjust
    this.
>
```

The input to `facets` should be a formula; were you to change the call to
`facets = . ~ mode`, the histograms would have appeared next to each
other horizontally, instead of vertically. Figure 5.4 shows a faceted histogram.

   If the histogram is the most popular univariate plot, then the scatterplot is
the most popular plot for understanding the relations between pairs of variables. Following are two identical ways to produce a scatterplot, one using the
full syntax and the other relying on the `qplot()` function:

```
> ggplot(data = d, aes(x = x, y = y)) + geom_point()
> qplot(x, y, data = d)
>
```

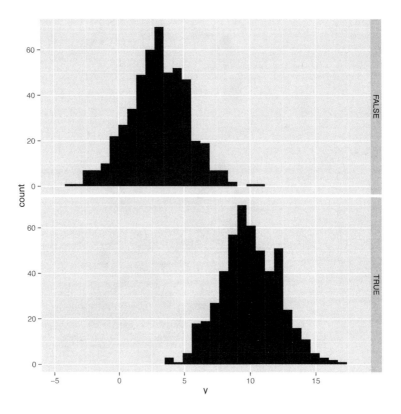

Figure 5.4: Faceted Histogram

By now the `ggplot` logic should be somewhat familiar. All the action occurs inside the `aes()` function; the points are used to represent each datum (see Figure 5.5). Notice how elegant and concise the shorter implementation is.

Although you can use `facets` on scatterplots, sometimes a better way to visualize differences between subsets of data is to use a single plot with symbols in different shapes and sizes:

```
> qplot(x, y, data = d, shape = mode, size = mode)
>
```

By using symbols in different sizes and shapes (see Figure 5.6), you can potentially represent four variables in a two-dimensional plot.

Although much more could be written about plotting graphs in R, most of it is best learned by doing.

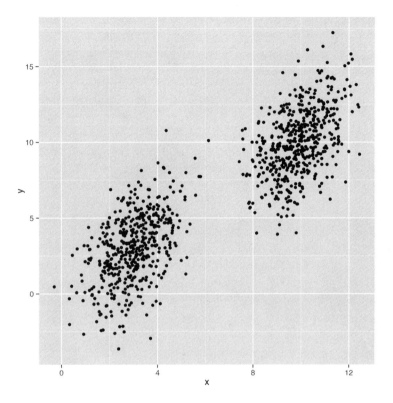

Figure 5.5: First Scatterplot

5.4.9   Regressions

In part, R is popular among both applied statisticians and machine learners because virtually every existing algorithm has been implemented inside one of R's many packages (or will be soon). Functions to estimate (train) simple empirical models (such as linear and logistic regression) are provided in the `stats` package, which is loaded by default. In the following, we use the simulated data of the previous section to demonstrate how you can fit models to data in R.

Method of Least-Squares Regression

Although the method of least squares was first reported by the French mathematician Adrien-Marie Legendre in 1805, and then by the German

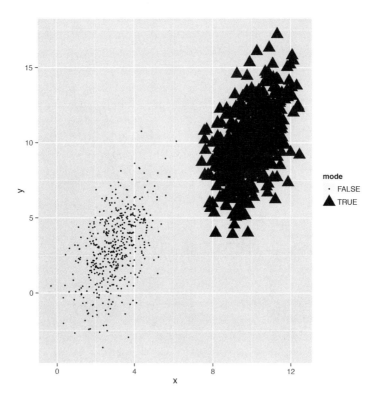

Figure 5.6: Second Scatterplot

mathematician Johann Carl Friedrich Gauss in 1809, Sir Francis Galton made the technique popular under the name regression. In fact, today the method of least-squares regression or least-squares estimation is the most popular empirical technique used by scientists. We present the material in this section as a review. The material will also allow you to appreciate the definition of the Python class in Chapter 6.

   The linear regression model is used to discover a relation between the *dependent variable* (*regressand* or *output*), denoted by Y, and a collection of variables, the *covariates* (*regressors* or *features*), collected in the $(1 \times K)$ vector of features denoted by $\mathbf{x}$. Now, the observed value of the dependent variable Y can be decomposed linearly into an unknown mean value that depends on $\mathbf{x}$, which we denote $\mu(\mathbf{x})$, and an unobserved variable U, which is assumed to be a random variable that has mean zero by construction. Suppose it has a constant variance

σ^2, too. In symbols,

$$Y = \mu(\mathbf{x}) + U,$$

where

$$\mathbb{E}(U|\mathbf{x}) = 0.$$

The linear regression model rests on two additional important assumptions: First, the U and the elements of the vector $\mathbf{x}$ have no covariation. In symbols,

$$\mathbb{E}(Ux_k) = 0 \quad k = 1, 2, \ldots, K.$$

Second, the conditional mean function is linear in unknown parameters $\beta_1, \beta_2, \ldots, \beta_K$, that is,

$$\mu(\mathbf{x}) = \beta_1 x_1 + \beta_2 x_2 + \cdots + \beta_K x_K \equiv \mathbf{x}\boldsymbol{\beta},$$

where $\boldsymbol{\beta}$ is a $(K \times 1)$ vector that is conformable to $\mathbf{x}$. Consequently,

$$Y = \mu(\mathbf{x}) + U = \mathbf{x}\boldsymbol{\beta} + U. \tag{5.1}$$

Typically, an empirical specification is assumed to have an intercept, so $\mathbf{x} = (1, x_2, x_3, \ldots, x_K)$.

In practice, in empirical work, you are typically given (or have created) a sample of N observations concerning the $(\mathbf{x}, Y)$s, which is often denoted by $\{(\mathbf{x}_n, y_n)\}_{n=1}^N$ where the lowercase y_n denotes a realized value of Y_n. Here, the index n is mnemonic for individual, but it could also represent time, in which case the subscript t is often used. Writing equation (5.1) observation by observation yields

$$\mathbf{y} \equiv \begin{bmatrix} y_1 \\ y_2 \\ \vdots \\ y_N \end{bmatrix} = \begin{bmatrix} 1 & x_{1,2} & x_{1,3} & \cdots & x_{1,K} \\ 1 & x_{2,2} & x_{2,3} & \cdots & x_{2,K} \\ \vdots & \vdots & \vdots & \ddots & \vdots \\ 1 & x_{N,2} & x_{N,3} & \cdots & x_{N,K} \end{bmatrix} \begin{bmatrix} \beta_1 \\ \beta_2 \\ \beta_3 \\ \vdots \\ \beta_K \end{bmatrix} + \begin{bmatrix} u_1 \\ u_2 \\ \vdots \\ u_N \end{bmatrix} \equiv \mathbf{X}\boldsymbol{\beta} + \mathbf{u},$$

where $\mathbf{u}$ is a vector of realized errors, which are unobserved.

Researchers seek to estimate $\boldsymbol{\beta}$ using the information in $\mathbf{X}$ and $\mathbf{y}$. As mentioned, the most commonly used empirical strategy to estimate a regression model is the method of least squares. Least-squares estimation involves choosing $\boldsymbol{\beta}$ to minimize the sum of squared residuals $S(\boldsymbol{\beta})$, which can be written in matrix notation as

$$S(\boldsymbol{\beta}) \equiv (\mathbf{y} - \mathbf{X}\boldsymbol{\beta})^\top (\mathbf{y} - \mathbf{X}\boldsymbol{\beta}) = \mathbf{y}^\top \mathbf{y} - 2\boldsymbol{\beta}^\top \mathbf{X}^\top \mathbf{y} + \boldsymbol{\beta}^\top \mathbf{X}^\top \mathbf{X}\boldsymbol{\beta}.$$

In particular, the method involves decomposing the observed y into two parts, one that can be "explained" by the $\mathbf{X}$ and another, denoted by $\hat{e}$, that is orthogonal to the $\mathbf{X}$, that is, "unexplained" by the $\mathbf{X}$. Specifically, the least-squares estimator is the solution to the following minimization problem:

$$\min_{\beta} S(\beta) = \min_{\beta} y^\top y - 2\beta^\top \mathbf{X}^\top y + \beta^\top \mathbf{X}^\top \mathbf{X}\beta,$$

whence derive the first-order conditions of the minimum of $S(\beta)$ with respect to β:

$$\nabla_\beta S(\hat{\beta}) = -2\mathbf{X}^\top y + 2\mathbf{X}^\top \mathbf{X}\hat{\beta} - 2\mathbf{X}^\top(y - \mathbf{X}^\top \mathbf{X}\hat{\beta}) \equiv -2\mathbf{X}^\top \hat{e} = \mathbf{0}_K.$$

These linear equations, sometimes called the *normal equations*, define the least-squares estimator $\hat{\beta}$:

$$(\mathbf{X}^\top \mathbf{X})\hat{\beta} = \mathbf{X}^\top y$$
$$\hat{\beta} = (\mathbf{X}^\top \mathbf{X})^{-1}\mathbf{X}^\top y.$$

Hence,

$$y = \mathbf{X}\hat{\beta} + \hat{e} = \hat{y} + \hat{e}.$$

If the vector U is distributed jointly normal, which is often denoted as

$$U \sim \mathcal{N}(\mathbf{0}_N, \sigma^2 \mathbf{I}_N),$$

then

$$\hat{\beta} \sim \mathcal{N}\left[\beta^0, \sigma^2(\mathbf{X}^\top \mathbf{X})^{-1}\right],$$

where β^0 denotes the true value of β. Also,

$$\frac{\hat{e}^\top \hat{e}}{\sigma^2} \sim \chi^2(N - K).$$

Under normality, linear hypotheses of the form

$$H_0 : \mathbf{R}\beta^0 = \mathbf{r}$$
$$H_1 : \text{not } H_0$$

can be tested, where **R** is a $(Q \times K)$ matrix and **r** is a $(Q \times 1)$ vector of known constants. For example, the hypothesis that none of the covariates explains a significant portion of the variation in the dependent variable

$$H_0 : \beta_2^0 = \beta_3^0 = \cdots = \beta_K^0 = 0$$
$$H_1 : \text{not } H_0$$

can be written in this way, and tested using Fisher's F statistic

$$\text{calc. } F = \frac{(N-K)}{(K-1)} \frac{\left[\sum_{n=1}^{N}(y_n - \bar{y})^2 - \hat{e}^\top \hat{e}\right]}{\hat{e}^\top \hat{e}} \sim F(K-1, N-K).$$

Example of Regression

We begin with an example of the linear regression of y on x, which is carried out using the lm() function (from "linear model"):

```
> ls.model <- lm(y ~ x, data = d)
> ls.model

Call:
lm(formula = y ~ x, data = d)

Coefficients:
(Intercept)            x
  -0.008825     1.012867

>
```

As might be expected, lm() returns a list. (Technically, it is an object of class lm; under the hood, however, it is a list.) The default printout is minimal; only the least-squares estimates are shown. To obtain more detailed regression output, you can use the following summary() function:

```
> summary(ls.model)

Call:
lm(formula = y ~ x, data = d)

Residuals:
    Min       1Q   Median       3Q      Max
-6.6894  -1.2866   0.0705   1.3123   6.3505
```

```
Coefficients:
             Estimate Std. Error t value Pr(>|t|)
(Intercept) -0.008825   0.128460  -0.069    0.945
x            1.012867   0.017332  58.438   <2e-16 ***
---
Signif. codes:  0 '***' 0.001 '**' 0.01 '*' 0.05 '.' 0.1 ' ' 1

Residual standard error: 1.967 on 998 degrees of freedom
Multiple R-squared:  0.7739,    Adjusted R-squared:  0.7736
F-statistic:  3415 on 1 and 998 DF,  p-value: < 2.2e-16


>
```

This code shows that least-squares regression permits recovering estimates of the true values of parameters that are quite accurate. Basically, the estimated intercept is near 0 and the estimated slope is near 1. The exact structure and contents of the `ls.model` object can be examined by studying the output of `str(ls.model)`.

Here you can see signs of R's memory management problems: the object `ls.model[["model"]]` contains a copy of the entire input data frame, that is, *all* the data. Typically, you only need the model's estimated coefficients, the object `ls.model[["coefficients"]]`, and the variance-covariance matrix, the object `vcov(ls.model)`. Fitted values can be calculated using the `predict()` function, to which the model object is passed. To exclude the intercept term from the model, you can modify the formula as follows: `y ~ x - 1`. We agree, it's dorky.

To fit other kinds of models to data is no more complicated. In fact, the `glm()` function fits the family of generalized linear models, which includes logistic, Poisson, and negative-binomial regression. Discussing the details of these models and interpreting the output of R is reserved for econometrics or statistics courses.

5.4.10   Batch Scripts

One attractive feature of R is that the language permits you to play interactively with your data easily, therefore allowing you to find potentially interesting patterns quickly. However entertaining that activity may be, we encourage you to use batch scripts to collect commands, and then to execute those scripts in the console or from the command line in a terminal window. By now the reasons must be clear: batch scripts provide a written record of what was done, which you can double- and triple-check; this written record can be shared with others. We simply cannot stress these two points enough.

Suppose you have collected the relevant R commands in the following file `BatchScript.R`:

```
x <- 1:4
print(x)
```

You can execute `BatchScript.R` from inside the console by typing the following:

```
> source("BatchScript.R")
[1] 1 2 3 4
>
```

You can also execute `BatchScript.R` in a terminal window on the command line using the standard input-output redirection commands that are supported by every shell:

```
$ R --save < BatchScript.R > BatchOutput.out
```

a practice we recommend for large, time-consuming jobs. In this case, the contents of the `BatchOutput.out` file are as follows:

```
R version 3.1.2 (2014-10-31) -- "Pumpkin Helmet"
Copyright (C) 2014 The R Foundation for Statistical Computing
Platform: x86_64-apple-darwin10.8.0 (64-bit)

R is free software and comes with ABSOLUTELY NO WARRANTY.
You are welcome to redistribute it under certain conditions.
Type 'license()' or 'licence()' for distribution details.

  Natural language support but running in an English locale

R is a collaborative project with many contributors.
Type 'contributors()' for more information and
'citation()' on how to cite R or R packages in publications.

Type 'demo()' for some demos, 'help()' for on-line help, or
'help.start()' for an HTML browser interface to help.
Type 'q()' to quit R.
```

```
> x <- 1:4
> print(x)
[1] 1 2 3 4
>
```

Listing 5.1: Contents of `BatchOutput.out` File

Having to look at the preamble each time can become a bit tedious. To suppress the preamble, type

```
$ R --save --silent < BatchScript.R > SilentBatchOutput.out
```

If you type the following at the command line, you will see

```
$ more SilentBatchOutput.out
> x <- 1:4
> print(x)
[1] 1 2 3 4
>
```

Alternatively, R supports the following syntax, which might be easier for some to follow:

```
$ R CMD BATCH [options] inputFile [outputFile]
```

where `inputFile` should be a path to the script that you seek to run in batch mode, namely, `BatchScript.R`. An example of an option would be the usage of `--silent`, and if the `outputFile` is not specified, it will default to `inputFile.Rout`.

We should also mention that when you install R, another executable is created, `Rscript`, which is usually placed in `/usr/bin/Rscript` on a UNIX-based system. Its sole purpose is to simplify execution of batch R scripts, hence the name. You can use this executable in two ways: first, as an executable for an existing R script, that is,

```
$ echo 'print("Hello World!")' > test.R
$ cat test.R
print("Hello World!")
$ Rscript test.R
[1] "Hello World!"
$ rm test.R
```

Here, we created a small R script named `test.R` in the current directory and used the built-in UNIX command `echo` to write an R command into it. The command prints a string "Hello World!" to the screen. We then used `Rscript` to execute this script; we observed its output on the screen. We cleaned up by deleting the R script.

Second, you can make the R script executable and instruct UNIX to use `Rscript` to execute it. While illustrating how to do this, we demonstrate another UNIX technique.

```
$ cat > test.R << endOfInput
#! /usr/bin/Rscript
print("Hello World!")
endOfInput
$ cat test.R
#! /usr/bin/Rscript
print("Hello World!")
$ chmod 744 ./test.R
$ ./test.R
[1] "Hello World!"
$ rm test.R
```

This may appear cryptic at first, but let's work through it together. The first line should be read as "create file `test.R`, overwriting one if it exists already, and redirect into this file everything starting from next line, until encountering the `endOfInput` character combination." The file creation part is handled by the `> test.R` code, and the `<<` forces the `cat` command to start capturing output from next line onward. The `endOfInput` marker is arbitrary, but without it, `cat` would not know where to stop. The next two lines are placed into the `test.R` file as is, a fact illustrated by the `cat test.R` output. The second line of the R script is familiar by now, and the first line instructs UNIX shell how this file must be executed—this is how the `#!` combination is interpreted. We use the `chmod` command to make the script executable, and then use the `./test.R` command to run it. The output is the same as in the previous code. We clean up by removing the file when we are done; otherwise, with time, the current working directory will be full of test scripts that clutter and prevent you from finding the files you want to use.

5.5   Useful R Packages

However powerful base R may be, its real strength derives from its collection of other packages. In Section 5.4.6, we demonstrated how to install `package.name` using `install.packages("package.name")` and then loading that package using `library(package.name)`. Two subtle points relating to R packages should be mentioned. First, on a Linux machine, R installs packages in your home directory, specifically, in `/home/username/R`. Should you decide to share your code with another user, even someone who uses the same computer as you, then that person will likely have to install the R packages you used on his home directory. Second, most (if not all) R packages are specific to particular versions of R. Whenever you upgrade R, you will typically need to reinstall all the packages again. Although this may appear to be straightforward (how hard can it be to run the `install.packages()` command once more) it is sometimes quite disruptive. This is because R packages depend on each other, and when R is updated, some of the changes in the new version can cause a subset of these packages to stop working unexpectedly. In turn, other packages that consume them as dependencies may stop working as well, and tracing these issues back to the root cause can take some time and effort. This fact is perhaps not surprising; coordination is not usually an outcome of decentralized crowdsourcing.

Alternatively, in R, you can run the following command:

```
> update.packages(checkBuilt = TRUE, ask = FALSE)
```

to update all outdated packages and refresh all packages that were built under earlier versions of R.

In January 2016, over 7,500 CRAN packages were available. Several other useful R packages that did not make it onto CRAN also exist, which can be installed and used. In what follows, we briefly describe about 30 packages that we think you should know about; we group them into sets of tasks that these packages can help you to accomplish.

R enthusiasts have put together several lists, *CRAN Task Views*, which can be found at `http://cran.us.r-project.org/web/views/`, where short descriptions pertaining to the packages are also available. The task views are organized by use case, for instance, machine learning, survival analysis, time series, and so on.

5.5.1 Reading in Data

We have already mentioned how to load plain text data into R from disk (see Section 5.4.5). In Section 5.6, we describe how to connect to a SQLite database. Similar packages exist to connect R to other database engines. Given their self-describing names, the `RMySQL` and `RPostgreSQL` packages accomplish exactly what you would expect; the `RODBC` package uses the Open Database Connectivity protocol, which works with several database engines.

Many people use Microsoft Excel to store and to manipulate data. In fact, in Chapter 3, we recommended the spreadsheet as the first tool to use. Because Excel is the most common implementation of the spreadsheet, the `xlsx` package is particularly useful. In short, you can, in principle, connect to Excel workbooks from within R; in practice, we have found that most packages with that functionality fail to work as expected, at least some of the time. Generally, in the long run, you will be much better off saving your Excel files as comma-separated plain text files instead.

The `foreign` package enables R to read data sets stored in native SAS, SPSS, and Stata formats, which can sometimes be quite handy. Unfortunately, as of the version 13 release of Stata, the binary data file format has been changed, and currently the newest Stata data sets are no longer readable using `read.dta()` function in `foreign`. Although we have had limited exposure to various types of SAS binary files, we believe that `foreign` does not handle all of them equally well. This is why we mentioned the proprietary StatTransfer program that can be quite useful in dealing with issues of data format.

For data that do not readily conform to the relational model, the `XML` and `jsonlite` packages can be used to read XML and JSON files, respectively.

Finally, the `httr` package implements the most common functions you may wish to employ when reading data directly from servers on the Internet. No, `httr` is *not* a typo.

5.5.2 Manipulating Data

Manipulating data into the format necessary to perform data analysis usually takes considerably more time than the actual analysis itself. We mentioned that the most common R package for manipulating data is `plyr`. Several other packages are definitely worth mentioning as well.

First, the recently released `dplyr` package is an improved and updated version of `plyr`; it is claimed to be several times faster at doing most common data manipulations. We chose to describe `plyr` because the package is well established; for example, `plyr` is the most commonly downloaded R package from CRAN. Therefore, you are more likely to run into code that uses `plyr` constructs than `dplyr` constructs. In addition, `dplyr` can only perform a subset of what `plyr` can: `dplyr` is built and optimized for use with data frames only, whereas the `plyr` can also manipulate lists and arrays. That `dplyr` has a different syntax from `plyr` is indeed unfortunate. We have the following suggestion for novice R users. If you have no experience with either `plyr` or `dplyr`, then opt for `dplyr` because it usually provides an easier way to solve most of the data manipulation problems that challenge an average user.

Second, the package `reshape2` is useful when converting data back and forth between *wide* and *long* formats. These two terms are best explained using an example. Consider the following data concerning the annual revenues of Amazon and Google (in billions of U.S. dollars):

```
year    company    revenue
2012    Amazon     61.09
2012    Google     50.18
2013    Amazon     74.45
2013    Google     59.83
```

This data set is in the long format, the most common format to store data; data stored within relational databases are in this format. Sometimes, however, it is useful to analyze the data in the wide format, as in the following:

```
year    revenue_amazon    revenue_google
2012    61.09             50.18
2013    74.45             59.83
```

This format makes it easier to compare Amazon to Google at different dates. Alternatively, if you want to see how individual companies perform over time, a different wide data set can be used:

```
company    revenue_2012    revenue_2013
Amazon     61.09           74.45
Google     50.18           59.83
```

You can now compare the performances of Amazon and Google in 2012 to their performances in 2013 with no extra work. The economists among you will recognize that the original data set is often referred to as a *panel data set*, the first transformation as a *time-series data set,* and the second transformation as a *cross-sectional data set.* The `reshape2` package excels at performing such transformations to large R data sets. A newer and simpler version of `reshape2` is also available on CRAN under a completely different name: `tidyr`. Again, for those with no prior R experience, learning `tidyr` instead of `reshape2` might be a solid long-term strategy. As with the `plyr-dplyr` dichotomy, `tidyr` cannot do everything that `reshape2` can, but `tidyr` usually provides an easier way to solve most problems of this type that challenge an average user.

In addition to these three packages, a few others are worth mentioning because they are quite efficient at solving specific, well-defined problems. We have already mentioned the package `lubridate` for working with data concerning dates. A similar package exists for manipulating strings in R: `stringr`. Given the prevalence of text-based data, the `stringr` package is another popular R package. For those seeking intermediate and advanced functionality for working with text data, the `tm` package (an abbreviation of "text mining") is the de facto standard toolbox for natural language processing in R.

We should also mention the `data.table` package, which is designed primarily to read large data files into R from disk and then subsequently to manipulate them faster and more efficiently than the tools contained in base R. In fact, we already mentioned its superb `fread()` function. The `data.table` package is implemented in C++ and relies primarily on in-place modifications of the data rather than copying them over and over again, as most base R functions do. One drawback of this package is the learning curve: the `data.table` syntax is daunting—different from everything else in R. Consider the following simple example:

```
> # First, we will use base R
>
> # We will load one of the built-in R data sets into memory:
> data(mtcars)
> str(mtcars)
'data.frame':    32 obs. of  11 variables:
 $ mpg : num  21 21 22.8 21.4 18.7 18.1 14.3 24.4 22.8 19.2 ...
 $ cyl : num  6 6 4 6 8 6 8 4 4 6 ...
 $ disp: num  160 160 108 258 360 ...
 $ hp  : num  110 110 93 110 175 105 245 62 95 123 ...
 $ drat: num  3.9 3.9 3.85 3.08 3.15 2.76 3.21 3.69 3.92 3.92 ...
 $ wt  : num  2.62 2.88 2.32 3.21 3.44 ...
 $ qsec: num  16.5 17 18.6 19.4 17 ...
```

```
$ vs  : num  0 0 1 1 0 1 0 1 1 1 ...
$ am  : num  1 1 1 0 0 0 0 0 0 0 ...
$ gear: num  4 4 4 3 3 3 3 4 4 4 ...
$ carb: num  4 4 1 1 2 1 4 2 2 4 ...
>
> # we want to add another column to the data frame
> # it will contain square of car's mpg
> mtcars[["mpg.squared"]] <- mtcars[["mpg"]]^2
> head(mtcars)
                   mpg cyl disp  hp drat    wt  qsec vs am gear carb
Mazda RX4         21.0   6  160 110 3.90 2.620 16.46  0  1    4    4
Mazda RX4 Wag     21.0   6  160 110 3.90 2.875 17.02  0  1    4    4
Datsun 710        22.8   4  108  93 3.85 2.320 18.61  1  1    4    1
Hornet 4 Drive    21.4   6  258 110 3.08 3.215 19.44  1  0    3    1
Hornet Sportabout 18.7   8  360 175 3.15 3.440 17.02  0  0    3    2
Valiant           18.1   6  225 105 2.76 3.460 20.22  1  0    3    1
                  mpg.squared
Mazda RX4              441.00
Mazda RX4 Wag          441.00
Datsun 710             519.84
Hornet 4 Drive         457.96
Hornet Sportabout      349.69
Valiant                327.61
>
> # now we will delete the horsepower (hp) column from the data frame
> # and select only cars that have six cylinders
> mtcars[["hp"]] <- NULL
> mtcars[mtcars[["cyl"]] == 6, ]
                   mpg cyl  disp drat    wt  qsec vs am gear carb mpg.
                       squared
Mazda RX4         21.0   6 160.0 3.90 2.620 16.46  0  1    4    4
    441.00
Mazda RX4 Wag     21.0   6 160.0 3.90 2.875 17.02  0  1    4    4
    441.00
Hornet 4 Drive    21.4   6 258.0 3.08 3.215 19.44  1  0    3    1
    457.96
Valiant           18.1   6 225.0 2.76 3.460 20.22  1  0    3    1
    327.61
Merc 280          19.2   6 167.6 3.92 3.440 18.30  1  0    4    4
    368.64
Merc 280C         17.8   6 167.6 3.92 3.440 18.90  1  0    4    4
    316.84
Ferrari Dino      19.7   6 145.0 3.62 2.770 15.50  0  1    5    6
    388.09
```

How are the same operations performed on `data.tables` instead of `data.frames`?

```
> library(data.table)
> data(mtcars)
> mtcars <- data.table(mtcars)
>
> # creating new column
> mtcars[, mpg.squared := mpg^2]
> head(mtcars)
    mpg cyl disp  hp drat    wt  qsec vs am gear carb mpg.squared
1: 21.0   6  160 110 3.90 2.620 16.46  0  1    4    4      441.00
2: 21.0   6  160 110 3.90 2.875 17.02  0  1    4    4      441.00
3: 22.8   4  108  93 3.85 2.320 18.61  1  1    4    1      519.84
4: 21.4   6  258 110 3.08 3.215 19.44  1  0    3    1      457.96
5: 18.7   8  360 175 3.15 3.440 17.02  0  0    3    2      349.69
6: 18.1   6  225 105 2.76 3.460 20.22  1  0    3    1      327.61
>
> # removing a column
> mtcars[, hp := NULL]
>
> # selecting a subset of the resulting data
> setkey(mtcars, cyl)
> mtcars[J(6)]
   cyl  mpg  disp drat    wt  qsec vs am gear carb mpg.squared
1:   6 22.0 160.0 3.90 2.620 16.46  0  1    4    4      441.00
2:   6 21.0 160.0 3.90 2.875 17.02  0  1    4    4      441.00
3:   6 21.4 258.0 3.08 3.215 19.44  1  0    3    1      457.96
4:   6 18.1 225.0 2.76 3.460 20.22  1  0    3    1      327.61
5:   6 19.2 167.6 3.92 3.440 18.30  1  0    4    4      368.64
6:   6 17.8 167.6 3.92 3.440 18.90  1  0    4    4      316.84
7:   6 19.7 145.0 3.62 2.770 15.50  0  1    5    6      388.09
>
```

Although you would not see any meaningful speed improvements on a data set of just 32 observations, they would be apparent if data set had 32 million records. The strange-looking operator `:=` uses *assignment by reference* to perform operations blazingly fast, particularly when it comes to deleting columns; it takes the same constant amount of time to delete a column from a data table of *any* size. Subsetting in data tables is also much faster: the standard `mtcars[mtcars[["cyl"]] == 6, ]` operation requires computer resources that are linear in the input size because the entire `cyl` column must be scanned and each value is compared with 6.

In contrast, the `mtcars[J(6)]` operation performs a binary search on values of `cyl` (which are declared as *key* using the `setkey()` function call) with resources that are logarithmic in the input size. (Logarithmic performance is *much* faster than linear performance, at least when the input size is large.) In short, data tables are powerful, but in order to reap their full potential you must learn some syntax.

5.5.3 Plotting Figures

Several packages are available to create figures and graphs, for example, the package `lattice`, but the most commonly used packages is `ggplot2`. A few other packages exist to manipulate color themes and other settings, but most of them are beyond the scope of this book.

5.5.4 Time-Series Data

Within R, basic functionality involving time-series data is provided by the `ts` class, but it can only deal with regularly spaced data. The `zoo` package (an example of a non-self-describing name) is designed to solve this problem, whereas the `xts` package provides a more user-friendly interface to the same functionality. The `tseries` package provides stationarity tests, and the `forecast` package implements many common univariate time-series models, such as ARIMA models as well as exponential smoothers. The `vars` package enables users to fit multivariate time-series models such as VARs and ECMs.

A subtle issue exists with the built-in `ts` class in R that surfaces when you try to apply lag operators to time-series objects. Consider the following code:

```
> rm(list = ls())
> set.seed(123457)
> x.raw <- round(5 + rnorm(4), digits = 3)
> x.ts <- ts(x.raw)
> x.ts
Time Series:
Start = 1
End = 4
Frequency = 1
[1] 4.759 4.919 4.859 4.452
```

```
> x.lag.wrong <- lag(x.ts, k = 1)
> x.lag.wrong
Time Series:
Start = 0
End = 3
Frequency = 1
[1]  4.759 4.919 4.859 4.452
>
```

Notice that the indices of observations in `x.lag.wrong` are moved back relative to the ones in `x.ts`—not what most time-series econometricians expect as an output from a lag operator function. Fortunately, you can use the `Lag()` function from the `quantmod` package to solve this problem:

```
> # let's do the lags correctly now
> library(zoo)
> library(quantmod)
> x.zoo <- zoo(x.raw)
> x.lag.correct <- Lag(x.zoo, k = 1)
> x.lag.correct
  Lag.1
1    NA
2 4.759
3 4.919
4 4.859
```

Note the uppercase L instead of the lowercase one in the previous code.

5.5.5 Improving Code Performance

In order to decide whether the performance of an R script can be improved, you must know where bottlenecks exist. This sort of analysis, which is referred to as *profiling*, was mentioned in conjunction with Python scripts in Chapter 4, page 183. Profiling allows you to examine, for example, the amount of memory used as well as the frequency and duration of function calls.

In R the command to use when profiling is `Rprof`. As a useful illustration of how you would profile R code, consider an example where you have decided to implement your own R function to multiply two matrices. This can be accomplished using the following simple R function:

```
MultiplyMatrices <- function(A, B) {
  # Given two matrices A and B, return their product.
  # Check for conformability of matrices and return an error
```

```
    # if column dimension of A is not equal to row dimension of B

    row.dim.A <- dim(A)[1]
    col.dim.B <- dim(B)[2]
    inner.dim <- dim(A)[2]
    if (dim(B)[1] != inner.dim) stop("Matrices are not conformable!")
    # start multiplication
    product <- matrix(0, nrow = row.dim.A, ncol = col.dim.B)
    for (i in 1:row.dim.A) {
      for (j in 1:col.dim.B) {
        for (k in 1:inner.dim) {
          product[i, j] = product[i, j] + A[i, k] * B[k, j]
        }
      }
    }
    return(product)
}
```

This code implements the textbook definition of matrix multiplication. As such, it will work, but it will be relatively inefficient computationally because R is required to evaluate nested loops. To demonstrate how this function performs, consider using it to compute the least-squares regression estimates using simulated data. To generate some random data for the regression, use the following:

```
> rm(list = ls())
> set.seed(123457)
> # define data size
> n <- 100000
> # generate random regressor
> Xcol <- rnorm(n)
> # create a matrix of regressors with a constant
> X <- cbind(rep(1, n), Xcol)
> # generate regression errors
> U <- rnorm(n, sd = 2)
> # fix "true" values of coefficients
> true.betas <- c(-1, 2)
> # generate dependent variable, %*% means "matrix multiplication"
> y <- X %*% true.betas + U
> # put generated data into a data frame for later
> df <- data.frame(y = y, x = Xcol)
>
```

Here, a column of standard normal pseudo-random values of X and a column of $Y = -1 + 2X + U$ are formed, where U follows the normal distribution having mean 0 and variance 4. By using 100,000 observations two points will be illustrated: first, the true values of regression coefficients will almost surely be recovered; second, the bottlenecks in the calculations will be clear.

To find the bottlenecks, profiling is used. Thus, the temporary data are written to a file, and then those contents are retrieved. To implement least-squares estimation manually, the following is calculated:

$$\hat{\beta} = (\mathbf{X}^\top \mathbf{X})^{-1} \mathbf{X}^\top y.$$

Subsequently, the same calculation is performed using `lm()`, the built-in R function for fitting linear regressions. Finally, the results are compared. Here's how to proceed:

```
> profileFilename <- "testProfile.out"
> # turn on profiling
> Rprof(profileFilename)
> # doing least squares by hand
> XprimeX <- MultiplyMatrices(t(X), X)
> XprimeXinv <- solve(XprimeX) # solve means inverse in R
> XprimeY <- MultiplyMatrices(t(X), y)
> ls.betas <- MultiplyMatrices(XprimeXinv, XprimeY)
> # Now let's do the same procedure via lm()
> ls.model <- lm(y ~ x, data = df)
> ls.coef   <- ls.model[["coefficients"]]
> # turn off profiling
> Rprof(NULL)
> # compare results
> ls.betas <- as.vector(ls.betas)
> dist(rbind(ls.betas, ls.coef))
            ls.betas
ls.coef 1.688853e-14
>
```

As you can see, numerically the two ways of computing the least-squares estimates are less than 10^{-13} apart. The difference arises because direct matrix multiplication can result in some round-off errors, and the `lm()` function is designed to handle such issues. For illustrative purposes, however, pretend that the results are the same.

Now, let's look at the following results of profiling the code:

```
> summaryRprof(profileFilename)[["by.total"]]
                       total.time total.pct self.time self.pct
"MultiplyMatrices"          4.84     96.03      4.14    82.14
"+"                         0.38      7.54      0.38     7.54
"*"                         0.32      6.35      0.32     6.35
"lm"                        0.20      3.97      0.04     0.79
".External2"                0.08      1.59      0.04     0.79
"as.character"              0.04      0.79      0.04     0.79
"[.data.frame"              0.04      0.79      0.02     0.40
"["                         0.04      0.79      0.00     0.00
"<Anonymous>"               0.04      0.79      0.00     0.00
"eval"                      0.04      0.79      0.00     0.00
"lm.fit"                    0.04      0.79      0.00     0.00
"model.frame.default"       0.04      0.79      0.00     0.00
"model.matrix"              0.04      0.79      0.00     0.00
"model.matrix.default"      0.04      0.79      0.00     0.00
"model.response"            0.04      0.79      0.00     0.00
"na.omit"                   0.04      0.79      0.00     0.00
"na.omit.data.frame"        0.04      0.79      0.00     0.00
"anyDuplicated.default"     0.02      0.40      0.02     0.40
"c"                         0.02      0.40      0.02     0.40
"list"                      0.02      0.40      0.02     0.40
"anyDuplicated"             0.02      0.40      0.00     0.00
>
```

This output may look intimidating, but you need only concentrate on the first few rows and the first three columns. What you see is a complete list of functions that R executed after `Rprof(profileFilename)` ran, but before `Rprof(NULL)` was invoked. Function names are in the first column, while the second column tells you how much time was spent in each function, and the third one expresses time in percentage terms. In general, you can ignore the last two columns, since they provide essentially the same information. About 96 percent of total profiled run time was spent in the function `MultiplyMatrices()`, which employs three nested loops; nested loops are known to be incredibly slow in R. You are encouraged to replace the calls to `MultiplyMatrices()` with `%*%` to see how the profiling results will change.[7]

---

[7]In R everything is a function call, so you can write either A + B or `+`(A, B), and the results will be the same. An excellent source of information concerning these advanced R details is the book by Wickham (2014).

Most of R's source code is written in C++. Naturally, a package like `Rcpp` must exist. As the name suggests, this package allows you to call compiled C++ code from within R, which is sometimes unavoidable when dealing with an application where code cannot be optimized any further using vectorization. We suggest the following rule of thumb: If it becomes clear that you cannot avoid nested loops within R, then consider using `Rcpp` and implementing the inner loops in a compiled language. A similar package, which has the self-describing name `rJava`, allows you to call Java code from within R.

In addition, several packages make it possible to speed up R code using parallel computing techniques. Although this topic is beyond the scope of this book, we note that several packages have been developed to simplify this process. For an introduction to parallel computing, we recommend the `doParallel` and `foreach` duo of packages. The former does the work of creating the infrastructure, while the latter allows the user to execute `foreach` loops that, unlike normal `for` loops in R, can peform multiple iterations in parallel.

5.5.6 Estimating Various Models

One reason why R is so popular among statisticians is that virtually every new algorithm gets implemented in R. Consequently, you can find packages that allow you to fit virtually any kind of model to an appropriate data set. We have mentioned the `lm` and `glm` packages for linear and generalized-linear models, respectively. The `rpart` package implements the CART algorithm for fitting classification and regression trees; the `randomForest` package builds on `rpart`, enabling users to build ensembles of trees, which are commonly referred to as *random forests*.

Despite the non-self-describing name, the `e1071` package is an implementation of algorithms for classification and regression problems using support vector machines.

Algorithms to train neural networks have been implemented in the package `kernlab`.

The `survival` package allows you to estimate empirical specifications referred to as *duration* or *survival* or *waiting time* models with a minimum of bother. Such research is sometimes referred to as *failure time analysis*.

The `quantreg` package allows you to estimate quantile regressions.

The packages `nlme` and `lme4` allow you to fit fixed-, mixed-, and random-effect specifications of linear models using longitudinal data sets. The recently developed package `lfe` is a better implementation of methods to estimate fixed-effect models.

The `robustbase` package is an implementation of several techniques from robust statistics, for instance, least trimmed squares regression.

Although not quite related to model fitting, the `sandwich` package provides implementations of some estimators of the variance-covariance matrix.

Finally, we mention `quadprog`, an R package to solve quadratic programming problems. We acknowledge, however, that many other, better programs exist to solve mathematical optimization problems. In fact, as noted in Chapter 7, serious optimization problems will probably require that you purchase a state-of-the-art solver (such as MINOS or SNOPT) along with a modeling language (such as AMPL). In short, serious optimization requires more firepower than `quadprog` can provide. That said, for a one-off project, particularly if the problem is relatively small, the `quadprog` package may be useful.

5.5.7 Reporting Results

Several R packages are available to create dynamic reports. The package `Sweave` is designed to integrate R with LaTeX, a document preparation system and markup language that uses the typsetting program TeX to create beautiful documents, as seamlessly as possible (see Chapter 10). Instead of writing a LaTeX document, and then copying and pasting R source code and output into it, `Sweave` allows you to create a `.Swv` file that combines both LaTeX and R source code, and then evaluates all of it at run time. `Sweave` is particularly effective when used in tandem with the `xtable` package that generates LaTeX tables from raw R outputs.

A similar package, `knitr`, exists for creating HTML documents with examples of R code, referred to as *R markdown files*. R markdown files are similar in spirit and performance to IPython Notebooks. In fact, `knitr` can do everything that `Sweave` can, using a simpler syntax. You must, however, install `knitr` separately, whereas the `Sweave` package is part of the base R and LaTeX installations.

5.5.8 Other Packages

The `Hmisc` package contains several useful functions, for instance, the `describe()` function (see Section 5.4.6). The `Matrix` package is useful for operating on matrices, particularly sparse ones. The `formatR` package is invaluable for sticklers (like the authors of this book) combing through R source code and formatting it according to predetermined specifications.

5.6 Connecting R to SQLite

The Achilles' heel of R is memory management, an artifact of R's heritage. R was conceived and developed by statisticians. Historically, statistics was the art and science of extracting as much information as possible from small data sets, mostly because it was typically very costly to obtain large data sets. To this day, R remains a great tool for manipulating small and even moderate-size data sets, those having megabytes or perhaps tens of megabytes of information. The recent deluge of information that is Big Data exposed weaknesses in the R system; when data sets contain gigabytes of information, R stumbles, badly. Fortunately, alternative methods have been developed to circumvent these challenges.

In Chapter 3 we described the SQLite DBMS, an incredibly useful tool for manipulating large amounts of data. Rather than loading the raw data into R, we instead connect R to SQLite and then perform all necessary data manipulations from within R.

To be able to do this, you must perform a one-time installation of the `RSQLite` package using the following command:

```
> install.packages("RSQLite")
>
```

You may be asked to select a CRAN mirror for your session. Although it is, in general, advisable to choose a location that is physically close to you, the choice often does not matter much in practice.

Once the installation concludes, the following command loads the package:

```
> library(RSQLite)
>
```

In the next example, we use the SQLite database developed in Chapter 3. Specifically, we demonstrate how you would run a query against that database and then extract the query output into an R data frame. The R code to accomplish this task is quite concise.

```
> # Define paths to database and query files
> database.name <- "Data/Auctions_DataBase.db"
> query.file <- "Code/ComputeAverageForBidderAndCompetitors.sql"
> # open up a connection with the database
> database.connection <- dbConnect(drv = "SQLite", dbname = database.
    name)
> # read the query file into a single long character string
> query.text <- readChar(query.file, file.info(query.file)[["size"]])
> # execute the query
> query.object <- dbSendQuery(database.connection, query.text)
> # load query results into a data frame
> average.bids <- fetch(query.object)
> str(average.bids)
'data.frame':    7 obs. of  4 variables:
 $ FirstName          : chr  "Adam" "Bryan" "Charles" "David" ...
 $ LastName           : chr  "Cooper" "Dykstra" "Elan" "Forester"
     ...
 $ AverageBid         : num  13.5 11.4 10.6 12.3 10.1 ...
 $ AverageCompetitorBid : num  12 13.7 14.5 15.6 12.3 ...
>
```

Most of this code is self-describing, particularly because helpful comments were introduced. First, the paths to the database file and the query file are assigned. Of course, it is possible to supply the SQL query as part of the call to SQLite from R. Given that the query had already been developed, that code was reused. In general, reusing code that you know works is a time-saving practice.

In the next line, a connection from within R to SQLite is opened; in what follows, this connection is used to tell SQLite explicitly against which database to execute a query. After this, the contents of the .sql file containing the query are read into a character string query.text. Once a connection to the database has been established, and the query is available, the query against the database is executed using the function dbSendQuery(). This function returns the object SQLiteResult, which can be used to retrieve the actual query output using the fetch() function. All of this produces a data frame whose contents are identical to the output of the query described in Chapter 3. SQLite automatically closes the connection once the query succeeds, so nothing further is required.

At this juncture, two points should be made: first, the process of opening a connection, constructing a query object, and fetching its results can quickly become tedious. Ideologically, the correct way to do this in R would be to develop a function that takes care of this for you, like the following:

```
RunSQLiteQuery <- function(database, query) {
  # Use the built-in functions from RSQLite package to execute
  # supplied query against an existing SQLite database, and
  # return the results in a data frame.

  require(RSQLite)
  connection <- dbConnect(drv = "SQLite", dbname = database)
  query.object <- dbSendQuery(connection, query)
  query.data <- fetch(query.object)
  return(query.data)
}
```

The only exceptional line in this code is `require(RSQLite)`, which ensures the `RSQLite` package gets installed and loaded if that had not yet been done.

Second, it is unnecessary to read the query SQL code from a file on disk. You could instead provide it as a part of the R script. The correct way to do this involves using the `paste()` function. Consider the following, where the previously defined function is used:

```
> database.name <- "Data/Auctions_DataBase.db"
> simple.query <- "SELECT
                    bidders.First_Name
                  , bidders.Last_Name
                  , bids.Bid

                  FROM Bids

                  INNER JOIN Bidders
                    ON bids.Bidder_ID = bidders.Bidder_ID

                  WHERE bids.Bidder_ID = 1;")
> RunSQLiteQuery(database.name, simple.query)
  First_Name Last_Name    Bid
1       Adam    Cooper  12.10
2       Adam    Cooper  12.27
3       Adam    Cooper  19.21
```

```
4        Adam    Cooper 12.59
5        Adam    Cooper 14.16
6        Adam    Cooper 10.86
>
```

Maintaining a query written this way is inconvenient. In addition to the correct R syntax, you also have to keep track of the proper SQL syntax. Therefore, we recommend storing longer SQL queries in separate files and using the `read-Char()` function.

5.7   Python Library `pandas`

However attractive and useful R may be, poor memory management is a major drawback: the program simply gobbles up memory until either the task is completed or your computer crashes. For serious practitioners of data science, this is an unattractive feature, but it really only matters when data sets are larger than, say, one-half of the main memory of your computer. As computer memory increases progressively over time, this restriction may become relatively unimportant. We have discussed one strategy for dealing with large data sets: querying databases maintained under SQLite using R. Another is to use the Python library `pandas`.

The `pandas` library was developed by Wes McKinney to simplify routine data manipulation tasks for Python users; `pandas` was designed to bridge the gap between R and Python, that is, to make working with data in Python easy. Together with `matplotlib`, numpy, `scipy`, and `ipython`, `pandas` constitutes a respectable software ecosystem for working with data in Python. Although Golyaev is not fully convinced that this gap has been completely eliminated, `pandas` does make it noticeably easier to manipulate large volumes of data. In short, `pandas` is a valuable addition to a data scientist's toolbox. When illustrating how to use the `pandas` library, we assume that you have also invoked `ipython`, that is, the following:

```
$ ipython
```

The console will then look like this:

```
Python 2.7.9 |Anaconda 2.0.1 (x86_64)| (default, Dec 15 2014,
    10:37:34)
Type "copyright", "credits" or "license" for more information.
```

```
IPython 2.3.1 -- An enhanced Interactive Python.
Anaconda is brought to you by Continuum Analytics.
Please check out: http://continuum.io/thanks and https://binstar.org
?          -> Introduction and overview of IPython's features.
%quickref -> Quick reference.
help      -> Python's own help system.
object?   -> Details about 'object', use 'object??' for extra details.
%guiref   -> A brief reference about the graphical user interface.

In [1]:
```

Python for Data Analysis (McKinney 2013) uses `ipython`. If you adopt this strategy, you will find reading that book easier. In addition, you will be introduced to the power and the elegance that is `ipython`.

The heart of the `pandas` library is the `DataFrame` object, which is modeled after its R counterpart. The easiest way to understand this object, however, is to understand the core building block, the `Series` object. Here, the word *series* simply refers to a set of data points. In the vocabulary of econometrics, a `pandas` series can contain either time-series or cross-sectional data, depending on the application. Internally, `pandas` `Series` is stored as a Python dictionary, that is, a collection of key-value pairs. For example,

```
In [0]: from pandas import Series

In [1]: revenue2012 = Series({'Amazon' : 61.09, 'Google' : 50.18})
In [2]: revenue2013 = Series({'Amazon' : 74.45, 'Google' : 59.83})
In [3]: revenueAmazon = Series({2012 : 61.09, 2013 : 74.45})
In [4]: revenueGoogle = Series({2012 : 50.18, 2013 : 59.83})

In [5]: revenue2012
Out[5]:
Amazon    61.09
Google    50.18
dtype: float64

In [6]: revenue2013
Out[6]:
Amazon    74.45
Google    59.83
dtype: float64
```

```
In [7]: revenueAmazon
Out[7]:
2012    61.09
2013    74.45
dtype: float64

In [8]: revenueGoogle
Out[8]:
2012    50.18
2013    59.83
dtype: float64
```

In this example, four `Series` objects were created, two of which are cross-sectional, representing annual revenue for Amazon and Google in 2012 and 2013, respectively, and two of which are time-series, representing revenue for each of these companies for 2012 and 2013. Yes, the same information was effectively recorded twice, for illustrative purposes. The `Series` interprets keys as entry indices, and values as entry values:

```
In [1]: revenueGoogle.index
Out[1]: Int64Index([2012, 2013], dtype='int64')

In [2]: revenueGoogle.values
Out[2]: array([ 50.18,  59.83])
```

Indexing observations in `Series` makes operations on several `Series` seamless, an incredibly powerful property.

```
In [1]: revenueAmazon + revenueGoogle
Out[1]:
2012    111.27
2013    134.28
dtype: float64

# Let's make up a longer series, and demonstrate another way of
# creating the Series object

In [2]: emptyData = Series([0, 0, 0], index = [2011, 2012, 2013])

In [3]: emptyData
Out[3]:
2011    0
2012    0
2013    0
```

```
dtype: int64

In [4]: revenueAmazon + emptyData
Out[4]:
2011      NaN
2012    61.09
2013    74.45
dtype: float64
```

Because no value for Amazon revenue in 2011 exists, `pandas` created a missing value in the corresponding cell of the last output. The point here is to remove the burden of aligning data from the person doing the analysis, and make the software handle it instead. Note, too, how you can create a `Series` object simply by passing an array of values and an array of indices to the constructor function instead of a dictionary.

Now that you understand the basic idea behind `Series`, it is time to focus on the `DataFrame` construct. If `Series` is a dictionary, then `DataFrame` is a dictionary of dictionaries. Alternatively, `DataFrame` is a collection of `Series` that are all of the same length and that all share the same index. Consider the previous example concerning Amazon and Google:

```
In [1]: revenues = DataFrame({'Company' : ['Amazon', 'Amazon', \
                                           'Google', 'Google'], \
                              'Year'    : [2012,     2013, \
                                           2012,     2013], \
                              'Revenue' : [61.09,    74.45, \
                                           50.18,    59.83]})

In [2]: revenues = revenues.set_index(['Company', 'Year'])

In [3]: revenues
Out[3]:
               Revenue
Company Year
Amazon  2012     61.09
        2013     74.45
Google  2012     50.18
        2013     59.83

[4 rows x 1 columns]
```

The second command is necessary; otherwise columns `Company` and `Year` will be interpreted as data columns rather than as indices. Preserving the columns as data and having them used as indices is possible, as is supplying the `drop = False` argument to the `set_index()` function. When a `DataFrame` has an index that consists of several variables, this is referred to as a *hierarchical index* in `pandas`. The hierarchical index allow you to wrangle data into appropriate shape with ease:

```
In [1]: revenues.unstack(level = 0)
Out[1]:
         Revenue
Company  Amazon   Google
Year
2012       61.09    50.18
2013       74.45    59.83

[2 rows x 2 columns]

In [2]: revenues.unstack(level = 1)
Out[2]:
         Revenue
Year        2012     2013
Company
Amazon     61.09    74.45
Google     50.18    59.83

[2 rows x 2 columns]
```

The first command created a time-series data set from the *stacked* version of the data, while the second command created a cross-sectional data set. Of course, the hierarchical index can have more than two levels. With a properly defined index, wrangling large data sets into desired shapes using several hierarchies can be almost trivial.

We now return to the auction example to demonstrate how you can use `pandas` to perform the data manipulations previously implemented using R. Throughout the remaining part of this section, we assume that the following commands were executed:

```
import pandas as pd
import numpy as np
from pandas import Series, DataFrame
pd.set_option('html', False)
```

```
pd.set_option('max_columns', 30)
pd.set_option('max_rows', 20)
```

The first three commands are self-explanatory (see Chapter 4). The last three lines set up how the output from `pandas` will be formatted.

As usual, the first thing to do is to load the raw data from disk into Python. For reasonably well-formatted data files, the following built-in `pandas` commands exist:

```
In [1]: bidsData = pd.read_csv("Data/BidsTable.csv",      \
                     names     = ['BidID', 'AuctionID', \
                                  'BidderID', 'Bid'],    \
                     index_col = ['AuctionID', 'BidderID'])
In [2]: del bidsData['BidID']
In [3]: bidsData.head()

Out[3]:
                       Bid
AuctionID BidderID
1         1          12.10
          2          12.38
          3          11.63
          5           8.84
          6           8.37

[5 rows x 1 columns]
```

First, the bid data are read using the `read_csv()` function in `pandas`. The `names` option allows you to name data frame columns, and the `index_col` option specifies the set of columns that, together, constitute the data frame index. In this example, a bidder can only bid once per auction; together, the `AuctionID` and `BidderID` uniquely identify each bid, which makes the `BidID` superfluous. The `del` command deletes that column from the data frame, and the `head()` function that every data frame object possesses prints the top five rows just to illustrate the structure of the data.

Next, the auctions and bidders data sets are loaded using the following commands:

```
In [1]: auctionsData = pd.read_csv("Data/AuctionsTable.csv", \
                     names     = ['AuctionID', 'Volume', \
                                  'District', 'Date'],    \
```

```
                              index_col = 'AuctionID')
In [2]: auctionsData['Date'] = auctionsData['Date'].apply(str)
In [3]: auctionsData['Date'] = pd.to_datetime(auctionsData['Date'])
In [4]: auctionsData
Out[4]:
          Volume   District        Date
AuctionID
1            1234          1  2011-10-03
2             345          3  2011-11-07
3            2346          2  2011-12-05
4            1278          4  2012-01-09
5             789          7  2012-02-06
6             934          6  2012-03-05
7             269          9  2012-04-02
8             357          8  2012-05-07
9            1503          4  2012-06-04
10            239          7  2012-07-09


[10 rows x 3 columns]

In [5]: biddersData = pd.read_csv("BiddersTable.csv", \
                  names = ['BidderID', 'FirstName', 'LastName', \
                           'Address1', 'Address2', 'Town', \
                           'Province', 'PostalCode',\
                           'Telephone','Email', 'Preferred'], \
                  index_col = 'BidderID')
In [6]: biddersData
Out[6]:
          FirstName    LastName     Address1 Address2       Town
              Province
BidderID
1              Adam      Cooper   12 Fern Rd      #1   Qualicum
     BC
2             Bryan     Dykstra   23 Gorge Rd     #2    Victoria
     BC
3           Charles        Elan   34 Hall St      #3    Alberni
     BC
4             David    Forester   45 New Ln       #4    Clinton
     BC
5            Edward      Gulden   56 East Cr      #5   Qualicum
     BC
6             Frank   Hollister   67 West Cr      #6   Qualicum
     BC
```

```
7            George     Ivanov     2 Main St      #7   Vancouver
     BC


          PostalCode    Telephone              Email Preferred
BidderID
1            V9K 1S2  2507529922       cooper@gmail.com      Yes
2            V8W 1L0  2503878309  bdykstra@hotmail.com        No
3            V9Y 1A5  2507249807     charlee@yahoo.com        No
4            V0K 1K0  2504592437      dforeste@trex.com      Yes
5            V9K 1S2  2507529685       gulden@telus.ca       Yes
6            V9K 1S2  2507526934   fhollister@shaw.ca        Yes
7            V6B 4C7  6047324919       gsi@ivanov.ca          No

[7 rows x 10 columns]
```

The only new thing to point out concerning this code is how the auction dates were handled in the auctions data set. Because the dates are recorded in the yyyyMMdd format, pandas incorrectly guesses that this column should be numeric and not string, which is what you would like. Thus, the apply() function is used: every data frame column has to apply another built-in function, str() to each element in the column. After that, the built-in pandas function to_datetime() is used to convert the string column into a Python datetime object.

You can examine the distribution of bids in the data using the function describe() on the data frame:

```
in [1]: bidsData.describe()
Out[1]:
             Bid
count  37.000000
mean   11.155676
std     2.781688
min     7.140000
25%     8.840000
50%    10.880000
75%    12.760000
max    19.210000

[8 rows x 1 columns]
```

You can also compute summary statistics by auction by levering the definition of index and the `groupby()` method:

```
In [1]: averageBids = bidsData.groupby(level = 'AuctionID').mean()
In [2]: averageBids
Out[2]:
                   Bid
AuctionID
1             10.218333
2              9.760000
3             12.250000
4             12.068000
5             12.777500
6             10.460000
7             11.775000
8             10.168000
9             11.100000
10            11.420000

[10 rows x 1 columns]
```

Note, too, that the result of this operation is also a data frame. To combine this information with the original bid data, you would only need to merge these two data frames. Although it is possible to use indices of data frames to define merge semantics, it is generally easier to use actual data frame columns. This means you will need to do a bit of work before merging:

```
In [1]: bidsDataFull = bidsData.reset_index().set_index(['AuctionID',
    'BidderID'], drop = False)
In [2]: bidsDataFull.head()
Out[2]:
                    AuctionID  BidderID    Bid
AuctionID BidderID
1         1                 1         1   12.10
          2                 1         2   12.38
          3                 1         3   11.63
          5                 1         5    8.84
          6                 1         6    8.37

[5 rows x 3 columns]
```

The `reset_index()` function moves the index columns back into the data frame. The `set_index()` function does the reverse, and the `drop = False` parameter ensures that the index variables are preserved within the data frame, as the call to `head()` illustrates.

You will also need to rename the column in the `averageBids` data frame for the purposes of disambiguation:

```
In [1]: averageBids.columns = 'AverageBid'
In [2]: averageBids = averageBids.reset_index().set_index('AuctionID',
    drop = False)
In [3]: mergedBidsData = pd.merge(bidsDataFull, averageBids)
In [4]: mergedBidsData = mergedBidsData.set_index(['AuctionID', \
                            'BidderID'], drop = False)
In [5]: mergedBidsData.head(10)
Out[5]:
                        AuctionID  BidderID    Bid  AverageBid
AuctionID BidderID
1         1                    1         1  12.10   10.218333
          2                    1         2  12.38   10.218333
          3                    1         3  11.63   10.218333
          5                    1         5   8.84   10.218333
          6                    1         6   8.37   10.218333
          7                    1         7   7.99   10.218333
2         5                    2         5   9.80    9.760000
          6                    2         6   7.14    9.760000
          7                    2         7  12.34    9.760000
3         2                    3         2  12.84   12.250000
```

Note how `pandas` automatically figures out on which variables to join two data frames, in this case, the variable `AuctionID`. By default, `pandas` return an inner join, but this can be changed by supplying the `how` parameter to the `merge()` function.

We have barely scratched the surface of `pandas`' functionality. For those interested in using this library, McKinney (2013) is the best place to start.

5.8   Python or R?

Given the choice between learning Python and learning R as a first programming language, which one should you choose? We are economists, so you should not be surprised that our only acceptable answer is, It depends. In general, the cleaner your data are, the more you should lean toward R over Python. Even though `pandas` was created to provide R-like functionality to

Python users, currently, the library does not provide the easy user experience
of R; novices are affected by this the most. We demonstrated how to perform a
number of common data manipulations using `pandas`. In our experience, however, many ways exist to accomplish the same task in `pandas`; they all make
intuitive sense, but only a couple of them typically work in practice, while the
others often throw cryptic error messages. To an experienced programmer, a
cryptic error message is catnip: I get to play. To a novice, that same message is
downright perplexing, and can induce an anxiety attack.

On the other hand, Python is much more useful than R when dealing with
messy raw data; unlike R, Python is a full-fledged, general-purpose programming language. As a research assistant, however, you may not have the luxury
of choosing the language you use, particularly if you are thrown into an ongoing project. For this reason, we provided enough information for you to be able
to pick up either language.

5.9   Training, Validation, and Testing

One of the major differences between the way social scientists estimate and
select models, and the way data miners and machine learners do, involves the
triad referred to as *training, validation, and testing*.

What are the differences? Initially, let's focus on the case of *supervised learning*, where observation labels (that is, values for the dependent variable) exist.
For example, suppose you are trying to predict whether a student will pass an
examination based on information you have concerning the student's grade-
point average, major, class year, and so forth. The data set will be composed of
labels, denoted by y, that are either `True` or `False` as well as some features
created from the information known for each student, collected in a vector denoted by $\mathbf{x}$. Among social scientists the variables in $\mathbf{x}$ are often referred to as
covariates, whereas among data miners and machine learners the variables in $\mathbf{x}$
are referred to as *features*. A data set having N observations for social scientists,
and examples for data miners and machine learners, is then $\{(\mathbf{x}_n, y_n)\}_{n=1}^{N}$.

The main difference between the way social scientists proceed and the way
data miners and machine learners proceed is as follows. Social scientists will
use all the data $\{(\mathbf{x}_n, y_n)\}_{n=1}^{N}$, whereas data miners and machine learners will
divide an existing data set into two (or three) subordinate data sets, depending on whether tuning parameters are used during the training stage. For the

time being, suppose no tuning parameters are used, in which case two subordinate data sets are created, one for training models, the other for testing them. Usually, about 60 percent of the data are used to train models, that is, are selected randomly for the *training set*, whereas the other 40 percent are reserved for evaluating the trained models, the *test set*.

In short, by construction (random assignment), two different data sets are used, one to train models, the other to test them. By proceeding in this way, you will avoid *overfitting*, which plagues models estimated by social scientists. Overfitting is a problem commonly encountered when estimating (training) models. The models are chosen to fit the data well, but they do not fit new data as well, that is, the models do not *generalize*. Thus, on the test set, using the feature variables available, you try to predict whether a student will pass. The virtue of the test set is that you know what actually happened, so you can see whether the predictions are, in fact, true.

When tuning parameters are used, the data set is divided into three subordinate data sets: a training set, a *validation set*, and a test set. In this case, usually half the data are randomly selected for the training set, and the remainder are randomly split between the validation and test sets. For example, in machine learning, particularly with large dimensioned feature vectors, a procedure referred to as *regularization* is undertaken using a parameter denoted, say, λ. The regularizaton parameter λ penalizes objective functions, such as the sum of squared residuals and thus limits which feature variables are included in the model. In such cases, for a particular λ, you would train models using the training set and choose the appropriate value of λ using the validation set. Having chosen the appropriate value for λ, you would then evaluate models using the test set.

Historically, social scientists have rarely implemented this triad, probably because they did not have enough data. With the advent of Big Data, however, no excuse exists for not following this protocol.

5.9.1 Precision and Recall; ROC Curves

In classification problems (problems where you need to assign an observation to a particular member of a finite set), data miners and machine learners use several techniques to evaluate models. By and large, these techniques have not been used by social scientists, but they should be, so we introduce one particular tool here.

Precision and Recall

Consider supervised learning, specifically, the case where you want to predict whether a student will pass an examination, given some observed features. Suppose there is a data set of N examples concerning a label y_n for example n as well as features contained in the $(K \times 1)$ vector $\mathbf{x}_n$ for example n. This is the simplest prediction problem possible—binary classification. In this case, y_n, the label for example n, can take on the value 1 if the student passes, and 0 otherwise. Using information in the feature vectors $\mathbf{x}$ from students whose outcomes you have observed, you would like to predict the outcomes of students you have not yet observed, that is, whether they will pass. Many different ways exist to train binary prediction models. How do you decide among competing models?

The outcomes and the predictions of labels can be divided into a two-by-two table like Table 5.1, where the columns are the label outcomes, and the rows are the predicted outcomes. Ironically, researchers refer to a table like this as a *confusion matrix*.

Let's denote the number of true positives by TP, the number of true negatives by TN, the number of false positives by FP, and the number of false negatives by FN. The total number of examples in the test set is N_{Test}, so

$$N_{\text{Test}} = TP + TN + FP + FN.$$

In binary prediction problems, the *accuracy* (ACC) is defined as the ratio of the total number of correct predictions to the total number of cases, so

$$ACC = \frac{TP + TN}{TP + TN + FP + FN} = \frac{TP + TN}{N_{\text{Test}}},$$

whereas the *sensitivity*, sometimes referred to as the *true positive rate* or the *hit rate*, or *recall*, is the ratio of the total number of true positive predictions to the total number of positive predictions, so

$$TPR = \frac{TP}{TP + FN},$$

	Passed	Failed
Passed	True Positive	False Positive
Failed	False Negative	True Negative

Table 5.1: Confusion Matrix

and the *specificity (SPC)*, or *true negative rate*, is the total number of correct negative predictions over the total number of negative predictions, or

$$SPC = \frac{TN}{FP + TN}.$$

The *precision*, or *positive predictive value (PPV)*, is the fraction of correct positive predictions, or

$$PPV = \frac{TP}{TP + FP}.$$

Similarly, the *negative predictive value (NPV)* is the fraction of correct negative predictions, or

$$NPV = \frac{TN}{TN + FN}.$$

The *false positive rate (FPR)* is the fraction of incorrectly classified positives relative to the total number of negatives

$$FPR = \frac{FP}{FP + TN},$$

whereas the *false discovery rate (FDR)* is the fraction of incorrectly classified positives relative to the total number of positive predictions, or

$$FDR = \frac{FP}{FP + TP}.$$

ROC Curves

In binary classification, you typically *score* (predict the outcome of) a new observation using an index that is a function of observed features $\mathbf{x}_m$ for that new observation. For example, having trained a logistic regression, you would calculate the index $\mathbf{x}_m\hat{\boldsymbol{\beta}}$, from which you could then estimate the likelihood of Y_m equaling 1 using the following logit transformation:

$$\Pr(\widehat{Y_m = 1}|\mathbf{x}) = \frac{\exp(\mathbf{x}_m\hat{\boldsymbol{\beta}})}{1 + \exp(\mathbf{x}_m\hat{\boldsymbol{\beta}})}.$$

Usually, the threshold determining whether you predict a 1 is whether $\Pr(\widehat{Y_m = 1}|\mathbf{x}_m)$ exceeds one-half, but there is nothing special about the value one-half. In fact, you could use any other real number τ contained in $(0, 1)$. Moreover, when the costs of false negatives and false positives differ, you would want to choose a different threshold. Thus, consider scoring data from a test data set using different thresholds, for example, at values for $\tau = 0.1, 0.2, \ldots, 0.9$. For each value, calculate the TPR (specificity) as well as the FPR, sometimes referred to as the *fall-out rate*.

One commonly used diagnostic tool of data miners and machine learners is referred to as the *receiver operating characteristic curve*, or the ROC curve. The ROC curve is created by plotting the TPR versus the FPR for different values of the tuning parameter τ. The ROC curve thus illustrates the performance of a binary classifier as its discrimination threshold is varied. Another way to think of the ROC curve is as a plot of the sensitivity of a classifier for a particular tuning parameter τ versus 1 minus the specificity. Figure 5.7 depicts the space with the FPR on the abscissa and the TPR on the ordinate.

The ROC curve provides a way to select among different competing classifiers. Specifically, classifiers whose ROC curves are further to the northwest in Figure 5.7, in the limit at point $(0, 1)$, are better than those to the southeast. In

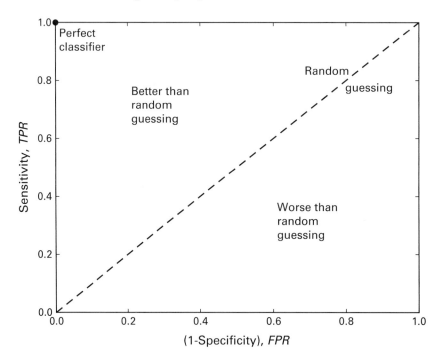

Figure 5.7: Space of ROC Curves

fact, classifiers whose ROC curves are below the 45 degree line are dominated by random guessing. Figure 5.8 shows the ROC curves for two classifiers, one of which is strictly better than the other, with both being better than random guessing. As such, the ROC curve is a useful diagnostic tool.

The accuracy of a predictor depends on how well it discriminates between the two classes being predicted. One summary measure of accuracy is the *area under the (ROC) curve*, often abbreviated as *AUC*. An AUC of 1 would be a perfect predictor, whereas an AUC of one-half is no better than random guessing, in short, a worthless predictor.[8] Note that the R package ROCR does most of the heavy lifting for calculating ROC curves given a trained binary classifier.

Depending on the field, you may encounter summary measures of performance named *F score* or *Youden's index* or *Youden's J statistic.*

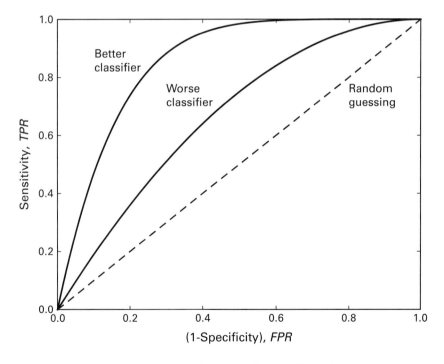

Figure 5.8: ROC Curves of Two Classifiers

---

[8]A predictor whose AUC is less than one-half can always be flipped around so its AUC is above one-half.

Introductions are at `http://en.wikipedia.org/wiki/F1_score` and `http://en.wikipedia.org/wiki/Youden's_J_statistic`.

5.10 Fixed-Effect Regressions

Angrist and Pischke (2009) have discussed at length the virtues of the following regression model, which includes fixed effects:

$$Y_{n,t} = \alpha_n + \mathbf{x}_{n,t}\boldsymbol{\beta} + U_{n,t} \quad n = 1, 2, \ldots, N; \; t = 1, 2, \ldots, T_n. \tag{5.2}$$

Under this specification, the dependent variable Y is assumed to have an intercept that varies with the index n, whereas the slope vector $\boldsymbol{\beta}$, which is of dimension $(K \times 1)$ and equals $(\beta_1, \beta_2, \ldots, \beta_K)^\top$, is assumed constant across both the index n and the index t. Here, the index n is mnemonic for individual, while the index t is mnemonic for time. The $(1 \times K)$ vector $\mathbf{x}_{n,t} = (x_{1,n,t}, x_{2,n,t}, \ldots, x_{K,n,t})$ can vary across both the index n and the index t. In particular, $\mathbf{x}_{n,t}$ could include dummy variables for the different periods indexed by t, provided that the average effect on each individual is assumed the same. Although the fixed-effect regression model presented in equation (5.2) is not completely general, its principal virtue is that it can be estimated using modest computer hardware. Because of this virtue, it is used extensively in social science as well as in business.

Note that under this notation the index t has a variable range T_n, which is referred to in the literature as an *unbalanced panel*. Things simplify somewhat when T_n is the same for all $n = 1, 2, \ldots, N$ in the data set, which is called a *balanced panel*.

The α_ns, the $\boldsymbol{\beta}$, and the U_ns are unknown. From the observed data $\{\{(\mathbf{x}_{n,t}, Y_{n,t})\}_{t=1}^{T_n}\}_{n=1}^{N}$, you would like to estimate the unknown parameters of interest, namely, $(\alpha_1, \alpha_2, \ldots, \alpha_N)$ and $\boldsymbol{\beta}$, but often just the $\boldsymbol{\beta}$.

Estimating regression models when the number of fixed-effect parameters is extremely large, for example, in the hundreds of thousands or more, is computationally challenging because standard regression models have a computational complexity of $\mathcal{O}(P^3)$ where P is $(N + K)$, that is, the sum of the number of fixed-effect parameters and the number of other covariates in the regression model. When N is in the hundreds of thousands, many computers simply do not have the memory to hold the design matrix. Even for those computers that have enough memory, the calculations can take a very long time.

In the case of the fixed-effect regression model, the Frisch-Lovell-Waugh theorem allows you to exploit the sparse nature of the design matrix, which makes the estimation problem feasible (see Davidson and MacKinnon 2004, 62–75, or Frisch and Waugh 1933 or Lovell 1963). We illustrate how to speed up the estimation of β by exploiting the sparse nature of the design matrix in the model. Specifically, we go through the algebra involved in these calculations because we believe that understanding this algebra will help you understand why some regression calculations are easier than others.

Our analysis is not new. For example, SDEs who developed, say, Stata, improved on other implementations of the fixed-effect model by employing the Frisch-Lovell-Waugh decomposition. That is, the Stata command `areg` breaks estimating the fixed-effect parameters into two parts, first, estimating the response parameters of the other covariates included in the regression model, and then recovering estimates of the fixed-effect parameters.

To begin, we introduce some additional notation. Let $D_{n,t}$ denote an indicator variable which equals 1 for individual n in period t, and 0 otherwise. Equation (5.2) can then be written as

$$Y_{n,t} = \sum_{n=1}^{N} \alpha_n D_{n,t} + \mathbf{x}_{n,t}\boldsymbol{\beta} + U_{n,t}.$$

The reason for rewriting equation (5.2) this way will become clear.

Without loss of generality, you can order the data so that all the observations for the individual with index 1 come first, then the observations for the individual with index 2 come next, and so forth. Although such an ordering is unnecessary, we introduce it here to make the algebra clearer. Hence,

$$
\begin{bmatrix}
Y_{1,1} \\
Y_{1,2} \\
\vdots \\
Y_{1,T_1} \\
Y_{2,1} \\
\vdots \\
Y_{2,T_2} \\
\vdots \\
Y_{N,1} \\
\vdots \\
Y_{N,T_N}
\end{bmatrix}
=
\begin{bmatrix}
D_{1,1} & D_{2,1} & \cdots & D_{N,1} & x_{1,1,1} & x_{2,1,1} & \cdots & x_{K,1,1} \\
D_{1,2} & D_{2,2} & \cdots & D_{N,2} & x_{1,1,2} & x_{2,1,2} & \cdots & x_{K,1,2} \\
\vdots & \vdots & \ddots & \vdots & \vdots & \vdots & \ddots & \vdots \\
D_{1,T_1} & D_{2,T_1} & \cdots & D_{N,T_1} & x_{1,1,T_1} & x_{2,1,T_1} & \cdots & x_{K,1,T_1} \\
D_{1,1} & D_{2,1} & \cdots & D_{N,1} & x_{1,2,1} & x_{2,2,1} & \cdots & x_{K,2,1} \\
\vdots & \vdots & \ddots & \vdots & \vdots & \vdots & \ddots & \vdots \\
D_{1,T_2} & D_{2,T_2} & \cdots & D_{N,T_2} & x_{1,2,T_2} & x_{2,2,T_2} & \cdots & x_{K,2,T_2} \\
\vdots & \vdots & \ddots & \vdots & \vdots & \vdots & \ddots & \vdots \\
D_{1,1} & D_{2,1} & \cdots & D_{N,1} & x_{1,I,1} & x_{2,I,1} & \cdots & x_{K,I,1} \\
& & \ddots & \vdots & \vdots & \vdots & \ddots & \vdots \\
D_{1,T_N} & D_{2,T_N} & \cdots & D_{N,T_N} & x_{1,I,T_N} & x_{2,N,T_N} & \cdots & x_{K,N,T_N}
\end{bmatrix}
\begin{bmatrix}
\alpha_1 \\
\alpha_2 \\
\vdots \\
\alpha_N \\
\beta_1 \\
\beta_2 \\
\vdots \\
\beta_K
\end{bmatrix}
+
\begin{bmatrix}
U_{1,1} \\
U_{1,2} \\
\vdots \\
U_{1,T_1} \\
U_{2,1} \\
\vdots \\
U_{2,T_2} \\
\vdots \\
U_{N,1} \\
\vdots \\
U_{N,T_N}
\end{bmatrix}.
$$

We write this linear system compactly using the notation from matrix algebra as

$$Y = Z\theta + U,$$

where the Z can be written out explicitly as

$$
Z = \begin{bmatrix}
1 & 0 & \cdots & 0 & x_{1,1,1} & x_{2,1,1} & \cdots & x_{K,1,1} \\
1 & 0 & \cdots & 0 & x_{1,1,2} & x_{2,1,2} & \cdots & x_{K,1,2} \\
\vdots & \vdots & \ddots & \vdots & \vdots & \vdots & \ddots & \vdots \\
1 & 0 & \cdots & 0 & x_{1,1,T_1} & x_{2,1,T_1} & \cdots & x_{K,1,T_1} \\
0 & 1 & \cdots & 0 & x_{1,2,1} & x_{2,2,1} & \cdots & x_{K,2,1} \\
\vdots & \vdots & \ddots & \vdots & \vdots & \vdots & \ddots & \vdots \\
0 & 1 & \cdots & 0 & x_{1,2,T_2} & x_{2,2,T_2} & \cdots & x_{K,2,T_2} \\
\vdots & \vdots & \ddots & \vdots & \vdots & \vdots & \ddots & \vdots \\
0 & 0 & \cdots & 1 & x_{1,N,1} & x_{2,N,1} & \cdots & x_{K,N,1} \\
\vdots & \vdots & \ddots & \vdots & \vdots & \vdots & \ddots & \vdots \\
0 & 0 & \cdots & 1 & x_{1,N,T_N} & x_{2,N,T_N} & \cdots & x_{K,N,T_N}
\end{bmatrix}.
$$

The first column of Z is a vector D_1 which has T_1 1s in the first T_1 rows, and 0s elsewhere. The second column of Z is a vector D_2 which has T_2 1s in row $(T_1 + 1)$ to row $(T_1 + T_2)$, and 0s elsewhere. The Nth column of Z is a vector D_N which has T_N 1s in the last T_N rows, and 0s elsewhere. In general, the nth column of Z is a vector D_n which has T_n 1s from row $(\sum_{m=1}^{n-1} T_m + 1)$ to row $\sum_{m=1}^{n} T_m$. We denote the kth column vector of the $x_{k,n,t}$s as follows:

$$x_k = \left[x_{k,1,1}, x_{k,1,2}, \ldots, x_{k,1,T_1}, x_{k,2,1}, \ldots, x_{k,2,T_2}, \ldots, x_{k,N,1}, \ldots, x_{k,N,T_N} \right]^\top.$$

Hence, Z can be written in this vector notation as

$$Z = \begin{bmatrix} D_1 & D_2 & \ldots & D_N & x_1 & x_2 & \ldots & x_K \end{bmatrix} \equiv \begin{bmatrix} D_1 & D_2 & \ldots & D_N & X \end{bmatrix},$$

where the column vectors $x_1, x_2, \ldots, x_K$ are collected into into the matrix X.

5.10.1 Least-Squares Estimator of θ

Under this notation, $\hat{\theta}$, the least-squares estimator of the parameter vector θ, solves the following linear system of $(N + K)$ equations in $(N + K)$ unknowns:

$$\mathbf{Z}^\top \mathbf{Z} \hat{\theta} = \mathbf{Z}^\top Y$$
$$\hat{\theta} = (\mathbf{Z}^\top \mathbf{Z})^{-1} \mathbf{Z}^\top Y$$
$$\hat{\theta} \equiv \mathbf{M}^{-1} \mathbf{c}.$$

The first N elements of the vector $\hat{\theta}$ correspond to $\hat{\alpha}_1, \hat{\alpha}_2, \ldots, \hat{\alpha}_N$, which are the fixed-effect estimates. In many analyses, only $\hat{\beta}$ is of interest, that is, only the last K elements of the vector $\hat{\theta}$ are needed.

To this end, we decompose the matrix $\mathbf{M}$ as follows:

$$\mathbf{M} = \begin{bmatrix} \mathbf{M}_{11} & \mathbf{M}_{12} \\ \mathbf{M}_{21} & \mathbf{M}_{22} \end{bmatrix},$$

where $\mathbf{M}_{11}$ is the submatrix corresponding to the fixed effects, that is, an $(N \times N)$ matrix. Note that $\mathbf{M}_{22}$ is a $(K \times K)$ submatrix corresponding to the slope vector relating the covariate vector $\mathbf{x}$ to Y. Under this decomposition, $\mathbf{M}_{12}$ is an $(N \times K)$ matrix, while $\mathbf{M}_{21}$ is a $(K \times N)$ matrix. In general, the inverse of a partitioned matrix can be written as follows:

$$\mathbf{M}^{-1} = \begin{bmatrix} \left(\mathbf{M}_{11} - \mathbf{M}_{12}\mathbf{M}_{22}^{-1}\mathbf{M}_{21} \right)^{-1} & -\mathbf{M}_{11}^{-1}\mathbf{M}_{12} \left(\mathbf{M}_{22} - \mathbf{M}_{21}\mathbf{M}_{11}^{-1}\mathbf{M}_{12} \right)^{-1} \\ -\mathbf{M}_{22}^{-1}\mathbf{M}_{21} \left(\mathbf{M}_{11} - \mathbf{M}_{12}\mathbf{M}_{22}^{-1}\mathbf{M}_{21} \right)^{-1} & \left(\mathbf{M}_{22} - \mathbf{M}_{21}\mathbf{M}_{11}^{-1}\mathbf{M}_{12} \right)^{-1} \end{bmatrix}.$$

Because $\mathbf{M}$ is symmetric, this simplifies further to the following:

$$\mathbf{M}^{-1} = \begin{bmatrix} \left(\mathbf{M}_{11} - \mathbf{M}_{12}\mathbf{M}_{22}^{-1}\mathbf{M}_{21} \right)^{-1} & -\mathbf{M}_{11}^{-1}\mathbf{M}_{12} \left(\mathbf{M}_{22} - \mathbf{M}_{21}\mathbf{M}_{11}^{-1}\mathbf{M}_{12} \right)^{-1} \\ -\left(\mathbf{M}_{22} - \mathbf{M}_{21}\mathbf{M}_{11}^{-1}\mathbf{M}_{12} \right)^{-1} \mathbf{M}_{21}\mathbf{M}_{11}^{-1} & \left(\mathbf{M}_{22} - \mathbf{M}_{21}\mathbf{M}_{11}^{-1}\mathbf{M}_{12} \right)^{-1} \end{bmatrix}.$$

5.10.2   What to Do with It All

The first thing to note is that $\mathbf{D}_n^\top \mathbf{D}_m$ is zero for $n \neq m$. That is, for any $n \neq m$, the vector $\mathbf{D}_n$ is orthogonal to the vector $\mathbf{D}_m$. Also, $\mathbf{D}_n^\top \mathbf{D}_n$ equals T_n. Thus,

$$
\mathbf{M} = \begin{bmatrix}
T_1 & 0 & \cdots & 0 & \mathbf{D}_1^\top \mathbf{X} \\
0 & T_2 & \cdots & 0 & \mathbf{D}_2^\top \mathbf{X} \\
\vdots & \vdots & \ddots & \vdots & \vdots \\
0 & 0 & \cdots & T_N & \mathbf{D}_N^\top \mathbf{X} \\
\mathbf{X}^\top \mathbf{D}_1 & \mathbf{X}^\top \mathbf{D}_2 & \cdots & \mathbf{X}^\top \mathbf{D}_N & \mathbf{X}^\top \mathbf{X}
\end{bmatrix}.
$$

Now, $\mathbf{D}_n^\top \mathbf{X}$ is a $(1 \times K)$ vector where a representative element is the sum of the elements of the $\mathbf{x}_k$ for individual n. That is,

$$
\mathbf{D}_n^\top \mathbf{X} = \left[\sum_{t=1}^{T_n} x_{1,n,t}, \sum_{t=1}^{T_n} x_{2,n,t}, \ldots, \sum_{t=1}^{T_n} x_{K,n,t} \right],
$$

while

$$
\mathbf{X}^\top \mathbf{D}_n = \left[\sum_{t=1}^{T_n} x_{1,n,t}, \sum_{t=1}^{T_n} x_{2,n,t}, \ldots, \sum_{1}^{T_n} x_{K,n,t} \right]^\top,
$$

so

$$
\mathbf{M} = \begin{bmatrix}
T_1 & 0 & \cdots & 0 & \sum_{t=1}^{T_1} x_{1,1,t} & \sum_{t=1}^{T_1} x_{2,1,t} & \cdots & \sum_{t=1}^{T_1} x_{K,1,t} \\
0 & T_2 & \cdots & 0 & \sum_{t=1}^{T_2} x_{1,2,t} & \sum_{t=1}^{T_2} x_{2,2,t} & \cdots & \sum_{t=1}^{T_2} x_{K,2,t} \\
\vdots & \vdots & \ddots & \vdots & \vdots & \vdots & \ddots & \vdots \\
0 & 0 & \cdots & T_N & \sum_{t=1}^{T_N} x_{1,N,t} & \sum_{t=1}^{T_N} x_{2,N,t} & \cdots & \sum_{t=1}^{T_N} x_{K,N,t} \\
\sum_{t=1}^{T_1} x_{1,1,t} & \sum_{t=1}^{T_2} x_{1,2,t} & \cdots & \sum_{t=1}^{T_N} x_{1,N,t} & & & & \\
\sum_{t=1}^{T_1} x_{2,1,t} & \sum_{t=1}^{T_2} x_{2,2,t} & \cdots & \sum_{t=1}^{T_N} x_{2,N,t} & & \mathbf{X}^\top \mathbf{X} & & \\
\vdots & \vdots & \ddots & \vdots & & & & \\
\sum_{t=1}^{T_1} x_{K,1,t} & \sum_{t=1}^{T_2} x_{K,2,t} & \cdots & \sum_{t=1}^{T_N} x_{K,N,t} & & & &
\end{bmatrix}.
$$

Noting that the sum of T_n variables can be written as T_n times the sample mean of those variables implies that $\mathbf{M}$ can be written as

$$
\mathbf{M} =
\left[
\begin{array}{ccccccccc}
T_1 & 0 & \cdots & 0 & T_1\bar{x}_{1,1} & T_1\bar{x}_{2,1} & \cdots & T_1\bar{x}_{K,1} \\
0 & T_2 & \cdots & 0 & T_2\bar{x}_{1,2} & T_2\bar{x}_{2,2} & \cdots & T_2\bar{x}_{K,2} \\
\vdots & \vdots & \ddots & \vdots & \vdots & \vdots & \ddots & \vdots \\
0 & 0 & \cdots & T_N & T_N\bar{x}_{1,N} & T_N\bar{x}_{2,N} & \cdots & T_N\bar{x}_{K,N} \\
T_1\bar{x}_{1,1} & T_2\bar{x}_{1,2} & \cdots & T_N\bar{x}_{1,N} & & & & \\
T_1\bar{x}_{2,1} & T_2\bar{x}_{2,2} & \cdots & T_N\bar{x}_{2,N} & & & & \\
\vdots & \vdots & \ddots & \vdots & & \mathbf{X}^\top\mathbf{X} & & \\
T_1\bar{x}_{K,1} & T_2\bar{x}_{K,2} & \cdots & T_N\bar{x}_{K,N} & & & &
\end{array}
\right],
$$

where $\bar{x}_{k,i}$ denotes the sample mean of the kth covariate of individual n, for which T_n observations exist.

Consider now the matrix $\left(\mathbf{M}_{22} - \mathbf{M}_{21}\mathbf{M}_{11}^{-1}\mathbf{M}_{12} \right)$, and examine each of its matrix parts in turn. First,

$$
\mathbf{M}_{22} = \mathbf{X}^\top\mathbf{X}
$$

is a $(K \times K)$ matrix, while

$$
\mathbf{M}_{11}^{-1} =
\begin{bmatrix}
T_1^{-1} & 0 & \cdots & 0 \\
0 & T_2^{-1} & \cdots & 0 \\
\vdots & \vdots & \ddots & \vdots \\
0 & 0 & \cdots & T_N^{-1}
\end{bmatrix}
$$

is an $(N \times N)$ matrix, and

$$
\mathbf{M}_{12} =
\begin{bmatrix}
T_1\bar{x}_{1,1} & T_1\bar{x}_{2,1} & \cdots & T_1\bar{x}_{K,1} \\
T_2\bar{x}_{1,2} & T_2\bar{x}_{2,2} & \cdots & T_2\bar{x}_{K,2} \\
\vdots & \vdots & \ddots & \vdots \\
T_N\bar{x}_{1,N} & T_N\bar{x}_{2,N} & \cdots & T_N\bar{x}_{K,N}
\end{bmatrix}
$$

is an $(N \times K)$ matrix, while $\mathbf{M}_{21}$ is simply $\mathbf{M}_{12}^\top$, so

$$
\mathbf{M}_{21}\mathbf{M}_{11}^{-1} =
\begin{bmatrix}
\bar{x}_{1,1} & \bar{x}_{2,1} & \cdots & \bar{x}_{K,1} \\
\bar{x}_{1,2} & \bar{x}_{2,2} & \cdots & \bar{x}_{K,2} \\
\vdots & \vdots & \ddots & \vdots \\
\bar{x}_{1,N} & \bar{x}_{2,N} & \cdots & \bar{x}_{K,N}
\end{bmatrix}.
$$

Hence,

$$
\mathbf{M}_{21}\mathbf{M}_{11}^{-1}\mathbf{M}_{12} =
\begin{bmatrix}
\sum_{n=1}^{N} T_n \bar{x}_{1,n}^2 & \sum_{n=1}^{N} T_n \bar{x}_{1,n}\bar{x}_{2,n} & \cdots & \sum_{n=1}^{N} T_n \bar{x}_{1,n}\bar{x}_{K,n} \\
\sum_{n=1}^{N} T_n \bar{x}_{2,n}\bar{x}_{1,n} & \sum_{n=1}^{N} T_n \bar{x}_{2,n}^2 & \cdots & \sum_{n=1}^{N} T_n \bar{x}_{2,n}\bar{x}_{K,n} \\
\vdots & \vdots & \ddots & \vdots \\
\sum_{n=1}^{N} T_n \bar{x}_{K,n}\bar{x}_{1,n} & \sum_{n=1}^{N} T_n \bar{x}_{K,n}\bar{x}_{2,n} & \cdots & \sum_{n=1}^{N} T_n \bar{x}_{K,n}^2
\end{bmatrix}.
$$

Practically speaking, this means that you need only solve the following $[K \times (N + K)]$ matrix multiplication problem:

$$
\hat{\beta} = \left[-\left(\mathbf{M}_{22} - \mathbf{M}_{21}\mathbf{M}_{11}^{-1}\mathbf{M}_{12}\right)^{-1} \mathbf{M}_{21}\mathbf{M}_{11}^{-1}, \ \left(\mathbf{M}_{22} - \mathbf{M}_{21}\mathbf{M}_{11}^{-1}\mathbf{M}_{12}\right)^{-1} \right] \mathbf{c}
$$

to calculate $\hat{\beta}$.

In some applications, N could be 100, 000 or 1 million, whereas K might only be 100, with the average T_n being, say, 10. Using this method can result in considerable time savings. In fact, in many cases, it is the only way not to run out of memory. Why? Note that the highest-order term relates to the inversion of a $(K \times K)$ matrix. Inverting a matrix requires resources that are approximately a cubic function of the number of parameter P, where P is $(N + K)$ under the complete estimation of the fixed-effect estimator, whereas P is K under the Stata command `areg`.

At this point, a numerical issue is worth mentioning. The matrix

$$
\mathbf{M}_{22} = \mathbf{X}^\top \mathbf{X}
$$

is difficult to form accurately on a computer because the diagonal elements, in particular, are the sums of squared numbers. When these elements are created in a do-loop, the cumulative sum up to observation t can be several orders of magnitude larger than the squared term being added to that cumulative sum. In short, round-off error can be a serious problem. If $\mathbf{M}_{22}$ is at all ill-conditioned, then this round-off error can be important. A similar problem exists for the matrix

$$
\mathbf{M}_{21}\mathbf{M}_{11}^{-1}\mathbf{M}_{12}.
$$

What to do?

Consider a representative diagonal element of the matrix $\mathbf{M}_{21}\mathbf{M}_{11}^{-1}\mathbf{M}_{12}$. To reduce the clutter, suppose K is 1 and N is 2. Under these assumptions, there is no need to use a k subscript. Let $\bar{x}_1$ denote the mean of x for the first T_1 observations (those for individual 1) and $\bar{x}_2$ denote the mean for the second T_2 observations (those for individual 2). One can then write the matrix as

$$\mathbf{M}_{22} - \mathbf{M}_{21}\mathbf{M}_{11}^{-1}\mathbf{M}_{12} = \sum_{t=1}^{T_1}(x_t - \bar{x}_1)^2 + \sum_{t=T_1+1}^{T_1+T_2}(x_t - \bar{x}_2)^2$$

$$= \sum_{t=1}^{T_1}(x_t^2 - 2\bar{x}_1 x_t + \bar{x}_1)^2 + \sum_{t=T_1+1}^{T_1+T_2}(x_t^2 - 2\bar{x}_2 x_t + \bar{x}_2)^2$$

$$= \sum_{t=1}^{T_1}x_t^2 - 2\bar{x}_1\sum_{t=1}^{T_1}x_t + T_1\bar{x}_1^2 + \sum_{t=T_1+1}^{T_1+T_2}x_t^2 - 2\bar{x}_2\sum_{t=T_1+1}^{T_1+T_2}x_t + T_2\bar{x}_2^2$$

$$= \sum_{t=1}^{T_1}x_t^2 - 2T_1\bar{x}_1^2 + T_1\bar{x}_1^2 + \sum_{t=T_1+1}^{T_1+T_2}x_t^2 - 2T_2\bar{x}_2 + T_2\bar{x}_2^2$$

$$= \sum_{t=1}^{T_1+T_2}x_t^2 - T_1\bar{x}_1^2 - T_2\bar{x}_2^2$$

$$= \sum_{t=1}^{T_1+T_2}x_t^2 - (T_1\bar{x}_1^2 + T_2\bar{x}_2^2).$$

In short, a representative (i,j) element of the matrix $[\mathbf{M}_{22} - \mathbf{M}_{21}\mathbf{M}_{11}^{-1}\mathbf{M}_{12}]$ is

$$\sum_{n=1}^{N}\sum_{t=1}^{T_n}(x_{i,n,t} - \bar{x}_{i,n})(x_{j,n,t} - \bar{x}_{j,n}) \quad i = 1, 2, \ldots, K; \; j = 1, 2, \ldots, K$$

where

$$\bar{x}_{i,n} = \frac{1}{T_n}\sum_{t=1}^{T_n}x_{i,n,t}.$$

For each individual n and for each covariate k, find the squared variation of covariate k about the mean for that covariate and that individual. Similarly, for each individual n, and for each pair of covariates i and j that are different, find the sum of the cross variation of covariates i and j about the means for those covariates and that individual.

We now have all the moving parts necessary to calculate $\hat{\beta}$, save for the column vector $\mathbf{c}$, which is $\mathbf{Z}^\top \mathbf{Y}$. Here,

$$\mathbf{c} = \mathbf{Z}^\top \mathbf{Y} = \begin{bmatrix} \mathbf{D}_1^\top \mathbf{Y} \\ \mathbf{D}_2^\top \mathbf{Y} \\ \vdots \\ \mathbf{D}_N^\top \mathbf{Y} \\ \mathbf{x}_1^\top \mathbf{Y} \\ \mathbf{x}_2^\top \mathbf{Y} \\ \vdots \\ \mathbf{x}_K^\top \mathbf{Y} \end{bmatrix} = \begin{bmatrix} T_1 \bar{Y}_1 \\ T_2 \bar{Y}_2 \\ \vdots \\ T_N \bar{Y}_N \\ \sum_{n=1}^N \sum_{t=1}^{T_n} x_{1,n,t} Y_{n,t} \\ \sum_{n=1}^N \sum_{t=1}^{T_n} x_{2,n,t} Y_{n,t} \\ \vdots \\ \sum_{n=1}^N \sum_{t=1}^{T_n} x_{K,n,t} Y_{n,t} \end{bmatrix} \equiv \begin{bmatrix} c_1 \\ c_2 \\ \vdots \\ c_N \\ c_{N+1} \\ c_{N+2} \\ \vdots \\ c_{N+K} \end{bmatrix} \equiv \begin{bmatrix} \mathbf{c}_N \\ \mathbf{c}_K \end{bmatrix},$$

where $\bar{Y}_n$ is the average of the response variable for the T_n observed values of the dependent variable $Y_{n,t}$, that is,

$$\bar{Y}_n = \frac{1}{T_n} \sum_{t=1}^{T_n} Y_{n,t}.$$

The least-squares estimates of the fixed-effect parameters can be calculated using the following formula:

$$\hat{\alpha}_n = \bar{Y}_n - \bar{\mathbf{x}}_n \hat{\beta} \quad n = 1, 2, \ldots N,$$

where the vector $\bar{\mathbf{x}}_n$ collects the sample means of the covariate values for individual n.

In practice, this means that calculations do not need to be undertaken using the large matrix $\mathbf{Z}$. Instead, you can calculate the arithmetic means of $\mathbf{x}_{n,t}$ and $Y_{n,t}$ for each n over the relevant value of t, and then write the regression model in terms of deviations from those means, namely,

$$Y_{n,t} - \bar{Y}_n = (\mathbf{x}_{n,t} - \bar{\mathbf{x}}_n)\beta + \varepsilon_{n,t},$$

which only involves inverting a $(K \times K)$ matrix when estimating β. If needed, then you can recover estimates of the $(\alpha_1, \ldots, \alpha_N)$ later. This problem illustrates that with the advent of Big Data some empirical specifications may require more memory than even the largest of computers can supply, so you will need to be clever to get around such problems.

Somaini and Wolak (2014) described how the Frisch-Lovell-Waugh decomposition can be applied to other estimation strategies as well.

6

Geek Stuff

OUR DESCRIPTIONS THUS far have focused on some basic tools and techniques for effective computing, but it is difficult to proceed much further without discussing the engineering reality of hardware or the rich body of theory concerning algorithms. Thus, in this chapter, we describe some practical features of computing hardware and present some abstract material concerning algorithms. We also discuss computing paradigms and related languages—in short, geek stuff.

6.1 Hardware

Virtually all modern computers have the following seven components: first, and foremost is the central processing unit (CPU) where the calculations are completed.[1] Second is the volatile memory, or *random-access memory* (RAM); this main memory is only available when the computer is turned on. Third is nonvolatile memory, made up of a small amount of *read-only memory* (ROM), which is accessed when the computer is initially turned on, as well as a hard disk drive or a solid state drive. Nonvolatile memory is more or less permanent in the sense that data residing in this form of memory do not disappear when the computer is turned off; thus, such memory is sometimes referred to as *permanent memory* even though it can disappear. Fourth is a keyboard, which allows you to key information into the computer's memory. Fifth is a mouse,

---

[1] The CPU is actually made up of two parts, the controller and the arithmetic/logic unit (ALU).

which allows you to manipulate input to and output from programs living on the computer. Sixth is a monitor, which allows you to see computer output. Seventh is a graphics card, which can render information quickly in a form that can be viewed on most monitors.[2]

Most of this information is common knowledge. We have introduced it to establish a common set of terms for our discussion.

Perhaps the most common perception people have concerning computers is that they just keep getting better and better, and will continue to do so into the future. Although we hope this optimistic view turns out to be true, we are not sanguine. Here's why. The CPU is an integrated circuit—a set of electronic circuits on one small *chip*, which is typically made of silicon. In 1965, Intel co-founder Gordon E. Moore (1965) described an empirical regularity, predicting that the number of transistors on integrated circuits would double approximately every year for the next decade or so. The prediction, dubbed Moore's law in his honor, has been adjusted over the past 40 years to be a doubling every two years. Recently, Intel executive David House updated the prediction: the doubling will now occur, on average, every eighteen months.[3] Suffice it to say, the CPUs of computers are becoming faster.

Clearly, the doubling predicted by Moore's law is a good thing, particularly for those whose research involves brute-force calculations, provided that those calculations can be completed solely in the main memory of the computer; problems that took three months to solve in 1985 will take less than a minute in 2015.

Even though Moore's law has proven remarkably robust for over five decades, there are signs that diminishing returns are setting in. Despite the fact that it may be possible to make transistors even smaller than before, so more can be put on a microchip, the heat produced by their functioning is increasingly becoming a problem. Too much heat can cause transistors to malfunction. Brynjolfsson and McAfee (2014) pointed out, however, that Moore's law is not solely for one technology. In fact, innovation has been continual during the past 50 years or so, suggesting that the process can continue.

---

[2]Most new computer have a *graphical processing unit*, which is a specialized processor that completes the calculations necessary in rendering three-dimensional graphics, thus releasing the main CPU for other tasks.

[3]From http://en.wikipedia.org/wiki/Moore's_law.

An example might be the following: Because of the heat generated by faster processors, there has been a move to distributed and parallel computing, that is, using many commodity microprocessors in tandem. Initially, because CPUs were expensive, only one was used in each computer; for most modern computers, the number is at least two, but often more than that. In addition, with the advent of fast communication between computers, it has also become possible to deploy thousands of commodity computers together. Although distributed and parallel computing will continue to be an important, the field is changing rapidly so it is difficult to predict.

Like Moore's law, a similar empirical regularity has been observed for the capacity and density of hard disk drives (HDDs). This regularity is sometimes referred to as *Kryder's law*, in honor of Mark Kryder, a senior vice president and chief technical officer at Seagate Corporation, one of three major manufacturers of HDDs. Kryder's law predicts even faster growth than Moore's law—a doubling every fourteen months perhaps.[4]

Faster and more microprocessors as well as larger and denser HDDs must seem like a boon to those analyzing Big Data. Unfortunately, getting the data from the HDD into the computer's main memory is the bottleneck. During the past 30 years, the improvements in the speed of reading from and writing to HDDs have not kept pace with the improvements in microprocessors or the density or size of HDDs. For example, in 1980, the average time to find something on an HDD, often referred to as the average *seek time*, was about 20 milliseconds, whereas in 2010 that time was about 1 millisecond. (Table 6.1 presents a list of the International System of Units as well as their abbreviations.) In any other industry, a 20-fold improvement over 30 years would be outstanding, but not the computer industry. By contrast, during the same period, under Moore's law, the speed of a microprocessor increased approximately 2^{15}-fold. In other words, microprocessors were some $32,000$ times faster in 2010 than they were in 1980.

Faced with this bottleneck, engineers have developed a variety of alternatives. The easiest to understand is the solid state drive (SSD), which is an alternative medium to the magnetic disk used in an HDD. SSDs store the data on microchips, an alternative that has several attractive features, not the least of which is speed. Whereas in 2013 HDDs could read between 50 and 120

---

[4]From http://en.wikipedia.org/wiki/Mark_Kryder.

Factor	Name	Symbol	Factor	Name	Symbol
10^1	deka	da	10^{-1}	deci	d
10^2	hecto	h	10^{-2}	centi	c
10^3	kilo	k	10^{-3}	milli	m
10^6	mega	M	10^{-6}	micro	μ
10^9	giga	G	10^{-9}	nano	n
10^{12}	tera	T	10^{-12}	pico	p
10^{15}	peta	P	10^{-15}	femto	f
10^{18}	exa	E	10^{-18}	atto	a
10^{21}	zetta	Z	10^{-21}	zepto	z
10^{24}	yotta	Y	10^{-24}	yocto	y

Table 6.1: International System of Units

Factor	Name	Symbol
1	byte	B
2^{10}	kilobyte	KB
2^{20}	megabyte	MB
2^{30}	gigabyte	GB
2^{40}	terabyte	TB
2^{50}	petabyte	PB
2^{60}	exabyte	EB

Table 6.2: Data Units

megabytes per second, SSDs could read between 200 and 500 megabytes per second. What do these units mean?

When applied in computing, particularly to data, the International System of Units has a slightly different meaning. The minimal basic unit is the binary digit, or *bit*, a term coined by John W. Tukey. A bit can take on one of two values: 0 or 1. A byte is 8 bits, that is, 2^3 bits. A kilobyte is 2^{10}, or $1,024$ bytes; a megabyte is $1,024$ kilobytes; a gigabyte is $1,024$ megabytes; a terabyte is $1,024$ gigabytes; a petabyte is $1,024$ terabytes; and an exabyte is $1,024$ petabytes. Table 6.2 summarizes these relationships, and provides the conventional abbreviations.

In 2013, HDDs had two major advantages over SSDs—capacity and price. For example, in June 2013, you could get 1 GB of HDD storage for about $7\frac{1}{2}$

cents, whereas the same amount of SSD storage would cost about a dollar. HDDs of 1 TB were available in 2013, but the largest SSDs only had capacities of about 512 GB. With time, SSD prices will fall and capacities will increase.

One major strength of SSD storage is reliability. Because SSD storage is on microchips, no physical *arm* is used to read or write. An HDD is a *platter*, which spins when accessed; the arm directs the *head* to read from (or write to) a particular part of the platter. In short, SSDs are less likely to fail than HDDs. Moreover, even if a part of an SSD does fail, it is not as catastrophic as the crash of an HDD, for example, when the head scratches the platter and destroys data. Early SSDs, however, had fairly short lives; the expected number of reads from a location was relatively small, a feature that has been changing. In any case, SSDs use less energy, do not generate as much heat, do not vibrate, and make less noise, so HDDs will likely become obsolete.

Because HDD access is relatively slow, to reduce delays, or *latencies*, computer manufacturers have gone to considerable lengths to keep important data near the CPU. In addition, to the extent possible, SDEs try to read the data from the HDD and then keep them in RAM for the duration of computation. With the increasing sizes of RAM, historically this has been possible, but with the advent of huge data sets, reading all the data into volatile memory will be impossible.

In any case, in addition to a small amount (less than 1 KB) of storage available as part of a CPU, which is referred to as the *processor registers*, other types of fast-access storage have evolved, specifically, the Level 1 (L1) cache and the Level 2 (L2) cache. A third type of cache has existed as well—the Level 3 (L3) cache—but it is no longer available on new computers because its function has been replaced by the L2 cache. A final kind of relatively fast memory is the Level 4 (L4) cache.

Table 6.3 presents some rough estimates of access times for the hierarchy of data storage possibilities taken from various computers, many of which are probably out-of-date now. Also included are SSD, HDD, and tertiary storage access times to put things into perspective.

For extremely large amounts of information, the only alternative is tertiary storage, where a robot mounts a removable storage device and reads the information from it onto either an HDD or an SSD. Although reading tertiary storage device can be relatively fast, mounting the devices can take several seconds, which is an eternity in terms of access time.

Memory Type	Read Volume/Unit of Time	Typical Size
Registers	more or less instantaneous	under 1 KB
L1 Cache	700 GB per second	64–128 KB per CPU
L2 Cache	200 GB per second	up to 1 MB per CPU
L3 Cache	100 GB per second	$\approx$ 6 MB per microchip
L4 Cache	40 GB per second	$\approx$ 128 MB per microchip
Main memory	10 GB per second	4–32 GB per computer
SSD	up to 500 MB per second	512 GB per SSD
HDD	up to 120 MB per second	up to 1 TB per HDD
Tertiary storage	less than 120 MB per second	up to 1 EB per device

Table 6.3: Data Access Time and Typical Size

To increase the speed of data throughput, high-speed L1 cache memory has been introduced between the CPU and RAM; except for processor registers, L1 cache memory is the fastest memory and is usually part of the CPU itself. Some CPUs have two L1 caches, one for instructions, the other for data. L1 cache memory uses high-speed SRAM (static RAM) instead of the slower, cheaper DRAM (dynamic RAM) used in the main volatile memory. Even though the L1 cache is quite fast, it is also relatively small, between 64 KB and 128 KB; older computers probably have substantially less than this.

The L2 cache is located between the L1 cache and the main memory RAM, so CPU–L1–L2–RAM. The L2 cache is larger than the L1 cache (for example, between 128 KB and 4 MB), but the L2 cache can be twice as slow as the L1 cache, yet ten times faster than the DRAM of the volatile memory. Obviously, reading from an HDD is even slower: it could take thousands of times longer to read from the HDD, but just one-quarter of that time for an SSD. Nevertheless, accessing an SSD still takes several hundreds of times longer than accessing the L2 cache.

In the future, faster and larger HDDs and SSDs will surely be built; for example, Western Digital has built a prototype where the HDD lives in helium to reduce friction. In the meantime, however, the reigning alternative way to store a huge amount of data is via distributed computing.

In the distributed computing model, data are kept on many cheap commodity computers. Calculations are only done on those data maintained on the local HDD; a *master* computer sends out instructions to the other *slave* computers that are distributed spatially. Inevitably, however, the answers have to be collected and analyzed, which involves transmitting information back to the master. Therein lies the rub: moving large amounts of data around the Internet is costly. In other words, with distributed computing, distance becomes an issue; physical constants (in particular, the speed of light) determine how fast data can be moved, even under ideal conditions.

6.1.1 What Does It All Mean?

First, Moore's law will inevitably peter out: the atomic size of components will eventually prevent engineers from making transistors any smaller. In short, improvements in speed are going to decelerate. Second, with the advent of Big Data, the access times of HDDs and SSDs put upper bounds on how much information can be processed. Third, although distributed computing is a boon, the physical distance between CPUs and data limits improvements. In sum, even though computing has made amazing strides using the Atanasoff-Zuse-Eckert-Mauchly-von Neumann model, diminishing returns are setting in. The rates of improvements seen in the past 50 years are unlikely to continue. In the absence of a new technological paradigm, this makes learning how to use this existing technology effectively even more important than when everything appeared to be improving all the time.

6.1.2 Raspberry Pi

Perhaps the best way to learn how a computer really works is to buy the parts for a small one and assemble them. It worked for Dale Whiteman (see page 184); it could work for you, too. By proceeding in this way, you could see all the moving parts and play with them.

In the United Kingdom, the Raspberry Pi Foundation has developed a credit-card sized computer to promote the teaching of basic computer science in schools. The computer, named the *Raspberry Pi*, can be purchased from a number of vendors, including some third-party vendors on Amazon.com.[5]

---

[5]Another alternative is the *BeagleBone Black*, which is a development platform for SDEs intent on creating applications for mobile devices, such as smartphones and tablet computers. Produced by Texas Instruments in association with Digi-Key and Newark element14 and priced at about $45, the BeagleBone Black runs the Linux operating system, but can also be used as a platform for Android development. Android is an operating system based on the Linux kernel, but

At the time of this writing, two models of the Raspberry Pi existed: Model A cost about $25, whereas Model B cost about $35.[6] The Raspberry Pi is is really just a motherboard, not a working computer. What is a *motherboard*? It is the main circuit board of a computer, on which most of the crucial electronic components of the system reside. These include the CPU and the volatile memory as well as the connectors to other peripherals, such as a keyboard, a mouse, a video device, and the nonvolatile storage. In short, you have to buy the other peripherals in order for the Raspberry Pi to be functional.[7]

Once you have purchased a wireless keyboard with mouse, a memory card, a USB hub, a clear-plastic case in which to embed the motherboard, and some books to help you figure out what to do, we know from personal experience that the total will be closer to $150 than to $100.[8] Moreover, at this point, you will either have to use your television as a monitor or `ssh` into the Raspberry Pi from, say, your desktop or laptop computer.

The CPUs on both models of Raspberry Pi are modest, having a *clock speed* of just 700 megahertz. Hertz is an international measure of units, abbreviated Hz, that is defined as the number of cycles per second. Thus, 700 MHz is 700 million cycles per second. The clock speed of a CPU is determined by the frequency of an oscillating crystal that produces a fixed sine wave. Under parity of architecture, the clock speed limits how many instructions can be executed in a fixed period of time—in short, the speed of the computer.

The RAM of Model A is 256 MB, whereas for Model B it is 512 MB, a standard amount of volatile memory on an Apple PowerBook in, say, 2004 or 2005.

Each model also has a graphical processing unit (GPU).

Neither model comes with either an HDD or an SSD. Instead, a secure digital (SD) memory card is used for storage. You may already be familiar with SD

---

designed for mobile devices; Android is owned by Google. As such, BeagleBone Black is more of a commercial venture than an educational one. In fact, the documentation available for the BeagleBone Black is not as easy to read as that for the Raspberry Pi.

[6]In July 2014, Model B+ was released. Although this model does more than Model B, it cost $35 at that time. With time, other models will be released. For example, in early 2015, Model 2 was released; it cost $35, too. You should consult the relevant web page for up-to-date information.

[7]From http://en.wikipedia.org/wiki/Raspberry_Pi.

[8]For a small margin, some vendors sell the components for a Raspberry Pi bundled together. The virtue of purchasing the parts bundled is that it partly insures you against purchasing parts that are incompatible with one another. We say "partly" because not all vendors are equal when it comes to service; some may inadvertently bundle together incompatible parts.

memory cards because they are used as nonvolatile storage in portable devices such as digital cameras, mobile phones, and tablet computers.

At `http://www.raspberrypi.org`, the Raspberry Pi Foundation website, you can download either the Debian or the Arch ARM distributions of the Linux operating system; Python is the main programming language.

What can you do with this device? By following the instructions in, say, the book by Upton and Halfacre (2012), you can learn an amazing amount about where bottlenecks in computing can arise. For example, we mentioned that the L1 cache is much faster than RAM. On a Raspberry Pi, it is possible to control whether the L1 cache is used for the GPU or the CPU. In particular, you can allocate none or all of the 128 KB in the L1 cache to the CPU. You can then create a small Python script that uses different amounts of memory, which will allow you to see how that script's performance is affected by whether it uses just RAM, or the L1 cache memory and RAM.

6.2 Algorithmics

The famous academic computer scientist Edsger W. Dijkstra is reported (disputedly) to have quipped once that "computer science is no more about computers than astronomy is about telescopes." It has also been reported that Dijkstra did not even use a computer in his research. He communicated by writing letters to friends using a fountain pen, indexing each missive by his initials EWD plus a number, for example, EWD443.[9]

Apparently, Dijkstra believed that computer science should be concerned with the analysis and evaluation of algorithms—in that sense an extension of mathematics rather than a part of engineering.

Similarly, many academic computer scientists believe that programming languages have about as much to do with computer science as English grammar has to do with English literature. In *Algorithmics: The Spirit of Computing*, Harel (1992) argued convincingly that a major portion of computer science, perhaps the most important portion, is not concerned with writing computer code. Instead, it deals with developing as well as analyzing and evaluating the algorithms that are then implemented in computer code.

---

[9]The online archive `http://www.cs.utexas.edu/~EWD/` at the University of Texas contains copies of some 1,300 such documents.

Bixby (2002) reported that in 1988 to solve a benchmark set of linear programming problems using hardware current to that time as well as implementations of algorithms current to the late 1980s would have taken 82 years. In contrast, in 2002, the same benchmark set of problems would have taken one minute using hardware and algorithms current to the early 2000s. Of this 43 million-fold speedup, however, only about 1,000-fold obtained because of Moore's law; the other 43,000-fold obtained because of improvements in algorithms.[10]

At the September 2013 Dagstuhl Seminars, Professor Bixby presented more recent evidence concerning mixed-integer programs (MIPs). He reported that between 1991 and 2008 the improvements arising from better algorithms and implementations have resulted in about a 29,000-fold speedup; hardware held constant.[11]

In light of this evidence, you will probably not be surprised to learn that many academic computer scientists believe that computer science is primarily concerned with algorithms, not with designing sophisticated hardware (that is, computer engineering), or implementing efficient computer code (that is, software engineering).

To some, the notion that algorithms need to be analyzed and evaluated may seem odd. Valiant (2013) noted that most of the algorithms taught in schools are the practical ones, and with good reason. Given limited class time as well as the brief attention spans of students, teachers focus on those algorithms that would be useful to students in later life, for instance, the one used in long division.

Valiant deplores this exclusive focus on the simple, useful algorithms, however, because it has led many to believe that successful computation is possible for *any* problem, a belief that is patently false. In fact, the set of problems that can be solved using computers is relatively small, at least when compared to the set of all problems. (As well, the set of problems that can be solved using machine learning is a proper subset of those that can be solved on a computer.)

If some problems are amenable to solution on a computer, and others are not, then what are the features of the amenable problems? Moreover, can you

---

[10]This result, which is attributed to Martin Grötschel, was reported on page 71 of *Designing a Digital Future: Federally Funded Research and Development in Networking and Information Technology* (2010), a report prepared by the President's Council of Advisors on Science and Technology. In personal email from Professor Grötschel, we learned that this citation is from Bixby (2002) and Bixby et al. (2004).

[11]We thank Professor Bixby for providing us the slides from this seminar.

determine *ex ante* (that is, before beginning implementation) which problems can be solved using a computer, and which ones are just too hard? The short answer is yes. In fact, during the past 50 years, computer scientists have developed a rich and powerful theory to analyze and to evaluate algorithms. The analysis and evaluation of algorithms is referred to as *algorithmics*.

6.2.1 Analysis and Evaluation

What does it mean to analyze and to evaluate an algorithm? Beginning with the pathbreaking research of Alan M. Turing (1936), analyzing an algorithm has typically involved attributing some resource cost to each action that the computer takes when executing a program. At least two dimensions to resource costs exist: time and space. Historically, by and large, issues of space have been assumed away, probably because the rapid growth in cheap storage has implied that constraints of space were not as binding as constraints of time. In short, implicitly, computer scientists have assumed either that computers have infinite amounts of memory or that the finite-memory constraints do not bind. Thus, the dimension of time use is explored.

The problem with using time is that different computers have different clock speeds. In other words, different computers process information at different rates. Completing a specific instruction on one computer will typically take a different amount of time than completing it on another. For example, reading in data will depend on the device—HDD or SSD. Moreover, even on a particular computer, different instructions take different amounts of time. For example, assigning a value to an integer variable takes less time than adding two integer values, which takes less time than multiplying two floating-point values, which takes less time than calculating the logarithm of a floating-point variable, and so forth.

Faced with such heterogeneity, what to do? Computer scientists have chosen to abstract from these specifics, and to focus on the number of basic instructions that must be completed. For example, consider the assignment of a variable in Python:

```
>>> x = 3
```

This assignment instruction would take some resource time, say, α. A fixed resource cost of Δ could also exist, for example, to invoke the Python interpreter. Thus, the total resource cost would be $(\alpha + \Delta)$.

As a second example, consider calculating the sum of the floating-point elements in a list y having length `len(y)`, which we denote by n below to signify that n may vary among applications.

```
>>> ySum = 0.
>>> for i in range( 0, len(y) ):   ySum = ySum + y[i]
...
>>>
```

Suppose that the instruction to take the sum of two numbers uses, say, β resources. This code would take α for the assignment `ySum = 0.`, α for each update of `ySum`, and β for each time that `y[i]` was added to `ySum`. Thus, calculating this sum would take $[\alpha(n+1) + \beta n]$ resources, plus the fixed cost Δ, which can be written as $[\alpha + \Delta + (\alpha + \beta)n]$, a linear function of list length n.

As a third example, consider searching for a particular string (say, `'On Watch List'`) through a dictionary of lists `dictOfLists`. In this example, we imagine that airline flight numbers are the keys, and the contents of each list are predictions concerning the risk status of a ticketed passenger having a particular index of the list, `id`.

In the following Python code, the number of keys is 3, and each list has a variable number of elements. In general, let's denote the number of keys by n and the number of elements in each list by m_i for $i = 1, 2, \ldots, n$.

```
dictOfLists = {'CP123': ['Medium', 'Low', 'On Watch List', 'High'],
               'TW345': ['Medium', 'Low', 'Low'],
               'EA987': ['High', 'Low']}

potentialBadGuys = []
for flight in dictOfLists.keys():
  for id in range(0, len(dictOfLists[flight])):
    if (dictOfLists[flight][id] == 'On Watch List'):
      addToList = (flight, id)
      potentialBadGuys.append(addToList)
```

Assigning data to the dictionary of lists will cost approximately $\alpha \sum_{i=1}^{n} m_i$ resources. Why approximately? Some overhead exists in creating the dictionary and the lists beyond what is used when assigning them values to the various locations in memory. Also, each pass through a loop will take γ resources, and a comparison will take δ resources. Each assignment to `addToList` will take 2α resources. Why? Two pieces of information must be loaded. Finally, the data must be appended to the list, which uses, say, η resources each time.

Thus, for each `flight` key, of which there are n, for each list which has length $m_{\texttt{flight}}$, a comparison is made. Depending on the outcome of the comparison, two assignments and an append will occur. In the best-case scenario, when no one is on the watch list, total resource use (in effect computer time used) is approximately

$$\alpha + \alpha \sum_{i=1}^{n} m_i + (\gamma + \delta) \sum_{i=1}^{n} m_i + \Delta.$$

This is a lower bound on the amount of resources that will be used. To get an upper bound on resource use (computer time used), imagine that everyone is on the watch list, in which case total resource use is approximately

$$\alpha \sum_{i=1}^{n} m_i + (2\alpha + \gamma + \delta + \eta) \sum_{i=1}^{n} m_i + \Delta.$$

The lower- and upper-bound expressions are somewhat difficult to interpret, mainly because of the term $\sum_{i=1}^{n} m_i$. It seems reasonable to assume that each flight has a maximum upper bound, say, $\bar{m}$ for the number of seats available. When m_i is the same (and $\bar{m}$) for each key,

$$\sum_{i=1}^{n} \bar{m} = \overbrace{\bar{m} + \bar{m} + \ldots + \bar{m}}^{n \text{ times}} = n\bar{m}.$$

Thus, an upper bound for the amount of resources used is approximately

$$(3\alpha + \gamma + \delta + \eta)n\bar{m} + \Delta.$$

Because it is typically easier to establish an upper bound on total resource use, by considering the worst-case scenario, computer scientists focus almost exclusively on worst-case total resource use, the most computer time that will be used.

In this example, a natural upper bound (cap) exists on the m_is—the finite number of seats in an aircraft. In other cases, the m_is may grow approximately with n, for example, say, proportionally

$$m_i \approx \rho n,$$

in which case worst-case total resource use would be

$$\rho(3\alpha + \gamma + \delta + \eta)n^2 + \Delta,$$

which is a quadratic function of the number of keys n.

As you can see from these examples, an algorithm can be broken down into a series of basic instructions, each of which has some resource cost. You can then aggregate these expressions to get an estimate of the total resource cost—in short, a total resource cost function that depends on the size of the input, n in the examples. Such expressions can be complicated functions of both the inputs and the cost parameters. In general, a worst-case total resource cost function might look something like

$$T(n) = t_0 + t_1 n + t_2 n^2 + \cdots + t_p n^p.$$

That is, the worst-case total resource cost function is a polynomial of order p in the input argument n.

For large n, the term $t_p n^p$ will dominate the other terms in the sum that are of order smaller than n^p. Moreover, across computer models, the parameter t_p will vary because the cost of basic operations varies across computer architectures. Thus, computer scientists ignore the terms

$$t_0 + t_1 n + t_2 n^2 + \cdots + t_{p-1} n^{p-1}.$$

They then refer to the order of worst-case total resource costs using the *Big O notation*, $\mathcal{O}$. In short, $T(n)$ is $\mathcal{O}(n^p)$ when n gets very large, that is, asymptotically. Thus, as in the case of guesstimation (see Section 5.1), computer scientists are really just trying to get an order-of-magnitude estimate of an algorithm's worst-case total resource use, the most computer time that will be used.

So far, so good. As a fourth example, suppose you have to store some information in a binary tree. Figure 6.1 depicts the graph of a binary tree. The tree begins at the top, at the root node 0, and branches to left and right. At the second level, each of the left and right leaves can go left and right. Continuing on, at the third level, each of these leaves can go left and right. Suppose there are n values, indexed according to a binary sequence, where left is 0 and right is 1. How deep must the binary tree be in order to store the n values? The depth of the binary tree is k, the smallest integer such that n is less than 2^k; that is,

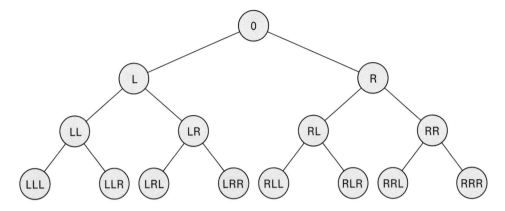

Figure 6.1: Binary Tree $k = 3$, $n = 2^k$

k equals $\lceil \lg(n) \rceil$, namely, the ceiling of $\lg(n)$, where $\lg$ is the base-2 logarithmic function.[12]

To find a specific value in the binary tree, you just travel down its leaves until you find that value. How long does it take to find a particular value? You need to make k, that is $\lg(n)$, decisions. How is $\lg(n)$ related to $\log(2^k)$? The function $\lg$ is proportional to the function $\log$ because

$$\lg(2^k) = k \propto k \log(2).$$

In the $\mathcal{O}$ notation, the worst-case total resource cost is $\mathcal{O}(\log n)$. Note that the function $\log(n)$ grows much more slowly than the linear function n. Even the function $n \log(n)$ grows relatively slowly, at least when compared to the quadratic function n^2.

As a fifth example, consider calculating the number of subsets in the set $\{a_1, a_2, \ldots, a_n\}$, which contains n members. One strategy is to proceed by induction. First, consider a set having just one element $\{a_1\}$. In this case, there are two subsets: the empty set $\{\}$ and the entire set $\{a_1\}$. Next, consider a set having two elements $\{a_1, a_2\}$. Four subsets exist: the empty set $\{\}$, two singletons $\{a_1\}$ and $\{a_2\}$, and the entire set $\{a_1, a_2\}$. Then, consider a set having three elements $\{a_1, a_2, a_3\}$. Now eight subsets exist: the empty set $\{\}$; three singletons $\{a_1\}$ $\{a_2\}$ $\{a_3\}$; three sets of doubles $\{a_1, a_2\}$, $\{a_1, a_3\}$, and $\{a_2, a_3\}$; and the

---

[12]This convention is used by many computer scientists, but lb is the ISO31-11 international standard for the base-2 logarithmic function, whereas the base-10 logarithmic function is lg, and the base-e logarithmic function is ln. See http://en.wikipedia.org/wiki/ISO_31-11.

entire set $\{a_1, a_2, a_3\}$. Finally, consider a set having four elements $\{a_1, a_2, a_3, a_4\}$. In this case, 16 subsets exist

$1 : \{\}$

$4 : \{a_1\}, \{a_2\}, \{a_3\}, \{a_4\}$

$6 : \{a_1, a_2\}, \{a_1, a_3\}, \{a_1, a_4\}, \{a_2, a_3\}, \{a_2, a_4\}, \{a_3, a_4\}$

$4 : \{a_1, a_2, a_3\}, \{a_1, a_2, a_4\}, \{a_1, a_3, a_4\}, \{a_2, a_3, a_4\}$

$1 : \{a_1, a_2, a_3, a_4\}.$

Is there a pattern? Yes. For $n = 1, 2, 3, 4$, we see $2(= 2^1)$, $4 = (2^2)$, $8(= 2^3)$, and $16(= 2^4)$ subsets. Therefore, in general, for a set having n members $\{a_1, a_2, \ldots, a_n\}$, there are 2^n subsets. This is not a polynomial function of n; it is an exponential function of n.

As a sixth example, again consider the set $\{a_1, a_2, \ldots, a_n\}$, but now find the number of permutations of members of this set. As with the subset example, consider proceeding by induction. For $\{a_1\}$, there is just one, that is, $\{a_1\}$. For $\{a_1, a_2\}$, there are two: $\{a_1, a_2\}$ and $\{a_2, a_1\}$. For $\{a_1, a_2, a_3\}$, there are six: $\{a_1, a_2, a_3\}, \{a_2, a_1, a_3\}, \{a_2, a_3, a_1\}, \{a_1, a_3, a_2\}, \{a_3, a_1, a_2\}$, and $\{a_3, a_2, a_1\}$. Now let's try to figure out the pattern:

$1 : 1$

$2 : 2 \times 1 = 2$

$3 : 3 \times 2 \times 1 = 6$

$\vdots \quad \vdots$

$n : n \times (n - 1) \times \cdots \times 2 \times 1 = n!$

This is not a polynomial function of n, either. It is the factorial function of n.

To provide you with some notion of how the functions like $\log(n)$, n, $n \log(n)$, n^2, 2^n, and $n!$ behave, Figure 6.2 depicts graphs of each versus n. We chose these functions because they are often found to characterize the worst-case total resource use of many commonly used algorithms. As you can see, the factorial and exponential functions increase very quickly with input size, whereas the others increase more slowly. Practically speaking, you can see that the factorial and exponential functions mean that algorithms having this behavior are not realistic alternatives to solve problems when n is large: such algorithms will take too long.

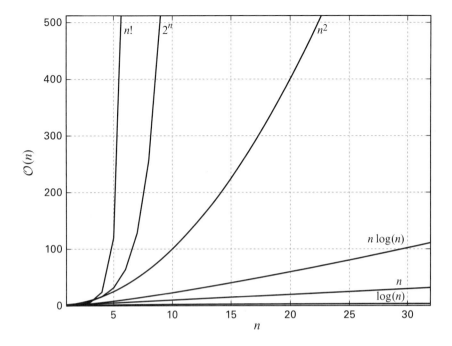

Figure 6.2: $\mathcal{O}$ Functions for Various Algorithms

6.2.2 Sorting Algorithms

In computer science, sorting a sequence of names or numbers is the canonical example often used to illustrate the importance of algorithmic choice. Because sorting is such an important task in computing, many different algorithms have been invented—referred to by such colorful names as *bubble sort, heapsort, insertion sort, merge sort, quicksort,* and *selection sort,* to name six of some three dozen.[13] Sometimes, the name of the algorithm provides a hint regarding the strategy used (for example, in the cases of insertion and merge sort), but in others (for example, quicksort) it does not. As in the preceding analysis, the main way to classify sorting algorithms is by their worst-case resource use. For example, for a vector of numbers of length n, bubble sort is among the worst behaved algorithms, being $\mathcal{O}(n^2)$, whereas heapsort is among the best behaved, being $\mathcal{O}(n \log n)$. Indeed, computer scientists have shown that this is the best

---

[13]From http://en.wikipedia.org/wiki/Sorting_algorithm.

you can do in the case of sorting; that is, no better algorithm exists, at least not asymptotically.

Sorting algorithms also allow us to illustrate that best-case performance can vary between $\mathcal{O}(n)$ and $\mathcal{O}(n^2)$, and average-case performance can vary between $\mathcal{O}(n \log n)$ and $\mathcal{O}(n^2)$. In addition, although we have not discussed this, algorithms can be compared by the amounts of memory each uses. Memory use is an important consideration in the era of Big Data. Algorithms that use only one memory location are better than those that require n. Sorting algorithms can be compared using considerations like stability as well. In short, making good choices when selecting an algorithm to solve a problem involves balancing a variety of considerations.

6.2.3   Complexity Classes

With all these factors, problems can in fact be divided into two groups according to the worst-case total resource cost functions of their algorithms, sometimes referred to as *complexity classes*. In the first group are algorithms referred to as *polynomial-time* algorithms, and in the second group are *exponential-time* algorithms.

Polynomial-time algorithms—algorithms that use resources according to a small-order polynomial of the input n as well as $\log(n)$ and $n \log(n)$, which are not polymials of n—can be used when n is large. Polynomial-time problems are often referred to as *tractable* problems. On the other hand, if the order of the total resource cost polynomial is greater than 3, then even a polynomial-time algorithm is of little use when n is large.

Exponential-time algorithms—algorithms whose total resource cost function is exponential in the input size—can only be used when n is small. These problems are often referred to as *intractable* problems, or *infeasible* problems.

We have met people who believe that exponential resource use is just an economic constraint, that is, a hardware constraint. In other words, if you just bought bigger (or more) computers, then the problem could be surmounted. But we disagree. Bigger (or more) computers *cannot* solve the resource requirements of exponential-time algorithms. When the size of the input is large, there just are not enough computers in the universe to solve problems that require exponential amounts of input. It is not a question of being clever or working harder; it is a physical reality.

Among computer scientists, problems for which the best-known algorithms have polynomial-time resource use are said to live in the *P class* (an abbreviation of "polynomial time"). Problems for which the best-known algorithms have exponential-time resource use are broken down into several other classes.

One of those classes (in fact, the class one up from P) is referred to as *NP* (an abbreviation of "nondeterministic polynomial time"). NP problems are decision problems, ones for which either a yes or a no answer can be given for a candidate solution. In short, for such problems, the best-known solution algorithms require worst-case total resource use that is exponential in the input size n.

Among the problems within the NP class is a very interesting class referred to as *NP-complete*. No known algorithm exists that provides a solution to an NP-complete problem in polynomial time. The hallmark of problems that live within the NP-complete class is that if you solve any one problem within the class in polynomial time, then you have solved them all. Among academic computer scientists, solving an NP-complete problem in polynomial time is the holy grail: by solving a single problem, you have also solved many others. The number of problems within the NP-complete class is unknown at this time.

The next class up from NP-complete is referred to as *NP-hard*, which means that such problems are at least as difficult to solve as NP-complete problems, but they are not decision problems. Obviously, NP-complete problems are also NP-hard problems, but not vice versa. You may have heard of the following two NP-hard problems:

- Knapsack problem. Given a knapsack of fixed volume $\bar{v}$ and a set of items $\{v_1, v_2, \ldots, v_n\}$, where v_i denotes, say, the volume of item i, determine which items to pack using the maximum packed volume as the objective function, often referred to as a *combinatorial optimization problem*.

- Traveling saleman problem. Given a list of cities and the distances between each pair of cities, find the shortest possible route that visits each city exactly once and returns to the origin city.

An outstanding question in computer science is whether the class P and the class NP are, in fact, the same. That is, can every problem whose solution can be verified in polynomial time be solved in polynomial time? This problem was first investigated by Cook (1971). Demonstrating that P=NP is a problem for which the Clay Mathematics Institute of Cambridge, Massachusetts, will pay a one million dollar prize to resolve.

The Clay Mathematics Institute was incorporated in 1998 by Landon T. Clay, a successful businessman, to endorse and support the belief that mathematical knowledge is valuable. To celebrate mathematics in the new millennium, the Clay Mathematics Institute established seven prize problems in 2000. Prizes of one million dollars each are to be awarded for a solution to any one of what are viewed as the seven most difficult mathematical problems in 2000. The P=NP problem is one of the seven. (In fact, the television drama *Elementary* featured this problem and the prize as the backdrop for a murder investigation.) If P=NP, then humankind is golden. But most computer scientists do not believe that this equality is true.[14]

Even more difficult problems exist than those within the NP-hard class. A class referred to as #*P* (pronounced "sharp-P") exists, containing problems that are conjectured to be even more difficult than those contained in the NP-complete class. For example, Valiant (1979) demonstrated that the problem of calculating the permanent of a square matrix is in the #P class.[15]

We would wager that most of the algorithms you know and use are for problems within the P class. You may also know some algorithms that require exponential resource use, but you only use them on problems with small input sizes, for instance, Laplace's expansion to calculate the determinant of an $(n \times n)$ matrix is an $\mathcal{O}(n!)$ algorithm.

So what is a computer scientist to do? Much current research focuses on approximation algorithms, namely, algorithms that provide what is referred to as *provably good* approximate solutions to difficult problems, but do so in polynomial time. One notion of provably good is that the solution is bounded within the optimum by a small factor. In essence, under these solution strategies, you are trading off the quality of the solution for the speed with which an approximate solution is found. Practically speaking, wouldn't you rather accept a solution to the traveling salesman problem that is no worse than 10 percent of the optimum, provided you could obtain that solution quickly rather than wait years? Thus, under approximation strategies, correct solutions are abandoned in favor of good approximations.

---

[14]From http://en.wikipedia.org/wiki/Clay_Mathematics_Institute.

[15]In linear algebra, the permanent of a square matrix is a function of the matrix elements, similar to the determinant, except the signs in the expansion by minors are all positive. From http://en.wikipedia.org/wiki/Permanent.

According to Valiant (2013), machine learning problems live in the *probably, approximately correct class* (PAC class), which is a proper subset of the P class. You can now appreciate the following two claims:

- The set of problems that can be solved on a computer is relatively small.

- The set of problems that can be solved using machine learning is a proper subset of those that can be solved on a computer.

In other words, computers cannot solve all problems, and machine learning can solve even fewer problems than that.

In fact, in order for any analysis of computational complexity to be at all meaningful, you must first demonstrate that the answer is computable. Computer scientists have determined conditions under which some questions cannot be answered. One such problem is the so-called *Entscheidungsproblem*, which is roughly translated from German as the *decision problem*. Initially posed by Gottfried Wilhelm von Leibniz, and then recast in the modern form by David Hilbert, the problem is as follows: Does an algorithm exist whose input is a statement of first-order logic and whose answer is either yes or no depending on whether the statement is universally valid? Alonzo Church (1936) and Alan M. Turing (1936) each proved independently that such an algorithm cannot exist.[16]

By the way, in 2010 the Clay Mathematics Institute announced that one of the seven Millenium Prize Problems had been solved: Grigoriy Perelman proved the Poincaré conjecture. (Maybe P does equal NP?)

6.2.4 Exploiting Complexity in Computer Security

Perhaps the most important feature of computing in the twenty-first century is the Internet. The ability to transfer huge amounts of information over large distances almost instantly is unparalleled in history. But, as anyone who has had his identity stolen can attest, transferring information over the Internet is not without peril. Because privacy is so important to banking, e-commerce, and finance as well as international relations and national security, much effort has been expended to ensure that the Internet is secure to use. Despite these efforts, lapses in security seem to occur almost daily. What can be done?

---

[16]From http://en.wikipedia.org/wiki/Halting_problem.

On the one hand, complexity is the bane of a scientist's existence. Problems whose solutions involve algorithms that have exponential resource use are impossible to solve at scale. On the other hand, exponential resource use also means that others cannot solve those problems either. At the heart of modern computer security is a set of algorithms that require exponential resource use to break their codes. Currently, an important class of algorithms used to ensure that information transfer on the Internet is secure is referred to as *public-key encryption.*

Public-key encryption algorithms require two different numbers, *keys.* One is referred to as the *private key;* this key is secret and known only to the party seeking privacy. The other is referred to as the *public key;* that key is known to all. These two keys are generated algorithmically, specifically, as two very large prime numbers. The public key is used to encrypt the message, while the private key is used to decrypt it.

Several different public-key encryption algorithms exist, but the most commonly used one is referred to as *RSA,* an acronym formed from the first letters of the surnames of the three inventors, Ronald Rivest, Adi Shamir, and Leonard Adelman.[17] RSA public-key encryption exploits the fact that factoring a very large number as a product of primes has no known polynomial-time algorithm. In other words, trying to break the encryption using brute-force calculation requires exponential resource use—in short, it is impractical.[18] Hence, complexity is a two-edged sword. Solving problems in your research life can be impossible to do at scale, but violating your privacy is made virtually impossible for others, too.

6.2.5   What Does It Mean?

Knowing whether a problem is within a particular complexity class can save you a lot of time. To wit, trying to solve a problem within the NP-hard class is doomed to failure, at least for large-dimensioned inputs. Even trying to solve a problem within the P class could be doomed to failure if the best-known algorithm has a total resource cost that is a high-order polynomial in the input size.

---

[17]From `http://en.wikipedia.org/wiki/RSA_(cryptosystem)`.
[18]From `http://simple.wikipedia.org/wiki/RSA_(algorithm)`.

With Big Data, realistic computing restricts you to problems whose solution algorithms have worst-case total resource use of $\mathcal{O}(\log n)$, $\mathcal{O}(n)$, or $\mathcal{O}(n \log n)$, and maybe $\mathcal{O}(n^2)$, but $\mathcal{O}(n^3)$ or higher are out of the question. Hence, the common claim by machine learners that you should never invert a matrix. (Hint: To appreciate this comment, see Chapter 7.)

Certain models of computing are also ruled out with Big Data. For example, pushing lots of data around the Internet is costly, so distributed computing is essentially not in the cards if huge amounts of data need to be transmitted long distances; except for local consumption, you won't see many cloud computing facilities in Australia. On the other hand, in situ computing using many instances in a server farm is well suited to distributed computing.[19]

6.2.6 Further Reading

We have provided a gentle introduction to algorithmics. Harel (1992) and Stuart (2013) have gone further. Moore and Mertens (2011) developed the topic in great detail. The Nobel Prize winner Alvin E. Roth (2015) reported on a fascinating application of algorithms to kidney transplantation: medicine, economics, and algorithmics were used in tandem to invent kidney exchanges.

In order to become at all proficient at analyzing, evaluating, and using algorithms, you need to read about this from experts. At least two excellent texts exist. Sedgewick and Wayne (2011) proceed at a more leisurely pace than Kleinberg and Tardos (2006).

The mathematical methods required to analyze and to evaluate algorithms have been developed by Graham et al. (1994). You should initially consider this as a reference, but aspire to read it all. A standard reference concerning complexity is by Papadimitriou (1994), which should also be considered as a reference initially.

6.2.7 Approaches to Algorithmic Design

Is there a systematic way in which to design algorithms? Yes and no. Yes, in the sense that three basic approaches to algorithmic design exist: (1) the greedy approach; (2) the dynamic programming approach; and (3) the

---

[19]A server farm is collection of computers maintained by a company or an organization to satisfy computing needs beyond those of an individual machine.

divide-and-conquer approach. No, in the sense that recipes for using these approaches do not exist. In short, except in rare cases, constructing an algorithm that solves a nontrivial problem requires considerable ingenuity, which is why most researchers use existing algorithms. Using intuition to develop algorithms is probably doomed to failure: If intuition had been such a powerful tool, humankind would have never invented logic and mathematics.

Greedy Approach

Perhaps the most natural approach to algorithmic design involves greed: get as much done as you can with little regard for how it is done. For some problems, this is a fine approach; for others, it is simply the worst thing you can do.

In general, for a problem to be amenable to the greedy approach, several features must be present: First, you must be able to build the solution set incrementally; second, you must have a formal function to use as the criterion to determine the best candidate to add to the solution set; third, you must be able to determine whether a candidate solution is feasible; fourth, you must have a way to determine whether you are done.

A classic example of the greedy approach applied to algorithmic design was reported by Denardo (2003, 6–11). In his example, Denardo imagined that you are trying to find the fastest route from your home to your work. He depicted the various routes from home to work using the circles with numbers in them and the lines connecting the circles with values near them (see Figure 6.3). This object is referred to as a *graph*. (We discuss graph theory in section 6.4.)

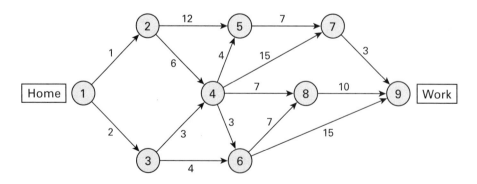

Figure 6.3: Routes from Home to Work

In Figure 6.3 you begin at the circle marked 1 (the root node) and seek the destination node, the circle marked 9. The lines with arrows (the edges) depict the various routes, while the numbers near the edges denote the times in, say, minutes. For example, it takes one minute from node 1 to node 2, but two minutes from node 1 to node 3.

Using the greedy approach to solve this problem, find the lowest-cost path out of node 1 to its neighbors, which means go to node 2. From that neighbor, then find the lowest-cost path to the next neighbor, and so forth. Thus, at node 2, the greedy route is to node 4; from node 4, go to node 6; from node 6, go to node 8, and then to node 9. According to this greedy approach, the total time is 27 minutes. We depict this solution in Figure 6.4.

Is this the best you can do? Does an alternative, better algorithm exist? Yes.

Dynamic Programming

Dynamic programming is perhaps the most difficult algorithmic strategy for many people to understand; dynamic programming is also the most powerful strategy, so avoiding it is really not an option. For although you can get through graduate school on partial credit, it is difficult to get through life that way, even though Woody Allen claims that "eighty percent of success is showing up," quoted by Safire (1992, 32).

In describing how dynamic programming proceeds algorithmically, we employ the example from Denardo (2003). He imagined that you are trying to find the fastest route from your home to your work (see Figure 6.3). The main idea

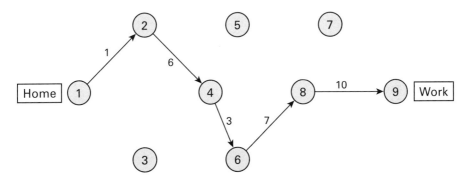

Figure 6.4: Getting to Work Using a Greedy Approach

behind finding the route that takes the shortest time from home to work is referred to as *backward induction*. Start at the destination node, in this case 9, and
work backward, finding the best route as you go. In dynamic programming
problems with a finite horizon like this one, backward induction is the way to
construct the optimal solution.

In this example, denote the time between two adjacent nodes, i and j, by $t_{i,j}$;
for example, $t_{7,9} = 3$, $t_{8,9} = 10$, and $t_{6,9} = 15$. Denote the minimum travel time
from node i to the destination node, node 9, by V_i. Now,

$$V_i = \min_j \; t_{i,j} + V_j \quad i \neq 9.$$

By definition, $V_9 = 0$; you are already at the office, so no time is required.

Because no choice is possible at the nodes just before the destination node,
$V_7 = 3$, $V_8 = 10$, and $V_6 = 15$. Similarly, $V_5 = 10$ because it is just $(t_{5,7} + V_7)$.
The most interesting nodes are the ones where a choice can exist. For example,
consider node 6, where

$$\begin{aligned} V_6 &= \min(V_6, t_{6,8} + V_8) \\ &= \min(t_{6,9}, t_{6,8} + V_8) \\ &= \min(15, 17) = 15. \end{aligned}$$

In words, it is better to go from node 6 directly to node 9 than to go from node 6
to nodes 8 and then 9. This is not a foregone conclusion. Suppose $t_{6,8}$ had been
1 instead of 7; then it would be faster to go through node 8 than to go directly
to node 9.

Even more interesting than node 6 is node 4, where

$$\begin{aligned} V_4 &= \min(t_{4,5} + V_5, t_{4,6} + V_6, t_{4,7} + V_7, t_{4,8} + V_8) \\ &= \min(4 + 10, 3 + 15, 15 + 3, 7 + 10) \\ &= \min(14, 18, 18, 17) = 14. \end{aligned}$$

In short, if you are at node 4, then don't go to nodes 6, 7 or 8, but rather go to
node 5; it's faster.

Next come the minimum times for nodes 2 and 3, which are calculated by
solving the following:

$$\begin{aligned} V_2 &= \min(t_{2,5} + V_5, t_{2,4} + V_4) \\ &= \min(12 + 10, 6 + 14) \\ &= \min(22, 20) = 20, \end{aligned}$$

and

$$V_3 = \min(t_{3,4} + V_4, t_{3,6} + V_6)$$
$$= \min(3 + 14, 4 + 15)$$
$$= \min(17, 19) = 17.$$

Finally, the root node, node 1, has the following minimum cost:

$$V_1 = \min(t_{1,2} + V_2, t_{1,3} + V_3)$$
$$= \min(1 + 20, 2 + 17)$$
$$= \min(21, 19) = 19.$$

In words, the fastest time to work is 19 minutes, which is achieved by going from 1 to 3 to 4 to 5 to 7 and to 9. Figure 6.5 depicts the optimal path to work from any node on the graph. For each node, in the box adjacent to it, we list the shortest time V_i.

Contrast the dynamic programming solution in Figure 6.5 with the greedy solution in Figure 6.4; the difference is quite stark. For problems with this structure, the greedy approach is an inappropriate strategy for designing a useful algorithm. You would fail to find the optimal solution if you applied the greedy approach to the knapsack problem (see section 6.2.3). To solve the knapsack problem, you would also need to use the dynamic programming approach. For

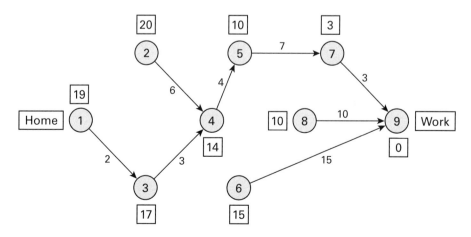

Figure 6.5: Shortest Times and Routes to Work

the knapsack problem, the greedy approach does not work because how you combine the various objects matters when you have to satisfy the feasibility constraint—namely, the total capacity of the knapsack.

Constructing the optimal solutions to problems like these using dynamic programming is an industry in engineering as well as economics and finance. Other factors may be important, too. In cases where the path from node 1 to node 9 is time rather than space, discounting may be introduced, particularly in economics, so accommodations must be made. Often, too, with the passage of time, randomness intervenes, and that risk must be accommodated as well. Finally, in some problems, no terminal node exists; that is, time goes on forever. Modifications to accommodate this reality must be introduced, too. Suffice it to say, however, that the method of dynamic programming is one of the most powerful optimization techniques available, which makes the information in the next paragraph quite disheartening.

Despite being an incredibly powerful solution strategy, many of the algorithms that implement dynamic programming require worst-case total resource uses that are exponential functions of the inputs. This occurs because of a phenomenon known as the *curse of dimensionality*, a term coined by Richard Bellman. Dynamic programming is a brute-force approach where you have to calculate the value of all possible paths. The number of paths can be exponentially large. That is, many problems that rely on the dynamic programming approach for the best algorithm lie within the NP-hard class.

As an aside, statements like "Oh, we can use machine learning to solve these dynamic programs" are utter nonsense. Machine learning problems lie within the PAC class, which is a proper subset of the P class. In short, machine learning cannot solve NP-hard problems. Machine learning might be used to construct a *heuristic* but not to solve dynamic programming problems in general. A heuristic is a technique for solving problems that derives from experience with the problem.

Divide-and-Conquer Approach

Some problems have a particular structure that allows you to break up solving the entire problem into solving a sequence of smaller problems. For such problems, the divide-and-conquer approach is a boon. To apply the divide-and-conquer approach, work done on one part of the problem cannot depend on whether work done elsewhere in the problem is completed or done optimally. In other words, the problem must have a separable structure. When the optimality of the solution to one part depends on the optimality of the solutions to other parts, the dynamic programming approach should be used.

Recursion

As mentioned in Section 4.3.14 recursion is one way of implementing the divide-and-conquer strategy in a programming language. There we used calculating $n!$, the factorial of n, as an example. Under the divide-and-conquer strategy, the solution to a problem depends on solutions to smaller instances of the same problem. For example,

$$n! = \prod_{i=1}^{n} i = n \prod_{i=1}^{n-1} i = n(n-1)!.$$

When the divide-and-conquer strategy is implemented, a function will often call itself—recursion—as we demonstrated in coding the Python function `Factorial` on page 165.

6.3 Some Programming Paradigms

Although it is unnecessary to know what a programming paradigm is when writing a Python script, knowing some vocabulary can be useful. Also, by having a basic idea of what a particular programming paradigm emphasizes, you can decide whether some languages or programs are suited to a particular task.

6.3.1 Imperative Programming

For historical reasons, by far the most common programming paradigm is *imperative programming*. Within this paradigm, computer instructions (statements) change the state of the computer. What is the state? Broadly speaking, you can think of the computer's memory as a large collection of pigeonholes, say, N of them, with data of various sorts in each pigeonhole. Collect the contents of all the pigeonholes into the vector $\mathbf{x}_t = (x_{1,t}, x_{2,t}, \ldots, x_{N,t})$, which describes the contents, or state, at time t. In imperative programming, an instruction u_t

changes the state of the system so that in the next period, however defined, the state is now x_{t+1}. Thus, an imperative program defines sequences of commands that the computer executes. This paradigm is closest to what Harel (1992) described in his introduction to algorithmics.

On early computers, imperative programming was implemented in a language referred to as *assembly*. Writing programs in assembly literally involved moving information from register to register, an exercise that required a deep understanding of a computer's architecture. In short, assembly languages were not versatile. Writing computer code in assembly is also very exacting; only certain human beings have the ability to do this task well. Because assembly languages were intimately tied to the hardware of a particular computer, programs were typically not portable. Consequently, higher-level languages, like FORTRAN, were created.

6.3.2   Procedural Programming

The demand for computing required a more flexible paradigm than the imperative paradigm, one in which computer code created previously could be reused. Maurice Wilkes, David Wheeler, and Stanley Gill are credited with having invented the construct referred to as the *subroutine*, which ushered in the *procedural paradigm*.[20] Procedural programming is really just an extension of imperative programming. As noted, depending on the language, a subroutine is referred to as a subprogram, routine, procedure, method, or in Python, function.

In Python a function is a sequence of instructions, packaged as a single logical bundle, that typically completes a specific task. The function can then be used in other programs whenever that particular task needs to be completed. When trying to complete a large, complicated project, the idea is to divide the project into smaller tasks: divide-and-conquer is the algorithmic strategy (see Section 6.2.7). For each smaller task, write a function to complete that task.

For example, in analyzing some data, you might break the entire project into the following. First, read in the data; second, check to ensure that no missing data or unusual data exist; third, calculate the statistics desired; fourth, output the results to a file in a nice format. Some natural limits exist concerning how small each task (and therefore, how small each function) should be because a

---

[20]From http://en.wikipedia.org/wiki/Subroutine.

fixed cost is incurred with each function call. In Section 9.1, we discuss how to use the Python profiler to get an imperfect measure of these fixed costs.

In imperative programming you would have a long sequence of instructions, whereas in procedural programming you would break up tasks that are frequently done (or thematically related) into smaller functions. Procedural programming is sometimes referred to as *structural programming*; considerable structure is imposed on the computing exercise. Procedural/structural programming specifies the steps the program must take to reach a particular outcome.

Often, functions (subroutines) that perform related tasks are collected in libraries. In Python functions can be collected in modules or in packages or in classes. Later, we discuss the Python construct `class` in conjunction with the object-oriented programming paradigm.

6.3.3 Declarative Programming

Because both imperative and procedural programming require that the user play an active role in designing and implementing algorithms, only a small fraction of the population can really do this sort of work. In many cases, however, designing and implementing an algorithm need only be done once; then the analyst is free to use the code in a variety of circumstances, sometimes referred to as *use cases*. In an effort to allow the user to avoid the low-level parts of the code, an extra layer is created on top of the implemented algorithms, with an expressive language that helps the user, at a high level, think through logically what he is doing, not specifically how he is doing it.

For example, implementations of Codd's RA as SQLs are examples of declarative programming. When using the `SELECT ... FROM ... WHERE ...`, the user is really quite removed from the actual code that is implementing the RA. Nevertheless, the user has considerable control; as we have seen, SQL is a very flexible language. In SQL the user does not write the instructions that he wants the computer to execute but rather sketches the logic at a higher level, and then the language/program decides how that logic will be executed. In fact, in Oracle Database, for example, the exact algorithm used for a particular `SELECT ... FROM ... WHERE ...` may depend on the number of records in the table being queried.

Similarly, when R is used to analyze data, it's not necessary to know the nitty gritty of implementation when using the regression command `lm()`, only how to interpret the output.

6.3.4　Object-Oriented Programming

What is object-oriented programming? In an object-oriented programming language, collections of objects are manipulated. The computer language C++ is an object-oriented language; Python supports object-oriented programming through the construct `class`.

Python `class`

We have advocated a structural approach to programming, the procedural programming paradigm: break up tasks into related calculations and then collect in the Python construct `function`. Related functions can be collected into modules, or packages. Often, however, considerable redundancy in inputs can exist in related functions. In this case, rather than having the same arguments in many different functions, you might want to collect the functions that all share the same inputs into the Python construct `class`. Thus, a `class` is just another data type packaged with associated functions to manipulate it; you might hear someone claim that an object is of type class. These functions, which are referred to as *methods*, are simply Python functions having a special relation to the object of the specified type. That object is `self`.

In the following code, we demonstrate how to define a `class` using an example. Specifically, suppose you want to conduct an empirical analysis of some multivariate data using the least-squares regression technique. To this end, we have written the Python class definition named `Regression` which resides in the file `RegressionClass.py`. (Had we named the file `Regression.py`, Python would have treated it as a module.)

In the `Regression` class definition, the kind of information that would be relevant when undertaking an empirical analysis using the method of least-squares regression is calculated from the inputs. We use this script to demonstrate how a class in Python might be employed.

Readers unfamiliar with regression and who skipped that part of Chapter 5, should perhaps go back and read that material.

With that basic review in mind, we can now work through the Python script that defines the `Regression` class.

```
import numpy
import sys
# A class to do multivariate linear regression.
class Regression:
  def __init__(self, y, X):
    try:
      self.y = numpy.asarray(y)
      self.X = numpy.asarray(X)
    except:
      print "There is an error with the input data."
      sys.exit(0)

    self.N         = numpy.shape(self.X)[0]
    self.K         = numpy.shape(self.X)[1]
    if (numpy.shape(self.y)[0] != self.N):
      print "Regressand vector and feature matrix are nonconformable!"
      sys.exit(0)

    self.DegOfFree = self.N - self.K
    self.yBar      = numpy.mean(self.y)
    self.xBar      = numpy.mean(self.X, axis=0)
    XpX = numpy.dot(numpy.transpose(self.X), self.X)
    self.betaHats = \
    numpy.linalg.solve(XpX, numpy.dot(numpy.transpose(self.X),self.y))
    self.yHat = numpy.dot(self.X, self.betaHats)
    self.eHat = self.y - self.yHat
    self.RSS  = numpy.sum(self.eHat*self.eHat)
    self.sHatSquared = self.RSS / self.DegOfFree
    self.seRegression = numpy.sqrt(self.sHatSquared)
    self.vcMatrix = numpy.linalg.inv(numpy.matrix(XpX))
    self.vcMatrix = self.sHatSquared * self.vcMatrix
    self.stdErrs = numpy.zeros(self.K)
    for k in range(0, self.K):
      self.stdErrs[k] = numpy.array(numpy.sqrt(self.vcMatrix[k, k]))

    self.ESS = numpy.sum((self.yHat-self.yBar)*(self.yHat-self.yBar))
    self.TSS = numpy.sum((self.y-self.yBar)*(self.y-self.yBar))
    self.rSquared = self.ESS / self.TSS
    self.tStats = self.betaHats / self.stdErrs
    self.calcF = (self.ESS/self.K) / (self.TSS / self.DegOfFree)
```

Listing 6.1: Python `class` Definition `Regression`

Lines 1 and 2 import `numpy` and `sys`, which will be used throughout, whereas line 3 is simply a comment describing the purpose of the class. Line 4 highlights the main structure of a `class` definition. First, a class definition always begins with the keyword `class` and begins in the first column. Second, the class definition line always ends with a colon `:`. Third, the first line of class, line 5, has a particular structure:

```
def __init__(self, y, X):
```

The command `def __init__` initializes the object, which is an instance of the class, and the keyword `self` refers to that object (it is a pointer to a location in memory). Here, `y` and `X` are inputs, the two kinds of data that are necessary to run a regression: the regressand `y` and the regressors `X`. On entering the class definition, after initialization, in line 6, we first `try:` to make sure that both `self.y` and `self.X` are set to `numpy` arrays. If the elements of either `y` or `X` fail this assignment, then the exception will direct the script to `except:`, and the user will be alerted to the error.

In line 13 the sample size `self.N` is derived from the row dimension of `self.X`, while the number of covariates is derived from the column dimension of `self.X` in line 14. A check is made in line 15 to ensure that the regressand vector `self.y` is `self.N` long; if not, then the whole operation is terminated and an error message printed.

Next, we calculate the degrees of freedom `self.DegOfFree`; see line 19. Using the `numpy.mean` function, we then calculate the mean of the dependent variable `self.ybar` as well as the mean vector of the covariates `self.xbar`; see lines 20 and 21. In line 22 the matrix $\mathbf{X}^\top\mathbf{X}$ is formed, but because it is not necessary for output, it is not related to `self`; it is a local variable. The least-squares estimate $\hat{\beta}$ is assigned to `self.betaHats` in lines 23 and 24, and then used to calculate $\hat{y}$, which is assigned to `self.yHat` in line 25. Then, in line 26, $\hat{e}$ is assigned to `self.eHat`, and in line 27 we calculate the sum of squared residuals $\hat{e}^\top\hat{e}$, which is assigned to `self.RSS`. In line 28 we calculate an estimate of σ^2 and assign this to `self.sHatSquared`, and in line 29 we calculate an estimate of σ, assigning it to `self.seRegression`. In line 30 the first part of an estimate of the variance-covariance matrix $\sigma^2(\mathbf{X}^\top\mathbf{X})^{-1}$, that is, the inverse of `XpX`, is formed. Note that here we convert the `numpy` array to a `numpy` matrix because matrix inversion is easier to understand for `numpy` matrices. Line 31 just completes that exercise. In lines 32–35, the standard errors of the regression coefficient estimates are calculated; these are central to Student *t* tests.

In lines 36 and 37 the explained sum of squares `self.ESS` and the total sum of squares `self.TSS` are calculated. Lines 38–40 calculate some statistics of interest, for example, R^2 and calc *F* as well as Student *t* statistics.

To see how flexible classes can be, in the script `ClassTest.py`, we generate some artificial regression data in Python, which we then pass through the `Regression` class, and then access some of the output, specifically, `regressionObject.betaHats`.

```
from RegressionClass import Regression
import numpy
# Set up the data for the test using data
# simulated within Python.
# Set up the seed for replicability.
numpy.random.seed(123457)
N = 100
K =    3
# Set all of the coefficients to zero.
beta0 = numpy.zeros(K)
sigma = 1.
# Create the constant feature.
ones = numpy.ones(N)
# Create N(0,1) features.
X      = numpy.random.normal(0., 1., [N, K-1])
X      = numpy.column_stack((ones, X))
y      = numpy.dot(X, beta0) + sigma * numpy.random.normal(0., 1., N)
# Instantiates the Regression class.
regressionObject = Regression(y, X)
print "You can obviously improve on the format:\n"
print "Regression Coefficient Estimates:" + str(regressionObject.
    betaHats)
```

Listing 6.2: Python Script to Use `Regression` class

If you execute `python ClassTest.py` in a terminal window, then the following:

```
$ python ClassTest.py
You can obviously improve on the format:

Regression Coefficient Estimates:[ 0.18036748 -0.07007819 -0.08201033]
$
```

will appear in that terminal window. Obviously, this is not at all what the output would look like ideally, but you get the idea. In fact, you could create a method that would render the output in a nice format; we leave that as an exercise for you to complete.

6.3.5   Functional Programming

Another computing paradigm, *functional programming*, is a style of building computer programs. In functional programming, a problem is decomposed into a set of functions. The functions only take inputs and then produce outputs. Unlike in object-oriented programming, no internal state exists. Functional programming is really the opposite of object-oriented programming. Objects are bundles containing some internal state along with a collection of method calls that let you modify this state; programs consist of making the right set of state changes. Functional programming seeks to avoid state changes as much as possible and works with data flowing between functions.

Why is this interesting? In some other programming paradigms, such as object-oriented programming, the state of the computing system can change because other processes on the computer may affect the program you are running. In functional programming, correctly specified functions take a known input and produce an output. Thus, the output value of a function will always be the same given a particular input value. Mathematicians would claim that these are pure mathematical functions.

Functional programming is founded on the λ calculus developed by Alonzo Church in the 1930s in conjunction with the *Entscheidungsproblem*. In fact, in Python the word `lambda` is a keyword used when implementing functional programs.

Python `lambda`

Python allows the creation of small anonymous functions using the construct `lambda`. Even though the Python `lambda` construct is not the same as the lambda in functional programming, it is nonetheless a very powerful feature. Although `lambda` functions can be used wherever function objects are

required, they are restricted to a single expression. For example, consider the
following code:

```
>>> def f(x): return x ** 2
...
>>> g = lambda x: x ** 2
>>> print f(4.), g(4.)
16.0 16.0
>>> xList = range(0, 11)
>>> print filter(lambda x: x % 2 == 0, xList)
[0, 2, 4, 6, 8, 10]
>>> map(lambda i: i * i * i, range(0,5))
[0, 1, 8, 27, 64]
>>> reduce(lambda i, j: i + j, range(1, 10))
45
```

This code illustrates the difference between the standard function definition f
and the `lambda` function definition g. It also illustrates how you can use the
functions `filter()`, `map()`, and `reduce()`.

6.3.6 Programming Languages and Paradigms

Different programming languages have been developed with different programming paradigms in mind. For example, FORTRAN-77 is a procedural
programming language, whereas C++ is an object-oriented programming language. It is impossible to execute in FORTRAN many features available in C++.
Oracle Database as well as MySQL, PostgreSQL, and SQLite are all examples
of dialects of a declarative programming language. Lisp is the Big Daddy of
functional programming languages, but today many use a descendant Clojure,
yet others swear by Haskell. R is a functional programming language, too.

Python is an attractive programming language because it supports several
different programming paradigms: procedural, object-oriented, and functional.
Although Python is definitely not a declarative programming language, you
can use `sqlite3` as an API to SQL.

6.4 Graph Theory

By now, you will probably have noticed one of the hallmark features of computer science, namely, the relations among sets of discrete elements. Graph the-

ory is a branch of mathematics used to investigate the relations among a set of discrete elements. Graphs have been used successfully in many fields of science, for example, biology and physics as well as computer science. Graphs have also been used by social scientists, like economists and sociologists. Because graph theory is so important in computer science, in this section we present a brief introduction to the vocabulary and outline some of the problems and methods. Even though this material is unnecessary to understanding the material in Chapter 7 (so you could skip this section), we encourage you to read the section eventually.

A graph, denoted $\mathcal{G} = (\mathcal{V}, \mathcal{E})$, is a nonempty set $\mathcal{V}$ with a set $\mathcal{E}$ of two-element subsets of $\mathcal{V}$. The elements of $\mathcal{V}$ are referred to as *vertices* (or in network theory the *nodes*), and the elements of $\mathcal{E}$ are referred to as *edges* (or in network theory the *arcs*). In Figure 6.6, the set of vertices $\mathcal{V}$ is $\{v_1, v_2, v_3, v_4, v_5, v_6, \}$; the concept of edge is used to describe a link between two vertices. For example, in Figure 6.6, the set $\mathcal{E}$ contains $\{(v_1, v_2), (v_1, v_5), (v_2, v_3), (v_2, v_4), (v_2, v_5), (v_3, v_4), (v_4, v_5), (v_4, v_6)\}$. The vertices in Figure 6.6 could represent warehouses in a network: the distance from warehouse v_1 to warehouse v_2 is the same as the distance from warehouse v_2 to warehouse v_1. Because direction does not matter in this example, the graph is referred to as an *undirected graph*.

Edges that connect the same pair of distinct vertices are referred to as *multiple edges*. These will be important when investigating the Internet where one web page may link to another, but not the other way around. In short, with multiple edges direction matters.

A *self-loop* (sometimes called a *self-edge*) is an edge that connects a vertex to itself; this is illustrated three times in Figure 6.7—at nodes 1, 5, and 6. When a

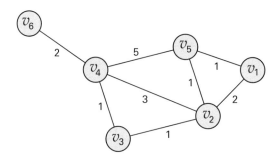

Figure 6.6: Example of Undirected Graph

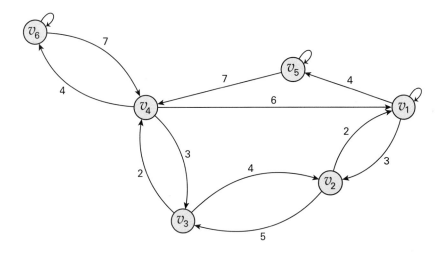

Figure 6.7: Example of Multigraph

vertex loops back to itself or if two or more edges connect the same two vertices, this is referred to as a *multigraph*, or sometimes a *pseudograph*. A graph like Figure 6.6, which has no multiple edges and no self-loops, is referred to as a *simple graph*.

In the graph of Figure 6.6, the distance from, say, v_1 to v_2 is the same as the distance from, say, v_2 to v_1—namely, 2 in the figure. When each vertex in a graph can be either an origin or a destination, or both, the graph is referred to as a *directed graph* or sometimes *digraph*. In short, in a directed graph, arrows of direction exist. Figure 6.7 depicts a multigraph where direction matters.

The number of vertices in a graph is referred to as its *cardinality* and de-noted $|\mathcal{V}|$; in Figure 6.6 the cardinality is 6. For undirected graphs, the number of edges from a particular vertex, say, vertex i, is referred to as its *degree* and de-noted $\deg(v_i)$; for example, in Figure 6.6 $\deg(v_1)$ is 2, $\deg(v_2)$ is 4, and so forth. In a directed graph, a distinction is made between the number of vertices that originate from a specific vertex and the number of edges that have that vertex as a destination—the *outdegree* and the *indegree* of a vertex, respectively. The sum of the outdegree and the indegree would then be the degree of that vertex. For instance, in Figure 6.7 the indegree of vertex 4 is 3, whereas the outdegree of that vertex is also 3, and the degree of vertex 4 is 6.

Many different ways can exist to represent the same information in a graph, a property referred to as *isomorphism*.

Another way to summarize a graph is using an *adjacency list*. For the graph in Figure 6.6, the adjacency list would be the following:

$$v_1 : v_2, v_5$$
$$v_2 : v_1, v_3, v_4, v_5$$
$$v_3 : v_2, v_4$$
$$v_4 : v_2, v_3, v_5, v_6$$
$$v_5 : v_1, v_2, v_4$$
$$v_6 : v_4.$$

Perhaps the most common way to summarize a graph is using an *adjacency matrix*, like the following one for the example in Figure 6.6:

$$\mathbf{A} = \begin{bmatrix} 0 & 1 & 0 & 0 & 1 & 0 \\ 1 & 0 & 1 & 1 & 1 & 0 \\ 0 & 1 & 0 & 1 & 0 & 0 \\ 0 & 1 & 1 & 0 & 1 & 1 \\ 1 & 1 & 0 & 1 & 0 & 0 \\ 0 & 0 & 0 & 1 & 0 & 0 \end{bmatrix}.$$

In the matrix $\mathbf{A}$, the rows correspond to the six vertices $v_1, v_2, v_3, v_4, v_5,$ and v_6 in order, and the six columns correspond to the six vertices $v_1, v_2, v_3, v_4, v_5,$ and v_6, again in order. Since vertex v_1 does not loop, it has a value of zero in the $(1,1)$ entry of $\mathbf{A}$, while vertex v_2 has edges with $v_1, v_3,$ and v_5, so it has a value of 1 in the $(1,2)$, $(2,3)$, and $(2,4)$ as well as the $(2,1)$, $(3,2)$, and $(4,2)$ elements of $\mathbf{A}$. Note that an undirected graph will always have a symmetric adjacency matrix. A directed graph, on the other hand, may have a nonsymmetric adjacency matrix.

As a practical matter, most large graphs are stored as adjacency lists because many nodes exist, but most nodes are not connected to each other. In short, an adjacency list is a parsimonious store.

In graph theory, a *walk* of length k is a sequence of vertices $v_1, v_2, \ldots, v_{k+1}$ such that v_i and v_{i+1} are adjacent to each i, often written as $v_i \sim v_{i+1}$. A *closed walk* of length k is a walk where $v_1 = v_{k+1}$. A *cycle* is a closed walk where none of the vertices repeats except for the first and the last. A *complete graph* on N vertices is a graph where $v_i \sim v_j$ for all $i \neq j$. In other words, every vertex is adjacent to every other vertex. A graph is connected if for all pairs (v_i, v_j) there exists a walk that begins at v_i and ends at v_j.

A path that starts at some point and ends at that same point, passing through each vertex exactly once, is referred to as an *Eulerian cycle*, in honor of Leonard Euler, who was first to consider this notion concerning the Seven Bridges of Königsberg.

6.4.1 Some Theorems

In fact, the following theorem tells you when an Eulerian cycle exists:

Theorem 1 *An undirected graph has an Eulerian cycle if and only if*

1) *every node degree is even;*

2) *the graph is connected (that is, there is a path from each node to each other node).*

Thus, according to this theorem, no Eulerian cycle exists in the graph of Figure 6.6 because not every node has an even degree. In fact, two of the vertices have odd degrees; to see this, sum the row values of the adjacency matrix; this yields 2, 4, 2, 4, 3, and 1.

Sociologists have used graphs to study *cliques*, groups of individuals who interact with each other more regularly and intensely than others. One definition of a clique is the following:

Definition 1 *A clique in a digraph is a subset $\mathcal{S}$ of the vertices satisfying the following three properties:*

(1) $\mathcal{S}$ *contains three or more vertices.*

(2) *If v_i and v_j are in $\mathcal{S}$, then v_i has access to v_j, and v_j has access to v_i.*

(3) *There is no larger subset containing $\mathcal{S}$ that satisfies properties 1 and 2.*

Although defining a clique is straightforward, identifying cliques in a large group is another matter. One way to identify a clique is to examine powers of the adjacency matrix. In fact, the following theorem provides an easy-to-use rule:

Theorem 2 *Let* $\mathbf{A}$ *denote the adjacency matrix of a digraph, and let* $\mathbf{C}$ *denote the matrix whose entries are defined by*

$$c_{ij} = \begin{cases} 1 & \text{if } [a_{ij}] = [a_{ji}] = 1; \\ 0 & \text{otherwise.} \end{cases}$$

A vertex v_i *belongs to a clique if and only if* (i, i) *element of* $\mathbf{A}^3$ *is nonzero.*

For example, consider the previous adjacency matrix

$$\mathbf{A} = \begin{bmatrix} 0 & 1 & 0 & 0 & 1 & 0 \\ 1 & 0 & 1 & 1 & 1 & 0 \\ 0 & 1 & 0 & 1 & 0 & 0 \\ 0 & 1 & 1 & 0 & 1 & 1 \\ 1 & 1 & 0 & 1 & 0 & 0 \\ 0 & 0 & 0 & 1 & 0 & 0 \end{bmatrix}.$$

whence

$$\mathbf{A}^2 = \begin{bmatrix} 2 & 1 & 1 & 2 & 1 & 0 \\ 1 & 4 & 1 & 2 & 2 & 1 \\ 1 & 1 & 2 & 1 & 2 & 1 \\ 2 & 2 & 1 & 4 & 1 & 0 \\ 1 & 2 & 2 & 1 & 3 & 1 \\ 0 & 1 & 1 & 0 & 1 & 1 \end{bmatrix} \quad \text{and} \quad \mathbf{A}^3 = \begin{bmatrix} 2 & 6 & 3 & 3 & 5 & 2 \\ 6 & 6 & 6 & 8 & 7 & 2 \\ 3 & 6 & 2 & 6 & 3 & 1 \\ 3 & 8 & 6 & 4 & 8 & 4 \\ 5 & 7 & 3 & 8 & 4 & 1 \\ 2 & 2 & 1 & 4 & 1 & 0 \end{bmatrix}.$$

Thus, vertex v_6 is not a member of the clique because the $(6, 6)$ element of $\mathbf{A}^3$ is zero.

7

Numerical Methods

THE MOST DIFFICULT tasks that a research assistant will face typically involve applying numerical methods. Some of the difficulties arise simply because many research assistants have little training (let alone experience) in numerical methods, but others arise because implementing numerical methods in a programming language can sometimes be complicated. Fortunately, Python has several useful modules and packages that are well-suited to implementing numerical methods with a minimum of bother.

In this chapter, we do four things: First, we describe how the discrete nature and finite precision of computers induce errors. Next, we illustrate how the algorithmic strategies described in Chapter 6 are used to solve problems involving numerical methods. Third, we use the tools from that chapter to get some notion of how efficient a particular algorithm is. Fourth, we outline some algorithms designed to solve specific problems commonly encountered by research assistants.

7.1   Round-off and Truncation Errors

In numerical analysis, two important and related notions exist. The first is *accuracy*, that is, how close a computed value is to its true value. The second is *precision*, that is, how closely individual computed values agree with one another.

Scientists often speak in terms of errors. For example, the *true error* is the difference between the true value and the approximated value, while the *absolute error* is just the absolute value of the true error. Also the *relative error* is the absolute error divided by the absolute value of the true value.

Now, round-off errors arise because computers cannot represent some numbers exactly, whereas truncation errors arise because computers cannot represent such numbers as infinity. Why? The CPUs of computers come in different sizes. For example, many old personal computers were 16-bit machines. A bit is a bin where a number, either a 0 or a 1, can be stored. Computers represent (encode) numbers in sequences of 0s and 1s, that is, in binary. This means that any number in base 10 is first converted to base 2 (and encoded in that form), before any computations are done. Thus, the integer -1 would appear as the sequence

$$1000000000000001$$

on a 16-bit computer. Note that the first bit (bin) is often used for the sign of the number: a 1 is the negative sign $-$, whereas a 0 is the positive sign $+$.[1] Hence, the integer 2 would appear as

$$0000000000000010$$

the integer 3 as

$$0000000000000011$$

and the integer 9 as

$$0000000000001001$$

Therefore, under this convention, the largest integer that can be represented on a 16-bit computer is $(2^{15} - 1)$:

$$0111111111111111$$

This largest number is referred to as *machine limit*. Anything larger than machine limit cannot fit in the available bins and will result in an *overflow*, which is typically a fatal error in any programming language. Most modern computers are 32-bit machines, at least, or even 64-bit machines. Hence, on a 32-bit computer the largest integer is $(2^{31} - 1)$ or $2,147,483,647$, and $(2^{63} - 1)$ or about 9.2234×10^{18} is the largest integer on a 64-bit computer.[2]

---

[1] In some programming languages (for instance, C) an unsigned integer type is possible.

[2] Locations in computer memory are addressed using integers. One reason new computers have a 64-bit architecture is because referencing more than about four gigabytes of memory requires integers that exceed $(2^{32} - 1)$, or $4,294,967,294$. The sign is not used to reference address locations.

Scientific computing is typically not conducted using integers. Instead, numbers having decimal places are used. Such real numbers are referred to as *floating-point numbers*, or *floats*, for short. However, the floating-point numbers that can be represented on a computer are really just a small subset of the real numbers.

Early programming languages, like FORTRAN, made a distinction between *single precision* and *double precision* when defining two different types of floating-point numbers. The word *double* points to the fact that a double-precision float uses twice as many bits as a single-precision float. For example, if a single-precision float required 32 bits, then its double-precision counterpart would require 64 bits. The extra bits increase not only the precision of the number (that is, the number of significant digits), but also the largest number that can be represented.

Python has adopted as default the IEEE double-precision format in which 8 bytes (64 bits) are used to represent a floating-point number.[3] Thus, any floating-point number f is decomposed into three basic parts: the sign $\pm$, the mantissa m, and the exponent e. In short,

$$f = \pm m \times 2^e.$$

As with integers, the sign $\pm$ is determined by the first bit; e is determined by an 11-bit binary number, from which $1,023$ is subtracted to get e; and the mantissa m is determined by a 52-bit binary number. Thus,

```
seeeeeeeeeeemmmmmmmmmmmmmmmmmmmmmmmmmmmmmmmmmmmmmmmmmmmmmmmmmmmmmmmmmmmmmmmmm
```

where s is the sign bit, e is the exponent, and m is the mantissa. In this way, all the bins are exhausted. Why is $1,023$ subtracted? Consider $(2^{11} - 1)$, which equals $2,047$. Now, $0, 1, 2, \ldots, 1,023$ involves $1,024$ integers, whereas $-1,023, -1,022, \ldots, -1$ involves another $1,023$ integers. Together, these exhaust the available spaces. On the Internet, several websites provide converters, so you can practice seeing how this conversion works; see, for example, http://www.binaryconvert.com.

---

[3]The Institute of Electrical and Electronics Engineers (IEEE, pronounced "I-triple-E") is a professional association dedicated to advancing technological innovation and excellence in electrical and electronic engineering, and a leading standards-making organization in the world; see http://en.wikipedia.org/wiki/Institute_of_Electrical_and_Electronics_Engineers.

The Python floating-point numbers are a subset of the rational numbers. The real numbers contain both the rational and the irrational numbers. In short, Python floating-point numbers are a proper subset of the rational numbers and therefore a small subset of the real numbers.

On a finite-precision computer, the upper bound on the relative error due to rounding in floating-point arithmetic is referred to as *machine epsilon*, or *macheps*, or sometimes *unit roundoff*. The value of machine epsilon is important in computer arithmetic in general, and in the field of numerical analysis in particular. On standard hardware, with double-precision floating-point arithmetic, machine epsilon is 2^{-52}, about 2.22×10^{-16}, in the base-10 number system.[4]

Note, too, that the spacing between two consecutive Python floating-point numbers is 2^{-1123}. Ken Judd refers to this number as *machine zero*; anything smaller than this number will result in an *underflow*, which is typically not a fatal error in any programming language (the number is set equal to zero).

Knowing the spacing in the neighborhood of a floating-point number can help avoid round-off errors, which can occur in several circumstances other than just storing numbers. First, when the number of computations is large, round-off errors can accumulate and become significant. Second, when adding a large number to a small number, the small number's mantissa is shifted to the right to have the same scale as the large number, and so digits are lost during this operation. For example, suppose instead of having a mantissa that is 52 digits wide, we only had a mantissa that is 16 digits wide. Consider adding 1.01×2^5 and $1.111111111111111 \times 2^{-5}$. Roughly speaking, these would be represented as

$$1.0100000000000000 \times 2^5$$

$$0.0000000001111111 \times 2^5$$

so the trailing ten 1s would be lost. Third, whenever the individual terms in a summation are larger in magnitude than the summation itself, something referred to as *smearing* occurs. Smearing also occurs when two large numbers of the same magnitude are used in a subtraction operation. For example, consider the series representation of e^x, which is

$$e^x = 1 + x + \frac{x^2}{2!} + \frac{x^3}{3!} + \cdots.$$

---

[4]From http://en.wikipedia.org/wiki/Machine_epsilon.

If x is positive, then no problem arises, but when x is negative, the second and third, fourth and fifth, and so on, terms differ in sign but can be quite large, so digits will be lost when the accumulation is done from left to right.

7.1.1 Classic Example of Smearing

To illustrate the importance of smearing, consider calculating the sample variance of a sequence of N sample observations $\{y_1, y_2, \dots, y_N\}$ concerning the random variable Y. An estimator of the population mean $\mathbb{E}(Y)$ based on the *analogy principle* involves using the sample analog of the population measure, namely, the sample mean

$$\bar{y} = \frac{1}{N} \sum_{n=1}^{N} y_n.$$

For additional information concerning this estimation strategy, see the book by Manski (1988). An analog estimator of the population variance $\mathbb{V}(Y)$ is

$$s^2 = \frac{1}{N} \sum_{n=1}^{N} (y_n - \bar{y})^2$$

$$= \frac{1}{N} \sum_{n=1}^{N} (y_n^2 - 2y_n\bar{y} + \bar{y}^2)$$

$$= \frac{1}{N} \left(\sum_{n=1}^{N} y_n^2 - 2N\bar{y}^2 + N\bar{y}^2 \right)$$

$$= \frac{1}{N} \left(\sum_{n=1}^{N} y_n^2 - N\bar{y}^2 \right)$$

$$= \frac{1}{N} \sum_{n=1}^{N} y_n^2 - \bar{y}^2.$$

At least two different algebraic ways exist to calculate s^2, one based on the sum of squares $\sum_{n=1}^{N}(y_n - \bar{y})^2$, the other based on a rewriting of that expression $\left[\left(\sum_{n=1}^{N} y_n^2 / N \right) - \bar{y}^2 \right]$. In terms of algebra, the two quantities are identical, but numerically, because of smearing, they are different. For example, consider the following R code:

```
1 > # Classic example of smearing: calculating the sample variance.
2 > rm(list = ls())
```

```
3  > set.seed(123457)
4  > # Use a sample of a billion to get rid of sampling variability.
5  > N <- 1000000000
6  > shift <- 1000000
7  > # N uniform random numbers between 1,000,000 and 1,000,001.
8  > y <- runif(N) + shift
9  > true.Mean <- shift + 0.5
10 > true.Variance <- 1/12
11 > builtin.Variance <- var(y)
12 > okay.Variance <- 1/N * sum((y - true.mean)^2)
13 > smearing.Variance <- ((1/N) * sum(y^2)) - ((sum(y)/N)^2)
14 > results <- list(truth   = true.Variance,
15 +                 builtin = builtin.Variance,
16 +                 okay    = okay.Variance,
17 +                 smear   = smearing.Variance)
18 > print(results)
19 $truth
20 [1] 0.08333333
21
22 $built.in
23 [1] 0.0833359
24
25 $okay
26 [1] 0.0833359
27
28 $smear
29 [1] 0.08288574
```

This R script illustrates the differences among different methods for calculating the sample variance. In this code, the first line is a comment describing the exercise, while the second cleans out R's memory. In line 3 the seed of the random number generator is set, while line 4 is a comment, and line 5 sets the sample size at 1 billion. The lower-bound support of the random variable is set in line 6, and the sample of vector y is assigned in line 8. The true population mean and variance are calculated in lines 9 and 10, respectively. In line 11 the built-in variance function var() is used to calculate the sample variance of y. In lines 12 and 13, two other methods are used to calculate the sample variance; lines 14–17 collect the results in the object results; and line 18 prints the results. Notice that both the built-in function var and the created function okay.Variance return similar estimates that are close to the population quantity, expected by the law of large numbers. On the other hand, the `smearing.Variance` function returns a value that is off by about 50 basis points, half a percent.

On his blog `http://www.johndcook.com/blog/standard_deviation/`, John D. Cook described accurate ways to calculate the sample variance. Chan, Golub, and LeVeque (1983) provided a rigorous analysis of the example, while in his book Monahan (2001) described the implications of these errors in various parts of statistics in general.

7.1.2 Summary

Round-off errors arise because computers cannot represent some numbers exactly. That is, round-off errors occur in calculations because computers are limited in the size of numbers as well as the precision with which those numbers can be represented. In addition, certain numerical calculations are sensitive to round-off errors. For example, ratios are particularly sensitive. Suppose the true value of x is 0.0001, but the absolute error is 10^{-5}, so an approximate value could be, say, either 0.00009 or 0.00011. Now, the reciprocal of 0.0001 is $10,000$, whereas the reciprocal of 0.00009 is $11,111.1111$, and the reciprocal of 0.00011 is $9,090.9091$. Suppose these were yearly stipends. Which one would you prefer?

Truncation errors result when an approximation is used in place of an exact mathematical expression. For example, consider calculating the exponential function e^x. Now, e^x can be represented by the following expansion in powers of x:

$$e^x = 1 + \sum_{n=1}^{\infty} \frac{x^n}{n!}.$$

In light of the preceding discussion, ∞ cannot be represented on a computer, so the series must be truncated at some point. When this happens, a difference is introduced between the true value of e^x and the approximated value. Errors of this sort can occur whenever you type the Python functions `math.exp(x)` or `math.log(x)` or `math.sqrt(x)`, for example, as well as others from the `math` module.

An Aside

Historically, typesetters found it easier to represent $e^{f(x)}$ by $\exp[f(x)]$ because if the exponent $f(x)$ had an exponent, the type size of the exponent of an exponent could become exceedingly small and hard to read. Therefore, we use the "exp" notation almost exclusively in the following text.

7.2 Linear Algebra

One of the most common problems encountered in numerical methods involves finding the solution to a system of K linear equations in K unknowns:

$$a_{11}x_1 + a_{12}x_2 + \cdots + a_{1K}x_K = b_1$$
$$a_{21}x_1 + a_{22}x_2 + \cdots + a_{2K}x_K = b_2$$
$$\vdots \qquad \vdots \qquad \qquad \vdots = \vdots$$
$$a_{K1}x_1 + a_{K2}x_2 + \cdots + a_{KK}x_K = b_K.$$

Here, the a_{ij}s and the b_ks are known numbers, whereas the x_ks are the unknowns. We seek $(\hat{x}_1, \hat{x}_2, \ldots, \hat{x}_K)$, where the left-hand side of each equation equals the right-hand side, that is, the *solution* to this system of linear equations.

Introducing the following $(K \times K)$ matrix $\mathbf{A}$ as well as $(K \times 1)$ vectors $\mathbf{x}$ and $\mathbf{b}$,

$$\mathbf{A} = \begin{bmatrix} a_{11} & a_{12} & \cdots & a_{1K} \\ a_{21} & a_{22} & \cdots & a_{2K} \\ \vdots & \vdots & \ddots & \vdots \\ a_{K1} & a_{K2} & \cdots & a_{KK} \end{bmatrix}, \quad \mathbf{x} = \begin{bmatrix} x_1 \\ x_2 \\ \vdots \\ x_K \end{bmatrix}, \quad \text{and} \quad \mathbf{b} = \begin{bmatrix} b_1 \\ b_2 \\ \vdots \\ b_K \end{bmatrix},$$

this linear system can be written in matrix notation as follows:

$$\mathbf{A}\mathbf{x} = \mathbf{b}. \tag{7.1}$$

If $\mathbf{A}$ is a nonsingular matrix, which means that no column of $\mathbf{A}$ can be expressed as a linear combination of the other columns of $\mathbf{A}$, then equation (7.1) has a unique solution, which mathematicians write as

$$\hat{\mathbf{x}} = \mathbf{A}^{-1}\mathbf{b}. \tag{7.2}$$

$\mathbf{A}^{-1}$ is referred to as the *inverse* of $\mathbf{A}$.

Because a computer is constrained to finite-precision arithmetic, the way in which you calculate the inverse of **A** on a computer matters. A simple example may make this clear. Suppose

$$\mathbf{A} = \begin{bmatrix} 1 & 1 \\ 1 & 1+\delta \end{bmatrix},$$

where δ does not equal zero. As you can see, the matrix **A** is nonsingular because its determinant is nonzero, that is,

$$|\mathbf{A}| = (1)(1+\delta) - (1)(1) = \delta \neq 0.$$

Now, the inverse of **A** is

$$\mathbf{A}^{-1} = \frac{1}{\delta} \begin{bmatrix} 1+\delta & -1 \\ -1 & 1 \end{bmatrix}.$$

Note, however, that as δ goes to zero, $\mathbf{A}^{-1}$ explodes. If δ is on the order of machine epsilon ε, then a nonsingular matrix will appear to be a singular one. Matrices of this sort are referred to as *ill-conditioned*. Seemingly equivalent ways of calculating the inverse of an ill-conditioned matrix can result in different results.

7.2.1 Condition Number

In general, it would be useful to have some sort of metric to decide whether a matrix is ill-conditioned. Unlike in the preceding example, however, determining whether a general matrix is ill-conditioned is not straightforward. For those who know some linear algebra, whether a matrix is ill-conditioned is closely related to whether that matrix is near-singular, which in turn is related to the singular values or the eigenvalues of the matrix. In short, the ratio of the absolute value of the largest eigenvalue to the absolute value of the smallest one provides some notion concerning how well-conditioned a matrix is. In fact, for normal matrices, the ratio of the absolute value of the largest eigenvalue to the absolute value of smallest eigenvalue of a matrix is referred to as the *condition number*.[5] In short, the smaller is the condition number, the better conditioned is the matrix. Clearly, the smallest condition number is 1, which obtains when matrices are proportional to the identity matrix. As a matrix becomes closer and closer to singular, the condition number gets larger and larger, eventually going to infinity when the matrix is singular.

At what point is a condition number too large to use numerical methods reliably? It depends on the computer, specifically, what machine epsilon is. One practical way to find an approximate value involves creating a matrix like $\mathbf{A}$, and calculating its inverse $\mathbf{A}^{-1}$ numerically. If $\mathbf{A}^{-1}$ is multiplied by $\mathbf{A}$, the identity matrix should be the result. When the identity matrix stops being returned, the inverse of δ is the condition number at which numerical problems are going to become an issue.

One rule of thumb says that one digit of accuracy in the solution is lost for every factor of 10 in the condition number. Thus, if the condition number were 1.23×10^5, about five digits of accuracy would be lost. How important this is depends on the accuracy of the underlying data. If the data are only accurate to 10^{-5}, then such a high condition number would be a problem. You should be wary of numerical results derived from matrices that have condition numbers near such upper bounds as well.

To demonstrate the practical importance of ill-conditioning, we examine a classic data set named the *Longley data* in honor of James W. Longley, who pointed out that different regression packages often yielded different answers: "With identical inputs, all except four programs produced outputs which differed from each other in every digit." (1967, 822) These differences obtained because different methods were used to solve the normal equations that define the least-squares estimates. The Longley data have a design matrix which, in a regression context, gives rise to normal equations that are extremely ill-conditioned—have a very large condition number. You can find the Longley

---

[5]Alternatively, more generally, the condition number is defined to be the ratio of the largest to the smallest singular values of the matrix. Going into the details of what singular values are would require knowing about the singular value decomposition (SVD), a topic more advanced than eigenvalues. To learn about the SVD, consult Golub and Van Loan (2013). Cleve B. Moler, one of the authors of LINPACK and EISPACK (FORTRAN libraries for numerical computing) and the inventor of MATLAB, created a film that used animation to depict the SVD; see the video on YouTube at https://www.youtube.com/watch?v=R9UoFyqJca8.

data in the R library of data, and calculate an estimate of the condition number
by executing the following instructions:

```
> require(stats)
> X <- data.matrix(longley[, 1:6])
> XpX <- t(X) %*% X
> kappa(XpX)
[1] 43018622
>
```

in the R console.

In the first line of this code, the R `stats` package is loaded, and in the next
line, the appropriate columns of the `longley` data matrix are assigned to the
matrix X. In the third line, the matrix $X^{\top}X$ is created, and in the fourth line, the
`kappa` function is used to calculate the condition number, which is $43,018,622$,
or 4.3018622×10^7. Given that the series in the Longley data are only known to
at most six significant digits, you can see why problems could arise.[6]

Introduced in conjunction with approximation theory (see Section 7.7), the
German mathematician David Hilbert proposed constructing a $(K \times K)$ matrix
$\mathbf{H}_K$ whose (i, j) element is defined as follows:

$$h_{ij} = \frac{1}{i+j-1} \quad i = 1, 2, \ldots, K; \; j = 1, 2, \ldots, K.$$

For example, when K is 4,

$$\mathbf{H}_4 = \begin{bmatrix} 1 & \frac{1}{2} & \frac{1}{3} & \frac{1}{4} \\ \frac{1}{2} & \frac{1}{3} & \frac{1}{4} & \frac{1}{5} \\ \frac{1}{3} & \frac{1}{4} & \frac{1}{5} & \frac{1}{6} \\ \frac{1}{4} & \frac{1}{5} & \frac{1}{6} & \frac{1}{7} \end{bmatrix}.$$

Named the *Hilbert matrix* in his honor, this matrix is the poster child for ill-
conditioning. Figure 7.1 presents a graph of the logarithm of the condition
numbers as K increases: according to this graph, an extra dimension increases
the condition number by a factor of 10. On the other hand, if the elements of a
$(K \times K)$ matrix $\mathbf{U}$ are generated by uniformly distributed random draws from
the $[0, 1]$ interval, then the average behavior of the condition number will be as
shown by the dashed line in Figure 7.1.

---

[6]If you add a column of 1s to the design matrix used above, the condition number will change,
but the new one will still be extremely large.

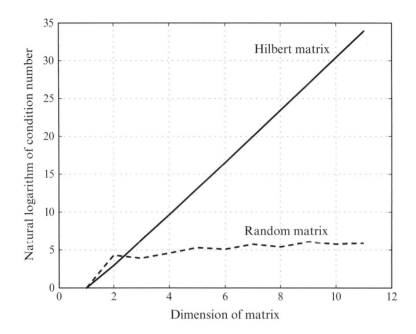

Figure 7.1: Condition Number versus Hilbert Matrix Dimension

To calculate the condition number using Python, do the following:

```
>>> import numpy
>>> numpy.random.seed(123457)
>>> uMatrix = numpy.random.uniform(0., 1., (100, 100))
>>> numpy.linalg.cond(uMatrix)
1163.8090503948172
>>>
```

The first instruction imports the `numpy` package, and the second instruction ensures that we are all starting at the same point. The third instruction generates a (100×100) matrix of random elements from the $[0, 1]$ interval and names it `uMatrix`, and the fourth instruction calculates the condition number of that matrix, which is 1163.8090503948172.

7.2.2   Solving a Linear System

In numerical analysis, in order to control round-off error and its interaction with the condition number of a matrix, you should never invert a matrix like **A** to solve for $\hat{\mathbf{x}}$. Instead, from linear algebra, note that $\mathbf{A}$ can be written as

$$\mathbf{A} = \mathbf{LU},$$

where $\mathbf{L}$ is a lower triangular matrix, while $\mathbf{U}$ is an upper triangular matrix; that is, all the elements above (below) the diagonal are zeros. This is known as the *LU decomposition*. To find $\hat{\mathbf{x}}$, note that

$$\mathbf{A}\hat{\mathbf{x}} = \mathbf{b}$$
$$\mathbf{LU}\hat{\mathbf{x}} = \mathbf{b}$$
$$\mathbf{L}\hat{\mathbf{z}} = \mathbf{b},$$

where $\hat{\mathbf{z}}$ equals $\mathbf{U}\hat{\mathbf{x}}$. This can be written out as

$$
\begin{aligned}
b_1 &= \ell_{11}\hat{z}_1 \\
b_2 &= \ell_{21}\hat{z}_1 + \ell_{22}\hat{z}_2 \\
\vdots &= \vdots \\
b_K &= \ell_{K1}\hat{z}_1 + \ell_{K2}\hat{z}_2 + \cdots + \ell_{KK}\hat{z}_K,
\end{aligned}
$$

so the elements of $\hat{\mathbf{z}}$ are found recursively as

$$
\begin{aligned}
\hat{z}_1 &= b_1/\ell_{11} \\
\hat{z}_2 &= (b_2 - \ell_{21}\hat{z}_1)/\ell_{22} = [b_2 - (\ell_{21}b_1/\ell_{11})]/\ell_{22} \\
\vdots &= \vdots \\
\hat{z}_K &= \left(b_K - \sum_{j=1}^{K-1} \ell_{Kj}\hat{z}_j\right)/\ell_{KK},
\end{aligned}
$$

which is referred to as *forward substitution*. Now, $\mathbf{U}\hat{\mathbf{x}} = \hat{\mathbf{z}}$, or

$$
\begin{aligned}
u_{11}\hat{x}_1 + u_{12}\hat{x}_2 + \cdots + u_{1K}\hat{x}_K &= \hat{z}_1 \\
u_{22}\hat{x}_2 + \cdots + u_{2K}\hat{x}_K &= \hat{z}_2 \\
\vdots &= \vdots \\
u_{KK}\hat{x}_K &= \hat{z}_K
\end{aligned}
$$

from which the elements of $\hat{\mathbf{x}}$ are found recursively using *back substitution*. Namely, solve for $\hat{x}_K$ first, then $\hat{x}_{K-1}$, and so forth:

$$\hat{x}_K = \hat{z}_K / u_{KK}$$
$$\hat{x}_{K-1} = (\hat{z}_{K-1} - u_{K-1,K}\hat{x}_K)/u_{K-1,K-1}$$
$$\vdots = \vdots$$
$$\hat{x}_1 = (\hat{z}_1 - \sum_{j=2}^{K} u_{1j}\hat{x}_j)/u_{11}.$$

Thus, consider the following example:

$$\mathbf{A} = \begin{bmatrix} 2 & 0 \\ 1 & 1 \end{bmatrix} \quad \text{and} \quad \mathbf{b} = \begin{bmatrix} 1 \\ 1 \end{bmatrix}.$$

In Python, the following code,

```
>>> import numpy
>>> A = numpy.array([[2, 0], [1, 1]])
>>> b = numpy.array([[1], [1]])
>>> xHat = numpy.linalg.solve(A, b)
>>> xHat
array([[ 0.5],
       [ 0.5]])
>>>
```

would implement the LU decomposition as well as forward substitution and back substitution to yield the solution $\hat{\mathbf{x}} = (0.5, 0.5)^\top$. As you can see, this method is very simple to implement.

We have described how the most common method is implemented. Others, of course, exist as well. Perhaps the best reference for numerical linear algebra is Golub and Van Loan (2013). Algorithmically, the complexity of using the LU decomposition to solve a linear system of equations is $\mathcal{O}(K^3)$.

7.2.3 Cholesky Decomposition

If a $(K \times K)$ matrix $\mathbf{A}$ is symmetric (so $\mathbf{A}^\top = \mathbf{A}$) and positive definite (all its eigenvalues are strictly positive), then the LU decomposition has a special form. In particular, the matrix $\mathbf{A}$ can be written as

$$\mathbf{F}\mathbf{F}^\top = \mathbf{A},$$

where $\mathbf{F}$ is a lower triangular matrix; that is, all the values above its diagonal are zero. In short,

$$\mathbf{FF}^\top \equiv \begin{bmatrix} f_{11} & 0 & 0 & \cdots & 0 \\ f_{21} & f_{22} & 0 & \cdots & 0 \\ \vdots & \vdots & \vdots & \ddots & \vdots \\ f_{K1} & f_{K2} & f_{K3} & \cdots & f_{KK} \end{bmatrix} \begin{bmatrix} f_{11} & f_{21} & f_{31} & \cdots & f_{K1} \\ 0 & f_{22} & 0 & \cdots & f_{K2} \\ \vdots & \vdots & \vdots & \ddots & \vdots \\ 0 & 0 & 0 & \cdots & f_{KK} \end{bmatrix}$$

$$= \begin{bmatrix} a_{11} & a_{12} & a_{13} & \cdots & a_{1K} \\ a_{12} & a_{22} & a_{23} & \cdots & a_{2K} \\ \vdots & \vdots & \vdots & \ddots & \vdots \\ a_{1K} & a_{1K} & a_{1K} & \cdots & a_{KK} \end{bmatrix} = \mathbf{A}.$$

This decomposition is known as the *Cholesky decomposition*. Under the conditions assumed, the Cholesky decomposition always exists and is unique. Furthermore, computing the Cholesky decomposition is more efficient than computing other LU decompositions; it is about twice as fast. The Cholesky decomposition is also numerically more stable than other LU decompositions. Implementing the Cholesky decomposition in single precision attains the same degree of accuracy as implementing the LU decomposition in double precision.[7] Put another way, if the Cholesky and the other LU decompositions were all implemented in Python, then the Cholesky would be twice as accurate as the other LU decompositions. In short, when a matrix is symmetric as well as positive definite, use the Cholesky decomposition rather than another LU decomposition.

When does such a situation arise? Consider the following linear regression model, introduced on page 267:

$$Y = \mathbf{X}\beta + U.$$

In this model, $Y = (Y_1, Y_2, \ldots, Y_N)^\top$, $\mathbf{X} = [\mathbf{X}_1, \mathbf{X}_2, \ldots, \mathbf{X}_K]$ with $\mathbf{X}_k = (X_{1,k}, X_{2,k}, \ldots, X_{N,k})^\top$, $\beta = (\beta_1, \beta_2, \ldots, \beta_K)^\top$, and $U = (U_1, U_2, \ldots, U_N)^\top$. Here, the dependent variable Y and the covariates $\mathbf{X}$ are observed, while the U is an unobserved random variable, and the β is unknown. Researchers seek to estimate β using the information in $\mathbf{X}$ and Y. Perhaps the most commonly used

---

[7]Paarsch found this last result in his lecture notes from graduate school for a course on computing in statistics that was taught by Gene H. Golub in the autumn of 1982.

empirical strategy to estimate a regression model is the method of least squares. Least-squares estimation involves choosing β to minimize the sum of squared residuals $S(\beta)$, which can be written in matrix notation as

$$S(\beta) \equiv (Y - X\beta)^\top (Y - X\beta) = Y^\top Y - 2\beta^\top X^\top Y + \beta^\top X^\top X\beta.$$

In particular, the method involves decomposing the observed Y into two parts, one that can be explained by the X and the other that is orthogonal to the X, unexplained by the X. Specifically, the least-squares estimator is the solution to the following optimization problem:

$$\min_{\beta} S(\beta) = \min_{\beta} Y^\top Y - 2\beta^\top X^\top Y + \beta^\top X^\top X\beta$$

whence derive the following first-order conditions of the minimum of $S(\beta)$ with respect to β:

$$\nabla_\beta S(\hat{\beta}) = -2X^\top Y + 2X^\top X\hat{\beta} = 0_K.$$

These linear equations, which we referred to as the normal equations in Chapter 5, define the least-squares estimator $\hat{\beta}$:

$$(X^\top X)\hat{\beta} = X^\top Y$$

where the matrix $(X^\top X)$ is symmetric as well as positive definite. Hence, we can write the normal equations as

$$(X^\top X)\hat{\beta} = X^\top Y$$
$$(FF^\top)\hat{\beta} = X^\top Y.$$

As with the LU decomposition, we can then apply forward substitution and back substitution to solve for the least-squares estimator $\hat{\beta}$. The Cholesky decomposition is also $\mathcal{O}(K^3)$, but uses about one-half of the resources.

To use the Cholesky decomposition in Python, do the following:

```
>>> import numpy
>>> A = numpy.array([[1., 1.],[1., 2.]])
>>> F = numpy.linalg.cholesky(A)
>>> F
array([[ 1.,   0.],
       [ 1.,   1.]])
>>>
```

7.3 Finding the Zero of a Function

Often, the solution to an equation is defined only implicitly because the function is nonlinear. For example, the first-order condition for a maximum (or minimum) at the point $\hat{x}$ is

$$g(\hat{x}) = 0,$$

where no closed-form solution need exist. If the function $g(x)$ is reasonably well-behaved (typically, this means that it is a continuous, monotonic function of x), then a number of methods exist to solve for $g(x)$ equal to zero.

7.3.1 Bisection Method

Perhaps the most commonly known and intuitively obvious method for finding a zero of a continuous, monotonic function is the method of *bisection*. This method is easy to understand. To begin, we introduce $\underline{x}_0$ and $\overline{x}_0$, which are the lower and upper values, that bound $\hat{x}$, so $g(\underline{x}_0)g(\overline{x}_0)$ is negative because of monotonicity.[8] Thus, $\hat{x} \in [\underline{x}_0, \overline{x}_0]$. Clearly, you need to use care in defining $\underline{x}_0$ and $\overline{x}_0$.

Now, construct a new set of lower and upper bounds $\underline{x}_1$, which equals $\underline{x}_0$; and $\overline{x}_1$, which equals $[(\underline{x}_0 + \overline{x}_0)/2]$. Evaluate $g(\cdot)$ at the new lower and upper bounds. Suppose $g(\underline{x}_1)$ is positive. If $g(\overline{x}_1)$ is negative, then set $\underline{x}_2$ equal to $\underline{x}_1$ and set $\overline{x}_2$ equal to $[(\underline{x}_1 + \overline{x}_1)/2]$. On the other hand, if, say, $g(\overline{x}_2)$ is positive, when $g(\overline{x}_1)$ was negative, then set $\underline{x}_2$ equal to the new $\overline{x}_2$ and update $\overline{x}_2$ to be $[(\underline{x}_2 + \overline{x}_1)/2]$. Continue to iterate until $|\underline{x}_r - \overline{x}_r|$ is less than some tolerance, ε equal to 10^{-4}, for example.[9]

To see how this would work in practice, consider the function

$$g(x) = \log(x),$$

which we know has solution $g(\hat{x})$ equals zero when $\hat{x}$ equals 1. Let $\underline{x}_0 = 0.4$ and $\overline{x}_0 = 2.2$. Table 7.1 presents the values of $\underline{x}_r$ and $\overline{x}_r$ as the algorithm proceeds, and Figure 7.2 depicts the first few iterates on the path to the solution.

---

[8] The function $g(x)$ is assumed to cross the abscissa once, so it must be positive at one end of the interval and negative at the other. Consequently, the product of the function at the ends of the interval must be negative.

[9] Notation alert: This ε is different from the one used to refer to machine limit. Because the Greek and Roman alphabets are limited in size, we must reuse letters here, and again several times later.

r	$\underline{x}_r$	$\overline{x}_r$
0	0.4000	2.2000
1	0.4000	1.3000
2	0.8500	1.3000
3	0.8500	1.0750
4	0.9625	1.0750

Table 7.1: Bisection Applied to $\log(x) = 0$

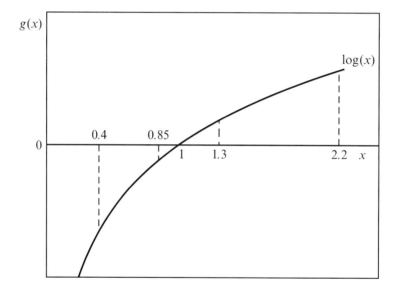

Figure 7.2: Solving $\log(x) = 0$ Using the Method of Bisection

Although the method of bisection works fairly well in this example, the method is the poster child for why intuition is a bad way in which to derive numerical methods. For a particular tolerance, bisection can take some time to achieve convergence. In addition, it does not generalize to higher dimensions.

7.3.2 Newton-Raphson Method

Another method, which is more sophisticated than the bisection method and which is used often in numerical optimization, is sometimes referred to as

Newton's method. We refer to it as the *Newton-Raphson method*, in honor of both Sir Isaac Newton and Joseph Raphson who invented it.

The Newton-Raphson method involves finding successively better approximations to $\hat{x}$, the root of $g(x)$; the method is relatively simple to implement, provided that the derivative of the function can be calculated reliably.

Consider $g(x)$, any differentiable, monotonic function of x, where $g(\hat{x})$ equal to zero exists. From Taylor's theorem, we can write $g(x)$ as

$$g(x) = g(x_0) + g'(x_0)(x - x_0) + R_2$$

where x_0 is a starting point contained in the interval $[\underline{x}_0, \overline{x}_0]$ as defined, and R_2 is a remainder term. If we ignore R_2, because it will be negligible near the solution, and impose the solution $g(x)$ equal to zero, then we can solve the preceding equation for x. In particular,

$$g(x_0) + g'(x_0)(x - x_0) = 0$$
$$g'(x_0)(x - x_0) = -g(x_0)$$
$$(x - x_0) = -[g'(x_0)]^{-1}g(x_0)$$
$$x = x_0 - [g'(x_0)]^{-1}g(x_0).$$

In general, the recursion relation is

$$x_{r+1} = x_r - [g'(x_r)]^{-1}g(x_r) \qquad r = 0, 1, \dots .$$

If $g(x)$ is a well-behaved function, and if x_0 is in a neighborhood of the solution $\hat{x}$, then the recursion will converge to $\hat{x}$. In symbols,

$$\lim_{r \to \infty} x_r = \hat{x}.$$

We present the iterative solution starting from x_0 equal to 2 in Table 7.2; Figure 7.3 illustrates the path to the solution. As you can see, convergence to 1 at four digits is attained in four iterations. How many times you must iterate depends on the function and the starting point. The numbers for this example were computed using the following Python script:

```
# Script:   NewtonRaphson.py
# Author:   Harry J. Paarsch
# Date:     14 July 2013
""" This program uses the Newton-Raphson method to solve
    for the zero of the function log(x).
```

r	x_r	$g(x_r)$	$g'(x_r)$	x_{r+1}
0	2.0000	0.6931	0.5000	0.6137
1	0.6137	−0.4882	1.6294	0.9133
2	0.9133	−0.0906	1.0949	0.9961
3	0.9961	−0.0039	1.0039	1.0000
4	1.0000	−0.0000	1.0000	1.0000

Table 7.2: Newton-Raphson Iterations Applied to $\log(x) = 0$

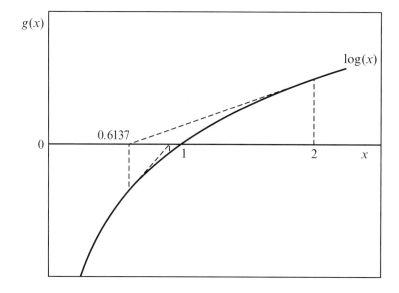

Figure 7.3: Solving $\log(x) = 0$ Using Newton-Raphson Method

```
"""
import math
xnot    = 2.
epsilon = 0.000001
delta   = 0.000001
gnot    = math.log(xnot)
diff    = xnot
norm    = math.fabs(gnot)
iguess  = 0
maxIter = 100
```

```
print "At guess %.4f for x^*, the function is %.4f.\n" %\
        (xnot, gnot)
print "Guess\txnot\tFunc\tSlope\txhat\n"
while ( (norm > epsilon) & (diff > delta) & (iguess < maxIter) ):
    gnot = math.log(xnot)
    hnot = 1./xnot
    xhat = xnot - (gnot/hnot)
    print "%3d\t%.4f\t%.4f\t%.4f\t%.4f" % \
          (iguess, xnot, gnot, hnot, xhat)
    ghat = math.log(xhat)
    diff = math.fabs(xhat-xnot)
    norm = math.fabs(ghat)
    xnot = xhat
    iguess = iguess + 1

iguess = iguess - 1
print "\nThe estimate of  x^*  is %.4f." % xhat
print "At that value the function is %.4f." % ghat
print "%d iterations were used to calculate this estimate." % iguess
```

Listing 7.1: Python Script for Newton-Raphson Example

Sometimes, too, it can take many iterations to attain convergence. Note that a poor starting point can also cause Newton's method to blow up, even when the function $g(x)$ appears nicely behaved. That is, the monotonicity of $g(x)$ in x is not a sufficient condition to guarantee that the Newton-Raphson method is well behaved. For example, let x_0 equal 10 in this example. Listing 7.2 shows what happens in the output file Newton.out,

```
At guess 10.0000 for x^*, the function is 2.3026.

Guess xnot  Func  Slope xhat

  0 10.0000 2.3026  0.1000  -13.0259
```

Listing 7.2: Output of NewtonRaphson.py

and Listing 7.3 shows the errors that would appear in the terminal window:

```
Traceback (most recent call last):
  File "Code/Newton.py", line 17, in <module>
    ghat = math.log(xhat)
ValueError: math domain error
```

Listing 7.3: Error Log for NewtonRaphson.py

7.4   Solving Systems of Nonlinear Equations

Solving systems of nonlinear equations arises naturally in a number of situations. For example, in economics, a model of an economy is typically represented as a nonlinear system of equations, in which case the solution is often an equilibrium price vector; Judd (1998) provided a discussion of various other situations in economics. In optimization, the nonlinear system of equations could be the first-order conditions for the extremum of an objective function.

7.4.1   Newton-Raphson Method

One natural way to solve for K nonlinear equations in K unknowns involves generalizing the Newton-Raphson method, except now consider $\mathbf{g}(\mathbf{x})$, a $(K \times 1)$ vector of real-valued functions of $\mathbf{x} = (x_1, x_2, \ldots, x_K)^\top$, another $(K \times 1)$ vector. In symbols,

$$\mathbf{g}(\mathbf{x}) \equiv \begin{bmatrix} g_1(x_1, x_2, \ldots, x_K) \\ g_2(x_1, x_2, \ldots, x_K) \\ \vdots \\ g_K(x_1, x_2, \ldots, x_K) \end{bmatrix} = \begin{bmatrix} 0 \\ 0 \\ \vdots \\ 0 \end{bmatrix} \equiv \mathbf{0}_K. \tag{7.3}$$

From a numerical standpoint, the easiest way to proceed is again to linearize $\mathbf{g}(\mathbf{x})$ about some initial point $\mathbf{x}_0 = (x_{1,0}, x_{2,0}, \ldots, x_{K,0})^\top$. How does that work?

To begin, consider expanding the first equation $g_1(x_1, x_2, \ldots, x_K)$ in a Taylor series expansion about $\mathbf{x}_0$. Thus,

$$\begin{aligned} g_1(x_1, x_2, \ldots, x_K) =& g_1(x_{1,0}, x_{2,0}, \ldots, x_{K,0}) + \\ & \frac{\partial g_1(x_{1,0}, x_{2,0}, \ldots, x_{K,0})}{\partial x_1}(x_1 - x_{1,0}) + \\ & \frac{\partial g_1(x_{1,0}, x_{2,0}, \ldots, x_{K,0})}{\partial x_2}(x_2 - x_{2,0}) + \cdots + \\ & \frac{\partial g_1(x_{1,0}, x_{2,0}, \ldots, x_{K,0})}{\partial x_K}(x_K - x_{K,0}) + R_{1,2}, \end{aligned}$$

where $R_{1,2}$ represents the sum of the second- and higher-order remainder terms that arise when approximating $g_1(\cdot)$ by a hyperplane. Doing this for each of the other equations $k = 2, 3, \ldots, K$ yields

$$\mathbf{g}(\mathbf{x}) = \mathbf{g}(\mathbf{x}_0) + \mathbf{J}(\mathbf{x}_0)(\mathbf{x} - \mathbf{x}_0) + \mathbf{R}_2, \tag{7.4}$$

where

$$
\mathbf{J}(\mathbf{x}) =
\begin{bmatrix}
\dfrac{\partial g_1(\mathbf{x})}{\partial x_1} & \dfrac{\partial g_1(\mathbf{x})}{\partial x_2} & \cdots & \dfrac{\partial g_1(\mathbf{x})}{\partial x_K} \\
\dfrac{\partial g_2(\mathbf{x})}{\partial x_1} & \dfrac{\partial g_2(\mathbf{x})}{\partial x_2} & \cdots & \dfrac{\partial g_2(\mathbf{x})}{\partial x_K} \\
\vdots & \vdots & \ddots & \vdots \\
\dfrac{\partial g_K(\mathbf{x})}{\partial x_1} & \dfrac{\partial g_K(\mathbf{x})}{\partial x_2} & \cdots & \dfrac{\partial g_K(\mathbf{x})}{\partial x_K}
\end{bmatrix},
\tag{7.5}
$$

with $\mathbf{J}$ being a mnemonic for *Jacobian*, as in Jacobian matrix.

Ignoring the remainder $\mathbf{R}_2$ vector and setting the right-hand side of equation (7.4) equal to $\mathbf{0}_K$, we can then use linear algebra to solve for a new $\mathbf{x}$, which we denote $\mathbf{x}_1$. That is, in symbols,

$$
\begin{aligned}
\mathbf{0}_K &= \mathbf{g}(\mathbf{x}_0) + \mathbf{J}(\mathbf{x}_0)(\mathbf{x} - \mathbf{x}_0) \\
-\mathbf{J}(\mathbf{x}_0)(\mathbf{x} - \mathbf{x}_0) &= \mathbf{g}(\mathbf{x}_0) \\
(\mathbf{x} - \mathbf{x}_0) &= - \left[\mathbf{J}(\mathbf{x}_0) \right]^{-1} \mathbf{g}(\mathbf{x}_0) \\
\mathbf{x} &= \mathbf{x}_0 - \left[\mathbf{J}(\mathbf{x}_0) \right]^{-1} \mathbf{g}(\mathbf{x}_0) \equiv \mathbf{x}_1.
\end{aligned}
$$

Under certain conditions,

$$
\mathbf{x}_{r+1} = \mathbf{x}_r - \left[\mathbf{J}(\mathbf{x}_r) \right]^{-1} \mathbf{g}(\mathbf{x}_r) \qquad r = 0, 1, \ldots.
$$

will converge to the point $\hat{\mathbf{x}}$, which satisfies equation (7.3).

Because solving nonlinear equations builds on numerical linear algebra, some practioners advocate using other numerical methods that have been successful in solving linear equations under certain conditions. Two such methods are the *Jacobi method* and the *Gauss-Seidel method*.

7.4.2 Jacobi Method

In numerical linear algebra, the Jacobi method is an algorithm for approximating the solution to a system of linear equations. It is named in honor of the German mathematician Carl Gustav Jakob Jacobi.

Consider the system

$$
\mathbf{A}\mathbf{x} = \mathbf{b}.
$$

The ith row

$$
a_{i1}x_1 + a_{i2}x_2 + \cdots + a_{i,i-1}x_{i-1} + a_{ii}x_i + a_{i,i+1}x_{i+1} + \cdots + a_{iK}x_K = b_i
$$

can be written as

$$x_i = \frac{1}{a_{ii}}(b_i - a_{i1}x_1 - a_{i2}x_2 - \cdots - a_{i,i-1}x_{i-1} - a_{i,i+1}x_{i+1} - \cdots - a_{iK}x_K). \quad (7.6)$$

Given an initial vector x_0, we can use the information in the guess to update x_i, equation by equation, until we have x_1, and then do it again and again. Convergence may obtain. In general, under the Jacobi method (as well as the Gauss-Seidel method),

$$\hat{x} = P\hat{x} + q$$
$$(I_K - P)\hat{x} = q$$
$$\hat{x} = (I_K - P)^{-1}q.$$

If the spectral radius of P (which is the largest eigenvalue of the matrix P) is less than 1, then $(I - P)^{-1}$ exists, and the infinite sum in the expression

$$(I_K - P)^{-1} = I_K + P + P^2 + \cdots = \sum_{i=0}^{\infty} P^i$$

converges. Of course, calculating the eigenvalues of P requires some computational effort. Are there any shortcuts? One of the maintained assumptions of the Jacobi method is that the matrix in question possesses the property of *diagonal dominance*: for each row of the matrix, the absolute value of the diagonal element exceeds the sum of absolute values of the other elements in that row—a strong restriction indeed.

Why is this procedure interesting? Before electronic computers, calculations were carried out by humans. Inverting matrices that are (10×10) or more is time consuming and error prone. On the other hand, solving one equation in one unknown is relatively straightforward.

In matrix notation, the preceding calculations can be carried out by introducing three matrices where

$$A = D - L - U$$

with

$$D = \begin{bmatrix} a_{11} & 0 & 0 & \cdots & 0 \\ 0 & a_{22} & 0 & \cdots & 0 \\ 0 & 0 & a_{33} & \cdots & 0 \\ \vdots & \vdots & \vdots & \ddots & \vdots \\ 0 & 0 & 0 & \cdots & a_{KK} \end{bmatrix}$$

and

$$
\mathbf{L} = \begin{bmatrix} 0 & 0 & \cdots & 0 & 0 \\ -a_{21} & 0 & \cdots & 0 & 0 \\ -a_{31} & -a_{32} & \cdots & 0 & 0 \\ \vdots & \vdots & \ddots & \vdots & \vdots \\ -a_{K1} & -a_{K2} & \cdots & -a_{K,K-1} & 0 \end{bmatrix}
$$

and

$$
\mathbf{U} = \begin{bmatrix} 0 & -a_{12} & -a_{1,3} & \cdots & -a_{1,K} \\ 0 & 0 & -a_{2,3} & \cdots & -a_{2,K} \\ \vdots & \vdots & \vdots & \ddots & \vdots \\ 0 & 0 & \cdots & 0 & -a_{K-1,K} \\ 0 & 0 & \cdots & 0 & 0 \end{bmatrix}.
$$

Note that the **L** and **U** defined here are slightly different from those defined in Section 7.2.2: the diagonal elements of both **L** and **U** are all zeros, and the nonzero elements below and above the diagonals are the negative of their counterparts introduced previously. Thus,

$$
\mathbf{Ax} = (\mathbf{D} - \mathbf{L} - \mathbf{U})\mathbf{x} = \mathbf{b},
$$

so

$$
\mathbf{Dx} = (\mathbf{L} + \mathbf{U})\mathbf{x} + \mathbf{b}
$$
$$
\mathbf{x} = \mathbf{D}^{-1}(\mathbf{L} + \mathbf{U})\mathbf{x} + \mathbf{D}^{-1}\mathbf{b} \equiv \mathbf{Mx} + \mathbf{c}.
$$

Now, **c**, the vector $\mathbf{D}^{-1}\mathbf{b}$, and **M**, the matrix $[\mathbf{D}^{-1}(\mathbf{L} + \mathbf{U})]$, need only be calculated once, so

$$
\mathbf{x}_{r+1} = \mathbf{Mx}_r + \mathbf{c} \quad r = 0, 1, \ldots
$$

Continue until, say,

$$
\frac{\|\mathbf{x}_{r+1} - \mathbf{x}_r\|_2}{\|\mathbf{x}_r\|_2} < \varepsilon
$$

where ε could be 10^{-8}. We could also stop when there are no differences in, say, the eighth decimal place of each element of the approximate solution.[10]

---

[10]For the vector $\mathbf{x} = (x_1, x_2, \ldots, x_K)$, the Euclidean distance is defined as follows:

$$
\|\mathbf{x}\|_2 = \sqrt{\sum_{k=1}^{K} x_k^2}.
$$

7.4.3   Gauss-Seidel Method

The Gauss-Seidel method is a refinement of the Jacobi method in the sense that information from elements of the iterate already solved is used to find an approximate solution to the next element of the iterate. Consider equation (7.6); for the ith variate, $(i-1)$ previous candidate solutions have already been calculated at iteration $(r+1)$, whereas $(K-i)$ remain to be solved. Let's distinguish between the rth and $(r+1)^{st}$ iterates by placing an extra subscript after a comma. Hence, a Gauss-Seidel iteration would involve

$$x_{i,r+1} = \frac{1}{a_{ii}} \left(b_i - \sum_{j=1}^{i-1} a_{j1} x_{j,r+1} - \sum_{j=i+1}^{K} a_{j1} x_{j,r} \right), \tag{7.7}$$

where $i = 1, 2, \ldots, K$ and $r = 0, 1, \ldots$. In matrix notation,

$$(\mathbf{D} - \mathbf{L})\mathbf{x}_{r+1} = \mathbf{U}\mathbf{x}_r + \mathbf{b}$$
$$\mathbf{x}_{r+1} = (\mathbf{D} - \mathbf{L})^{-1}\mathbf{U}\mathbf{x}_r + (\mathbf{D} - \mathbf{L})^{-1}\mathbf{b}$$
$$\mathbf{x}_{r+1} \equiv \mathbf{N}\mathbf{x}_r + \mathbf{d} \quad r = 0, 1, \ldots.$$

That is, $\mathbf{d}$, the vector $(\mathbf{D} - \mathbf{L})^{-1}\mathbf{b}$, and $\mathbf{N}$, the matrix $(\mathbf{D} - \mathbf{L})^{-1}\mathbf{U}$, need only be calculated once.

To see how this would work in practice, consider the following numerical example:

$$5x_1 - 2x_2 + 3x_3 = -1$$
$$-3x_1 + 9x_2 + x_3 = 2$$
$$2x_1 - x_2 - 7x_3 = 3.$$

The Euclidean distance is sometimes referred to as the L_2 *distance*. Other norms exist as well. One commonly used alternative is the L_1 norm, or L_1 distance, sometimes called the *Manhattan distance*, or the *taxi-cab distance*, a name that derives from the distance a taxi would drive on a rectangular street grid to get from the origin to the point (x_1, x_2) on the plane.

$$\|\mathbf{x}\|_1 = \sum_{k=1}^{K} |x_k|.$$

The L_p norm is defined by

$$\|\mathbf{x}\|_p = \left(\sum_{k=1}^{K} |x_k|^p \right)^{\frac{1}{p}}.$$

For this example,

$$\mathbf{A} = \begin{bmatrix} 5 & -2 & 3 \\ -3 & 9 & 1 \\ 2 & -1 & -7 \end{bmatrix} \quad \text{and} \quad \mathbf{b} = \begin{bmatrix} -1 \\ 2 \\ 3 \end{bmatrix},$$

so

$$\hat{\mathbf{x}} = \mathbf{A}^{-1}\mathbf{b} = \begin{bmatrix} 0.18611987 \\ 0.33123028 \\ -0.42271293 \end{bmatrix}$$

with

$$\mathbf{D} = \begin{bmatrix} 5 & 0 & 0 \\ 0 & 9 & 0 \\ 0 & 0 & -7 \end{bmatrix}, \mathbf{L} = \begin{bmatrix} 0 & 0 & 0 \\ 3 & 0 & 0 \\ -2 & 1 & 0 \end{bmatrix}, \quad \text{and} \quad \mathbf{U} = \begin{bmatrix} 0 & -2 & 3 \\ 0 & 0 & 1 \\ 0 & 0 & -7 \end{bmatrix}.$$

Starting from an initial guess $\mathbf{x}_0$ equal to $\mathbf{0}_3$, we collect the first six iterations in Table 7.3. Notice that the Gauss-Seidel method yields an estimate that is identical to the truth (row ∞ in the table) in the first five decimal places, whereas the Jacobi method is only identical to the truth in the first three decimal places. This may suggest that the Gauss-Seidel method always dominates the Jacobi method, which is unfortunately false. Examples exist where the Jacobi method dominates the Gauss-Seidel method.

r	Jacobi	Gauss-Seidel
1	$(-0.200000, 0.222222, -0.428571)$	$(-0.200000, 0.155556, -0.507937)$
2	$(\ 0.146032, 0.203175, -0.517460)$	$(\ 0.166984, 0.334321, -0.428622)$
3	$(\ 0.191746, 0.328395, -0.415873)$	$(\ 0.190901, 0.333481, -0.421668)$
4	$(\ 0.180881, 0.332346, -0.420700)$	$(\ 0.186393, 0.331205, -0.422631)$
5	$(\ 0.185359, 0.329261, -0.424369)$	$(\ 0.186061, 0.331202, -0.422726)$
6	$(\ 0.186326, 0.331160, -0.422649)$	$(\ 0.186116, 0.331230, -0.422714)$
∞	$(\ 0.186120, 0.331230, -0.422713)$	$(\ 0.186120, 0.331230, -0.422713)$

Table 7.3: Jacobi and Gauss-Seidel Solutions

7.4.4   Using the Methods

Consider the following linearization of the nonlinear system:

$$\mathbf{g}_0 + \mathbf{J}_0\mathbf{x} - \mathbf{J}_0\mathbf{x}_0 \equiv \mathbf{g}(\mathbf{x}_0) + \mathbf{J}(\mathbf{x}_0)(\mathbf{x} - \mathbf{x}_0) = \mathbf{0}_K,$$

which can be rewritten as

$$\mathbf{A}\mathbf{x} \equiv \mathbf{J}_0\mathbf{x} = \mathbf{J}_0\mathbf{x}_0 - \mathbf{g}_0 \equiv \mathbf{b}.$$

In order for the Jacobi method to work, the diagonal dominance condition must hold for the linearized version of the nonlinear system of equations. Although it might be possible to guarantee this property at, say, the initial value $\mathbf{x}_0$, it can be difficult to guarantee it at every iteration of the entire path to a solution. Even though this is perhaps an obvious point, we mention it because the problem arises frequently in practice. A similar problem exists with the Gauss-Seidel method. In short, in the nonlinear case, because the $\mathbf{A}$ matrix changes as each equation is solved in turn, it is difficult to know whether the spectral radius of $\mathbf{M}$ or $\mathbf{N}$ will be less than 1.

To illustrate these problems, consider the following three equations in three unknowns:

$$\mathbf{g}(\mathbf{x}) = \begin{bmatrix} g_1(x_1, x_2, x_3; \ell_1, k_1, q_1) \\ g_2(x_1, x_2, x_3; \ell_2, k_2, q_2) \\ g_3(x_1, x_2, x_3; \ell_3, k_3, q_3) \end{bmatrix} = \begin{bmatrix} \exp(x_1)\ell_1^{x_2}k_1^{x_3} - q_1 \\ \exp(x_1)\ell_2^{x_2}k_2^{x_3} - q_2 \\ \exp(x_1)\ell_3^{x_2}k_3^{x_3} - q_3 \end{bmatrix} = \mathbf{0}_3,$$

where the values for the ℓ_is, k_is, and q_is are provided in Table 7.4.[11] In this example, we can find an exact solution using linear algebra. Notice that

$$\exp(x_1)\ell_1^{x_2}k_1^{x_3} = q_1$$

$$\exp(x_1)\ell_2^{x_2}k_2^{x_3} = q_2$$

$$\exp(x_1)\ell_3^{x_2}k_3^{x_3} = q_3$$

---

[11]Economists will recognize this as a Cobb-Douglas production function, which is often used in empirical work.

so

$$x_1 + x_2 \log(\ell_1) + x_3 \log(k_1) = \log(q_1)$$
$$x_1 + x_2 \log(\ell_2) + x_3 \log(k_2) = \log(q_2)$$
$$x_1 + x_2 \log(\ell_3) + x_3 \log(k_3) = \log(q_3).$$

For the values provided in Table 7.4, this linear system can be written in matrix notation as follows:

$$\mathbf{Ax} \equiv \begin{bmatrix} 1 & 2 & 3 \\ 1 & 3 & 2 \\ 1 & 4 & 4 \end{bmatrix} \begin{bmatrix} x_1 \\ x_2 \\ x_3 \end{bmatrix} = \begin{bmatrix} 2 \\ \frac{7}{4} \\ 3 \end{bmatrix} \equiv \mathbf{b},$$

whence $\hat{\mathbf{x}} = (0.00, 0.25, 0.50)^\top$, so

$$q_i = \ell_i^{\frac{1}{4}} k_i^{\frac{1}{2}} \quad i = 1, 2, 3.$$

The Jacobian associated with this nonlinear system is as follows:

$$\mathbf{J}(\mathbf{x}) = \begin{bmatrix} \frac{\partial g_1(\mathbf{x})}{\partial x_1} & \frac{\partial g_1(\mathbf{x})}{\partial x_2} & \frac{\partial g_1(\mathbf{x})}{\partial x_3} \\[2mm] \frac{\partial g_2(\mathbf{x})}{\partial x_1} & \frac{\partial g_2(\mathbf{x})}{\partial x_2} & \frac{\partial g_2(\mathbf{x})}{\partial x_3} \\[2mm] \frac{\partial g_3(\mathbf{x})}{\partial x_1} & \frac{\partial g_3(\mathbf{x})}{\partial x_2} & \frac{\partial g_3(\mathbf{x})}{\partial x_3} \end{bmatrix}$$

$$= \begin{bmatrix} \exp(x_1)\ell_1^{x_2}k_1^{x_3} & \exp(x_1)\log(\ell_1)\ell_1^{x_2}k_1^{x_3} & \exp(x_1)\ell_1^{x_2}\log(k_1)k_1^{x_3} \\ \exp(x_1)\ell_2^{x_2}k_2^{x_3} & \exp(x_1)\log(\ell_2)\ell_2^{x_2}k_2^{x_3} & \exp(x_1)\ell_2^{x_2}\log(k_2)k_2^{x_3} \\ \exp(x_1)\ell_3^{x_2}k_3^{x_3} & \exp(x_1)\log(\ell_3)\ell_3^{x_2}k_3^{x_3} & \exp(x_1)\ell_3^{x_2}\log(k_3)k_3^{x_3} \end{bmatrix},$$

i	ℓ_i	k_i	q_i
1	e^2	e^3	e^2
2	e^3	e^2	$e^{\frac{7}{4}}$
3	e^4	e^4	e^3

Table 7.4: Example Values for Gauss-Seidel Example

which is fairly well-behaved as matrices go. Unfortunately, trying to iterate to a solution using either the Jacobi method or the Gauss-Seidel method is destined to failure. Try it on the following:

$$\mathbf{J}(\hat{\mathbf{x}}) = \begin{bmatrix} 7.3890561 & 14.7781122 & 22.1671683 \\ 5.7546027 & 17.2638080 & 11.5092054 \\ 20.0855369 & 80.3421477 & 80.3421477 \end{bmatrix},$$

just to see if you understand what is going on.

In general, although the Jacobi and Gauss-Seidel methods are sometimes used to solve nonlinear equations, considerable domain knowledge is needed to be confident that either will work for a particular application. In short, if someone suggests that you use these methods, be wary of the advice, unless you know that the person is an expert.

7.4.5   Solving Nonlinear Equations Using Python

The simplest way to solve K equations in K unknowns in Python is to use the `fsolve()` function in the module `scipy.optimize`. For example, consider the following pair of functions:

$$\mathbf{g}(\hat{\mathbf{x}}) = \begin{bmatrix} g_1(\hat{x}_1, \hat{x}_2) \\ g_2(\hat{x}_1, \hat{x}_2) \end{bmatrix} = \begin{bmatrix} x_1 x_2 - 4 \\ x_2 - \exp(x_1) \end{bmatrix} = \mathbf{0}_2.$$

With the following Python instructions,

```
>>> from scipy.optimize import fsolve
>>> import math
>>> def Equations(vecX):
...     x1, x2 = vecX
...     return (x1*x2-4., x2-math.exp(x1))
>>>
>>> x1Hat, x2Hat = fsolve(Equations, (1., 1.))
>>> print x1Hat, x2Hat, Equations((x1Hat, x2Hat))
1.2021678732 3.3273223226 (1.8278711877428577e-12, -4.7828407900851744
    e-13)
>>>
```

the solution is relatively effortless to calculate.[12]

---

[12]Note that the function `fsolve` is just a wrapper around MINPACK's `hybrd` and `hybrj` algorithms. What is MINPACK? A library of FORTRAN subroutines for solving systems of non-linear equations, or the least-squares minimization of the residual of a set of linear or nonlinear equations.

For the preceding examples, we did not make use of information concerning the Jacobian matrix, which we should have done. The Python solver did the work, approximating the Jacobian matrix numerically. For one-off solutions, where the equations are well-behaved, this won't matter very much, but in problems where you may need to calculate the solution many, many times or where the solution is not well-behaved, supplying the Jacobian matrix is important. In general, when speed is an issue, you should supply the Jacobian matrix if possible; making the computer calculate it numerically is slow.

If you are having trouble finding a solution, one reason could be that you did not supply the Jacobian matrix, or that the Jacobian matrix you supplied is in error. In other words, you have made a mistake in differentiation.

7.5 Unconstrained Optimization

In science in general and in engineering in particular, optimization problems arise naturally in the course of theory. In the natural and social sciences, except perhaps for economics, optimization problems arise more in empirical work than in theory. In empirical work, researchers are often faced with the task of maximizing (or minimizing) an objective function $f(\theta)$ with respect to the unknown parameter vector θ. The solution to this sort of problem defines a statistical estimator. Because problems like this are common, we use this framework to organize our discussion of unconstrained optimization.

Numerical analysts treat maximization and minimization as the same problem because maximizing $f(\theta)$ is equivalent to minimizing $-f(\theta)$. Therefore, although we only discuss minimizing a function, our discussion applies to maximizing one as well. In fact, the numerical optimization solvers in the Python module `scipy.optimize` all presume that you are minimizing an objective function.

In empirical work, perhaps the most common way in which an optimization problem arises is when choosing parameter estimates to maximize the likelihood of observing a random sample of data. We employ this example to illustrate the unconstrained optimization of a continuous and twice-differentiable multivariate function.

Suppose that for the nth observation the endogenous variable Y has a conditional probability density function $f_{Y|X}(y_n|\mathbf{x}_n, \theta)$ where $\mathbf{x}_n$ is a $(K \times 1)$ vector of covariates and θ is a $(P \times 1)$ vector of unknown parameters. For a random sample of size N, the likelihood function is then

$$\mathcal{L}(\boldsymbol{\theta}|\mathbf{X}, \boldsymbol{y}) = \prod_{n=1}^{N} f_{Y|X}(\boldsymbol{\theta}|\mathbf{x}_n, y_n), \tag{7.8}$$

where $\boldsymbol{y}$ equals $(y_1, \ldots, y_N)^\top$, and $\mathbf{X}$ equals $(\mathbf{x}_1, \ldots, \mathbf{x}_N)^\top$.

The optimal value $\hat{\boldsymbol{\theta}}$ is defined by the following:

$$\hat{\boldsymbol{\theta}} = \operatorname*{argmax}_{\boldsymbol{\theta}} \ \mathcal{L}(\boldsymbol{\theta}|\mathbf{X}, \boldsymbol{y}).$$

When $\mathcal{L}(\boldsymbol{\theta}|\mathbf{X}, \boldsymbol{y})$ is a continuous, differentiable function of the $(P \times 1)$ vector $\boldsymbol{\theta}$, at a local optimum $\hat{\boldsymbol{\theta}}$, the vector of first derivatives of the function in equation (7.8) is zero, and the matrix of second derivatives is negative definite at that point.

Maximizing a function like that given in equation (7.8) is awkward because it involves repeated applications of the chain rule. In addition, evaluating the products required when calculating the derivatives of the function can be an unstable calculation. In short, linear combinations are cheaper and more stable to calculate on a computer than products. Also, as mentioned, most optimization software is created to minimize a function. What to do?

Recall that the stationary points of functions are preserved under monotonic transformations. Thus, take the negative of the logarithm of both sides of the equality in equation (7.8). In other words, focus on the following function:

$$f(\boldsymbol{\theta}|\mathbf{X}, \boldsymbol{y}) = -\log[\mathcal{L}(\boldsymbol{\theta}|\mathbf{X}, \boldsymbol{y})],$$

which can be written out further as

$$f(\boldsymbol{\theta}|\mathbf{X}, \boldsymbol{y}) \equiv \sum_{n=1}^{N} \ell(\boldsymbol{\theta}|\mathbf{x}_n, y_n) \equiv - \sum_{n=1}^{N} \log f_{Y|X}(\boldsymbol{\theta}|\mathbf{x}_n, y_n).$$

Minimizing $f(\boldsymbol{\theta})$ with respect to $\boldsymbol{\theta}$ is a well-defined optimization problem when $f(\boldsymbol{\theta})$ is convex in $\boldsymbol{\theta}$, that is, when the likelihood function is concave in $\boldsymbol{\theta}$. Hereafter, we assume this property holds.

When minimizing $f(\boldsymbol{\theta})$ with respect to vector $\boldsymbol{\theta}$, find a value $\hat{\boldsymbol{\theta}}$ for which the gradient vector satisfies the following:

$$\mathbf{g}(\hat{\boldsymbol{\theta}}) \equiv \frac{\partial f(\hat{\boldsymbol{\theta}})}{\partial \boldsymbol{\theta}} \equiv \nabla_{\boldsymbol{\theta}} f(\hat{\boldsymbol{\theta}}) = \mathbf{0}_P \tag{7.9}$$

and for which the *Hessian matrix*

$$\mathbf{H}(\hat{\boldsymbol{\theta}}) \equiv \frac{\partial^2 f(\hat{\boldsymbol{\theta}})}{\partial \boldsymbol{\theta} \partial \boldsymbol{\theta}^\top} \equiv \nabla_{\boldsymbol{\theta}\boldsymbol{\theta}} f(\hat{\boldsymbol{\theta}})$$

is positive definite. Here, the Hessian matrix is just the Jacobian matrix of Section 7.3.2. In the case of this optimization problem, however, the Jacobian (Hessian) matrix has more structure: by Clairaut's theorem, the Hessian matrix is symmetric, whereas the Jacobian matrix need not have that structure. For a concave function, the Hessian is also negative definite, whereas a convex function has a positive definite Hessian. For a negative definite matrix, all eigenvalues are negative, whereas for a positive definite matrix, all eigenvalues are positive.

7.5.1 Newton-Raphson Method

From a numerical standpoint, the easiest way to proceed is to linearize $\mathbf{g}(\boldsymbol{\theta})$ about some initial estimate $\boldsymbol{\theta}_0$

$$\mathbf{g}(\boldsymbol{\theta}) \approx \mathbf{g}(\boldsymbol{\theta}_0) + \mathbf{H}(\boldsymbol{\theta}_0)(\boldsymbol{\theta} - \boldsymbol{\theta}_0). \tag{7.10}$$

Setting the right-hand side of equation (7.10) equal to the zero vector and solving for a new $\boldsymbol{\theta}$, which we denote $\boldsymbol{\theta}_1$, yields

$$\boldsymbol{\theta}_1 = \boldsymbol{\theta}_0 - [\mathbf{H}(\boldsymbol{\theta}_0)]^{-1} \mathbf{g}(\boldsymbol{\theta}_0).$$

When f is globally convex, the sequence

$$\boldsymbol{\theta}_{r+1} = \boldsymbol{\theta}_r - [\mathbf{H}(\boldsymbol{\theta}_r)]^{-1} \mathbf{g}(\boldsymbol{\theta}_r) \qquad r = 0, 1, \dots \tag{7.11}$$

will typically converge to a point, satisfying equation (7.9). We hedge our bets here because the initial value of $\boldsymbol{\theta}_0$ can be important in determining whether the sequence in (7.11) converges. We illustrated this in one dimension using the method of Newton-Raphson in Section 7.3.2 on page 379.

Virtually all numerical routines adopt a strategy similar to equation (7.11) but very often use different approximations to $\mathbf{H}$, instead of the actual $\mathbf{H}$, or just use a constant, which we later denote by α.

When to Stop

Practically speaking, how do you determine whether convergence has obtained? The best way involves deciding whether the norm of the first partial derivative vector (the gradient vector) is less than some prescribed accuracy criterion. For example, if the Euclidean distance is used, then when

$$\|\mathbf{g}(\boldsymbol{\theta}_r)\|_2 < \varepsilon,$$

where the convergence criterion ε could be 10^{-6}, you might claim that convergence has obtained.

In industry, a second way to evaluate convergence is to calculate the distance of the difference between two successive iterates from zero, and to stop when it is less than some prescribed accuracy criterion. For example, if the Euclidean distance is again used, this reduces to

$$\|\boldsymbol{\theta}_r - \boldsymbol{\theta}_{r-1}\|_2 < \epsilon,$$

where ϵ need not be the same as ε. Alternatively, calculate

$$\frac{\|\boldsymbol{\theta}_r - \boldsymbol{\theta}_{r-1}\|_2}{\|\boldsymbol{\theta}_{r-1}\|_2} \quad \text{or} \quad \frac{\|\boldsymbol{\theta}_r - \boldsymbol{\theta}_{r-1}\|_2}{\|\boldsymbol{\theta}_r\|_2},$$

and stop iterating when the relative changes are small.

A third way to evaluate convergence, also used in industry, is to calculate the relative improvement in the objective function evaluated at adjacent iterates. For example,

$$\left| \frac{f(\boldsymbol{\theta}_r | \mathbf{X}, \mathbf{y}) - f(\boldsymbol{\theta}_{r-1} | \mathbf{X}, \mathbf{y})}{f(\boldsymbol{\theta}_{r-1} | \mathbf{X}, \mathbf{y})} \right| < \Delta,$$

where Δ might be 10^{-4}. In words, when changes in the objective function are less than a basis point, convergence has been attained.

You will notice that we use different values to evaluate convergence, depending on the criterion used—norm of the gradient vector, changes in the iterate values, or changes in the function values—as well as the data being used. Some believe that the criterion to use depends on the application.

For example, when the optimal solution characterizes a statistical estimator, the gradient vector should be as close to the zero vector as possible because the Hessian matrix is typically used to get some notion of sampling variability.

Evaluating the Hessian matrix at a point where the gradient vector is not small will not provide a reliable measure of sampling variability.

On the other hand, in industry, the solution may represent some monetary measure whose units are in dollars. Going beyond the third or the fourth decimal place probably won't improve a decision, or so the argument goes. Let's just say that we are unconvinced by this argument; we still prefer to use the norm-of-the-gradient-vector criterion.

Finally, sometimes the objective function is itself important to some other purpose or task, so the third criterion is used. We counsel against using this third criterion. For on the path to a minimum, the function value may not change much, but the optimum still remains some distance away and is yet to be found. Thus, even though some practioners think that the appropriate criterion to use should be informed by the problem at hand, we recommend always using the norm-of-the-gradient-vector criterion.

Rates of Convergence

Suppose a sequence $\{\theta_r\}$ converges to the number θ^0. This sequence is said to *converge linearly* to θ^0 if there exists a number $\kappa \in (0,1)$ such that

$$\lim_{r \to \infty} \frac{|\theta_{r+1} - \theta^0|}{|\theta_r - \theta^0|} = \kappa,$$

where κ is referred to as the *rate of convergence*. If the sequence converges and κ is zero, then the sequence is said *to converge superlinearly*, whereas if the sequence converges and κ is 1, then the sequence is said *to converge sublinearly*. When the sequence converges sublinearly and

$$\lim_{r \to \infty} \frac{|\theta_{r+2} - \theta_{r+1}|}{|\theta_{r+1} - \theta_r|} = 1,$$

then the sequence is said *to converge logarithmically*. Logarithmic convergence *bad*; superlinear convergence *good*. If

$$\lim_{r \to \infty} \frac{|\theta_{r+1} - \theta^0|}{|\theta_r - \theta^0|^q} = \kappa > 0, \, q > 1,$$

then the sequence is said *to converge with order* q. When q is 2, this is referred to as *quadratic convergence*.

If the objective function $f(\boldsymbol{\theta})$ is a convex function of $\boldsymbol{\theta}$, then in a neighborhood of the extremum of the function, the method of Newton-Raphson converges quadratically. Quadratic convergence in numerical optimization is rare; this is why the method of Newton-Raphson is the gold standard of optimization.

Outer Product of the Gradient Approximation

Perhaps the most difficult part of implementing the Newton-Raphson method involves calculating the Hessian matrix **H**, the matrix of second partial derivatives. In the case of a likelihood function, researchers have found ways to approximate this matrix that involve less calculation. Specifically, Berndt, Hall, Hall, and Hausman (1974) showed that the so-called *outer product of the gradient* (OPG) matrix

$$\sum_{n=1}^{N} \left[\frac{\partial \ell(\boldsymbol{\theta}|\mathbf{x}_n, y_n)}{\partial \boldsymbol{\theta}} \right] \left[\frac{\partial \ell(\boldsymbol{\theta}|\mathbf{x}_n, y_n)}{\partial \boldsymbol{\theta}} \right]^\top$$

is often a good approximation to $\mathbf{H}(\boldsymbol{\theta})$, particularly when N is quite large, say, over $1,000$. This is sometimes referred to as the *BHHH trick*.

One drawback with using either the Hessian matrix or its OPG approximation is that solving a system of linear equations to take a Newton-Raphson step is an $\mathcal{O}(P^3)$ calculation, where P is the dimension of the column vector $\boldsymbol{\theta}$. When P is large, the Newton-Raphson method of optimization can be prohibitively expensive, in both time and memory, so alternatives must be sought.

7.5.2   Quasi-Newton Methods

The greatest contributions to computation costs (in both instructions and storage) of the Newton-Raphson method involves solving a system of linear equations. Because the BHHH trick cannot be used in all cases, researchers have sought alternative ways of approximating the Hessian. But solving a system of linear equations is also costly, so researchers have sought alternatives for this, too. Thus, the methods discussed in this section all provide alternative ways around this bottleneck. For the most part, we do not present formulae but just describe the contributions of each set of researchers.

Davidon-Fletcher-Powell

Constructing the Hessian matrix can be expensive, so William C. Davidon as well as Roger Fletcher and Michael J. D. Powell independently sought to reduce this burden. Although his research was completed in the late 1950s, Davidon (1991) was not published until long after the one by Fletcher and Powell (1963). Nevertheless, Davidon still receives credit for the method known as *Davidon-Fletcher-Powell* (DFP).

The Newton-Raphson method relies on an expression for the Hessian matrix. Beginning in the 1950s, and continuing through the 1960s, researchers sought ways to approximate the Hessian numerically. A building block in these approaches is the so-called *secant method*. To see how this works, consider in one dimension the following Newton-Raphson iteration:

$$\theta_{r+1} = \theta_r - [g'(\theta_r)]^{-1} g(\theta_r),$$

where

$$g'(\theta_r) = \frac{dg(\theta_r)}{d\theta} \equiv h(\theta_r).$$

In this case, the scalar function $g'(\theta)$ is the Hessian matrix. Approximate $g'(\theta)$ using the first difference between two values θ_r and θ_{r-1}. In symbols,

$$\frac{dg(\theta_r)}{d\theta} \approx \frac{[g(\theta_r) - g(\theta_{r-1})]}{(\theta_r - \theta_{r-1})} \equiv \tilde{h}(\theta_{r-1})$$

whence derives the following secant method iteration:

$$\theta_{r+1} = \theta_r - [\tilde{h}(\theta_{r-1})]^{-1} g(\theta_r) = \theta_r - \frac{g(\theta_r)(\theta_r - \theta_{r-1})}{[g(\theta_r) - g(\theta_{r-1})]}.$$

Clearly, implementing the secant method requires two initial conditions, say, θ_0 and θ_1, so $g(\theta)$ can be evaluated at those two points. Then you proceed as you would with the Newton-Raphson method.

As with the Newton-Raphson method, however, if the initial guesses θ_0 and θ_1 are not close to the root in question, then no guarantee exists that the secant method will converge—ever. The definition of *close* is nebulous, as with the Newton-Raphson method. Table 7.5 presents the results from applying the secant method to the Newton-Raphson example of Table 7.2 and Figure 7.3.

r	θ_r	$g(\theta_r)$	$\tilde{h}(\theta_{r-1})$
0	2.0000	0.6931	—
1	0.5000	−0.6931	−1.3862
2	1.2500	0.2231	0.3862
3	1.0674	0.0652	−0.1580
4	0.9920	−0.0080	−0.0732
5	1.0003	0.0003	0.0083
6	1.0000	0.0000	−0.0003

Table 7.5: Secant Iterations Applied to $\log(\theta) = 0$

The intuition behind DFP is to use changes in the gradient vector to approximate the Hessian matrix, using a modification of the secant method. Building on the work of Davidon, Fletcher, and Powell, Charles G. Broyden developed a numerical approximation to the Hessian matrix beyond the one-dimensional case. Broyden (1965) actually proposed estimating the Jacobian matrix for a system of nonlinear equations

$$\mathbf{g}(\hat{\boldsymbol{\theta}}) = \mathbf{0}_P$$

using a generalization of the secant method. In the case of the first-order conditions for an optimum, this Jacobian is the Hessian matrix. Specifically, he reasoned that a matrix $\mathbf{J}_r$ existed such that

$$\mathbf{J}_r(\boldsymbol{\theta}_r - \boldsymbol{\theta}_{r-1}) \approx [\mathbf{g}(\boldsymbol{\theta}_r) - \mathbf{g}(\boldsymbol{\theta}_{r-1})].$$

Unfortunately, trying to create a full-rank $(P \times P)$ matrix $\mathbf{J}_r$ from two $(P \times 1)$ vectors $(\boldsymbol{\theta}_r - \boldsymbol{\theta}_{r-1})$ and $[\mathbf{g}(\boldsymbol{\theta}_r) - \mathbf{g}(\boldsymbol{\theta}_{r-1})]$ will not work. However, given $\mathbf{J}_{r-1}$, an initial estimate of the Jacobian (Hessian) (for example, $\mathbf{I}_P$), you can find a matrix $\mathbf{J}_r$ that is in some sense close to $\mathbf{J}_{r-1}$; Broyden chose the Frobenius norm.[13] Under Broyden's choice of the Frobenius norm,

$$\mathbf{J}_r = \mathbf{J}_{r-1} + \frac{\mathbf{g}(\boldsymbol{\theta}_r) - \mathbf{J}_{r-1}(\boldsymbol{\theta}_r - \boldsymbol{\theta}_{r-1})}{\|(\boldsymbol{\theta}_r - \boldsymbol{\theta}_{r-1})\|_2} (\boldsymbol{\theta}_r - \boldsymbol{\theta}_{r-1})^{\top}.$$

---

[13] For the $(P \times P)$ matrix $\mathbf{A}$, the Frobenius norm is defined as

$$\|\mathbf{A}\|_F = \sqrt{\sum_{i=1}^{P} \sum_{j=1}^{P} |a_{ij}|^2}.$$

The method makes use of two properties of the Hessian matrix: it is symmetric, and it is positive definite.

Although the DFP method is quite effective, it nevertheless requires solving a system of linear equations. In a series of independent papers, Broyden (1970), Fletcher (1970), Goldfarb (1970) and Shanno (1970) improved on the method, resulting in the *Broyden-Fletcher-Goldfarb-Shanno* (BFGS) method, which has now superseded DFP. In fact, no DFP solver is available in the `scipy.optimize` module.

Broyden-Fletcher-Goldfarb-Shanno

BFGS is almost the same as DFP, with one important difference: instead of approximating the Hessian, the inverse of the Hessian is approximated. The advantage of BFGS over DFP is clear: by avoiding solving a system of linear equations, an $\mathcal{O}(P^3)$ calculation becomes unnecessary; only vector/matrix multiplication is required. BFGS is also reported to be more numerically stable than DFP, presumably in part because no (potentially ill-conditioned) matrix needs to be inverted.

7.5.3 Line Search versus Trust Region Methods

Consider a Newton-Raphson iteration $(r+1)$

$$\boldsymbol{\theta}_{r+1} = \boldsymbol{\theta}_r - [\mathbf{H}(\boldsymbol{\theta}_r)]^{-1}\mathbf{g}(\boldsymbol{\theta}_r)$$
$$\boldsymbol{\theta}_{r+1} - \boldsymbol{\theta}_r = -[\mathbf{H}(\boldsymbol{\theta}_r)]^{-1}\mathbf{g}(\boldsymbol{\theta}_r)$$
$$\mathbf{s}_{r+1} = -[\mathbf{H}(\boldsymbol{\theta}_r)]^{-1}\mathbf{g}(\boldsymbol{\theta}_r).$$

At iterate $\boldsymbol{\theta}_r$, the function $f(\boldsymbol{\theta})$ is modeled as the following quadratic form in the step $\mathbf{s}$:

$$\hat{f}(\mathbf{s};\boldsymbol{\theta}_r) = f(\boldsymbol{\theta}_r) + \mathbf{s}^\top\mathbf{g}(\boldsymbol{\theta}_r) + \frac{1}{2}\mathbf{s}^\top\mathbf{H}(\boldsymbol{\theta}_r)\mathbf{s},$$

whence

$$\nabla_{\mathbf{s}}\hat{f}(\mathbf{s};\boldsymbol{\theta}_r) = \mathbf{g}(\boldsymbol{\theta}_r) + \mathbf{H}(\boldsymbol{\theta}_r)\mathbf{s}$$

and

$$\mathbf{s}_{r+1} = -[\mathbf{H}(\boldsymbol{\theta}_r)]^{-1}\mathbf{g}(\boldsymbol{\theta}_r),$$

so

$$\boldsymbol{\theta}_{r+1} = \boldsymbol{\theta}_r + \mathbf{s}_{r+1} = \boldsymbol{\theta}_r - [\mathbf{H}(\boldsymbol{\theta}_r)]^{-1}\mathbf{g}(\boldsymbol{\theta}_r) \quad r = 0, 1, \ldots$$

Sometimes a Newton-Raphson step is so large that it fails to improve the function value. To prevent such overstepping, *line search* methods are employed. In short, for a given step $\mathbf{s}$, a line search method involves selecting an $\alpha \in [0, 1]$ such that

$$f(\boldsymbol{\theta} + \alpha \mathbf{s}) \le f(\boldsymbol{\theta}).$$

Several different line search methods exist, with names like *golden-section search*, *Fibonacci search*, and *Armijo backtracking search*. In short, line search methods involve taking a step proportional to the $[\mathbf{H}(\boldsymbol{\theta}_r)]^{-1}\mathbf{g}(\boldsymbol{\theta}_r)$ direction, where the step length α_r is chosen using one of these search methods.

Trust region methods are alternatives to line search methods. With trust region methods, the Newton direction is not necessarily chosen. Instead, the following problem is solved:

$$\min_{\mathbf{s}} \hat{f}(\mathbf{s}) \quad \text{subject to} \quad \|\mathbf{s}\|_2 \le \delta_r,$$

where the radius δ_r of the sphere $\|\mathbf{s}\|_2^2$ is referred to as the *trust radius*. Trust-region methods are sometimes called *restricted step* methods. Where line search methods first choose a step direction and then a step size, trust region methods first choose a step size (the trust radius) and then a step direction.

This ends our brief introduction to line search and trust region methods. Conn, Gould, and Toint (2000) wrote a comprehensive book describing trust region methods and their relationship to line search methods.

7.5.4 Adjusting a Hessian Matrix

In problems where the objective function is not globally convex, the Hessian matrix may not be positive definite at a candidate iterate. In such cases, adjusting the Hessian is important.

Kenneth Levenberg (1944) was the first to propose a method of adjusting the Hessian in conjunction with solving nonlinear least-squares problems; that method was then modified by Donald W. Marquardt (1963). Consequently, you often see reference to the *Levenberg-Marquardt algorithm* when adjustments to the Hessian matrix are discussed.

To establish the ideas in a notation consistent with our analysis, we consider the following nonlinear, least-squares objective function:

$$f(\boldsymbol{\theta}) = \sum_{n=1}^{N} \ell_n(\boldsymbol{\theta}) = \sum_{n=1}^{N} [y_n - \mu_n(\boldsymbol{\theta})]^2$$

where y_n is the response variable for observation $n = 1, 2, \ldots, N$ and $\boldsymbol{\theta}$ is a $(P \times 1)$ vector of unknown parameters that are chosen to minimize the objective function $f(\boldsymbol{\theta})$. By allowing the mean function $\mu_n(\boldsymbol{\theta})$ to vary with n, we are being quite general concerning the presence and type of feature variables.

The nonlinear, least-squares estimator $\hat{\boldsymbol{\theta}}$ solves the following system:

$$\nabla_{\boldsymbol{\theta}} f(\hat{\boldsymbol{\theta}}) = \mathbf{g}(\hat{\boldsymbol{\theta}}) = -2 \sum_{n=1}^{N} [y_n - \mu_n(\hat{\boldsymbol{\theta}})] \nabla_{\boldsymbol{\theta}} \mu_n(\hat{\boldsymbol{\theta}}) = \mathbf{0}_P. \tag{7.12}$$

By collecting the y_ns and the $\mu_n(\boldsymbol{\theta})$s in the $(N \times 1)$ vectors $\mathbf{y}$ and $\boldsymbol{\mu}(\boldsymbol{\theta})$, respectively, and the transposes of the $\nabla_{\boldsymbol{\theta}} \mu_n(\boldsymbol{\theta})$s in the matrix $\mathbf{J}(\boldsymbol{\theta})$, where

$$\mathbf{J}(\boldsymbol{\theta}) = \begin{bmatrix} \frac{\partial \mu_1(\boldsymbol{\theta})}{\partial \theta_1} & \frac{\partial \mu_1(\boldsymbol{\theta})}{\partial \theta_2} & \cdots & \frac{\partial \mu_1(\boldsymbol{\theta})}{\partial \theta_p} \\ \frac{\partial \mu_2(\boldsymbol{\theta})}{\partial \theta_1} & \frac{\partial \mu_2(\boldsymbol{\theta})}{\partial \theta_2} & \cdots & \frac{\partial \mu_2(\boldsymbol{\theta})}{\partial \theta_p} \\ \vdots & \vdots & \ddots & \vdots \\ \frac{\partial \mu_N(\boldsymbol{\theta})}{\partial \theta_1} & \frac{\partial \mu_N(\boldsymbol{\theta})}{\partial \theta_2} & \cdots & \frac{\partial \mu_N(\boldsymbol{\theta})}{\partial \theta_p} \end{bmatrix} = \begin{bmatrix} \nabla_{\boldsymbol{\theta}} \mu_1(\boldsymbol{\theta})^\top \\ \nabla_{\boldsymbol{\theta}} \mu_2(\boldsymbol{\theta})^\top \\ \vdots \\ \nabla_{\boldsymbol{\theta}} \mu_N(\boldsymbol{\theta})^\top \end{bmatrix},$$

conditional on iterate $\boldsymbol{\theta}_r$, the objective function can be approximated by

$$\hat{f}(\mathbf{s}; \boldsymbol{\theta}_r) = \|\mathbf{y} - \boldsymbol{\mu}(\boldsymbol{\theta}_r) - \mathbf{J}(\boldsymbol{\theta}_r)\mathbf{s}\|_2^2$$
$$= [\mathbf{y} - \boldsymbol{\mu}(\boldsymbol{\theta}_r)]^\top [\mathbf{y} - \boldsymbol{\mu}(\boldsymbol{\theta}_r)] - 2\mathbf{s}^\top \mathbf{J}(\boldsymbol{\theta}_r)^\top [\mathbf{y} - \boldsymbol{\mu}(\boldsymbol{\theta}_r)] +$$
$$\mathbf{s}^\top \mathbf{J}(\boldsymbol{\theta}_r)^\top \mathbf{J}(\boldsymbol{\theta}_r)\mathbf{s}.$$

Differentiating $\hat{f}(\mathbf{s}; \boldsymbol{\theta}_r)$ with respect to the direction $\mathbf{s}$ yields the following first-order condition at iterate $\boldsymbol{\theta}_r$:

$$[\mathbf{J}(\boldsymbol{\theta}_r)^\top \mathbf{J}(\boldsymbol{\theta}_r)]\mathbf{s}_{r+1} = \mathbf{J}(\boldsymbol{\theta}_r)^\top [\mathbf{y} - \boldsymbol{\mu}(\boldsymbol{\theta}_r)]$$
$$\mathbf{s}_{r+1} = [\mathbf{J}(\boldsymbol{\theta}_r)^\top \mathbf{J}(\boldsymbol{\theta}_r)]^{-1} \mathbf{J}(\boldsymbol{\theta}_r)^\top [\mathbf{y} - \boldsymbol{\mu}(\boldsymbol{\theta}_r)] \quad r = 0, 1, \ldots.$$

This recursion is referred to as the method of *Gauss-Newton*. An observant reader will notice that each step looks very much like solving the normal equations in the case of a least-squares regression. Therefore, the numerical methods employed for that case can be used in this one, too.

Sometimes, the matrix $[\mathbf{J}(\boldsymbol{\theta}_r)^\top \mathbf{J}(\boldsymbol{\theta}_r)]$ is ill-conditioned, which means that even when using the Cholesky decomposition for each step of the Gauss-Newton algorithm, numerical problems can arise.

Levenberg (1944) proposed adding a multiple λ of the identity matrix $\mathbf{I}_P$ to the Hessian matrix $\mathbf{H}(\boldsymbol{\theta}_r)$, so equation (7.12) becomes

$$[\mathbf{J}(\boldsymbol{\theta}_r)^\top \mathbf{J}(\boldsymbol{\theta}_r) + \lambda \mathbf{I}_P]\mathbf{s}_{r+1} = \mathbf{J}(\boldsymbol{\theta}_r)^\top [\mathbf{y} - \boldsymbol{\mu}(\boldsymbol{\theta}_r)]$$

at iterate $\boldsymbol{\theta}_r$. This modification often (but not always) has a damping effect and reduces the step size. This is referred to as *ridge regression* in the statistics literature, and *Tikhonov regularization* in the machine learning literature—in honor of Andrey N. Tikhonov, who presented the idea in a paper in Russian in 1943.

However useful Levenberg's idea may be, it does not always work well. When λ is large, the information in the Jacobian $\mathbf{J}(\boldsymbol{\theta}_r)$ is really not used; when λ is small, the Hessian is not sufficiently regularized. Thus, Marquardt (1963) proposed using a different λ in each direction, so equation (7.12) becomes

$$\left(\mathbf{J}(\boldsymbol{\theta}_r)^\top \mathbf{J}(\boldsymbol{\theta}_r) + \lambda \mathbf{I}_P \operatorname{diag}[\mathbf{J}(\boldsymbol{\theta}_r)^\top \mathbf{J}(\boldsymbol{\theta}_r)]\right) \mathbf{s}_{r+1} = \mathbf{J}(\boldsymbol{\theta}_r)^\top [\mathbf{y} - \boldsymbol{\mu}(\boldsymbol{\theta}_r)]$$

where, for a $(P \times P)$ matrix $\mathbf{A}$, $\operatorname{diag}(\mathbf{A})$ is a $(P \times 1)$ vector of the diagonal elements of $\mathbf{A}$.

Subsequently, Goldfeld, Quandt, and Trotter (1966) derived the optimal step size at each iteration.

7.5.5 Scaling

The closer the approximating function is to a bowl, the easier the actual function is to optimize numerically, that is, fewer computing resources will be required. What do we mean by a bowl? In two dimensions, the algebraic formula of a bowl is

$$\operatorname{Bowl}(\theta_1, \theta_2) = \theta_1^2 + \theta_2^2.$$

In short, the level sets of a bowl are circles. For example, consider projecting the bowl at height ρ^2 onto the (θ_1, θ_2) plane, as shown in Figure 7.4. The following level set would obtain:

$$\theta_1^2 + \theta_2^2 = \rho^2,$$

which is the formula for a circle of radius ρ. (Remember conic sections?) In any case, the Hessian matrix of a bowl is proportional to the identity matrix, which

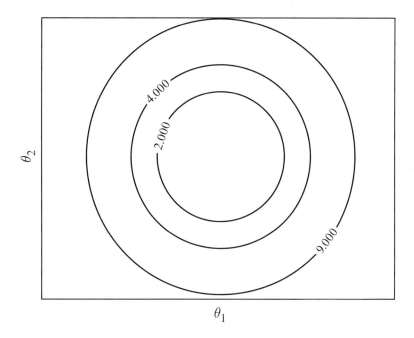

Figure 7.4: Level Sets of Bowl

is the best conditioned matrix you can find. In fact, try to demonstrate that the condition number is 1.

In two dimensions, the generalization of this bowl is the following:

$$\hat{f}(\theta_1, \theta_2; a_{11}, a_{12}, a_{22}, b_1, b_2) = a_{11}\theta_1^2 + 2a_{12}\theta_1\theta_2 + a_{22}\theta_2^2 - 2b_1\theta_1 - 2b_2\theta_2 + c$$
$$\equiv \theta^\top A\theta - 2\theta^\top b + c,$$

where

$$A = \begin{bmatrix} a_{11} & a_{12} \\ a_{12} & a_{22} \end{bmatrix}, \quad b = \begin{bmatrix} b_1 \\ b_2 \end{bmatrix}, \quad \text{and} \quad \theta = \begin{bmatrix} \theta_1 \\ \theta_2 \end{bmatrix},$$

with $a_{11} > 0$, $a_{22} > 0$, and $a_{11}a_{22} > a_{12}^2$. The level sets of this generalized function are ellipses centered about the minimum of this function, which is the point $\hat{\theta} = A^{-1}b$.

If the value of a_{11} is large relative to the value of a_{22} (for example, a_{11} is on the order of 10^5, whereas a_{22} is on the order of 10^{-5}), then numerical optimization can become difficult.

One general rule that applied mathematicians advocate is that, to the extent possible, the components of the solution to the system should be about 1 in absolute value.

In statistical problems, you can typically choose the units of feature variables to achieve this, but in general no rules exist to ensure that the Hessian in any given problem is approximately proportional to the identity matrix: you will need to use domain-specific knowledge to determine what the units should be.

In general, in unconstrained optimization, Nocedal and Wright (2006, 26–27) have referred to a problem as *poorly scaled* when changes to the variable vector θ in a certain direction produce much larger variations in the value of the objective function f than do changes to θ in other directions.

Because scaling by changing the units in which data are measured is relatively straighforward, some commercial software performs the task automatically. For other optimization software, problems with unusual or unbalanced scaling may cause difficulties, so it is typically worthwhile to consider transforming choice variables, the objective function, or the constraints required.[14]

In Section 7.5, we discussed a particular scaling of the objective function. There, the initial objective function, a product, was transformed using the natural logarithm to produce a sum, which is much better behaved numerically, and whose derivatives are easier to calculate and also better behaved numerically than those of products. Other forms of scaling the objective function can exist as well.

In the case of constrained optimization problems (see Section 7.6), scaling can also involve the constraints. In this vein, some researchers advocate tranforming a constraint so that it is approximately linear in the choice variables. For example, consider the constraint

$$x^{\theta_1} y^{\theta_2} \leq z,$$

where θ_1 and θ_2 are variables, while x, y, and z are data. By taking logarithms, you can obtain the following linear constraint:

$$\theta_1 \log(x) + \theta_2 \log(y) \leq \log(z).$$

In short, for some problem, you may need to scale not only the data relating to the choice variables, but the objective function and any constraints as well,

---

[14]From `http://www.nag.com/techtips/techtip004.asp`.

or some combination of the three. Nocedal and Wright (2006) and Gill, Murray, and Wright (1981) provide good discussions of the issues.

Note that scaling is both an art and a science. That said, if you are having trouble optimizing a multivariate function, we suggest that you print out the diagonal elements of the Hessian matrix and calculate the condition number of the Hessian as well. If the values of the diagonal elements of the Hessian are quite different in magnitude, then scaling could solve the problem. (At this point, you would be well served by doing some additional research in the domain of your problem to discover what might help.) On the other hand, if the elements of the diagonal elements are all about the same magnitude, but the condition number is large, you may want to regularize the Hessian matrix along the lines proposed by Levenberg (1944), Marquardt (1963), or Goldfeld et al. (1966).

7.5.6 Gradient Descent

When P is large, the Newton-Raphson and the quasi-Newton methods may be impractical. Perhaps the most computationally straightforward way to solve equation (7.9) when P is large is a method referred to as *gradient descent*, and sometimes as *steepest descent*. Under this method, the direction $-\mathbf{g}(\boldsymbol{\theta})$ is chosen. Updating the $\boldsymbol{\theta}_r$ then involves calculating the following sequence iteratively:

$$\boldsymbol{\theta}_{r+1} = \boldsymbol{\theta}_r - \alpha \mathbf{g}(\boldsymbol{\theta}_r) \quad r = 0, 1, 2, \ldots,$$

where α is a positive parameter (which may be indexed by r) that controls the rate of descent. When α is indexed by r, the α_rs sequence typically decreases as r increases. Unfortunately, the method of gradient descent can often be slow to converge, probably because it ignores curvature information embedded in the Hessian matrix. As illustrated in the following sections, the method meanders in some problems. The Levenberg-Marquardt algorithm can be interpreted as a hybrid between the quasi-Newton methods and the gradient descent method, but because it involves inverting a matrix this is not as helpful as some might think.

7.5.7 Conjugate Gradient

One way to prevent the method of gradient descent from meandering is to use past information to smooth the path to the optimum. The *conjugate gradient* method does just that. The best way to see how this smoothing obtains is to examine the formulae that define the conjugate gradient method.

Introduce the direction vector $\mathbf{d}(\boldsymbol{\theta})$, where

$$\mathbf{d}(\boldsymbol{\theta}) = -\frac{\mathbf{g}(\boldsymbol{\theta})}{\|\mathbf{g}(\boldsymbol{\theta})\|_2}.$$

In words, the direction vector is the negative of the gradient vector but scaled to have length 1. When evaluated at $\boldsymbol{\theta}_r$, denote these vectors by $\mathbf{d}_r$ and $\mathbf{g}_r$. Thus, for an initial estimated $\boldsymbol{\theta}_0$, you would obtain

$$\mathbf{d}_0 = -\frac{\mathbf{g}_0}{\|\mathbf{g}_0\|_2}.$$

For $r = 0, 1, 2, \ldots$ and for a positive definite matrix $\mathbf{Q}_r$, which could just be the identity matrix $\mathbf{I}_P$, when $\mathbf{g}_r \neq \mathbf{0}_P$, calculate the following sequence:

$$\alpha_r = \frac{\mathbf{g}_r^\top \mathbf{g}_r}{\mathbf{d}_r^\top \mathbf{Q} \mathbf{d}_r}$$

$$\boldsymbol{\theta}_{r+1} = \boldsymbol{\theta}_r + \alpha_r \mathbf{d}_r$$

$$\mathbf{g}_{r+1} = \mathbf{g}_r - \alpha_r \mathbf{d}_r$$

$$w_r = \frac{\mathbf{g}_{r+1}^\top \mathbf{g}_{r+1}}{\mathbf{g}_r^\top \mathbf{g}_r}$$

$$\mathbf{d}_{r+1} = \mathbf{g}_{r+1} + w_r \mathbf{d}_r.$$

In `scipy.optimize`, one of the solvers, `newton_cg()`, uses the Hessian at the most recent iterate for $\mathbf{Q}_r$.

As you can see, the new direction depends on the old direction and information contained in the gradient vector evaluated at the latest iterate; in addition, the line search parameter α_r is permitted to evolve as the method proceeds.

7.5.8 Stochastic Gradient Descent

In machine learning training exercises as well as estimation exercises in econometrics and in statistics, the minimand objective function typically has the following structure:

$$f(\boldsymbol{\theta}|\mathbf{X}, \mathbf{y}) = \sum_{n=1}^{N} \ell_n(\boldsymbol{\theta}|\mathbf{x}_n, y_n),$$

where in the case of estimation by the method of least squares

$$\ell(\boldsymbol{\theta}|\mathbf{x}_n, y_n) = (y_n - \mathbf{x}_n\boldsymbol{\theta})^2,$$

whereas in the case of estimation by the method of maximum likelihood

$$\ell(\boldsymbol{\theta}|\mathbf{x}_n, y_n) = -\log\left[f_{Y|X}(\boldsymbol{\theta}|\mathbf{x}_n, y_n)\right].$$

We demonstrated how to use all the data in a sample of size N to obtain an estimate of $\boldsymbol{\theta}$. Machine learners refer to this as *batch learning*. Specifically, under the method of gradient descent, the direction $-\mathbf{g}(\boldsymbol{\theta})$ is chosen. Updating the $\boldsymbol{\theta}_r$ then involves calculating the following sequence iteratively:

$$\boldsymbol{\theta}_{r+1} = \boldsymbol{\theta}_r - \alpha\mathbf{g}(\boldsymbol{\theta}_r) \quad r = 0, 1, 2, \ldots,$$

where α is a positive parameter (which may be indexed by r) that controls the rate of descent.

Instead of using all the data, just use the gradient of observation $n = 1, 2, \ldots, N$ to update $\boldsymbol{\theta}_n$. That is, fix an initial guess at, say, $\boldsymbol{\theta}_0$, and then update according to

$$\boldsymbol{\theta}_n = \boldsymbol{\theta}_{n-1} - \alpha_n\mathbf{g}_n(\boldsymbol{\theta}_{n-1}) \quad n = 1, 2, \ldots, N,$$

where

$$\mathbf{g}_n(\boldsymbol{\theta}_{n-1}) = \nabla_{\boldsymbol{\theta}}\ell(\boldsymbol{\theta}_{n-1}|\mathbf{x}_n, y_n).$$

Using results from the theory of stochastic approximation, Robbins and Monro (1951) and Kiefer and Wolfowitz (1952) demonstrated that under certain regularity conditions, as n gets very large (goes to infinity), $\boldsymbol{\theta}_n$ will converge to $\boldsymbol{\theta}^0$, the true value of $\boldsymbol{\theta}$.

Perhaps an example can make the mathematics clearer. Suppose Y_n is distributed normally, having mean θ and variance 1. Assume $\alpha_n = n^{-1}$. Now,

$$\ell(\theta|Y_n) = 0.5\log(2\pi) + \frac{(Y_n - \theta)^2}{2}$$

and

$$\frac{d\ell(\theta|Y_n)}{d\theta} = -(Y_n - \theta) = g_n(\theta).$$

You can interpret $(Y_n - \theta)$ as the mean-zero, unit-variance random variable Z_n. Suppose θ_0 is zero; then

$$\theta_1 = Y_1$$

$$\theta_2 = \theta_1 + \frac{(Y_2 - \theta_1)}{2} = \frac{\theta_1}{2} + \frac{Y_2}{2}$$

$$\theta_3 = \theta_2 + \frac{(Y_3 - \theta_2)}{2} = \frac{2\theta_2}{3} + \frac{Y_3}{3}$$

$$\vdots \qquad \vdots$$

$$\theta_n = \theta_{n-1} + \frac{(Y_n - \theta_{n-1})}{n} = \frac{(n-1)\theta_{n-1}}{n} + \frac{Y_n}{n}.$$

In this example, stochastic gradient descent (stochastic approximation) delivers the intuitive result that the sample mean should be updated by weighting the previous sample-mean estimate by $[(n-1)/n]$ and then adding it to the new observation Y_n, which is weighted by $(1/n)$. What delivered this result was presciently assuming that α_n should equal n^{-1}. How can the assumption of prescience be circumvented?

Choosing the Learning Rate Schedule

When the step size α_n (sometimes referred to as the *learning rate schedule*) is too large, the gradient steps can actually increase the objective function. On the other hand, if the step size is too small, then convergence can be very slow; in fact, it may not even obtain.

A common choice of learning rate is the constant schedule, which gives an exponentially larger weight to recent examples. In nonstationary environments, the constant schedule can be useful, but in stationary environments the schedule does not always work.

To guarantee convergence asymptotically, Robbins and Monro (1951) demonstrated that the learning rate schedule must satisfy the following conditions:

$$\sum_{n=1}^{\infty} \alpha_n = \infty \tag{7.13}$$

$$\sum_{n=1}^{\infty} \alpha_n^2 < \infty. \tag{7.14}$$

In the example of this section, we chose

$$\alpha_n = \frac{1}{n}.$$

Another, more general, alternative is

$$\alpha_n = \frac{\alpha_0}{\tau_0 + n},$$

which satisfies equations (7.13) and (7.14). A disadvantage is that two additional hyperparameters α_0 and τ_0 have been introduced; a poor choice of either can result in slow convergence.[15] Yet, a third proposed schedule is

$$\alpha_n = \frac{\alpha_0}{(\tau_0 + n)^{\tau_1}},$$

which depends on three hyperparameters, complicating matters even further.

So, too large an α_n and the function can actually increase; too small an α_n and convergence may never obtain. Perhaps not surprisingly, considerable effort has been devoted to investigating the optimal choice, especially in the machine learning literature where hand-tuning the learning schedule is not feasible at scale. What to do?

Ideally, you would like to learn from the past. To the extent that the past is representative of the future, this should work reasonably well. On the other hand, in nonstationary environments, it may not work at all. Thus, it should be clear that using domain-specific knowledge is important.

Because the off-diagonal elements of the Hessian are not used when implementing stochastic gradient descent, you can focus on a representative individual updating equation of the gradient vector $\mathbf{g}_n(\boldsymbol{\theta})$. Thus, to cement the ideas, we focus on just one parameter θ and write

$$(\theta_{n+1} - \theta_n) \equiv \Delta\theta_n = -\alpha_n g_{n+1}(\theta_n).$$

Rumelhart, Hinton, and Williams (1986) proposed the following alternative:

$$\Delta\theta_n = \rho\Delta\theta_{n-1} - \alpha_0 g_{n+1}(\theta_n)$$

---

[15]Hyperparameters in this context are parameters that need to be chosen by the user in some way, perhaps by the methods of *cross-validation*. You can learn more about hyperparameter optimization at http://en.wikipedia.org/wiki/Hyperparameteri_optimization.

where $0 < \rho < 1$. In this case, ρ smooths past values of the changes in θ_n; such changes are sometimes referred to as *momentum*. Any one familiar with time-series analysis recognizes this as an autoregressive model in the momentum of the parameter estimates $\Delta\theta$ having a mean-zero error term $-\alpha_0 g_{n+1}(\theta)$.

Duchi, Hazan, and Singer (2011) proposed a second alternative, referred to as *ADAGRAD*, which has the following form:

$$\Delta\theta_n = -\frac{\alpha_0}{\sum_{i=1}^{n} g_i^2} g_{n+1}(\theta_n).$$

In this case, the attempt is to build an estimate of the inverse of the diagonal element of the Hessian matrix empirically. When N is large, however, the sum of squares in the denominator can become huge, so learning effectively stops.

Matthew D. Zeiler (2012) proposed yet a third alternative,

$$\Delta\theta_n = -\frac{\alpha_0}{\text{RMS}_n(g)} g_{n+1}(\theta_n),$$

which he called the *ADADELTA* method. Here,

$$\text{RMS}_n(g) = \sqrt{\overline{g_n^2} + \epsilon},$$

where the ϵ is a tuning parameter with

$$\overline{g_n^2} = \beta \overline{g_{n-1}^2} + (1-\beta)g_n(\theta_n)^2 \qquad (7.15)$$

and $0 < \beta < 1$. In short, equation (7.15) represents an exponential smoothing of past squared gradient values.[16] The estimate is used to eliminate the noise that can plague getting a reliable estimate of the diagonal element of the Hessian.

Zeiler (2012) proposed a fourth method as well:

$$\Delta\theta_n = -\frac{\text{RMS}_n(\Delta\theta)}{\text{RMS}_n(g)} g_{n+1}(\theta_n),$$

where

$$\text{RMS}_n(\Delta\theta) = \sqrt{\overline{\Delta\theta_n^2} + \nu}$$

with

$$\overline{(\Delta\theta_n)^2} = \gamma\overline{(\Delta\theta_{n-1})^2} + (1-\gamma)(\Delta\theta_n)^2$$

---

[16]See http://en.wikipedia.org/wiki/Exponential_smoothing.

and $0 < \gamma < 1$ and $\nu > 0$. Thus, in addition to an exponential smoothing of past squared gradient values, there is an exponential smoothing of the squared momentum. The object here is to get the units correct.

Schaul, Zhang, and LeCun (2013) presented a nice summary of the issues.

However well these above heuristics may work in practice, theoretical work documenting their behavior is scant. An exception, at least in the case of batch versions of stochastic gradient descent, is the research of Johnson and Zhang (2013).

7.5.9 Derivative-Free Methods

Sometimes, the partial derivatives of the objective function $f(\boldsymbol{\theta})$ are impossible to calculate, or just too difficult to calculate in a reasonable amount of time. But correct derivative information is needed for gradient-based methods to find the correct optimum.

One strategy to deal with this problem involves calculating *finite-difference derivative approximations*, sometimes referred to as *numerical first partial derivatives*. Under this approximating strategy, you would call the function $f(\cdot)$ at some point, say, $\boldsymbol{\theta}_0$, and then perturb the input vector element by element in some direction δ_p. In this way, you can approximate the pth element of the gradient vector $\mathbf{g}(\boldsymbol{\theta}_0)$ by

$$\hat{g}_p(\boldsymbol{\theta}_0) \approx \frac{f(\boldsymbol{\theta}_0 + \delta_p \mathbf{e}_p) - f(\boldsymbol{\theta}_0)}{\delta_p},$$

where $\mathbf{e}_p$ is a $(P \times 1)$ unit vector having a one in row p. Armed with an approximation to the gradient vector, you can then pursue a quasi-Newton method, such as BFGS.

In some circumstances, using numerical first partial derivatives may work. Often, however, researchers use numerical first partial derivatives when the objective function is derived from a statistical simulation, or when it is the output of some numerical integration. Either the statistical simulation or the numerical integration make calculating the true partial derivatives awkward. But it is exactly in these situations where using the finite-difference derivative approximations will be most problematic. In short, although the step size may be small, the error introduced by the approximation inherent in the integration or the simulation can be orders of magnitude larger, thus making it difficult (sometimes impossible) to obtain convergence using numerical first partial derivatives.

Even though optimization in the absence of derivatives is a challenge, during the past half century or so, several strategies have been pursued with some success.

Directional Search

Perhaps the most intuitive method of directional search involves starting at some point θ_0. For the pth element of θ_0, consider increasing the value by 1, or decreasing it by that amount. At each of these 2^P candidate values, calculate the objective function; from the 2^P new candidate objective-function values, choose the one that is the smallest, and go to that point. Begin the process all over again, continuing until convergence obtains.

Although this method is easy to understand and to explain, it has several drawbacks. First, why should the step be 1? It could be α, which can be any step size; for example, you could choose the step size using either line search or trust region methods. Second, why should the same step apply in each dimension? It need not; it can be allowed to vary with the particular element of θ. Again, the step size could be chosen using either line search or trust region methods. Third, because unaltered directional search involves many function evaluations, it can be quite wasteful computationally, so the step size must be chosen adaptively in a clever way. By clever adaptation of the step size, researchers have implementations of directed search that have proven useful in practice. For example, Le Digabel (2011) developed an algorithm based on the research of Audet and Dennis (2006) (see Abramson, Audet, Couture, Dennis, Le Digabel, and Tribes 2013). In turn, this research was used by Nie and Racine (2012) to develop the R package crs, which is a collection of functions for spline-based nonparametric estimation of regression functions with both continuous and categorical regressors.

However intuitive directional search may be, John A. Nelder and Roger Mead proposed a derivative-free algorithm based on a model of the objective function (subsequently named to honor them) that is used frequently.

Nelder-Mead Algorithm

Nelder and Mead (1965) developed perhaps the most attractive alternative to directed search by building on the work of Hooke and Jeeves (1961) and

Spendley, Hext, and Himsworth (1962). Unfortunately, the Nelder-Mead algorithm is sometimes confusingly referred to as the *downhill simplex algorithm*, in contrast to *Dantzig's simplex algorithm*. For this reason, some refer to the Nelder-Mead algorithm as the *polytope method*. Under any name, the Nelder-Mead algorithm is a common way to minimize a function for which derivative information is either unavailable or costly.

The basic idea of Nelder-Mead is to approximate the function by a hyperplane that goes through $(P+1)$ points, and then to take a step appropriately chosen in the direction of steepest descent. A brief graphical description of the method can perhaps provide some insights concerning its behavior. If $\boldsymbol{\theta}$ is a $(P \times 1)$ vector, then the polytope method requires $(P+1)$ initial values. Most implementations of the algorithm, including the one in the Python module `scipy.optimize`, require just one initial value from which the other P guesses are generated, usually by perturbing them element by element. For example, suppose $P = 2$, so $\boldsymbol{\theta}^\top = (\theta_1, \theta_2)$, and $\boldsymbol{\theta}_0^\top$ is, say, $(1,1)$, then for some δ, $\boldsymbol{\theta}_1^\top$ will be $(1+\delta, 1)$, whereas $\boldsymbol{\theta}_2^\top$ will be $(1, 1+\delta)$.

In order to simplify the description, we focus on the trivial sum-of-squares function

$$f(\theta_1, \theta_2) = \theta_1^2 + \theta_2^2$$

of just two variables (θ_1, θ_2). The level sets of this function are depicted in Figure 7.5. We provide three initial vectors, $\boldsymbol{\theta}_0^\top = (1,1)$, $\boldsymbol{\theta}_1^\top = (0,-2)$, and $\boldsymbol{\theta}_2^\top = (-3,0)$. As is common in explanations of two-dimensional examples of the Nelder-Mead algorithm, these three vectors are labeled B(est), G(ood), and W(orst), respectively, because $f_B \equiv f(1,1) = 2 < f_G \equiv f(0,-2) = 4 < f_W = f(-3,0) = 9$.

In the first step of the polytope method, the center of mass for the P best points is found. In this example, this is the sample average of the B vector and the G vector, or

$$\frac{1}{2}\left(\begin{bmatrix} 1 \\ 1 \end{bmatrix} + \begin{bmatrix} 0 \\ -2 \end{bmatrix} \right) = \begin{bmatrix} \frac{1}{2} \\ -\frac{1}{2} \end{bmatrix},$$

which we denote M(ean) because the center of mass is the arithmetic mean.

At this point, the algorithm will *reflect* the vector at W about M to get the point R in Figure 7.6. In this case, we have simply added the distance between W and M to the vector at M, but in general you could use a multiple, say, ρ, where $\rho > 0$.

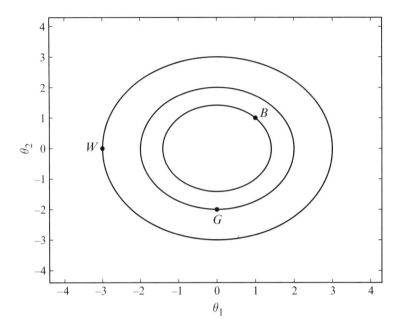

Figure 7.5: Level Sets and Three Initial Guesses

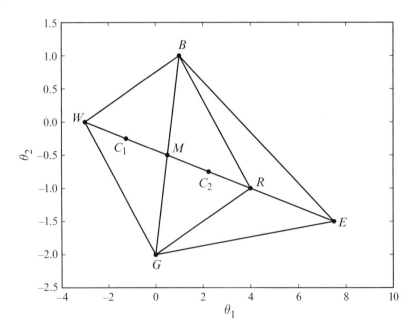

Figure 7.6: Initial Nelder-Mead Simplex

This vector is then *extended* yet again, by some multiple χ, to the point E in the figure; in this case, the distance from R to E is just the distance from M to R; that is, χ is just 2, twice the distance from W to M. The function is now evaluated at the R vector $(4, -1)^\top$ and the E vector $(7.5, -1.5)$. For the example considered in this case,

$$f(4, -1) = 17 \quad \text{and} \quad f(7.5, -1.5) = 58.5.$$

Because the function has not improved in the direction of E, the algorithm then contracts, creating two points C_1 and C_2. In this case, the two points are halfway between W and M as well as M and R, respectively, but one could use a constant ψ that is anywhere in the interval $(0, 1)$.

The C_1 vector is $(-1.25, 0.25)^\top$, and the C_2 vector is $(2.25, -0.75)^\top$. Therefore, in this example

$$f(-1.25, 0.25) = 1.625 \quad \text{and} \quad f(2.25, -0.75) = 5.625.$$

Sometimes, the Nelder-Mead algorithm fails to improve during a contraction of the simplex. In such cases, the polytope method must *shrink* the simplex. Doing this requires yet another parameter, often denoted σ, which is often set to one-half. In this case, the face between W and G is then shifted in parallel toward the point B, as in Figure 7.7.

Hence, at the beginning of the second iteration, the three points of the simplex (triangle) are now the B_2 vector $(-1.25, 0.25)^\top$, the G_2 vector $(1, 1)^\top$, and the W_2 vector $(0, -2)^\top$, as depicted in Figures 7.8 and 7.9.

The new center of mass M_2 vector is $(-0.125, 0.625)$, while the new reflected R_2 vector is $(-0.25, 3.25)$. We do not include the extended E_2 vector because you can see immediately, at least in this example, that the function is not improved at that point. Now,

$$f(-0.125, 0.625) = 0.4065 \quad \text{and} \quad f(-0.25, 3.25) = 10.625.$$

The W_2 vector will now be dropped from the triangle, and the new three points will be B_3 vector $(-0.125, 0.625)^\top$, G_3 vector $(-1.25, 0.25)^\top$, and W_3 vector $(1, 1)^\top$. The process continues until a convergence criterion obtains, or the specified maximum number of iterations is exceeded.

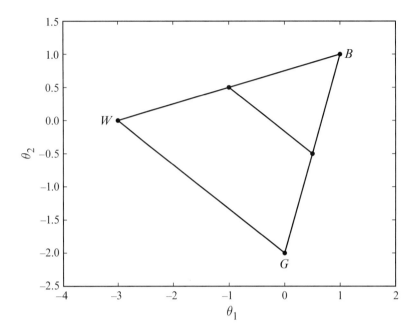

Figure 7.7: Shrinking the Nelder-Mead Simplex

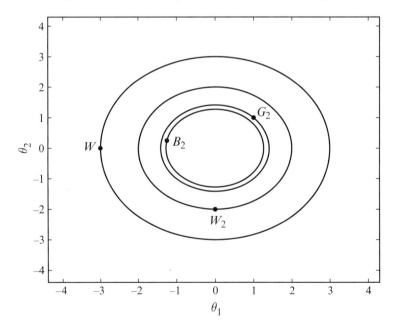

Figure 7.8: Level Sets and Three New Guesses

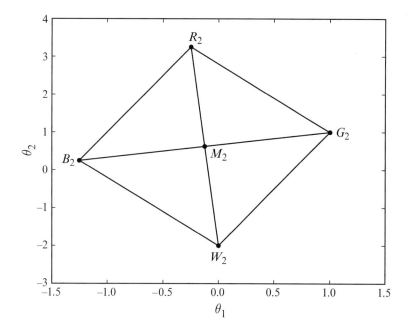

Figure 7.9: Second Iteration of Nelder-Mead Simplex

Genetic Algorithms

One strategy that practioners of optimization have pursued is to mimic nature.
The idea is that, in nature, evolution is a holistic process of optimization, for
example, survival of the fittest. If it works for nature, then why not have a go
with optimization problems? Thus, in the field of artificial intelligence, a *genetic
algorithm* (GA) is a search heuristic that mimics the process of natural selection.
GAs belong to the larger class of methods referred to as *evolutionary algorithms*
(EAs) that have been used to provide approximate solutions to optimization
problems using techniques inspired by inheritance, mutation, selection, and so
forth.

The key word is heuristic. Although using domain knowledge concerning
a problem is one of the most important characteristics of successful research,
search heuristics in optimization have no guarantee of being the most effective
or efficient method, or even of finding the optimum. Thus, we do not recommend GAs or EAs.

Simulated Annealing

Related to EAs and GAs is perhaps the most popular search heuristic, *simulated annealing* (SA), whose name derives from the process of annealing in metallurgy. Annealing involves heating and cooling, say, a steel bar to alter its physical properties by changing the internal structure of the metal. For SA, a *temperature variable* exists that simulates heating. The temperature variable is initially set high but is then allowed to fall—cool. When the temperature variable is high, the algorithm has a higher probability of accepting candidate solutions that are worse than the current best solution than when the temperature variable is low. By accepting a worse solution, the algorithm has the ability to jump out of the region around a local optimum where the SA algorithm could get stuck. As the temperature variable falls, however, the chances of accepting a worse solution fall; this allows the SA algorithm to refine solutions in the part of the search space that are promising. The schedule determining the temperature variable is what makes SA work.

In this field, the main theorem states that for an appropriately-chosen temperature function (cooling schedule), the SA algorithm will find the global optimum. Another interpretation of the theorem is that if all the points in the domain are sampled, the optimum will be found, which is not really surprising but could also take a long time, that is, forever. We mention this heuristic because in the `scipy.optimize` module one of the solvers offered is SA, `anneal()`.

Using examples, we compare the performance of the various optimization strategies.

Model-Based Methods

Another approach is to put structure on how points in the domain are exploited; such techniques are referred to as *model-based derivative-free optimization* methods (model-based DFO methods). Conn, Scheinberg, and Vincente (2009) wrote a very readable introduction to DFO methods. Here, we hope to provide you with some intuition concerning how these methods work.

Basically, in many areas of science, the objective function is expensive to calculate, and can be plagued with noise. For example, two common sources of this noise are integration error and simulation error. Cost and noise make using gradient-based methods of optimization either impractical or impossible. Also, neither directed search nor EAs or SA are reasonable alternatives. Under the Nelder-Mead algorithm, the gradient of a hyperplane is used to decide on a direction to proceed, but the hyperplane is a very simple model of the objective function. Perhaps a more refined model of the objective function can improve on Nelder-Mead. What is one step up from a hyperplane? A quadratic form.

Let's see how this would work using an example described by Conn et al. (2009), namely, choosing the tuning parameters in an optimization routine. For example, suppose you work in a firm that must solve many millions of optimization problems each day. Although these optimization problems are different, they all have the same basic structure. Suppose, further, that you use the Nelder-Mead algorithm. Recall that the Nelder-Mead algorithm relies on four *tuning* parameters that we referred to by $(\rho, \chi, \psi, \sigma)$, the default values for which are typically $(1, 2, 0.5, 0.5)$. Let's collect these four parameters in the vector η. Although the default values in η are sometimes useful, many times they are not. What to do?

Let's try to choose them optimally. Choosing the tuning parameters optimally requires an objective function. What would be the objective function in this case? Imagine that each problem n (where $n = 1, 2, \ldots, N$) has an objective function $f_n(\hat{\theta}_n | \eta)$ (for example, how long it takes to find an optimum at $\hat{\theta}_n$ when the tuning parameters are η) and that you are comfortable with using some objective function as a metric to evaluate your choice of η. For example, the following average-objective function

$$F(\eta) = \frac{1}{N} \sum_{n=1}^{N} f_n(\hat{\theta}_n | \eta)$$

could be one such metric. Alternatively, if $f_n > 0$, then

$$F(\eta) = \prod_{n=1}^{N} f_n(\hat{\theta}_n | \eta)^{\frac{1}{N}}$$

could be another, which can be rewritten as

$$F(\eta) = \frac{1}{N} \sum_{n=1}^{N} \log[f_n(\hat{\theta}_n | \eta)]$$

for reasons outlined.

You can see immediately that finding the derivatives of the objective function in this case is very difficult. Thus, let's try model-based DFO. For each $n = 1, 2, \ldots, N$, and for the default tuning values $\boldsymbol{\eta}_0$, solve each of the N problems using the Nelder-Mead algorithm. Aggregate these solutions to obtain $F(\boldsymbol{\eta}_0)$, which we denote by $\tilde{F}_0$ for short. Change the tuning parameters in some way and do this again, and again. In fact, do it $m = 1, 2, \ldots, M$ times to obtain $\{(\boldsymbol{\eta}_m, \tilde{F}_m)\}_{m=0}^{M}$.

The objective function $F(\boldsymbol{\eta})$ can be approximated by a quadratic form:

$$\hat{F}(\boldsymbol{\eta}) = p + \boldsymbol{\eta}^\top \mathbf{q} + \frac{\boldsymbol{\eta}^\top \mathbf{R} \boldsymbol{\eta}}{2}.$$

In short, when $\boldsymbol{\eta}$ is a $(K \times 1)$ vector, then $\hat{F}(\boldsymbol{\eta})$ has $\frac{(K+1)(K+2)}{2}$ unique parameters. Why? One for p, K for $\mathbf{q}$, and $\frac{K(K+1)}{2}$ for $\mathbf{R}$ because it is a symmetric matrix. Thus, in this case where four Nelder-Mead tuning parameters exist, evaluate $F(\boldsymbol{\eta})$ at 15 points, so $M = 14$; that is,

$$\tilde{F}_m = p + \boldsymbol{\eta}_m^\top \mathbf{q} + \frac{\boldsymbol{\eta}_m^\top \mathbf{R} \boldsymbol{\eta}_m}{2} \quad m = 0, 1, \ldots, 14.$$

Now, these 15 equations in 15 unknowns can be solved for $\tilde{p}_0$, $\tilde{\mathbf{q}}_0$, and $\tilde{\mathbf{R}}_0$. Calculate the minimum of the quadratic form, which obtains at

$$\tilde{\boldsymbol{\eta}}_0 = -\tilde{\mathbf{R}}_0^{-1} \tilde{\mathbf{q}}_0.$$

Based on this value, some of the previous values of $(\boldsymbol{\eta}_m, \tilde{F}_m)$ can be eliminated, and new ones incorporated. Continue until some notion of convergence has obtained.

7.5.10 Numerical Optimization in Python

For many Python users, `scipy` is the main environment within which to conduct numerical optimization, in particular, the `optimize` module. The `optimize` module has several functions that implement many of the algorithms and methods, specifically, the Nelder-Mead algorithm, Powell's (1964) method (which we did not describe), BFGS, and the Newton conjugate gradient method, where the Hessian matrix $\mathbf{H}$ is used instead of a general weighting matrix $\mathbf{Q}$ as in the formula on page 404.

To demonstrate how to use `scipy.optimize`, we first present graphs of solution paths for a very simple function under different algorithms. We use a function for which we know the exact solution as well as the value of the objective function at that solution. Specifically, the function we consider is a sum of squared variables

$$f(\theta_1, \theta_2) = 5\theta_1^2 + 10\theta_2^2,$$

the level sets for which are depicted in Figure 7.10. Notice that the global optimum of $f(\theta_1, \theta_2)$ obtains at $(0,0)$, and the function equals zero at that point. This function is one example of a *quadratic form*, having the following general form:

$$f(\boldsymbol{\theta}) = c + \boldsymbol{\theta}^\top \mathbf{b} + \boldsymbol{\theta}^\top \mathbf{A}\boldsymbol{\theta},$$

where $\mathbf{A}$ is a symmetric, positive definite matrix,

$$\mathbf{A} = \begin{bmatrix} a_{11} & a_{12} \\ a_{21} & a_{22} \end{bmatrix},$$

with $a_{11} > 0$, $a_{22} > 0$, $a_{21} = a_{12}$ and $a_{11}a_{22} > a_{12}^2$ as well as $\mathbf{b}^\top = (b_1, b_2)$. To simplify illustrations, we have made $a_{12} = b_1 = b_2 = a_{21} = c = 0$, which changes nothing qualitatively but simplifies arithmetic.

Naïve directed search—taking one step to the north, south, east, and west of an initial starting value, for example $(-10, 5)$ in Figure 7.10, and then choosing the best function outcome and moving to it—results in the sample path illustrated. Moreover, for this globally convex function, the optimum would be found in about 15 steps. The rate of convergence is sped up by the fact that the optimum is an integer, and the steps are integers as well. In short, this is about as good as things get for directed search.

In Figure 7.11, starting from the same initial point $(-10, 5)$, we present the solution path of the Nelder-Mead algorithm, which makes no use of derivative information. In the case of this well-behaved problem, the Nelder-Mead algorithm does quite well, too, taking about 20 iterations to attain the optimum with a tolerance of 10^{-4}; that is, successive function and iterate values are within 10^{-4} of one another.

In Figure 7.12, we present the solution paths of the methods of gradient descent and Newton-Raphson. In this case, the Newton-Raphson method takes

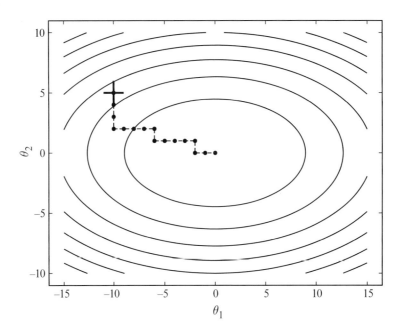

Figure 7.10: Sum-of-Squares Function and Directed Search

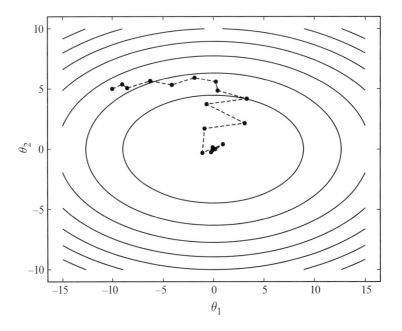

Figure 7.11: Nelder-Mead Solution Path

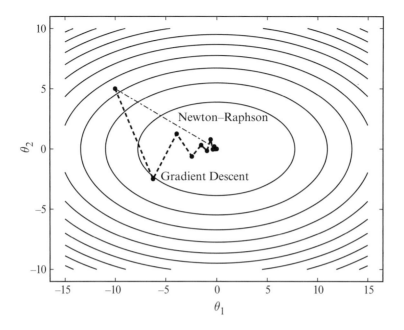

Figure 7.12: Gradient Descent and Newton-Raphson Paths

only one iteration, regardless of the starting value, because the gradient vector can be written as

$$\mathbf{g}(\hat{\boldsymbol{\theta}}) \equiv \begin{bmatrix} 10\hat{\theta}_1 \\ 20\hat{\theta}_2 \end{bmatrix} = \mathbf{0}_2,$$

whence $(\hat{\theta}_1, \hat{\theta}_2) = (0,0)$, and $f(0,0) = 0$, which is the global minimum for a sum of squares. For a general quadratic form, however, the first-order conditions characterizing the optimum would be

$$\mathbf{g}(\hat{\boldsymbol{\theta}}) = \begin{bmatrix} 2a_{11}\hat{\theta}_1 + 2a_{12}\hat{\theta}_2 + b_1 \\ 2a_{21}\hat{\theta}_1 + 2a_{22}\hat{\theta}_2 + b_2 \end{bmatrix} = \mathbf{0}_2,$$

which is a linear system and can be solved in one iteration to obtain

$$\hat{\boldsymbol{\theta}} = -0.5\mathbf{A}^{-1}\mathbf{b}.$$

However useful the sum-of-squares function (the quadratic form) may be in illustrating the mechanics of numerical optimization, the function is not particularly demanding of an algorithm; most algorithms will do well with a quadratic form. In fact, if an algorithm cannot do well with a quadratic form, then it is probably of no practical value. Thus, researchers of the theory of numerical optimization have contrived various functions to challenge the performance of algorithms. See examples at `http://en.wikipedia.org/wiki/Test_functions_for_optimization`.

One such function is referred to as the *Rosenbrock function*, named in honor of Howard H. Rosenbrock (1960), who first proposed the function. Many other functions exist for testing purposes as well. We consider another of those functions, the *Himmelblau function*, named in honor of David M. Himmelblau (1972), who proposed it.

Although the Rosenbrock function is a nonconvex function, it does have a unique, global minimum. This function is commonly used to test the performance of numerical optimization algorithms. In two dimensions (θ_1, θ_2), the Rosenbrock function has the following formula:

$$f(\theta_1, \theta_2) = (1 - \theta_1)^2 + 100(\theta_2 - \theta_1^2)^2.$$

We depict the level sets of the function in Figure 7.13, and in Figure 7.14 a surface plot of the function's two dimensions.

The hallmark of the Rosenbrock function is the banana-shaped valley, the floor of which has very little curvature—it is relatively flat. The global minimum of the Rosenbrock function is at $(1,1)$ where $f(1,1)$ equals zero—the point • near the top of the parabolic-shaped flat valley, as depicted in Figure 7.13. It is this flat valley floor that challenges many algorithms, and is presumably the reason Rosenbrock proposed the function in the first place. Although finding the valley is trivial, converging to the global minimum can be difficult; not all algorithms can do it, which is why the function is such a useful test function.

In the following listings, we illustrate how Python can be used to create both contour and surface plots of functions. First, consider the script `Contour-Plot.py`. Most of the instructions in this script are straightforward. The interesting ones are in lines 17–19, where a grid of points is laid down in the θ_1 and θ_2 dimension, as well as lines 21 and 23, where the grid of points is used to create a mesh, and then the function values are calculated on that mesh. The only other really interesting instruction is in line 31, where the command to label the contour sets is provided. We did not use this command because it cluttered the figure, but in other applications you may find it useful, so we included it and then commented it out.

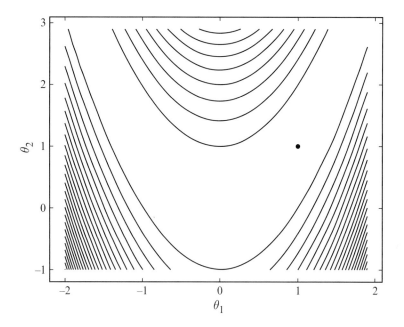

Figure 7.13: Contour Plot of Rosenbrock Function

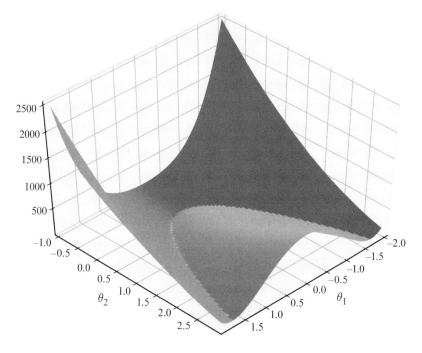

Figure 7.14: Surface Plot of Rosenbrock Function

```
   # Script:  ContourPlot.py
   # Author:  Harry J. Paarsch
   # Date:    7 February 2014
   """This script creates a contour plot of the
      Rosenbrock function, a classic function in
      the theory of numerical optimization.
   """
   import matplotlib.pyplot
   import numpy
10 # Use the TeX fonts.
   matplotlib.pyplot.rc('text', usetex=True)
   # Use fonts with serifs.
   matplotlib.pyplot.rc('font', family='serif')
   # Create variables for the figures, first by
   # calculating two vectors with grid spaced by
   # delta.
   delta = 0.1
   t1 = numpy.arange(-2.0, 2.0, delta)
   t2 = numpy.arange(-1.0, 3.0, delta)
20 # Create the mesh from the vectors t1 and t2.
   t1X, t2Y = numpy.meshgrid(t1, t2)
   # On the grid, evaluate the Rosenbrock function.
   fF = (1.-t1X)*(1.-t1X) + 100*(t2Y-t1X*t1X)*(t2Y-t1X*t1X)
   # Create a simple contour plot with labels in black.
   # The inline argument to clabel will control whether the
   # labels are drawn over the line segments of the contour,
   # removing the lines beneath the label.
   matplotlib.pyplot.figure()
   contourSet = matplotlib.pyplot.contour(t1X, t2Y, fF, 30, colors='k')
30 # Include the next line if you want the contour sets labelled.
   #matplotlib.pyplot.clabel(contourSet, inline=1, fontsize=10)
   matplotlib.pyplot.scatter(1., 1., facecolor='k')
   matplotlib.pyplot.xlabel(r'$\theta_1$', fontsize=14)
   matplotlib.pyplot.ylabel(r'$\theta_2$', fontsize=14)
   matplotlib.pyplot.savefig("ContourPlot.eps")
   matplotlib.pyplot.savefig("ContourPlot-eps-converted-to.pdf")
   matplotlib.pyplot.show()
```

Listing 7.4: Python Script `ContourPlot.py`

The script `SurfacePlot.py` is a prototype that you can use as a model when creating a rendition of the surface of a function in two dimensions. The important instructions begin in line 27 and continue to line 31. The key instruction in this case is in line 31, where the perspective is determined. Getting this correct can involve some trial-and-error, so persevere.

```
# Script:   SurfacePlot.py
# Author:   Harry J. Paarsch
# Date:     7 February 2014
"""This script creates a surface plot of the
    Rosenbrock function, a classic function in
    the theory of numerical optimization.
"""
from    mpl_toolkits.mplot3d import Axes3D
import matplotlib.pyplot
import numpy
# Use the TeX fonts.
matplotlib.pyplot.rc('text', usetex=True)
# Use fonts with serifs.
matplotlib.pyplot.rc('font', family='serif')
# Calculate two vectors with grid spaced by delta
delta = 0.005
t1 = numpy.arange(-2.0, 2.0, delta)
t2 = numpy.arange(-1.0, 3.0, delta)
# Create the mesh from the vectors t1 and t2.
t1X, t2Y = numpy.meshgrid(t1, t2)
# On the grid, evaluate the Rosenbrock function.
fF = (1.-t1X)*(1.-t1X) + 100*(t2Y-t1X*t1X)*(t2Y-t1X*t1X)
# Create surface of the Rosenbrock function in gray,
# label it, and then save it.
gray = (0.7, 0.7, 0.7)
figure = matplotlib.pyplot.figure()
axes   = Axes3D(figure)
axes.plot_surface(t1X, t2Y, fF, linewidth=0.0, color=gray)
matplotlib.pyplot.xlabel(r'$\theta_1$', fontsize=14)
matplotlib.pyplot.ylabel(r'$\theta_2$', fontsize=14)
axes.view_init( 45, 45)
matplotlib.pyplot.savefig("SurfacePlot.eps")
matplotlib.pyplot.savefig("SurfacePlot-eps-converted-to.pdf")
matplotlib.pyplot.show()
```

Listing 7.5: Python Script `SurfacePlot.py`

The Himmelblau function is multimodal and has the following formula in two dimensions:

$$f(\theta_1, \theta_2) = (\theta_1^2 + \theta_2 - 11)^2 + (\theta_1 + \theta_2^2 - 7)^2.$$

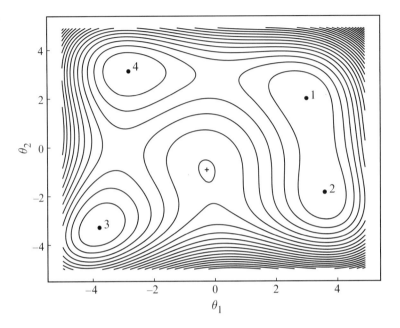

Figure 7.15: Contour Plot of Himmelblau Function

The Himmelblau function has one local maximum at $\theta_1 = -0.270845$ and $\theta_2 = -0.923039$, which is identified by the "+" in Figure 7.15. At this point, the objective function takes on the value 181.617. Four identical local minima, identified by the numbered dots in Figure 7.15, exist:

$$
\begin{aligned}
f(3.0, 2.0) &= f(3.584428, -1.848126) \\
&= f(-3.779310, -3.283186) \\
&= f(-2.805118, 3.131312) = 0.
\end{aligned}
$$

We use both of these functions to illustrate how different optimization functions within the `scipy.optimize` module work. To this end, we have written two modules that live in the files `Rosenbrock.py` and `Himmelblau.py`. From these two modules, we then import the functions `RosenFunc`, `RosenGrad`, and `RosenHess`

```
# Script:   RosenFunc.py
# Author:   Harry J. Paarsch
# Date:     11 February 2014
"""The following returns the classic Rosenbrock
```

```
    function in two dimensions.
"""
def RosenFunc(x):
  import numpy
  return (1.-x[0])**2 + 100.*(x[1]-x[0]*x[0])**2


# Script:  RosenGrad.py
# Author:  Harry J. Paarsch
# Date:     11 February 2014
"""The following returns the gradient vector
   of the classic Rosenbrock function in two
   dimensions.
"""
def RosenGrad(x):
  import numpy
  g = numpy.zeros(len(x))
  g[0] = -2.*(1.-x[0]) - 400.*(x[1]-x[0]*x[0])*x[0]
  g[1] = 200.*(x[1]-x[0]*x[0])
  return g


# Script:  RosenHess.py
# Author:  Harry J. Paarsch
# Date:     11 February 2014
"""The following returns the Hessian matrix
   of the classic Rosenbrock function in two
   dimensions.
"""
def RosenHess(x):
  import numpy
  H = numpy.zeros([len(x),len(x)])
  H[0][0] = 2.*x[0] - 400.*x[1] + 1200.*x[0]*x[0]
  H[0][1] = -400.*x[0]
  H[1][0] = H[0][1]
  H[1][1] = 200.
  return H
```

Listing 7.6: `Rosenbrock.py` Module Functions

as well as `HimmelFunc`, `HimmelGrad`, and `HimmelHess`

```
# Script:  HimmelFunc.py
# Author:  Harry J. Paarsch
# Date:     11 February 2014
"""The following returns the classic Himmelblau
   function in two dimensions.
"""
```

```
def HimmelFunc(x):
  import numpy
  f = (x[0]*x[0] + x[1] - 11.) * (x[0]*x[0] + x[1] - 11.)
  f = f + (x[0] + x[1]*x[1] - 7.) * (x[0] + x[1]*x[1] - 7.)
  return f

# Script:  HimmelGrad.py
# Author:  Harry J. Paarsch
# Date:      11 February 2014
"""The following returns the gradient vector
   of the classic Himmelblau function in two
   dimensions.
"""
def HimmelGrad(x):
  import numpy
  g = numpy.zeros(len(x))
  t1 = 2.*(x[0]*x[0] + x[1] - 11.)
  t2 = 2.*(x[0] + x[1]*x[1] -  7.)
  g[0] = 2. * x[0] * t1 + t2
  g[1] = t1 + 2. * x[1] * t2
  return g

# Script:  HimmelHess.py
# Author:  Harry J. Paarsch
# Date:      11 February 2014
"""The following returns the Hessian matrix
   of the classic Himmelblau function in two
   dimensions.
"""
def HimmelHess(x):
  import numpy
  H = numpy.zeros([len(x),len(x)])
  H[0][0] = 12. * x[0]*x[0] + 4. * x[1] - 42.
  H[0][1] = 4. * (x[0] + x[1])
  H[1][0] = H[0][1]
  H[1][1] = 12. * x[1]*x[1] + H[0][1] - 28.
  return H
```

Listing 7.7: `Himmelblau.py` Module Functions

    We first use the Rosenbrock function to test the following routines within the `optimize` module of `scipy`: fmin(), fmin_powell(), fmin_cg(), fmin_bfgs(), fmin_ncg(), and fmin_anneal().

```
# Script:   RosenbrockExample.py
# Author:   Harry J. Paarsch
# Date:     11 February 2014
"""This script drives the SciPy optimization
   module, for the Rosenbrock function, a
   classic function in numerical optimization.
"""
from Rosenbrock import RosenFunc, RosenGrad, RosenHess
import numpy
import scipy.optimize
# Get some starting values so the comparisons can begin.
P = int(raw_input("Number of Parameters: "))
x0 = numpy.zeros(P)
for p in range(0, P):
  x0[p] = float(raw_input("Input value for %i:  " % p))

print "========================================", '\n'
print "Comparing different scipy.optimize solvers"
print "using the Rosenbrock test objective function"
print "for the initial value:  ", x0              , '\n'
print "========================================", '\n'
# Using Nelder-Mead algorithm
results = scipy.optimize.fmin(RosenFunc, x0, ftol=0.0001)
print 'Nelder-Mead', results, '\n'
# Using Powell's algorithm
results = scipy.optimize.fmin_powell(RosenFunc, x0, ftol=0.0001)
print 'Powell', results, '\n'
# Using conjugate gradient algorithm
results = scipy.optimize.fmin_cg(RosenFunc, x0, RosenGrad, gtol
    =0.0001)
print 'Conjugate Gradient', results, '\n'
# Using Broyden-Fletcher-Goldfarb-Shanno algorithm
results = scipy.optimize.fmin_bfgs(RosenFunc, x0, RosenGrad, gtol
    =0.0001)
print 'BFGS', results, '\n'
# Using Newton-CG algorithm
results = scipy.optimize.fmin_ncg(RosenFunc, x0, RosenGrad, fhess=
    RosenHess, maxiter=1000)
print 'Newton-CG', results, '\n'
# Using annealing
results = scipy.optimize.anneal(RosenFunc, x0, schedule='cauchy')
print 'Simulated Annealing', results, '\n'
```

Listing 7.8: RosenbrockExample.py Test Driver

The Nelder-Mead, Powell, BFGS, conjugate gradient, and Newton conjugate gradient methods all did reasonably well on the Rosenbrock function, regardless of the starting values. On the other hand, SA did very poorly, even when the starting values were very close to the optimium.

```
================================================

Comparing different scipy.optimize solvers
using the Rosenbrock test objective function
for the initial value:   [ 5.   5.]


================================================


Optimization terminated successfully.
        Current function value: 0.000000
        Iterations: 106
        Function evaluations: 201
Nelder-Mead [ 0.99998936  0.9999766 ]

Optimization terminated successfully.
        Current function value: 0.000000
        Iterations: 25
        Function evaluations: 719
Powell [ 1.   1.]

Optimization terminated successfully.
        Current function value: 0.000000
        Iterations: 31
        Function evaluations: 100
        Gradient evaluations: 73
Conjugate Gradient [ 1.00001158  1.00002314]

Optimization terminated successfully.
        Current function value: 0.000000
        Iterations: 54
        Function evaluations: 72
        Gradient evaluations: 72
BFGS [ 1.00001813  1.00003619]

Optimization terminated successfully.
        Current function value: 0.000000
        Iterations: 72
        Function evaluations: 115
        Gradient evaluations: 72
```

```
                Hessian evaluations: 72
Newton-CG [ 0.99999957   0.99999913]

Simulated Annealing (array([ 0.4486194 ,   7.27943998]), 0)
```

Listing 7.9: Terminal Output from `RosenbrockExample.py`

In the case of the Himmelblau function, the Nelder-Mead, Powell, BFGS, conjugate gradient, and Newton conjugate-gradient methods typically found the local minimum that was nearest to the starting values, although the following output listing illustrates that some heterogeneity existed as well. For example, when starting at the value $(0,0)$ the Newton conjugate gradient method appeared to get stuck, whereas the other four methods converged to the point $(3,2)$, one of the local optima labeled 1 in Figure 7.15. On the other hand, with the initial value $(-0.5, 0.0)$, the Powell method converged to $(3,2)$, whereas the other three methods converged to $(-2.8051, 3.1313)$. In all cases, SA again did very poorly, even when starting values were very close to one of the optima.

```
================================================

Comparing different scipy.optimize solvers
using the Himmelblau test objective function
for the initial value:   [ 0.  0.]

================================================

Optimization terminated successfully.
        Current function value: 0.000000
        Iterations: 81
        Function evaluations: 157
Nelder-Mead [ 3.00000632   1.99996853]

Optimization terminated successfully.
        Current function value: 0.000000
        Iterations: 7
        Function evaluations: 232
Powell [ 3.   2.]

Optimization terminated successfully.
        Current function value: 0.000000
        Iterations: 11
        Function evaluations: 36
        Gradient evaluations: 25
```

```
Conjugate Gradient [ 2.99999997  1.99999998]

Optimization terminated successfully.
        Current function value: 0.000000
        Iterations: 10
        Function evaluations: 16
        Gradient evaluations: 16
BFGS [ 2.99999989  1.99999996]

Optimization terminated successfully.
        Current function value: 169.999976
        Iterations: 1
        Function evaluations: 5
        Gradient evaluations: 1
        Hessian evaluations: 1
Newton-CG [   5.03043120e-07   7.90496332e-07]

Simulated Annealing (array([-9.95323968, -5.02335818]), 0)
```

Listing 7.10: Terminal Output from `HimmelblauExample.py`

What points did we hope to make with this exercise? First, if the function has many potential local optima, then the starting value will be very important in determining which local optimum an algorithm will find. Second, when available, curvature information is really helpful. One of the reasons why gradient descent wanders, even in a well-behaved problem, is that the choice of the parameter α is very important. If α is too large, then the method will overshoot. On the other hand, when α is too small, the algorithm will take a very long time to converge. The Newton-Raphson and quasi-Newton methods do well because the α parameter in those cases is different for each element of θ and is adaptive, reacting to the local curvature of the function either through the inverse of the Hessian matrix or through an approximation to that matrix.

7.6   Constrained Optimization

In many fields, particularly in economics and engineering, the sets in which choice variables live are bounded—constrained. Thus, the optimization problems in these fields are constrained ones. During the past century, mathematicians have made considerable headway in solving particular kinds of constrained optimization problems. At the low end are the linear programming problems, that is, problems in which the objective functions are linear functions of the continuous choice variables, and the constraints are, too. Next come the quadratic programming problems, where the objective functions are now quadratic functions of the continuous choice variables, but the constraints remain linear functions of the continuous choice variables. Even more general than the quadratic programming problems are the convex optimization problems, where the objective functions are convex functions of the continuous choice variables, and the constraints characterize convex choice sets.[17] Finally come the nonlinear programming problems where neither the objectives nor the constraints need be either smooth or continuous, for example, integer programming problems.

7.6.1 Linear Programming

A large class of problems in business and science can be cast in the following form:

$$\min_{\mathbf{x}} \ \mathbf{c}^{\top}\mathbf{x} \quad \text{subject to} \quad \mathbf{A}\mathbf{x} \leq \mathbf{b}, \ \mathbf{x} \geq \mathbf{0}_K, \tag{7.16}$$

where $\mathbf{x}$ is a $(K \times 1)$ vector of choice variables, and $\mathbf{c}$ is a $(K \times 1)$ vector of cost parameters. The matrix $\mathbf{A}$ is of dimension $(J \times K)$ and contains parameters that represent how much of each x_k is required, and $\mathbf{b}$ is a $(J \times 1)$ vector of parameters that represents constraints on factors used to make up the x_ks. Within this framework, it is assumed that the choice variables can only take on weakly positive values.

Casting optimization problems as linear programs was developed by the Soviet mathematician Leonid Kantorovich in the 1930s, but because his research was undertaken for the military, it was kept secret and was unknown

---

[17]*Convex* is used in two ways here. First, a univariate function $f(x)$ is convex if for any two points x_0 and x_1 in its domain $\mathcal{X}$, the cord between $f(x_0)$ and $f(x_1)$ is weakly above the function itself. In symbols,

$$\lambda f(x_0) + (1 - \lambda)f(x_1) \geq f(x) \quad \forall x_0, x_1 \in \mathcal{X} \text{ and } \lambda \in [0,1].$$

The concept generalizes to the case where the $(K \times 1)$ vector $\mathbf{x} \in \mathbb{R}^K$. Second, a set $\mathcal{X} \in \Re^K$ is convex if for any two points $\mathbf{x}_0$ and $\mathbf{x}_1$ in $\mathcal{X}$ the point

$$\lambda \mathbf{x}_0 + (1 - \lambda)\mathbf{x}_1$$

is also in $\mathcal{X}$.

to the American operations researcher George B. Dantzig, who developed an algorithm to solve linear programs in the mid-1940s. Dantzig's algorithm is often referred to as the *simplex method*. Klee and Minty (1972) proved that the simplex algorithm has a worst-case total resource use that is exponential. That said, vast practical experience suggests that the average-case behavior of Dantzig's method is polynomial. Because of this efficient behavior, the simplex algorithm has been used to solve literally billions of linear programming problems since its invention.

In Python the most straightforward way to calculate solutions to linear programs is to use the CVXOPT package, which was developed by Martin Andersen, Joachim Dahl, and Lieven Vandenberghe and is located at http://cvxopt.org/examples/tutorial/lp.html. Below, we demonstrate how to use CVXOPT to solve the following prototypical linear program:

$$\min_{x_1, x_2} 2x_1 + x_2 \quad \text{subject to} \quad 4x_1 + x_2 \geq 4$$

$$x_1 + x_2 \geq 2$$
$$x_1 + 3x_2 \geq 3$$
$$x_1 \geq 0$$
$$x_2 \geq 0.$$

Figure 7.16 depicts the constraint set for this problem by the gray shaded area to the northeast of the origin. As you can see, the constraint set is convex: each half space defined by one of the five inequalities defines a convex set, and the intersection of convex sets is convex. In this problem, the objective is to get as close to the origin $(0,0)$ as possible, yet still satisfy the five constraints. Clearly, this means being somewhere along the sequence of lines from $(0,4)$ to $(\frac{2}{3}, \frac{4}{3})$ to $(\frac{3}{2}, \frac{1}{2})$ to $(3,0)$.

Which vertex is chosen will depend on the relative slope of the objective function $\mathbf{c}^\top \mathbf{x}$. When the objective function is very steep, having a slope less than -4 in this example, the optimal solution will obtain at $(0,4)$. As the objective function flattens, $(0,4)$ will remain a solution until the slope is greater than -4 but less than -1. In this case, the optimal solution will obtain at $(\frac{2}{3}, \frac{4}{3})$. When the slope exceeds -1 but is less than -3^{-1}, the optimal solution will obtain at $(\frac{3}{2}, \frac{1}{2})$. Finally, for any slope greater than -3^{-1}, the optimal solution is at $(3,0)$. When the slope is exactly equal to -1, an indeterminacy exists, that is, the optimal solution is not unique, being any point along the ray between $(\frac{2}{3}, \frac{4}{3})$ and $(\frac{3}{2}, \frac{1}{2})$.

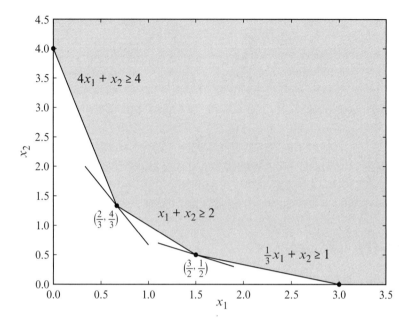

Figure 7.16: Optimal Solution to Linear Program

Dantzig's simplex algorithm provides an efficient way to decide which of the kinked points along the outer edge of the constraint set should be visited. Although, as the number of variables and constraints increases, an exponentially increasing number of these points exists, the average-case behavior of the simplex algorithm is polynomial.

When $\mathbf{c}^\top = (1, 2)$, the solution $\hat{\mathbf{x}} = (\frac{3}{2}, \frac{1}{2})$, whereas if $\mathbf{c}^\top = (2, 1)$, then the solution $\hat{\mathbf{x}} = (\frac{2}{3}, \frac{4}{3})$. Specifically,

```
>>> import cvxopt
>>> import cvxopt.solvers
>>> A = cvxopt.matrix([[-4.00, -1.00, -1.00, -1.00,  0.00],
...                    [-1.00, -1.00, -3.00,  0.00, -1.00]])
>>> b = cvxopt.matrix([[-4.00, -2.00, -3.00,  0.00,  0.00]])
>>> c = cvxopt.matrix([1., 2.])
>>> solution = cvxopt.solvers.lp(c, A, b)
     pcost       dcost       gap    pres   dres   k/t
 0:  2.1364e+00  1.0197e+01  1e+01  7e-01  4e+00  1e+00
 1:  2.4669e+00  4.0222e+00  9e-01  1e-01  6e-01  4e-01
 2:  2.3372e+00  2.9083e+00  4e-01  4e-02  2e-01  2e-01
 3:  2.4992e+00  2.5142e+00  1e-02  1e-03  6e-03  3e-03
```

```
  4:  2.5000e+00  2.5001e+00  1e-04  1e-05  6e-05  3e-05
  5:  2.5000e+00  2.5000e+00  1e-06  1e-07  6e-07  3e-07
  6:  2.5000e+00  2.5000e+00  1e-08  1e-09  6e-09  3e-09
Optimal solution found.
>>> print solution['x']
[ 1.50e+00]
[ 5.00e-01]
>>>
```

An alternative to CVXOPT is PuLP, which is a linear programming modeler for Python. A modeler is a declarative language that allows you to create input files that can then be processed by various solvers.

7.6.2 Dual Representation

In the preceding section, we wrote out the linear programming problem in a notation that mapped easily to CVXOPT, but the canonical representation of linear programming problems typically has the following form:

$$\max_{\mathbf{x}} \ \mathbf{c}^{\top}\mathbf{x} \quad \text{subject to} \quad \mathbf{A}\mathbf{x} \leq \mathbf{b}, \ \mathbf{x} \geq \mathbf{0}_K, \qquad (7.17)$$

which is referred to as the *primal* representation. Here, $\mathbf{x}$ is a $(K \times 1)$ vector of choice (control) variables, and $\mathbf{c}$ is a $(K \times 1)$ vector of known parameters, with $\mathbf{A}$ and $\mathbf{b}$ being an $(M \times K)$ matrix and an $(M \times 1)$ vector of known parameters, respectively.

We introduce this representation because the *dual* representation of this linear program then has the following form:

$$\min_{\mathbf{y}} \ \mathbf{b}^{\top}\mathbf{y} \quad \text{subject to} \quad \mathbf{A}^{\top}\mathbf{y} \geq \mathbf{c}, \ \mathbf{y} \geq \mathbf{0}_M. \qquad (7.18)$$

In this representation, $\mathbf{y}$ is an $(M \times 1)$ vector that will correspond to the Lagrange multipliers (shadow prices) that would obtain in the solution to problem (7.17).

For linear programs, the solutions to problems (7.17) and (7.18) have the following structure:

$$\mathbf{c}^{\top}\mathbf{x}^{*} \leq \mathbf{b}^{\top}\mathbf{y}^{*}, \qquad (7.19)$$

which is referred to as the *weak duality property*.

The most important point to note is that a duality exists between the two formulations. Sometimes, it will be more convenient to solve the dual of a problem than its primal representation. This duality also carries over to other convex optimization problems, such as the quadratic programming problems. In Chapter 8 we mention this duality when describing how large-scale optimization problems involving support vector machines can be solved.

7.6.3 Quadratic Programming

The next step up from linear programming problems is quadratic programming problems. Quadratic programming problems have the following basic structure:

$$\min_{\mathbf{x}} \frac{1}{2}\mathbf{x}^{\top}\mathbf{Q}\mathbf{x} + \mathbf{x}^{\top}\mathbf{p} \quad \text{subject to} \quad \mathbf{G}\mathbf{x} \leq \mathbf{h}, \ \mathbf{A}\mathbf{x} = \mathbf{b} \tag{7.20}$$

where $\mathbf{x}$ is again a $(K \times 1)$ vector of choice variables. For most quadratic programming problems, $\mathbf{Q}$ is a $(K \times K)$ matrix that is symmetric as well as positive definite, and $\mathbf{p}$ is a $(K \times 1)$ vector whose elements are unconstrained. The matrices $\mathbf{G}$ and $\mathbf{A}$ as well as the vectors $\mathbf{h}$ and $\mathbf{b}$ contain known parameters. In general, $\mathbf{G}$ and $\mathbf{A}$ both have K columns, but the row dimension of each will depend on the application. Thus, the dimensions of $\mathbf{h}$ and $\mathbf{b}$ depend on the row dimensions of $\mathbf{G}$ and $\mathbf{A}$, respectively.

At http://cvxopt.org/examples/tutorial/qp.html, sample code to solve the following quadratic program is available:

$$\min_{x_1, x_2} 2x_1^2 + x_2^2 + x_1 x_2 + x_1 + x_2 \quad \text{subject to} \quad x_1 \geq 0$$
$$x_2 \geq 0$$
$$x_1 + x_2 = 1.$$

In particular,

```
>>> from cvxopt import matrix, solvers
>>> Q = 2*matrix([ [2, .5], [.5, 1] ])
>>> p = matrix([1.0, 1.0])
>>> G = matrix([[-1.0,0.0],[0.0,-1.0]])
>>> h = matrix([0.0,0.0])
>>> A = matrix([1.0, 1.0], (1,2))
>>> b = matrix(1.0)
>>> solution = solvers.qp(Q, p, G, h, A, b)
     pcost        dcost        gap      pres     dres
```

```
 0:   1.8889e+00   7.7778e-01   1e+00   3e-16   2e+00
 1:   1.8769e+00   1.8320e+00   4e-02   1e-16   6e-02
 2:   1.8750e+00   1.8739e+00   1e-03   2e-16   5e-04
 3:   1.8750e+00   1.8750e+00   1e-05   1e-16   5e-06
 4:   1.8750e+00   1.8750e+00   1e-07   3e-16   5e-08
Optimal solution found.
>>> print(solution['x'])
[ 2.50e-01]
[ 7.50e-01]
>>>
```

The geometry of the solution is depicted in Figure 7.17. The objective function increases the further from the origin you are because the numbers on the level sets increase away from the origin. The feasible set is the quadrant where both x_1 and x_2 are weakly positive. Within this set, the solution must satisfy $x_1 + x_2 = 1$, which occurs at the tangency of this line and the objective function, point $(0.25, 0.75)$, which is identified by the $\bullet$ in the figure. The $\bullet$ at the origin in the figure denotes the global minimum of the function.

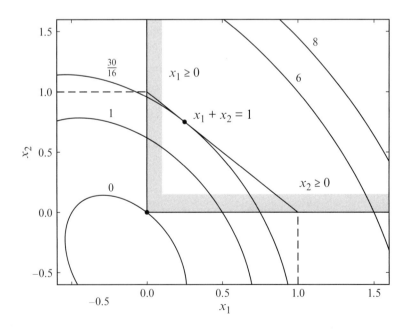

Figure 7.17: Solution to Quadratic Program

When **Q** is positive definite, the complexity of the best algorithms to solve quadratic programming problems is polynomial. If **Q** is not positive definite, then the quadratic programming problem lives within the NP-hard class.

7.6.4 Convex Optimization

Convex optimization is a further step up from quadratic programming. Within this subfield of optimization theory, mathematicians have constrained themselves to the problem of minimizing a convex function subject to a convex set. The convexity properties of both the objective function and the constraint set make the problem easier to solve because any local minimum is a global minimum.

Sundaram (1996) has provided a good introduction to optimization theory, but others exist as well. For example, the book by Boyd and Vandenberghe (2004) concerned convex optimization and contained many solved examples from a variety of fields; the Python CVXOPT package was written to supplement that book.

In general, a convex optimization problem has the following form:

$$\min_{\mathbf{x}} f(\mathbf{x}) \quad \text{subject to} \quad \mathbf{g}(\mathbf{x}) \leq \mathbf{0}_J, \tag{7.21}$$

where **x** is a $(K \times 1)$ vector. When $f(\mathbf{x})$ is a quasi-concave function of **x**, and the set of points defined by the constraint set is convex, mathematicians have characterized the optimum of $f(\mathbf{x})$. In addition, if $\mathbf{g}(\mathbf{x})$ is sufficiently smooth, the method of Lagrange, suitably modified, can be used to find the optimum. Associated with equation (7.21) is the following Lagrangian:

$$\mathcal{L}(\mathbf{x}, \boldsymbol{\lambda}) = f(\mathbf{x}) - \boldsymbol{\lambda}^\top \mathbf{g}(\mathbf{x}),$$

where $\boldsymbol{\lambda}$ is a $(J \times 1)$ vector of Lagrange multipliers. The complexity of the best algorithms to solve convex optimization problems is polynomial.

The CVXOPT package is useful for small to medium-size problems. For large-scale convex optimization problems, use IPOPT (Interior Point Optimizer), an open-source software package written in C++ and designed for large-scale optimization problems in general. Python has a package named iptopt, which is a cython wrapper for the IPOPT optimization solver.

7.6.5   Nonlinear Programming

A step up from the convex optimization problem is the nonlinear programming problem. Stating a nonlinear programming problem as

$$\min_{\mathbf{x}\in\mathcal{X}} f(\mathbf{x}) \quad \text{subject to} \quad g_j(\mathbf{x}) \leq 0, \quad j = 1, 2, \dots, J$$
$$h_i(\mathbf{x}) = 0, \quad i = 1, 2, \dots, I$$

is typically not the difficult part; solving it is. Which solution algorithm to use depends to a large extent on the structure of the set defined by the constraints as well as the structure of the objective function. A somewhat dated but well-written description of the issues is contained in Gill, Murray, and Wright (1981). In short, solving nonlinear programming problems involves considerable skill, a science to be sure, but some art is involved as well. The practical problem is that Python really does not have any good solvers for general nonlinear programming problems. What to do?

When the objective function and the constraints are smooth, the program MINOS (Modular In-core Nonlinear Optimization System) is well-suited to solving nonlinear programming problems. MINOS is particularly powerful at solving nonlinear programs where the objective function is smooth and non-linear in the choice variables, but the constraints are linear. MINOS works best when the gradient vector of the objective function and the Jacobian matrix of the constraints have closed-form expressions. For additional information, see the technical report by Murtagh and Saunders (2003), who created the program.

SNOPT (Sparse Nonlinear OPTimizer), a program for solving large-scale optimization problems, is another option (see Gill et al. 2002). The SNOPT program is especially effective for nonlinear problems whose objective functions and gradient vectors are expensive to evaluate, so it is an alternative to MINOS. The objective functions should be smooth but need not be convex.

Both MINOS and SNOPT are written in FORTRAN–77, which makes them difficult to integrate with Python. Because programming languages like FORTRAN impose entry barriers to researchers using high-quality solvers, a number of modeling languages have been developed. Modeling languages are declarative languages that remove the user from the low-level code used to perform the calculations. One example of a modeling language is AMPL (A Mathematical Programming Language); AMPL is a comprehensive and powerful algebraic modeling language for linear and nonlinear optimization problems in discrete or continuous variables. Like UNIX and C, AMPL was developed at AT&T Bell Labs, so you can be sure that it is of high quality. Fourer, Gay, and Kernighan (2002) wrote a step-by-step guide to using AMPL effectively.

An approach to solving a particular class of nonlinear programming problems, referred to as *mathematical programming with equilibrium constraints* (MPEC), was developed by Luo, Pang, and Ralph (1996). Su and Judd (2012) were the first to advocate employing the MPEC approach in economics. Hubbard and Paarsch (2009) and Hubbard, Kirkegaard, and Paarsch (2013) demonstrated how effective AMPL can be in solving auction problems that have been cast in the MPEC form.

Another example of a modeling language is GAMS (General Algebraic Modeling System), a high-level modeling system for mathematical programming and optimization. GAMS consists of a language compiler and a stable of integrated high-performance solvers. In fact, GAMS/MINOS is the oldest nonlinear programming solver available within GAMS. In short, the two modeling languages AMPL and GAMS call MINOS and SNOPT, among other solvers, under the hood, and are well-suited to solving large-scale linear, mixed integer, and nonlinear optimization problems. Unfortunately, neither AMPL nor GAMS is free.

Coopr (Common optimization Python repository), a suite of open-source optimization-related Python packages that supports a diverse set of optimization capabilities for formulating and analyzing optimization models, is available for free for the three major operating systems, Linux, OS X, and Windows. The Python Optimization Modeling Objects (`Pyomo`) package is an open-source tool for modeling optimization applications in Python that drives Coopr. `Pyomo` can be used to define symbolic problems, create problem specification files, and solve these problems using standard solvers. Coopr supports dozens of solvers, both open source and commercial, and *all* of the solvers supported by AMPL are included as well. Thus, `Pyomo` can incorporate solvers from AMPL and GAMS, but `Pyomo`'s modeling objects are embedded within Python and supported by the rich infrastructure within that language. In addition to integrating with Python, Coopr/`Pyomo` is free, available at `http://software.sandia.gov/trac/coopr`. Hart, Laird, Watson, and Woodruff (2012) have provided a useful discussion.

What's not to like about `Pyomo`? Incorporating the solvers (such as MINOS or SNOPT) from AMPL and GAMS requires a site license. In other words, they must be purchased.

Thus, solving large-scale nonlinear programming problems is a costly enterprise. Paarsch has had good experiences with AMPL as well as the solvers MINOS and SNOPT, either by themselves or when called from AMPL.

7.7 Approximation Methods

Often, a researcher is interested in approximating a function $f^0(x)$ using a simpler function $\hat{f}(x)$. Under certain conditions, $f^0(x)$ can be represented exactly by a Taylor series expansion of the following form:

$$f^0(x) = f^0(x_0) + \sum_{j=1}^{\infty} \frac{\mathrm{d}^{(j)} f^0(x_0)}{\mathrm{d}x^j} \frac{(x - x_0)^j}{j!}.$$

This polynomial is troublesome in practice. Since ∞ cannot be represented on a digital computer, truncation errors will occur. In many cases, the derivatives of $f^0(x)$ are unknown because $f^0(x)$ is unknown and must be estimated. What to do?

Suppose you are willing to truncate $f^0(x)$ at some high-order K, so

$$f^0(x) = f^0(x_0) + \sum_{k=1}^{K} \frac{\mathrm{d}^{(k)} f^0(x_0)}{\mathrm{d}x^k} \frac{(x - x_0)^k}{k!} + U(x_0).$$

Suppose the values of $f^0(x)$ are known at a finite set of $(K + 1)$ points $(x_1, \ldots, x_{K+1})$; denote them $y_k = f^0(x_k)$. The derivatives can be estimated from the following linear system:

$$y_1 = \alpha_0 + \alpha_1(x_1 - x_0) + \alpha_2(x_1 - x_0)^2 \ldots + \alpha_K(x_1 - x_0)^K + U_1$$
$$y_2 = \alpha_0 + \alpha_1(x_2 - x_0) + \alpha_2(x_2 - x_0)^2 \ldots + \alpha_K(x_2 - x_0)^K + U_2$$

$$\vdots = \qquad \vdots$$

$$y_{K+1} = \alpha_0 + \alpha_1(x_{K+1} - x_0) + \alpha_2(x_{K+1} - x_0)^2 \ldots + \alpha_K(x_{K+1} - x_0)^K + U_{K+1},$$

or in matrix notation,

$$\mathbf{y} = \mathbf{X}\boldsymbol{\alpha} + \mathbf{U},$$

so

$$\hat{\alpha} = (\mathbf{X}^\top \mathbf{X})^{-1} \mathbf{X}^\top \mathbf{y}.$$

Suppose x_0 is zero. A matrix of the following form

$$\mathbf{X} = \begin{bmatrix} 1 & x_1 & x_1^2 & \cdots & x_1^K \\ 1 & x_2 & x_2^2 & \cdots & x_2^K \\ \vdots & \vdots & \vdots & \ddots & \vdots \\ 1 & x_{K+1} & x_{K+1}^2 & \cdots & x_{K+1}^K \end{bmatrix}$$

is referred to as a *Vandermonde matrix*. When K is quite large, solving for $\hat{\alpha}$ is a delicate problem numerically because the matrix $(\mathbf{X}^\top \mathbf{X})$ will be ill-conditioned. This occurs because the column of x_k^js and the column of x_k^{j+1}s are almost collinear, that is, nearly linear combinations of one another. Consider Figure 7.18, where we present the natural logarithm of the average condition number of square matrices having $k = 1, 2, \ldots, 10$ dimensions where the columns of each such matrix are made up of powers of a $(k \times 1)$ random vector

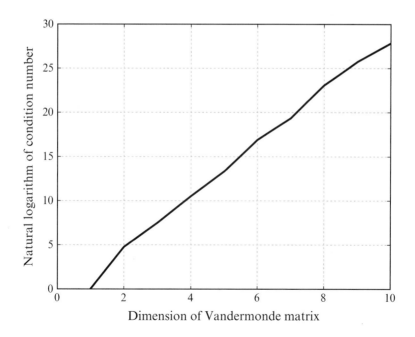

Figure 7.18: Condition Numbers of Vandermonde Matrices

drawn uniformly from the interval $[0, 1]$. As you can see, such matrices are very ill-conditioned.

Numerical analysts suggest using an alternative basis, and replacing the x_k^js with orthogonal polynomials; see Judd (1998). A variety of different orthogonal bases exist. For example, when x is contained on $[-1, 1]$, Chebyshev polynomials are used, whereas when x is contained on $[0, \infty)$, Laguerre polynomials are used, and when x is contained on $(-\infty, \infty)$, Hermite polynomials are used. In general, $f^0(x)$ can be approximated by a polynomial

$$\hat{f}_K(x) = \sum_{k=0}^{K} \alpha_k P_k(x).$$

Typically, the polynomial terms $\{P_k(x)\}_{k=0}^{\infty}$ can be constructed recursively. For example, in the case of Chebyshev polynomials $C_0(x)$ is 1, and $C_1(x)$ is x. Subsequently,

$$C_{k+1}(x) = 2xC_k(x) - C_{k-1}(x) \quad k = 1, 2, \dots .$$

Graphs of Chebyshev $C_k(x)$ polynomials for $k = 1, 2, 3, 4$ are presented in Figure 7.19.

In the case of Laguerre polynomials $L_0(x)$ is 1 and $L_1(x)$ is $(1 - x)$, and

$$L_{k+1}(x) = \frac{1}{k+1}(2k + 1 - x)L_k(x) - \frac{k}{k+1}L_{k-1}(x) \quad k = 1, 2, \dots .$$

Graphs of Laguerre $L_k(v)$ polynomials for $k = 1, 2, 3, 4$ are presented in Figure 7.20.

In the case of Hermite polynomials, $H_0(x)$ is 1 and $H_1(x)$ is $2x$, and

$$H_{k+1}(x) = 2xH_k(x) - 2kH_{k-1}(x) \quad k = 1, 2, \dots .$$

Graphs of Hermite $H_k(x)$ polynomials for $k = 1, 2, 3, 4$ are presented in Figure 7.21.

How can you use these methods? Consider approximating the function

$$f(x) = \log(1 + x)$$

on the interval $[0, 10]$. The following listing constructs an approximation to this function using a tenth-order Chebyshev's polynomial at 11 points, and then evaluates the approximation at 100 other points. (The weights are effectively

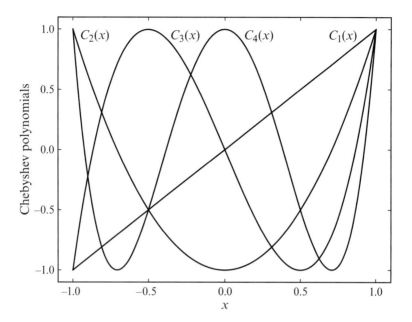

Figure 7.19: First Four Chebyshev Polynomials

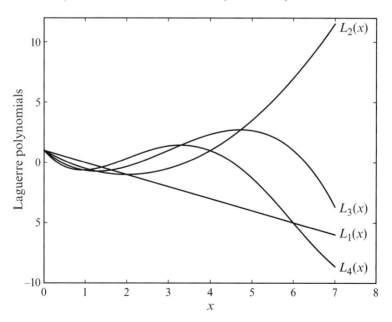

Figure 7.20: First Four Laguerre Polynomials

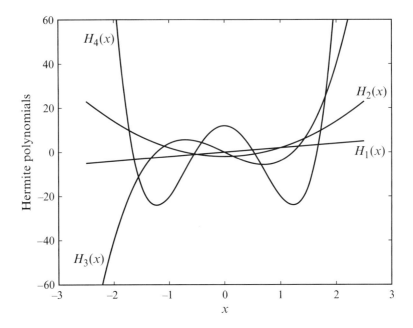

Figure 7.21: First Four Hermite Polynomials

zero in double-precision arithmetic if a polynomial of order higher than 10 is used.) The script then plots the approximating function at the 100 points as well as the function at those points; this is depicted in Figure 7.22. The approximation is so close in levels that it is very difficult to see any differences. Therefore, in Figure 7.23, we plot the natural logarithm of the ratio of the approximation to the truth at various points, which provides a notion of the percentage differences at those points.

```
# Script:   LSFit
# Author:   Harry J. Paarsch
# Date:     11 February 2014
def  LSFit(y, bT, M):
  """ The function  LSFit   returns the least-squares
      estimate of the parameters obtained from the inputs
      (y, bT, M) where   y   is the response variable,    bT
      is the design matrix, and   M   is the row dimension
      of   bT.   The rows of the design matrix are assumed
      orthogonal by construction because the are Chebyshev
      polynomials.
```

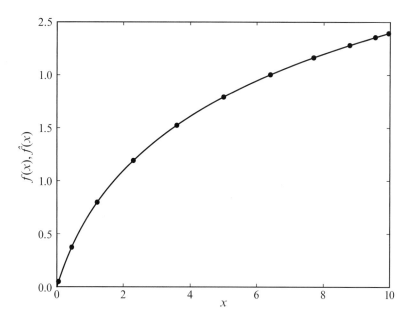

Figure 7.22: Chebyshev Approximation of $\log(1 + x)$

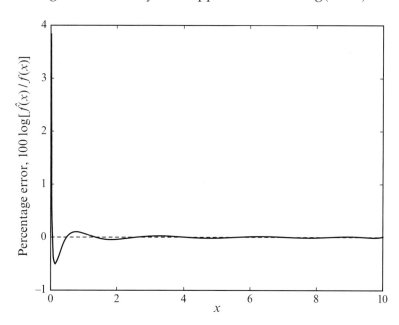

Figure 7.23: Percentage Error in Chebyshev Approximation

```
"""
import numpy
a = numpy.zeros(M)
for m in range(0, M):
    a[m] = sum(y*bT[m,:])/sum(bT[m,:]*bT[m,:])


return a

# Script:  Chebyshev.py
# Author:  Harry J. Paarsch
# Date:     11 February 2014
""" The scripts illustrates how to approximate a function
    using Chebyshev polynomials.
"""
import math
import numpy
import matplotlib.pyplot
# Use the TeX fonts.
matplotlib.pyplot.rc('text', usetex=True)
# Use fonts with serifs.
matplotlib.pyplot.rc('font', family='serif')
# Set total number of Chebyshev nodes  N  as well as the
# node  N  as well.  From these calculate the Chebyshev
# nodes  z.
N = 11
n = numpy.array(range(1, N+1))
z = -numpy.cos(math.pi*(2.*n-1.)/2./N)
# Set the lower and upper value for the variable x.
xlo =  0.
xup = 10.
x   = xlo + ((z+1.)*(xup-xlo)/2.)
M = 10
# Initialize the matrix of Chebyshev polynomials.
bT = numpy.ones((M,N))
# Create the second row of the matrix
bT[1,:] = z
# Build the other rows recursively according to the
# appropriate formula.
for m in range(2, M):
    bT[m,:] = 2. * z * bT[m-1,:] - bT[m-2,:]


#Evaluate the function at the Chebysheve nodes.
y = numpy.log(1. + x)
# Using the conjectured values as well as the
```

```python
# Chebyshev polynomials, fit the coefficients by the
# method of least squares.
aHat = LSFit(y, bT, M)
# Create some non-node points, to see how things fit.
K  = 101
k  = numpy.array(range(1, K+1))
kZ = -numpy.cos(math.pi*(2.*k-1.)/2./K)
# Set the lower and upper value for the variable  x.
kX = xlo + ((kZ+1.)*(xup-xlo)/2.)
#Evaluate the function at a richer set of points.
kY = numpy.log(1. + kX)
# Initialize the matrix of Chebyshev polynomials.
bKT = numpy.ones((M,K))
# Create the second row of the matrix
bKT[1,:] = kZ
# Build the other rows recursively according to the
# appropriate formula.
for m in range(2, M):
  bKT[m,:] = 2. * kZ * bKT[m-1,:] - bKT[m-2,:]


fHat   = numpy.dot(aHat, bT)
fTilde = numpy.dot(aHat, bKT)
# Let's make some figures, okay?
figure1 = matplotlib.pyplot.figure()
matplotlib.pyplot.plot(x, fHat,'ko')
matplotlib.pyplot.plot(kX, kY, color='k')
matplotlib.pyplot.plot(kX, fTilde, linestyle='--', color='k')
matplotlib.pyplot.xlabel('$x$', fontsize=14)
matplotlib.pyplot.ylabel('$f(x),\ \hat{f}(x)$', fontsize=14)
matplotlib.pyplot.savefig("Chebyshev.eps")
matplotlib.pyplot.savefig("Chebyshev-eps-converted-to.pdf")
# Let's make another figure.
figure2 = matplotlib.pyplot.figure()
matplotlib.pyplot.plot(kX[2:], 100.*numpy.log(fTilde[2:]/kY[2:]),
                       linewidth=2, color='k')
matplotlib.pyplot.plot([0., 10.], [0., 0], linestyle='--', color='k')
matplotlib.pyplot.xlabel('$x$', fontsize=14)
matplotlib.pyplot.ylabel('Percentage Error, $100\log[\hat{f}(x)/f(x)]$
    ', fontsize=14)
matplotlib.pyplot.savefig("PercentErrChebyshev.eps")
matplotlib.pyplot.savefig("PercentErrChebyshev-eps-converted-to.pdf")
matplotlib.pyplot.show()
```

Listing 7.11: Python Script to Approximate $\log(1+x)$

7.8   Numerical Integration

Sometimes, you need to calculate an integral

$$F(a,b) = \int_a^b f(u)\, du.$$

How is this done?

7.8.1   Newton-Cotes Formulae

One method, which students often learn in college and which is one of the Newton-Cotes formulae, is *trapezoidal quadrature*. This involves approximating $F(a,b)$ by an estimate, the area of a trapezoid,

$$\hat{F}_1(a,b) = (b-a)\frac{[f(b)+f(a)]}{2}.$$

This is depicted in Figure 7.24. An error, which equals the area labeled A between the straight line and the curved line connecting $f(a)$ and $f(b)$ exists.

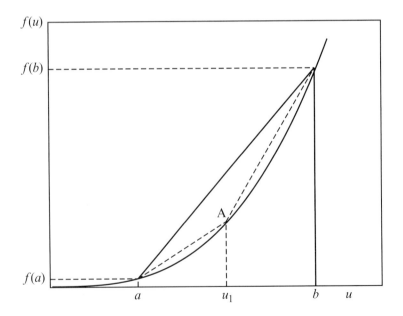

Figure 7.24: Error in Trapezoidal Quadrature

The area is bounded from above by

$$\frac{(b-a)^3}{12}\frac{\mathrm{d}^2 f(c)}{\mathrm{d}x^2},$$

where c is chosen to maximize the second derivative $\mathrm{d}^2 f(x)/\mathrm{d}x^2$ on the interval $[a,b]$. The error depends on $(b-a)$. If you break up the interval between a and b into J subintervals $[x_0,x_1], [x_1,x_2], \ldots, [x_{J-1},x_J]$, where $a = x_0 < x_1 < \ldots < x_J = b$, then you can refine this estimate by using

$$\hat{F}_J(a,b) = \sum_{j=1}^{J}(x_j - x_{j-1})\frac{[f(x_j) + f(x_{j-1})]}{2},$$

thus reducing the error. This, too, is illustrated in Figure 7.24 for the case of J equals 2. Under this approximation, the error is

$$\frac{\max[(x_j - x_{j-1})]^3}{12J^2}\frac{\mathrm{d}^2 f(c)}{\mathrm{d}x^2}.$$

Note, too, that

$$\lim_{J\to\infty}\hat{F}_J(a,b) = F(a,b).$$

Of course, for a fixed J, using a trapezoid to approximate the area is relatively inaccurate. For any three points x_{j-1}, x_j, and x_{j+1} you can approximate $f(u)$ by a polynomial, a parabola, and then integrate it to find the area between x_{j-1} and x_{j+1}. This is referred to by numerical analysts as *Simpson's rule*. When J is even, and the points are evenly spaced h units apart, Simpson's rule is represented by the estimate

$$\tilde{F}_J(a,b) = \frac{h}{3}\left[f(a) + \sum_{m=1}^{(J/2)-1}2f(x_{2m}) + \sum_{m=1}^{(J/2)}4f(x_{2m-1}) + f(b)\right].$$

The error associated with Simpson's rule is smaller than that associated with trapezoidal quadrature. Specifically,

$$\frac{h^4(b-a)}{180}\left|\frac{\mathrm{d}^{(4)}f(c)}{\mathrm{d}x^4}\right|,$$

where $c \in [a,b]$ and h, the step size, is $\frac{(b-a)}{J}$.

7.8.2   Monte Carlo Methods

Although an integral

$$F(a,b) = \int_a^b f(u)\, \mathrm{d}u$$

may sometimes have a closed-form solution that is straightforward to calculate, most of the time it will not. For univariate integrals, the quadrature methods discussed in the previous section can be used to approximate $F(a,b)$. Consider now the bivariate integral

$$F(a_1,b_1,a_2,b_2) = \int_{a_2}^{b_2} \int_{a_1}^{b_1} f(u_1,u_2)\, \mathrm{d}u_1 \mathrm{d}u_2.$$

Imagine dividing the intervals $[a_1,b_1]$ and $[a_2,b_2]$ into, say, J_1 and J_2 subintervals, evaluating the volume under $f(u_1,u_2)$ for each subinterval, and then adding up these volumes to find an approximation to $F(a_1,b_1,a_2,b_2)$. In contrast to quadrature, for multidimensional integrals, this class of methods is referred to as *cubature*. Note, too, that there would be $(J_1 \times J_2)$ points.

In higher dimensions, say, K (for example, three or more), for a fixed grid of points on an interval, the number of points that need to be evaluated grows quickly. If the dimension is K, and each dimension has J points, then the number of evaluations N is J^K. The number of function values needed to obtain an acceptable approximation increases exponentially in the number of dimensions K. Even for a modest number of dimensions, achieving adequate accuracy may be an intractable problem, another manifestation of the curse of dimensionality. For a fixed K, to make the computation feasible, J must be relatively small, in which case cubature can become numerically unreliable. Thus, for large K, implementing cubature with any precision is impossible.

When K is large, researchers often resort to Monte Carlo methods to simulate the integrals. Monte Carlo simulation involves sampling from a known distribution on the intervals $\{[a_k,b_k]\}_{k=1}^K$, for example the uniform, and then taking the average of $f(u_1,u_2,\ldots,u_K)$ evaluated over all the random draws. As the number of simulation draws N gets large (goes to infinity), this estimator converges to the truth. In the following, we show why this is a reasonable strategy.

To illustrate the differences between quadrature and simulation, we examine a univariate example and employ trapezoidal quadrature as well as Monte

Carlo simulation to evaluate

$$F(0,1) = \int_0^1 \exp(-u)\, du,$$

which is known to equal $[1 - \exp(-1)]$, or 0.6321.

We first approximate $F(0,1)$ by the area of a trapezoid defined by the points $(0,0)$, $(0,1)$, $(1,0)$, and $(1,e^{-1})$. The approximate value of the integral is 0.6839, so the absolute error associated with using this rule is 0.0518, which is a relative error of 8.2 percent. We next divide the interval $[0,1]$ up into $J = 10$ subintervals of the same width, and calculate the area for each trapezoid. The estimated area for $F(0,1)$, which is 0.6326, so the absolute error is now 0.0005, which is a relative error of 0.08 percent, that is, about 8 basis points.

Is there a formula for the estimation error as a function of the points a and b, the function $f(u)$ as well as the number of subintervals on $[a,b]$, assuming the trapezoid rule is used? Yes, in fact, the error is the following:

$$\frac{(b-a)^3}{12J^2} f''(c)$$

for some $c \in [a,b]$. Let's check what c must be using data. First, $(b-a)^3$ is 1 and, second, $f''(u)$ is $\exp(-u)$. Thus, $[f''(c)/12]$ or $[\exp(-c)/12]$ is approximately 0.0518, so c is about 0.4755, which is in the interval $[0,1]$, which is at least consistent with what the theory predicts.

Consider now drawing independently and identically distributed uniform random variables from the interval $[0,1]$. The expected value of $\exp(-U)$ on the interval $[0,1]$ is

$$\mathbb{E}\left[\exp(-U)\right] = \int_0^1 \exp(-u)\, du = 0.6321,$$

which just happens to be the integral we are trying to estimate. The variance of $\exp(-U)$ on the interval $[0,1]$ is

$$\begin{aligned}
\mathbb{V}\left[\exp(-U)\right] &= \mathbb{E}\left[\exp(-U)^2\right] - \left(\mathbb{E}\left[\exp(-U)\right]\right)^2 \\
&= \int_0^1 \exp(-2u)\, du - (0.6321)^2 \\
&= 0.4323 - 0.3996 \\
&= 0.0328,
\end{aligned}$$

which is finite. A finite variance is necessary to invoke the law of large numbers.

To estimate $F(0,1)$, introduce the following simulation estimator:

$$\tilde{F}_N(0,1) = \frac{1}{N} \sum_{n=1}^{N} f(U_n) = \frac{1}{N} \sum_{n=1}^{N} \exp(-U_n),$$

where N is the number of simulation draws. In words, for a random sample $\{U_n\}_{n=1}^{N}$ of uniform random variates from the $[0,1]$ interval, use the sample mean of the function $f(\cdot)$ evaluated at the draws.

Is $\tilde{F}_N(0,1)$ a good estimator of $F(0,1)$? We know that it is an unbiased estimator of $F(0,1)$ because

$$\mathbb{E}\left[\tilde{F}_N(0,1)\right] = \frac{1}{N} \sum_{n=1}^{N} \mathbb{E}\left[\exp(-U_n)\right] = \frac{N\mathbb{E}\left[\exp(-U)\right]}{N} = F(0,1).$$

In addition,

$$\mathbb{V}\left[\tilde{F}_N(0,1)\right] = \frac{\mathbb{V}\left[\exp(-U)\right]}{N} = \frac{0.0328}{N}.$$

Therefore, by the law of large numbers, the probability limit of $\tilde{F}_N(0,1)$ is $F(0,1)$. In symbols,

$$\operatorname*{plim}_{N\to\infty} \tilde{F}_N(0,1) = F(0,1).$$

Moreover, by the Lindeberg-Lévy central limit theorem,

$$\sqrt{N}\left[\tilde{F}_N(0,1) - F(0,1)\right] \xrightarrow{\text{d}} \mathcal{N}(0, 0.0328).$$

How large must N be before the root mean squared error of $\tilde{F}_N(0,1)$ equals the absolute error obtained using quadrature? First, what is the mean squared error?

For any estimator $\hat{\theta}$, the mean squared error of $\hat{\theta}$ is the average squared difference between the estimator and the truth θ^0. In symbols,

$$\mathrm{MSE}(\hat{\theta}) = \mathbb{E}\left[(\hat{\theta} - \theta^0)^2\right].$$

Now,

$$
\begin{aligned}
\mathbb{E}\left[(\hat{\theta}-\theta^0)^2\right] &= \mathbb{E}\left[(\hat{\theta}-\mathbb{E}(\hat{\theta})+\mathbb{E}(\hat{\theta})-\theta^0)^2\right] \\
&= \mathbb{E}\left([\hat{\theta}-\mathbb{E}(\hat{\theta})]^2\right)+2\mathbb{E}\left[\hat{\theta}-\mathbb{E}(\hat{\theta})\right]\left[\mathbb{E}(\hat{\theta})-\theta^0\right]+ \\
&\quad \left[\mathbb{E}\left(\hat{\theta}-\theta^0\right)\right]^2 \\
&= \mathbb{E}\left([\hat{\theta}-\mathbb{E}(\hat{\theta})]^2\right)+\left[\mathbb{E}(\hat{\theta}-\theta^0)\right]^2 \\
&= \mathbb{V}(\hat{\theta})+\operatorname{Bias}(\hat{\theta})^2
\end{aligned}
$$

because $\mathbb{E}\left[\hat{\theta}-\mathbb{E}(\hat{\theta})\right]$ equals zero; that is, the first central moment is zero. In words, the mean squared error of an estimator is the sum of the variance of that estimator plus the square of the bias of the estimator.

Applying the result to this problem, we know that $\tilde{F}_N(0,1)$ is an unbiased estimator of $F(0,1)$, so the Bias$(\cdot)^2$ term is zero. Also, the variance of $\tilde{F}_N(0,1)$ is $\mathbb{V}\left[f(u)\right]/N$, or $(0.0328/N)$. Consequently, the mean squared error is $(0.0328/N)$.

Researchers often focus on the square root of the mean squared error, sometimes referred to as the *root mean squared error*. Why? The root mean squared error has the same units as the absolute error of $\hat{F}_J(a,b)$. In this case, the absolute error associated with quadrature is

$$
\frac{1}{J^2}\frac{\exp(-0.4755)}{12}.
$$

The comparison is

$$
\begin{aligned}
\sqrt{0.0328/N} &= \frac{1}{J^2}\frac{\exp(-0.4755)}{12} \\
\frac{0.0328}{N} &= \frac{1}{J^4}\frac{\exp(-0.9510)}{144} \\
\frac{N}{0.0328} &= J^4\times 144\times \exp(0.9510) \\
N &= 0.0328\times J^4\times 144\times \exp(0.9510)
\end{aligned}
$$

which involves two unknowns J and N. If J is fixed at 10, then N is about $125,251$. Yikes!

The standard deviation of the Monte Carlo estimator is inversely proportional to $\sqrt{N}$. This is very slow even when compared to the trapezoidal rule, for which the absolute error is inversely proportional to N^2. To get one extra decimal place of accuracy using Monte Carlo simulation, you would need to increase the number of points by a factor of 100; to get three-digit accuracy, 1 million points might be required.

Thus, you would never want to use Monte Carlo simulation to evaluate a univariate integral or, in fact, to evaluate bivariate integrals, either. Evaluating an integral using Monte Carlo simulation only makes sense when the dimension K is 3 or larger.

Why? Monte Carlo simulation always has a root mean squared error that is $\mathcal{O}\left(\frac{1}{\sqrt{N}}\right)$, whereas cubature has an absolute error that is $\mathcal{O}\left(J^{\frac{-2}{K}}\right)$.

7.8.3   Quasi-Monte Carlo Methods

Even though Monte Carlo simulation has an error that is $\mathcal{O}\left(\frac{1}{\sqrt{N}}\right)$, you may still want to consider alternative methods. With Monte Carlo simulation, the integrand is evaluated at a sequence of points that are supposed to be a sample of independent random variables. In quasi-Monte Carlo methods, accuracy is enhanced by using specially chosen deterministic points; these sequences of points are constructed to be approximately equi-distributed over the region of integration. Two commonly used sequences are the so-called *Halton sequences* and the *Hammersley sequences*. This material is beyond the scope of this book, but you are encouraged to read about it on your own.

7.8.4   Gaussian Quadrature

As illustrated, quadrature (cubature) is a way of approximating a definite integral of a function using a weighted sum of the function evaluated at specified points within the domain of integration. Under Simpson's method, the function is approximated by a parabola; then proceed from there. *Gaussian quadrature*, named in honor of Carl Friedrich Gauss, is a more accurate way of constructing an approximation that yields exact results when the function is a polynomial (so of order higher than a parabola), but it often works well when the function to be integrated can be well approximated by a polynomial. We demonstrate this using an example from the exponential family of functions.

Gauss-Legendre Formulae

Consider the following integral:

$$F(a,b) = \int_a^b f(x)\,\mathrm{d}x. \tag{7.22}$$

Introduce

$$c = \frac{1}{2}(a+b), \quad d = \frac{1}{2}(b-a), \quad \text{and} \quad u = 2\left(\frac{x-a}{b-a}\right) + 1.$$

Now, equation (7.22) can be written as follows:

$$F(a,b) = \int_a^b f(x)\,\mathrm{d}x = \left(\frac{b-a}{2}\right)\int_{-1}^1 f(c+du)\,\mathrm{d}u.$$

We know from the theory of approximations that we can approximate a differentiable function $f(u)$ on the interval $[-1,1]$ using orthogonal polynomials of the appropriate kind. If the appropriate polynomial is used, then at an appropriate set of points (abscissae) $\{\ell_n\}_{n=1}^N$, an optimal set of weights $\{w_n\}_{n=1}^N$ can be derived, so

$$\frac{(b-a)}{2}\int_{-1}^1 f(c+du)\,\mathrm{d}u \approx \frac{(b-a)}{2}\sum_{n=1}^N w_n f(c+d\ell_n).$$

In Table 7.6 we present the abscissae and the weights for different orders of polynomial. Abscissae and weights for other Ns are given in the handbook by Abramowitz and Stegun (1972), but the best way to generate them in Python is by using the `polynomial.legendre` module in the `numpy` package (see Section 8.5 for an example, albeit one applied to Hermite polynomials). With this notation, when N is 3, ℓ_1 is -0.77459667 and w_1 is 0.55555556; ℓ_2 is 0. and w_2 is 0.88888889; ℓ_3 is 0.77459667 and w_3 is 0.55555556.

Often, however, integrals involve either ∞ or $-\infty$, or both.

Gauss-Laguerre Formulae

If the following integral arises,

$$\int_0^\infty f(x)\exp(-x)\,\mathrm{d}x, \tag{7.23}$$

N	ℓ_n	w_n
2	± 0.57735027	1.0
3	0.0	0.88888889
	± 0.77459667	0.55555556
4	± 0.33998104	0.65214515
	± 0.86113631	0.34785485
5	0.0	0.56888889
	± 0.53846931	0.47862867
	± 0.90617985	0.23692689
6	± 0.23861918	0.46791393
	± 0.66120939	0.36076157
	± 0.93246951	0.17132449
7	0.0	0.41795918
	± 0.40584515	0.38183005
	± 0.74153119	0.27970539
	± 0.94910791	0.12948497
8	± 0.18343464	0.36268378
	± 0.52553241	0.31370065
	± 0.79666648	0.22238103
	± 0.96028986	0.10122854
10	± 0.14887434	0.29552422
	± 0.43339539	0.26926672
	± 0.67940957	0.21908636
	± 0.86506337	0.14945135
	± 0.97390653	0.06667134

Table 7.6: Gauss-Legendre Abscissae and Weights

then there exist abscissae $\{\ell_n\}_{n=1}^{N}$ and weights $\{w_n\}_{n=1}^{N}$ such that

$$\int_0^\infty f(x)\exp(-x)\,\mathrm{d}x \approx \sum_{n=1}^{N} w_n f(\ell_n).$$

In this case, ℓ_n is the nth root of a Laguerre polynomial $L_N(x)$ (see Section 7.7), with

$$w_n = \frac{\ell_n}{(N+1)^2 [L_{N+1}(\ell_n)]^2}.$$

In Table 7.7 we present the abscissae and weights for N from 2 to 7. Abscissae and weights for other Ns can be found in Abramowitz and Stegun (1972), but the best way to generate them in Python is using the `polynomial.laguerre` module in the `numpy` package. We show some values here to assist you in figuring out how the functions within the `polynomial` module work.

Novices often complain that these are very special integrals, they are not. Even if the integral is not in the form of equation (7.23), it can be written that way by redefining the integrand, that is,

$$\int_0^\infty g(x)\, dx = \int_0^\infty g(x) \exp(x) \exp(-x)\, dx \equiv \int_0^\infty f(x) \exp(-x)\, dx.$$

Gauss-Hermite Formulae

The integral

$$\int_{-\infty}^\infty f(x) \exp(-x^2)\, dx \tag{7.24}$$

arises naturally in science as well as in economics and finance. In this case, abscissae $\{\ell_n\}_{n=1}^N$ and weights $\{w_n\}_{n=1}^N$ exist, so

$$\int_{-\infty}^\infty f(x) \exp(-x^2)\, dx \approx \sum_{n=1}^N w_n f(\ell_n),$$

where ℓ_n is the nth root of a Hermite polynomial $H_N(x)$ and

$$w_n = \frac{2^{N-1} N! \sqrt{\pi}}{N^2 [H_{N-1}(\ell_n)]^2}.$$

In Table 7.8 we present the abscissae and weights for N from 2 to 7. Other abscissae and weights can be found in Abramowitz and Stegun (1972), but using the `polynomial.hermite` module in the `numpy` package is the best way to generate them in Python.

To illustrate with an example, suppose Y is distributed normally, having mean μ and variance σ^2, and you want to find the expected value of $g(Y)$. Now,

$$\mathbb{E}[g(Y)] = \int_{-\infty}^\infty g(y) \frac{1}{\sqrt{2\pi}\sigma} \exp\left[-\frac{(y-\mu)^2}{2\sigma^2}\right] dy.$$

Note, too, that

$$x = \frac{y-\mu}{\sqrt{2\sigma}} \quad \text{or} \quad y = \mu + \sqrt{2}\sigma x \quad \text{and} \quad dy = \sqrt{2}\sigma dx.$$

N	ℓ_n	w_n
2	0.5857864376	0.8535533906
	3.4142135624	0.1464466094
3	0.4157745568	0.7110930099
	2.2942803603	0.2785177336
	6.2899450829	0.0103892565
4	0.3225476896	0.6031541043
	1.7457611012	0.3574186924
	4.5366202969	0.0388879085
	9.3950709123	0.0005392947
5	9.3950709123	0.0005392947
	0.2635603197	0.5217556106
	1.4134030591	0.3986668111
	3.5964257710	0.0759424497
	7.0858100059	0.0036117587
	12.6408008443	0.0000233700
6	0.2228466042	0.4589646739
	1.1889321017	0.4170008308
	2.9927363261	0.1133733820
	5.7751435691	0.0103991975
	9.8374674184	0.0002610172
	15.9828739806	0.0000008985
7	0.2228466042	0.4589646739
	0.1930436766	0.4093189517
	1.0266648953	0.4218312778
	2.5678767450	0.1471263487
	4.9003530845	0.0206335145
	8.1821534446	0.0010740101
	12.7341802918	0.0000158654
	19.3957278623	0.0000000317

Table 7.7: Gauss-Laguerre Abscissae and Weights

Consequently,

$$\mathbb{E}[g(Y)] = \int_{-\infty}^{\infty} \frac{1}{\sqrt{\pi}} \exp(-x^2) g(\mu + \sqrt{2}\sigma x) \, \mathrm{d}x,$$

N	ℓ_n	w_n
2	± 0.7071067812	0.8862269255
3	0.0	1.1816359006
	± 1.2247448714	0.2954089752
4	± 0.5246476233	0.8049140900
	± 1.6506801239	0.0813128354
5	0.0	0.9453087205
	± 0.9585724646	0.3936193232
	± 2.0201828706	0.0199532421
6	± 0.4360774119	0.7246295952
	± 2.3506049737	0.1570673203
	± 1.3358490740	0.0045300099
7	0.0	0.8102646176
	± 0.8162878829	0.4256072526
	± 1.6735516288	0.0545155828
	± 2.6519613568	0.0009717813
8	± 0.3811869902	0.6611470126
	± 1.1571937125	0.2078023258
	± 1.9816567567	0.0170779830
	± 2.9306374203	0.0001996041

Table 7.8: Gauss-Hermite Abscissae and Weights

which can then be approximated by

$$\frac{1}{\sqrt{\pi}} \sum_{n=1}^{N} w_n g(\mu + \sqrt{2}\sigma\ell_n).$$

To quantify the accuracy, suppose, for example, $g(y)$ is $\exp(y)$, and Y is a normal random variable having mean μ and variance σ^2, which means the pdf of Y has the following form:

$$\frac{1}{\sqrt{2\pi\sigma^2}} \exp\left[-\frac{(y-\mu)^2}{2\sigma^2}\right].$$

We know from statistics that

$$\mathbb{E}[\exp(Y)] = \exp(\mu + 0.5\sigma^2).$$

Parameters	$N = 2$	$N = 8$	$N = 12$	Truth
$\mu = 0, \sigma^2 = 1$	1.6487	1.6487	1.6487	1.6487
$\mu = 1, \sigma^2 = 1$	4.4816	4.4817	4.4817	4.4817
$\mu = 1, \sigma^2 = 2$	7.3844	7.3981	7.3981	7.3981
$\mu = 1, \sigma^2 = 4$	19.8480	20.0854	20.0855	20.0855

Table 7.9: Gauss-Hermite Approximate and Exact Values

In Table 7.9, for different values of μ and σ^2 as well as N, we present the approximate value of the integral as well as the true value. Notice that the approximation error depends on the parameter values: for some values of the parameters, a larger N is necessary in order to achieve the same relative error.

Consider now, for example, a value function $V(p)$, which arises in stochastic dynamic programming, where the logarithm of the state variable P is normally distributed, having mean μ and variance σ^2, and pdf $f_P(p)$. Introduce

$$z = \frac{(\log p - \mu)}{\sqrt{2}\sigma}$$

$$dz = \frac{dp}{p\sqrt{2}\sigma}.$$

In this case,

$$
\begin{aligned}
\mathbb{E}[V(P)] &= \int_0^\infty V(p) f_P(p) \, dp \\
&= \int_0^\infty V(p) \frac{1}{p\sqrt{2\pi\sigma^2}} \exp\left[-\frac{(\log p - \mu)^2}{2\sigma^2}\right] dp \\
&= \int_{-\infty}^\infty \frac{V\left[\exp(\mu + \sqrt{2}\sigma z)\right]}{\sqrt{\pi}p\sqrt{2}\sigma} p\sqrt{2}\sigma \exp(-z^2) \, dz \\
&= \int_{-\infty}^\infty \frac{V\left[\exp(\mu + \sqrt{2}\sigma z)\right]}{\sqrt{\pi}} \exp(-z^2) \, dz.
\end{aligned}
$$

The Gauss-Hermite approximation to $\mathbb{E}[V(P)]$ involves

$$\widehat{\mathbb{E}[V(P)]} = \sum_{n=0}^N w_n \frac{V\left[\exp(\mu + \sqrt{2}\sigma \ell_n)\right]}{\sqrt{\pi}}.$$

What about a function $V(P_1, P_2)$ that depends on two independent random variables, where $\log P_1$ and $\log P_2$ are jointly normally distributed having means μ_1 and μ_2 as well as variances σ_1^2 and σ_2^2? Collect $(P_1, P_2)^\top$ in the vector P, which has joint density function $f_P(p)$. In this case,

$$
\begin{aligned}
\mathbb{E}[V(P)] &= \int_0^\infty \int_0^\infty V(p_1, p_2) f_P(p) \, dp_1 dp_2 \\
&= \int_0^\infty \int_0^\infty V(p) \frac{1}{p_1 \sqrt{2\pi\sigma_1^2} p_2 \sqrt{2\pi\sigma_2^2}} \\
&\quad \exp\left[-\frac{(\log p_1 - \mu_1)^2}{2\sigma_1^2}\right] \exp\left[-\frac{(\log p_2 - \mu_2)^2}{2\sigma_2^2}\right] dp_1 dp_2 \\
&= \int_{-\infty}^\infty \frac{V\left[\exp(\mu_1 + \sqrt{2}\sigma_1 z_1), \exp(\mu_2 + \sqrt{2}\sigma_2 z_2)\right]}{\pi p_1 \sqrt{2}\sigma_1 p_2 \sqrt{2}\sigma_2} \\
&\quad p_1 \sqrt{2}\sigma_1 p_2 \sqrt{2}\sigma_2 \exp(-z_1^2)\exp(-z_2^2)\, dz_1 dz_2 \\
&= \int_{-\infty}^\infty \frac{V\left[\exp(\mu_1 + \sqrt{2}\sigma_1 z_1), \exp(\mu_2 + \sqrt{2}\sigma_2 z_2)\right]}{\pi} \\
&\quad \exp(-z_1^2)\exp(-z_2^2)\, dz_1 dz_2.
\end{aligned}
$$

The Gauss-Hermite approximation to $\mathbb{E}[V(P)]$ now involves

$$
\widehat{\mathbb{E}[V(P)]} = \sum_{n=1}^N \sum_{m=1}^N w_n w_m \frac{V\left[\exp(\mu_1 + \sqrt{2}\sigma_1 z_n), \exp(\mu_2 + \sqrt{2}\sigma_2 z_m)\right]}{\pi}.
$$

Let's now introduce some dependence between the two random variables, so, for example,

$$
\log(P) \sim \mathcal{N}(\mu, \Sigma)
$$

where μ equals $(\mu_1, \mu_2)^\top$, and

$$
\Sigma = \begin{bmatrix} \sigma_1^2 & \sigma_{12} \\ \sigma_{12} & \sigma_2^2 \end{bmatrix}.
$$

Using the Cholesky decomposition, write

$$
\Sigma = FF^\top \quad \text{where} \quad F = \begin{bmatrix} f_{11} & 0 \\ f_{21} & f_{22} \end{bmatrix}.
$$

Here,

$$f_{11} = \sigma_1, \quad f_{21} = \frac{\sigma_{12}}{\sigma_1}, \quad \text{and} \quad f_{22} = \sqrt{\sigma_2^2 - \frac{\sigma_{12}^2}{\sigma_1^2}}.$$

In this case, the joint density of $\boldsymbol{P}$ is

$$f_P(\boldsymbol{p}) = \frac{1}{2\pi |\boldsymbol{\Sigma}|^{\frac{1}{2}} p_1 p_2}$$

$$\exp\left(-\begin{bmatrix}(\log p_1 - \mu_1) & (\log p_2 - \mu_2)\end{bmatrix} \frac{\boldsymbol{\Sigma}^{-1}}{2} \begin{bmatrix}(\log p_1 - \mu_1)\\ (\log p_2 - \mu_2)\end{bmatrix}\right).$$

The Gauss-Hermite approximation to $\mathbb{E}[V(\boldsymbol{P})]$ then involves

$$\widehat{\mathbb{E}[V(\boldsymbol{P})]} =$$

$$\sum_{n=1}^{N} \sum_{m=1}^{N} w_n w_m \frac{V\left[\exp(\mu_1 + \sqrt{2}f_{11}z_n), \exp(\mu_2 + \sqrt{2}f_{21}z_n + \sqrt{2}f_{22}z_m)\right]}{\pi}.$$

Finally, consider the following:

$$(\log \boldsymbol{P}_{t+1} - \boldsymbol{\mu}) \equiv \begin{bmatrix}(\log P_{1,t+1} - \mu_1)\\ (\log P_{2,t+1} - \mu_2)\end{bmatrix}$$

$$= \begin{bmatrix}\rho_{11} & \rho_{12}\\ \rho_{21} & \rho_{22}\end{bmatrix} \begin{bmatrix}(\log p_{1,t} - \mu_1)\\ (\log p_{2,t} - \mu_2)\end{bmatrix} + \begin{bmatrix}\varepsilon_{1,t}\\ \varepsilon_{2,t}\end{bmatrix}$$

$$\equiv \mathbf{R}(\log \boldsymbol{p}_t - \boldsymbol{\mu}) + \varepsilon_t,$$

which is often referred to as a *bivariate autoregressive model of order* 1. Assume that

$$\varepsilon \sim \mathcal{N}(\mathbf{0}_2, \boldsymbol{\Sigma}).$$

Here, the upper and lower case $\boldsymbol{P}$ and $\boldsymbol{p}$ distinguish between the random variables $(P_1, P_2)^\top$ and the realizations $(p_1, p_2)^\top$. Rewriting this system yields

$$\log \boldsymbol{P}_{t+1} = [\mathbf{I}_2 - \mathbf{R}]\boldsymbol{\mu} + \mathbf{R} \log \boldsymbol{p}_t + \varepsilon_t \equiv \begin{bmatrix}\theta_{1,t}\\ \theta_{2,t}\end{bmatrix} + \varepsilon_t.$$

The Gauss-Hermite approximation to $\mathbb{E}[V(\boldsymbol{P})]$ in this case involves

$$\widehat{\mathbb{E}[V(\boldsymbol{P})]} =$$

$$\sum_{n=1}^{N} \sum_{m=1}^{N} w_n w_m \frac{V\left[\exp(\theta_{1,t} + \sqrt{2}f_{11}z_n), \exp(\theta_{2,t} + \sqrt{2}f_{21}z_n + \sqrt{2}f_{22}z_m)\right]}{\pi}.$$

7.9 Solving Differential Equations

A differential equation is a relation between an unknown function u and its derivatives. If the function $u(x)$ depends on only one variable $x \in \mathbb{R}$, then the differential equation is an *ordinary differential equation* (ODE). The order of the differential equation is determined by the order of the highest derivative of the function u that appears in the equation. Suppose F is a function of x and u as well as the derivatives of u. An equation of the form

$$F\left[x, u, u', u'', \cdots, u^{(n)}\right] = 0$$

is an *implicit* ODE of order n, whereas an equation of the form

$$u^{(n)} = F\left[x, u, u', \cdots, u^{(n-1)}\right]$$

is an *explicit* ODE of order n. An ODE is referred to as *linear* when F can be written as a linear combination of the derivatives of u. For example, the following:

$$\frac{d^2 u}{dx^2} + p(x)\frac{du}{dx} + q(x)u = u'' + p(x)u' + q(x)u = r(x)$$

is a second-order linear ODE.

When the function depends on more than one variable, as in $u(x, t)$, and the derivatives with respect to more than one variable are present in the equation, the differential equation is a *partial differential equation* (PDE). A PDE having the following form

$$u_t(x, t) + u_{xx}(x, t) = 0$$

is a *homogeneous* PDE of the second order. Even though just the first partial derivative of u with respect to t is present $u_t(x, t)$, the second partial derivative of u with respect to x is also present $u_{xx}(x, t)$. That the two partial derivatives sum to zero is the condition required for this PDE to qualify as homogeneous. In short, a linear PDE is homogeneous if all (nonzero) terms contain the function u or one of its derivatives.

On the other hand,

$$u_{xx}(x, y) + u_{yy}(x, y) = f(x, y)$$

is a *nonhomogeneous* PDE of the second order because the sum of the two partial derivative functions does not equal zero and each partial derivative function is of the second order.[18]

A solution to a differential equation is a function $u(x)$ or $u(x,t)$ or $u(x,y)$ such that when the equation is differentiated appropriately, the differential equation obtains. Thus, solving a differential equation is just like integrating it.

In general, however, a solution u cannot be expressed in terms of elementary functions, so numerical methods are the only way to solve the differential equation. In short, provided certain conditions hold, the solutions to differential equations are approximate, having been calculated using a computer.

One family of ODEs that has a closed-form solution is the following:

$$\frac{\mathrm{d}u}{\mathrm{d}x} + p(x)u = q(x),$$

in which case

$$u(x) = \frac{1}{r(x)}\left[k + \int_x q(z)r(z)\,\mathrm{d}z\right], \tag{7.25}$$

where

$$r(x) = \exp\left[\int_x p(z)\,\mathrm{d}z\right] \tag{7.26}$$

and k is chosen to satisfy an appropriate boundary condition. We mention this family because you may want to employ it to compare numerical solutions obtained to closed-form ones provided by equations (7.25) and (7.26) in an effort to determine the accuracy of solution algorithms.

With regard to the numerical solution of differential equations, we investigate two main approaches: *finite difference methods* and *finite element methods*. Finite difference methods are the oldest. Roughly speaking, they involve using a local Taylor series expansion to approximate the differential equation, thus approximating the solution values on a grid of points. Finite element methods are newer. Again roughly speaking, they involve approximating the solution

---

[18]We thought long and hard about this notation. It is common in many introductory books on differential equations to refer to ODEs as follows:

$$\frac{\mathrm{d}y}{\mathrm{d}t} + p(t)y = q(t),$$

but the notation does not carry over well to partial differential equations defined on the plane (x,y), so we chose the letter u instead.

by a polynomial function, thus approximating the solution function on a grid of points. Historically, both methods were infeasible for scientists to use because of the computational burden they impose. During the past half century, however, with the advent of ever-faster digital computers, finite difference and finite element methods have become part of every scientist's toolbox. We do not discuss a third approach, referred to as *finite volume methods*, but you should be aware that these methods exist, too. Such methods are typically used on certain families of partial differential equations, specifically, the elliptical, parabolic, and hyperbolic families.

7.9.1 Initial- and Boundary-Value Problems

When solving differential equations, a distinction is made between an *initial-value problem* and a *boundary-value problem*.

An initial-value problem involves the solution to an ODE where a specified value, referred to as the *initial condition*, of the unknown function u at a given point in the domain of the solution is known. For example,

$$u'(x) = x \quad \text{with} \quad u(0) = 1$$

implies

$$u(x) = 1 + \frac{x^2}{2}.$$

Boundary-value problems have more constraints on them than initial-value problems. Where an initial-value problem has all the conditions specified at the same value of the independent variable and that value is the lower boundary of the domain, a boundary-value problem has conditions specified at the extremes of the independent variable in the equation. For example, for $x \in [0,1]$,

$$u''(x) = -10x \quad \text{where} \quad u(0) = u(1) = 0.$$

When the boundary gives a value to the derivative of the function, it is a *Neumann boundary condition*, whereas when the boundary gives a value to the function, it is a *Dirichlet boundary condition*, and when the boundary has the form of a curve or surface that gives a value to the derivative and the variable itself, it is a *Cauchy boundary condition*.

7.9.2   Finite Difference Methods

Consider the following first-order ODE for u as a function of x:

$$\frac{du(x)}{dx} = \frac{du}{dx} = D(x, u). \tag{7.27}$$

Several different numerical methods exist to solve differential equations like equation (7.27). The simplest of the finite difference methods is *Euler's method*. Starting at x_0, an initial x where $u(x_0)$ is u_0, the value of $u(x_0 + h)$ can be approximated by u_0, plus the step h multiplied by the slope of the function, which is the derivative of u, evaluated at x_0. This is simply a first-order Taylor series expansion, so

$$u(x + h) \approx u_0 + h \frac{du}{dx}\bigg|_{x=x_0} = u_0 + hD(x_0, u_0).$$

Denoting this approximate value by u_1,

$$u_1 = u_0 + hD(x_0, u_0)$$
$$= u_0 + hD_0.$$

Calculating the value of du/dx at x_0 using equation (7.27), you can then generate an approximation for the value of u at x equal to $(x_0 + h)$ using the preceding approximation. You can then use this new value of u, at $(x_0 + h)$, to find du/dx (at the new x) and repeat. When $D(x, u)$ does not change too quickly, the method can generate an approximate solution of reasonable accuracy. For example, on an infinite-precision computer, the local truncation error is $\mathcal{O}(h^2)$, while the global error is $\mathcal{O}(h)$—first-order accuracy.

If the differential equation changes very quickly in response to a small step h, it is referred to as a *stiff* differential equation. To solve stiff differential equations accurately using Euler's method, h must be very small, which means that Euler's method will take a long time to compute an accurate solution. Although this may not be an issue when doing this once, in empirical work, the differential equation may need to be solved thousands (even millions) of times.

Perhaps the best-known generalization of Euler's method is a family of methods referred to collectively as *Runge-Kutta methods*. Of all the members in this family, the most commonly used is the fourth-order method, sometimes referred to as *RK4*. Under RK4,

$$u_{k+1} = u_k + h\frac{1}{6}(d_1 + 2d_2 + 2d_3 + d_4),$$

where

$$d_1 = D\left(x_k, u_k\right)$$
$$d_2 = D\left(x_k + \frac{1}{2}h, u_k + \frac{1}{2}hd_1\right)$$
$$d_3 = D\left(x_k + \frac{1}{2}h, u_k + \frac{1}{2}hd_2\right)$$
$$d_4 = D\left(x_k + h, u_k + hd_3\right).$$

Thus, the next value u_{k+1} is determined by the current one u_k, plus the product of the step size h and an estimated slope. The estimated slope is a weighted average of slopes: d_1 is the slope at the left endpoint of the interval; d_2 is the slope at the midpoint of the interval, using Euler's method along with slope d_1 to determine the value of u at the point $(x_k + \frac{1}{2}h)$; d_3 is again the slope at the midpoint, but now the slope d_2 is used to determine u; and d_4 is the slope at the right endpoint of the interval, with its u value determined using d_3. Assuming the Lipschitz condition is satisfied, the local truncation error of the RK4 method is $\mathcal{O}(h^5)$, while the global truncation error is $\mathcal{O}(h^4)$, which is a huge improvement over Euler's method. Note, too, that if $D(\cdot)$ does not depend on u, so that the differential equation is equivalent to a simple integral, then RK4 is simply Simpson's rule, the well-known and commonly used quadrature rule (see Section 7.8.1).

What is the Lipschitz condition? A function $g : \mathbb{R}^d \to \mathbb{R}^d$ satisfies the Lipschitz condition on a d-dimensional interval I if there exists a Lipschitz constant $\lambda > 0$ such that

$$||g(\mathbf{y}) - g(\mathbf{x})|| \le \lambda ||\mathbf{y} - \mathbf{x}||$$

for a given vector norm $|| \cdot ||$ and for all $\mathbf{x} \in I$ and $\mathbf{y} \in I$. To get a better understanding of this, assume $g : \mathbb{R} \to \mathbb{R}$ and rewrite the Lipschitz condition as

$$\left| \frac{g(x+h) - g(x)}{h} \right| \le \lambda,$$

where y equals $(x + h)$ and we have chosen to use the L_1 distance.[19] If we assume that $g(\cdot)$ is differentiable and let $h \to 0$, then the Lipschitz condition means that

$$|g'(x)| \leq \lambda.$$

In words, the derivative is bounded by the Lipschitz constant.

Like Euler's method, however, Runge-Kutta methods do not always perform well on stiff problems; see Butcher (2003). Note, too, that neither the method of Euler nor the methods of Runge-Kutta use past information to improve the approximation as you work to the right.

In response to these limitations, numerical analysts have pursued a variety of other strategies. For a given h, these alternative methods are more accurate than Euler's method and may have a smaller error constant than Runge-Kutta methods as well. Some of the alternative methods are referred to as *multistep methods*. Under multistep methods, you again start from an initial point x_0 and then take a small step h forward in x to find the next value of u. The difference is that, unlike Euler's method (which is a single-step method that refers only to one previous point and its derivative at that point to determine the next value), multistep methods use some intermediate points to obtain a higher-order approximation of the next value. Multistep methods gain efficiency by keeping track of and using the information from previous steps rather than discarding it. Specifically, multistep methods use the values of the function at several previous points as well as the derivatives (or some of them) at those points.

Linear multistep methods are special cases in the class of multistep methods. As the name suggests, under these methods, a linear combination of previous points and derivative values is used to approximate the solution. Denote by m the number of previous steps used to calculate the next value. Denote the desired value at the current stage by u_{k+m}. A linear multistep method has the following general form:

$$u_{k+m} + \lambda_{m-1} u_{k+m-1} + \lambda_{m-2} u_{k+m-2} + \cdots + \lambda_0 u_k$$
$$= h \left[\kappa_m D(x_{k+m}, u_{k+m}) + \kappa_{m-1} D(x_{k+m-1}, u_{k+m-1}) + \cdots + \kappa_0 D(x_k, u_k) \right].$$

---

[19] All norms are equivalent in finite-dimensional spaces, so if a function satisfies the Lipschitz condition in one norm, it satisfies the Lipschitz condition in all norms. The Lipschitz constant λ, however, does depend on the choice of norm.

The values chosen for $\lambda_0, \ldots, \lambda_{m-1}$ and $\kappa_0, \ldots, \kappa_m$ determine the solution method. Often, many of the coefficients are set to zero. Sometimes, a numerical analyst chooses the coefficients so they will interpolate $u(x)$ exactly when $u(x)$ is a kth order polynomial. When κ_m is nonzero, the value of u_{k+m} depends on the value of $D(x_{k+m}, u_{k+m})$, and the equation for u_{k+m} must be solved iteratively, using fixed-point iteration when the problem is not stiff or using variants of the method of Newton-Raphson when it is stiff.

A simple linear, multistep method is the *Adams-Bashforth two-step method*. Under this method,

$$u_{k+2} = u_{k+1} + h\frac{3}{2}D(x_{k+1}, u_{k+1}) - h\frac{1}{2}D(x_k, u_k).$$

That is, λ_1 is -1, κ_2 is zero, κ_1 is $\frac{3}{2}$, and κ_0 is $-\frac{1}{2}$. To implement Adams-Bashforth, however, two values (u_{k+1} and u_k) are needed to compute the next value u_{k+2}. In a typical initial-value problem, only one value is provided, for example, $u(x_0)$ equals u_0 is the only condition provided. One way to circumvent this lack of information is to use the u_1 computed by Euler's method as the second value. With this choice, the Adams-Bashforth two-step method yields a candidate approximating solution.

For other values of m, Butcher (2003) provided explicit formulae to implement the Adams-Bashforth methods. Again, assuming the Lipschitz condition is satisfied, the local truncation error of the Adams-Bashforth two-step method is $\mathcal{O}(h^3)$, while the global truncation error is $\mathcal{O}(h^2)$. (Other Adams-Bashforth methods have local truncation errors that are $\mathcal{O}(h^5)$ and global truncation errors that are $\mathcal{O}(h^4)$, and they are thus competitive with RK4.)

In addition to Adams-Bashforth, two other families are also used: Adams-Moulton methods and backward differentiation formulae (BDFs). Like Adams-Bashforth methods, the Adams-Moulton methods have λ_{m-1} equal to -1 and the other λ_is equal to zero. Where Adams-Bashforth methods are explicit, Adams-Moulton methods are implicit. For example, when m is zero, under Adams-Moulton,

$$u_k = u_{k-1} + hD(x_k, u_k), \tag{7.28}$$

which is sometimes referred to as the *backward Euler method*. When m is 1

$$u_{k+1} = u_k + h\frac{1}{2}\left[D(x_{k+1}, u_{k+1}) + D(x_k, u_k)\right], \tag{7.29}$$

which is sometimes referred to as the *trapezoidal rule*. Note that these equations only define the solutions implicitly; that is, equations (7.28) and (7.29) must be solved numerically for u_k and u_{k+1}, respectively.

BDFs constitute the main other way to solve ordinary differential equations. BDFs are linear multistep methods that are especially useful when solving stiff differential equations. From the preceding, we know that given equation (7.27), for step size h, a linear multistep method can, in general, be written as

$$u_{k+m} + \lambda_{m-1} u_{k+m-1} + \lambda_{m-2} u_{k+m-2} + \cdots + \lambda_0 u_k$$
$$= h \left[\kappa_m D(x_{k+m}, u_{k+m}) + \kappa_{m-1} D(x_{k+m-1}, u_{k+m-1}) + \cdots + \kappa_0 D(x_k, u_k) \right].$$

BDFs involve setting κ_i to zero for any i other than m, so a general BDF is

$$u_{k+m} + \lambda_{m-1} u_{k+m-1} + \lambda_{m-2} u_{k+m-2} + \cdots + \lambda_0 u_k = h b_m D_{k+m}$$

where D_{k+m} denotes $D(x_{k+m}, u_{k+m})$. Note that, like Adams-Moulton methods, BDFs are implicit methods as well: the nonlinear equations must be solved at each step, again, using fixed-point iteration when the problem is stiff or using variants of the method of Newton-Raphson when it is not stiff. Thus, the methods can be computationally burdensome. Evaluating u at x_{k+m} in $D(\cdot)$ is an effective way to discipline approximate solutions to stiff differential equations.

Perhaps an example will make the things simpler to understand. One of the canonical examples in this literature is the following two-point, boundary-value problem on the unit interval $[0, 1]$:

$$u''(x) = f(x)$$
$$u(0) = u(1) = 0$$

which arises naturally in physics, for example, when weight is applied to an elastic bar or when heat conducts in a single dimension through a medium. This differential equation is simple enough to solve in closed form:

$$\frac{d^2 u(x)}{dx^2} = f(x)$$

$$\frac{du(x)}{dx} = \int_0^x f(y)\, dy + k_1$$

$$\frac{du(x)}{dx} \equiv F(x) + k_1$$

$$u(x) = \int_0^x F(y)\, dy + k_1 x + k_0.$$

For example, if $f(x) = \kappa x$, then

$$u(x) = \frac{\kappa x^3}{6} - \frac{\kappa x}{6}.$$

Under finite difference methods, you would lay down a grid of $(N + 1)$ points; for example, you could do it equispaced using $x_n = nh$ with $h = (1/N)$, where $n = 0, 1, \ldots, N$, but that is unnecessary. The second derivative function $u''(x)$ is then approximated by the difference in the first differences. In symbols,

$$u''(x_n) \approx \frac{[u(x_{n+1}) - u(x_n)] - [u(x_n) - u(x_{n-1})]}{(\Delta x_n)^2}. \tag{7.30}$$

In short, equation (7.30) can be rewritten as

$$\frac{u_{n+1} - 2u_n + u_{n-1}}{h^2}.$$

Because u_0 and u_N are both zero, by the boundary conditions $u(0)$ and $u(1)$ being both zero, you can then write the second-difference approximation as the following system of linear equations in the unknown vector $(u_1, u_2, \ldots, u_{N-1})^\top$:

$$-2u_1 + u_2 = f(x_1)h^2$$
$$u_1 - 2u_2 + u_3 = f(x_2)h^2$$
$$u_2 - 2u_3 + u_4 = f(x_3)h^2$$
$$\vdots \qquad \vdots$$
$$u_{N-3} - 2u_{N-2} + u_{N-1} = f(x_{N-2})h^2$$
$$u_{N-2} - 2u_{N-1} = f(x_{N-1})h^2,$$

which can be written in matrix notation as

$$\mathbf{Au} = \mathbf{b},$$

where

$$\mathbf{A} = \begin{bmatrix} -2 & 1 & 0 & \dots & 0 & 0 & 0 \\ 1 & -2 & 1 & \dots & 0 & 0 & 0 \\ \vdots & \vdots & \vdots & \ddots & \vdots & \vdots & \vdots \\ 0 & 0 & 0 & \dots & 1 & -2 & 1 \\ 0 & 0 & 0 & \dots & 0 & 1 & -2 \end{bmatrix} \quad \text{and} \quad \mathbf{u} = \begin{bmatrix} u_1 \\ u_2 \\ u_3 \\ \vdots \\ u_{N-3} \\ u_{N-2} \\ u_{N-1} \end{bmatrix}$$

as well as

$$\mathbf{b} = \begin{bmatrix} f(x_1)h^2 \\ f(x_2)h^2 \\ f(x_3)h^2 \\ \vdots \\ f(x_{N-3})h^2 \\ f(x_{N-2})h^2 \\ f(x_{N-1})h^2 \end{bmatrix},$$

whence an approximate solution can be calculated using linear algebra:

$$\hat{\mathbf{u}} = \mathbf{A}^{-1}\mathbf{b}.$$

In Figure 7.25, we depict the exact solution to the specific case where

$$u''(x) = \kappa x$$

with $u(0) = u(1) = 0$ and $\kappa = -10$. In that figure, we also depict the solution obtained via the method of finite differences where $N = 10$, so $h = 0.1$. Values of $u(x)$ between the grid points are presumably approximated using linear interpolation (the dashed lines in the figure). Therefore, between $[x_n, x_{n+1}]$ use

$$\breve{u}(x; \hat{u}_n, \hat{u}_{n+1}) = \hat{u}_n + \frac{(\hat{u}_{n+1} - \hat{u}_n)}{(x_{n+1} - x_n)}(x - x_n) \quad n = 0, 1, \dots, N-1.$$

This is in fact how we backfilled the points between $(0,0)$ and the solution $(0.1, \hat{u}_1)$ as well as between the solution $(0.9, \hat{u}_{N-1})$ and the boundary condition $(1,0)$ in that figure.

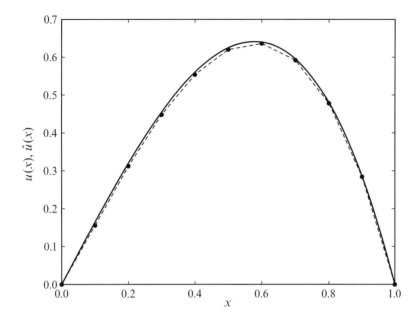

Figure 7.25: Exact and Finite Difference Solution

7.9.3 Finite Element Methods

Where finite difference methods attempt to approximate the values of $u(x)$ well at a finite set of points, finite element methods attempt to approximate the function $u(x)$. Researchers of finite element methods use the calculus of variations to derive functions that minimize a specified error function. This research is related to that concerning approximation theory (see Section 7.7). Zienkiewicz and Morgan (2006) and Johnson (2009) wrote helpful books on this topic.

In contrast to the finite difference method used, imagine approximating $u(x)$ by a polynomial.

$$\tilde{u}(x) = \alpha_0 + \sum_{k=1}^{K} \alpha_k P_k(x),$$

where the vector $(\alpha_0, \alpha_1, \dots, \alpha_K)$ is chosen so that

$$\tilde{u}''(x) = \sum_{k=1}^{K} \tilde{\alpha}_k P_k''(x) \approx f(x)$$

for all $x \in [0, 1]$. Here, $\tilde{\alpha}_0$ is chosen to satisfy the boundary conditions, $u(0) = u(1) = 0$.

For example, we suggested previously that on a compact interval like $[0, 1]$ you could use Chebyshev polynomials. Here, borrowing from Zienkiewicz and Morgan (2006), we consider members of the Bernstein family of polynomials. To illustrate the idea without overwhelming the computation, let's just use $K = 2$ where the following two Bernstein polynomials are used:

$$B_{1,1}(x) = x(1-x)$$
$$B_{2,1}(x) = x^2(1-x),$$

so

$$\tilde{u}(x) = \alpha_0 + \sum_{k=1}^{2} \alpha_k B_{k,1}(x) = \alpha_0 + \alpha_1 x(1-x) + \alpha_2 x^2(1-x).$$

Since $u(0) = u(1) = 0$, $\tilde{\alpha}_0 = 0$. Now, choose $\tilde{\alpha}_1$ and $\tilde{\alpha}_2$ to satisfy the following:

$$\int_0^1 \left[\frac{d^2 \tilde{u}(y)}{dx^2} - f(y) \right] dy = 0.$$

Consider two points, say $x_1 = \frac{1}{3}$ and $x_2 = \frac{2}{3}$, in which case

$$\mathbf{K}\boldsymbol{\alpha} \equiv \begin{bmatrix} 2 & 0 \\ 2 & 2 \end{bmatrix} \begin{bmatrix} \alpha_1 \\ \alpha_2 \end{bmatrix} = \begin{bmatrix} f(x_1) \\ f(x_2) \end{bmatrix} \equiv \mathbf{f}.$$

The perceptive reader will have noticed that the approximating function $\tilde{u}(x)$ corresponds exactly to the closed-form solution, where $\tilde{\alpha}_1 = -\tilde{\alpha}_2 = \frac{5}{3}$, so this is really not that much of a test of finite element methods.

Therefore, suppose that instead of being a constant, κ depends on u, for example,

$$\kappa(u) = -10 + \rho u.$$

Implementing the method of finite differences can be quite complicated. On the other hand, although the $\boldsymbol{\alpha}$ vector must be solved for iteratively, the basic idea of solving

$$\int_0^1 \left[\frac{d^2 \tilde{u}(y)}{dx^2} - \rho \tilde{u}(y)y + 10y \right] dy = 0$$

remains. In short, iterate

$$\tilde{\boldsymbol{\alpha}}_{r+1} = [\mathbf{K}(\tilde{\boldsymbol{\alpha}}_r)]^{-1}\mathbf{f} \quad r = 0, 1, \dots$$

until $\|\tilde{\alpha}_{r+1} - \tilde{\alpha}_{r-1}\| < \varepsilon$, where ε is some convergence criterion. Alternatively, you could stop once successive iterates differed only in digits beyond, say, the fourth decimal place.

In dimensions greater than 1, finite difference methods expand to points on a lattice, whereas finite element methods are more general than that but usually form triangles that are often referred to as *simplices,* which is the plural of *simplex.* For solving many partial differential equations, finite element methods are considered superior to finite difference methods. In addition, finite element methods can admit complicated boundary conditions that are often difficult to impose with finite difference methods. For these reasons, many engineers and scientists prefer finite element to finite difference methods.

What we have presented here barely scrapes the surface of these methods, but you should now have a basic appreciation of the choices you need to make when solving ODEs and PDEs.

7.10 Simulation

Throughout the sciences, fast computing has made simulation a viable alternative to mathematics when investigating the stochastic behavior of systems. In Python, the `random` module of the `numpy` package makes conducting simulation analyses relatively straightforward. Before we discuss how to implement the functions in the module `random`, we outline briefly some important facts about simulation in general.

7.10.1 Distribution of the cdf

Consider a continous random variable V having support on some interval that need not be bounded. Let $F_V(v)$ denote the cumulative distribution function of V and $f_V(v)$ denote the accompanying probability density function, where

$$f_V(v) = \frac{dF_V(v)}{dv} \geq 0.$$

A very special transformation of a continuous random variable is the cdf itself. Recall that

$$\Pr(V \leq v) = F_V(v) = \int_{-\infty}^{v} f_V(u) \, du.$$

Note that $F_V(v)$ is an increasing, monotonic function of v because

$$\frac{\mathrm{d}F_V(v)}{\mathrm{d}v} = f_V(v) \geq 0.$$

Since $F_V(V)$ is a monotonic function of the random variable V, it is natural to ask what its distribution is. In particular, letting U equal $F_V(V)$, you can find the pdf of U by

$$f_U(u) = f_V(v)\frac{\mathrm{d}v}{\mathrm{d}u}.$$

Because $F_V(v)$ is monotonic in v, you can invert $F_V(v)$ to get

$$v = F_V^{-1}(u)$$

where $F_V^{-1}(\cdot)$ is the inverse function of $F_V(v)$ having the property

$$v = F_V^{-1}\big[F_V(v)\big].$$

Now,

$$\mathrm{d}u = f_V(v)\mathrm{d}v,$$

so

$$\frac{\mathrm{d}v}{\mathrm{d}u} = \frac{1}{f_V(v)}.$$

Thus,

$$f_U(u) = f_V(v)\frac{1}{f_V(v)} = 1.$$

Although the random variable V is potentially supported on the interval $(-\infty, \infty)$, the cdf U is contained on the interval $[0,1]$, and the cdf is a random variable having a pdf equaling 1 everywhere on the interval $[0,1]$: it is distributed uniformly on the unit interval.

This result has direct implications for the simulation method of approximating the pdf of a random variable that is a function of another random variable. In particular, if you can devise a way of generating independently and identically distributed random variables from the uniform distribution on the interval $[0,1]$, then using the inverse function $F_V^{-1}(\cdot)$, which exists for any continuous random variable, you can generate a wide variety of random variables. Thus, you have saved a lot of work; instead of having to devise a method for each and every probability distribution, you only have to devise a method for the uniform and then apply the inverse mapping. Also, in many cases, uniform random variables can be used to generate discrete random variables.

7.10.2 Generating Random Numbers

In the previous section, we demonstrated that the cdf of any continuous random variable is distributed uniformly on the interval $[0, 1]$. Thus, if you could devise a way of generating uniform random numbers, then using the inverse function $F_V^{-1}(\cdot)$ you can generate random numbers according to any continuous law. For example, suppose you wanted Weibull random numbers given the parameter values θ_1 equal to 10 and θ_2 equal to 3.5, but all you had were uniform random numbers U, then you would use the following transformation:

$$F_V(V) = [1 - \exp(-\theta_1 V^{\theta_2})] = U$$
$$\exp(-\theta_1 V^{\theta_2}) = (1 - U)$$
$$-\theta_1 V^{\theta_2} = \log(1 - U)$$
$$\theta_1 V^{\theta_2} = -\log(1 - U)$$
$$V^{\theta_2} = \frac{-\log(1 - U)}{\theta_1}$$
$$V = \left[\frac{-\log(1 - U)}{\theta_1} \right]^{1/\theta_2}$$
$$V = \left[\frac{-\log(1 - U)}{10} \right]^{1/3.5}$$

to generate the Weibull Vs. The following code in Python generates ten uniform random variates on the interval $[0, 1]$ and then converts them to Weibull variates that have the parameters $(\theta_1, \theta_2) = (10, 3.5)$:

```
>>> import numpy
>>> N = 10
>>> theta1 = 10.0
>>> theta2 =  3.5
>>> U = numpy.random.uniform(0., 1., [N, 1])
>>> V = (-numpy.log(1.-U)/theta1)**(1./theta2)
>>>
```

This method can also be used for some discrete random variables, too. Suppose that V is distributed Bernoulli with parameter θ equal to 0.6. Thus, if a U is generated that is greater than 0.4, then set V equal to 1, otherwise set V to zero. Formally,

$$V = \begin{cases} 0 & \text{if } U \leq 0.4 \\ 1 & \text{if } U > 0.4. \end{cases} \tag{7.31}$$

The following Python code implements this

```
>>> import numpy
>>> N = 10
>>> theta = 0.6
>>> U = numpy.random.uniform(0., 1., [N, 1])
>>> V = (U > (1.-theta)).astype(int)
>>>
```

when the `astype(int)` function converts the floating-point value to an integer value.

The key to this approach is the uniform distribution. Several different physical models for generating uniform numbers exist. For example, consider taking ℓ bingo balls and numbering them 0 to $(\ell - 1)$. Place the balls in an urn, and draw a ball at random. Divide the number on the ball by ℓ to obtain a uniform rational number on the interval $[0, (\ell - 1)/\ell]$. Note that as ℓ tends to infinity, the interval becomes packed with rational numbers and tends to $[0, 1]$. Of course, uncountably many of the irrational numbers that make up the interval $[0, 1]$ are missing, but those irrational numbers are typically approximated by rational numbers on computers anyway. In short, we hope their absence is unimportant. Now that you have some uniform Us, you can generate the Vs.

7.10.3   Pseudo-Random Numbers

The device described at the end of the last section for generating random numbers from the uniform distribution is built on a very concrete model of the data-generating process—the bingo urn. Often, however, it is inconvenient to use such devices. Moreover, such devices are not always foolproof; wear-and-tear can affect their properties. In addition, in experimental situations, researchers around the globe require random sequences that can be easily replicated, so that scientific findings can be reproduced. For these reasons, numerical analysts have sought to devise methods of generating random numbers according to deterministic rules. Obviously, if something is generated according to a deterministic rule, it cannot be random. Thus, random numbers generated according to deterministic rules are often referred to as *pseudo-random numbers* (PRNs).

We examine a class of rules, which can be implemented on a computer, that can generate sequences of numbers that appear random by a variety of measures. Such rules (devices) are called *pseudo-random number generators* (PRNGs) where *pseudo* is often suppressed.[20]

Historically, *congruential* PRNGs were the most commonly used class of PRNGs, probably because of their simple structure. Although these PRNGs are simple to understand, over time researchers have demonstrated their limitations. We begin with a brief description of congruential PRNGs in order to give a general understanding for how the tool works.

In particular, a random number u_i is generated by a congruential rule when

$$u_i = \frac{x_i}{\ell} \quad i = 1, 2, \ldots$$

where ℓ is an integer and

$$x_i = \text{mod}(\alpha + \beta x_{i-1}, \ell) \quad i = 1, 2, \ldots \text{ with } x_0 \text{ a known integer.}$$

Here, "mod" is the modulus function. The modulus is the remainder from dividing $(\alpha + \beta x_{i-1})$ by ℓ. Since the x_is can take on the values from the set $\{0, 1, 2, \ldots, \ell - 1\}$, the u_is will take on the rational values $\{0, 1/\ell, 2/\ell, \ldots, (\ell - 1)/\ell\}$. If the x_is are distributed randomly on the integers $\{0, 1, \ldots, \ell - 1\}$, then the u_is will be distributed randomly on the lattice of rational numbers $\{0, 1/\ell, \ldots, (\ell - 1)/\ell\}$. Moreover, the larger is ℓ, the closer will the u_i approximate the true uniform distribution. It turns out that when the modulus function is implemented on a digital computer, the x_is appear to be distributed randomly on the lattice of points $\{0, 1, \ldots, \ell - 1\}$.

Note that congruential PRNGs depend on the choice of constants $(x_0, \ell, \alpha, \beta)$. What should they be? x_0 is referred to as the *seed*; it must be provided by the researcher. No rules for the choice of x_0 appear to exist. What is ℓ? Typically, ℓ is the largest integer that can be represented on a computer—machine limit. Currently, ℓ is either $(2^{31} - 1)$ or $(2^{63} - 1)$, since most computers are either 32- or 64-bit machines. The numbers α and β are referred to as the *increment* and the *multiplier*, respectively. No consensus appears to have emerged on the choice of α, and often α is set to zero. When α is zero, the generator falls within the class of *multiplicative congruential* PRNGs. Some consensus appears

---

[20]We describe only a small part of the work involving PRNGs in this section. For more details, see Gentle (2010).

to have emerged concerning the choice of the multiplier β. In particular, β equal to 397,204,094 has been shown by Fishman and Moore (1982) to provide a reasonable combination of randomness and speed.

All congruential PRNGs have a common failing: eventually, they will cycle. Thus, a limit exists to how many PRNs can be generated by this rule. Because of this failing and others, a variety of other PRNGs have been developed over the years. A large literature exists concerning PRNGs; see, for example, Gentle (2010). Here, we describe briefly the default PRNG in the Python module `random` as well as in R, which is referred to as *Mersenne Twister*.

Matsumoto and Nishimura (1998) created Mersenne Twister. The mathematics behind its construction is both deep and subtle, but the name refers to the fact that the period length is chosen to be a Mersenne prime number. All you really need to know is that the Mersenne Twister PRNG is fast and generates high-quality numbers with an almost uniform distribution in the range $[0, 2^k - 1]$, where k is the word size of the computer; for example, k would be 32 on a 32-bit computer. Also, the period length is $2^{19937} - 1$. Finally, the Mersenne Twister PRNs pass numerous tests for statistical randomness, including the Diehard tests, which were developed by George Marsaglia in 1995 and published on a compact disk (CD).[21] The Mersenne Twister PRNs also passed most, but not all, of the TestU01 tests of randomness.[22]

7.10.4   Seeding the PRNG

Because every PRNG is basically some sort of difference equation, you must provide an initial condition, x_0, as the seed (see Section 7.10.3).

If you do not, then the PRNG will provide the initial condition for you, often using the time on the system clock of your computer; that is, the PRNG will query the system clock, and then convert that string into an integer that it uses as the seed. By using the system clock to determine the seed, you will almost surely get a different sequence of PRNs every time you call the PRNG, which is a problem if you are trying to compare, say, different methods of estimation in

---

[21]George Marsaglia was a American computer scientist who in 1968 discovered that PRNGs generated according to the linear congruential method lie in planes. He reported this result in Marsaglia (1968), and then spent his career improving on the generation of PRNs. You can get the CD at http://stat.fsu.edu/pub/diehard/.

[22]See http://www.iro.umontreal.ca/~simardr/testu01/tu01.html.

different programs. When comparing two methods, you would like to use the same sequence. In addition, if other researchers elsewhere in the world would like to replicate your work, then they need to know the seed, too. Consequently, it is important to seed the PRNG, and to record what that seed is. The following command seeds the Mersenne Twister PRNG in Python:

```
>>> import numpy
>>> numpy.random.seed(123457)
>>> numpy.random.uniform()
0.4347450610414807
>>> numpy.random.uniform()
0.013851115175644302
>>> numpy.random.seed(123457)
>>> numpy.random.uniform()
0.4347450610414807
>>> numpy.random.uniform()
0.013851115175644302
>>>
```

As you can see, if you begin with `123457` and generate one uniform variate, you will get `0.4347450610414807`; if you call the PRNG again, then you will get `0.013851115175644302`. By resetting the seed to `123457`, you can start the process all over again. You should note that on different computer chips it is possible for the same seed to result in different sequences, but this has more to do with the compiler than the chip set per se.

7.10.5 Introducing Dependence

Although independence is a useful starting point in any analysis, dependence among random variables is the norm. The simplest extension from independence is linear dependence, where the random variables are related linearly. To this end, consider a random variable Y that has expected value $\mathbb{E}(Y)$ denoted μ and variance $\mathbb{V}(Y)$ denoted σ^2. Introduce the random variable Z that has mean zero and variance 1. Write Y in terms of Z as follows:

$$Y = \mathbb{E}(Y) + \sqrt{\mathbb{V}(Y)}Z = \mu + \sigma Z.$$

Now, introduce $\mathbf{Z} = (Z_1, Z_2, \ldots, Z_K)^\top$, a $(K \times 1)$ vector of independent random variables, where each Z_k has expected value zero and variance 1. In this case, the vector $\mathbb{E}(\mathbf{Z})$ is the zero vector $\mathbf{0}_K$. What is the matrix equivalent of the scalar variance? It is the *variance-covariance matrix* and has the following form:

$$\mathbb{V}(\mathbf{Z}) = \mathbb{E}\left([\mathbf{Z} - \mathbb{E}(\mathbf{Z})][\mathbf{Z} - \mathbb{E}(\mathbf{Z})]^\top \right)$$

or, in its full glory,

$$\mathbb{V}(\mathbf{Z}) = \begin{bmatrix} \mathbb{E}(Z_1 Z_1) & \mathbb{E}(Z_1 Z_2) & \mathbb{E}(Z_1 Z_3) & \cdots & \mathbb{E}(Z_1 Z_K) \\ \mathbb{E}(Z_2 Z_1) & \mathbb{E}(Z_2 Z_2) & \mathbb{E}(Z_2 Z_3) & \cdots & \mathbb{E}(Z_2 Z_K) \\ \vdots & \vdots & \vdots & \ddots & \vdots \\ \mathbb{E}(Z_K Z_1) & \mathbb{E}(Z_K Z_2) & \mathbb{E}(Z_K Z_3) & \cdots & \mathbb{E}(Z_K Z_K) \end{bmatrix} = \mathbf{I}_K.$$

In words, in this case, the variance-covariance matrix of $\mathbf{Z}$ is the identity matrix. Why? By independence, the covariance between any (i, j) where i does not equal j is zero. For (i, j) pairs where i equals j, the expectation of the square of a mean-zero random variable is calculated, which is its variance, and equals 1 in this case.

Introduce the random vector $\mathbf{Y}$, the mean vector $\boldsymbol{\mu} = (\mu_1, \mu_2, \ldots, \mu_K)^\top$, and the variance-covariance matrix $\boldsymbol{\Sigma}$. How can $\mathbf{Y}$ be written in terms of $\boldsymbol{\mu}$, $\boldsymbol{\Sigma}$, and $\mathbf{Z}$? Clearly, taking the square root of each element of $\boldsymbol{\Sigma}$ is out of the question (although we both remember at least one classmate in graduate school who attempted to do this). What to do? Use the Cholesky decomposition. Let $\mathbf{F}$ denote the Cholesky matrix associated with $\boldsymbol{\Sigma}$; that is,

$$\boldsymbol{\Sigma} = \mathbf{F}\mathbf{F}^\top.$$

Then write $\mathbf{Y}$ as follows:

$$\mathbf{Y} = \boldsymbol{\mu} + \mathbf{F}\mathbf{Z}.$$

You can verify that this is, in fact, true. Specifically, calculate the first two central moments of $\mathbf{Y}$ under this linear transformation. Note that

$$\mathbb{E}(\mathbf{Y}) = \boldsymbol{\mu} + \mathbb{E}(\mathbf{F}\mathbf{Z}) = \boldsymbol{\mu} + \mathbf{F}\mathbb{E}(\mathbf{Z}) = \boldsymbol{\mu} + \mathbf{F}\mathbf{0}_K = \boldsymbol{\mu}.$$

Also,

$$\begin{aligned}
\mathbb{V}(Y) &= \mathbb{E}[(Y-\mu)(Y-\mu)^\top] \\
&= \mathbb{E}[(\mathbf{F}Z)(\mathbf{F}Z)^\top] \\
&= \mathbb{E}(\mathbf{F}ZZ^\top\mathbf{F}^\top) \\
&= \mathbf{F}\mathbb{E}(ZZ^\top)\mathbf{F}^\top \\
&= \mathbf{F}\mathbf{I}_K\mathbf{F}^\top \\
&= \mathbf{F}\mathbf{F}^\top \\
&= \Sigma.
\end{aligned}$$

How is this relevant to simulation? Suppose you want to simulate two jointly normal random variables $Y = (Y_1, Y_2)^\top$, often written as

$$Y \sim \mathcal{N}(\mu, \Sigma)$$

with

$$\mu = \begin{bmatrix}1\\2\end{bmatrix} \quad \text{and} \quad \Sigma = \begin{bmatrix}1 & 1\\1 & 2\end{bmatrix}.$$

In this case,

$$\mathbf{F} = \begin{bmatrix}1 & 0\\1 & 1\end{bmatrix}.$$

(Check whether this is true.) Generating two independent normal random variables having mean zero and variance 1 is trivial in either Python or R. Generating $Y \sim \mathcal{N}(\mu, \Sigma)$ when μ and Σ are known is trivial, too. Thus, consider the following Python code:

```
>>> import numpy
>>> N = 100
>>> mu = numpy.array([1.0, 2.0])
>>> Sigma = numpy.array([[1.0, 1.0], [1.0, 2.0]])
>>> F = numpy.linalg.cholesky(Sigma)
>>> numpy.random.seed(123457)
>>> Z = numpy.random.normal(0., 1., [N, 2])
>>> Y = numpy.dot(Z, F) + mu
```

The simulated data that are generated are depicted in Figure 7.26.

Linear forms of dependence are not the only forms. In fact, general forms of dependence can be introduced using a device referred to as the *copula*. Nelsen (1999) wrote a very readable introduction to nonlinear forms of dependence.

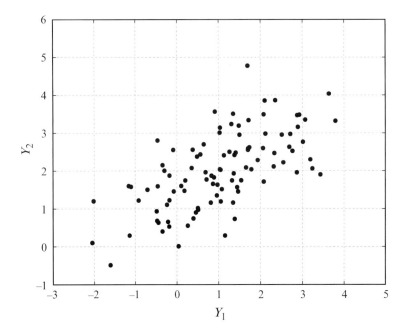

Figure 7.26: Scatterplot of Jointly Normal, Simulated Data

7.10.6 Antithetic Variates

Reducing the variance in Monte Carlo simulation is an important task. Because the variance of the simple arithmetic average is inversely proportional to the number of simulations undertaken, increasing the number of simulations is the most obvious way to reduce the variance, but such an approach is costly. Other techniques exist that are not as computationally expensive. One such variance reduction technique is the *method of antithetic variates*.

Suppose you are interested in calculating the expected value of some random variable U. To this end, consider taking the arithmetic average of two random draws U_1 and U_2, that is, $0.5(U_1 + U_2)$. In general, the variance of this sum is

$$\mathbb{V}[0.5(U_1 + U_2)] = 0.5^2\mathbb{V}(U_1) + 0.5^2\mathbb{V}(U_2) + 2 \times 0.5^2\text{cov}(U_1, U_2).$$

When two random variables U_1 and U_2 are independent as well as distributed identically, the $\text{cov}(U_1, U_2)$ is zero, and $\mathbb{V}(U_1)$ equals $\mathbb{V}(U_2)$, so the variance is one-half of the common variance of U. If, however, the covariance between U_1 and U_2 were negative, then you could get an even more precise estimate of the expected value. The method of antithetic variates involves choosing a second sample so that a negative covariance exists.

In general, under any Monte Carlo simulation, you must first generate a sequence of uniform random variables $\{U_n\}_{n=1}^{N}$. These uniform random variables may, of course, be subsequently transformed, for example using the inverse cdf transformation $Y_n = F_Y^{-1}(U_n)$, to obtain some other random variables, but it suffices here just to focus on the U_ns.

Under the method of antithetic variates, for every U_n, use its antithetic value $(1 - U_n)$ as well; that is, invert $(1 - U_n)$, too. For each U_n, you now have two values of the outcome, which are negatively correlated: average them.

The method has at least two advantages. First, it reduces by one-half the number of random numbers that need to be generated, which was an important consideration in the past but is not so important today. Second, it reduces the variance of the resulting estimate—for a fixed number of simulations N, the accuracy of the estimate is improved, which is important, even today.

7.10.7   Control Variates

Another variance reduction technique is the *method of control variates*. Under the method of control variates, information concerning errors made in known quantities is used to reduce the error of an estimate of an unknown quantity.

Consider the random variable $h(U)$, which is a nonlinear function of the random variable U. Suppose $h(U)$'s expected value is unknown and must be estimated. If $h(u)$ is small outside of some region $\mathcal{R}$ where $f_U(u)$, the pdf of U, is also small, then you can approximate $\mathbb{E}[h(U)]$ using a simple average like

$$\bar{h}_N = \frac{1}{N} \sum_{n=1}^{N} h(U_n),$$

where $\{U_n\}_{n=1}^{N}$ are independently and identically distributed random variables. (Roughly speaking, these conditions are used to ensure that the expectation of $h(U)$ exists.) For example, h could be $\exp(-U)$ and U could be uniform, as in the example from Section 7.8.2.

Suppose you calculate another statistic $g(U)$ whose expected value is known to be exactly, say, θ^0. The estimator

$$\hat{h}_N = \frac{1}{N} \sum_{n=1}^{N} \left(h(U_n) + \gamma \left[g(U_n) - \theta^0 \right] \right).$$

is also an unbiased estimator $\mathbb{E}[h(U)]$ for any choice of the constant γ. The variance of $\hat{h}_N$ is

$$\mathbb{V}(\hat{h}_N) = \frac{\mathbb{V}[h(U)]}{N} + \gamma^2 \frac{\mathbb{V}[g(U)]}{N} + 2\gamma \text{cov}[g(U), h(U)]. \qquad (7.32)$$

This quadratic form can be minimized with respect to γ, which yields

$$\hat{\gamma} = -\frac{\text{cov}[g(U), h(U)]}{\mathbb{V}[g(U)]}.$$

Substituting $\hat{\gamma}$ into equation (7.32), and rearranging terms yields

$$\mathbb{V}(\hat{h}_N) = (1 - \rho^2) \mathbb{V}(\bar{h}_N),$$

where ρ is the linear correlation coefficient between the two random variables $g(U)$ and $h(U)$. Since you get to choose $g(U)$, you get to choose ρ, which means you can reduce the variance of the estimator $\hat{h}_N$. For example, if $h(U)$ were $\exp(-U)$, then let $g(U)$ be U. Now, $g(U)$ and $h(U)$ are negatively correlated, so $\hat{\gamma}$ will be positive.

An Example

To demonstrate the improvements possible with the methods of antithetic variates and control variates, we conducted a small simulation experiment using the following function:

$$h(U) = \exp(-U),$$

where U is distributed uniformly on the $[0, 1]$ interval. This is the function we used in Section 7.8.2, that is,

$$\mathbb{E}[h(U)] = \int_0^1 \exp(-u) \, du.$$

From Section 7.8.2, we know that $\mathbb{E}[h(U)]$ equals $[1 - \exp(-1)]$, about 0.6321. In Section 7.8.2, we also demonstrated that the variance of $h(U)$ equals

$(0.5[1 - \exp(-2)] - [1 - \exp(-1)]^2)$, about 0.0328. Consequently, the variance of the sample mean

$$\bar{h}_N = \frac{1}{N} \sum_{n=1}^{N} h(U_n)$$

is then $(\mathbb{V}[h(U)]/N)$, around $(0.0328/N)$. Although deriving the variance of the method of antithetic variates estimator

$$\hat{h}_N = \frac{2}{N} \sum_{n=1}^{\frac{N}{2}} [h(U_n) + h(1 - U_n)]$$

is feasible in this example, we do not do this. Instead, in Table 7.10, we just present the variance of the realized $h(u_n)$s. For the method of control variates estimator

$$\tilde{h}_N = \frac{2}{N} \sum_{n=1}^{\frac{N}{2}} [h(U_n) + \gamma(U_n - 0.5)],$$

we cycled through different values for γ from 0.1 to 0.9 by steps of size 0.1. To reduce clutter, we present a subset of these outcomes in the table. As you can see from the table, the method of antithetic variates reduces the variation substantially; for some values of γ, the method of control variates does so as well. A problem with the method of control variates is that γ is typically unknown, which is an obvious limitation.

Estimator	Estimate	Variance
Sample Mean	0.62578961	0.03123373
True Expectation	0.63212056	0.03275596
Antithetic	0.63169936	0.00050431
Control, $\gamma = 0.1$	0.62092786	0.02197111
Control, $\gamma = 0.4$	0.62707423	0.00419697
Control, $\gamma = 0.5$	0.62912301	0.00153488
Control, $\gamma = 0.6$	0.63117180	0.00050410
Control, $\gamma = 0.7$	0.63322059	0.00110464
Control, $\gamma = 0.9$	0.63731817	0.00719964

Table 7.10: Comparison of Simulation Methods, $N = 1,000$

7.10.8   Importance Sampling

In some applications, you may be required to calculate the expected value of a function h of a $(K \times 1)$ vector of random variables Y. In symbols,

$$\mathbb{E}[h(Y)] = \int_{-\infty}^{\infty} \cdots \int_{-\infty}^{\infty} h(y) f_Y(y) \, \mathrm{d}y.$$

When K is large (for example, greater than five), cubature is ruled out because of the curse of dimensionality, so Monte Carlo simulation is one alternative. Again, if $h(y)$ is small outside of some region $\mathcal{R}$ where $f_Y(y)$ is also small, then you can approximate the expectation using a simple average like

$$\bar{h}_N = \frac{1}{N} \sum_{n=1}^{N} h(y_n),$$

where y_n is a random draw from $f_Y(y_n)$. Except in cases like the preceding Gaussian distribution, drawing from the joint distribution $f_Y(y)$ is often either infeasible or difficult. What to do?

Sometimes, you can sample from another distribution, which we denote here by $g_Y(y)$. In this case, by calculating

$$\mathbb{E}[h(Y)] = \int_{-\infty}^{\infty} \cdots \int_{-\infty}^{\infty} h(y) \frac{f_Y(y)}{g_Y(y)} g_Y(y) \, \mathrm{d}y$$

instead, you can simulate values from the joint distribution $g_Y(y)$ and approximate the expectation using

$$\hat{h}_N = \frac{1}{N} \sum_{n=1}^{N} h(y_n) \frac{f_Y(y_n)}{g_Y(y_n)},$$

which is referred to as *importance sampling*.

Given that you could not simulate from the joint distribution $f_Y(y)$, or only at a high cost, you would probably be willing to give up some efficiency when using importance sampling. Thus, it comes as a pleasant surprise that the variance of $\hat{h}_N$ can, in fact, be less than the variance of $\bar{h}_N$. Whether the variance in the estimate of the expectation is reduced depends on whether the variance of the object $[h(Y)f_Y(Y)/g_Y(Y)]$ under the law $g_Y(\cdot)$ is smaller than the variance of $h(Y)$ under the law $f_Y(\cdot)$.

Importance sampling is helpful when $h(\cdot)$ is largest for values of Y that are unlikely under the law $f_Y(\cdot)$. In such cases, you seek a law $g_Y(\cdot)$ that puts more weight on the most important (for the expected value of h) values of Y. Identifying the most important values of Y is the key to successful importance sampling, but that can sometimes be difficult. Even when those values can be identified, however, constructing $g_Y(\cdot)$ can be even more difficult. That said, importance sampling is a useful approach to solving sampling problems that arise when simulating rare events.

7.10.9 Markov Chain Monte Carlo

As mentioned, in some applications, sampling from the joint distribution $f_Y(y)$ is either infeasible or difficult. Moreover, constructing a useful alternative distribution $g_Y(y)$ that can be used in importance sampling need not be any easier. What to do?

Markov chain Monte Carlo (MCMC) involves algorithms that use simulation to construct approximations to $f_Y(y)$ in several different ways, but as the name suggests, the principal device is the Markov chain.

A Markov chain is a stochastic process for which, given the current state, future states of the random variable Y are independent of past states. To simplify matters, let's assume a finite number of states. In that case, the pdf $f_Y(y)$ becomes a probability mass function (pmf). Introducing a sequence of periods (or stages) indexed by $t = 1, 2, \ldots$, we can state the Markovian assumption in terms of the pmf as follows:

$$\Pr(Y_{t+1} = y | y_t, y_{t-1}, \ldots) = \Pr(Y_{t+1} = y | y_t).$$

A simple example of a Markov chain is the *mover-stayer model*. In this model, the random variable Y can take on one of two values, for instance, $\{1, 2\}$. For a sequence of periods indexed by $t = 1, 2, \ldots$, the transition from state to state is determined by the value of the present state y_t. Thus,

$$\Pr(Y_{t+1} = 1 | y_t = 1) = p_{11} \quad \text{and} \quad \Pr(Y_{t+1} = 2 | y_t = 1) = p_{12} = 1 - p_{11},$$

and

$$\Pr(Y_{t+1} = 2 | y_t = 2) = p_{22} \quad \text{and} \quad \Pr(Y_{t+1} = 1 | y_t = 2) = p_{21} = 1 - p_{22},$$

where p_{12} need not equal p_{22}. (Independence would require that p_{12} equal p_{22}.) A Markov chain can be represented by the following *transition matrix*:

$$\mathbf{P} = \begin{bmatrix} p_{11} & 1 - p_{11} \\ 1 - p_{22} & p_{22} \end{bmatrix}.$$

That is, the $(1, 1)$ element of the matrix $\mathbf{P}$ characterizes the probability of staying in state 1 in the next period, given that the current state is 1.

Now, if we take the matrix $\mathbf{P}$ to some large power, for example, infinity, we can find the steady-state distribution, which we denote by π here. In symbols, the steady-state distribution is a fixed-point when post-multiplied by the transition matrix $\mathbf{P}$, that is,

$$\pi = \pi \mathbf{P}.$$

For example, if

$$\mathbf{P} = \begin{bmatrix} 0.7 & 0.3 \\ 0.2 & 0.8 \end{bmatrix}, \quad \text{then} \quad \mathbf{P}^{\infty} = \begin{bmatrix} 0.4 & 0.6 \\ 0.4 & 0.6 \end{bmatrix} \quad \text{and} \quad \pi = [0.4 \, 0.6].$$

In short, by simulating an appropriately constructed Markov chain for a long enough time, an approximation to the desired distribution will obtain as an equilibrium outcome. Although the theory behind MCMC may not be easily accessible, implementing two commonly used methods is relatively straightforward.

Gibbs Sampling

Perhaps the simplest MCMC method to understand is *Gibbs sampling*, which was named in honor of the American physicist Josiah Willard Gibbs, an allusion to the analogy between the sampling algorithm and statistical physics. The method, first described by Geman and Geman (1984), can be implemented as follows. Assume that for $f_{XY}(x, y)$, the joint distribution of (X, Y), you can simulate from the conditional distributions $f_{X|Y}(x|y)$ and $f_{Y|X}(y|x)$. Our illustration of the Gibbs sampling algorithm follows the example presented by Casella and George (1992). There, the joint distribution of (X, Y) is sought when X can take on the integer values $0, 1, \ldots, N$, whereas Y is contained in the unit interval $(0, 1)$—in short, a potentially intractable distribution from which to sample.

Suppose that the distribution of X conditional on Y is binomial, so the pmf of X given $Y = y$ is

$$f_{X|Y}(x|y) = \binom{N}{x} y^x (1-y)^{N-x} \quad x = 0, 1, \ldots, N; \ 0 < y < 1,$$

whereas the distribution of Y conditional on X is beta, so the pdf of Y given $X = x$ is

$$f_{Y|X}(y|x) = \frac{y^{x+\alpha-1}(1-y)^{N-x+\beta-1}}{B(x+\alpha, N-x+\beta)} \quad x = 0, 1, \ldots, N; \ 0 < y < 1;$$

where

$$B(v, w) = \frac{\Gamma(v)\Gamma(w)}{\Gamma(v+w)}$$

and

$$\Gamma(v) = \int_0^\infty u^{v-1} \exp(-u) \, du.$$

Presumably, the example was chosen by Casella and George because the marginal pmf of X is known to be the following:

$$f_X(x|\alpha, \beta, N) = \binom{N}{x} \frac{\Gamma(\alpha+\beta)}{\Gamma(\alpha)\Gamma(\beta)} \frac{\Gamma(x+\alpha)\Gamma(N-x+\beta)}{\Gamma(N+\alpha+\beta)}, \tag{7.33}$$

which makes it easy to compare the Gibb sampling output with the truth.

Thus, Gibbs sampling begins by choosing an initial value for y_0, say, 0.5. Based on that value, now simulate x_0 from the binomial distribution having the parameter pair (N, y_0). Using that x_0, now generate y_1, a random variable from the beta distribution having parameters (α, β, N, x_0). With y_1, generate x_1, and so forth.

After some time, often referred to as the *burn-in period*, the draws will be from the marginal distributions $\hat{f}_X(x)$ and $\hat{f}_Y(y)$. In words, if the Gibbs sampler is allowed to proceed for, say, M iterations, then the values of the last, say, L iterations will be from equilibrium distributions that are close to the true marginal distributions. Thus, using either $f_{X|Y}(x|y)$ and $\hat{f}_Y(y)$ or $f_{Y|X}(y|x)$ and $\hat{f}_X(x)$, you can now get random draws from the joint distribution.

To demonstrate Gibbs sampling, we present in Listing 7.12 the Python script.

```
# Script:  Gibbs.py
# Author:  Harry J. Paarsch
# Date:    28 March 2014
from numpy import random, zeros
# Set up the parameters of the Gibbs sampling.
nObs    =       10
alpha   =       2.
beta    =       4.
sLow    =     9000
S       =    10000
xGibbs = zeros(S+1)
yGibbs = zeros(S+1)
random.seed(123457)
yGibbs[0] = 0.5
for s in range(0, S):
  xGibbs[s]   = random.binomial(nObs, yGibbs[s])
  yGibbs[s+1] = random.beta(alpha+xGibbs[s],nObs-xGibbs[s]+beta)

# You can now use the last (S-sLow) realizations.
xHat = xGibbs[sLow:S]
yHat = yGibbs[sLow:S]
```

Listing 7.12: Casella-George Gibbs Sampling Python Script

In this example, we set N to be 10, α to be 2, and β to be 4. We simulated the system 10,000 times but only used the last 1,000 realizations to estimate the marginal distributions. In other words, the burn-in period was 9,000 iterations. In Figure 7.27 we present the expected number of outcomes concerning $x = 0, 1, \ldots, 10$ predicted in 1,000 draws by equation (7.33) versus the number that obtained under Gibbs sampling. That the pairs of points lie close to the 45-degree line supports the claim that Gibbs sampling is approximating the relevant distribution well.

Clearly, some dependence will exist among the pairs of draws across successive iterates (after all, the stochastic process is Markovian), but a law of large numbers will still apply, so the expectation of some function $h(X, Y)$ can be approximated by calculating the average of the function at the pairs $\{(x_\ell, y_\ell)\}_{\ell=M-L+1}^{M}$ using

$$\frac{1}{L} \sum_{\ell=M-L+1}^{M} h(x_\ell, y_\ell).$$

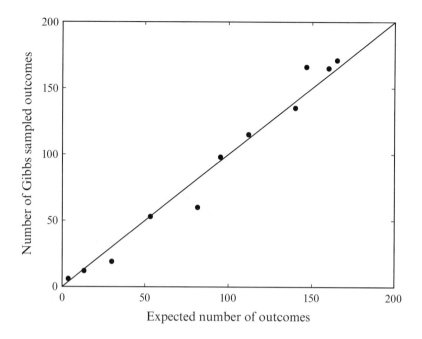

Figure 7.27: Expected versus Gibbs Sampled Outcomes

When more than two random variables exist, the updating of the Gibbs sampling algorithm follows the notion that is used in the Gauss-Seidel algorithm (see Section 7.4.3). For example, suppose Y is a (3×1) vector, where sampling from each of the following three conditional distributions is easy. In this case, the following would work:

$$\text{draw } y_1^{(1)} \text{ from } f_{1|23}(y_1|y_2^{(0)}, y_3^{(0)})$$
$$\text{draw } y_2^{(1)} \text{ from } f_{2|13}(y_2|y_1^{(1)}, y_3^{(0)})$$
$$\text{draw } y_3^{(1)} \text{ from } f_{3|12}(y_3|y_1^{(1)}, y_2^{(1)}).$$

Of course, the question is how to order the draws. It shouldn't matter after the burn-in period. Put another way, if it does matter, then the equilibrium has not obtained, so keep drawing.

Metropolis-Hastings

Another MCMC method is the *Metropolis-Hastings algorithm*, named in honor of two of its inventors, Nicholas Metropolis and W. Keith Hastings (see Metropolis, Rosenbluth, Rosenbluth, Teller, and Teller 1953, and Hastings 1970).

The key to implementing the Gibbs sampling algorithm is that the conditional distributions of each random variable can be expressed in terms of the others in a way that can be simulated easily. Sometimes that is impossible, or at best difficult. In such cases, the Metropolis-Hastings algorithm is a useful alternative. The Metropolis-Hastings algorithm is more expensive to implement than the Gibbs sampling algorithm, and somewhat more complicated to describe. Chib and Greenberg (1995) wrote an excellent introduction to this topic.

7.11   Figures and Graphs

Research assistants are often asked to create figures and graphs that are then incorporated into a paper or presentation. As mentioned, the final use of a figure or graph really determines its format. In Chapter 4, we provided explicit Python instructions concerning how to control the appearance of fonts and their sizes. Because of heterogeneity in format requirements, it is difficult to provide concrete instructions concerning how to use Python or R to produce figures and graphs, but we can provide you with some advice concerning how to store them; several formats exist.

Because we have committed to using LaTeX (see Chapter 10), our preferred format is as an encapsulated PostScript (EPS) file. An EPS file, it is almost like a program instructing the computer in how the image should be rendered. In that sense, an EPS file can be extremely unwieldy; if you have a figure is constructed from lots of data, then the file containing it can become huge, sometimes literally hundreds of megabytes. Publishers like EPS files because the format affords them maximal flexibility in the production process.

For day-to-day use, however, a figure or graph in either Portable Document Format (PDF) or Portable Network Graphics (PNG) format is probably best. As the name implies, PDF allows documents to be stored in a way that is independent of applications, for example, hardware or software as well as operating systems. In a PDF file, a complete description of how the fonts, graphics, and text are laid out is included. For this reason, using PDF files is quite common.

PNG is a graphics file format that supports *lossless data compression*. Lossless data compression is a class of data compression algorithms that allows the original data to be perfectly reconstructed from the compressed data. By contrast, *lossy data compression* permits reconstruction only of an approximation of the original data, but this usually admits improved compression rates, smaller files.[23] PNG was created as a replacement for the Graphics Interchange Format (GIF) when patent issues arose concerning GIF.

Another format is PGF (Portable Graphics Format). PGF is a low-level language, which you may want to avoid until you have more experience computing; TikZ is a collection of high-level macros that uses PGF.[24] The top-level PGF and TikZ commands are invoked as TeX macros, but in contrast to PSTricks (a set of macros used to include PostScript figures and graphs into LaTeX), the PGF/TikZ graphics themselves are described in a language that resembles METAPOST.

If you continue with an academic career, you will almost certainly encounter these software tools, particularly if you publish, so it is worth at least knowing what the acronyms mean.

---

[23]From `http://en.wikipedia.org/wiki/Lossless_compression`.

[24]The name TikZ is a recursive acronym for *TikZ ist kein Zeichenprogramm* (TikZ is not a drawing program).

8

Solved Examples

SOLVING PROBLEMS SIMILAR to those that arise often in research is the only way to gain the experience necessary to hone your craft. Thus, in this chapter, we present a sequence of solved examples that illustrate some of the methods we described in Chapter 7.

8.1 Linear Algebra: Portfolio Allocation Problem

Consider an investor who faces a $(K \times 1)$ vector of assets whose returns Y are distributed jointly normal having mean μ and variance-covariance matrix Σ, often referred to as *following the Gaussian law*. Assume the investor can go either long or short, that is, have positive amounts (long) or negative amounts (short) in any asset and must invest all his resources in at least some of the assets.

One investment strategy the investor might want to investigate is to find the variance-minimizing portfolio allocation $\hat{\mathbf{a}}$ for final wealth

$$W(\mathbf{a}) = \mathbf{a}^\top Y.$$

Here, wealth W is a function of a vector of allocations $\mathbf{a} = (a_1, \ldots, a_K)^\top$. The sum of the allocations must equal 1, that is, $\mathbf{a}^\top \iota_K = 1$ where ι_K is a $(K \times 1)$ vector of 1s.

When Y follows the Gaussian law, often denoted $Y \sim \mathcal{N}(\mu, \Sigma)$, the distribution of $W(\mathbf{a})$ is normal, having mean $\mathbf{a}^\top \mu$ and variance $\mathbf{a}^\top \Sigma \mathbf{a}$. The investor seeks to minimize the variance of $W(\mathbf{a})$—or alternatively, $0.5 \times W(\mathbf{a})$—subject to the constraint that the sum of the shares of wealth in each asset equals 1;

that is, $\mathbf{a}^{\top}\iota_K$ is one. Here, the one-half on the objective function is introduced to avoid having to carry around a 2 that will obtain after differentiation. This is perfectly fine; as noted in Section 7.5, the stationary points of functions are preserved under monotonic transformations. The corresponding Lagrangian for this problem is

$$\mathcal{L}(\mathbf{a}, \lambda) = \frac{\mathbf{a}^{\top}\Sigma\mathbf{a}}{2} + \lambda(1 - \mathbf{a}^{\top}\iota_K)$$

whence derive the first-order conditions that can be solved for $\hat{\mathbf{a}}$:

$$\frac{\partial\mathcal{L}(\hat{\mathbf{a}}, \hat{\lambda})}{\partial\mathbf{a}} = \mathbf{0}_K = \Sigma\hat{\mathbf{a}} - \hat{\lambda}\iota_K$$

$$\frac{\partial\mathcal{L}(\hat{\mathbf{a}}, \hat{\lambda})}{\partial\lambda} = 0 = 1 - \hat{\mathbf{a}}^{\top}\iota_K = 1 - \iota_K^{\top}\hat{\mathbf{a}}.$$

Thus,

$$\hat{\mathbf{a}} = \hat{\lambda}\Sigma^{-1}\iota_K = \frac{\Sigma^{-1}\iota_K}{\iota_K^{\top}\Sigma^{-1}\iota_K},$$

since

$$\hat{\lambda} = \frac{1}{\iota_K^{\top}\Sigma^{-1}\iota_K}.$$

Now suppose instead that the investor has preferences U over wealth W of the following form:

$$U(W) = -\exp(-\eta W) \quad \eta > 0.$$

Such preferences are often referred to as *constant absolute risk aversion* (CARA) preferences because a measure of risk aversion known as absolute risk aversion is a constant. CARA preferences are used in the field of finance, especially in conjunction with normal (Gaussian) returns because the expected utility function has a particularly tractable, closed-form expression.

To see this, first consider a scalar normal random variable W having expectation μ and variance σ^2. The expected value of $\exp(\tau W)$ has the following functional form:

$$\exp(\tau\mu + 0.5\tau^2\sigma^2).$$

With this in mind, calculating the expected utility–maximizing portfolio allocation $\tilde{\mathbf{a}}$ involves solving the following problem:

$$\max_{\mathbf{a}} \mathbb{E}\left(U[W(\mathbf{a})]\right) \text{ subject to } \mathbf{a}^{\top}\iota_K = 1,$$

where

$$\mathbb{E}\left(U[W(\mathbf{a})]\right) = \mathbb{E}\left[U(\mathbf{a}^\top Y)\right] = -\exp\left(-\eta\mathbf{a}^\top\boldsymbol{\mu} + \eta^2\frac{\mathbf{a}^\top\boldsymbol{\Sigma}\mathbf{a}}{2}\right).$$

The function $\mathbb{E}\left[U(\mathbf{a}^\top Y)\right]$ is awkward to differentiate with respect to $\mathbf{a}$, but a monotonic function of it, such as $\log\left(-\mathbb{E}\left[U(\mathbf{a}^\top Z)\right]\right)$, is relatively easy to differentiate. Thus, consider the following Lagrangian:

$$\mathcal{L}(\mathbf{a},\lambda) = \log\left[-\mathbb{E}\left(U[W(\mathbf{a})]\right)\right] + \lambda(1 - \mathbf{a}^\top\iota_K)$$

$$= -\eta\mathbf{a}^\top\boldsymbol{\mu} + \eta^2\frac{\mathbf{a}^\top\boldsymbol{\Sigma}\mathbf{a}}{2} + \lambda(1 - \mathbf{a}^\top\iota_K)$$

whence derive the first-order conditions that can be solved for $\tilde{\mathbf{a}}$:

$$\frac{\partial\mathcal{L}(\tilde{\mathbf{a}},\tilde{\lambda})}{\partial\mathbf{a}} = \mathbf{0}_K = -\eta\boldsymbol{\mu} + \eta^2\boldsymbol{\Sigma}\tilde{\mathbf{a}} - \tilde{\lambda}\iota_K$$

$$\frac{\partial\mathcal{L}(\tilde{\mathbf{a}},\tilde{\lambda})}{\partial\lambda} = 0 = 1 - \tilde{\mathbf{a}}^\top\iota_K = 1 - \iota_K^\top\tilde{\mathbf{a}}.$$

Thus,

$$\tilde{\mathbf{a}} = \frac{\boldsymbol{\Sigma}^{-1}\iota_K}{\iota_K^\top\boldsymbol{\Sigma}^{-1}\iota_K} - \frac{\iota_K^\top\boldsymbol{\Sigma}^{-1}\boldsymbol{\mu}\boldsymbol{\Sigma}^{-1}\iota_K}{\eta\iota_K^\top\boldsymbol{\Sigma}^{-1}\iota_K} + \frac{\boldsymbol{\Sigma}^{-1}\boldsymbol{\mu}}{\eta}$$

since

$$\tilde{\lambda} = \frac{\eta^2 - \eta\iota_K^\top\boldsymbol{\Sigma}^{-1}\boldsymbol{\mu}}{\iota_K^\top\boldsymbol{\Sigma}^{-1}\iota_K}.$$

When η equals 2, $\boldsymbol{\mu} = (1,2)^\top$, and

$$\boldsymbol{\Sigma} = \begin{bmatrix} 2 & 1 \\ 1 & 4 \end{bmatrix},$$

calculating $\hat{\mathbf{a}}$ and $\tilde{\mathbf{a}}$ as well as the expected value and the variance of $W(\hat{\mathbf{a}})$ and $W(\tilde{\mathbf{a}})$, and the expected utilities of $W(\hat{\mathbf{a}})$ and $W(\tilde{\mathbf{a}})$, can be done by hand. To this end, note that

$$\boldsymbol{\Sigma}^{-1} = \frac{1}{7}\begin{bmatrix} 4 & -1 \\ -1 & 2 \end{bmatrix},$$

so $\Sigma^{-1}\iota_2 = (3/7, 1/7)^\top$ and $\iota_2^\top \Sigma^{-1}\iota_2 = 4/7$, whereas $\Sigma^{-1}\mu = (2/7, 3/7)^\top$ and $\iota_2^\top \Sigma^{-1}\mu = 5/7$. Hence, $\hat{\mathbf{a}} = (0.75, 0.25)^\top$, whereas $\tilde{\mathbf{a}} = (0.625, 0.375)^\top$, so $\hat{\mathbf{a}}^\top \mu = 1.25$ and $\tilde{\mathbf{a}}^\top \mu = 1.375$. Therefore, $\mathbb{V}[W(\hat{\mathbf{a}})] = 1.75$ and $\mathbb{V}[W(\tilde{\mathbf{a}})] = 1.8125$, while

$$\mathbb{E}\left(U[W(\hat{\mathbf{a}})]\right) = -\exp\left(-\eta\hat{\mathbf{a}}^\top\mu + \eta^2\frac{\hat{\mathbf{a}}^\top\Sigma\hat{\mathbf{a}}}{2}\right)$$

$$= -2.7183$$

and

$$\mathbb{E}\left(U[W(\tilde{\mathbf{a}})]\right) = -\exp\left(-\eta\tilde{\mathbf{a}}^\top\mu + \eta^2\frac{\tilde{\mathbf{a}}^\top\Sigma\tilde{\mathbf{a}}}{2}\right)$$

$$= -2.3989.$$

Suppose instead that μ equals $(1, 2, 3, 4)^\top$ and

$$\Sigma = \begin{bmatrix} 2 & 1 & 1 & 1 \\ 1 & 4 & 2 & 2 \\ 1 & 2 & 6 & 3 \\ 1 & 2 & 3 & 8 \end{bmatrix},$$

then calculations by hand, although feasible, are tedious as well as error prone and time consuming, so use Python. The Python code to calculate $\hat{\mathbf{a}}$ and $\tilde{\mathbf{a}}$, the expected value and the variance of $W(\hat{\mathbf{a}})$ and $W(\tilde{\mathbf{a}})$, and the expected utilities of $W(\hat{\mathbf{a}})$ and $W(\tilde{\mathbf{a}})$ is presented in Listing 8.1, and the output of that program is presented in Listing 8.2.

```
# Script: PortAllo.py
# Author: Harry J. Paarsch
# Date:    25 July 2013
import numpy as np
#
# Assign the data for the problem given in the text.
#
eta   = 2.;
mu    = np.array([1., 2., 3., 4.])
iota  = np.array([1., 1., 1., 1.])
sigma = np.array
        ([[2.,1.,1.,1.],[1.,4.,2.,2.],[1.,2.,6.,3.],[1.,2.,3.,8.]])
#
```

```
# Do some intermediate calculations to get the various moving parts.
# Note that no inverses were used in the construction of these parts.
#
sigInvIo   = np.linalg.solve(sigma, iota)
ioSigInvIo = np.dot(iota, sigInvIo)
sigInvMu   = np.linalg.solve(sigma, mu)
ioSigInvMu = np.dot(iota, sigInvMu)
#
# Calculate the variance-minimizing portfolio-allocation vector ahat.
# Then calculate the expected-utility maximizing portfolio-allocation
# vector atil.
#
ahat    = sigInvIo / ioSigInvIo
atil    = ahat - (ioSigInvMu*sigInvIo/eta/ioSigInvIo) + (sigInvMu/eta)
#
# Calculate the mean and the variance of wealth under ahat and atil.
#
muWahat = np.dot(ahat, mu)
vWahat  = np.dot(ahat, np.dot(sigma, ahat))
muWatil = np.dot(atil, mu)
vWatil  = np.dot(atil, np.dot(sigma, atil))
#
# Calculate the expected utility of wealth under ahat and atil.
#
eUWahat = -np.exp(-eta*muWahat+(0.5*eta*eta*vWahat))
eUWatil = -np.exp(-eta*muWatil+(0.5*eta*eta*vWatil))
#
# Output the results.
#
print 'Solutions to Portfolio Allocation Problem\n'
print 'ahat =    ', ahat
print 'atil =    ', atil
print 'muWahat = ', muWahat
print 'vWahat = ', vWahat
print 'muWatil = ', muWatil
print 'vWatil = ', vWatil
print 'eUWahat = ', eUWahat
print 'eUWatil = ', eUWatil
```

Listing 8.1: Python Script to Solve Portfolio Allocation Problem

```
Solutions to Portfolio Allocation Problem

ahat =     [ 0.68548387  0.18548387  0.08064516  0.0483871 ]
atil =     [ 0.43951613  0.18951613  0.16935484  0.2016129 ]
```

```
muWahat =   1.49193548387
vWahat  =   1.68548387097
muWatil =   2.13306451613
vWatil  =   2.0060483871
eUWahat =  -1.47269900364
eUWatil =  -0.775666780134
```

Listing 8.2: Solutions to Portfolio Allocation Problem

8.2   Unconstrained Optimization: Duration Model

Problems that involve modeling the waiting time until some event occurs arise naturally in both business and science. We use this class of problems to provide a nontrivial example of unconstrained optimization. Specifically, as the working example, we consider a model developed by Han and Hausman (1990) and by Singer and Willet (1993).

In what follows, we assume that this waiting time can be represented as a random draw from the population of a positive random variable T that has a probability density function denoted by $f_T(t)$ and a cumulative distribution function denoted by $F_T(t)$. Here, $F_T(t)$ is the probability that T is less than or equal to t, or

$$F_T(t) = \Pr(T \le t) = \int_0^t f_T(z)\, \mathrm{d}z.$$

In words, $F_T(t)$ represents the proportion of events that will occur within the first t periods of time.

It is standard in the literature concerned with waiting times to use techniques from a subfield of statistics referred to by several different names, including *duration analysis, failure time analysis,* and *survival analysis.* We use the term *duration analysis.*

8.2.1   Putting Structure on $f_T(t)$

A number of different models can be employed to put structure on the probability law governing event arrivals, the pdf $f_T(t)$, but in duration analysis the three most common ones are the exponential law, for which

$$f_T(t) = \lambda \exp(-\lambda t) \quad \lambda > 0,\ t > 0,$$

and two generalizations of the exponential law, the Weibull law, for which

$$f_T(t) = \lambda p t^{p-1} \exp(-\lambda t^p) \quad \lambda > 0, \ p > 0, \ t > 0,$$

and the gamma law, for which

$$f_T(t) = \frac{\lambda^q}{\Gamma(q)} t^{q-1} \exp(-\lambda t) \quad \lambda > 0, \ q > 0, \ t > 0.$$

Here, the parameters λ, p, and q are unknown and must be estimated.

In the case of the exponential law, λ is often referred to as the *hazard rate*; in that case, the inverse of λ is the average waiting time to the event.

In the case of the Weibull distribution, p is sometimes referred to as the *shape parameter*.

When q is an integer, one interpretation of a gamma-distributed random variable is as the sum of q independent, exponentially distributed random variables, each having hazard rate λ.

A model that encompasses all three specifications is the generalized gamma law, for which

$$f_T(t) = \frac{\lambda^q p}{\Gamma(q/p)} t^{q-1} \exp(-\lambda^p t^p) \quad \lambda > 0, \ p > 0, \ q > 0, \ t > 0.$$

In Figure 8.1 we present plots of the pdfs of the Weibull and gamma as well as generalized gamma laws for specific values of the parameter, namely, $\lambda = 1$, $p = 0.9$, and $q = 3$.

Now, an event has either occurred before time t or it has not, so

$$\Pr(T \leq t) + \Pr(T > t) = 1,$$

or

$$\Pr(T > t) = [1 - \Pr(T \leq t)].$$

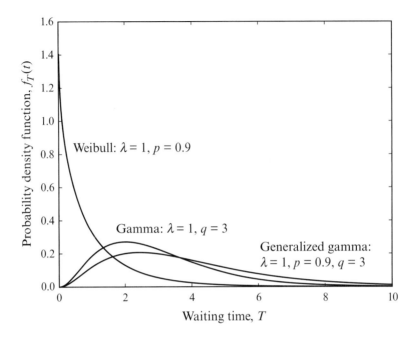

Figure 8.1: Examples of Probability Density Functions

If $F_T(t)$ is the fraction of events that has occurred by time t, then the fraction that has not is $[1 - F_T(t)]$, which we denote by $S_T(t)$. For various reasons, $S_T(t)$ is referred to as the *survivor function* of T. Note, too, that

$$S_T(t) = \int_t^\infty f_T(z)\,\mathrm{d}z.$$

Given that an event has not occurred, the conditional probability of its occurring in the next instant is

$$\frac{f_T(t)}{\Pr(T > t)} = \frac{f_T(t)}{S_T(t)} = \frac{f_T(t)}{[1 - F_T(t)]} = h_T(t),$$

the hazard rate (or hazard function) of T.

A number of relations exist between the pdf $f_T(t)$ and the cdf $F_T(t)$ as well as the hazard rate $h_T(t)$ and the survivor function $S_T(t)$. For example,

$$f_T(t) = h_T(t)S_T(t) = h_T(t)[1 - F_T(t)].$$

Also,

$$\frac{f_T(t)}{[1 - F_T(t)]} = h_T(t)$$

$$\int_0^t \frac{f_T(z)}{[1 - F_T(z)]} \, dz = \int_0^t h_T(z) \, dz$$

$$-\log[1 - F_T(t)] = \int_0^t h_T(z) \, dz$$

$$[1 - F_T(t)] = \exp\left[-\int_0^t h_T(z) \, dz\right]$$

$$S_T(t) = \exp\left[-\int_0^t h_T(z) \, dz\right]$$

$$F_T(t) = 1 - \exp\left[-\int_0^t h_T(z) \, dz\right]$$

$$\frac{dF_T(t)}{dt} = f_T(t) = h_T(t) \exp\left[-\int_0^t h_T(z) \, dz\right].$$

In short, an assumption concerning the hazard rate $h_T(t)$ is an assumption concerning the pdf $f_T(t)$. For example, if the hazard rate is assumed to be a constant $\lambda > 0$, then

$$h_T(t) = \lambda$$

$$S_T(t) = \exp\left(-\int_0^t \lambda \, dz\right)$$

$$F_T(t) = 1 - \exp(-\lambda t)$$

$$f_T(t) = \lambda \exp(-\lambda t),$$

which is the pdf of an exponentially distributed random variable T.

Now introduce a generalization of the exponential hazard rate, one for which

$$h_T(t) = \lambda p t^{p-1}.$$

When p is 1, an exponential random variable obtains. If p is greater than 1, then a hazard rate that is an increasing function of time t obtains, which is sometimes referred to as *positive duration dependence*. When p is less than 1, the hazard rate is a decreasing function of t, which is sometimes referred to as *negative duration dependence*. In this case,

$$h_T(t) = \lambda p t^{p-1}$$

$$S_T(t) = \exp\left(-\int_0^t \lambda p z^{p-1}\, dz\right)$$

$$F_T(t) = 1 - \exp(-\lambda t^p)$$

$$f_T(t) = \lambda p t^{p-1} \exp(-\lambda t^p),$$

which is the pdf of a Weibull random variable. Each of these probability laws translates into a particular structure concerning the conditional probability of an event's arriving at some future date, given that it has yet to arrive. That is, the conditional probability of T, given that the event has not occurred, is

$$\frac{f_T(t)}{\Pr(T > t)} = \frac{f_T(t)}{[1 - \Pr(T \le t)]} = \frac{f_T(t)}{[1 - F_T(t)]} \equiv \frac{f_T(t)}{S_T(t)} \equiv h_T(t).$$

This conditional pdf is the hazard rate or the hazard function. In Figure 8.2 we depict the hazard rates for Weibull random variables when p is greater than, less than, and equal to 1, labeled increasing, decreasing, and constant, respectively.

In Figure 8.3 we contrast the hazard rate of a Weibull random variable, which exhibits increasing duration dependence, with the hazard rates of random variables following the gamma as well as the generalized gamma laws. The point of this graph is to demonstrate that relatively small changes in the parameters of the generalized gamma law can have quite different hazard rate behavior. An important point to note is that an assumption concerning the hazard rate is an assumption concerning the pdf, and vice versa.

Often data are not gathered in continuous time but rather at, say, the daily frequency. Thus, we construct a discrete-time hazard rate model of duration. The building block in this case is the geometric distribution.

The geometric distribution can be motivated by considering a sequence of independent Bernoulli draws. For example, suppose that on each of a sequence of days an event can fail to occur, so the Bernoulli random variable B takes on the value zero, which has probability $(1 - \pi)$, or the event can occur, so B takes on the value 1 which has probability π. Under this notation, the probability mass function of B is

$$f_B(b; \pi) = \pi^b (1 - \pi)^{1-b} \quad b = 0, 1;\ 0 < \pi < 1.$$

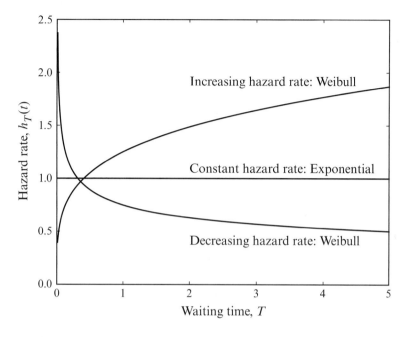

Figure 8.2: Weibull Hazard Rates

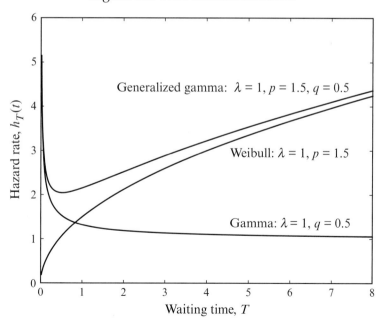

Figure 8.3: Examples of Other Hazard Rates

Consider now a sequence of independently and identically distributed Bernoulli random variables $\{B_1, B_2, \ldots, B_t, \ldots\}$. How many days must we wait until B equals 1—an event occurs? It could be one day, two days, even three or more. In general, the duration time T is random, having the pmf

$$f_T(t; \pi) = (1 - \pi)^{t-1}\pi \quad t = 1, 2, \ldots,$$

which is known as the geometric distribution. The geometric distribution is the discrete-time analog of the exponential distribution. Like an exponentially distributed random variable, its discrete cousin has a constant hazard rate; that is, given that an event has not occurred in the first $(t - 1)$ days, the probability of its arriving on day t is just π.

8.2.2 Loosening the Structure on $f_T(t)$

Empirically, we would like to loosen the constant hazard assumption in several ways. First, we would like the hazard rate to vary with time-invariant covariates, or *features* in the machine learning literature. Second, we would like the hazard rate to vary with time, but perhaps not in the monotonic way admitted by the Weibull distribution or the restrictive U-shaped way admitted by some generalized gamma distributions. Third, we would like the hazard rate to be able to vary with events that evolve over time, sometimes referred to as *time-varying covariates*. In short, if a feature changes during the duration of the process, then this change can affect the conditional probability. Including all these requirements in a continuous-time model of duration can be challenging, mostly for computational reasons. The model that we present here is designed to be computationally tractable and therefore scalable, yet it addresses (at least to the first order) each of these three requirements.

To introduce observation-specific characteristics, we assume that a $(1 \times I)$ vector of features $\mathbf{u}$ exists for each order and that these features influence the hazard rate π through a conformable $(I \times 1)$ vector of unknown parameters $\boldsymbol{\beta}$. That is, for observation n,

$$\pi_n = h(\mathbf{u}_n\boldsymbol{\beta}) \equiv \frac{\exp(\mathbf{u}_n\boldsymbol{\beta})}{1 + \exp(\mathbf{u}_n\boldsymbol{\beta})}.$$

We make the logit assumption for analytical and computational tractability. The logit transformation constrains π_n to the unit interval; the parameters contained in $\boldsymbol{\beta}$ (sometimes called *weights* in the machine learning literature) have a clear interpretation; and the partial derivatives of h with respect to the elements of β have convenient closed-form expressions. Typically, the first element of the vector $\mathbf{u}$ contains a 1; the first element of the weight vector β is referred to as the *bias* in the machine learning literature and the *constant* in other literatures. We omit the 1 and, thus, the constant; they enter elsewhere.

Next, to introduce a time-varying hazard rate, we assume that

$$\pi_{n,t} = h(\mathbf{u}_n\beta + \mathbf{v}_{n,t}\gamma) \equiv \frac{\exp(\mathbf{u}_n\beta + \gamma_t)}{1 + \exp(\mathbf{u}_n\beta + \gamma_t)} \equiv \frac{\exp(\mathbf{u}_n\beta + \mathbf{v}_{n,t}\gamma)}{1 + \exp(\mathbf{u}_n\beta + \mathbf{v}_{n,t}\gamma)},$$

where $\mathbf{v}$ is a $(1 \times J)$ vector that has zeros for all elements except the tth one, which equals 1, and γ is a conformable $(J \times 1)$ vector of unknown parameters. These covariates represent the 1s omitted in the $\mathbf{u}$; the corresponding elements of γ become the bias (constant) for each period.

Finally, to introduce time-varying, observation-specific characteristics, we assume that

$$\pi_{n,t} = h(\mathbf{x}_{n,t}\theta) \equiv \frac{\exp(\mathbf{u}_n\beta + \mathbf{v}_{n,t}\gamma + \mathbf{w}_{n,t}\delta)}{1 + \exp(\mathbf{u}_n\beta + \mathbf{v}_{n,t}\gamma + \mathbf{w}_{n,t}\delta)} \equiv \frac{\exp(\mathbf{x}_{n,t}\theta)}{1 + \exp(\mathbf{x}_{n,t}\theta)},$$

where $\mathbf{w}$ is a $(1 \times K)$ vector of features that can vary with time, with δ a conformable $(K \times 1)$ vector of unknown parameters. Thus, $\mathbf{x}$ is a $[1 \times (I + J + K)]$ dimensional feature vector, with θ a $[(I + J + K) \times 1]$ dimensional vector of unknown parameters. As a shorthand, we denote $(I + J + K)$ by M, and index the elements of $\mathbf{x}$ and θ by $m = 1, 2, \ldots, M$.

As with any exercise in data science, the power of the empirical analysis is largely determined by the covariates (features) used. In this case, three different kinds of features exist, which we denote $\mathbf{u}$, $\mathbf{v}$, and $\mathbf{w}$. The elements of $\mathbf{u}$ are static; for the most part, these will be qualitative variables, perhaps indicator variables. On the other hand, the elements of $\mathbf{v}$ are generated features; these elements are binary outcomes, which for a given n vary with the duration of the event.

What about the elements of $\mathbf{w}$? How might they obtain? Assume that J is 9. Table 8.1 shows that the duration until the event for the first observation is 5, whereas the duration for the second observation is 9. In the case of the first observation, the column on the far right of Table 8.1, a feature in $\mathbf{w}$ is initially 7, but decreases by 1 each period. For the second observation, the feature was initially 5, and then changed to 4 after three days.

The first observation can be represented as the input to a logit, where four of the labels are zero, whereas on the event day (day five) the label is 1. The

n	t_n	$y_{n,t}$	$\mathbf{u}$	$v_{n,1}$	$v_{n,2}$	$v_{n,3}$	$v_{n,4}$	$v_{n,5}$	$v_{n,6}$	$v_{n,7}$	$v_{n,8}$	$v_{n,9}$	$w_{n,t}$
1	1	0	$\mathbf{u}_1$	1	0	0	0	0	0	0	0	0	6
1	2	0	$\mathbf{u}_1$	0	1	0	0	0	0	0	0	0	5
1	3	0	$\mathbf{u}_1$	0	0	1	0	0	0	0	0	0	4
1	4	0	$\mathbf{u}_1$	0	0	0	1	0	0	0	0	0	3
1	5	1	$\mathbf{u}_1$	0	0	0	0	1	0	0	0	0	2
2	1	0	$\mathbf{u}_2$	1	0	0	0	0	0	0	0	0	4
2	2	0	$\mathbf{u}_2$	0	1	0	0	0	0	0	0	0	3
2	3	0	$\mathbf{u}_2$	0	0	1	0	0	0	0	0	0	2
2	4	0	$\mathbf{u}_2$	0	0	0	1	0	0	0	0	0	4
2	5	0	$\mathbf{u}_2$	0	0	0	0	1	0	0	0	0	3
2	6	0	$\mathbf{u}_2$	0	0	0	0	0	1	0	0	0	2
2	7	0	$\mathbf{u}_2$	0	0	0	0	0	0	1	0	0	1
2	8	0	$\mathbf{u}_2$	0	0	0	0	0	0	0	1	0	0
2	9	1	$\mathbf{u}_2$	0	0	0	0	0	0	0	0	1	-1

Table 8.1: Table of Feature Variables for the Stylized Example

second observation has a similar structure: eight of the labels are zero, but on the event day (day nine) the label is 1. Notice that the features in $\mathbf{v}_1$ have a very regular pattern: for the first day $v_{1,1}$ is 1, but the remaining features of this kind are zero, and on the second day $v_{1,2}$ is 1, with the remaining features of this kind being zero, and so forth. Clearly, the parameter J, which in this case is 9, will be determined by the data. If there are waiting times that have not obtained after, say, 90 days, then J will be at least 90. Of course, a trade-off exists: if J is too large, then the model may be overfit.

In the machine learning literature, it is common to normalize feature variables, that is, to subtract out the mean of a feature variable, and then to scale by the standard deviation of that variable, so that the newly created feature vector has elements having mean zero and Euclidean length 1—in other words, to scale the data. We have not done that here.

8.2.3   Cox Proportional Hazard Rate Model

All of the analysis concerning the continuous duration model was done in the absence of feature heterogeneity. Feature heterogeneity can confound empirical results. One practical way to deal with the problem of feature heterogeneity is to include it in the empirical model. For example, suppose that a vector of time-invariant features $\mathbf{u}$ is observed, and the analyst can condition on them. Denote the conditional pdf of T given $\mathbf{U}$ by $f_{T|\mathbf{U}}(t|\mathbf{u})$. In duration analysis, the most commonly used empirical model to accommodate time-invariant feature heterogeneity is the *Cox proportional hazard rate* (CPH) model; see Cox (1972).

In a CPH model, the feature vector $\mathbf{u}$ influences $h_{T|\mathbf{U}}(t|\mathbf{u})$, the conditional hazard rate of the duration time T, according to the following structure:

$$h_{T|\mathbf{U}}(t|\mathbf{u}) = \exp(\mathbf{u}\boldsymbol{\beta})h_0(t),$$

where $\boldsymbol{\beta}$ is a vector of unknown parameters conformable to $\mathbf{u}$, and $h_0(t)$ is the baseline hazard rate where $\mathbf{u}$ is a vector of zeros. Thus, the features shift the baseline hazard rate proportionally up or down, depending on the sign of the parameters in the vector $\boldsymbol{\beta}$. This empirical specification is particularly attractive because the individual parameters in the vector $\boldsymbol{\beta}$ can be interpreted in percentage terms. For example, if the ith element of $\boldsymbol{\beta}$ is, say, 0.0123, then that feature increases the hazard rate by about 1.23 percent for a one-unit increase in u_i relative to the case when u_i equals zero. Note that both $\boldsymbol{\beta}$ and $h_0(t)$ must be estimated using $\{\{(t_n, \mathbf{u}_n)\}_{n=1}^{N}$, data from all events during the observation period.

Now, the baseline survivor function $S_0(t)$ is related to the baseline hazard rate $h_0(t)$ according to

$$S_0(t) = \exp\left[-\int_0^t h_0(z)\,dz\right],$$

so the conditional survivor function can be written as

$$
\begin{aligned}
S_{T|\mathbf{U}}(t|\mathbf{u}) &= \exp\left[-\exp(\mathbf{u}\boldsymbol{\beta})\int_0^t h_0(z)\,dz\right] \\
&= \exp\left[-\int_0^t h_0(z)\,dz\right]^{\exp(\mathbf{u}\boldsymbol{\beta})} \\
&= S_0(t)^{\exp(\mathbf{u}\boldsymbol{\beta})},
\end{aligned}
$$

whence

$$f_{T|\mathbf{U}}(t|\mathbf{u}) = h_{T|\mathbf{U}}(t|\mathbf{u})S_{T|\mathbf{U}}(t|\mathbf{u}) = \exp(\mathbf{u}\boldsymbol{\beta})h_0(t)S_0(t)^{\exp(\mathbf{u}\boldsymbol{\beta})}.$$

If a parameteric assumption is made concerning $h_0(t)$, we can derive $S_0(t)$, and from that construct $f_{T|U}(t|\mathbf{u})$. Hazard rates observed in real data are not always regular in the shape of parametric models, such as the generalized gamma. In addition, introducing time-varying covariates into this framework is somewhat complicated. Thus, we have pursued the discrete-time, semiparametric empirical model.

Following the research of Han and Hausman (1990), we next illustrate the link between that model and the one we implemented. After that, we present the loss function used when training the empirical model.

To begin, introduce

$$H_0(t) = \int_0^t h_0(z) \, \mathrm{d}z,$$

which is often referred to as the *integrated hazard rate*, as well as

$$\Lambda_0(t) = \log[H_0(t)].$$

In a CPH model,

$$\Lambda_0(t) - \mathbf{u}_n\boldsymbol{\beta} = \log[H_0(t)] - \mathbf{u}_n\boldsymbol{\beta} = \Psi_n,$$

where Ψ is a random variable. The probability of the event obtaining in period t is then given by

$$\Pr(\text{event in period } t) = \int_{\Lambda_0(t-1)-\mathbf{u}_n\boldsymbol{\beta}}^{\Lambda_0(t)-\mathbf{u}_n\boldsymbol{\beta}} f_\Psi(\psi) \, \mathrm{d}\psi.$$

The logarithm of the likelihood function (which is a function of $\boldsymbol{\beta}$ as well as $[\Lambda_0(1),\dots,\Lambda_0(J)]$) can be written as

$$\sum_{n=1}^N \sum_{t=1}^J y_{n,t} \log\left[\int_{\Lambda_0(t-1)-\mathbf{u}_n\boldsymbol{\beta}}^{\Lambda_0(t)-\mathbf{u}_n\boldsymbol{\beta}} f_\Psi(\psi) \, \mathrm{d}\psi\right],$$

where $y_{n,t}$ is zero if the event has not occurred in period t and 1 if it has. The logit model has this flavor, but also admits time-varying covariates, which are difficult to include in the continuous-time model.

8.2.4 Training the Model

For the time being, ignore observation- and date-specific information, and focus on just one index, n. Denote the label for observation n by y_n, which can take on one of two values, zero or 1. Interpret 1 as the event has occurred and zero as the event has not occurred. Under the logit assumption,

$$\Pr(y_n = 1 | \mathbf{x}_n \boldsymbol{\theta}) = h(\mathbf{x}_n \boldsymbol{\theta}) = \frac{\exp(\mathbf{x}_n \boldsymbol{\theta})}{1 + \exp(\mathbf{x}_n \boldsymbol{\theta})},$$

and

$$\Pr(y_n = 0 | \mathbf{x}_n \boldsymbol{\theta}) = 1 - h(\mathbf{x}_n \boldsymbol{\theta}) = \frac{1}{1 + \exp(\mathbf{x}_n \boldsymbol{\theta})}.$$

For observation n, the loss function is often referred to as the *cross-entropy* loss function, and it is simply the negative of the contribution to the logarithm of the likelihood function for observation n. In symbols, the loss function for observation n is

$$\ell(\boldsymbol{\theta} | \mathbf{x}_n, y_n) = -y_n \log[h(\mathbf{x}_n \boldsymbol{\theta})] - (1 - y_n) \log[1 - h(\mathbf{x}_n \boldsymbol{\theta})]$$
$$= -y_n \mathbf{x}_n \boldsymbol{\theta} + \log[1 + \exp(\mathbf{x}_n \boldsymbol{\theta})],$$

and the sample-averaged loss function when N observations exist is

$$f(\boldsymbol{\theta} | \mathbf{X}, \mathbf{y}) = \frac{1}{N} \sum_{n=1}^{N} \ell(\boldsymbol{\theta} | \mathbf{x}_n, y_n) = \frac{1}{N} \sum_{n=1}^{N} \{-y_n \mathbf{x}_n \boldsymbol{\theta} + \log[1 + \exp(\mathbf{x}_n \boldsymbol{\theta})]\},$$

where $\mathbf{y}$ is an $(N \times 1)$ vector that collects the labels of the N observations, and $\mathbf{X}$ is the $[N \times (I + J + K)]$ matrix concerning the features.

Estimating the unknown parameters of the empirical model involves calculating

$$\hat{\boldsymbol{\theta}} = \operatorname*{argmin}_{\boldsymbol{\theta}} f(\boldsymbol{\theta} | \mathbf{X}, \mathbf{y}). \tag{8.1}$$

Because the objective function in equation (8.1) is continuous, convex, and differentiable in the argument vector $\boldsymbol{\theta}$, the unique minimizer $\hat{\boldsymbol{\theta}}$ is characterized by the following vector of first-order conditions:

$$\nabla_{\boldsymbol{\theta}} f(\hat{\boldsymbol{\theta}} | \mathbf{X}, \mathbf{y}) = \mathbf{0}_M, \tag{8.2}$$

where $M = I + J + K$. The individual elements of the gradient vector $\nabla_\theta f(\theta|\mathbf{X}, \mathbf{y})$ have convenient, closed-form expressions. In particular,

$$\frac{\partial f(\theta|\mathbf{X}, \mathbf{y})}{\partial \theta_m} = \frac{1}{N} \sum_{n=1}^{N} \frac{\partial \ell(\theta|\mathbf{x}_n, y_n)}{\partial \theta_m} \quad m = 1, 2, \ldots, M$$

and

$$\frac{\partial \ell(\theta|\mathbf{x}_n, y_n)}{\partial \theta_m} = -y_n x_{n,m} + \frac{\exp(\mathbf{x}_n \theta)}{1 + \exp(\mathbf{x}_n \theta)} x_{n,m}$$

$$= [h(\mathbf{x}_n \theta) - y_n] x_{n,m}$$

$$\equiv E(\theta|\mathbf{x}_n, y_n) x_{n,m}.$$

Collecting the E_ns, which is a shorthand notation for $E(\theta|\mathbf{x}_n, y_n)$, in the $(N \times 1)$ vector $E(\theta|\mathbf{X}, \mathbf{y})$, or E for short, equation (8.2) can be written as

$$\frac{\mathbf{X}^\top E(\hat{\theta}|\mathbf{X}, \mathbf{y})}{N} = \mathbf{0}_M,$$

whose solution can be found iteratively using numerical methods. Specifically, let

$$\mathbf{g}(\theta) \equiv \frac{\mathbf{X}^\top E(\theta|\mathbf{X}, \mathbf{y})}{N}.$$

Given θ_0, an initial guess for θ, we can then use the recursion defined by equation (7.11) to find $\hat{\theta}$, provided we have an expression for $\mathbf{H}(\theta)$. Fortunately, in this case, the (i, j) element of the Hessian has the following simple form:

$$\left[\sum_{n=1}^{N} x_{n,i} x_{n,j} h(\mathbf{x}_n \theta)[1 - h(\mathbf{x}_n \theta)] \right].$$

If it did not have a closed-form expression, then the OPG approximation could be used. In that case, the (i, j) element of the Hessian has the following form:

$$\left[\sum_{n=1}^{N} x_{n,i} x_{n,j} [h(\mathbf{x}_n \theta) - y_n]^2 \right].$$

On the surface, these two formulae look quite different, until we recognize that

$$\mathbb{E}\left([Y_n - h(\mathbf{x}_n \theta^0)]^2 \big| \mathbf{x}_n, \theta^0 \right) = h(\mathbf{x}_n \theta^0)[1 - h(\mathbf{x}_n \theta^0)] = \mathbb{V}(Y_n | \mathbf{x}_n, \theta^0),$$

where θ^0 is the true value of θ. In words, conditional on the covariates and the true parameter vector, the expected value of the squared deviation of Y_n from its mean $h(\mathbf{x}_n \theta^0)$ is the conditional variance of Y_n.

8.2.5 Putting It All Together

In solving this example, we use the algorithmic strategy of divide-and-conquer. Specifically, five steps exist:

1. Read in the data.

2. Form logarithm of likelihood function, gradient vector, and Hessian matrix.

3. Take Newton-Raphson step.

4. Continue until some convergence criterion is met.

5. Output convergent results.

For the first step, we created our data using simulation methods, so you can replicate our results easily. In Python the objective function as well as its gradient vector Hessian matrix are all calculated using the function in Listing 8.3. (The code in the docstring is included so that you can convince yourself of the virtues of vectorization. In short, if you take out the docstring quotes, then you will find that without vectorization the code may not even have enough memory to run.)

```python
# Function:  FuncGradHess
# Author:    Harry J. Paarsch
# Date:      24 July 2013
def FuncGradHess(theta, y, designX, N, p):
  """ Function FuncGradHess returns the cross-entropy cost function
      in Logit regression model plus its gradient vector and Hessian
      matrix, given the input vector  y  as well as the matrix
      designX  and a parameter vector  theta where  N  and  p  are
      the number of instances and the number of features,
      respectively.
  """
  import numpy as np
  xTheta        = np.dot(designX, theta)
  hXTheta       = np.exp(xTheta)/(1.+np.exp(xTheta))
  sXTheta       = 1. - hXTheta
  function      = sum(sXTheta - y*xTheta)
  gradientVector = np.dot(designX.T, (hXTheta-y))
  hSXTheta      = hXTheta * sXTheta
```

```
   innerH          = hSXTheta * designX
   hessianMatrix   = np.dot(designX.T, innerH)
   """
   hMatrix = np.zeros((p,p))
   for i in xrange(0, p):
     for j in xrange(0, i+1):
       for n in xrange(0, N):
         hMatrix[i,j] += hXTheta[n]*(1.-hXTheta[n])*designX[n,i]*
             designX[n,j]
       hMatrix[j,i] = hMatrix[i,j]
   """
   return  function, gradientVector, hessianMatrix
```

Listing 8.3: Python Function `FuncGradHess`

These Python functions were then called by the following driver program:

```
# Script:   Duration.py
# Author:   Harry J. Paarsch
# Date:     24 July 2013
#
""" This program reads in the data, and then estimates a
    discrete-time, duration model using a Logit hazard.
"""
import math
import numpy as np
import time
#
# Set up the parameters of the system
#
N         = 3881
J         =   12
p         = J - 1
theta     = np.zeros((p,1))
inputData = np.loadtxt('./DuraData.dat')
idNo      = np.zeros((N,1))
u         = np.zeros((N,1))
y         = np.zeros((N,1))
v         = np.zeros((N,J-2))
for n in range(0,N):
  idNo[n] = inputData[n,0]
  u[n]    = inputData[n,1]
  y[n]    = inputData[n,4]
  v[n,:]  = inputData[n,5:5+J-2]
```

```
X = np.column_stack((u,v))
#
# Describe model.
#
title    = '*** This is discrete-time, duration model of a waiting
    time.'
subtitle = '*** The hazard rate is a Logit with a time-varying
    constant.\n'
print title
print subtitle
#
# Find the value of the cost function.
#
f, g, H = FuncGradHess(theta, y, X, N, p)
print 'At the initial parameter estimates, the cost function is:  %f\n
    ' % f
print 'The initial parameter estimates are:\n'
print theta.T
#
# Set tolerance criterion as well as initial value of norm.
#
epsilon = 1.e-6
norm    = math.fabs(f)
that    = theta
itern   = 1
start   = time.time()
while (norm > epsilon):
  theta   = that
  f, g, H = FuncGradHess(theta, y, X, N, p)
  # print itern, norm, theta, g
  dTheta  = np.linalg.solve(H, g)
  that    = theta - dTheta
  itern   = itern + 1
  norm    = math.sqrt(np.dot(g.T, g))

#
# Make sure everything is current before calculating the
# standard errors.
#
f, g, H = FuncGradHess(theta, y, X, N, p)
infMat  = np.linalg.inv(H)
stErr   = np.sqrt(np.diagonal(infMat))
#
# Make up some names, so the output is pretty.
```

```
#
names   = ['u']
names.append('v01')
names.append('v02')
names.append('v03')
names.append('v04')
names.append('v05')
names.append('v06')
names.append('v07')
names.append('v08')
names.append('v09')
names.append('v10+')
print '\nAt the convergent estimates, the cost function is:   %f\n'  %
    f
print 'Norm of the gradient vector is %f.\n' % norm
print '%d iterations were used to obtain tolerance %f.\n' % (itern,
    epsilon)
print 'Final parameter estimates, standard errors, and gradient values
    .\n'
print 'Variable\tEstimates\tStd.Err.\tGradient\n'
for i in range(0,p):
  print '%s\t\t%f\t%f\t%f' % (names[i], theta[i], stErr[i], g[i])

end = time.time()
print '\n %f seconds were used to complete this task.' % (end - start)
```

Listing 8.4: Python Script Duration.py

The script created the following output:

```
*** This is discrete-time, duration model of a waiting time.
*** The hazard rate is a Logit with a time-varying constant.

At the initial parameter estimates, the cost function is:  1940.500000

The initial parameter estimates are:

[[ 0.  0.  0.  0.  0.  0.  0.  0.  0.  0.  0.]]

At the convergent estimates, the cost function is:  3523.462043

Norm of the gradient vector is 0.000000.

8 iterations were used to obtain tolerance 0.000001.
```

```
Final parameter estimates, standard errors, and gradient values.

Variable  Estimates Std.Err.  Gradient

u      0.012119  0.137681   0.000000
v01    -2.757707 0.150521   0.000000
v02    -1.575299 0.111251  -0.000000
v03    -0.886740 0.105438   0.000000
v04    -0.449593 0.111547  -0.000000
v05    0.035721  0.129272   0.000000
v06    0.465692  0.175740   0.000000
v07    -0.101601 0.262192  -0.000000
v08    0.298846  0.359962   0.000000
v09    1.292440  0.655957   0.000000
v10+    0.689836  1.225323   0.000000

 0.122011 seconds were used to complete this task.
```

Listing 8.5: Output of `Driver.py`

8.3 Linear Programming: LAD-Lasso Estimator

Since at least the time of Edgeworth (1885), empirical workers have known that the sample mean is sensitive to outliers. In the vocabulary summarized by Huber (1981), the sample mean has a *breakdown point* of $(1/N)$, where N is the sample size. If just one of the N observations is an outlier from a pathologically different distribution, then the optimal properties of the mean (for example, unbiasedness as well as minimum variance) can disappear. The sample median is referred to as a *robust* estimate of location because its breakdown point is 50 percent: up to one-half of the sample can be contaminated before the attractive properties of the sample median disappear.

For the data $\{y_n\}_{n=1}^{N}$, the sample mean

$$\hat{\mu} = \frac{1}{N} \sum_{n=1}^{N} y_n$$

solves the optimization problem

$$\min_{\mu} \sum_{n=1}^{N} (y_n - \mu)^2, \tag{8.3}$$

and the sample median

$$\tilde{\mu} = \begin{cases} 0.5[y_{(0.5N:N)} + y_{(0.5N+1:N)}] & N \text{ even;} \\ y_{(0.5[N+1]:N)} & N \text{ odd;} \end{cases}$$

solves the optimization problem

$$\min_{\mu} \sum_{n=1}^{N} |y_n - \mu|. \tag{8.4}$$

Here, the nth order statistic $y_{(n:N)}$ is defined by

$$y_{(1:N)} \le y_{(2:N)} \le \cdots \le y_{(N:N)}.$$

When features related to the dependent variable Y exist, which are collected in the $(1 \times K)$ vectors $\{\mathbf{x}_n\}_{n=1}^{N}$, the sample equivalent of equation (8.3) is

$$\min_{\beta} \sum_{n=1}^{N} (y_n - \mathbf{x}_n \beta)^2. \tag{8.5}$$

Here, β is a $(K \times 1)$ vector of unknown parameters. Often, the first element is the constant by convention, which means that the first element of $\mathbf{x}_n$ is then always a 1. The sample equivalent of equation (8.4) is

$$\min_{\beta} \sum_{n=1}^{N} |y_n - \mathbf{x}_n \beta|. \tag{8.6}$$

Estimators of β that solve problems (8.5) and (8.6) can be derived in a straightforward way. They are the *least-squares regression* and the *least-absolute-deviations* (LAD) *regression* estimators, respectively.

When K, the dimension of the feature vector $\mathbf{x}$, is large relative to N, the number of observations, statisticians as well as machine learners often try to penalize those features that add little to the prediction exercise using a process referred to as *regularization*. One way to regularize problem (8.5) is to minimize the following objective function:

$$\sum_{n=1}^{N} (y_n - \mathbf{x}_n \beta)^2 + \lambda \sum_{k=1}^{K} \beta_k^2, \tag{8.7}$$

where the parameter λ is called the *complexity* or *regularization* or *shrinkage parameter*. With the notation from Chapter 5, the solution to this problem results in an estimator known as *ridge regression*. Where the least-squares estimator is

$$\hat{\beta} = (\mathbf{X}^\top \mathbf{X})^{-1} \mathbf{X}^\top y,$$

the ridge regression estimator is

$$\check{\beta} = (\mathbf{X}^\top \mathbf{X} + \lambda \mathbf{I}_K)^{-1} \mathbf{X}^\top y.$$

Another way to regularize problem (8.5) is to introduce a different penalty to the objective function, that is, to minimize the following objective function:

$$\sum_{n=1}^{N} (y_n - \mathbf{x}_n \beta)^2 + \lambda \sum_{k=2}^{K} |\beta_k|. \tag{8.8}$$

This procedure, proposed by Tibshirani (1996), is referred to as *lasso* (least absolute shrinkage and selection operator). In Tibshirani's original formulation, the objective function was written as the following quadratic programming problem:

$$\min_{\beta} \sum_{n=1}^{N} (y_n - \mathbf{x}_n \beta)^2 \quad \text{subject to} \quad \sum_{k=2}^{K} |\beta_k| \le \tau, \tag{8.9}$$

where τ is a *tuning parameter*. For suitably chosen λ and τ, the solutions to problems (8.8) and (8.9) are the same.

A natural extension to these problems considered is the LAD-Lasso estimator proposed by Wang et al. (2007). The LAD-Lasso estimator solves the following problem:

$$\min_{\beta} \sum_{n=1}^{N} |y_n - \mathbf{x}_n \beta| + N \sum_{k=1}^{K} \lambda_k |\beta_k|. \tag{8.10}$$

Computationally, solving for the LAD-Lasso estimator involves applying methods of linear programmming, but we need to be somewhat clever in specifying the linear program. To demonstrate how to proceed, we first illustrate how to solve the LAD estimator of problem (8.6) as a linear program and then proceed to the LAD-Lasso estimator.

Introducing the vector $e = (e_1, e_2, \ldots, e_N)^\top$, where $e_n = y_n - \mathbf{x}_n\beta$, we write problem (8.6) as the linear program

$$\min_{\beta} \sum_{n=1}^{N} e_n \quad \text{subject to} \quad e_n \geq y_n - \mathbf{x}_n\beta$$

$$e_n \geq \mathbf{x}_n\beta - y_n \quad n = 1, 2, \ldots, N.$$

In canonical form, the linear program is specified as follows:

$$\min_{e^*} \mathbf{c}^\top e^* \quad \text{subject to} \quad \mathbf{A}e^* \leq \mathbf{b},$$

where

$$\mathbf{c} = (\overbrace{1, 1, \ldots, 1}^{N}, \overbrace{0, 0, \ldots, 0}^{K})^\top$$
$$e^* = (e_1, e_2, \ldots, e_N, \beta_1, \beta_2, \ldots, \beta_K)^\top$$

and

$$\mathbf{A} = \begin{bmatrix} -1 & 0 & 0 & \cdots & 0 & -\mathbf{x}_1 \\ -1 & 0 & 0 & \cdots & 0 & \mathbf{x}_1 \\ 0 & -1 & 0 & \cdots & 0 & -\mathbf{x}_2 \\ 0 & -1 & 0 & \cdots & 0 & \mathbf{x}_2 \\ 0 & 0 & -1 & \cdots & 0 & -\mathbf{x}_3 \\ 0 & 0 & -1 & \cdots & 0 & \mathbf{x}_3 \\ \vdots & \vdots & \vdots & \ddots & \vdots & \vdots \\ 0 & 0 & 0 & \cdots & -1 & -\mathbf{x}_N \\ 0 & 0 & 0 & \cdots & -1 & \mathbf{x}_N \end{bmatrix} \quad \text{and} \quad \mathbf{b} = \begin{bmatrix} -y_1 \\ y_1 \\ -y_2 \\ y_2 \\ \vdots \\ -y_N \\ y_N \end{bmatrix}.$$

With the trick introduced by Wang et al. (2007), the LAD-Lasso estimator solves the following linear program:

$$\min_{\beta} \sum_{n=1}^{N+K} e_n^* \quad \text{subject to} \quad e_n^* \geq y_n^* - \mathbf{x}_n^*\beta$$

$$e_n^* \geq \mathbf{x}_n^*\beta - y_n^* \quad n = 1, 2, \ldots, N + K$$

where

$$(\mathbf{x}_n^*, y_n^*) = \begin{cases} (\mathbf{x}_n, y_n) & n = 1, 2, \ldots, N; \\ (N\lambda_k \mathbf{e}_k, 0) & n = N + k, \ k = 1, 2, \ldots, K. \end{cases}$$

Here, $\mathbf{e}_k$ is different from e_n^*: the latter represents the nth element of the vector e^*, whereas the former represents a $(1 \times K)$ vector of zeros except for the kth element, which is a 1, often referred to as a *unit vector*. This optimization problem can be written in the canonical form of a linear program as follows:

$$\min_{e^*} \mathbf{c}^\top e^* \quad \text{subject to} \quad \mathbf{A} e^* \le \mathbf{b},$$

where

$$\mathbf{c}^\top = (\overbrace{1, 1, \ldots, 1}^{(N+K)})$$

and

$$\mathbf{A} = \begin{bmatrix} -1 & 0 & \cdots & 0 & 0 & \cdots & 0 & -\mathbf{x}_1 \\ -1 & 0 & \cdots & 0 & 0 & \cdots & 0 & \mathbf{x}_1 \\ 0 & -1 & \cdots & 0 & 0 & \cdots & 0 & -\mathbf{x}_2 \\ 0 & -1 & \cdots & 0 & 0 & \cdots & 0 & \mathbf{x}_2 \\ \vdots & \vdots & \ddots & \vdots & \vdots & \ddots & \vdots & \vdots \\ 0 & 0 & \cdots & -1 & 0 & \cdots & 0 & -\mathbf{x}_N \\ 0 & 0 & \cdots & -1 & 0 & \cdots & 0 & \mathbf{x}_N \\ 0 & 0 & \cdots & 0 & -1 & \cdots & 0 & -N\lambda_1\mathbf{e}_1 \\ 0 & 0 & \cdots & 0 & -1 & \cdots & 0 & N\lambda_1\mathbf{e}_1 \\ \vdots & \vdots & \ddots & \vdots & \vdots & \ddots & \vdots & \vdots \\ 0 & 0 & \cdots & 0 & 0 & \cdots & -1 & -N\lambda_K\mathbf{e}_K \\ 0 & 0 & \cdots & 0 & 0 & \cdots & -1 & N\lambda_K\mathbf{e}_K \end{bmatrix} \quad \text{and} \quad \mathbf{b} = \begin{bmatrix} -y_1 \\ y_1 \\ -y_2 \\ y_2 \\ \vdots \\ -y_N \\ y_N \\ 0 \\ 0 \\ \vdots \\ 0 \\ 0 \end{bmatrix}.$$

Given the Python CVXOPT code supporting Figure 7.16 in Section 7.6.1, the only code that needs to be written is a function that takes $(\mathbf{X}, y)$ and returns $\mathbf{c}$, $\mathbf{A}$, and $\mathbf{b}$, where $\mathbf{X}$ is the stacked matrix of $(1 \times K)$ feature vectors $\{\mathbf{x}_n\}_{n=1}^N$, and y is an $(N \times 1)$ vector of the dependent variable.

The following is one implementation of this function:

```
# Function:   MakeLPMatrix
# Author:     Harry J. Paarsch
# Date:       12 November 2014
def MakeLPMatrix(X, y, lamda):
  """This function takes in a feature matrix  X, a vector of
     dependent variables  y, and tuning vector  lamda  and
     returns the cost vector  c, the matrix  A  associated with
     the constraints, and the vector  b  associated with the
     right-hand side of the constraints in the case of the
     LAD-LASSO estimator.  (Note the misspelling of  lamda.)
  """
  # Find dimensions of y and X; check for consistency.
  N = len(y)
  Nx, K = X.shape
  if (Nx!=N):
    print "y-vector and X-matrix are not conformable."
    return

  # Now start to build A, b, and c
  P = N + K
  c = cvxopt.matrix(np.ones(P))
  EK = np.identity(K)
  XE = np.concatenate( (X, lamda*N*EK), axis=0)
  minusI = -np.identity(P)
  minusA = np.concatenate( (minusI, -XE), axis=1)
  plusA  = np.concatenate( (minusI,  XE), axis=1)
  A = cvxopt.matrix(np.concatenate( (minusA, plusA), axis=0) )
  bMinus = np.concatenate( (-y, np.zeros(K)), axis=0)
  bPlus  = np.concatenate( ( y, np.zeros(K)), axis=0)
  b = cvxopt.matrix(np.concatenate( (bMinus, bPlus), axis=0) )
  return c, A, b
```

Listing 8.6: Python Function for LAD-Lasso LP

This function simply reformats the user-supplied feature matrix X, the vector of dependent variables y, and the tuning vector lamda (which is intentionally misspelled because Python has a native keyword lambda) and then returns the cost vector c as well as the matrix A and vector b associated with the linear program, which are consumed by the solvers.lp function in the CVXOPT package. Note that to make this function somewhat elegant but without loss of generality, we reordered the rows of the constraints.

8.4 Quadratic Programming: Support Vector Machines

In some applications of classification, for some data sets, perfect separation can occur; for a given feature vector, you can predict exactly which label will obtain. Figure 8.4 depicts data $\{(x_{n,1}, x_{n,2}, y_n)\}_{n=1}^{N}$ where this has happened. In this example, y_n can take on either the value -1 (denoted by ▼) or the value $+1$ (denoted by ▲). This is a different convention from what is used in other models of classification where 0s and 1s are used instead, but it is no less informative. In short, whether the random variable Y takes on the values 0 and 1, or -1 and $+1$, does not matter to the approach; only the estimated intercepts of the two specifications will be different; estimates of the slope coefficients will be the same.

In this case, X_1 and X_2 are two feature variables used to train a predictor of whether Y is -1 or $+1$. We collect realizations of these feature variables in the vector **x** so that you can see that the approach is fully general but impossible to depict graphically in dimensions greater than 2.

In cases like this, the logistic regression classifier becomes undefined. Because infinitely many different hyperplanes exist to separate the two sets of observations, some criterion must be used to break the apparent ties.

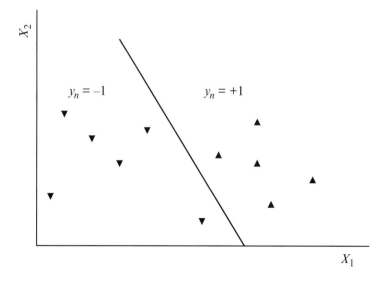

Figure 8.4: Complete Separation in Classification Data

Support vector classifiers (SVCs) use one such criterion, which involves selecting a hyperplane that maximizes the margin of separation between the two labeled samples.

The original SVC algorithm was invented by Vladimir N. Vapnik and reported in Russian in a monograph published in 1979.[1] Subsequently, the research was described in English by Boser et al. (1992). Were SVCs only useful in the case of perfect separation, then we would not have too much to say. As we demonstrate, however, SVCs are also useful when perfect separation is impossible, the case examined by Cortes and Vapnick (1995). Shalev-Shwartz and Ben-David (2014) provide a good introduction to methods of machine learning, and Rajaraman and Ullman (2011) give many practical insights into analyzing Big Data.

To cement the ideas, let's begin with the case of perfect separation. With SVCs, the convex hulls of the feature variables for labels that are equal to -1 and $+1$, respectively, are determined. These are depicted as the polygons to the left and right of the solid line in Figure 8.5.[2] In general, the two polygons are closest at two points on their boundaries. In this figure, the leftmost boundary of the $+1$ polygon is determined by just a hyperplane $\mathbf{x}\mathbf{w} - b = +1$ through a point, but the rightmost boundary of the -1 polygon is determined by a line (the two-dimensional name for a hyperplane) through $\mathbf{x}\mathbf{w} - b = -1$.

The notation adopted here is that of machine learners. In short, the vector β is now $(b, w_1, w_2)^\top$, while the feature vector $\mathbf{x}$ is now the covariate vector introduced above, *without* the 1 as the first element.

The optimal hyperplane is orthogonal to the shortest line between the two convex hulls; it is depicted by the vector $\hat{\mathbf{w}}$ in the figure. The optimal vector $\hat{\mathbf{w}}$ creates two hyperplanes: one where the dot product of $\hat{\mathbf{w}}$ and a representative feature vector $\mathbf{x}$, minus a constant b, equals -1; and another where the dot product of $\hat{\mathbf{w}}$ and a representative feature vector $\mathbf{x}$, minus a constant b, equals $+1$. In machine learning, the $\mathbf{w}$ vector is typically referred to as the *weight vector*, whereas the constant b is typically referred to as the *bias*.

The distance between the two hyperplanes is $(2/\|\mathbf{w}\|_2)$. Therefore, maximizing the margins between the two samples involves solving the optimization

---

[1] We thank Denis Nekipelov for this information.
[2] This figure is borrowed from Schölkopf (1998).

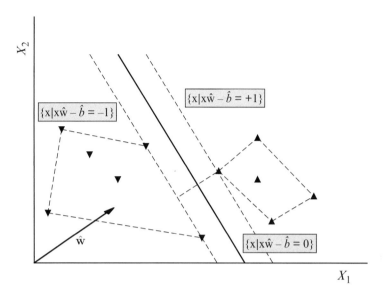

Figure 8.5: Schölkopf's (1998) Toy Problem Graph

problem

$$\min_{\mathbf{w},b} 0.5\|\mathbf{w}\|_2^2 \quad \text{subject to} \quad y_n(\mathbf{x}_n\mathbf{w} - b) \geq 1,$$

which can be written in the canonical form of a quadratic programming problem as follows:

$$\min_{\theta} \frac{1}{2}\theta^\top \mathbf{Q}\theta + \theta^\top \mathbf{p} \quad \text{subject to} \quad \mathbf{G}\theta \leq \mathbf{h}, \ \mathbf{A}\theta = \mathbf{b},$$

where in the case of K features,

$$\mathbf{Q} = \begin{bmatrix} 1 & 0 & 0 & \dots & 0 & 0 \\ 0 & 1 & 0 & \dots & 0 & 0 \\ 0 & 0 & 1 & \dots & 0 & 0 \\ \vdots & \vdots & \vdots & \ddots & \vdots & \vdots \\ 0 & 0 & 0 & \dots & 1 & 0 \\ 0 & 0 & 0 & \dots & 0 & 0 \end{bmatrix} \equiv \begin{bmatrix} \mathbf{I}_K & \mathbf{0}_K \\ \mathbf{0}_K^\top & 0 \end{bmatrix}.$$

In words, $\mathbf{Q}$ is a $(K \times K)$ identity matrix $\mathbf{I}_K$ bordered by two zero vectors. Also, $\mathbf{p}$ is equal to $\mathbf{0}_{K+1}$, and $\mathbf{h}$ is $-\iota_K$. The θ vector and the $\mathbf{G}$ matrix have the following structure:

$$\theta = \begin{bmatrix} w_1 \\ w_2 \\ \vdots \\ w_K \\ b \end{bmatrix} \quad \text{and} \quad \mathbf{G} = \begin{bmatrix} -y_1 x_{1,1} & -y_1 x_{1,2} & \cdots & -y_1 x_{1,K} & y_1 \\ -y_2 x_{2,1} & -y_2 x_{2,2} & \cdots & -y_2 x_{2,K} & y_2 \\ \vdots & \vdots & \ddots & \vdots & \vdots \\ -y_N x_{N,1} & -y_N x_{N,2} & \cdots & -y_N x_{N,K} & y_N \end{bmatrix}.$$

In this case, $\mathbf{A}$ and $\mathbf{b}$ are a zero matrix and a zero vector, respectively.

What happens if perfect separation cannot obtain, for example, as in Figure 8.6? In that figure, one observation from the $y_n = -1$ labels in Figure 8.4 has been exchanged with an observation from the $y_n = +1$ labels. A linear-in-features predictor of the form $\mathbf{xw}$ cannot achieve perfect separation. Under these circumstances, Cortes and Vapnick (1995) proposed introducing a *soft margin*.

Thus, each of the linear constraints becomes

$$y_n(\mathbf{x}_n \mathbf{w} - b) \geq 1 - s_n, \; s_n \geq 0 \quad n = 1, 2, \dots, N,$$

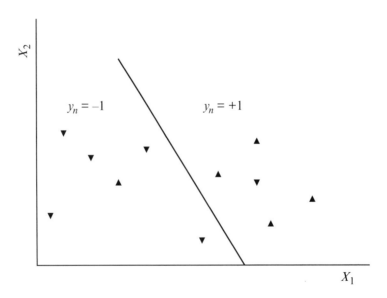

Figure 8.6: No Separation with Linear-in-Features Classifier

where the s_n are interpreted as *slack variables*, a term from mathematical programming. In canonical form, the quadratic programming problem then becomes

$$\min_{\theta} \frac{1}{2}\theta^{\top}\mathbf{Q}\theta + \theta^{\top}\mathbf{p} \quad \text{subject to} \quad \mathbf{G}\theta \leq \mathbf{h}, \ \mathbf{A}\theta = \mathbf{b},$$

where in the case of K features

$$\mathbf{Q} = \begin{bmatrix} \mathbf{I}_K & \mathbf{0}_{K,N+1} \\ \mathbf{0}_{N+1,K} & \mathbf{0}_{N+1,N+1} \end{bmatrix},$$

where $\mathbf{0}_{L,M}$ is an $(L \times M)$ matrix of zeros. Also, $\mathbf{p}$ is equal to $(\mathbf{0}_{K+1}^{\top}, \tau \iota_N^{\top})^{\top}$, where τ is some tuning parameter. Now, $\mathbf{h}$ is equal to $(-\iota_K^{\top}, \mathbf{0}_N^{\top})^{\top}$. The θ vector is then $\theta = (\mathbf{w}^{\top}, b, s_1, s_2, \ldots, s_N)^{\top}$, whereas the $\mathbf{G}$ matrix has the following structure:

$$\mathbf{G} = \begin{bmatrix} -y_1 x_{1,1} & -y_1 x_{1,2} & \cdots & -y_1 x_{1,K} & y_1 & -1 & 0 & \cdots & 0 \\ -y_2 x_{2,1} & -y_2 x_{2,2} & \cdots & -y_2 x_{2,K} & y_2 & 0 & -1 & \cdots & 0 \\ \vdots & \vdots & \ddots & \vdots & \vdots & \vdots & \vdots & \ddots & \vdots \\ -y_N x_{N,1} & -y_N x_{N,2} & \cdots & -y_N x_{N,K} & y_N & 0 & 0 & \cdots & -1 \end{bmatrix}.$$

If the number of observations N is relatively small and the number of features K even smaller, then the solution to this quadratic programming problem is not particularly arduous. Recall that when $\mathbf{Q}$ is positive definite, the complexity is $\mathcal{O}\left((N+K+1)^3\right)$. Therefore, the `solvers.qp` function from the CVXOPT package can be used to train this SVC. Small N and smaller K is not, however, typical in Big Data.

8.4.1 Hinge Loss Function

Although it is common to use the maximized margin as a way to motivate SVCs, another way to define an SVC is as the solution to an optimization problem for a particular loss function, the *hinge loss function*.

For data $\{(\mathbf{x}_n, y_n)\}_{n=1}^N$, the most commonly used contribution to the objective function, often referred to as the *cost function*, of observation n is the *squared loss function*

$$\ell(\mathbf{w}, b|\mathbf{x}_n, y_n) = (y_n - b - \mathbf{x}_n \mathbf{w})^2,$$

which is related to the Euclidean distance, the L_2 distance. Another contribution to the cost function is the *absolute loss function*

$$\ell(\mathbf{w}, b|\mathbf{x}_n, y_n) = |y_n - b - \mathbf{x}_n \mathbf{w}|,$$

which is related to the Manhattan distance, the L_1 distance. In the case of logistic regression, the cross-entropy loss function in this notation is

$$\ell(\mathbf{w}, b|\mathbf{x}_n, y_n) = -\mathbb{1}(y_n = +1) \log[h(\mathbf{x}_n \mathbf{w} - b)] - \\ \mathbb{1}(y_n = -1) \log[1 - h(\mathbf{x}_n \mathbf{w} - b)],$$

where

$$h(\mathbf{x}_n \mathbf{w} - b) = \frac{\exp(\mathbf{x}_n \mathbf{w} - b)}{1 + \exp(\mathbf{x}_n \mathbf{w} - b)}.$$

Consider modifying the L_1 loss function so that positive errors count, but negative ones do not (they are set to zero). Thus,

$$\ell(\mathbf{w}|\mathbf{x}_n, y_n) = \max(0, 1 - y_n \mathbf{x}_n \mathbf{w}),$$

which looks like the hinge of a door. This loss function is shown in Figure 8.7.

8.4.2 Support Vector Machines

The mean function (be it in a regression framework or a prediction context) is often not linear in the feature variables. The *support vector machine* (SVM) allows us to extend the numbers of dimensions of the feature variables to get very large, in principle, go to infinity.[3] For example, in Figure 8.8, we illustrate an example that was chosen because perfect separation is possible in this classification problem; it is just in a different set of feature variables. In this case, nonlinear functions of the feature variables yield perfect separation as is shown in Figure 8.9. We have used products of the feature variables, $(x_1, x_2, x_1^2, x_1 x_2, x_2^2)$ instead of just (x_1, x_2).

In principle, we could use other higher-order terms, but as noted that would result in an ill-conditioned design matrix—in short, numerical problems (see Section 7.7). Thus, machine learners have chosen other transformations of the

---

[3]Often, however, no distinction is made between the SVC and the SVM classifier. In fact, the SVC is often just referred to as an SVM.

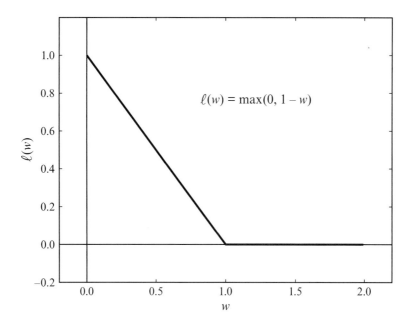

Figure 8.7: Hinge Loss Function

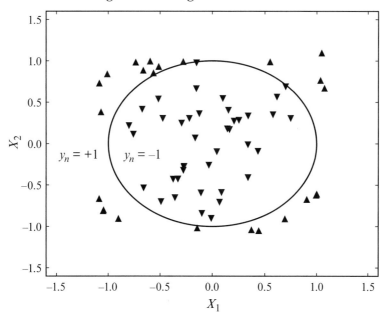

Figure 8.8: Nonlinear Functions of Features Classification

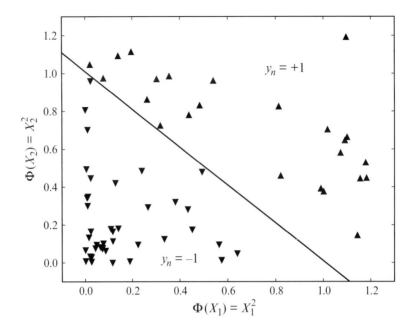

Figure 8.9: Linear Separation with Nonlinear Features

feature vectors, the most commonly used one being the *kernel*. Among kernels, the one used most is the *radial basis function* (RBF), which is what statisticians would refer to as the *Gaussian kernel*. For the two vectors $\mathbf{x}_1 = (x_{1,1}, x_{1,2})$ and $\mathbf{x}_2 = (x_{2,1}, x_{2,2})$, the RBF kernel $\kappa(\mathbf{x}_1, \mathbf{x}_2)$ would have the following formula:

$$\kappa(\mathbf{x}_1, \mathbf{x}_2) = \exp\left(\gamma\|\mathbf{x}_1 - \mathbf{x}_2\|_2^2\right),$$

where $\gamma = (-1/h^2)$ with h being sometimes referred to as the *bandwidth parameter*.

8.4.3   Implementing SVM in Python

As illustrated, one way to calculate the optimal weights for the SVM involves solving a quadratic programming problem. To demonstrate how to do this, we used the Python package CVXOPT.[4] In Listing 8.7 we present a skeleton script that uses simulated data so that you can compare your solution to ours.

---

[4]We are extremely grateful to Jack H.S. Chua for his helpful advice and useful guidance with the Python script presented here.

```
 1  # Script:       SVM-CVXOPT.py
 2  # Author:       Jack H.S. Chua
 3  # Revised by:   Harry J. Paarsch
 4  # Date:         14 November 2014
 5  """ This script trains a SVM predictor by solving the QP of the
 6      dual representation using the solver from the CVXOPT package.
 7      Simulated data are created to make testing by the user easy.
 8  """
 9  import numpy as np
10  import time
11  from cvxopt import matrix, solvers
12  from optparse import OptionParser
13  # In order to be able to replicate the results, create a utility
14  # function to construct a binary y variable and two independent,
15  # standard-normally distributed features.
16  def MakeData(n=100):
17    np.random.seed(123457)
18    y = 2*np.random.binomial(1, 0.5, n)
19    y = y - 1
20    X = np.column_stack((np.random.randn(n), np.random.randn(n)))
21    return (y, X)
22
23  # Create a utility function to construct kernel matrix, given the
24  # features and a kernel function.
25  def KernelMatrix(X, kernel):
26    (N,k) = np.shape(X)
27    tmp = np.ndarray((N, N))
28    for idx1, x in enumerate(X):
29      for idx2, y in enumerate(X):
30        tmp[idx1][idx2]=kernel(x, y)
31    return tmp
32
33  def LinearSVM(y, X, C=1, tol=0.0001):
34    # Construct kernel matrix using a linear kernel.
35    # You could use others kernels by changing this.
36    linearKernel = lambda x1,x2: np.dot(x1, x2)
37    K = KernelMatrix(X, linearKernel)
38    # Define the quadratic program.
39    (N,k) = np.shape(X)
40    Q = matrix(np.outer(y,y)*K, tc='d')
41    p = matrix(-1*np.ones(N), tc='d')
42    G = matrix(np.row_stack((-1*np.diag(np.ones(N)),
43                             np.diag(np.ones(N)))), tc='d')
44    h = matrix(np.concatenate((np.zeros(N),
```

```
45                    C*np.ones(N))), tc='d')
46      A = matrix(y, tc='d').trans()
47      b = matrix(0, tc='d')
48      # Now, solve the QP and compute results.
49      soln = solvers.qp(Q, p, G, h, A, b)['x']
50      # Obtain the support vectors.
51      soln = np.ravel(soln)
52      svIndices = np.where(soln>tol)[0]
53      svData = { 'svs' : soln[svIndices],
54                    'y' : y[svIndices],
55                    'X' : X[svIndices] }
56      # Finally, compute the weights.
57      weights = np.dot(np.transpose(
58                        np.multiply(svData['svs'],
59                        svData['y'])),
60                  svData['X'])
61      # And then return the results.
62      return {'weights':weights}
63
64  if __name__=="__main__":
65          # Fancy stuff to parse size.
66          parser = OptionParser()
67          parser.add_option("--N", action="store", default="", dest="N")
68          (options, args) = parser.parse_args()
69          N = int(options.N)
70
71          # Create data set to test the code.
72          (y, X) = MakeData(N)
73
74          # Now, let the games begin.
75          startTime = time.time()
76          SVC = LinearSVM(y, X)
77          elapsedTime = time.time() - startTime
78
79          # Let's see some output, shall we?
80          print "Time elapsed: %s" % elapsedTime
81          print "***** CVXOPT SOLUTION SVM *****"
82          print SVC
```

Listing 8.7: Training SVM Using CVXOPT QP Solver

The script, named SVM-CVXOPT.py, has the following structure. First, in lines 1–12, we include our usual preamble to a Python script, where the script's name, author(s), and date are listed and any required modules as well as packages are imported.

In order to make the script self-contained (so that you can replicate the output), in lines 13–22, using simulation methods, we generate some simulated data in the function `MakeData`; the argument `n=100` ensures that a default sample size of 100 is used should none be otherwise provided. The instruction in line 17 simply seeds the PRNG at a particular place to ensure replicability. The sample data are trivial: a two-state dependent variable is collected in the vector `y`; two feature variables are collected in the array `X`. The dependent variable is first created from a Bernoulli (a binomial having just one draw) random variable where the probability of success (the dependent variables taking on the value 1) is 0.6, and then transformed from the set of outcomes $\{0,1\}$ to the set $\{-1,1\}$, which is the input required for an SVC. The two feature variables are independent, standard normal random variables.

By construction, the features are independent of the dependent variable. Therefore, the training exercise should yield `weights` on those features that are very close to zero. Finding small weights (for example, on the order of 10^{-7}, particularly if the number of observations is relatively large, say, $1,000$) is a crude test of the script. Another test would be to use an SVM package to train the model, for example, that from `scikit-learn`, an open-source machine learning library for Python.

In lines 23–32, a function is created to define the kernel matrix of the SVM, while in lines 33–63, the linear SVM is defined. Note the use of the `lambda` function line 36 to define the dot product of the feature vectors. The various matrices and vectors relevant to solving the quadratic program are defined using variable names that correspond to the notation we used to define the SVM optimization problem as a quadratic program.

Finally, in lines 64–82, the `main()` part of the script is defined. Lines 65–70 are introduced so that you can use parameters to guide the script; their use is demonstrated below.

In line 72 the data set is created, while in line 75 the "games begin": in order to know how long things take, we first record the `startTime`, then train the the support vector classifier `SVC`, and finally calculate the `elapsedTime`. Lines 80–82 simply output the results.

Perhaps the only remaining puzzle is `tc='d'` (in lines 40–47), which means "double-precision numbers in the matrix."

To train the SVC, we simply execute the following on the command line, where the `-N 1000` parameter creates $1,000$ observations,

```
$ python SVM-CVXOPT.py --N 1000
```

whence the following output appears in the terminal window:

```
     pcost          dcost          gap     pres    dres
 0: -9.9510e+02 -2.1347e+03    5e+03   2e+00   3e-14
 1: -7.9732e+02 -1.4473e+03    7e+02   3e-14   3e-14
 2: -9.2483e+02 -1.0191e+03    9e+01   6e-15   3e-14
 3: -9.3220e+02 -9.3893e+02    7e+00   5e-15   3e-14
 4: -9.3398e+02 -9.3405e+02    7e-02   6e-14   3e-14
 5: -9.3400e+02 -9.3400e+02    7e-04   2e-14   3e-14
Optimal solution found.
Time elapsed: 5.44436383247
***** CVXOPT SOLUTION SVM *****
{'weights': array([ -1.82276128e-07,    2.48285050e-07])}
$
```

8.4.4   Alternative Solution Strategies

One problem with SVMs is that the optimization problem can involve matrices that are potentially huge. For example, when written in terms of maximizing the margins, the optimization problem is

$$\min_{\mathbf{x},b,\mathbf{s}} \; 0.5\|\mathbf{w}\|_2^2 + \tau \sum_{n=1}^{N} s_n \quad \text{subject to} \quad y_n(\mathbf{x}_n\mathbf{w} - b) \geq 1 - s_n, \; s_n \geq 0$$

$$n = 1, 2, \ldots, N,$$

where $\mathbf{s}$ collects the N slack variables in an $(N \times 1)$ vector. This problem has $P = (N + K + 1)$ variables.

Unfortunately, if the dimension of the weight vector is P, then solving the QP problem has complexity $\mathcal{O}(P^3)$ when $\mathbf{Q}$ is positive definite. Specialized algorithms for solving the QP problem have been developed, but many of these algorithms rely on heuristics, for example, breaking the problem into smaller, manageable chunks. One such method is *Platt's sequential minimal optimization* (SMO) algorithm, in honor of John C. Platt (1999). Under this algorithm, the problem is broken into two-dimensional subproblems that may be solved analytically, thus eliminating the need for a numerical optimization algorithm.

Ferris and Munson (2002) proposed an alternative approach. Instead of solving a sequence of smaller problems, they proposed solving the whole problem; they avoided solving the large linear system involving the large kernel matrix by introducing a low rank approximation.

As you have probably noted, solving real-world problems often involves balancing conflicting goals.

8.5   Numerical Integration: Gauss-Hermite Quadrature

In many Internet marketplaces, vendors vie to purchase items (such as used books or smartphones), which they then resell. Economic theorists refer to this as the *common-value paradigm*: even though none of the vendors may know what the resale value is, it is probably the same regardless of which vendor wins the good.

Suppose that you believe that each vendor has an unbiased estimator of a good's value, but that different vendors have different and independent realizations of that estimator. In some marketplaces, transfer prices are determined at auction, where the highest bidder typically wins and then pays what he bid. As a participant at such auctions, you worry that when you win it is because you have made an (excessively) optimistic estimate of the good's true value. In short, you worry about a phenomenon referred to by economists as the *winner's curse*.

Thus, one calculation necessary to avoid the winner's curse requires evaluating the expected value of the maximum of, say, N independent random variables. How to proceed? Introduce the random variable X whose cdf is $F_X(x)$ and pdf is $f_X(x)$. Consider a random sample of N independent draws concerning X, collected in $\{X_1, X_2, \ldots, X_N\}$. Let

$$Y = \max(X_1, X_2, \ldots, X_N).$$

What is the expected value of Y? It is

$$\mathbb{E}(Y) = \int_{-\infty}^{\infty} y f_Y(y)\, \mathrm{d}y.$$

Thus, you need to find the pdf of Y, which you can typically get by differentiating the cdf of Y. The cdf of Y is

$$\Pr(Y \le y) = F_Y(y) = \Pr\left[(X_1 \le y) \cap (X_2 \le y) \cap \ldots \cap (X_N \le y)\right]$$

$$= \prod_{n=1}^{N} \Pr(X_n \le y)$$

$$= F_X(y)^N,$$

so the pdf of Y is

$$f_Y(Y) = \frac{dF_Y(y)}{dy} = NF_X(y)^{N-1}f_X(y)$$

whence the expected value of Y is

$$\mathbb{E}(Y) = \int_{-\infty}^{\infty} yf_Y(y)\, dy = N\int_{-\infty}^{\infty} yF_X(y)^{N-1}f_X(y)\, dy.$$

Suppose X comes from the location-scale family of distributions, such as the Gaussian family. In short, the estimators are normally distributed, an approximation supported by the central limit theorem. In this case,

$$X = \mu + \sigma Z,$$

where $\mathbb{E}(X) = \mu$ and $\mathbb{V}(X) = \sigma^2$. Introduce the order statistics

$$Z_{(1:N)} \geq Z_{(2:N)} \geq \cdots \geq Z_{(N:N)},$$

so

$$Y = \mu + \sigma Z_{(1:N)}.$$

Suppose Z is, in fact, a standard normal random variable. Denoting the cdf and pdf of Z by $F_Z(z)$ and $f_Z(z)$, respectively,

$$f_Z(z) = \frac{1}{\sqrt{2\pi}} \exp\left(-z^2/2\right)$$

and

$$F_Z(z) = \frac{1}{\sqrt{2\pi}} \int_{-\infty}^{z} \exp\left(-u^2/2\right)\, du.$$

Furthermore,

$$\mathbb{E}\left[Z_{(1:N)}\right] = N\int_{-\infty}^{\infty} zF_Z(z)^{N-1}f_Z(z)\, dz$$

$$= \frac{1}{\sqrt{\pi}} \int_{-\infty}^{\infty} g\left(\sqrt{2}z\right) \exp\left(-z^2\right)\, dz]$$

where

$$g\left(\sqrt{2}z\right) = N\sqrt{2}zF_Z\left(\sqrt{2}z\right)^{N-1}.$$

```python
# Script:   GaussHermiteExample.py
# Author:   Harry J. Paarsch
# Date:     12 March 2014
""" Script to implement Gauss-Hermite quadrature when
    calculating the expected value of maximum of  N
    draws concerning a standard normal random variate.
"""
def Integrand(z, N):
  """ Integrand for the expected value of the
      maximum of  N  standard normal variates.
  """
  from scipy.stats import norm
  return N*z*(norm.cdf(z)**(N-1))

from math import sqrt
from math import pi
import numpy
# Define the abscissae and weights for the Gauss--Hermite
# quadrature with M nodes.
M         = 80
# The abscissae are ell and the weights are w.
[ell, w] = numpy.polynomial.hermite.hermgauss(M)
# Define the maximum number of draws.
maxN      = 20
# Introduce  N  as number of draws and  zeta  as the
# expectation of the maximum of  N  draws.
N         = numpy.zeros(maxN)
zeta      = numpy.zeros(maxN)
for n in range(1, maxN+1):
  N[n-1] = n
  for m in range(0, M):
    zeta[n-1] = zeta[n-1] + w[m]*Integrand(sqrt(2.)*ell[m], N[n-1])

zeta = zeta / sqrt(pi)
# Print out the results
print "Draws, N\t Expectation, zeta\n"
for n in range(0, maxN):
  print "%d\t\t%18.15f" % (N[n], zeta[n])
```

Listing 8.8: Python Script for Gauss-Hermite Quadrature

If you run this script in a terminal window and pipe the output through `more -10`, you will see something like the following:

```
Draws, N           Expectation, zeta

1                  -0.000000000000000
2                   0.564189583547756
3                   0.846284375321634
4                   1.029375373003964
5                   1.162964473640519
6                   1.267206360611472
7                   1.352178375606909
8                   1.423600306044959
--More--
```

At least on the surface, the results make sense: the maximum of one draw is just the draw, which has expectation zero, and is calculated to be so, at least to 15 decimal places. The expected value of the maximum of two standard normal variates is calculated to be about one-half; of three, about 0.85; and so forth. In fact, you can double-check these results using other sources, for example, Abramowitz and Stegun (1972).

8.6   Simulation: Demand for Change

Did you ever wonder why you have more of one type of coin in change than another? Because the bags of wrappers for pennies, nickels, dimes, and quarters always have an equal number for each type of coin, you inevitably end up with too many wrappers for nickels and dimes, and not enough for pennies and quarters. What determines the distribution of coinage in change? Presumably, the prices for objects at each sale. In this section, we demonstrate how Monte Carlo simulation can be used to investigate the effect of pricing practices by store owners on the demand for coins of particular denominations. In addition, we investigate what might happen to the demand for quarters, nickels, and dimes if pennies were abolished.

Finding the distributions for pennies, nickels, dimes, and quarters in these applications is an example of finding the distributions of transformations of random variables. In general, the distributions of these transformations would be very time consuming and tedious to evaluate. Moreover, the results would be sensitive to the choice of the underlying change distribution.

A researcher might be interested in investigating the effects of altering the change distribution and would therefore be interested in trying several alternatives. In such cases, it is relatively easy to approximate accurately and quickly the distribution of transformations using simulation methods.

To begin, assume we are only interested in the distributions of coinage, not the distributions of bills that might obtain as a result of a transaction. Also, assume that one-dollar coins, if they exist (as they do in Canada, for example), are counted as bills. The analysis we perform could be modified to introduce dollar coins, but such modifications would not alter the treatment of small change.

In order to find the distributions for pennies, nickels, dimes, and quarters, we first need to know the distribution of change. A natural distribution for change might be the discrete uniform, where the potential values are $0, 1, \ldots, 99$ cents. Later, we examine another distribution for change.

To find the distributions for coinage that makes up change, we must model the transformation function. But first a few words about integer division. Consider two integers i and j. If $i < j$, then (i/j) equals zero, but if $i > j$, then (i/j) equals the largest integer k that divides i by j. This is the *floor*. For example, when $i = 78$ and $j = 25$, then $(i/j) = (78/25) = 3 = k$, whereas if $i = 4$ and $j = 5$, then $(i/j) = (4/5) = 0 = k$. Next, assume that the minimum number of coins is always given in change. Thus, if the change is 26 cents, then one quarter and one penny are given, not two dimes, a nickel, and a penny or five nickels and a penny. Then the distribution of coinage for the nth transaction can be determined by the following rules which must be executed in order:

```
# Function:     MakeChange
# Written by:   Harry J. Paarsch
# Date:         28 January 2014
def MakeChange(change):
    """ This function makes change from an input change producing an
        output list coins where the first element is the number of
        quarters, the second element is the number of dimes, the
        third is the number of nickels and the fourth is the number
        of pennies.
    """
    quarters = change / 25
    change   = change % 25
    dimes    = change / 10
    change   = change % 10
    nickels  = change / 5
```

```
pennies  = change % 5
coins    = [quarters, dimes, nickels, pennies]
return coins
```

Here, `change` is the amount of change in a transaction, `quarters` is the number of quarters in the transaction, `dimes` is the number of dimes, `nickels` is the number of nickels, and `pennies` is the number of pennies. Also, `%` is the modulus operator, that is, the integer remainder from dividing, say, `change` by 25. Thus, 78 % 25 would equal 3. The first line of the rules determines the number of quarters in the change, and the next line finds the remaining change after the quarters have been taken out. In the third line, the number of dimes is calculated, and in the fourth line the change after dimes and quarters is calculated. In the fifth line, the number of nickels is calculated, and in the last line the number of pennies is calculated.

To implement this on a computer you would need to generate a vector of N uniform pseudo-random integers `change` using the `numpy` module `random` and the function `randint`. The script to do this is as follows:

```
# Script:  SimChange.py
# Author:  Harry J. Paarsch
# Date:    28 January 2014
""" This script sets up the simulation code in order to simulate
    the demand for coins.
"""
import matplotlib.pyplot
import numpy
from MakeChange import MakeChange
# Determine the simulation sample size.
N = 10000
# Set the initial seed for replicability.
numpy.random.seed(123457)
# Generate the change for random integers from 0-99
change = numpy.random.randint(0, 99, size=N)
# Old guys initialize arrays.
quarters = numpy.zeros([N, 1]).astype(int)
dimes    = numpy.zeros([N, 1]).astype(int)
nickels  = numpy.zeros([N, 1]).astype(int)
pennies  = numpy.zeros([N, 1]).astype(int)
# Let the games begin.
for n in range(0, N):
  coins = MakeChange(change[n])
  quarters[n] = coins[0]
```

```
 dimes[n]    = coins[1]
 nickels[n]  = coins[2]
 pennies[n]  = coins[3]

# Use the TeX fonts.
matplotlib.rc('text', usetex=True)
# Use fonts with serifs.
matplotlib.rc('font', family='serif')
# Define the color gray.
gray = (0.7, 0.7, 0.7)
# Create the histograms of the quarters.
matplotlib.pyplot.hist(quarters, bins=numpy.arange(0, 5)-0.5,\
                    normed=1, facecolor=gray, alpha=0.75)
matplotlib.pyplot.xlabel("Number of Quarters", fontsize=30)
matplotlib.pyplot.ylabel("Relative Frequency", fontsize=30)
matplotlib.pyplot.xticks(numpy.arange(0, 4), ('0', '1', '2', '3') )
matplotlib.pyplot.yticks(numpy.arange(0., 0.30, 0.05))
# Save the resulting figure in eps and pdf formats.
matplotlib.pyplot.savefig('HistogramQuarters.eps')
matplotlib.pyplot.savefig('HistogramQuarters-eps-converted-to.pdf')
matplotlib.pyplot.close()
```

Listing 8.9: Python Script `SimChange.py`

In Figure 8.10 the histograms for quarters, dimes, nickels, and pennies based upon $10,000$ replications from the uniform distribution of change are presented. Notice that the estimates of the pmfs for the numbers of pennies and quarters given in change are uniform over the integers $\{0, 1, 2, 3, 4\}$ and $\{0, 1, 2, 3\}$, respectively. Sixty percent of the time no nickels are given in change, and 40 percent of the time only one nickel is given in change. Twenty percent of the time two dimes are given in change, and 40 percent of the time, no dimes or only one dime is given in change.

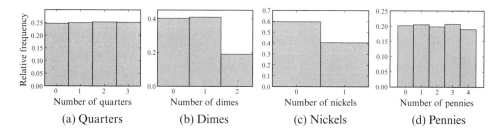

(a) Quarters   (b) Dimes   (c) Nickels   (d) Pennies

Figure 8.10: Simulated Demand for Coins—Uniform Change

Suppose now that instead of a uniform distribution, the distribution of change is a power distribution. An example of the power distribution for a continuous random variable V is

$$f_V(v) = \begin{cases} \theta(1-v)^{\theta-1} & 0 \le v \le 1 \text{ and } 1 < \theta; \\ 0 & \text{otherwise.} \end{cases}$$

What this means is that more store owners use prices that have change that is closer to the 10s than to the 90s, based on the notion that a price of $24.99 appears more enticing to a consumer than a price of $25.01. We ignore any sales taxes to obtain the final price. In addition, the fact that customers often buy more than one item changes the distribution. We leave the investigation of those problems to the reader as an exercise.

In any case, the cdf of V for the power distribution is

$$F_V(v) = 1 - (1-v)^\theta \quad v \in [0,1], \ \theta > 1.$$

Suppose $\theta = 3$, then v can be generated from uniform u via the rule

$$v = F_V^{-1}(u) = 1 - (1-u)^{1/3}.$$

Assuming that the continuous cdf is a good approximation to the discrete cdf for change, we can implement this rule using the transformation formula

```
U      = numpy.random.uniform(0., 1., [N, 1])
change = (100*(1.-((1.-U)**(1./theta)))).astype(int)
```

and then use the transformations to find the numbers of quarters, nickels, dimes, and pennies.

Figure 8.11 collects the histograms for quarters, dimes, nickels, and pennies based upon $10,000$ replications from the power distribution of change. Notice that the estimates of the pmfs for the numbers of pennies and nickels remain unchanged. Under the power distribution of change, no dimes are given in change 50 percent of the time, one dime is given in change 40 percent of the time, and two dimes 10 percent of the time. The distribution of quarters is skewed to the right. No quarters are given in change nearly 60 percent of the time, but three quarters are given in change less than 5 percent of the time. One and two quarters change are given just over 30 and 10 percent of the time, respectively.

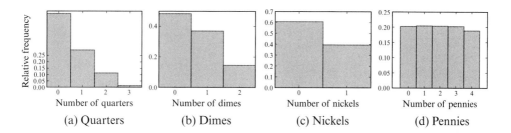

Figure 8.11: Simulated Demand for Coins—Power-Law Change

What would happen if pennies were abolished? Let's assume that all change is rounded to the nearest nickel. Thus, 72 cents becomes 70 cents, but 73 cents becomes 75 cents. Under this assumption, the following rules determine change:

```
def MakeChangeNoPennies(change):
    """ This function makes change from an input change producing
        an output list coins where the first element is the number
        of quarters, the second element is the number of dimes, and
        the third is the number of nickels.  It has been assumed
        that pennies have been abolished.
    """
    check  = change % 5
    change = change / 5
    change = change * 5
    if (check > 2):
      change = change + 5

    quarters = change / 25
    change   = change % 25
    dimes    = change / 10
    change   = change % 10
    nickels  = change / 5
    pennies  = change % 5

    if (pennies > 0):
      print "We have a problem:  pennies are positive!"

    coins    = [quarters, dimes, nickels]
    return coins
```

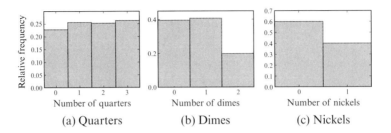

Figure 8.12: Demand for Coins—No Pennies, Uniform Change

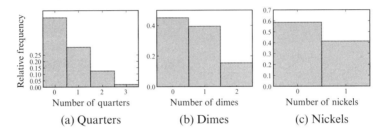

Figure 8.13: Demand for Coins—No Pennies, Power-Law Change

Here, `check` determines how many pennies should be given in change, if pennies were not abolished. The first line defines `check`, and the next three lines determine how to round off change. When `check` is less than 3, changes is rounded down, whereas when `check` is greater than 2, change is rounded up. The remaining rules determine change in the same way as before.

In Figures 8.12 and 8.13, histograms for quarters, dimes, and nickels are presented. Notice that the abolition of pennies does not affect the pmfs of quarters, dimes, and nickels under the uniform distribution of change, but does change those pmfs slightly under the power distribution of change.

8.7 Resampling: Quantifying Variability

With the advent of cheap and powerful computing, alternative methods of estimation and inference have evolved. A subset of these methods is often referred to as *resampling methods*.

Perhaps the most influential idea in the latter two decades of the twentieth century is due to Efron (1979, 1982). It is referred to as the *bootstrap*. Efron and Tibshirani (1993) provided an elementary introduction to this method.

We believe it is safe to say that this idea has revolutionized the practice of statistics. Salsburg (2001) placed the history of the research endeavor in perspective, in layman's terms.

Other statistical procedures related to the bootstrap include an earlier invented technique referred to as the *jackknife*, which is due to Quenouille (1949, 1956) and Tukey (1958).

In addition, Politis and Romano (1994) invented a method referred to as *subsampling*; Politis et al. (1999) described the method in detail.

Together, the jackknife and the bootstrap as well as subsampling represent resampling methods. We outline the mechanics of resampling methods with a solved example using the exponential distribution as the case study. Before proceeding with this analysis, however, we outline the statistical framework that existed before the jackknife, the bootstrap, and subsampling.

8.7.1 First-Order Asymptotic Methods

For the first half of the twentieth century, researchers assumed that $F_Y(y)$, the cumulative distribution function of a random variable Y, belonged to specific families of distributions indexed by the scalar parameter θ or a vector of parameters $\boldsymbol{\theta}$. This was usually denoted by either $F_Y(y; \theta)$ or $F_Y(y; \boldsymbol{\theta})$, depending on the dimension of the parameter vector. The parameters of the distribution function $F_Y(y; \boldsymbol{\theta})$ are typically unobserved by the researcher and must be estimated from data.

Consider a random sample of N observations $\{Y_1, Y_2, \ldots, Y_N\}$ from $F_Y(\cdot)$. Perhaps the most important property of these estimates is parameter consistency; that is, as the sample gets large, the parameter estimate gets close to the truth θ^0. Knowing the sampling distribution is also important, particularly to conduct inference—test hypotheses concerning θ.

In order to highlight what the resampling methods can do, we review tools that were used to investigate parameter consistency and asymptotic distribution before the advent of resampling methods. Such tools were referred to as *first-order asymptotic methods*. These are important tools for evaluating the large-sample properties of estimators.

Parameter Consistency: Laws of Large Numbers

Several definitions of parameter consistency exist. One notion is convergence in probability. That is, for a sample of size N, an estimator $\hat{\theta}_N$ is parameter consistent if it converges to the true value θ^0 in probability as the sample gets very large. In symbols,

$$\lim_{N\to\infty} \Pr(|\hat{\theta}_N - \theta^0| \le \varepsilon) = 1$$

for any ε greater than zero. Thus, consider any small distance ε from the true value θ^0, the probability that $\hat{\theta}_N$ lies within the interval $[\theta^0 - \varepsilon, \theta^0 + \varepsilon]$ must be arbitrarily close to 1 as the sample size N increases. In such cases, the *probability limit* or the plim of $\hat{\theta}_N$ is θ^0. This is often written as

$$\operatorname*{plim}_{N\to\infty} \hat{\theta}_N = \theta^0 \quad \text{or} \quad \hat{\theta}_N \xrightarrow{\mathrm{P}} \theta^0.$$

To demonstrate our methods, we use the following example concerning $\{Y_n\}_{n=1}^N$ an independently and identically distributed sample of size N from an exponential distribution. For the parameter θ, the data-generating process is

$$f_Y(y;\theta) = \theta \exp(-\theta y) \quad y > 0,\ \theta > 0,$$

so the kth raw population moment is

$$\mathbb{E}(Y^k) = \mu_k(\theta) = \frac{k!}{\theta^k} \quad k = 1, 2, \dots .$$

By a *law of large numbers*, the sample mean

$$\bar{Y}_N = \frac{1}{N} \sum_{n=1}^N Y_n$$

converges to the population mean $\mu_1(\theta^0)$ with probability 1 as the sample size gets very large, goes to infinity. We outline a proof of a law of large numbers as an example of convergence in probability using *Chebyshev's inequality*.

For the preceding sample, note that $\mathbb{E}(\bar{Y}_N)$ equals $\mathbb{E}(Y)$ or $\mu_1(\theta^0)$ or $(1/\theta^0)$, whereas $\mathbb{V}(Y)$ equals $[1/(\theta^0)^2]$, with $\mathbb{V}(\bar{Y}_N)$ equaling $\mathbb{V}(Y)/N$. Both $\mathbb{E}(Y)$ and $\mathbb{V}(Y)$ are finite when θ^0 is greater than zero.

Chebyshev's inequality states that

$$\Pr\left[|\bar{Y}_N - \mathbb{E}(Y)| \ge d\sqrt{\mathbb{V}(\bar{Y}_N)}\right] \le \frac{1}{d^2} \quad d > 1.$$

In words, less than d^{-2} of the mass is contained outside of d standard deviations from the mean. For some ε larger than zero, consider

$$\Pr\left[\left|\bar{Y}_N - (1/\theta^0)\right| \le \varepsilon\right] = 1 - \Pr\left[\left|\bar{Y}_N - (1/\theta^0)\right| \ge \varepsilon\sqrt{\mathbb{V}(\bar{Y}_N)}/\sqrt{\mathbb{V}(\bar{Y}_N)}\right]$$

$$\ge 1 - \frac{1}{\left[\varepsilon/\sqrt{\mathbb{V}(Y)/N}\right]^2} = 1 - \frac{\mathbb{V}(Y)}{N\varepsilon^2}.$$

Thus, for an arbitrary ε greater than zero,

$$\lim_{N\to\infty} \Pr\left[\left|\bar{Y}_N - \mathbb{E}(Y)\right| \le \varepsilon\right] \ge \lim_{N\to\infty}\left[1 - \frac{\mathbb{V}(Y)}{N\varepsilon^2}\right] = 1,$$

or

$$\plim_{N\to\infty} \bar{Y}_N = \mathbb{E}(Y) = \mu_1(\theta^0).$$

Using this example, the kth raw sample moment is

$$M_k = \frac{1}{N}\sum_{n=1}^{N} Y_n^k \quad k = 1, 2, \ldots,$$

so, by a law of large numbers,

$$\plim_{N\to\infty} M_k = \mu_k(\theta^0) \quad k = 1, 2, \ldots.$$

Asymptotic Normality: Central Limit Theorems

Frequently, the estimators we see are functions of the sample mean $\bar{Y}_N$. Sometimes, we can find the exact distribution of the sample mean; for example, when the estimators are linear in $\bar{Y}_N$ and the samples are from the Bernoulli, Poisson, exponential, or normal laws. In other cases, typically when the estimators are nonlinear functions of $\bar{Y}_N$, we may only be able to find the approximate distribution as the sample size gets very large—the asymptotic distribution. The idea behind asymptotic (or large-sample) theory can be formalized by the notion of *convergence in distribution*.

A sequence of random variables Y_N is said to converge in distribution to Y if for any bounded continuous function $g(\cdot)$ and for all y such that the cdf of $g(Y)$ is continuous at y,

$$\lim_{N \to \infty} \Pr[g(Y_N) \leq y] = \Pr[g(Y) \leq y].$$

This is often written as $Y_N \overset{d}{\to} Y$. The notation $\overset{d}{\to}$ means "is approximately distributed" according to the term following it when the sample is large. If Y is a constant μ, then $Y_N \overset{d}{\to} Y$ implies $Y_N \overset{p}{\to} \mu$. When Y_N is a suitably normalized function of the sample mean, and Y is a normal random variable, results concerning conditions under which $Y_N \overset{d}{\to} Y$ are called *central limit theorems*. Y_N is said to be *asymptotically normal* in this case.

If the sample is from the Bernoulli law, then by the de Moivre-Laplace central limit theorem, an appropriately chosen transformation of $\bar{Y}_N$ will be normally distributed, asymptotically

$$\frac{\sqrt{N}[\bar{Y}_N - \mathbb{E}(Y)]}{\sqrt{\mathbb{V}(Y)}} \overset{d}{\to} \mathcal{N}(0,1).$$

The notation $\mathcal{N}(0,1)$ means "normally distributed with mean zero and variance 1."

The Lindeberg-Lévy central limit theorem is a more general central limit theorem than the deMoivre-Laplace central limit theorem. For any $\{Y_n\}_{n=1}^{N}$, an independent- and identically-distributed sample of size N from $f_Y(y; \theta)$ where the mean $\mathbb{E}(Y)$ and variance $\mathbb{V}(Y)$ are finite and the so-called Lindeberg condition is satisfied, this central limit theorem states that

$$\frac{\sqrt{N}[\bar{Y}_N - \mathbb{E}(Y)]}{\sqrt{\mathbb{V}(Y)}} \overset{d}{\to} \mathcal{N}(0,1).$$

This is a major step forward since we can now consider the sample mean from *any* distribution satisfying the fairly weak conditions (not just the Bernoulli law) and thus conclude that it is distributed normally, asymptotically. In our example,

$$\sqrt{N}\big[M_k - \mu_k(\theta^0)\big] \overset{d}{\to} \mathcal{N}\big[0, \mathbb{V}(Y^k)\big],$$

where

$$\mathbb{V}(Y^k) = \frac{(2k)! - (k!)^2}{(\theta^0)^{2k}}$$

by the Lindeberg-Lévy central limit theorem.

Figure 8.14 presents the exact pdf of the sample mean of five independently and identically distributed uniform random variables having support on the interval $[0, 1]$—the solid line. Superimposed on this graph is the pdf of the normal approximation to this distribution where the normal has mean $(1/2)$ and variance $(1/60)$—the dashed line. Notice how accurate this approximation is, even for a sample of size 5. Much of this accuracy obtains from the symmetry of the pdf of the uniform.

In Figure 8.15 consider the exact pdf of the sample mean of 25 independently and identically distributed exponential random variables having parameter θ^0 of 1, a mean and variance of 1—the solid line. Even though each exponential is skewed to the right, the pdf of the normal approximation for

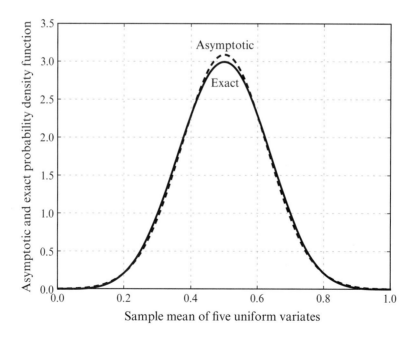

Figure 8.14: Density of Sample Mean—Five Uniforms

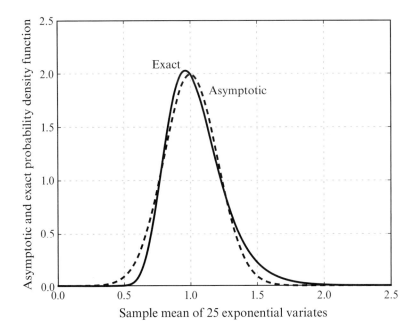

Figure 8.15: Density of Sample Mean—25 Exponentials

this statistic, where the normal has mean 1 and variance (1/25)—the dashed line superimposed on this graph—is quite accurate, but still slightly skewed.

Continuous Mapping Theorem

Suppose that $g(Y)$ is a continuous function of Y with probability 1, and that the Y_N converges in distribution to Y. Thus,

$$Y_N \xrightarrow{d} Y.$$

The *continuous mapping theorem* allows us to find the limiting distribution of $g(Y_N)$. In particular,

$$g(Y_N) \xrightarrow{d} g(Y).$$

When Y is a constant (for example, μ), this implies that the operation of $g(\cdot)$ and calculating probability limits can be exchanged:

$$\underset{N\to\infty}{\text{plim}}\ g(Y_N) = g\left(\underset{N\to\infty}{\text{plim}}\ Y_N\right)$$
$$= g(\mu).$$

This is a very powerful result, since we need only evaluate the function $g(\cdot)$ at μ to calculate its probability limit.

In practice, we can analyze a random vector $\mathbf{Y}_N$, which has a random scalar Y_{1N}, which converges to a constant μ, and a subvector of $\mathbf{Y}_{2N}$, which converges to a random vector $\mathbf{Y}_2$. If

$$\underset{N\to\infty}{\text{plim}}\ \mathbf{Y}_N = \underset{N\to\infty}{\text{plim}}\ \begin{bmatrix} Y_{1N} \\ \mathbf{Y}_{2N} \end{bmatrix} = \begin{bmatrix} \mu \\ \mathbf{Y}_2 \end{bmatrix}$$

then the continuous mapping theorem states that

$$g(\mathbf{Y}_N) \xrightarrow{d} g(\mu, \mathbf{Y}_2).$$

Several special cases of the continuous mapping theorem are often referred to as *Slutsky's theorem*:

Theorem 3 *If* $\mathbf{Y}_{2N} \xrightarrow{d} \mathbf{Y}_2$ *and* $\text{plim}_{N\to\infty}\ Y_{1N} = \mu$, *then*

(a) $\mathbf{Y}_{2N} \pm Y_{1N} \xrightarrow{d} \mathbf{Y}_2 \pm \mu$;

(b) $\mathbf{Y}_{2N} \times Y_{1N} \xrightarrow{d} \mathbf{Y}_2 \times \mu$;

(c) *when* $\mu \neq 0$, $\frac{\mathbf{Y}_{2N}}{Y_{1N}} \xrightarrow{d} \frac{\mathbf{Y}_2}{\mu}$.

Delta Method

Suppose that $g(Y_N)$ is a continuous and differentiable function of Y_N, where the random variable converges in probability to μ, and that for some sequence of normalizing constants a_N,

$$a_N(Y_N - \mu) \xrightarrow{d} Y.$$

When Y_N is a sample mean, this usually follows from a law of large numbers and a central limit theorem and a_N equals $\sqrt{N}$. By Slutsky's theorem,

$$\underset{N \to \infty}{\text{plim}} \; g(Y_N) = g(\mu).$$

In addition, take a first-order Taylor series expansion of $g(Y_N)$ about μ to get

$$a_N[g(Y_N) - g(\mu)] = g'(\mu)a_N(Y_N - \mu) + o[a_N(Y_N - \mu)],$$

where $o(y)$ indicates a term that is smaller in magnitude than y, in the sense that $[o(y)/y]$ tends to zero as y goes to zero. Slutsky's theorem then implies that

$$\underset{N \to \infty}{\text{plim}} \; o[a_N(Y_N - \mu)] = 0.$$

Another application of Slutsky's theorem implies that

$$a_N[g(Y_N) - g(\mu)] \xrightarrow{\text{d}} g'(\mu)Y.$$

This is referred to as the *delta method*. It is commonly used to show that smooth functions of sample averages are also asymptotically normally distributed. In particular, if Y_N satisfies a central limit theorem, so

$$\sqrt{N}(Y_N - \mu) \xrightarrow{\text{d}} \mathcal{N}[0, \mathbb{V}(Y)],$$

then by the delta method,

$$\sqrt{N}[g(Y_N) - g(\mu)] \xrightarrow{\text{d}} \mathcal{N}\left[0, g'(\mu)\mathbb{V}(Y)g'(\mu)\right].$$

8.7.2 Bootstrap

For a random sample of N observations $\{Y_1, Y_2, \ldots, Y_N\}$, one way to view an estimator is as a rule that maps the N values into a number. Because the N values can vary from sample to sample, so too will the estimate, hence the sampling variability in estimators. For a realized sample of N measurements $\{y_1, y_2, \ldots, y_N\}$, it is impossible to get any variation in the estimate since the y_ns do not change. If, however, we think of $\{y_1, y_2, \ldots, y_N\}$ as an urn that represents well the true cdf $F_Y^0(y)$, then we can sample from $\{y_1, y_2, \ldots, y_N\}$ with replacement and thus create variability in an estimate—sampling variation, so to speak.

Treating $\{y_1, y_2, \ldots, y_N\}$ as an urn that represents $F_Y^0(y)$ and then resampling from it is the essential idea behind the bootstrap and the jackknife as well as subsampling; the differences among the methods arise in how the resampling is done. Resampling only became feasible with the advent of cheap and fast computation.

To motivate the bootstrap, we continue with our example. In this case, the mean of Y is

$$\mathbb{E}(Y) = \mu_1(\theta^0) = \frac{1}{\theta^0},$$

and the variance of Y is

$$\mathbb{V}(Y) = \frac{1}{(\theta^0)^2}.$$

One estimator of θ^0 is

$$\hat{\theta} = \frac{N}{\sum_{n=1}^{N} Y_n} = g(M_1),$$

where $g(M_1)$ is a continuous and differentiable function of M_1, which is defined by

$$M_1 = \frac{\sum_{n=1}^{N} Y_n}{N}.$$

Notice that this estimator is a nonlinear function of the data. Such nonlinearities often make it difficult to find either the mean or the variance of $\hat{\theta}_N$. Using first-order asymptotic methods, we approximated the sampling variability and asymptotic distribution of $\hat{\theta}_N$ by

$$\sqrt{N}(\hat{\theta}_N - \theta^0) \xrightarrow{d} \mathcal{N}\left[0, (\theta^0)^2\right].$$

For $\{y_1, y_2, \ldots, y_N\}$, a realization of $\{Y_1, Y_2, \ldots, Y_N\}$, $(N/\sum_{n=1}^{N} y_n)$, an estimate of θ^0, has standard error $(\sqrt{N}/\sum_{n=1}^{N} y_n)$.

If you suspect that the remainder in a delta method expansion is not negligible, then the bootstrap is a useful way to investigate the sampling behavior of estimators like $\hat{\theta}_N$. For instance, first-order methods may not work well when the sample size N is small. Thus, you can think of the bootstrap as something between finite-sample and large-sample theory. In fact, one interpretation of the bootstrap is that it takes into account terms ignored under first-order asymptotic methods.

In general, the bootstrap can be used to evaluate variability, to estimate bias, and to calculate tables of test statistics. In the following, we demonstrate how to implement the *nonparametric* bootstrap standard error of an estimator $\hat{\theta}_N$ of θ^0 for $\{Y_1, Y_2, \ldots, Y_N\}$, an independently and identically drawn sample of size N from some family of distributions $F_Y^0(y) = F_Y(y; \theta^0)$.

The mechanics we describe are often referred to as the *plug-in formula* for the nonparametric bootstrap standard error. Denote the data vector $\{Y_1, Y_2, \ldots, Y_N\}$ by $\mathbf{Y}$. Suppose you want to calculate the standard error of $\hat{\theta}_N = \hat{\theta}(\mathbf{Y})$. Calculating the nonparametric bootstrap standard error involves the following steps:

1. For y, the sample realization of $\mathbf{Y}$, calculate $\hat{\theta}(y)$, an estimate of θ^0.

2. From y take random samples of size N with replacement weighting each y_n equally by $(1/N)$. For the jth bootstrap sample y_j^*, which equals $\{y_{1j}^*, y_{2j}^*, \ldots, y_{Nj}^*\}$, where $j = 1, \ldots, J$, calculate the estimator $\hat{\theta}(y_j^*)$ to get $\hat{\theta}_j^*$.

3. To calculate the nonparametric bootstrap standard error of $\hat{\theta}_N$, use the following formula:

$$\text{se}_B(\hat{\theta}_N) = \sqrt{\frac{\sum_{j=1}^{J}(\hat{\theta}_j^* - \overline{\hat{\theta}^*})^2}{(J-1)}},$$

where

$$\overline{\hat{\theta}^*} = \frac{\sum_{j=1}^{J} \hat{\theta}_j^*}{J}.$$

Carrying out the steps outlined above requires calculating the estimator $\hat{\theta}(\mathbf{Y})$ and sampling randomly from y. Presumably, if you are interested in calculating the standard error of $\hat{\theta}_N$, an estimate of θ^0, then you know the structure of $\hat{\theta}(\mathbf{Y})$ and have implemented this on a computer. An example Python function is as follows:

```
def MoMHRExponential(sample):
    """ This function produces the method-of-moments
        estimate of the hazard rate for exponentially
```

```
        distributed data.
    """
    import numpy
    return 1. / numpy.mean(sample)
```

Listing 8.10: Python Function `MoMHRExponential`

Central to the bootstrap is selecting randomly from y with replacement. To do this, random numbers are required. We discussed how to generate uniform pseudo-random numbers from either a discrete or a continuous distribution. But how can these uniform pseudo-random numbers be used to sample randomly with replacement from y using weights $(1/N)$?

Introduce an integer variable `itag` that marks which of the integers $1, 2, \ldots, N$ has been randomly chosen with replacement. In lines 34–36 of the following Python script, we demonstrate one way to bootstrap resample:

```
   # Script:  Bootstrap.py
 2 # Author:  Harry J. Paarsch
   # Date:    31 January 2014
   """ This script implements the bootstrap as
       an alternative to first-order asymptotics
       in evaluating the method-of-moments estimator
       of the hazard rate in an exponential model.
   """
   import numpy
   # Bring in an external function to calculate the
   # estimator for a given sample.
12 from Estimators import MoMHRExponential
   # Set the seed of the PRNG
   numpy.random.seed(123457)
   # Set the parameters of the process.
   theta = 1.0
   # Set the number of simulations.
   M = 1000
   # Set the sample size.
   N =    9
   # Set the bootstrap sample size.
22 J =  625
   # Old guys initialize vectors
   thetaHat    = numpy.zeros([M, 1])
   seThetaHat  = numpy.zeros([M, 1])
   bootstrapSE = numpy.zeros([M, 1])
   for m in range(0, M):
     U = numpy.random.uniform(0., 1., [N, 1])
```

```
      y = -numpy.log(1.-U) / theta
      thetaHat[m] = MoMHRExponential(y)
      thetaHatStar = numpy.zeros([J,1])
32    # Begin a bootstrappin'
      for j in range(0, J):
        itag = numpy.random.randint(0, len(y), len(y))
        yStar = y[itag]
        thetaHatStar[j] = MoMHRExponential(yStar)

      bootstrapSE[m] = numpy.sqrt(numpy.var(thetaHatStar))
      seThetaHat[m]  = thetaHat[m] / numpy.sqrt(1.*N)

   meanBootstrapSE = numpy.mean(bootstrapSE)
42 meanSEThetaHat   = numpy.mean(seThetaHat)

   print "When the hazard rate parameter is %3.2f;"      % theta
   print "For a sample size of %3i;"                      % N
   print "And %3i bootstrap resamplings for each sample;" % J
   print "And %3i simulation samples.\n"                  % M
   print "Mean of bootstrap standard errors is:   %6.4f"  %
      meanBootstrapSE
   print "Mean of asymptotic standard errors is:  %6.4f"  %
      meanSEThetaHat
```

Listing 8.11: Python Script `Bootstrap.py`

The output of this program, for sample size 9, is presented in the terminal window:

```
$ python Bootstrap
When the hazard rate parameter is 1.00;
For a sample size of   9;
And 625 bootstrap resamplings for each sample;
And 1000 simulation samples.

Mean of bootstrap standard errors is:   0.4529
Mean of asymptotic standard errors is:  0.3785
$
```

Notice that the first-order asymptotics are far too optimistic, which is probably not a big surprise since 9 is not very large sample size. You can try other samples sizes as well, to see when the asymptotics kick in, and to improve on the way input and output are done.

8.7.3 Jackknife

Another useful statistical tool is the jackknife. Quenouille (1956) derived the jackknife estimate of the bias, and Tukey (1958) derived the jackknife estimate of the variance. Because it is such a useful statistical tool, Tukey coined the name *jackknife*, an analogy to a child's handy jackknife.

Although an analysis of the jackknife's statistical behavior is beyond the scope of this book, we can describe how to implement it in a relatively straightforward way. Consider the random sample of N observations collected in the vector y, where $\hat{\theta}_N$ is the full-sample estimate of θ^0. Now, imagine dropping the nth observation from y; denote that vector by y_{-n}. Consider estimating θ^0 using this new sample y_{-n}; denote this $\hat{\theta}_{-n}$. It has been shown that under certain regularity conditions, the average of N jackknife estimates can be used to estimate the bias in $\hat{\theta}_N$, that is,

$$\text{Bias}(\hat{\theta}_N) = (N-1)\left(\frac{\sum_{n=1}^{N}\hat{\theta}_{-n}}{N} - \hat{\theta}_N\right).$$

The variability of $\hat{\theta}_N$ can be estimated using

$$\mathbb{V}(\hat{\theta}_N) = \frac{\sum_{n=1}^{N}(\hat{\theta}_{-n} - \overline{\hat{\theta}_N})^2}{N},$$

where

$$\overline{\hat{\theta}_N} = \frac{1}{N}\sum_{n=1}^{N}\hat{\theta}_{-n}.$$

The following Python script provides estimates of the bias of the method-of-moments estimator of the hazard rate parameter for an exponential random variable. Most of the Python commands are straightforward to understand, but the command `numpy.delete(y, n)` is an especially elegant way of dropping one observation from a `numpy` array vector `y`. Note, too, how we reused the function `MoMHRExponential`, from Listing 8.10.

```
# Script:  JackKnife.py
# Author:  Harry J. Paarsch
# Date:    29 January 2014
import numpy
from Estimators import MoMHRExponential
# Seed PRNG
```

```
numpy.random.seed(123457)
# M is number of simulations.
# N is sample size.
M = 10000
N =     25
theta = 1.
thetaHat = numpy.zeros([M, 1])
meanJackKnife = numpy.zeros([M, 1])
biasJackKnife = numpy.zeros([M, 1])
thetaHatJackKnife = numpy.zeros([N, 1])
for m in range(0, M):
  # Generate the sample.
  y = -numpy.log( (1.-numpy.random.uniform(0., 1., [N, 1])/theta) )
  # Estimate parameter by MoM
  thetaHat[m] = MoMHRExponential(y)
  # Now jackknife the bias.
  for n in range(0, N):
    yJackKnife = numpy.delete(y, n)
    thetaHatJackKnife[n] = MoMHRExponential(yJackKnife)

  meanJackKnife[m] = numpy.mean(thetaHatJackKnife)
  biasJackKnife[m] = (N-1) * (meanJackKnife[m] - thetaHat[m])

meanThetaHat          = numpy.mean(thetaHat)
meanMeanJackKnife     = numpy.mean(meanJackKnife)
meanBiasJackKnife     = numpy.mean(biasJackKnife)
biasCorrectThetaHat = meanThetaHat - meanBiasJackKnife

print "When the sample size is %3i,"               % N
print "And the true hazard rate is %3.1f,"         % theta
print "With %4i simulation samples,\n"             % M
print "Method-of-moments estimator mean is  %6.4f" % meanThetaHat
print "Mean of jackknife estimator means is %6.4f" % meanMeanJackKnife
print "Mean of bias-corrected estimator is  %6.4f" %
    biasCorrectThetaHat
```

Listing 8.12: Python Script `JackKnife.py`

The output of one experiment is presented in the terminal window:

```
$ python JackKnife.py
When the sample size is  25,
And the true hazard rate is 1.0,
With 10000 simulation samples,

Method-of-moments estimator mean is  1.0398
```

```
Mean of jackknife estimator means is 1.0416
Mean of bias-corrected estimator is  0.9963
$
```

By the way, in this example, we could have found the exact distribution of the method-of-moments estimator and then calculated its expectation. If we had done that, we would have found that the bias is (θ^0/N), which in this case is 0.04. In short, the jackknife did a good job at removing the first-order term in the bias.

8.7.4 Subsampling

However powerful the bootstrap may be, it does not work under all conditions. Put another way, the bootstrap is known to work under a set of fairly general regularity conditions. When those regularity conditions do not hold, the bootstrap is not guaranteed to work.[5] Statisticians have demonstrated that the method of subsampling works under more general regularity conditions than the bootstrap, provided that a limiting distribution of the estimator exists.

Under the method of subsampling, samples of size b are taken from the full sample of N observations. The size of b, often referred to as the *block size*, is determined by the rate of convergence of the estimator $\hat{\theta}_N$.

The mechanics of implementing the method of subsampling can be summarized as follows:

1. Draw $y_b^{s,*}$, a sample of size b without replacement from y. If the Y are independently and identically distributed, then take all $\binom{N}{b}$ such subsamples. If the Y is a stationary time series, then take all contiguous blocks of size b.

2. Calculate $\hat{\theta}_s^*$, which denotes $\hat{\theta}(y_b^{s,*})$; repeat until all the subsamples are exhausted.

3. Use the distribution of the simulated estimates $\{\hat{\theta}_s^*\}_{s=1}^S$ to estimate the distribution of $\hat{\theta}_N$ and its moments.

---

[5]An example of a regularity condition failing is the following. Consider a uniform random variable U having support on the interval $[0, \theta^0]$ where θ^0 is an unknown parameter that must be estimated. In this case, a consistent estimator of θ^0 is the maximum of the observed sample $\{U_1, U_2, \ldots, U_N\}$. Using the bootstrap to estimate the distribution of $\hat{\theta}_N = \max(U_1, U_2, \ldots, U_N)$ will fail in this case.

4. If the distribution is used to calculate standard errors or confidence intervals, then adjust by a scaling factor that depends on the rate of convergence; for example, if the rate of convergence is $\sqrt{N}$, then rescale by the factor $\sqrt{\frac{b}{N}}$.

As you can see, subsampling is really only viable because computing is cheap.

Note, too, that subsampling is related to the "b out of N bootstrap," a resampling plan under which a subsample of b is randomly drawn with replacement from y, and then $\hat{\theta}_b^{*,s}$ is calculated. When $(b^2/N) \to 0$ as $N \to \infty$, the b out of N bootstrap is asymptotically equivalent to subsampling.

8.8 `Makefile`: Dealing with Dependencies

In Chapter 2 we extolled the virtues of the `make` tool but deferred illustrating how to use it until there was a context within which to appreciate its power. In this section, we provide a simple `Makefile` that illustrates the power of the `make` tool, but first a few preliminaries.

By default, when invoked on the command line alone, `make` will search for a file named `makefile` in the current working directory and then execute it. If no such file exists, then `make` will return the following:

```
$ make
make: *** No targets specified and no makefile found.    Stop.
```

When several makefiles exist (or the only one is not named `makefile`), the name must be specified. For example, suppose the `Makefile` is named `ExampleMakefile`, then

```
$ make -f ExampleMakefile
```

is how you invoke `make`, where the flag `-f` is mnemonic for file. To find the relevant flags, use `man make`.

In Chapter 2 we noted that `make` is particularly useful when dependencies exist across tasks, that is, when the input of one program depends on the output of another and so forth. As the number of links in a chain increases, these dependencies can become crippling. Questions arise, such as, Will the output of program `X`, and subsequently program `Y`, depend on the new changes? A `Makefile` can determine which files have been changed, rerun those, and then determine which files depend on the changed files and rerun those, too. In short, `make` can save a lot of effort and time, at least when compared to doing things manually.

Now for a concrete example. Suppose you have an empirical project that involves first querying a database and writing a data set to a file; then postprocessing the data in that file to create another file; third, estimating an empirical specification using the postprocessed data; and finally, creating some output, either a table or a figure based on output concerning the empirical specification. Because querying the database and creating the data set may take some time, you do not want to be redoing that work unless it is absolutely necessary. On the other hand, you do want the latest data to be used in the estimation and when the final results are presented.

Suppose you have the following five Python scripts:

`QuerySQLite.py;`

`PostProcessData.py;`

`EstimateModel.py;`

`OutputLaTeXTable.py;`

`Histogram.py.`

In this example, each script creates an output from an input, which depends on the output of previous scripts. Suppose that

1. `QuerySQLite.py` creates `QueriedOutput.dat`;

2. using `QueriedOutput.dat` as input, `PostProcessData.py` creates `Estimation.dat`;

3. using `Estimation.dat` as input, `EstimateModel.py` creates `EstimateModel.out`;

4. using `EstimateModel.out` as input, `OutputLaTeXTable.py` redirects output to the file `LaTeXTable.tex`;

5. using `Estimation.dat` as input, `Histogram.py` creates the figure `Histogram.eps`.

For example, if neither QueriedOutput.dat nor Estimation.dat has
changed, but EstimateModel.py did not converge, then only (3) and (4) need
to be rerun; (5) would not need to be rerun because it only depends on (2),
which has not been changed.

In Listing 8.13, we present the Makefile that deals with these
dependencies.

```
# By default, update/create the Histogram and the LaTeX table,
# which are the only two files you really care about.
all: Histogram.eps LaTeXTable.tex

# Produce Histogram.eps from Estimation.dat,
# first ensuring Estimation.dat is up to date.
Histogram.eps: Estimation.dat
  @echo "Creating Histogram.eps from Estimation.dat"
  @python Histogram.py

# Produce Estimation.dat from QueriedOutput.dat,
# first ensuring QueriedOutput.dat is up to date.
Estimation.dat: QueriedOutput.dat
  @echo "Creating Estimation.dat from QueriedOutput.dat"
  @python PostProcessData.py

# Produce EstimateModel.out from Estimation.dat,
# first ensuring Estimation.dat is up to date.
EstimateModel.out: Estimation.dat
  @echo "Creating EstimateModel.out from Estimation.dat"
  @python EstimateModel.py

# Produce LaTexTable.tex from EstimateModel.out,
# first ensuring EstimateModel.out is up to date.
LaTeXTable.tex: EstimateModel.out
  @echo "Creating LaTeXTable.tex from EstimateModel.out"
  @python OutputLaTeXTable.py

# Obtain QueriedOutput.dat from the database.
QueriedOutput.dat:
  @echo "Creating QueriedOutput.dat"
  @python QuerySQLite.py

clean:
  @rm *dat *eps *out
```

Listing 8.13: Example Makefile

Let's see how this `Makefile` will work. First, imagine that nothing has been done, and the default name is used. Executing `make` will yield the following:

```
$ make
Creating QueriedOutput.dat
Creating Estimation.dat from QueriedOutput.dat
Creating Histogram.eps from Estimation.dat
Creating EstimateModel.out from Estimation.dat
Creating LaTeXTable.tex from EstimateModel.out
```

Now, if you deleted `EstimateModel.out`, executing `make` would yield

```
$ rm EstimateModel.out
$ make
Creating EstimateModel.out from Estimation.dat
Creating LaTeXTable.tex from EstimateModel.out
```

Note how `make` just does what is required to ensure that the file containing LaTeX table file `LaTeXTable.tex` is up-to-date.

Consider now another example where `Estimation.dat` has been deleted.

```
$ rm Estimation.dat
$ make
Creating Estimation.dat from QueriedOutput.dat
Creating Histogram.eps from Estimation.dat
Creating EstimateModel.out from Estimation.dat
Creating LaTeXTable.tex from EstimateModel.out
```

Here, the dependencies ensured that both the figure `Histogram.eps` and the table `LaTeXTable.tex` were remade once `Estimation.dat` was reconstructed. Suppose now that just `Histogram.eps` was deleted, so

```
$ rm Histogram.eps
$ make
Creating Histogram.eps from Estimation.dat
```

In this case, only the last step needed redoing.

You can, of course, introduce parameters into a `Makefile`, for example, from the UNIX operating system. To learn about the power of `make`, read the book *Managing Projects with GNU Make* by Mecklenburg (2005).

8.9   Git: Version Control

Except in trivial cases, developing computer code involves trial and error: the final code is the result of many iterations over an initial try. Having the ability to track significant code revisions and switch between versions can be extremely valuable. When you are working on a project with several collaborators, each of whom develops features in parallel independently, the importance of tracking and switching increases. In principle, a diligent and organized person could keep track of all code modifications he introduces, but as the number of collaborators increases, coordinating the efforts of other collaborators becomes impossible to track reliably. SDEs were forced to face these challenges long before other scientists, so version control systems (VCSs) were developed.

As mentioned in Chapter 2, we chose Git as the VCS for this book. In this section, we illustrate how to use Git with a simple project that has just two R scripts. The R scripts are trivial to follow, but if you are unfamiliar with R, we encourage you to study Chapter 5.

Before illustrating the specifics of Git, we describe briefly some alternative strategies to carry out version control. For example, the simplest VCS would involve the following: whenever a change is made to one of the files in the project, a time-stamped backup of all project files is created. Such a strategy guarantees that every revision will work, and it is quite easy to implement without any additional software. There are drawbacks to this strategy, however. First, you must be diligent and consistent in performing such backups. Second, with many files, storing several copies of the same unmodified files will quickly become wasteful, particularly if only a few files change from one revision to the next. Third, with many collaborators, the approach is infeasible.

Formal VCSs address all these challenges. Of course, users must still *check in* revised versions of files, but VCSs keep track of change dates and never accidentally overwrite existing data. Most VCSs store incremental differences in files rather than full copies, so in a project with thousands of revisions, none of which pertain to a particular file, that file will be stored as is. To coordinate among several collaborators, VCSs use objects referred to as *repositories* and *branches*.

As we mentioned in Chapter 2, several different implementations of VCSs exist. Historically, the most popular VCS was Subversion, abbreviated as SVN. Another example is Perforce, commonly referred to as P4. P4 and SVN are *centralized* VCSs. At any point in time, a single centralized server hosts the entire project repository; the complete history of all files concerning the project are maintained in that repository. A user can *checkout* certain files from the repository to his local machine, make any changes he wants, and then check in the revised versions to the repository. Today, most people think about version control in these terms.

Centralized VCSs have two disadvantages: First, the central repository is a single point of failure; if the main server should go down for any reason, then all work is interrupted. Second, it is typically tedious to create branches because you need to obtain physical copies of most files in the dependency tree.

An alternative to a centralized VCS is a *distributed* VCS. Today, the most popular VCS is Git. In Git the notion of a remote repository that can be accessed by several users exists; the work flow of collaborators, however, does not depend on the remote repository because every user maintains a replica of the entire repository on his local machine. Periodically, that local repository is synchronized with the remote server. Clearly, the one-time cost of cloning the remote repository can be large, but nearly all subsequent operations are done locally, quickly. If, for whatever reason, the remote server fails unexpectedly, then every collaborator maintains an entire project history on his local machine. Therefore, it is unlikely that the entire project will be lost forever.

Of course, this is a double-edged sword. Git is primarily designed to undertake version control of source code; unlike SVN, Git is not optimized to handle large binary objects. Another disadvantage of Git is that at first it may be somewhat intimidating to learn. Fortunately, only a relatively small subset of Git's commands need to be understood in order to use it for small projects that have only a few collaborators—the most common case in research. Overall, Git has become the standard VCS. Thus, even though Git is relatively new (that is, not mature), we chose to use it.

Consider `Functions.R` and `Main.R`, two R scripts:

```
#############################
###    Functions.R       ###
#############################

AddArguments <- function(x, y) {
  return(x + y)
} # end AddArguments
```

Listing 8.14: `Functions.R`

```
#############################
###    Main.R              ###
#############################

rm(list = ls())
source("Functions.R")

x <- 3
y <- 4
z <- AddArguments(x, y)
print(z)
```

Listing 8.15: `Main.R`

These files are self-explanatory. The file `Functions.R` contains the function `AddArguments()`, which returns the sum of two inputs; the file `Main.R` deletes everything, loads the function `AddArguments()`, calls the function, and prints the result. We assume both of these files live in the `GitExample` subdirectory. Figure 8.16 shows the evolution of the files through the stages of a *VCS*.

8.9.1   Theory

Git is really just a file system, a subdirectory with a VCS laid on top of it. Most VCSs track individual states of version-controlled files. Figure 8.17 depicts the evolution of files in Git through the stages of a VCS. Suppose that the two files `Main.R` and `Functions.R` are checked into another VCS as well as Git; refer to these versions as *Stage A*.

Next, suppose that `Main.R` is modified, but `Functions.R` remains intact. Check the new version of `Main.R` back into the main repository; refer to this as stage B.

Files	Stage A	Stage B	Stage C
Main.R	Main.R (A)	Main.R (B)	
Functions.R	Functions.R (A)		Functions.R (C)

Figure 8.16: Evolution of Files through Stages of a VCS

Files	Stage A	Stage B	Stage C
`Main.R`	`Main.R` (A)	`Main.R` (B)	`Main.R` (B)
`Functions.R`	`Functions.R` (A)	`Functions.R` (A)	`Functions.R` (C)

Figure 8.17: Evolution of Files in Git through Stages of a VCS

With most VCSs, this second check includes no information concerning `Functions.R` because it has not been touched. Suppose you check out `Functions.R`, modify it, and check in the updated version; refer to this as stage C. No data concerning `Main.R` will exist in stage C.

Git stores all information concerning both `Main.R` and `Functions.R` for every stage—A, B, or C. To be efficient, if the R script `Functions.R` did not change between the stages A and B, Git will just store a pointer, not an actual replica of the file. Effectively, Git stores snapshots of the entire set of files for a project with every write to a repository.

Although Git is quite sophisticated, only a few important objects are critical to understanding the program. Once these objects are understood, Git is easy to use effectively.

The first important object is the *remote repository*, which is the location on an Internet server where the canonical versions of all project files are stored. Every person working on a project must be able to connect to that server and, at the very least, read files from it. In the example in Section 8.9.2, we assume that all users have full access to the remote repository, even though for large-scale projects this is rarely practical. Collaborators use the remote repository to synchronize their versions of files with each other.

Second, whenever a user begins working on a project, he must create what is referred to as a *local repository*, typically by *cloning* the then-current remote repository to the local machine in its entirety. Nearly everything in Git involves the local repository, except for commands that synchronize the local repository with its remote counterpart. Each user must have his own local repository, which will typically be slightly out of sync with its counterparts on other users' machines.

Next comes an object referred to as the *working directory*, which is used to check out specific versions of files from the local repository. The working directory is monitored by Git for any changes to these files. Files can be checked out to an arbitrary directory, but then Git will not monitor changes to them. Almost all the work is done within the working directory or within its subdirectories.

In addition, an object called the *staging area* is used; the staging area is an intermediate virtual space to which you write files from the working directory *after* you have modifed them, but *before* you record the modified versions into the local repository as a new snapshot. To understand the staging area, it is helpful to understand the final act, which is referred to as the *commit*.

At this point, an analogy may be helpful. Consider a digital photograph: Staging a file is equivalent to taking a digital photograph of its state, whereas committing the changed file is akin to saving the photograph to an external disk—one not on the camera. The labels stage A, stage B, or stage C represent Git commits. Typically, it is much easier to modify staged files that have not yet been committed. Once a new commit is created, subsequent modifications are by default expected to be stored as the next commit. If by accident the latest version of a file in the working directory is deleted or overwritten, it is always possible to recover a committed file in Git; recovering staged but uncommitted files is much more difficult; recovering modified but unstaged files is impossible.

We now introduce some objects important to understanding Git's internal structure—the *possible states* of project files. Understanding these, together with the preceding objects, will allow you to understand around 80 percent of the important objects in Git.

In Git five possible states of project files exist, as illustrated in Figure 8.18.

First, the file can be *untracked*, which happens every time a new file is added to a project by putting it in the working directory. Git is aware of new untracked files but will not explicitly monitor them. Unless explicitly instructed to start tracking the file, Git will not process any changes made to this new file.

Second, a file can be *unmodified*, which is the default state every time a tracked file is checked out from the local repository. As the name suggests, an unmodified file is tracked by Git, but it has not been modified since the last commit, that is, since the last time the state was recorded in the local repository.

Third, a file can be *modified*, which means it is a tracked file that has been modified since the last commit. Git has not yet been told to record any changes,

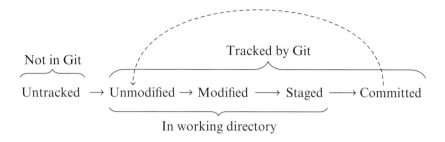

Figure 8.18: Five Stages of Files in Git

so any modifications are in limbo. Such modifications can be as minor as an extra space having been added or as major as the entire contents of the file having been deleted. Changes in the file state from unmodified to modified happen automatically, without your having to interact with Git, provided the action takes place in the working directory.

Fourth, a file can be *staged*. By staging a file, you instruct Git to record all changes that were made to the file since the last commit. This is a snapshot of the current state of the file that Git is told to remember, but such changes have not yet been commited. In short, they are unrecorded in the local repository.

New users of Git often become confused by the following. Suppose you have a tracked file, and a version of it has been committed. Imagine that you edit the file and stage it. You can modify it again, but at that point, the file exists in two states: staged and modified. Any changes to the file after it has last been staged will *not* automatically be known to Git. This is where the digital photograph analogy is useful. Once a photograph has been taken (that is, once a file has been staged), subsequent changes to the file will not be automatically reflected in the photograph (that is, the staged version). For this to occur, you need to stage these later changes again, in which case Git will record all changes into one stage, not two.

Fifth, a file can be *committed*. If you are satisfied with the modifications made to the file, then you can commit the changes, that is, record the modified version into the local repository. In general, only the staged files can be committed, although it is possible to stage all modified files and commit them with a single Git command. If a file is committed, then the latest commit will represent the current state of the file. When the file is now checked out, Git will provide the most recent commit of the file. Once checked out, the file becomes unmodified again. Of course, it is possible to check out any arbitrary commit, not just the latest one; we discuss this later.

8.9.2   Example

In order to understand the working example, especially if you have never used Git before, you first need to set up a few configuration parameters.

Basics

Thus, we introduce the following:

```
$ git config --global user.name "Konstantin Golyaev"
$ git config --global user.email "konstantin.golyaev@gmail.com"
$ git config --global core.editor emacs
```

The first two commands are necessary; otherwise Git will ask for your identity every time you attempt to commit anything. Git will use the requested information to identify everyone who iteracts with repositories. Strictly speaking, the third command is unnecessary; without it, Git will use the default text editor (which in UNIX is usually identified by the contents of the $EDITOR environmental variable).

Next, you have to create a directory where the version-controlled files will live:

```
$ mkdir ~/GitExample
$ cd ~/GitExample
$ git status
```

When using Git, the `git status` command is your friend: use it *frequently*.[6] The preceding invocation will produce the following output:

```
fatal: Not a git repository (or any of the parent directories): .git
```

---

[6]To speed up frequent use, create a shell alias using `alias gs="git status"`. You can also use internal Git commands to create aliases that are internal to Git only. For example, suppose you want to abbreviate the `git status` command to `git s`, then you can use the following: `git config --global alias.s status`.

Why? Git has not been instructed to track the contents of the subdirectory Gi-
tExample, so its status is undefined. You need to put the .R files into this
subdirectory, and instruct Git to track them:

```
$ git init
Initialized empty Git repository in ~/GitExample/.git/
$ git status
# On branch master
#
# Initial commit
#
# Untracked files:
#   (use "git add <file>..." to include in what will be committed)
#
# Functions.R
# Main.R
nothing added to commit but untracked files present (use "git add" to
    track)
```

The git init command instructs Git to create a local repository in the
/GitExample subdirectory. Another way to create a local repository is to use
the git clone command, which instructs Git to retrieve a full copy of a remote repository and to create a local counterpart. After that, the git status
command presents a very different output, which is typically what you would
see. Specifically, you are told that you are in the master branch of the local
repository, that no prior commits were created in this repository, and that you
have two untracked files: Functions.R and Main.R. Git is now aware of the
files you want it to track, but so far you have not explicitly told it to keep track
of them. To do this, use the git add command:

```
$ git add Functions.R Main.R
$ git status
# On branch master
# Changes to be committed:
#   (use "git reset HEAD <file>..." to unstage)
#
# new file:   Functions.R
# new file:   Main.R
#
```

Notice how the output of git status changed. You staged the first version
of your R scripts. You took the digital photograph of the contents of these files,

but you have not yet saved the photographs. To record the current state of files, use `git commit`:

```
$ git commit -m "First commit, both files added, initial version"
[master (root-commit) 21c4f20] First commit, both files added, initial
    version
 2 files changed, 20 insertions(+)
 create mode 100644 Functions.R
 create mode 100644 Main.R
$ git status
# On branch master
nothing to commit (working directory clean)
```

The −m flag passed to `git commit` supplies the commit description. Without this option, Git will start up the default editor and force you to provide a description, aborting the commit attempt otherwise. The `git status` invocation after committing files shows that all the files in your working directory are tracked but unmodified, that is, their contents matches exactly whatever is stored in the latest Git commit.

By now, you have seen files in four of the five states; the only one that remains is modified. Let's change the contents of both files and call `git status` again:

```
$ git status
# On branch master
# Changes not staged for commit:
#   (use "git add <file>..." to update what will be committed)
#   (use "git checkout -- <file>..." to discard changes in working
    directory)
#
# modified:    Functions.R
# modified:    Main.R
#
no changes added to commit (use "git add" and/or "git commit -a")
```

Both files are now modified, but the exact modifications are unknown to Git. Using `git add Main.R Functions.R`, you stage them:

```
$ git add Main.R Functions.R
$ git status
# On branch master
# Changes to be committed:
```

```
#      (use "git reset HEAD <file>..." to unstage)
#
# modified:     Functions.R
# modified:     Main.R
#
```

Now Git knows the exact differences that were made to each of the files, but you have not yet instructed Git to record them. You can see a file may be in several states by changing one of the R scripts again before committing any changes:

```
$ emacs Functions.R
$ git status
# On branch master
# Changes to be committed:
#   (use "git reset HEAD <file>..." to unstage)
#
# modified:     Functions.R
# modified:     Main.R
#
# Changes not staged for commit:
#   (use "git add <file>..." to update what will be committed)
#   (use "git checkout -- <file>..." to discard changes in working
    directory)
#
# modified:     Functions.R
#
```

The contents of Functions.R were changed since the last call to git add; Git warns you about this. Suppose you want to discard the latest, unstaged set of modifications to Functions.R. To do this, you must check out the previous version of that file from the local directory:

```
$ git checkout Functions.R
$ git status
# On branch master
# Changes to be committed:
#   (use "git reset HEAD <file>..." to unstage)
#
# modified:     Functions.R
# modified:     Main.R
#
```

The `git checkout` command overwrites the specified file in the working directory with the most recently committed version from the current branch. For completeness, consider unstaging the file:

```
$ git reset HEAD Main.R
Unstaged changes after reset:
M   Main.R
$ git status
# On branch master
# Changes to be committed:
#   (use "git reset HEAD <file>..." to unstage)
#
# modified:   Functions.R
#
# Changes not staged for commit:
#   (use "git add <file>..." to update what will be committed)
#   (use "git checkout -- <file>..." to discard changes in working
     directory)
#
# modified:   Main.R
#
```

The `git reset HEAD` command unstages the `Main.R` file. The `HEAD` part of the command is an internal Git term referring to the latest commit of the current branch. To conclude the example of Git basics, commit all changes, bypassing the staging step entirely:

```
$ git commit -a -m "Modified whitespace"
[master 7f9f428] Modified whitespace
 2 files changed, 2 deletions(-)
$ git status
# On branch master
nothing to commit (working directory clean)
$ git log --graph
* commit 7f9f42891cfe390b11cdd87c192a6b16473a6d40
| Author: Konstantin Golyaev <konstantin.golyaev@gmail.com>
| Date:   Sun Mar 16 11:51:51 2014 -0700
|
|     Modified whitespace
|
* commit 21c4f207a435d1f81c6ba0efd07bc69df2686b73
  Author: Konstantin Golyaev <konstantin.golyaev@gmail.com>
  Date:   Mon Mar 10 00:45:12 2014 -0700

      First commit, both files added, initial version
```

The `-a` flag passed to `git commit` instructs Git to stage all modified files and commit them. Subsequent invocation of `git status` shows that all files are now unmodified. You can also see the entire history of the local repository via the `git log --graph` command, which is currently quite simple since there is only one branch and two commits. You can alter the output of the `git log` command in many ways, but most are beyond the scope of this example.

You can instruct Git not to track certain files in the working directory, which can be useful for several reasons. First, most editors produce backup versions of files you edit; for example, `emacs` will create a file named `Main.R~` should you edit the `Main.R` file. Second, Git works best when you track plain text files, such as source code, rather than compiled binary files. For example, the source code of a LATEX document in `.tex` files should be tracked, but the final `.pdf` output should not be, unless you have a really good reason for doing this. For instance, you may want to keep drafts at particular dates, in which case you could use the suffix `.PDF` instead and employ a prefix that involves a self-describing date.

The easiest way to tell Git what not to track is to create a file named `.git-ignore` and place it into the root folder of the working directory, making Git track its contents. The `.gitignore` file can be used to specify patterns of files that you want Git to ignore. For example, the `*.*~` pattern will instruct Git to ignore any files that have a suffix that ends with a tilde, `~`. Another example is `*.pdf`—this will make Git ignore all `.pdf` files. Blank lines are ignored, the hash symbol `#` is a comment for `.gitignore`, and the exclamation mark `!` can be used to define exceptions for patterns. If, for some reason, you need to track versions of a particular `.pdf` file, then you could make Git do so by adding a line `!Exception.pdf` to `.gitignore`.

Branches

Thus far, the benefits of using Git may not be obvious, particularly if you rarely develop code collaboratively with others. The most powerful feature of Git is, however, its ability to create and to use branches.

A code branch is nothing more than a replica of the entire local repository. It is virtual in a sense that only pointers to unmodified files are stored rather than actual copies. Once a branch is created, however, you can modify some or all the files and store the changes in Git under this branch. In short, by committing the same file to different branches, you can maintain several concurrent versions. For example, consider a project that involves regression analysis; suppose the baseline model specification has been selected. You can create a new branch, modify the code that supplies model specification, save it under the new branch, and test the implications of such changes, all the while certain that your main results are preserved. Coupling this with the development practice of modularizing code into separate files, you can see how branching enables agile experimentation without the risk of breaking a current working implementation; that is, branching allows you to experiment, all the while protecting the current, working implementation.

To illustrate, suppose you are in the process of estimating a structural model in which a key latent (that is, unobservable) process is assumed to evolve according to a first-order autoregressive model, also known as AR(1). In a sufficiently complex model, it is possible to inadvertently organize one's code in such a way that a subsequent estimation step would implicitly rely on the latent process to be AR(1). Creating an experimental code branch would allow you to see how your result would change in case the latent process is instead parametrized as AR(2). In addition, it would help you isolate the parts of your code that may be assuming an AR(1) specification and fix them accordingly. At the same time, switching back to the main branch will preserve all the code that worked under the AR(1) latent model in case the AR(2) experiment proves to be unsuccessful.

Consider Main.R and Functions.R as currently implemented. Executing the former produces the following output:

```
$ Rscript Main.R
[1] 7
```

The Rscript command is a shorthand notation for executing R scripts in batch mode. We explained how to read raw R output in Chapter 5, but now you would just like to get rid of the [1]   part, which is internal to how R prints raw output. To do this, create a new branch in Git and switch to it:

```
$ git branch cat
$ git branch
  cat
* master
$ git checkout cat
Switched to branch 'cat'
$ git branch
* cat
  master
```

The first command creates the branch `cat`. The second command lists all branches and marks the current branch. The third command switches to the new branch, whereas the final command confirms that you are now in the new branch. Using the Git command `git checkout -b cat`, you could have accomplished all of this, but that would have been more difficult to follow.

We now modify `Main.R` by changing the following line:

```
print(z)
```

to

```
cat(z, fill = TRUE)
```

Saving the modified `Main.R` and executing it as before yields the following:

```
$ Rscript Main.R
7
```

Having made all the necessary changes and obtained desirable results, it is now time to save the modified code:

```
$ git status
# On branch cat
# Changes not staged for commit:
#   (use "git add <file>..." to update what will be committed)
#   (use "git checkout -- <file>..." to discard changes in working
     directory)
#
# modified:   Main.R
#
no changes added to commit (use "git add" and/or "git commit -a")
$ git commit -a -m "Replaced print() with cat()"
[cat 76ad98c] Replaced print() with cat()
 1 file changed, 1 insertion(+), 1 deletion(-)
```

We have added and committed the modifed code to the `cat` branch. The history of commits now becomes a bit complicated, so it is helpful to visualize it. Fortunately, you can do this using

```
$ git log --graph --decorate  --color --all --oneline
* 76ad98c (HEAD, cat) Replaced print() with cat()
* 7f9f428 (master) Modified whitespace
* 21c4f20 First commit, both files added, initial version
```

This command has several flags, so it is also instructive to go through the output carefully. You have already seen the output from `git log --graph` command, and the flags `--decorate` `--color` are for purely aesthetic purposes. The `--all` flag lists all branches, not just the current one, and the `--oneline` flag forces the output to be compact and fit on as few lines as possible. Next, go through the output, keeping in mind that the commits are listed with newest on top and oldest at the bottom. The alphanumeric gibberish `76ad98c` is the commit identifier (in fact, the hash key in a dictionary) and can be safely ignored, but the following is important: First, the `(HEAD, cat)` part means this is the currently checked-out of branch `cat` and this commit only exists on this branch. The second commit, `7f9f428`, is the latest commit on the `master` branch, which is the default main branch for all Git projects. The third commit has no branch designations and is thus identical for both existing branches, `master` and `cat`. This is the *root* of the tree with all code branches and commits, the starting point for all subsequent iterations over the code. Here is how this output would look were you to switch branches:

```
$ git checkout master
$ git log --graph --decorate  --color --all --oneline
* 76ad98c (cat) Replaced print() with cat()
* 7f9f428 (HEAD, master) Modified whitespace
* 21c4f20 First commit, both files added, initial version
```

The commit keys are all the same, but notice that the HEAD pointer has moved to the latest commit on the `master` branch. At this point, using the `git checkout` command will result in a different version of `Main.R` in the working directory, depending on the branch:

```
$ git branch
* cat
  master
$ cat Main.R
############################
###    Main.R           ###
############################

rm(list = ls())
source("Functions.R")

x <- 3
y <- 4
z <- AddArguments(x, y)
cat(z, fill = TRUE)
$ git checkout master
```

```
Switched to branch 'master'
$ cat Main.R
############################
###    Main.R            ###
############################

rm(list = ls())
source("Functions.R")

x <- 3
y <- 4
z <- AddArguments(x, y)
print(z)
```

For example, if you had committed an extra file to the `cat` branch, then it would automatically appear in the working directory every time that branch is checked out, and disappear once you switch to a new branch. This seamless transition between branches makes Git very powerful: it is difficult or even impossible to achieve using other means.

Merges

Although maintaining different branches of code is useful, you may also need to be able to *merge* several branches. For example, suppose you are satisfied with replacing `print()` by `cat()` and would like to abandon the former implementation entirely. With Git, that is easy to do using the following:

```
$ git checkout master
$ git merge cat
Updating 7f9f428..76ad98c
Fast-forward
 Main.R |    2 +-
 1 file changed, 1 insertion(+), 1 deletion(-)
$ cat Main.R
############################
###    Main.R            ###
############################

rm(list = ls())
source("Functions.R")

x <- 3
y <- 4
```

```
z <- AddArguments(x, y)
cat(z, fill = TRUE)
$ git log --graph --decorate  --color --all --oneline
* 76ad98c (HEAD, master, cat) Replaced print() with cat()
* 7f9f428 Modified whitespace
* 21c4f20 First commit, both files added, initial version
```

The `git merge` command replaces the contents of Main.R from the master branch with that stored in the cat branch. The two branches are now synchronized, which you can see clearly from the commit graph. This is an example of a *fast-forward merge*: Git understands that you have replaced one line of code with another and guessed correctly that you want to keep the latter version instead of the former. This is an easy and painless merge. Unfortunately, sometimes merges are more complicated, and you have to resolve merge conflicts.

Consider the following example, where we again make a change on the cat branch. Specifically, you replace the `fill = TRUE` in the last line with `fill = FALSE`, and commit. At the same time, you advance the master branch further via an even simpler edit: replacing `fill = TRUE` with `fill = T`. After committing this change, the commit history will look like this:

```
$ git log --graph --decorate  --color --all --oneline
* 06e88b5 (HEAD, master) abbreviated TRUE to T
| * 7a63c8b (cat) do not fill line in cat()
|/
* 76ad98c Replaced print() with cat()
* 7f9f428 Modified whitespace
* 21c4f20 First commit, both files added, initial version
```

The two branches have diverged, and attempts to merge them directly will fail because the same file has been edited twice. Git cannot decide which change to keep:

```
$ git merge cat
Auto-merging Main.R
CONFLICT (content): Merge conflict in Main.R
Automatic merge failed; fix conflicts and then commit the result.
```

Because situations like this arise somewhat frequently, tools have been created to handle them. By default, Git uses `vimdiff`, which is great if you are familiar with the `vim` text editor, but can be incredibly confusing otherwise.

For most users, a simpler alternative would be KDiff3, a program that works on any platform. To instruct Git to use it, type the following:

```
$ git config --global merge.tool kdiff3
$ git checkout master
```

Then the `git mergetool` command will start KDiff3 (see Figure 8.19).

You will see three versions of the `Main.R` file. KDiff3 was invoked while on the `master` branch, so KDiff3 will refer to its version as `Local`. In this case, the `cat` branch is being merged, so its version of `Main.R` will be called `Remote`. Finally, there is a version labeled `Base` on the very left, which is the latest version on which the `Local` and the `Remote` branches agreed. The merge

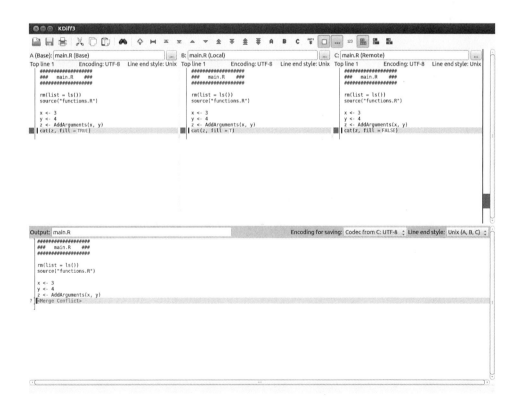

Figure 8.19: Illustration of KDiff3

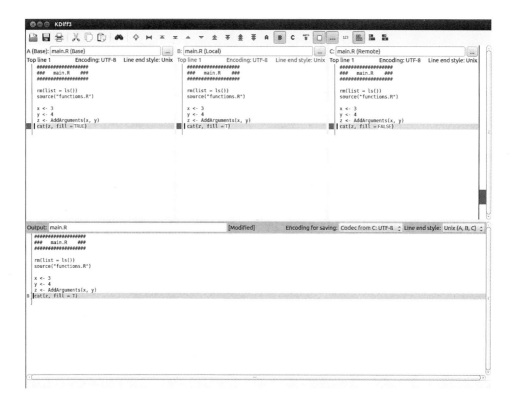

Figure 8.20: KDiff3 after Resolving a Merge Conflict

tool highlights the rows that differ across files, and is usually smart enough to handle minor differences in whitespace. At the bottom is the output file, which is what will be saved once you manually resolve the differences across files. The KDiff3 tool is quite powerful; it is impossible to cover all its features within this example. Suppose that you decided the Local implementation works best, and the Remote representation is not good enough. You can simply click on the B button in the upper toolbar to pick the Local implementation for the output (see Figure 8.20).

You then save the result and exit KDiff3. Now the only thing remaining is to commit changes made by KDiff3:

```
$ git commit -m "Resolved merge diff for 'fill = T'"
[master b0e9be1] Resolved merge diff for 'fill = T'
$ git log --graph --decorate  --color --all --oneline
```

```
*   b0e9be1 (HEAD, master) Resolved merge diff for 'fill = T'
|\
| *  7a63c8b (cat) do not fill line in cat()
* |  06e88b5 abbreviated TRUE to T
|/
*  76ad98c Replaced print() with cat()
*  7f9f428 Modified whitespace
*  21c4f20 First commit, both files added, initial version
```

The graph demonstrates that the `master` and `cat` branches have been merged successfully.

Until now, we only discussed dealing with a local Git repository. Although this covers over 90 percent of what a novice user needs to know in order to increase his productivity by using Git, for the sake of completeness, we briefly mention how to deal with remote repositories.

First, a remote repository must exist for you to interact with it. A remote Git repository is nothing more than a separate computer that has Git installed on it, and to which you can connect in order to read and write files. Two popular online platforms exist that provide exactly this kind of functionality to anyone free of charge: GitHub and Bitbucket. The former is arguably more popular but requires users to make contents of their repositories publicly available unless you are willing to get a paid account. The latter allows users to have private repositories but limits the number of users who can interact with them concurrently; for small research-oriented projects, this may well be an ideal solution.

Both GitHub and Bitbucket have excellent step-by-step guides to creating an account and starting a repository. Since the exact steps that must be taken can change over time, we direct you to those guides rather than attempting to recreate them here. Moreover, connecting to the repositories hosted by these websites will generally require you to create and use an *ssh identity*. An ssh identity is just a really long password that your computer uses to authenticate itself when connecting to a remote server such as Bitbucket. By creating the identity and uploading it to your Bitbucket account, you can then connect seamlessly whenever needed.

To keep the focus of this discussion on Git, we fast-forward to a point where a remote version of a repository exists and can be accessed. By default Git will refer to the remote repository as `origin`, particularly if you did not create the local repository from scratch but instead used `git clone` to obtain it. To verify the setup, use the `git remote -v` command.

Suppose that you work jointly with colleagues who notify you that they have developed a newer version of code and have pushed it to the remote repository that all of you employ to stay in sync. Your local repository and the remote repository are now out of sync, and you want to rectify this. First, you use the `git fetch` command to download the latest commits from the remote repository. Fetching the latest remote code does not synchronize it with the local counterpart, so the next step is to do the `git merge` command and resolve all the conflicts that may have arisen as the result of remote changes. Once the merge is complete, your local repository is synchronized with its remote counterpart. The "fetch and merge" sequence is so commonly used that a built-in shorthand command exists in Git to accomplish these two actions: `git pull`.

Finally, suppose you have developed an updated version of the code and would like to make it available to your colleagues. Assuming that your local repository is in sync with the remote one—something that you should be now be able to ensure—the command `git push` will upload the latest commits from your local repository to the remote one. Git is smart enough to refuse the push if somebody has advanced ahead the remote repository and made it out of sync with your local one. You could pass many options to the `fetch`, `pull`, and `push` commands that would instruct Git in detail what exactly to fetch, to pull, or to merge; at this point, however, you are better off exploring a book on Git.

In this brief example, we have not covered many other things that can be done using Git, specifically, erasing commits from history and amending the latest commit, rebasing branches instead of merging them, stashing intermediate work or pull and push requests from and to multiple remote repositories. The material we presented should, however, provide you with enough informaton to use Git effectively in your research. Swicegood (2010) has written an easy-to-read and complete guide to Git. Another excellent book on Git is the one by Chacon (2009).

9

Extensions to Python

HOWEVER POWERFUL THE Python language may be, its Achilles' heel is cycle time. Cycle time refers to the amount of time required to complete one cycle of an operation, that is, to complete a function, job, or task from start to finish. Run time, on the other hand, refers to the total elapsed time it takes for a computer program to return an answer. Cycle time is a commonly used metric to evaluate productivity because the total duration of a process is much more informative and representative of resource use than the run time; the latter can be affected by the number and type of tasks running on the computer at the time a program was executed.

Aruoba and Fernández-Villaverde (2014) solved the stochastic neoclassical growth model (the workhorse of modern macroeconomics) using the method of dynamic programming, implementing their algorithm (value function iteration with grid search) in the programming languages C++, FORTRAN, Java, Julia, MATLAB, Mathematica, Python, and R. In other words, they coded the same algorithm in each of the languages and reported cycle times for the Apple Mac with OS X and a Microsoft Windows-based computer. We converted that metric to *relative cycle time*.

Suppose the C++ executable image created using the Intel C++ compiler takes 100 seconds of cycle time to complete a task; that would be defined as relative cycle time of 1.00. In their test cases, the GNU C++ executable had a relative cycle time of 0.73; in other words, it took 73 seconds to solve the same problem using the same algorithm. Table 9.1 presents relative cycle times calculated for several programming languages on the Apple Mac OS X operating system.[1] It is evident, at least in terms of cycle time, there is a high cost to using Python or R. A task that would take about 18 hours to complete in FORTRAN could take almost nine months to complete in Python and almost two years in R. Of course, the trade-off is the reduction in developer time when writing Python or R scripts.

Language	Time
GNU C++	0.73
FORTRAN	0.75
MATLAB	7.91
Python	195.87
R	517.53

Table 9.1: Estimates of Relative Cycle Time Apple Mac OS X

Aruoba and Fernández-Villaverde (2014) demonstrated that if parts of the Python script were optimized or the R script was compiled, improvements could occur. For example, when they used the numba package for Python, the relative cycle time fell to 1.18; compiling the R code halved the relative cycle time.[2] In short, even though using either Python or R right out of the box is convenient, for computationally intensive projects you will need to find alternatives.

For R, two packages have been developed to improve the performance of scripts: {compiler}, which creates *just-in-time* (JIT) byte code, and {jit}, which provides just-in-time compilation of R loops and arithmetic expressions in loops.[3] Although both packages are reported to make code between two and twenty times faster, neither achieves the efficiencies that the package numba does in Python. In short, at present, optimizing R scripts does not appear to be a productive use of time.

In Python bottlenecks can arise when a part of a script that is not well written is executed many times. Because Python code is not optimized, such

---

[1]Our table is drawn from Table 1 of Aruoba and Fernández-Villaverde (2014). Although they did not use the programming language C, they conjectured that the relative cycle times would be comparable to C++.

[2]By the way (for the MATLAB aficionados among you) mexing the MATLAB code resulted in a relative cycle time of 1.19.

[3]JIT takes bytecode and creates instructions understood by the computer on the fly.

bottlenecks are often difficult to circumvent: rewriting native Python will not solve the problem. Poor performance of Python scripts arises when `for` or `while` loops that evaluate each element of a `numpy` array are used. For example, the following `for` loop

```
for n in range(1, N}:
  v[n] = Value(n)
```

could be extremely slow in Python, depending on how large N is, and what is being executed within the function `Value`. The degradation introduced by nested loops is worse, often much worse. The order analysis of Chapter 6 shows why: one loop of length N uses $\mathcal{O}(N)$ resources, but two nested loops (each of length N) use $\mathcal{O}(N^2)$ resources; three nested loops would use $\mathcal{O}(N^3)$ resources, and so forth.

One strategy to reduce cycle time is to eliminate the bottleneck by importing compiled computer code written in programming languages like C or FORTRAN. Compiled code typically runs much faster than interpreted code. Compiled code from certain languages can be integrated or imported into a Python script in a straightforward way. The imported code is typically referred to as an *extension*, which is why we prefer the word *suffix* when referring to the last three letters of a filename.

For example, Python can be extended using code written in C; the extension is nothing more than a normal C library. On UNIX-based machines, these libraries usually end in the suffix `.so`, an abbreviation for "shared object." On Windows-based machines, the suffix is `.dll`, an abbreviation for "dynamic link library." Python can be extended using code written in FORTRAN, too.

Thus, after discussing the profiling of Python scripts in the next section (to determine where bottlenecks exist), we look at the elements of the C and FORTRAN programming languages in the following four sections and provide examples of how to create simple extensions to Python in these programming languages. Our examples are simple; they are intended to provide some notion of the complexity of this work. In the final section of the chapter, we discuss using the Python package `numba`, which is at once easy and difficult to use. On the one hand, `numba` only requires annotating native Python code appropriately; on the other hand, `numba` requires installing the LLVM (low level virtual machine) compiler infrastructure, which some may find difficult to do.

The main question still remains. How do you know whether extensions are worth the effort? Although you can always determine how long a particular program (for example, one named `MyProgram`) takes to execute by using the UNIX `time` command, as in

```
$ time MyProgram
```

that approach gives very little information concerning what bottlenecks may exist in the internal running of the code. The only way to determine whether extensions will improve cycle time is to profile the Python code. Profiling reveals which functions in a script sojourn the most and the longest. Based on this information, you can then decide whether to introduce extensions. Which programming language to use is a separate question. The "wrong" choice may enrage some people; among people who compute, strong opinions are common.

9.1   Profiling Python Code

Profiling is a tricky business. Simply running the profiling program can change the way in which a piece of software performs because the profiler itself occupies memory and uses time. That said, Python has two profiling tools, `profile` and `cProfile`. The module `profile` is written solely in Python, whereas the module `cProfile` is written mostly in C. The interface of each is virtually the same as the other in that both `profile` and `cProfile` export the same data, which can be accessed by the module `pstat`. Because `cProfile` is written in C, it is faster and also uses less overhead than `profile`. In general, either of these tools provides an estimate of the total time used, but they also produce separate estimates of the time each function uses; neither tool, however, bores down to the level of an instruction. In any case, both tools can tell how many times each function was called, making it easy to determine (at a high level) where an extension could help.

Either `profile` or `cProfile` can be invoked from inside the Python interpreter, from within the code, or on the command line. For example, on the command line, for a program named `MyCode.py`, you would type `python -m cProfile MyCode.py`. You could also create a shell script, perhaps named `profile`, that has the following structure:

```
python -m cProfile %1
```

Put this in a pathed subdirectory, and then type the following:

```
$ profile MyCode.py
```

Note, however, that by default cProfile only works on the main thread: you will get no information concerning other threads. What is a thread? A *thread* is a task, for example, a function call. Typically, a thread is used when the execution of a task involves some waiting. If a CPU is being used fully, then threading will not provide any improvements: you will need to use other processors, if you have them, and compute in parallel.

Although we believe that both distributed and parallel computing will be very important in the future, because the technology involved in this sort of computing is changing rapidly, we only mention these topics in passing. For the time being, you probably do not need to be concerned about the fact that profile and cProfile only work on the main thread.

9.2 C Programming Language

Initially developed by Dennis M. Ritchie at AT&T Bell Labs around 1972, C is a general-purpose programming language, often referred to as a *low-level imperative programming language* because even the most basic of operations, which are part of the Python language, need to be programmed separately in C.[4] This is actually not as bad as it sounds. Because C is a mature language, chances are that someone has already created the code for any task that you might need to accomplish. In short, C is supported by a rich set of libraries. Because C is available for many different computer architectures and operating systems (specifically, Linux, OS X, and Windows), the language has been and is still widely used. In fact, most of the numerical parts of Python are derived from code written in C, for example, the functions in the numpy package. Thus, knowing how to incorporate C code into Python can be a useful skill. To get anywhere in such an endeavor, however, you must know at least the grammar of C.

The classic book by Kernighan and Ritchie (1988), *The C Programming Language*, is the C bible for many SDEs. We base a good portion of our introduction to C grammar on this book. Be careful to read the 1988 version, the ANSI C version. Since that book was written, many others at many different levels have appeared.

---

[4]Perhaps not surprisingly, C is also tied closely to the UNIX operating system. For example, the original UNIX operating system was written in C.

9.2.1 Basic Grammar

Like Python, C has a small vocabulary. In fact, the C vocabulary is even smaller than that of Python. However, C has none of the pleasant features of Python. For example, basic C does not even allow you to print your results to a terminal window; you need to include that function from a library when the program is compiled. To inform the compiler of that function's calling conventions, you must include a *header* directive. Header files have the .h suffix. If the header files are part of the installation, then they typically live between the < and > characters, which act as quotation marks of sorts; user-created header files live between double quotes when included. Including headers in C is, however, no more complicated than importing modules and packages in Python.

Hello World!

Without question, the best-known piece of code in C is the "Hello World!" program. Although the program is no more than six lines, it is what people remember most about their first encounter with C. In memory of Ritchie, in Chapter 4 we began our description of Python using a similar script. Here is an example of the C counterpart:

```
1 # include <stdio.h>
2
3 main()
4 {
5   printf("Hello World!\n");
6 }
```

Listing 9.1: `HelloWorld.c` Program

Line 5 prints the sentence "Hello World!", but the structure of this simple program is important to note. In line 1, the compiler is informed of the calling conventions for a library of functions that support input and output, hence the header directive `# include <stdio.h>`.

Because C is remarkably austere, functions must typically be included from various libraries, which will require informing the C compiler that you are using a particular library by citing the appropriate `# include` directive for that library. Because libraries are linked in the last step, the header files tell the compiler what the functions in the libraries look like. By and large C is not that different from Python.

Like Python, C has a particular syntax to define logical structure. In Python this is achieved using indentation; in C the same is achieved using the opening and closing braces { and }. In C the end of a typical instruction is signified by the semicolon ; but obvious exceptions exist. We note explicitly when an instruction does not end in a semicolon. For example, after the main program is defined using `main()`, no semicolon is included. The logical beginning of the main program is determined by the open brace { in line 4; its logical end is determined by the closing brace } in line 6.

Because commands in a program are separated by the semicolon, there could in principle be one long string within the braces. For example,

```
1  # include <stdio.h>
2  main() {printf("Hello World!\n");}
```

Note, too, there is no indentation in the second example. In C indentation is a matter of style, not logic. This extends to blank lines as well; in line 2 of the first example program, the blank line is simply for style, to introduce some whitespace between the `# include` directive, and the remainder of the program. To be clear, the line with the `# include` directive and the line with `main` ... cannot appear on the same line. Whether instructions appear on separate lines or not is a matter of style, but clearly the first program is much easier to read and understand than the second one, so we counsel you to use indentation and blank lines liberally to improve the exposition of your code.

In line 5 of the first example program, the function `printf()` lives in the standard C library devoted to input and output; the header `stdio.h` directive informs the compiler of the calling conventions for the functions in the corresponding library.

Other functions have relations like this as well. For example, the function `strcpy()` (which copies a string into a variable) lives in a library whose header directive is `# include <string.h>`, and the exponential function `exp()` lives in a library whose header directive is `# include <math.h>`.

Running a C program is a bit more involved than running a Python script. A C program must first be compiled. In addition, if the compiled code depends on other compiled codes (sometimes referred to as *object modules*), then it must be linked; only then can it be executed. Because several steps can exist, which can have dependencies, the `make` tool described on page 46 of Chapter 2, for which an example was provided in Section 8.8 is well-suited to developing C code.

For the "Hello World!" program, the following steps are required:

```
1  $ gcc HelloWorld.c
2  $ ./a.out
3  Hello World!
4  $
```

The first line in the terminal window invokes the C compiler, in this case the GNU C compiler, where the input is the file `HelloWorld.c`. Even though this program depends on the `printf()` function in the library having the header directive `# include <stdio.h>`, you do not need to inform the compiler because this particular library is so commonly used that the default behavior is to link it always. This is true for functions in the library having the header directive `# include <stdlib>` as well. In general, however, when using functions from libraries, inform the compiler which libraries to link by using appropriate flags. Also, by default, the compiler creates the executable image `a.out`, which can be executed as in line 2. The resulting output appears in the next line of the terminal window. Recall that the notation `./` tells the operating system that `a.out` lives in the current working directory (see Section 2.3.10.)

In this example, you could also have directed the output of `gcc` to a specific file, such as `HelloWorld`, using the flag `-o`, an abbreviation of "output file." Then `./HelloWorld` could be executed. For example,

```
1  $ gcc HelloWorld.c -o HelloWorld
2  $ ./HelloWorld
3  Hello World!
4  $
```

Variable Types

Like Python, C supports the three most common variable types, that is, character, integer, and floating point; to get access to Boolean variables, use the header directive `# include <stdbool.h>`. Unlike in Python, however, a variable's type must be defined formally when it is introduced. For example,

```
/* This is a comment card, which can span lines.
   It always begins with forward slash asterisk.
   It always ends with asterisk forward slash.   */
char  letter;
int   i, j;
float celsius;
```

In C the number of bits used by a variable can be specified. For example,

```
short int i;           /* At least 16 bits in size.         */
unsigned short int j;  /* Can hold a larger value since no
                          negative values are admitted.     */
long int k;            /* At least 32 bits in size.         */
signed long int m;     /* Pedantic way of declaring long m. */
double millimetres;    /* Double-precision float, 64 bits.  */
long double revenues;  /* Double-precision, with 80 bits.   */
char filename[10];     /* Strings are arrays of characters. */
double y[20]           /* This is a double precision array, */
                       /* having length 20.                 */
int counts[20][4]      /* This is a two-dimensional array
                          of integers which is 20x4.        */
```

Note that vectors and matrices are another data type to be included. One alternative might be to include the header directives for the GNU Scientific Library, but since you will probably be concerned with creating extensions to Python, the header directives related to the data types in numpy are probably the best place to start. As in Python, C arrays begin with index [0] and go to the array length minus 1, for example, y[19] is the last element of the array of length 20.

In C access to the Boolean data type requires using the following header directives:

```
# include <stdio.h>
# include <stdbool.h>

int main()
{
  bool state = true;
  printf("The state is %d.\n", state);
}
```

What does the word int before the main() do? It provides the compiler with the data type of main(). What about the pair of parentheses after main? Usually, a function (and the main program is just a function) takes input(s) and returns output(s). By convention, the code would look like the following:

```
# include <stdio.h>
# include <stdbool.h>

int main (int argc, char *argv[])
{
  bool state = true;
```

```
  printf("The state is %d.\n", state);
}
```

where `argc` is the argument count from the command line and `argv` is an array of pointers to strings corresponding to the command line invocation of the compiled code. Thus, if the program were invoked as

```
$ a.out 1 2
```

then `argc = 3` where `argv[0] = "a.out"`, `argv[1] = "1"`, and `argv[2] = "2"`. In the beginning, most people do not include arguments in the definition of `main`; hence `int main()` is what you see most frequently.

When a function takes no arguments, the `void` data type can appear as the sole argument, to ensure that the reader and the compiler know exactly what is intended. When a function is defined without arguments, the compiler will not check whether the function is really called with no arguments; instead, a function call with arbitrary number of arguments is permitted. When used as a function return type, `void` means that the function does not return a value. For example,

```
# include <stdio.h>
# include <string.h>

void Gday(char *name);

int main()
{
  char name[5];
  strcpy(name, "Harry");
  Gday(name);
}

void Gday(char *name)
{
  printf("G\'day %s!\n", name);
}
```

To be clear, an argument is passed, the function is called, a line is printed from within the function, but nothing is returned.

Variable Assignment

In C values can be assigned to variables on declaration or later in the code, for example,

```
int main()
{
  int j = 1;
  float x;
  x = 1.;
}
```

Constants and Macros

In C the keyword `const` declares a variable to be a constant that does not change during the execution of the program. For example,

```
const int number = 123;
```

The value of `number` cannot be modified. If you try to change its value later in the code, the compiler will issue a warning or an error, depending on the compiler's settings.

Variables can also be set to be constants that cannot be changed during the execution of the program using the preprocessing header directive `#define`. Note that the `#define` directive does not end in a semicolon. In addition, only one token (the name of the constant) can be defined on each line. For example,

```
# define N 3
# define PI 3.141592654

int main()
{
  double x[N];
  x[0] = 1.;
  x[1] = 2.;
  x[2] = 3.;
  printf("Pi is %.9f", PI)
}
```

Where the `const` variable declaration declares an actual variable, which you can use like a variable (for example, take its address, pass the value around, use the value, convert it, and so forth), the `#define` directive replaces the macro by the contents of its body before the C compiler even sees the code. In short, the # define directive effectively searches and replaces that term in the source code. Is there a difference in performance between the const variable declaration and the # define directive? Probably not. An optimizing compiler will be able to make changes so that the differences are minimal.

define directives are sometimes referred to as *object-like* macros, in contrast to *function-like* macros. A function-like macro is a fragment of code that has been given a name. Whenever the name is invoked, that name is replaced by the contents of the macro. For example,

```
# include <stdio.h>
# define SUM(a, b)  (a + b)

int main()
{
  int a, b;
  a = 3;
  b = 4;
  printf("a + b = %d\n", SUM(a, b));
}
```

Defining Other Variable Types

Although C is relatively poor in terms of native data types, at least when compared to Python, enum permits you to define your own variable types, sort of. For example, suppose you wanted to define a logical variable type, like the Boolean but without including stdbool.h. You could use the # define directive to create the following:

```
# define FALSE   0
# define TRUE    1
```

For small sets, alternatives like this could work, but a better solution is needed. Fortunately, in C, the enum instruction provides such an alternative. For example, suppose the following lines of code were entered into the file Logical.c:

```
# include <stdio.h>

enum logical
{
  FALSE,
```

```
   TRUE
};

int main()
{
  enum logical state;
  state = TRUE;
  printf("This is a logical data type %d.\n", state);
}
```

When this code is compiled and executed, the following appears in the terminal window:

```
$ gcc Logical.c
$ ./a.out
This is a logical data type 1.
$
```

The `enum` statement always creates data types that start at zero and increments by 1, but you may want another convention. For example,

```
# include <stdio.h>

enum sign
{
  NEG   = -1,
  ZERO =   0,
  POS   =  1,
};

int main()
{
  enum sign state;
  state = NEG;
  printf("This is a sign data type %d.\n", state);
}
```

Collecting Variables

Often, variables are related to one another: where one is needed, the others will likely be needed as well. The `struct` command groups variables into a single record for ease of use later, basically defining another data type. Consider the following, where the `typedef` command in conjunction with the `struct` command creates the `information` structure that is referred to as the `cus-` `tomer` data type.

```
# include <stdio.h>
# include <string.h>

typedef struct information
{
  char firstName[25],
  char lastName[25],
  char address[25],
  char city[25],
  char state[2],
  int  zip
} customer;


int main()
{
  customer newone;
  strcpy(newone.firstName, "Jeff");
  /* And so forth. */
  newone.zip = 98105;
  printf("First Name: %s\n", newone.firstName);
  /* And so forth. */
  printf("Zip Code:   %d\n", newone.zip);
}
```

Notice that in order to assign the string `"Jeff"` to this new data type in lo-cation `newone.firstName`, the function `strcpy` from the header `string.h` was required, whereas the zip code could be assigned directly to `newone.zip`. Compiling and executing the above code gives the following output:

```
$ ./a.out
First Name: Jeff
Zip Code:   98105
$
```

Determining Space

Determining the amount of space that variables take as well as multiples of variables is important in C because memory must be allocated explicitly, something Python does automatically. For this purpose, the `sizeof` command is invaluable. For example,

```
# include <stdio.h>
# include <string.h>

int main()
{
  char letter;
  char name[5];
  int  number;

  number = 1234567890;
  printf("%zu\n", sizeof(number));
  letter = 'A';
  printf("%zu\n", sizeof(letter));
  strcpy(name, "Harry");
  printf("%zu\n", sizeof(name));
}
```

The output of this program would be the following:

```
$ ./a.out
4
1
5
```

which is the size of each variable in bytes.

As you can see in the `printf` instruction, format statements in C are richer than those in Python, mostly because C has a richer set of variable sizes. In this case, the form `%zu` is used because the format structures across 32-bit and 64-bit machines can vary; the `z` format avoids this problem.

Some useful formats include the following:

$%$`.nd` = integer (optional n = number of columns; if 0, pad with zeros)

$%$`m.nf` = float or double (optional m = number of columns, n = number of decimal places)

$%$`ns` = string (optional n = number of columns)

$%$`c` = character

Many of these are similar to those in Python, for example, \n introduces a new line, whereas \t introduces a tab.

for Loops

for loops in C bear some resemblance to their counterparts in Python. For example,

```
# include <stdio.h>
# define N 10

int main()
{
  int n;
  for(n=0; n<N; n++)
  {
   printf("%i\n", n);
  }
}
```

In this code, the counter n is set to zero, it is incremented by 1 each time through the loop (hence the n++), with this continuing until n gets to N, at which point control passes out of the for loop.

while Loops

Conditional iteration in C is completed in much the same way as in Python. For example,

```
# include <stdio.h>
# define MAXIT 5

int main()
{
  int iterNo = 1;
  while(iterNo<=MAXIT)
  {
      printf("Iteration number = %i\n", iterNo);
      iterNo++;
  }
}
```

In this code, the counter iterNo is set to one; it is incremented by 1 each time through the loop (hence the iterNo++), with this continuing until iterNo exceeds MAXIT, at which point control passes out of the while loop.

Conditional Control

Conditional control in C is executed in much the same way as in Python, except that no `elif` exists, but this is not a limitation because `if` can be embedded inside of `else`. For example, whereas in Python the code would be

```
if (x < 0.):
  x = x*x
  print 'x = %.4f\n' % x
elif (x == 0.):
  print 'x is zero.\n'
elif (x > 0.):
  x = x / 2.
  print 'x = %.4f\n' % x
else:
  print 'This should not occur!\n'
```

in C an `if/else` chain would accomplish the same thing:

```
if (x < 0.) {
  x = x*x;
  printf("x is %.4f.\n", x);
} else if (x == 0.) {
  printf("x is zero.\n");
} else if (x > 0.) {
  x = x / 2.;
  printf("x is %.4f.\n", x);
}
else {
  printf("This should not occur!");
}
```

Thus, you could write the following C code:

```
# include <stdio.h>
# define FEE 3.50
# define PENALTY 10.0

int main()
{
  float balance, deposit;
  balance  = 0.;
  deposit  = -10.;
  if(deposit >= 0.)
  {
```

```
    balance = balance + deposit;
  }
  else
  {
    balance = balance + deposit - FEE;
    if (balance < 0.)
    {
      printf("Account overdrawn.\n");
      balance = balance - PENALTY;
    }
  }
}
```

In this code, the sign of a variable `deposit` is checked. If the deposit is zero or greater, the `balance` is updated; if the deposit is negative (thus a withdrawal), the `balance` is updated and a fee is charged. If the resulting balance is negative, then a message is surfaced, and a penalty is assigned.

Branch Control

`switch` and `case` commands control complex conditional and branching operations. The `switch` command transfers control to an instruction within its body, depending on the value. For example,

```
# include <stdio.h>

int main()
{
  char letterGrade;
  letterGrade = 'D';

  switch(letterGrade)
  {
    case 'A':
      printf("Excellent!\n");
      break;
    case 'B':
      printf("Good.\n");
      break;
    case 'C':
      printf("Fair.\n");
      break;
    case 'F':
```

```
        printf("Fail.\n");
        break;
    default:
        printf("Invalid letter grade.\n");
        break;
  }
  printf("Student grade is:  %c\n", letterGrade);

  return 0;
}
```

In this case, the `letterGrade` of D would be considered an invalid grade.

Getting out of Places

The `break` command can only appear in the body of a loop or a switch. As in Python, the command terminates execution of the current enclosing switch or loop body. For example,

```
# include <stdio.h>

int main()
{
  int iteration;
  for(iteration=1; iteration <= 50 ; iteration++)
  {
    printf("%i\n", iteration);
    if( (iteration % 10) == 0)
      break;
  }
}
```

This was also used in the program implementing `switch`. Without the `break` instruction, in each `case`, the terminal window would display

```
Excellent!
Good.
Fair.
Fail.
Invalid letter grade.
```

every time the program went through the `switch`. Check it out.

Skipping Code

The `continue` statement can only appear in a loop body. It causes the rest of the statement body in the loop to be skipped. For example,

```
# include <stdio.h>

int main()
{
  int value;
  for(value=0; value<5; value++)
  {
    if(value==2)
    {
      continue;
    }
    else
    {
      printf("Value = %i.\n", value);
    }
  }
}
```

Input/Output

The command `printf` directs output to the terminal window. In C reading information from a file (or writing output to a file) is only slightly more complicated than in Python. First, you must define the file; second, you must open it; and third, after having read from or written to the file, you must close it. In the following program, we do all of this:

```
1  # include <stdio.h>
2
3  int main(void)
4  {
5    FILE *inFile, *outFile;
6    inFile  = fopen("UserID.dat", "r");
7    outFile = fopen("Usage.out", "w");
8    char    userID[10];
9    int     days;
10   float   usage;
11
12   if (inFile == NULL)
```

```
13  {
14     fprintf(stderr, "Cannot find input file.\n");
15     return -1;
16  }
17  if (outFile == NULL)
18  {
19     fprintf(stderr, "Cannot open output file.\n");
20     return -1;
21  }
22  while (fscanf(inFile, "%s %f %d", userID, &usage, &days) != EOF)
23  {
24     fprintf(outFile, "%10s %6.2f %3i\n", userID, usage/60., days);
25  }
26  return 1;
27 }
```

Listing 9.2: C Program to Read and Write

After line 1, where we include the necessary header, the next interesting line is 5, where pointers (signified by asterisks) to the files *inFile and *outFile are defined to type FILE. In line 6 the file UserID.dat is opened and assigned to the variable inFile with "r" (read-only) status, and in line 7 the file Usage.out is opened and assigned to the variable outFile with "w" (write-only) status. Three variables are defined in lines 8, 9, and 10, one a character of length up to ten characters for userID, another an integer for days, and the third a floating-point variable for usage.

Lines 12–16 are included to demonstrate how to deal with the case where the input file is nonexistent, using conditional control; lines 17–21 are included to demonstrate how to deal with the case where the output file is nonexistent. When the file is nonexistent (hence the constant NULL), an error is printed to stderr, and the integer −1 is returned, which is the standard return code. (Recall from Chapter 2 that stdin, stdout, and stderr are special files in UNIX, namely, standard input, standard output, and standard error.) This is also why the main function has type int.

In line 22 the program reads from the input file until the end-of-file; EOF is a special variable in C. Notice the ampersands, &; these are included to signal that spaces exist between the character variable userID and the floating-point variable usage as well as between usage and the integer variable days. Line 24 is included to demonstrate that some work would be done in this block of code, in this case, the input data are manipulated by scaling them by 60 (for

acos()	asin()	atan()	atan2()
ceil()	cos()	cosh()	exp()
fabs()	floor()	fmod()	frexp()
ldexp()	log()	log10()	modf()
pow()	sin()	sinh()	sqrt()
	tan()	tanh()	

Table 9.2: Functions of #include <math.h>

example, the number of seconds in a minute or the number of minutes in an hour) and then output to outFile. Finally, in line 26, on successful completion the integer 1 is returned.

Mathematical Functions

The header directive # include <math.h> is required in order to use the functions necessary in scientific computing; their names are listed in Table 9.2. What they do is documented in Table 4.1.

Compiling the C source code for these functions can be somewhat tricky, depending on the platform—OS X or Linux. To be on the safe side, always include a particular flag when invoking the gcc compiler.

Here, we list the C code

```
# include <stdio.h>
# include <math.h>

int main()
{
  double input, inter, output;
  inter = 1.;
  input = exp(inter);
  output = log(input);
  printf("log(%f) = %f\n", input, output);
}
```

Listing 9.3: Using the Math Functions

To compile this code, use the following command:

```
$ gcc MathFunctions.c -lm
$ ./a.out
```

```
log(2.718282) = 1.000000
$
```

Here, the flag -lm ensures that the math libraries are loaded. No flags were used with the Hello.c file because stdio.h (and stdlib.h) loaded by default.

Functions

Defining functions within C is straightforward, but using them requires understanding how to sequence the code. Consider a function Celsius that converts float fahr, temperature in Fahrenheit, into another float, temperature in Celsius. The definition of the function would have the following structure:

```
float Celsius(float fahr)
{
    return 5. * (fahr - 32.) / 9.;
}
```

but how the function is used is different from, say, in Python. Here is a working example of the sequence of code:

```
1  # include <stdio.h>
2  float Celsius(float);
3
4  main(void)
5  {
6      float fahr;
7      fahr = 12.34;
8      printf("%6.2f Fahrenheit is %6.2f Celsius.\n", fahr, Celsius(fahr));
9  }
10
11 float Celsius(float fahr)
12 {
13     return 5. * (fahr - 32.) / 9.;
14 }
```

Listing 9.4: Using a Function in C

In line 2 the external function Celsius is defined: the type(s) of the input(s) are listed, and the type of output is defined. In this case, both are float.

Alternatively, you could include the file Celsius.h, which has the following line,

```
float Celsius(float fahr);
```

using the following directive instead of line 2:

```
# include "Celsius.h"
```

provided that `Celsius.h` lives in the same working directory as the file to be compiled. If not, then explicit pathing will be necessary.

Lines 4–9 define the main program, and lines 11–14 define the function `Celsius`.

Storage Classes

In C variables can be stored for different lifetimes and in different places. Four storage classes exist: `auto`, `static`, `register`, and `extern`.

The most common storage class is `auto`. Because `auto` is the default storage class for local variables, it is unnecessary to specify it, which is why this declaration is not seen often.

Local variables disappear once a function is left, but in some cases permanence is needed. Thus, `static` permits variables to live during the entire lifetime of the program, everywhere. A `static` variable inside a function keeps its value between invocations, and it can only be changed within the function. For example,

```
 1  # include <stdio.h>
 2
 3  Increment(void);
 4
 5  int main()
 6  {
 7     Increment();
 8     Increment();
 9     Increment();
10  }
11
12  Increment(void)
13  {
14     static int counter = 0;
15     counter = counter + 1;
16     printf("The value of the counter is %d.\n", counter);
17  }
```

which would create the following output:

```
$ ./a.out
The value of the counter is 1.
The value of the counter is 2.
The value of the counter is 3.
$
```

Note that `static` global variables or `static` functions are only available in places where they have been declared.

Recall from Chapter 6 that register locations are faster to access than memory locations. The C `register` keyword provides a way to put variables in registers. Although, during the process of optimization, the C compiler will decide whether to place a variable in a register, declaring a variable with the `register` keyword signals to the compiler that this variable will be used often and should probably not be placed in memory.

By default any function that is defined in a C file is `extern`, an abbreviation of "external." This means that the function can be used in any other source file of the same code. Remember, in C the code for functions called within a main function does not need to be in the same file as the main function. In fact, such files can be compiled separately and then brought in at the link step to create the executable image. When access to a function is limited to the file in which it is defined, or if a function with same name is desired in some other file of the same code, then the function in C can be made `static`.

All C Keywords

Table 9.3 presents all of the key words of the C language. Of the 31 in this table, we have used all but the following three: `goto`, `union`, and `volatile`.

Dijkstra (1968) argued that the `goto` statement did not foster good programming habits; it allowed programmers to skip around, willy-nilly, without taking into account future readers of the code. Specifically, `goto` statements are often used when the programmer has not thought through the logic of the problem he is solving and relies on the `goto` to get him out of a predicament. In that sense, Dijkstra was correct: the `goto` is a bad statement, even though in some cases it is invaluable.

The `union` command is similar to the `struct` command, except `union` defines variables that share storage space. The `volatile` command is used to

auto	break	case	char	const
continue	default	do	double	else
enum	extern	float	for	goto
if	int	long	register	return
short	signed	sizeof	static	switch
typedef	union	unsigned	void	volatile
		while		

Table 9.3: Keywords in C

signal that a variable's value may change without anything being done to it. Both topics are beyond the scope of this book.

9.3   C Extensions to Python

In general, writing C extensions to Python is not difficult, but it can be complicated and requires painstaking attention to detail. Even a single C function that accepts a few inputs and returns an output requires several important parts. To demonstrate the details required just to create the simple `HelloWorld.c` extension to Python, we use an example from `http://www.tutorialspoint .com/python/python_further_extensions.htm`. Before going through C code, line by line, we first present the contents of the source code `HelloWorldExt.c` in its entirety:

```
1  # include <Python/Python.h>
2
3  static char helloworld_docstring[] =
4    "helloworld(): The simplest possible C extension to Python.\n";
5
6  static PyObject *helloworld(PyObject *self)
7  {
8    return Py_BuildValue("s",
9                         "Hello World! using C extension to Python.");
10 }
11
12 static PyMethodDef helloworld_funcs[] =
13 {
14   {"helloworld", (PyCFunction)helloworld, METH_NOARGS,
```

```
15    helloworld_docstring}, {NULL}
16 };
17
18 void inithelloworld(void)
19 {
20   Py_InitModule3("helloworld", helloworld_funcs,
21                  "C extension to Python module example!");
22 }
```

When creating C extensions to Python, you must first include the appropriate header directive(s). For example, in order for C to know about Python, you need to include the header `Python.h` in line 1. Why is the subdirectory `Python/` introduced before the `Python.h`? Sometimes, depending on the way Python is set up on the computer, the `#include` directives may require explicit pathing.

Second, to make the module and function understandable to others, you must create a docstring, hence lines 3 and 4. Once this code has been compiled, typing

```
$ pydoc helloworld
```

on the command line, produce the following:

```
Help on module helloworld:

NAME
    helloworld - C extension to Python module example!

FILE
    /Library/Frameworks/Python.framework/Versions/7.3/lib/python2.7/
        site-packages/helloworld.so

FUNCTIONS
    helloworld(...)
        helloworld(): The simplest possible C extension to Python.

(END)
```

The same would result within the Python interactive window by typing

```
>>> help(helloworld)
```

Up to this point, everything has been in C, but at some point Python must learn about variables as well as what needs to be done. Therefore, you need to declare the function in lines 6–10 and then describe it to Python in lines 12–16. (The type `PyObject` refers to all Python data types; all communication between the Python interpreter and the C code is done by passing `PyObject`s.) Finally, the function needs to be initialized, as in lines 18–22.

To create the extension, you must write the following Python script:

```
from distutils.core import setup, Extension
setup(name='helloworld', version='1.0',   \
      ext_modules=[Extension('helloworld', ['HelloWorldExt.c'])])
```

which we have named `BuildHelloWorld.py`. This script imports from the `distutils.core` module the `setup` and `Extension` functions that allow us to compile `HelloWorld.c` and to create the module `helloworld` containing the function `helloworld()`. Finally, on the command line, we invoke the following:

```
$ python BuildHelloWorld.py install
```

To use the function `helloworld()`, import the module `helloworld` into the Python interactive window as follows:

```
>>> import helloworld
>>> helloworld.helloworld()
'Hello World! using C extension to Python.'
>>>
```

Exercises like this are unforgiving; omitting even one argument will result in failure, signaled by a core dump to the terminal window. What is most distressing about this exercise, however, is that no inputs were provided, not a single output was returned, and only a single line was printed. The mappings required when inputs are supplied and outputs returned can be quite involved. Daniel Foreman-Mackey, on his web page, `http://dan.iel.fm/posts/python-c-extensions/` provided a detailed, illustrative example with a few inputs and one output that demonstrates the process. The script as well as its discussion go on for several pages.

In an effort to reduce such complications, alternatives have been developed. We describe one such alternative, the `numba` package, in Section 9.6.

9.4 FORTRAN Programming Language

Because FORTRAN is the oldest programming language used in scientific computing, a large stock of legacy code exists. Some of that code has been converted to C and then to Python libraries, but much useful code remains in its natural state. Therefore, in some circumstances, you may be required to use some legacy FORTRAN code in research. In other circumstances, you may want to increase the efficiency of a particular part of a Python script because evidence from profiling suggests that a bottleneck exists.

How can FORTRAN code be used in conjunction with Python? The `f2py` module, which is a part of the `numpy` package, makes incorporating FORTRAN code simple, but familiarity with some FORTRAN grammar is necessary in order to be effective in using `f2py`. In short, learning some FORTRAN is probably a good idea.

9.4.1 Basic Grammar

In this subsection, we introduce enough FORTRAN grammar so you can at least read and then incorporate extant code into your research. A diligent learner should also be able to cobble together simple subroutines to improve computational performance.

One of the major problems with FORTRAN is that, in an effort to stay current, additions to the language have been introduced. In short, several "new" versions of the language exist. However, these new versions, such as FORTRAN–90 and FORTRAN–95, are backward-compatible; that is, code written in ANSI FORTRAN–77 will compile under these new compilers.[5] This is not true of Python; code written in Version 2.7 will not necessarily work in Version 3.1. For example, `print` statements that work in Version 2.7 appear differently in Version 3.1, which is only a cosmetic feature, but other differences are more fundamental. At this time, the `numpy` package has yet to be ported to Version 3.1. Another problem with FORTRAN is that over time different vendors have added different features to compilers, much in the same way that different vendors of DBMSs have different features, for instance, Oracle Database is somewhat different from SQLite. Therefore, we limit ourselves to a syntax that is

---

[5]The numbers after FORTRAN (for example, 77) indicate the last two digits of the release date of the compiler, so 77 indicates 1977, 90 indicates 1990, and 95 indicates 1995.

portable across different versions of compilers, basically, old-style FORTRAN, that is, ANSI FORTRAN–77.

Lines of code in FORTRAN can be at most 80 characters wide, sometimes referred to as *cards* because the lines of code were initially keypunched onto paper cards that were 80 columns wide. In Figure 9.1 we present a photograph of a punch card that was used in FORTRAN programming. Because the punch card only has 80 columns, it was impossible to type information beyond that.

In FORTRAN all usable instructions need to begin in column 7 or later; this is a feature of the language, in much the same way that indentation is a feature of Python. Therefore, FORTRAN programmers overused the space bar on keyboards because they needed to hit it at least six times to get over to column 7 for each line entered.

In FORTRAN a line can be designated as a comment by putting a c or a C in the first column of that line and then typing in text thereafter. Hence, the first column is the *comment column*. Columns 73—80 are reserved for comments as well.

Columns 2–5 are reserved for label numbers. These four columns are *label columns*.

Column 6 is reserved for a continuation character that is used when an instruction is longer than 66 characters;anything typed in columns 73–80 is often ignored by the compiler. Column 6 is the *continuation column*. Even though any ASCII character can be used as a continuation character, it is customary to use

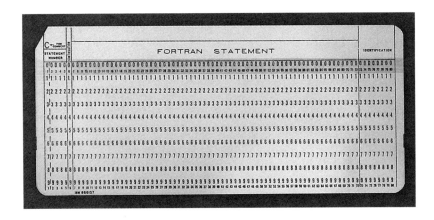

Figure 9.1: Example of Punch Card

the ampersand, that is, the letter &, which is a character typesetters invented for the Latin word *et*, the English translation of which is *and*.

In summary, column 1 is a comment column, columns 2–5 are label columns, column 6 is a continuation column, columns 7–72 are for instructions, and columns 73–80 are for additional comments.

Although FORTRAN initially required all instructions to be in uppercase letters, today's FORTRAN is case-insensitive; no distinction is made between `return` or `RETURN` or `Return`. In that sense, FORTRAN is very much like the dialects of SQL, or any program developed in the 1950s or 1960s. Consequently, in FORTRAN, the variable names `inch` and `Inch` and `INCH` will all refer to the same variable, even though you may think that these three names mean very different things. For example, in the following snippet of code:

```
inch = 1
Inch = 2
INCH = 3
```

after the first assignment statement the register containing `inch` has the integer value 1, whereas after the second assignment that same register contains the integer value 2, and after the third one that register contains the integer value 3.

The following code represents the bare minimum for a "Hello World!" FORTRAN program:

```
print *, "Hello World!"
end
```

where the keyword `end` is required to tell the compiler that the program ends. Even though it is not required, it is considered good practice to begin a FORTRAN program with the formal `program` declaration, followed by a user-supplied name, for example,

```
program hello
print *, "Hello World!"
end program
```

We also recommend that the program name be the prefix of the filename, the suffix being `f`. In short, this Ritchie FORTRAN program would be named `hello.f`.

Although `end` is sufficient to end the FORTRAN program, some SDEs use `end program` to distinguish the end of a program from the end of some other structure, such as a subroutine.

Executing a FORTRAN program is different from executing a Python script. To execute a FORTRAN program, you must first compile it to create an object module, and then link the object module to create an executable image, which can then be executed on the command line. In that sense, FORTRAN code is like C code. Thus, the following commands, executed on the command line, are required:

```
$ gfortran -c hello.f
$ gfortran -o hello hello.o
$ ./hello
 Hello World!
```

The first command takes the FORTRAN program input `hello.f` and compiles it (hence the flag `-c`) and then produces the object module `hello.o`; the second command takes the object module input `hello.o` and creates the executable image (hence the flag `-o`), which we have named `hello`, but which could have any name other name. Of course, all this is done in the current working directory. The third command runs the executable image from the current working directory and directs the output to `stdout`. Collecting these commands in a shell script (for example, one named `hello.sh` or `hello.com`) would be a natural way to reduce the amount of typing. (For simple programs, `gfortran hello.f` would produce `a.out`, which could then be run on the command line.)

Like Python, FORTRAN supports several different variable types, just not the rich variety supported in Python. In FORTRAN variable names can consist of a maximum of six characters chosen from the letters A to Z (as well as a to z) and the digits 0 to 9. In FORTRAN–90 and later, variable names can be of arbitrary length. Even, today, however, variable names cannot begin with a digit.

FORTRAN has five main variable types: logical, integer, real, complex, and character; these five variable types correspond, respectively, to the Boolean, integer, floating-point, complex, and string variable types in Python. Note, however, that some of the variable types come in different sizes, which is different from Python.

Only one size of `logical` variables exists, presumably because only one bit of space is required to represent the values `.true.` and `.false.` in memory, which are written out as T and F but are stored as 1 and 0 internally.

For integers and reals, two common variable sizes exist: `integer*2` and `integer*4` as well as `real*4` and `real*8`, but others can be declared. The number after the `*` specifies how many bytes are used to represent the number.

An `integer*4` variable in FORTRAN is just like an integer in Python. A `real*8` variable in FORTRAN is just like a floating-point number in Python. In FORTRAN `real*8` variables are sometimes referred to as *double-precision* variables.[6] In fact, in FORTRAN, the keywords `real*8` and `double precision` are synonyms.

Like C, FORTRAN imposes static typing, that is, each variable's type must be formally declared before it can be used. This is not strictly true because in FORTRAN there is the option to type variables implicitly using the following statement:

```
implicit integer*4 (i-n)
implicit real*8 (a-h,o-z)
```

which is placed at the very beginning of a function, program, or subroutine. These two statements declare that all variables beginning with the letters i through n are `integer*4` variable types, while all variables beginning with the letters a through h and o through z are `real*8` variable types. Historically, the convention in FORTRAN has been that variables beginning with the letters i through n are integers, whereas those beginning with the letters a through h and o through z are reals. The `implicit` statements can save some effort and time by not requiring a declaration of each variable's type. Many SDEs believe that this is sloppy and begin the programs with

```
implicit none
```

thereafter defining every variable explicitly. This would be a good thing to do when incorporating FORTRAN code into Python—the fewer places in which something can go pear-shaped, the better in the long run. In any case, the following two variable declarations of x and y each yield the `real*8` variable type:

```
real*8 x
double precision y
```

The keyword combination `double precision` is typically used in the definition of a function in FORTRAN, whereas `real*8` is often used in declarations

---

[6]Under this convention, a `real*16` variable is referred to as *quadruple-precision*; the more precision used when declaring a real variable, the more memory used to represent that variable.

of variables (and arrays). For example, consider the following double-precision FORTRAN function:

```
double precision function inches(centis)
real*8 centis
inches = centis / 2.54d0
return
end
```

In this case, the input variable `centis`, which is `real*8`, is converted to the output `inches`, which is also `real*8`, by dividing by the constant 2.54, the approximate number of centimetres in an inch. The `d0` after the `2.54` tells FORTRAN that this constant is in `d` (double precision), whereas just `2.54` would tell FORTRAN that the constant is in single precision. Newer compilers will often perform type conversions for you; older compilers did not. For example, the following FORTRAN `program` divides x, a `real*8`, by i, an `integer`. In one case, the `real*8` variable y is formally declared, whereas in the second `write` statement the value of `(x / i)` is defined implicitly in the statement.

```
      program typcon
      integer i
      real*8   x, y
      i = 10
      x = 2.54d0
      y = x / i
      write(6,11) i, x, y
   11 format(1x,i2,1x,f6.2,1x,f6.3)
      write(6,11)   i, x, (x / i)
      stop
      end
```

In the first case, along with i and x, the `real*8` variable y is written to unit 6, which by default is `stdout` in FORTRAN, according to a `format` determined by the label 11 instruction. In the second case, along with i and x, `(x / i)` are also written out to unit 6 in `format` determined by label 11. But, in this second `write`, the FORTRAN compiler uses an implicit type conversion, taking the `real*8` and the `integer` and representing it as a `real*8` variable.

In the case of character variables, the size of a variable must be formally declared in a variable declaration statement. For example, in the following declaration statement:

```
character*80 card
```

the variable `card` is defined to be 80 characters wide, just like a punch card.

Because a complex number has two parts (the real and the imaginary), it requires twice as much space. Thus, no `complex*4` exists in FORTRAN, but `complex*8` is a single-precision complex variable, whereas `complex*16` is a double-precision complex variable.

FORTRAN has an archaic way of reading data from input files and writing data to output files. In FORTRAN an input or an output file is referred to as a `unit`; typically, these files must be declared using an `open` statement, as in

```
open(unit=5,file='input.dat')
open(unit=6,file='output.out')
```

By convention, unit 5 is for input, and unit 6 is for output. If additional input or output units are needed, one convention is to use odd numbers for inputs and even ones for output, for example, 1, 3, and 7 for extra input units and 2, 4, and 8 for output units. By default `stdin` is unit 5 and `stdout` is unit 6.

The following simple program reads in some data, manipulates them, and then writes a subset of the data out to a file, much like the Python script on page 187 of Chapter 4.

```
1       program ioeg
2       parameter(n=8)
3       real*8 d,h,x,y
4       open(unit=5,file='inputf.dat')
5       open(unit=6,file='outputf.out')
6       do 1 i=1,n
7          read(5,*) x, y, h
8          d = sqrt(x*x + y*y)
9          write(6,11) d, h
10    1 continue
11   11 format(1x,2(f12.6))
12      stop
13      end
```

Listing 9.5: FORTRAN Program to Read and Write

In line 1 the program is named, while in line 2 the `parameter` n is defined. A parameter is different from a variable: it is immutable. Hereafter, in this program, whenever n is encountered, the value 8 will be associated with it. If you tried to change n using an assignment statement in the code, FORTRAN would throw an error something like the following:

```
Error: Named constant 'n' in variable definition context
```

The variables d, h, x, and y are declared as `real*8` in line 3, and then the input and output units are declared in lines 4 and 5 to be the files `inputf.dat` and `outputf.out`, respectively.

In line 6, the loop begins. A do-loop is very much like the `for`-loop in Python, although one can only iterate over integers. In lieu of the Python instruction `for i in range(1,n):`, the FORTRAN instruction would be `do 1 i=1, n`.

FORTRAN does not require indentation, but it is considered good programming practice to use it. In short, indentation is a stylistic choice in FORTRAN, just as in C, whereas in Python indentation is a logical feature of the language.

The `1` after the `do` specifies the label where the loop ends, in this case at line 10. Therefore, for each of n iterations, the data x, y, and h are read in, transformed to d, and then written out to unit 6 in the format determined by label 11, which is coincidentally in line 11. The loop ends with the continue statement, labeled 1.

The FORTRAN keyword `continue` is curious in that it really does very little but hold the place of a label. For a do-loop, `continue` is used to mark the end of the loop.

Finally, the process is formally stopped, and then the program ends. The keyword `stop` is different from the keyword `end`: the former can be used anywhere in a program, subroutine, or function, whereas the latter ends each of those structures.

Unlike Python, old-style FORTRAN does not support the list, tuple, or dictionary variable types, but arrays exist in FORTRAN; arrays can be made to behave like lists and tuples, sort of. To define an array in FORTRAN, use the `dimension` statement, but a variable type statement will work, too. For example, the integer vectors `itag` and `jtag`, each having length 10, could be declared in the following two ways:

```
integer, dimension(10) :: itag
integer jtag(10)
real*8 x(10)
real*8, dimension(10) :: y
```

and the two `real*8` vectors x and y could be defined in two similar ways as well. By default, FORTRAN arrays begin at 1, but they can begin at any index, for example `w(0:m)` as well as `z(-1:n,0:m)`, which is a two-dimensional array, a table or matrix.

FORTRAN stores numbers in multidimensional arrays in a different way from many other languages. Usually, in an $(m \times n)$ matrix **A**, a representative (i, j) element has the i indexing the row, whereas the j indexes the column. But in FORTRAN the matrix A is stored in columns in contiguous parts of memory. In Chapter 5, in the case of R, this was referred to as *column-major*. The way some people remember this is "left subscript varies most rapidly." Thus, for example, the `real*8 A(3,3)` matrix

$$\mathbf{A} = \begin{bmatrix} 1 & 2 & 3 \\ 4 & 5 & 6 \\ 7 & 8 & 9 \end{bmatrix}$$

would be stored in contiguous registers of memory as the following vector:

$$[1, 4, 7, 2, 5, 8, 3, 6, 9].$$

Why is this important? As we mentioned in the same way that Python has `for`-loops, FORTRAN has do-loops. Consider looping through the matrix `A(3,3)` using the following code:

```
      do 1 i=1,3
        do 2 j=1,3
      write(6,11) i, j, A(i,j)
   2     continue
   1 continue
  11 format(1x,i2,1x,i2,1x,f6.2)
```

The following is the output:

```
   1   1   1.00
   1   2   2.00
   1   3   3.00
   2   1   4.00
   2   2   5.00
   2   3   6.00
   3   1   7.00
   3   2   8.00
   3   3   9.00
```

which is as expected, but to access the vector

$$[1, 4, 7, 2, 5, 8, 3, 6, 9]$$

FORTRAN would have to jump back and forth through the vector, first element 1, then element 4, then element 7, and so forth. For a matrix as small as A(3,3), this is no problem, since it can probably be kept in the L1 cache.

Imagine, however, a `real*8` matrix `data(10000000,1000)`, which is 10 million observations concerning say 1,000 variables. Each element is eight bytes, so the matrix takes up about 75 GB, which cannot be fit into either the L1 or the L2 cache. On a computer with 100 GB of RAM, all the data can fit into memory. When the elements of `data` are accessed using the do-loop, they need not occur contiguously in L1 or L2 cache memory, which will require the data to be brought in from RAM; this will take considerably more time than if those data were read from cached memory.

On the other hand, with the following looping,

```
      do 1 j=1,n
        do 2 i=1,m
          trans = data(i,j) * data(i,j)
  2     continue
  1 continue
```

things will go much faster because the sequential accesses to the `data` matrix will be to registers that are contiguous in memory.

For example, suppose that the number of variables n is 1,000, and the number of observations m is 100,000. Under the first looping structure, on a particular computer, the time taken was 2.599 seconds, whereas under the second looping structure, on that same computer, the time taken was 0.437 seconds, in short, one-sixth of the time.

FORTRAN supports conditional branching (that is, the logical construct if ...then ...else), but not the `while`-loop of Python. But a `while`-loop can be fashioned using a labeled `continue` statement and an `if` statement. For example,

```
      program while
      integer i
      i = 0
 10 continue
      i = i + 1
      if (i .le. 10) goto 10
      print *, i
      stop
      end
```

In addition to illustrating how to fashion a `while`-loop, the program `while` also introduces the `goto` statement. Without the `goto` statement, some things just could not be done in old-style FORTRAN because the language was limited. In that sense, the `goto` statement, when used with care, is useful. As you have probably surmised by now, the `goto` statement can pass control to any label number in the code.

Although FORTRAN also has a structure referred to as a `function`, which we demonstrated, such functions are not as flexible or as useful as subroutines, which are most like the Python functions. As an example, consider the Euclidean (L_2) distance of the N-vector $x = (x_1, x_2, \ldots, x_n)$ from the origin.

$$\|x\|_2 = \sqrt{\sum_{i=1}^{n} x_i^2}.$$

The following subroutine takes in a double-precision vector x having length n, and returns a double-precision scalar `dnorm`, which is the Euclidean distance of the input vector:

```fortran
      subroutine norm2(x,n,dnorm)
      double precision dnorm
      double precision, dimension(n) :: x
      integer n
      dnorm = 0.d0
      do 1 i=1,n
         dnorm = dnorm + x(i)*x(i)
    1 continue
      dnorm = sqrt(dnorm)
      return
      end
```

```fortran
      program driver
      parameter(m=10)
      real*8 dnorm,y(m)
      do 1 i=1,m
         y(i) = 1.d0*i
    1 continue
      call norm2(y,m,dnorm)
      print *, "dnorm = ",dnorm
      end
```

Note that the subroutine `norm2` and the program `driver` have many instructions that are identical, specifically, many variable names that are identical.

But the instructions in the subroutine are *local* to norm2, basically invisible to the program driver. Note, too, that the vector x in the subroutine norm2 is just a placeholder and that the dimension of x within the subroutine norm2 is arbitrary, being determined by the argument n. When the subroutine norm2 is called in the program driver, the vector y is used, and the dimension is determined by the parameter m.

A number of books exist concerning the various versions of FORTRAN, but Nyhoff and Leestma (1995) is particularly attractive because it contrasts FORTRAN–77 with FORTRAN–90.

9.5   FORTRAN Extensions to Python

In the preceding definition of the subroutine norm2, without further inspection it is unclear what is an input and what is an output. That is, from the argument list (x, n, dnorm), it is unclear which arguments are inputs and which are outputs. By convention, in FORTRAN, the input arguments are first, and the output arguments second, but this is not a logical feature of the language—just good housekeeping. Herein lies some potential for confusion: Python does not know what is an input and what is an output, so it defaults to making all variables inputs. To get around this problem, you must formally define your intent at the top of the subroutine.

Consider the following listing, which is a modified version of the norm2 subroutine:

```
 1       subroutine norm2(x,n,dnorm)
 2 cf2py intent(out) :: dnorm
 3 cf2py intent(hide) :: n
 4 cf2py double precision :: x(n)
 5       double precision dnorm
 6       double precision, dimension(n) :: x
 7       integer n
 8       dnorm = 0.d0
 9       do 1 i=1,n
10         dnorm = dnorm + x(i)*x(i)
11     1 continue
12       dnorm = sqrt(dnorm)
13       return
14       end
```

Listing 9.6: FORTRAN Subroutine norm2.f

As you can see, we have explicitly noted in lines 2–4 that the variable `dnorm` is intended to be an output, hence the line

```
cf2py intent(out) :: dnorm
```

that the variable `n` is hidden, hence the line

```
cf2py intent(hide) :: n
```

and that the floating-point vector `x` is in double precision, hence the line

```
cf2py double precision :: x(n)
```

To do all this from within a Python script, use the following code:

```
import numpy.f2py as f2py
inputFile = open('norm2.f')
sourceCode = inputFile.read()
inputFile.close()
f2py.compile(sourceCode, modulename='norm2')
import norm2
```

9.6 Numba

Using the `numba` package can speed up Python scripts with high-performance functions written directly in Python. Aruoba and Fernández-Villaverde (2014) demonstrated that JIT compiling Python code to native machine instructions performed almost as well as compiled C or FORTRAN code. The `numba` package compiles Python code to run either on a CPU or on a GPU. Moreover, `numba` is designed to integrate with existing Python packages.

At `http://numba.pydata.org`, the following example is provided,

```
from numba import jit
from numpy import arange
# The  jit  decorator tells  numba  to compile this function.
# The argument types will be inferred by Numba when the function
# is called.
@jit
def sum2d(arr):
  M, N = arr.shape
  result = 0.0
  for i in range(M):
    for j in range(N):
```

```
        result += arr[i,j]
   return result

a = arange(9).reshape(3,3)
print sum2d(a)
```

which demonstrates how easy the `numba` package is to use.

Unfortunately, the `numba` package depends on the LLVM compiler infrastructure. The LLVM compiler infrastructure is a program designed to optimize code written in arbitrary programming languages. As such, LLVM requires that you install some code, a task that is not straightforward for everyone to do. If you need to use the LLVM compiler infrastructure, then instructions exist at `http://llvm.org`.

As you can see, extending Python is both feasible and desirable, but it is not for the novice. In short, before proceeding with extensions, you should seek to exploit other feasible avenues, such as using code written by more experienced programmers.

10

Papers and Presentations

SOMETIMES A RESEARCH assistant is asked to put together the first draft of a paper or to create the presentation for a conference or a seminar, using inputs from other researchers as well as other completed work. We do not provide any guidance on writing. If you do not write effectively, consider reading in the order listed the following excellent books:

William Strunk, Jr. and E. B. White (2009), *The Elements of Style*.

Deirdre N. McCloskey (2000), *Economic Writing*.

Lynne Truss (2003), *Eats, Shoots & Leaves*.

William K. Zinsser (2006), *On Writing Well*.

Jane E. Miller (2004), *The Chicago Guide to Writing about Numbers*.

Nicholas J. Higham (1998), *Handbook of Writing for the Mathematical Sciences*.

Although reading Strunk and White (2009) and the others may take a long time, it is well worth the effort, especially if you are planning on a scholarly career. Even if you do not plan to be a scholar, you will stand out in business or government if you write effectively.

In this chapter, we describe how you can bring together the output from all the tools used in this book to create a paper or a presentation. In short, we demonstrate how to complete the research project.

The main tool we chose to carry out this work is LaTeX, a document markup language and preparation system for the TeX typesetting program.[1] TeX was written by Donald E. Knuth (1984), and LaTeX was written in the TeX language by Leslie Lamport (1994). We augment TeX/LaTeX with BibTeX, a tool to manage bibliographic references, which was written by Oren Patashnik and Leslie Lamport. To create presentations, we chose the LaTeX class `Beamer`, which was developed by Till Tantau, Joseph Wright, and Vedran Miletić. In addition to using Python and R to produce figures and graphs, we also introduce a pair of languages, PGF and TikZ, which are closely related to TeX/LaTeX. Developed by Till Tantau and Christian Feuersaenger, PGF and TikZ create vector graphics from either geometric or algebraic descriptions; those PGF/TikZ files can then be imported into any LaTeX document, including `Beamer` presentations.

These tools augment one another remarkably well, but it is probably best to learn them in a particular sequence. First, start by creating a LaTeX document and then incorporate references using BibTeX. After that, you can incorporate figures and graphs created using either Python or R into LaTeX documents using standard macros. Once you have a document written in LaTeX, creating slides for presentations using `Beamer` will be trivial. Having gained some experience with the TeX family of tools, you can then try TikZ, and maybe even PGF, to create figures, but that can be exacting work.

---

[1]Although TeX and LaTeX are shipped with Linux distributions, neither is installed by default on the Apple Mac. Detailed instructions to install TeX/LaTeX on the Mac are available at a number of websites. The authoritative source is http://tug.org/mactex/

For computers on which native UNIX is the operating system, TeX and LaTeX are usually available. If not, you will have to ask your system administrator to install them for you. On the virtual machine we created for the Windows users among you, TeX/LaTeX and all related programs have been installed. In the short run, a time-constrained Mac user could just install the virtual machine, and then run TeX/LaTeX. However, that would be a bit like burning down the barn to get roast beef.

10.1   LaTeX

To some, LaTeX source code is mystifying, at least at first, mostly because introductory examples of LaTeX code often include many more commands than are necessary to demonstrate how simple TeX/LaTeX really is. The same is true of LaTeX source code generated by a GUI like Scientific WorkPlace. The following listing, Paper.tex, has the bare minimum of required commands as well as one sentence:

```
1 \documentclass{paper}
2 \begin{document}
3 This is a test.
4 \end{document}
```

Line 1 introduces the class of document class, in this case a paper. Other common document classes include article, book, report, and letter. A class for slides exists as well, but we recommend that you use the beamer class instead (see Section 10.3).

The document begins on line 2 and ends on line 4. The sole input sentence is in line 3. As you can see, the LaTeX language is self-describing: Paper.tex could not be any simpler.

Several options are available for compiling this source code using the LaTeX program. The oldest option involves two steps, which are illustrated in the following terminal window:

```
$ latex Paper.tex
$ xdvi Paper.dvi
```

The first command takes the LaTeX source code and compiles it to create the *device independent* (.dvi) file Paper.dvi. The second command invokes the dvi previewer to view the file in a graphics window. You do not need to use the suffix .tex or .dvi when invoking the commands latex and xdvi, but we include them to keep track of what each command is doing.

Other options exist as well. For example, on some systems, the tool `pdfla-tex` could be used to create a PDF file, which could then be viewed using, say, Adobe Reader, or printed on a linked printer.

```
$ pdflatex Paper
```

Note that if you include figures or graphs that are in EPS format, the `pdflatex` option will not work. The EPS figures would have to be preprocessed using the tool `epstopdf`, which is not very difficult. For example, suppose the figure is `Figure.eps`; you can get the PDF version of this figure using

```
$ epstopdf Figure.eps -o=Figure.pdf
```

Why not just export the figure as a PDF file from either Python or R? That does not always work with all applications. We encourage you to try to save figures and graphs as PDF files initially, but if that does not work, an alternative is to save in EPS format and postprocess the file using `epstopdf` to create a readable PDF file of the figure or graph. In Jutland, they would say that "in addition to having a belt you have also purchased suspenders." Many publishers prefer EPS files because figures in that format offer them the most flexibility. You can also use the PNG format with `pdflatex`.

When converting, say, the `Figure.eps` to PDF, you may sometimes need to use the following:

```
$ epstopdf Figures.eps > Figures-eps-converted-to.pdf
```

That is, you should extend the filename of the PDF file; otherwise, some versions of LaTeX will balk. Under either option, depending on your monitor, the output will appear something like the following page.

This example is a bit like the "Hello World!" example: it provides a proof of concept. What you would really like to have is a template that demonstrates the power of LaTeX and its supporting cast members BiBTeX as well as PGF/TikZ. Like Python, many packages exist that augment LaTeX; you just need to know the name of the package, and then import it using the command `\usepackage{package name}`. In the following example, we demonstrate how that would work. Rather than describe the script, which is a bit like watching paint dry, we annotate it with commands.

The following code includes some common commands (lines beginning with \) and comments (lines beginining with %) as well as some representative content for the file `Paper.tex`. After the listing follows the PDF output of what looks like the skeleton of a paper.

```
\documentclass[11pt,letterpaper]{paper}
% This is referred to as the preamble.
% Other arguments for font size could be 12pt; 10pt is the default.
% Other arguments for paper type could be a4paper.
% Other arguments instead of paper could be article, book, or report.
%
% Now bring in whatever packages you want to use.  Because we
% use BibTeX later in this chapter, we include the package natbib.
% To include figures, we include the package graphicx.  We also bring
% in the American Mathematical Society package amsmath.
%
\usepackage{amsmath}
\usepackage{natbib}
\usepackage{graphicx}
%
% That was the preamble, now begins the paper.
%
\begin{document}
%
% Create the titlepage with names and affiliations as well as
% acknowldgments and thanks.  You can also include an abstract
% as well as keyword and classification number information.
%
\title{The Title}
\author{Firstname M.~LastNameFirstAuthor%
\thanks{We thank ...
        }\\
        {\it Affiliation}\\
        Firstname M.~LastNameOtherAuthor(s)\\
        {\it Affiliation Other(s)}\\
        }

\maketitle

\begin{abstract}
This is an abstract of the paper ...
\end{abstract}

\begin{itemize}
```

```
\item[ ] \textsf{Keywords:} word1; word2; word3.

\item[ ] \textsf{Classification numbers:} C20, D44, L1.
\end{itemize}

\section*{Introduction and Motivation}
% The * after section means do not number this section.

\section{Theoretical Model}

George Box once wrote

\begin{quotation}
  All models are wrong, but some models are useful.
\end{quotation}

\subsection{A Solved Example}

An equation
$$U(x,y) = x^\alpha y^\beta.$$
Another one with a label
\begin{equation}
\label{prodeqn}
q = f(\ell,k) = A\ell^\gamma k^\delta.
\end{equation}
You can refer to equation (\ref{prodeqn}) here.

\section{Field Data}

Here we place a table, right after this text.

\begin{table}[h!] % Definitely put it right here.
\centering
\begin{tabular}{|l|r|r|r|}
\hline
Variable& Mean&Minimum&Maximum\\
\hline
Rain& 12.2&   0.0&   25.3\\
Sun &723.1& 134.5&1,113.8\\
\hline
\end{tabular}
\caption{Sample Descriptive Statistics}
\label{tab:SmplDStats}
\end{table}
```

```
You can the refer to Table \ref{tab:SmplDStats}.

\section{Statistical Model}

Here is a multilined equation:
\begin{align*}
 z&= (a + x) (b + y)\\
   &= ab + bx + ay + xy
\end{align*}

\section{Empirical Results}

Here we place a figure, but allow it to float to the top of a page.

\begin{figure}[t] % Float the figure at the top of a page.
\centering
\includegraphics[width=0.8\textwidth]{Figures/ksrexample.eps}
\caption{A Sample Figure}
\label{fig:EgFig}
\end{figure}

You can then refer to Figure \ref{fig:EgFig}.

\end{document}
```

Listing 10.1: Sample Paper Template in LATEX

10.1.1 Notation

Paarsch has very strong opinions concerning notation. He was not always this way. When he was a graduate student, he basically made up notation in real time—willy-nilly. The results were utter gibberish. A senior scholar offered him some pointers. After that, he developed notation *before* writing a paper, thinking about how the notation would be used and whether it would be easy to understand, that is, whether the notation would help the reader. His papers became easier to read and to understand.

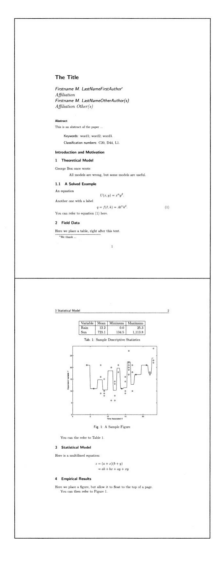

In *An Introduction to Mathematics*, Alfred N. Whitehead (1911, 59) summarized the importance of notation:

> By relieving the brain of all unnecessary work, a good notation sets it free to concentrate on more advanced problems, and in effect increases the mental power of the race.

We do not provide you with much guidance concerning notation because from discipline to discipline, and from field to field, differences in notation are huge. Thus, it is difficult to suggest a universal set of principles to guide notation choice because each discipline or field potentially has a different set of factors it is attempting to capture. Some have tried to develop notations. For example, in econometrics, Abadir and Magnus (2002) proposed a standard, with which some agree, but the standard has not been adopted widely, at least not to our knowledge.

Others have sought to teach the use of notation by example. For instance, Davidson and MacKinnon (2004) provided a fine notation, but it is really only relevant to econometrics and perhaps applied statistics. Some scholars, such as the economic theorist Kenneth Hendricks, put much effort into defining a notation well before writing a paper, and it shows. Often, however, researchers just follow in the tradition of the literature to which they want to contribute, which is a fine idea, provided the founding scholars in that field defined the initial notation in a consistent and helpful way.

In this section, we demonstrate how to define notation in LaTeX so that it is easy to change should the need arise. In TeX/LaTeX, the `\def` command should be used when defining complicated notation, that is, notation involving combinations of TeX characters. Using the `\def` command is a bit like creating aliases in UNIX. For example, suppose you want to introduce the boldface Greek lowercase vector θ, but you want a circumflex (hat) on it as well, $\hat{\theta}$. You could type the entire LaTeX sequence `\skew3\hat\boldsymbol{\theta}` each time, or you could introduce the following definition:

    \def\bthat{\skew3\hat\boldsymbol{\theta}}

and thereafter just use `\bthat` whenever you want to typeset $\hat{\theta}$. If you need to change your notation, then under the first option you would have to make many changes, whereas under the second only one definition would need to

be changed. In fact, we changed the notation of this book at least twice, but the
entire exercise took less than ten minutes because we only had to change the
definitions in the file `Notation.tex`.

Although you can introduce a definition at almost any point in the LATₑX
source code and have it apply thereafter, it is typically best to define notation in the preamble, that is, before the `\begin{document}` command. In
fact, you should collect all your definitions of notation in a file having a self-
describing filename, such as `Notation.tex`, and input the file in the preamble
of the LATₑX source code, typically after all the packages have been loaded. You
should load it after all the packages because you may rely on definitions in the
packages, for example, the `amsmath` fonts. If you have other definitions that
may not pertain to notation, you should collect them in a separate file, perhaps named `Macros.tex`, which would also be inputted in the preamble of
the LATₑX source code, just before or just after the `Notation.tex` file, depending on whether `Notation.tex` relies on definitions in `Macros.tex` or vice
versa.

10.2 BIBTₑX

BIBTₑX is a tool to manage bibliographic references that is typically used in conjunction with LATₑX. BIBTₑX makes it easy to cite sources in a consistent manner
by separating the bibliographic information from the presentation of this information in the completed document. Many publishers require that references be
in a format derived from a BIBTₑX database.

To use BIBTₑX, you need to input your references in a particular format into
a file with the suffix `.bib`, which serves as a database. Several options exist
when creating a BIBTₑX database. First, you can just type in the relevant data
by hand; second, you can convert information concerning references from the
files of old papers using the tool `text2bib`;[2] third, you can export references
in BIBTₑX format from a source like Google Scholar; fourth, you can use some
other resource on the Internet.

---

[2]Go to `http://www.ctan.org/tex-archive/biblio/bibtex/utils/text2bib`.

The first option is the most tedious—typing the bibliographic information yourself. This option is also error prone, but it does give you total control over the format of the BIBTEX database. Whether you choose this option or not, you should probably have a system. Clearly, bibliographic information is static, so no choice exists there, but the labels in the BIBTEX database admit some scope for choice. The labels are how you will refer to the article, book, chapter, and so forth in the LATEX source code. You should create a labeling system that is easy to remember, otherwise you will make a lot of errors, which can take time to correct. Having a consistent system for labels will be helpful not only to you, but to other researchers working with you on a project or to co-authors. For a labeling system to be useful to co-authors, it must be consistent, logical, and clear—free of idiosyncracies. Also, because you will have to type the labels many times, it is best that they have relatively few characters.

We adopt the following labeling convention: each label has two parts, separated by a colon. After the colon comes the date of the reference, for example, 1992. Before the colon comes a string based on the surname(s) of the author(s). For single-authored works, such as

> Paarsch, Harry J., "Deciding between the Common and Private Value Paradigms in Empirical Models of Auctions," *Journal of Econometrics*, 51 (1992), 191–215.

we include the entire surname, but in lowercase letters, for example, `paarsch:1992` as the label.

For works with two authors, such as

> Paarsch, Harry J. and Han Hong. *An Introduction to the Structural Econometrics of Auction Data*. Cambridge, Massachusetts: MIT Press, 2006.

we include the first four letters of each surname in lowercase, for example, `paarhong:2006`. If a surname has fewer than four letters, we just use the letters. Why four letters? One, two, or even three letters fail to be unique identifiers. For works with three authors or more, such as

> Davies, James B., David A. Green, and Harry J. Paarsch, "Economic Statistics and Social Welfare Comparisons: A Review." In *Handbook of Applied*

Economic Statistics, edited by David Giles and Aman Ullah. New York: Marcel Dekker, 1998, pages 1–38.

we include the first four letters of the first author's surname plus "etal", an abreviation of the Latin *et alia* (and others). Thus, `davietal:1998` would be the label for the reference to the *Handbook* chapter.[3] Some authors are so prolific that they have several publications in one year, for example, the economics Nobel Prize winner James J. Heckman. In such cases, we use `heckman:2000a`, `heckman:2000b`, and so on.

   We present some examples of these label formats along with the structure of various kinds of entries in a BIBTₑX database. Using a self-describing naming convention, we named this file `References.bib`. Note that the `.bib` suffix is important because BIBTₑX assumes it by default. Also, the suffix `.bib` is another example of a self-describing notation.

```
@article{paarsch:1992,
author   = "Harry J.~Paarsch",
title    = "Deciding between the Common and Private Value Paradigms in
            Empirical Models of Auctions",
journal = "Journal of Econometrics",
volume   = {51},
year     = {1992},
pages    = {191--215}
}

@book{paarhong:2006,
author    = "Harry J.~Paarsch and Han Hong",
title     = "An Introduction to the Structural Econometrics of
             Auction Data",
publisher = "MIT Press",
address   = "Cambridge, Massachusetts",
year      = {2006}
}
```

---

[3]The term *et alia* is the neutral plural, whereas *et alii* is the masculine plural and *et aliae* is the feminine plural. Thus, *et al.* avoids having to know the gender of all the authors.

```
@incollection{davietal:1998,
author    = "James B.~Davies and David A.~Green and
             Harry J.~Paarsch",
title     = "Economic Statistics and Social Welfare Comparisons:
             A Review",
booktitle = "Handbook of Applied Economic Statistics",
editor    = "David Giles and Aman Ullah",
publisher = "Marcel Dekker",
address   = "New York",
year      = {1998},
pages     = {1--38}
}


@inproceedings{codd:1974,
author    = "Edgar F.~Codd",
title     = "Recent Investigations into Relational Data Base
             Systems",
booktitle = "IFIP Congress, {\rm Volume 74}",
publisher = "North-Holland",
address   = "New York",
year      = {1974}
}


@misc{atheelli:2008,
author  = "Susan C.~Athey and Glenn D.~Ellison",
title   = "Position Auctions with Consumer Search, typescript,
           {D}epartment of {E}conomics, {H}arvard {U}niversity",
year    = {2008}
}
```

Listing 10.2: Examples of BIBTEX Formats

BIBTEX also allows cross-referencing, which is easier to explain using the following example:

```
@inproceedings{lastname:2015,
author    = "Firstname M.~Lastname",
title     = "Paper Title",
booktitle = "Title of Proceedings",
crossref  = {nameetal:2015},
```

```
pages      = {xx--yy}
}

@proceedings{nameetal:2015,
editor     = "Editor1 Name1 and Editor2 Name2 and Editor3 Name3",
title      = "Proceedings Title",
booktitle = "Title of Proceedings",
publisher = "Publisher Name",
address    = "Place",
year       = {2015}
}
```

The label `nameetal:2015` from `@proceedings` is mapped to the entry
`@inproceedings{lastname:2015}` via a cross-reference to the parameter
`crossref={nameetal:2015}`. Note, too, that the attribute `booktitle` is
used in both definitions. It is important to include this attribute in both records
of the database because otherwise BIBTₑX will return an error complaining that
the "booktitle is missing."

To use BIBTₑX in your paper, you will need to include the package `nat-
bib` via the command `\usepackage{natbib}` in the preamble of the file,
which we have named `BibTeXTest.tex`. In addition, at the bottom of `Bib-
TeXTest.tex`, just before the `\end{document}` command, you must include
the three `\bibliography` commands.

```
\documentclass[11pt]{paper}
\usepackage{natbib}

\begin{document}

\section{Demonstrating \BibTeX}

\index[subject]{\BibTeX!.bib file format}%
Here, we list a few \BibTeX\ references, for example, the paper
by \citet{paarsch:1992} as well as the book by
\citet{paarhong:2006} and the chapter by \citet{davietal:1998}
and the working paper by \citet{atheelli:2008}.
All of the other references in \texttt{References.bib} were left
```

```
untouched because they were not referred to by label in this
file.

% Choose the bibliography style here.
\bibliographystyle{plainnat}
%\bibliographystyle{plain} % This is another style.

% Include the file Reference.bib which must be in the
% current working directory.
\bibliography{References}
\end{document}
```

To compile the LaTeX code with the BIBTeX citations, you also need to do some precompiling using the tool `bibtex`. The sequence of commands, which you could collect in a shell script, is as follows:

```
1 $ latex BibTeXTest
2 $ latex BibTeXTest
3 $ bibtex BibTeXTest
4 $ latex BibTeXTest
5 $ pdflatex BibTeXTest
```

The first command uses LaTeX to compile source code. Often, you need to do this twice to get label numbers correct, hence line 2. Once a proper `BibTeX-Test.aux` exists, which is where label numbers reside, then invoking `bibtex` in line 3 will create the `BibTeXTest.bbl` file, which is referred to as the *bibliography file*. Sometimes, you need to invoke `latex` one more time, hence line 4. Finally `BibTeXTest.pdf` is produced in line 5.

Having completed these commands, the citations in your paper as well as in the list of references will be formatted consistently according to the style you have chosen. You can see what a sample of the output looks like on the following page.

1   Demonstrating BIBTEX

Here, we list a few BIBTEX references, for example, the paper by Paarsch [1992] as well as the book by Paarsch and Hong [2006] and the chapter by Davies et al. [1998] and the working paper by Athey and Ellison [2008]. All of the other references in `References.bib` were left untouched because they were not referred to by label in this file.

References

Susan C. Athey and Glenn D. Ellison. Position auctions with consumer search, typescript, Department of Economics, Harvard University, 2008.

James B. Davies, David A. Green, and Harry J. Paarsch. Economic statistics and social welfare comparisons: A review. In David Giles and Aman Ullah, editors, *Handbook of Applied Economic Statistics*, pages 1–38. Marcel Dekker, New York, 1998.

Harry J. Paarsch. Deciding between the common and private value paradigms in empirical models of auctions. *Journal of Econometrics*, 51: 191–215, 1992.

Harry J. Paarsch and Han Hong. *An Introduction to the Structural Econometrics of Auction Data*. MIT Press, Cambridge, Massachusetts, 2006.

In general, it is a good idea to enter the records in the BIBTEX database alphabetically. Also, it is easier to read the database if it has a regular structure. A friend of the authors, Benjamin S. Skrainka, wrote a Python script to organize the BIBTEX reference file in a consistent way.

```python
#!/usr/bin/env python2.7
# Script: FormatBibTeX.py
# Author: Benjamin S. Skrainka
# Date:    20 May 2010
"""
FormatBibTex - formats BibTex to conform to my conventions
"""
import sys
def ParseLine( line ) :
    """ Split line into LHS and RHS about '='
    """
    if -1 != line.find( '=' ) :
        # Handle case where there is a URL : I assume first '=' belongs
        #     to BibTeX
        vParts = line.strip().split( '=' )
        lhs = vParts[ 0 ]
        rhs = '='.join( vParts[ 1: ] )          # Put full RHS back
            together
        vRet = [ lhs.strip(), rhs.strip() ]
    else :
        vRet = line.strip()
    return( vRet )


def CalcSize( item ) :
    """ Computes the size of the LHS before the '='
    """
    nSize = 0 ;
    if 2 == len( item ) :
        nSize = len( item[ 0 ] )
    return( nSize )



# Process the input
if __name__ == '__main__' :
    if 1 == len( sys.argv ) :
        vLines = sys.stdin
    elif 2 == len( sys.argv ) :
        szInFile = sys.argv[ 1 ]
```

```
      vLines = open( szInFile, 'r' )
    else :
      raise SyntaxWarning

    # Process lines
#     vLines = open( '/Users/bss/tmp/Python/test.bib', 'r' )
    vLines = open( szInFile, 'r' )
    vParsed = [ ]
    for line in vLines :
      vParsed.append( ParseLine( line ) )
      vSizeLHS = map( CalcSize, vParsed )
      nMaxLHS  = max( vSizeLHS )

    vLines.close()

    # Nice Output

    cSpace  = ' '
    nIndent = 2
    for ( ix, item ) in enumerate( vParsed ) :
      if 0 == vSizeLHS[ ix ] :
        print item
      else :
        print nIndent * cSpace + item[ 0 ] + ( nMaxLHS - vSizeLHS[ ix ]
          ) * cSpace + ' = ' + item[ 1 ]
```

Listing 10.3: Python Script to Format BIBTEX Reference File

10.3 Beamer

Like much LATEX source code, Beamer source code is often needlessly complicated. We introduce the bare minimum of commands into the file Slides.tex
to create just one slide:

```
\documentclass{beamer}

\begin{document}

\begin{frame}
\begin{itemize}
\item[1)] First point.
\item[2)] Second point.
```

```
\item[3)] Third point.
\end{itemize}
\end{frame}

\end{document}
```

To compile this source code, type the following into a terminal window:

```
$ latex Slides
$ xdvi Slides
```

The first command compiles the source code to create `Slides.dvi`, and the second command invokes the dvi previewer so you can view the output. Depending on your monitor, the output will appear something like figure on the following page.

This is just a proof of concept, a prototype if you like. As with our example `Paper.tex`, we introduce some nontrivial commands so that `Slides.tex` actually does something.

The listing after the next page includes self-describing comments, but you can see what we did. First, we brought in the American Mathematical Society fonts that are useful for typesetting complicated mathematical expressions in LaTeX.

We also brought in the `enumerate` package, so that we would not have to number things: `Beamer` takes care of that for us. Sometimes, you want to have links to web pages, so we used the `hyperref` package.

Typically, you also want to depict figures and graphs, so we imported the `graphicx` package as well.

Because Paarsch has a tendency to create figures in EPS format, which often need to be translated into PDF files, he included `epstopdf` package.

Since the principal competitor to `Beamer` is Windows Powerpoint, which has color, the `xcolor` package is imported, too. Changing themes and colors is also possible—the `\usetheme{CambridgeUS}` and the `\usecolortheme[name=SlateGray]{structure}` commands.

The remaining commands are relatively self-explanatory, except perhaps for the one that brings in the figure, the one that makes a reference to a URL, and the one that includes a link. In general `Beamer` is easy to use, but you have to fiddle with these commands a bit—to get things to your tastes.

1. First point.
2. Second point.
3. Third point.

```
% Choose a nice font with serifs.   Include notes and compress.
\documentclass[xcolor=svgnames,serifs,notes,compress,professionalfont
    ]{beamer}
% Bring in the American Mathematical Society fonts.
\usepackage{amsfonts,amsmath}
% Admit the enumerating feature.
\usepackage{enumerate}
% Include the hyperlink feature.
\usepackage{hyperref}
% Include graphics.
\usepackage{graphicx}
% Convert Encapsulated PostScript to PDF
\usepackage{epstopdf}
% Let's have some color, shall we?
\usepackage{xcolor}
% Use a prepackaged theme.
\usetheme{CambridgeUS}
% Change colors.
\usecolortheme[named=SlateGray]{structure}
% Make bullets and items fancy balls.
\beamertemplateballitem
% Include the same notation as Paper.tex
\input Notation.tex

\begin{document}

\title{Presentation Title}
\author{Author(s)}
\institute{Affiliation}

\begin{frame}
  \titlepage
\end{frame}

\section{Introduction}
\begin{frame}
\frametitle{Roadmap of Talk}
  \begin{enumerate}[<+->]
    \item Background
    \item Data
    \item Results
    \item Conclusions
  \end{enumerate}
\end{frame}
```

```
\section{Background}
\begin{frame}
  \frametitle{Some Institutional Knowledge}
  \begin{itemize}
    \item First point.
    \item Second point.
  \end{itemize}
\end{frame}

\begin{frame}
  \frametitle{Additional Background Information}
  \begin{itemize}
    \item First point.
    \item Second point.
  \end{itemize}
\end{frame}

\section{Data}
\begin{frame}
  \frametitle{Where Did You Get Those Data?}
  \begin{itemize}
    \item First point.
    \item Second point.
  \end{itemize}
\end{frame}

\section{Results}
\begin{frame}
  \frametitle{What Did We Learn?}
  \begin{itemize}
    \item Using the empirical specification,
$$Y_n = \alpha + \beta x_n + U_n.$$
    \item Second point.
  \end{itemize}
\end{frame}

\begin{frame}
  \frametitle{A Picture is a Thousand Words}
  \begin{figure}
    \begin{center}
      \includegraphics[height=2in]{Figures/GaltonScatterplot.eps}
    \end{center}
  \end{figure}
```

```
\end{frame}

\begin{frame}
  \frametitle{Let's Put in Some Hyperlinks}
  \begin{center}
    \url{http://sites.google.com/site/hjpaarsch/}
  \end{center}
  \begin{center}
    \href{http://sites.google.com/site/hjpaarsch/paarsch-golyaev-book
        }{A Cool Book}
  \end{center}
\end{frame}

\section{Conclusions}
\begin{frame}
  \frametitle{Summary of Findings}
  \begin{itemize}
    \item First point.
    \item Second point.
  \end{itemize}
\end{frame}

\end{document}
```

Listing 10.4: Sample `Beamer` Presentation

The following listing is used to compile the PDF for the `Beamer` presentation.

```
1 latex      Slides
2 latex      Slides
3 latex      Slides
4 dvips -Ppdf Slides
5 ps2pdf     Slides.ps
```

Listing 10.5: Sample Shell Script to Process `Slides.tex`

The slides appear as follows:

10.4 Incorporating PGF/TikZ Figures

We have illustrated how easy it is to incorporate PostScript figures created by Python or R into LaTeX. A popular package for constructing PostScript figures in LaTeX is PSTricks, which was originally created by Timothy van Zandt but is now maintained by Denis Girou, Sebastian Rahtz, and Herbert Voss. PSTricks permits you to construct figures right in the LaTeX code, so no dependencies exist on other inputs. Goossens et al. (2007) provide an introduction to PSTricks. PostScript figures and PSTricks are not, however, as compatible with code that makes use of PDF files as well.

Another LaTeX package for creating figures is TikZ, which is much more compatible with the command `pdflatex`. The languages PGF and TikZ are incredibly rich and powerful. Crémer (2011) wrote a concise introduction to TikZ and highlighted its value to economists. We describe these tools in the hope that you will make use of them. A variety of templates are at http://www.texample.net/tikz/examples/. The following listing is based on the source code used to generate Figure 3.1, which is modeled on examples from that website.

```
% styles for ER diagram
\tikzstyle{attribute} = [circle, draw, text width=6em,
                         text centered, minimum width=3em]
\tikzstyle{entity}    = [rectangle, draw, text width=6em,
                         text centered, minimum width=5em,
                         minimum height=2.5em]
\tikzstyle{relation}  = [diamond, draw, text width=6em,
                         text centered, minimum width=6em,
                         aspect=2]

\begin{figure}[htp]
\begin{center}
\begin{tikzpicture}[node distance=0.5cm, auto, >=stealth]
{\footnotesize
% nodes
\node[relation]  (participates)
                 {\texttt{Attended}};
\node[entity]    (bidders)  [left =of participates]
                 {\texttt{Bidders}};
\node[entity]    (auctions) [right=of participates]
                 {\texttt{Auctions}};
\node[attribute] (date)     [right=of auctions]
```

```
                       {\texttt{Date}};
\node[attribute] (location) [below=of auctions]
                       {\texttt{Location}};
\node[attribute] (volume)   [above=of auctions]
                       {\texttt{Volume}};
\node[attribute] (name)    [left =of bidders]
                       {\texttt{Name}};
\node[attribute] (address)  [above=of bidders]
                       {\texttt{Address}};
\node[attribute] (type)      [below=of bidders]
                       {\texttt{Preferred}};
\node[entity]     (bids)       [above=of participates]
                       {\texttt{Bids}};
\node[attribute] (auctionid)  [above=of volume]
                       {\textsl{\texttt{AuctionID}}};
\node[attribute] (bidderid)    [above=of address]
{\textsl{\texttt{BidderID}}};
\node[attribute] (bid)         [above left=of auctionid]
                       {\texttt{Bid}};
\node[attribute] (bidid)        [above right=of bidderid]
                       {\underline{\texttt{BidID}}};
\node[attribute] (bidderskey) [below=of name]
                       {\underline{\texttt{BidderID}}};
\node[attribute] (auctionskey)  [below=of date]
                       {\underline{\texttt{AuctionID}}};
% edges
\draw[-] (date)          -- (auctions);
\draw[-] (location)      -- (auctions);
\draw[-] (volume)        -- (auctions);
\draw[-] (auctions)      -- (participates);
\draw[-] (participates) -- (bidders);
\draw[-] (participates) -- (bids);
\draw[-] (bids)          -- (bid);
\draw[-] (bids)          -- (bidid);
\draw[-] (bidders)      -- (name);
\draw[-] (bidders)      -- (address);
\draw[-] (bidders)      -- (type);
\draw[-] (bids)          -- (auctionid);
\draw[-] (bids)          -- (bidderid);
\draw[-] (bidders)      -- (bidderskey);
\draw[-] (auctions)      -- (auctionskey);
}
\end{tikzpicture}
\caption{Entity-Relationship Diagram}
```

```
\label{fig:ERDiagram}
\end{center}
\end{figure}
```

Listing 10.6: Sample Template of TikZ Code

10.5   Other TEX/LATEX Tricks

TEX and LATEX are languages that you continue to learn with time, and as you complete more complicated document structures. Perhaps the best way to learn tricks in both is to read the original sources Knuth (1984) and Lamport (1994). In particular, by working through the exercises set by Professor Knuth, you will learn an amazing number of useful tricks. And, of course, you can always ask questions and look for answers on the `StackExchange` website `TeX-LaTeX`—for users of TEX, LATEX, ConTEXt, and related typesetting systems at `stackoverflow.com`.

10.6   ConTEXt

Begun in 1990 by Hans Hagen, ConTEXt is another free markup language (distributed under GNU) for typesetting high-quality documents. Why not use ConTEXt instead of LATEX? Just as Python and Ruby are substitute scripting languages, the two markup languages ConTEXt and LATEX are also substitutes. Just as Python has more users than Ruby, LATEX has more users than ConTEXt. In short, the network externalities from using LATEX are greater than those for learning ConTEXt. If you already know LATEX, then incurring the costs of learning ConTEXt may not be worth it. Nevertheless, note that in some disciplines, such as computer science, ConTEXt is used by a good fraction of the profession; in addition, ConTEXt may make it easier to typeset languages not derived from Latin.

According to the ConTEXt website, this markup language supports colors, configurable page backgrounds, hyperlinks, presentations, figure-text integration, cross-references, bibliographies, indices, typesetting for chemistry and

physics, conditional compilation, non-Latin languages, and binding and impo-
sition. ConTEXt can also integrate MetaFun, a superset of METAPOST, which
allows drawing page backgrounds and ornaments. ConTEXt provides a mul-
tilingual user interface with support for markup in English, Dutch, German,
French, and Italian and support for output in many languages, including
western European languages, eastern European languages, Arabic, Chinese,
Japanese, and Korean. ConTEXt supports TEX engines such as `pdftex` without
changing the user interface.[4]

---

[4]From `http://wiki.contextgarden.net/What_is_ConTeXt`.

11

Final Thoughts

THUS ENDS OUR intellectual journey. We hope you enjoyed the ride; we did. We also hope you will continue to learn about distributed and parallel computing, which will be essential tools in scientific research in coming years.

Early computers had just one CPU and a limited amount of local storage in terms of main memory and HD storage as well as magnetic tapes. Because these computers were expensive, they were rarely left idle. Computers are now cheap and ubiquitous. Any particular computer might only be used a small fraction of the time.

Distributed computing is a way to harness the power of many small, cheap computers to solve a large, potentially complicated computing problem. In one popular paradigm, a central computer, often referred to as the *master*, breaks the computing up into *chunks*, which are then farmed out to other computers, which are referred to as the *slaves*. When a slave is done with a task, it returns the answer to the master, and awaits another task, an example of the algorithmic strategy divide-and-conquer. Distributed computing is practical when the data live on the separate computers, and little communication is required until the answer is sent to the master. Distributed computing makes use of cheap hardware but typically requires considerable programming effort and skill, which are costly.

Although Google is perhaps the best-known firm to adopt this strategy when crawling the Web for links to build PageRank, others have used distributed computing in equally imaginative ways. For example, in the search for extraterrestrial intelligence, scientists at the Space Sciences Laboratory on the campus of the University of California, Berkeley, have created an Internet-based volunteer computing project. The SETI@home program searches for possible evidence of radio transmissions from extraterrestrial intelligence using observational data from the Arecibo radio telescope. Data gathered by the telescope are digitized and sent to the SETI@home facility. From there, the data are farmed out to remote, volunteer computers to be analyzed using software that searches for signals. When done, results are reported back to the master computer at SETI@home.

As CPUs have become smaller, faster, and cheaper, putting many CPUs (sometimes referred to as *cores*) in the same computer has expanded computing possibilities. With a multicored computer that has substantial permanent storage you can implement the method of parallel computing. Under this strategy, the individual CPUs are used in tandem to solve a common computing problem. For example, consider solving for the optimal policy function in a Markov decision problem (MDP). Suppose that your computer has eight cores and that you can divide up the state space into eight mutually exclusive sets of values for the state variable. Allocate to a particular core a specific set of state variables and then solve for the optimal policy at each value of the set assigned to that core. When all the cores have completed their tasks, collect the optimal policies. Parallel computing requires expensive hardware (multiple cores or clusters) but typically less programming effort than distributed programming.

Thus, distributed computing typically refers to computing on many remote computers, whereas parallel computing typically refers to using many processors on a local computer. Distributed computing is an engineering possibility because of the Internet. However, if large volumes of data need to be passed, then distributed computing will be slow because of latencies.

Distributed and parallel computing will be central features of science in the future. Thus, knowing how to implement distributed and parallel methods of computing will be an important skill. This area of computing is changing rapidly, even as we write, so we limit ourselves to a brief discussion of MapReduce, a computing model that has matured substantially.

MapReduce is a computing model developed by Dean and Ghemawat (2008) at Google in the early part of the twenty-first century. MapReduce is used widely in industry to solve problems like the following: In Section 4.8.9, in the solved example involving regular expressions, we mentioned that computer servers often generate huge log files; for instance, whenever you go to a website, a record is made each time you access a web page (a file) on that server. Such log files typically contain the date and time of the visit, and the file touched as well as the operating system and the IP address of the visitor. To make the example concrete, suppose you would like to know how many users accessed a file from the same IP address on two consecutive days or more.

The problem itself can be solved on one computer, but there could be millions (billions) of hits to the server. The hits could be divided into 1,000 groups and the data for each group distributed to a different computer. Then the 1,000 computers would work on aggregating the hits. By spreading the entire task over many computers, the task will take less time. Whether the entire task takes 0.001 of the time or not really depends on the fixed costs of setting up each computer.

The best-known implementation of MapReduce is Apache Hadoop, an open-source program implemented in Java. Historically, most early users of Hadoop were well-versed in the Java programming language. Although Java is a flexible and powerful language, many novices find using it difficult. In short, the start-up costs associated with Hadoop to solve distributed computing problems have prevented many from exploiting the power of the MapReduce model. Third-party vendors, such as Amazon Web Services (AWS), have provided platforms that reduce these start-up costs, but computing on AWS using Elastic Cloud Computing (EC2) and Elastic MapReduce (EMR) is not free. Those who want to compute on the cloud using AWS will find the web pages and videos at `http://aws.amazon.com` useful in getting up to speed quickly.

You can implement parallel computing using Python by employing the IPython module (see Pérez and Granger 2007) along with the Notebook feature.

Although both distributed and parallel computing are feasible alternatives, each involves considerable fixed costs to implement. Therefore, it is important to recognize up front how much can be gained from either distributed or parallel computing.

11.1 Amdahl's Law

On the surface, it would appear that if it takes one computer a year to complete a task, then 365 computers should complete the same task in just one day.

This is referred to as *linear speedup*. Unfortunately, the engineering reality is that linear speedup is typically impossible because in every program a portion (maybe just a small portion) cannot be parallelized, and using multiple processors necessarily introduces a cost of communication. The portion that cannot be parallelized limits the overall speedup possible. If, say, some fraction α of the time is spent sojourning in parts of a program that cannot be parallelized, then $(1/\alpha)$ is the maximum speedup that can obtain through the parallelization of a program. This is often referred to as *Amdahl's law*, in honor of Gene Amdahl, who noted the fact in the 1960s.

To see how important Amdahl's law is, suppose that the sequential portion of a program accounts for 20 percent of the run time; then the maximum speedup is fivefold regardless of the number of processors used. Amdahl's law puts an upper limit on the usefulness of adding more processors in parallel. As Brooks (1995, 17) colorfully put it in *The Mythical Man Month* (albeit in the context of SDEs),

> When a task cannot be partitioned because of sequential constraints, the application of more effort has no effect on the schedule. The bearing of a child takes nine months, no matter how many women are assigned.

Thus, just as Harel (1992) outlined the limits to computation, so, too, did Amdahl and Brooks. Amdahl's law is useful because it gives a guesstimate of what can be gained from parallelization. Put another way, by using Amdahl's law you can decide whether it is worth your while to solve a problem using parallel computing.

11.2 MapReduce

In computer science, a programming paradigm is a fundamental style of computer programming. We mentioned in Chapter 4 that Python supports four of those paradigms: imperative, procedural, functional and object-oriented. Computer scientists refer to a *programming model* as an abstraction of a computer system. For example, the most common model is referred to as the *von Neumann model*, named in honor of John von Neumann, the principal architect of the modern computer. The von Neumann model refers to sequential computing. When referring to parallel computing, several possible models exist, each

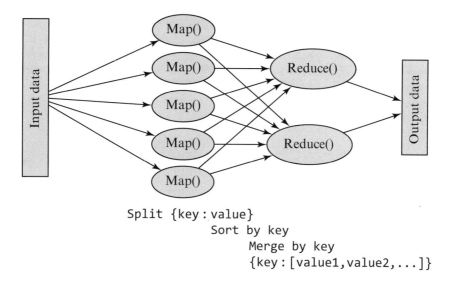

```
Split {key:value}
     Sort by key
        Merge by key
           {key:[value1,value2,...]}
```

Figure 11.1: High-Level MapReduce Diagram

capturing the different ways processors can be interconnected. Two common models are the shared-memory model, where many processors all have access to the same memory and the distributed-memory model, where each processor has only its private memory and communicates with the other processors using message passing. In practice, most used is some hybrid of the two.

Perhaps the best-known model of distributed/parallel computing is the MapReduce model. In Figure 11.1 we present a high-level MapReduce diagram, which describes what the mappers and the reducers do.

MapReduce Example

McKinney (2013, ch.2) illustrated how information can be processed from a relatively small log file, one that could fit into the memory of even a modest computer. An example of a few lines from such a log file is presented in Listing 11.1:

```
63.152.113.99 - segre [07/Dec/2014:08:10:55 -0600] "GET /~segre/myFTP/
    HTTP/1.1" 200 2016 "-" "Mozilla/5.0 (Windows NT 6.1; WOW64)
    AppleWebKit/537.36 (KHTML, like Gecko) Chrome/39.0.2171.71 Safari
    /537.36"
```

```
63.152.113.99 - segre [07/Dec/2014:08:11:02 -0600] "GET /~segre/myFTP/
    corpus1.zip HTTP/1.1" 200 3134440 "http://vinci.cs.uiowa.edu/~
    segre/myFTP/" "Mozilla/5.0 (Windows NT 6.1; WOW64) AppleWebKit/
    537.36 (KHTML, like Gecko) Chrome/39.0.2171.71 Safari/537.36"
66.249.69.83 - - [07/Dec/2014:08:13:22 -0600] "GET /redmine/issues?
    page=1&per_page=25&sort=tracker%2Cstatus%3Adesc%2Csubject HTTP/1.1
    " 404 511 "-" "Mozilla/5.0 (compatible; Googlebot/2.1; +http://www
    .google.com/bot.html)"
123.125.71.95 - - [07/Dec/2014:08:46:47 -0600] "GET / HTTP/1.1" 301
    546 "-" "Mozilla/5.0 (compatible; Baiduspider/2.0; +http://www.
    baidu.com/search/spider.html)"
186.153.108.164 - - [07/Dec/2014:08:49:27 -0600] "GET /~segre/ HTTP/
    1.1" 200 748 "http://www.amcs.uiowa.edu/faculty" "Mozilla/5.0 (
    Windows NT 5.1) AppleWebKit/537.36 (KHTML, like Gecko) Chrome/
    39.0.2171.71 Safari/537.36"
```

Listing 11.1: A Few Lines from a Log File

The problem is that log files can often be huge. What to do if a file is petabytes large?

To some extent, what you can do really depends on what you want to learn from the log file. In other words, it depends on the application. In many practical applications, however, what you seek to learn involves solving a problem that is referred to as an *embarrassingly parallel problem* or sometimes a *pleasingly parallel problem*. Such problems tend to require little or no communication of results between tasks. Embarrassingly parallel problems differ from distributed computing problems, which require communication between tasks, especially communication of intermediate results. Clearly, the range of problems lives, more or less, on a continuum from perfectly parallel problems to distributed computing problems.

In this section, we explore the solution to a problem using the MapReduce model for processing and generating large data sets with a parallel, distributed algorithm on a cluster of computers. We use the example mentioned previously, namely, how many users accessed a file from the same IP address on two consecutive days or more?

To begin, assume you just have one computer on which to do the calculations, and the log file is small enough to fit into memory. Perhaps the most straightfoward way to proceed is to use a dictionary to store the IP address as key and the access dates as values, and then to iterate through each IP address's date values, checking for consecutive dates. Simple enough.

Now, imagine that the log file is too large to fit into memory. If the list of customers fits into memory, then you can still find the customers who have visited the website on two consecutive days. To do this, create a dictionary, read the log file line by line, and add every new record to it. If the customer already exists in the dictionary, then add a new date, otherwise add the new customer.

When the list of customers is too large to fit into memory, an alternative computing strategy is required. In this case, we use MapReduce. The idea behind MapReduce is illustrated in Figure 11.1. A MapReduce solution involves each mapper emitting a key-value pair that a reducer consumes. Reducers then process the values (reduce them) for each key in a specific way.

We illustrate how that would work using pseudocode.

```
def Map(line):
  # parse line
  line = line.split("")
  ip = line[0]
  date = line[1]
  # emit customer id and date they visited
  emit (ip, date)

def Reduce(key, values):
  # combine results using a predefined function
  # checking to see if any consecutive dates exist
  emit (id, areDatesConsecutive(values))

# this is a utility function that takes all date values
# for a particular id and produces 1 if the customer
# returns, and 0 otherwise
def AreDatesConsecutive(dates):
  # cast date into datetime object
  dates = [datetime.strptime(d, ?%Y-%m-%d?) for d in dates]
  # sort dates
  dates = sorted(dates)
  # generate list of date differences
  dateDiffs = dates[1:len(dates)] - dates[0:-1]
  dateDiffs = [d.day for d in dateDiffs]
  # check to see if any date difference is 1
  if 1 in res: return 1 else return 0
```

11.3   Summary

This example provides only a crude outline of how MapReduce works. To learn how to implement MapReduce, consider reading the book by Miner and Shook (2012). They have provided templates for Hadoop for many commonly encountered problems. The practical problem is configuring a cluster on which to use Hadoop, which is why many people use third-party implementations, such as EMR on AWS.

Appendices

Appendix A

The Virtual Machine

A virtual machine (VM) is a computer program that simulates the behavior of one computer in the memory of another computer. Specifically, a VM can execute computer programs on one hardware configuration for a particular operating system that behave just like a different hardware configuration using a different operating system. For example, for those using a Microsoft Windows–based computer, we have created a VM that will mimic the OS X environment, albeit in the Linux environment, but you could install the VM we have created on an Apple Mac and have that computer behaves as if it were a Linux computer. Although this may sound odd to experienced users, we believe that for beginners the benefits will outweigh the costs; that is, installing all the software available on the VM separately on a Mac is not straightforward. Thus, by installing the VM on a Mac, a novice avoids becoming discouraged.

A.1   Installing the Virtual Machine

On the VM, we have chosen the Linux Ubuntu operating system, which is based on the Debian/GNU distribution, because it is free and because a large community supports this operating system.

We have also chosen Oracle's VM VirtualBox as the virtualization software, again because it is free. Thus, in order to run the VM, you must also install VM VirtualBox on your computer. For instructions concerning how to do this, go to `https://www.virtualbox.org`. *Be sure to install the version for your computer.* That is, if Windows is your operating system, then choose VM VirtualBox for that operating system.

A.2 Downloading the Virtual Machine

To download the VM for this book, go to its web page at the MIT Press `http://www.mitpress.mit.edu/books/gentle-intro` and follow the instructions.[1] The first thing to note about this file is its size—about 7 gigabytes. Once imported, however, the VM will create a 15-gigabyte file with its virtual hard drive. Therefore, it is very important that you have at least 23 gigabytes of free space, and preferably more, to use this VM. By default, the VM has 1024 MB of RAM, so your computer should have at least twice that amount of RAM, and preferably four times.

Second, in order for the download to have a good chance of success, you will also need a very stable Internet connection: using the Wi-Fi at Starbucks just won't cut it.

Assuming you have already installed the VM VirtualBox software, and downloaded the `.ova` file of the VM into the subdirectory of your choice, you should be able simply to double-click on it, which should then make VM VirtualBox open it. If you have done everything correctly, then the `Import VM Appliance` window will appear. You will see that the VM is named `PGBookVM`, uses the 64-bit version of Ubuntu, and has one CPU as well as 1024 MB of RAM. Check the `Reinitialize the MAC address of all network cards` box and then click on the `Import` button.

This process can take several minutes, after which you should be able to start the VM using the `Start` button. The default user name is `PGBook` and the default password is `pgbook`. Once the system boots, you should be able to begin your work by opening a terminal window.

---

[1]If, with time, web pages have moved around, and this is no longer a valid URL, then search for the expression "`paarsch golyaev vm`" which may help you find the appropriate link. If not, contact the MIT Press.

A.3 Special Instructions

What if this download doesn't work? Suppose you followed the instructions perfectly, so user error is not the reason. Although transmission over the Internet is remarkably error-free, it is still possible for corruptions (errors) to occur, especially when transmitting large files. How will you know whether a 7-gigabyte file has a corruption? Use a hash function with the entire file as an input, and calculate the hash value (see Chapter 3).

For the file that contains the image of the VM, the hash value returned by the `md5` hash function is available on the web page from which you downloaded the VM. Thus, after you have downloaded the VM, you should use the `md5` hash function on that file to see whether something went amiss in transmission. If the two hash values don't match, you will need to download the file again. On the other hand, if the hash values do match and the VM still does not work, the cause is likely user error.

Most of the time, when something does not work on a computer, it is some kind of user error. Sometimes, the error will be obvious; most of the time it won't. We actually prefer obvious errors to subtle ones, because finding the cause of a subtle error can often take days—even weeks.

It is unfortunate that such a complex task should be required at the beginning, before you have really learned much. But this is unavoidable because the alternative is for you to install many, many programs yourself, which would be even worse.

Appendix B

Recommended Reading

In this appendix, we collect the articles and books we think are most important for the reader to consult. Obviously, you cannot read them all, at least not in the next year or so. Which to read first? Those are marked with one asterisk, and those to read next, with two asterisks. Unmarked items are references. Full bibliographic information is given in the References list that follows this appendix.

B.1   Computers

* Barrett, N. (2006) *The Binary Revolution*.

** Ceruzzi, P. E. (2003) *A History of Modern Computing*.

B.2   Programming

* McConnell, S. C. (2004) *Code Complete: A Practical Handbook of Software Construction*.

Brooks, F. P. (1982) *The Mythical Man Month*.

B.3   Software Tools

*(1) Neil, D. (2012) *Practical Vim*.

*(2) Cameron, D., et al. (2005) *Learning GNU Emacs*.

*(3) Swicegood, T. (2010) *Pragmatic Guide to Git.*

*(4) Mecklenburg, R. (2005) *Managing Projects with GNU Make.*

*(5) Walkenbach, J. (2013) *Excel 2013 Bible.*

*(6) Fitzgerald, M. (2012) *Introducing Regular Expressions.*

**(1) Knuth, D. E. (1984) *The T$_E$Xbook.*

**(2) Lamport, L. (1994) *LaT$_E$X: A Document Preparation System.*

Kernighan B. W. and D. M. Ritchie. (1988) *The C Programming Language.*

Nyhoff, L. and S. Leestma. (1995) *FORTRAN 77 for Engineers and Scientists with an Introduction to FORTRAN 90.*

B.4 Databases

* Sanders, G. L. (1995) *Data Modeling.*

**(1) Garcia-Molina, H., et al. (2009) *Database Systems.*

**(2) Date, C. J. (2012a) *Database Design and Relational Theory.*

**(3) Date, C. J. (2012b) *SQL and Relational Theory.*

Codd, E. F. (1970) "A Relational Model for Shared Data Banks."

Codd, E. F. (1972) "Relational Completeness of Data Base Sublanguages."

Chen, P. (1976) "The Entity-Relationship Model: Towards a Unified View of Data."

B.5 Python

* Campbell, J., et al. (2009) *Practical Programming: An Introduction to Computer Science Using Python.*

Lutz, M. (2009) *Learning Python.*

McKinney, W. (2013) *Python for Data Analysis*.

Bird, S., et al. (2009) *Natural Language Processing with Python*.

B.6   Econometrics and Statistics

*(1) Salsburg, D. (2001) *The Lady Tasting Tea*.

*(2) Kabacoff, R. I. (2013) *R in Action*.

*(3) James, G., et al. (2013) *An Introduction to Statistical Learning: With Applications in R*.

*(4) Davidson, R. and J. G. MacKinnon. (2004) *Econometric Theory and Methods*.

**(1) Matloff, N. (2011) *The Art of R Programming*.

Chambers, J. M. (2009) *Software for Data Analysis: Programming with R*.

Angrist J. D. and J.-S. Pischke. (2009) *Mostly Harmless Econometrics*.

Frisch R. and F. V. Waugh. (1933) "Partial Time Regressions as Compared with Individual Trends."

Lovell, M. C. (1963) "Seasonal Adjustment of Economic Time Series and Multiple Regression Analysis."

B.7   Algorithmics

*   Harel, D. (1992) *Algorithmics: The Spirit of Computing*.

** Moore, C. and S. Mertens. (2011) *The Nature of Computation*.

Graham, R. L., et al. (1994) *Concrete Mathematics*.

Sedgewick, R. and K. Wayne. (2011) *Algorithms*.

Kleinberg, J. and E. Tardos. (2006) *Algorithm Design*.

Cook, S. A. (1971) "The Complexity of Theorem-Proving Procedures."

B.8   Numerical Methods

* Weinstein, L. (2012) *Guesstimation 2.0: Solving Today's Problems on the Back of a Napkin.*

** Hubbard, D. W. (2010) *How to Measure Anything: Finding the Value of "Intangibles" in Business.*

Golub, G. H. and C. F. Van Loan. (2013) *Matrix Computations.*

Scott, L. R. (2011) *Numerical Analysis.*

Monahan, J. F. (2001) *Numerical Methods of Statistics.*

Judd, K. L. (1998) *Numerical Methods in Economics.*

Boyd, S. and L. Vandenberghe. (2004) *Convex Optimization.*

Gill, P. E., et al. (1981) *Practical Optimization.*

Nocedal, J. and S. J. Wright. (2006) *Numerical Optimization.*

Conn, A. R., et al. (2009) *Introduction to Derivative-Free Optimization.*

Gentle, J. E. (2010) *Random Number Generation and Monte Carlo Methods.*

Marsaglia, G. (1968) "Random Numbers Fall Mainly in the Planes."

Matsumoto, M. and T. Nishimura. (1998) "Mersenne Twister: A 623-Dimensionally Equidistributed Uniform Pseudo-Random Number Generator."

B.9   Data Mining and Machine Learning

* Halevy, A., et al. (2009) "The Unreasonable Effectiveness of Data."

** Valiant, L. G. (2013) *Probably Approximately Correct.*

Shalev-Shwartz, S. and S. Ben-David. (2014) *Understanding Machine Learning.*

Dean, J. and S. Ghemawat. (2008) "MapReduce: Simplified Data Processing on Large Clusters."

Rajaraman, A. and J. D. Ullman. (2011) *Mining Massive Datasets*.

B.10 Information and Markets

Surowiecki, J. (2004) *The Wisdom of Crowds*.

McMillan, J. (2002) *Reinventing the Bazaar*.

Hubbard, T. P. and H. J. Paarsch. (2015) *Auctions*.

Roth, A. E. (2015) *Who Gets What — and Why*.

References

Abadir, K. M. and J. R. Magnus (2002). Notation in econometrics: A proposal for a standard. *Econometrics Journal 5*, 76–90.

Abramowitz, M. and I. A. Stegun (1972). *Handbook of Mathematical Functions, Tenth Printing with Corrections*. Mineola, NY: Dover Publications.

Abramson, M. A., C. Audet, G. Couture, J. E. Dennis, S. Le Digabel, and C. Tribes (2013). The NOMAD Project. https://www.gerad.ca/nomad/.

Angrist, J. D. and J.-S. Pischke (2009). *Mostly Harmless Econometrics*. Princeton, NJ: Princeton University Press.

Aruoba, S. B. and J. Fernández-Villaverde (2014). A comparison of programming languages in economics, typescript, Department of Economics, University of Pennsylvania, Philadelphia, Pa.

Audet, C. and J. E. Dennis (2006). Mesh adaptive direct search algorithms for constrained optimization. *SIAM Journal on Optimization 17*, 188–217.

Barrett, N. (2006). *The Binary Revolution*. London: Weidenfeld and Nicolson.

Becker, R. A., J. M. Chambers, and A. R. Wilks (1988). *The New S Language*. Pacific Grove, CA: Wadsworth and Brooks.

Berndt, E. R., Z. Griliches, and N. Rappaport (1995). Econometric estimates of price indexes for personal computers in the 1990s. *Journal of Econometrics 68*, 243–268.

Berndt, E. R., B. H. Hall, R. E. Hall, and J. A. Hausman (1974). Estimation and inference in nonlinear structural models. *Annals of Economic and Social Measurement 3*, 653–665.

Bird, S., E. Klein, and E. Loper (2009). *Natural Language Processing with Python.* Sebastopol, CA: O'Reilly.

Bixby, R. E. (2002). Solving real-world linear programs: A decade and more of progress. *Operations Research 50*, 3–15.

Bixby, R. E., M. Fenelon, Z. Gu, E. Rothberg, and R. Wunderling (2004). Mixed-integer programming: A progress report. In M. Grötschel (Ed.), *The Sharpest Cut: The Impact of Manfred Padberg and His Work*, pp. 309–325. Philadelphia: SIAM.

Boser, B. E., I. M. Guyon, and V. Vapnik (1992). A training algorithm for optimal margin classifiers. In *Proceedings of the Fifth Annual Workshop on Computational Learning Theory*, pp. 144–152. ACM.

Boyd, S. and L. Vandenberghe (2004). *Convex Optimization.* New York: Cambridge University Press.

Brooks, F. P. (1995). *The Mythical Man Month,* 2nd ed. Reading, MA: Addison-Wesley.

Broyden, C. G. (1965). A class of methods for solving nonlinear simultaneous equations. *Mathematics of Computation 19*, 577–593.

Broyden, C. G. (1970). The convergence of a class of double-rank minimization algorithms. *Journal of the Institute of Mathematics and Its Applications 6*, 76–90.

Brynjolfsson, E. and A. McAfee (2014). *The Second Machine Age: Work, Progress, and Prosperity in a Time of Brilliant Technologies.* New York: W. W. Norton.

Butcher, J. C. (2003). *Numerical Methods for Ordinary Differential Equations.* New York: Wiley.

Cameron, D., J. Elliott, M. Loy, E. Raymond, and B. Rosenblatt (2005). *Learning GNU Emacs,* 3rd ed. Sebastopol, CA: O'Reilly.

Campbell, J., P. Gries, J. Montojo, and G. Wilson (2009). *Practical Programming: An Introduction to Computer Science Using Python.* Dallas: Pragmatic Bookshelf.

Casella, G. and E. I. George (1992). Explaining the Gibbs sampler. *American Statistician 46*, 167–174.

Ceruzzi, P. E. (2003). *A History of Modern Computing*, 2nd ed. Cambridge, MA: MIT Press.

Ceruzzi, P. E. (2012). *Computing: A Concise History*. Cambridge, MA: MIT Press.

Chacon, S. (2009). *Pro Git*. New York: Apress.

Chambers, J. M. (2009). *Software for Data Analysis: Programming with R*. New York: Springer.

Chan, T. F., G. H. Golub, and R. J. LeVeque (1983). Algorithms for computing the sample variance: Analysis and recommendations. *American Statistician 37*, 242–247.

Chen, P. P. (1976). The entity-relationship model: Towards a unified view of data. *ACM Transactions on Database Systems 1*, 9–36.

Chib, S. and E. Greenberg (1995). Understanding the Metropolis-Hastings algorithm. *American Statistician 49*, 327–335.

Church, A. (1936). An unsolvable problem of elementary number theory. *American Journal of Mathematics 58*, 345–363.

Codd, E. F. (1970). A relational model for shared data banks. *Communications of the ACM 13*, 377–387.

Codd, E. F. (1972). Relational completeness of data base sublanguages. In R. J. Rustin (Ed.), *Database Systems, Courant Computer Science Symposia, Series 6*, Upper Saddle River, NJ. Prentice Hall.

Conn, A. R., N. I. M. Gould, and P. L. Toint (2000). *Trust Region Methods*. Philadelphia: SIAM.

Conn, A. R., K. Scheinberg, and L. N. Vincente (2009). *Introduction to Derivative-Free Optimization*. Philadelphia: SIAM.

Cook, S. A. (1971). The complexity of theorem-proving procedures. In *Proceedings of the Third Annual ACM Symposium on Theory of Computing*, pp. 151–158.

Cortes, C. and V. N. Vapnick (1995). Support-vector networks. *Machine Learning 20*, 273–297.

Cox, D. R. (1972). Regression models and life-tables. *Journal of the Royal Statistical Society:* Series B *34*, 187–220.

Crémer, J. (2011). A very minimal introduction to TikZ, typescript, Toulouse School of Economics, Toulouse, France.

Date, C. J. (2012a). *Database Design and Relational Theory*. Sebastopol, CA: O'Reilly.

Date, C. J. (2012b). *SQL and Relational Theory,* 2nd ed. Sebastopol, CA: O'Reilly.

Davidon, W. C. (1991). Variable metric method for minimization. *SIAM Journal on Optimization 1*, 1–17.

Davidson, R. and J. G. MacKinnon (2004). *Econometric Theory and Methods*. New York: Oxford University Press.

Dean, J. and S. Ghemawat (2008). MapReduce: Simplified data processing on large clusters. *Communications of the ACM 51*, 107–113.

Denardo, E. V. (2003). *Dynamic Programming: Models and Applicatons*. Mineola, NY: Dover Publications.

Dijkstra, E. W. (1968). Go to statement considered harmful. *Communications of the ACM 11*, 147–148.

Duchi, J., E. Hazan, and Y. Singer (2011). Adaptive subgradient methods for online learning and stochastic optimization. *Journal of Machine Learning 12*, 2121–2159.

Edgeworth, F. Y. (1885). Methods of statistics. *Journal of the Royal Statistical Society Jubilee Volume*, 181–217.

Efron, B. (1979). Bootstrap methods: Another look at the jackknife. *Annals of Statistics 7*, 1–26.

Efron, B. (1982). *The Jackknife, the Bootstrap, and Other Resampling Plans*. Philadelphia: SIAM.

Efron, B. (2010). *Large-Scale Inference: Empirical Bayes Methods for Estimation, Testing, and Prediction*. New York: Cambridge University Press.

Efron, B. and R. Tibshirani (1993). *An Introduction to the Bootstrap*. London: Chapman and Hall.

Ferris, M. C. and T. S. Munson (2002). Interior-point methods for massive support vector machines. *SIAM Journal on Optimization 13*, 783–804.

Fishman, G. S. and L. R. Moore (1982). A statistical evaluation of multiplicative congruential random number generators with modulus $2^{31} - 1$. *Journal of the American Statistical Association 77*, 129–136.

Fitzgerald, M. (2012). *Introducing Regular Expressions*. Sebastopol, CA: O'Reilly.

Fletcher, R. (1970). A new approach to variable metric algorithms. *Computer Journal 13*, 317–322.

Fletcher, R. and M. J. D. Powell (1963). A rapidly convergent descent method for minimization. *Computer Journal 6*, 163–168.

Fourer, R., D. M. Gay, and B. W. Kernighan (2002). *AMPL: A Modeling Language for Mathematical Programming*, 2nd ed. Pacific Grove, CA: Brooks/Cole.

Frisch, R. and F. V. Waugh (1933). Partial time regressions as compared with individual trends. *Econometrica 1*, 387–401.

Galton, F. (1907). Vox populi. *Nature 75*, 450–451.

Garcia-Molina, H., J. D. Ullman, and J. Widom (2009). *Database Systems*, 2nd ed. Upper Saddle River, NJ: Pearson Prentice Hall.

Geman, S. and D. Geman (1984). Stochastic relaxation, Gibbs distributions, and the Bayesian restoration of images. *IEEE Transactions on Pattern Analysis and Machine Intelligence 6*, 721–741.

Gentle, J. E. (2010). *Random Number Generation and Monte Carlo Methods*. New York: Springer.

Gilbert, S. L. and N. A. Lynch (2002). Brewer's conjecture and the feasibility of consistent, available, partition-tolerant web services. *ACM SIGACT News 33*, 51–59.

Gill, P. E., W. Murray, and M. A. Saunders (2002). SNOPT: An SQP algorithm for large-scale constrained optimization. *SIAM Journal on Optimization 12*, 979–1006.

Gill, P. E., W. Murray, and M. H. Wright (1981). *Practical Optimization*. San Francisco: Academic Press.

Goldfarb, D. (1970). A family of variable metric updates derived by variational means. *Mathematics of Computation 24*, 23–26.

Goldfeld, S. M., R. E. Quandt, and H. F. Trotter (1966). Maximization by quadratic hill-climbing. *Econometrica 34*, 541–551.

Golub, G. H. and C. F. Van Loan (2013). *Matrix Computations*, 4th ed. Baltimore: Johns Hopkins University Press.

Goossens, M., F. Mittelbach, S. Rahtz, D. Roegel, and H. Voss (2007). *The LaTeX Graphics Companion*, 2nd ed. Reading, MA: Addison-Wesley.

Graham, R. L., D. E. Knuth, and O. Patashnik (1994). *Concrete Mathematics*, 2nd ed. Reading, MA: Addison-Wesley.

Gray, J. (2009). A transformed scientific method. In T. Hey, S. Tansley, and K. Tolle (Eds.), *The Fourth Paradigm*. Redmond, WA: Microsoft Research.

Haddock, S. H. D. and C. W. Dunn (2011). *Practical Computing for Biologists*. Sunderland, MA: Sinauer Associates.

Halevy, A., P. Norvig, and F. Pereira (2009). The unreasonable effectiveness of data. *IEEE Intelligent Systems March/April*, 8–12.

Han, A. and J. A. Hausman (1990). Flexible parametric estimation of duration and competing risk models. *Journal of Applied Econometrics 5*, 1–28.

Hanley, J. A. (2004). 'Transmuting' women into men: Galton's family data on human stature. *American Statistician 58*, 237–243.

Harel, D. (1992). *Algorithmics: The Spirit of Computing*, 2nd ed. Reading, MA: Addison-Wesley.

Hart, W. E., C. Laird, J.-P. Watson, and D. L. Woodruff (2012). *Pyomo—Optimization Modeling in Python*. New York: Springer.

Hastings, W. K. (1970). Monte Carlo sampling methods using Markov chains and their applications. *Biometrika 57*, 97–109.

Higham, N. J. (1998). *Handbook of Writing for the Mathematical Sciences.* Philadelphia: SIAM.

Himmelblau, D. M. (1972). *Applied Nonlinear Programming.* New York: McGraw-Hill.

Hooke, R. and T. A. Jeeves (1961). "Direct search" solution of numerical and statistical problems. *Journal of the ACM 8*, 212–229.

Hubbard, D. W. (2010). *How to Measure Anything: Finding the Value of "Intangibles" in Business.* Hoboken, NJ: Wiley.

Hubbard, T. P., R. Kirkegaard, and H. J. Paarsch (2013). Using economic theory to guide numerical analysis: Solving for equilibria in models of asymmetric first-price auctions. *Computational Economics 42*, 241–266.

Hubbard, T. P. and H. J. Paarsch (2009). Investigating bid preferences at low-price, sealed-bid auctions with endogenous participation. *International Journal of Industrial Organization 27*, 1–14.

Hubbard, T. P. and H. J. Paarsch (2015). *Auctions.* Cambridge, MA: MIT Press.

Huber, P. J. (1981). *Robust Statistics.* New York: Wiley.

James, G., D. Witten, T. Hastie, and R. Tibshirani (2013). *An Introduction to Statistical Learning: With Applications in R.* New York: Springer.

Johnson, C. (2009). *Numerical Solution of Partial Differential Equations by the Finite Element Method.* Mineola, NY: Dover Publications.

Johnson, R. and T. Zhang (2013). Accelerating stochastic gradient descent using predictive variance reduction, typescript, Department of Statistics, Rutgers University, Newark, NJ.

Judd, K. L. (1997). Computational economics and economic theory: Substitutes or complements? *Journal of Economic Dynamics and Control 21*, 907–942.

Judd, K. L. (1998). *Numerical Methods in Economics.* Cambridge, MA: MIT Press.

Kabacoff, R. I. (2013). *R in Action,* 2nd ed. Shelter Island, NY: Manning Publications.

Kernighan, B. W. and D. M. Ritchie (1988). *The C Programming Language,* 2nd ed. Upper Saddle River, NJ: Prentice Hall.

Kiefer, J. and J. Wolfowitz (1952). Stochastic estimation of the maximum of a regression function. *Annals of Mathematical Statistics 23,* 462.

Klee, V. and G. J. Minty (1972). How good is the simplex algorithm. In O. Shisha (Ed.), *Inequalities III,* New York, pp. 159–175. Academic Press.

Kleinberg, J. and É. Tardos (2006). *Algorithm Design.* Reading, MA: Addison-Wesley.

Knuth, D. E. (1984). *The TEXbook.* Reading, MA: Addison-Wesley.

Kreibich, J. A. (2010). *Using SQLite.* Sebastopol, CA: O'Reilley.

Lamport, L. (1994). *LATEX: A Document Preparation System,* 2nd ed. Reading, MA: Addison-Wesley.

Le Digabel, S. (2011). Algorithm 909: NOMAD: Nonlinear optimization with the MADS algorithm. *ACM Transactions on Mathematical Software 37,* 44:1–44:15.

Levenberg, K. (1944). A method for the solution of certain non-linear problems in least squares. *Quarterly of Applied Mathematics 2,* 164–168.

Longley, J. W. (1967). An appraisal of least-squares programs from the point of view of the user. *Journal of the American Statistical Association 62,* 819–841.

Lovell, M. C. (1963). Seasonal adjustment of economic time series and multiple regression analysis. *Journal of the American Statistical Association 58,* 993–1010.

Luo, Z.-Q., J.-S. Pang, and D. Ralph (1996). *Mathematical Programs with Equilibrium Constraints.* Cambridge: Cambridge University Press.

Lutz, M. (2009). *Learning Python,* 4th ed. Sebastopol, CA: O'Reilly.

Manski, C. F. (1988). *Analog Estimation Methods in Econometrics.* London: Chapman and Hall.

Marquardt, D. W. (1963). An algorithm for least-squares estimation of nonlinear parameters. *SIAM Journal of Applied Mathematics 11*, 431–441.

Marsaglia, G. (1968). Random numbers fall mainly in the planes. *Proceedings of the National Academy of Sciences 61*, 25–28.

Matloff, N. (2011). *The Art of R Programming*. San Francisco: No Starch Press.

Matsumoto, M. and T. Nishimura (1998). Mersenne Twister: A 623-dimensionally equidistributed uniform pseudo-random number generator. *ACM Transactions on Modeling and Computer Simulation 8*, 3–30.

McCloskey, D. N. (2000). *Economic Writing*, 2nd ed. Long Grove, IL: Waveland Press.

McConnell, S. C. (2004). *Code Complete: A Practical Handbook of Software Construction*, 2nd ed. Redmond, Washington: Microsoft Press.

McKinney, W. (2013). *Python for Data Analysis*. Sebastopol, CA: O'Reilly.

McMillan, J. (2002). *Reinventing the Bazaar*. New York: W. W. Norton.

Mecklenburg, R. (2005). *Managing Projects with GNU Make*, 3rd ed. Sebastopol, CA: O'Reilly.

Metropolis, N., A. W. Rosenbluth, M. N. Rosenbluth, A. H. Teller, and E. Teller (1953). Equations of state calculations by fast computing machines. *Journal of Chemical Physics 21*, 1087–1092.

Miller, J. E. (2004). *The Chicago Guide to Writing about Numbers*. Chicago: University of Chicago Press.

Miner, D. and A. Shook (2012). *MapReduce Design Patterns: Building Effective Algorithms and Analytics for Hadoop and Other Systems*. Sebastopol, CA: O'Reilly.

Monahan, J. F. (2001). *Numerical Methods of Statistics*. New York: Cambridge University Press.

Moore, C. and S. Mertens (2011). *The Nature of Computation*. New York: Oxford University Press.

Moore, G. E. (1965). Cramming more components onto integrated circuits. *Electronics 38*, 114–117.

Murrell, P. (2006). *R Graphics*. Boca Ratan, FL: Chapman and Hall.

Murtagh, B. A. and M. A. Saunders (2003). MINOS 5.51 User's Guide. Technical Report SOL-83-20R, Systems Optimization Laboratory, Department of Management Science and Engineering, Stanford University, Stanford, Calif.

Neil, D. (2012). *Practical Vim*. Dallas: Pragmatic Bookshelf.

Nelder, J. A. and R. Mead (1965). A simplex method for function minimization. *Computer Journal 7*, 308–313.

Nelsen, R. B. (1999). *An Introduction to Copulas*. New York: Springer.

Nie, Z. and J. S. Racine (2012). The crs package: Nonparametric regression splines for continuous and categorical predictors. *R Journal 4*, 48–56.

Nocedal, J. and S. J. Wright (2006). *Numerical Optimization,* 2nd ed. New York: Springer.

Nyhoff, L. and S. Leestma (1995). *FORTRAN 77 for Engineers and Scientists with an Introduction to FORTRAN 90,* 4th ed. Upper Saddle River, NJ: Prentice Hall.

Paarsch, H. J. and H. Hong (2006). *An Introduction to Structural Econometrics of Auction Data*. Cambridge, MA: MIT Press.

Papadimitriou, C. H. (1994). *Computational Complexity*. Reading, MA: Addison-Wesley.

Pérez, F. and B. E. Granger (2007). IPython: A system for interactive scientific computing. *Computing in Science and Engineering 9*, 21–29.

Platt, J. C. (1999). Fast training of support vector machines using sequential minimal optimization. In *Advances in Kernel Methods*, Cambridge, MA, pp. 185–208. MIT Press.

Politis, D. N. and J. P. Romano (1994). Large sample confidence regions based on subsamples under minimal assumptions. *Annals of Statistics 22*, 2031–2050.

Politis, D. N., J. P. Romano, and M. Wolf (1999). *Subsampling*. New York: Springer.

Powell, M. J. D. (1964). An efficient method for finding the minimum of a function of several variables without calculating derivatives. *Computer Journal 7*, 155–162.

Quenouille, M. H. (1949). Problems in plane sampling. *Annals of Mathematical Statistics 20*, 355–375.

Quenouille, M. H. (1956). Notes on bias in estimation. *Biometrika 43*, 353–360.

Rajaraman, A. and J. D. Ullman (2011). *Mining Massive Datasets*. New York: Cambridge University Press.

Robbins, H. E. and S. Monro (1951). A stochastic approximation method. *Annals of Mathematical Statistics 22*, 400.

Rosenbloom, P. S. (2013). *On Computing: The Fourth Great Scientific Domain*. Cambridge, MA: MIT Press.

Rosenbrock, H. H. (1960). An automatic method for finding the greatest or least value of a function. *Computer Journal 3*, 175–184.

Roth, A. E. (2015). *Who Gets What — and Why*. New York: Houghton Mifflin Harcourt.

Rumelhart, D. E., G. E. Hinton, and R. J. Williams (1986). Learning representations by back-propagating errors. *Nature 323*, 533–536.

Safire, W. (1992). *The First Dissident: The Book of Job in Today's Politics*. New York: Random House.

Salsburg, D. (2001). *The Lady Tasting Tea*. New York: Henry Holt.

Sanders, G. L. (1995). *Data Modeling*. New York: Boyd and Fraser.

Schaul, T., S. Zhang, and Y. LeCun (2013). No more pesky learning rates, typescript, Courant Institute of Mathematical Science, New York University, New York.

Schölkopf, B. (1998). SVMs—a practical consequence of learning theory. *IEEE Intelligent Systems July/August*, 18–21.

Schutt, R. and C. O'Neil (2013). *Doing Data Science: Straight Talk from the Frontline*. Sebastopol, CA: O'Reilly.

Scott, L. R. (2011). *Numerical Analysis*. Princeton, NJ: Princeton University Press.

Sedgewick, R. and K. Wayne (2011). *Algorithms*, 4th ed. Reading, MA: Addison-Wesley.

Shalev-Shwartz, S. and S. Ben-David (2014). *Understanding Machine Learning*. New York: Cambridge University Press.

Shanno, D. F. (1970). Conditioning of quasi-Newton methods for function minimization. *Mathematics of Computation 24*, 647–656.

Shaw, Z. A. (2014). *Learn Python the Hard Way*, 3rd ed. Reading, MA: Addison-Wesley.

Singer, J. D. and J. B. Willet (1993). It's about time: Using discrete-time survival analysis to study duration and the time of events. *Journal of Educational Statistics 18*, 155–195.

Smiley, J. (2010). *The Man Who Invented the Computer*. New York: Doubleday.

Somaini, P. J. and F. A. Wolak (2014). An algorithm to estimate the two-way fixed effect model, typescript, Department of Economics, Massachusetts Institute of Technology, Cambridge, Mass.

Spendley, W., G. R. Hext, and F. R. Himsworth (1962). Sequential application of simplex designs in optimisation and evolutionary operation. *Technometrics 4*, 441.

Stachurski, J. (2009). *Economic Dynamics: Theory and Computation*. Cambridge, MA: MIT Press.

Strunk, Jr., W. and E. B. White (2009). *The Elements of Style*, 50th Anniversary Edition. New York: Pearson Longman.

Stuart, T. (2013). *Understanding Computation*. Sebastopol, CA: O'Reilly.

Su, C.-L. and K. L. Judd (2012). Constrained optimization approaches to estimation of structural models. *Econometrica 80*, 2213–2230.

Sundaram, R. K. (1996). *A First Course in Optimization Theory*. New York: Cambridge University Press.

Surowiecki, J. (2004). *The Wisdom of Crowds*. New York: Anchor Books.

Sweigart, A. (2015). *Automate the Boring Stuff with Python*. San Francisco: No Starch Press.

Swicegood, T. (2010). *Pragmatic Guide to Git*. Dallas: Pragmatic Bookshelf.

Tibshirani, R. (1996). Regression shrinkage and selection via the Lasso. *Journal of the Royal Statistical Society:* Series B *58*, 267–288.

Truss, L. (2003). *Eats, Shoots & Leaves*. New York: Gotham Books.

Tukey, J. W. (1958). Bias and confidence in not quite large samples. *Annals of Mathematical Statistics 29*, 64.

Turing, A. M. (1936). On computable numbers with an application to the *Entscheidungsproblem*. *Proceedings of the London Mathematical Society 42*, 230–265.

Upton, E. and G. Halfacre (2012). *Raspberry Pi User Guide*. Chichester, UK: Wiley.

Valiant, L. G. (1979). The complexity of computing the permanent. *Theoretical Computer Science 8*, 189–201.

Valiant, L. G. (2013). *Probably Approximately Correct*. New York: Basic Books.

Walkenbach, J. (2013). *Excel 2013 Bible*. New York: Wiley.

Wang, H., G. Li, and G. Jiang (2007). Robust regression shrinkage and consistent variable selection through the LAD-Lasso. *Journal of Business and Economic Statistics 25*, 347–355.

Weinstein, L. (2012). *Guesstimation 2.0: Solving Today's Problems on the Back of a Napkin*. Princeton, NJ: Princeton University Press.

Weinstein, L. and J. A. Adam (2008). *Guesstimation: Solving Today's Problems on the Back of a Napkin*. Princeton, NJ: Princeton University Press.

Whitehead, A. N. (1911). *An Introduction to Mathematics*. New York: Henry Holt.

Wickham, H. (2009). *ggplot2: Elegant Graphics for Data Analysis*. New York: Springer.

Wickham, H. (2011). The split-apply-combine strategy for data analysis. *Journal of Statistical Software 40*, 1–29.

Wickham, H. (2014). Advanced R. http://adv-r.had.co.nz/.

Wing, J. M. (2006). Computational thinking. *Communications of the ACM 49*, 33–35.

Zeiler, M. D. (2012). ADADELTA: An adaptive learning rate method, typescript, Department of Computer Science, New York University, New York.

Zienkiewicz, O. C. and K. Morgan (2006). *Finite Elements and Approximation*. Mineola, NY: Dover Publications.

Zinsser, W. K. (2006). *On Writing Well*, 7th ed. New York: Collins.

About the Authors

Harry J. Paarsch is an applied economist and data scientist who worked for Amazon.com, Inc., in Seattle from 2011 until 2014. Prior to joining Amazon, Paarsch was chair in economics at the University of Melbourne, where he remains a principal fellow. He has also held appointments at the University of British Columbia and the University of Western Ontario as well as the University of Iowa, and has been a visiting professor at Aarhus Universitet, Universitat Autònoma de Barcelona, Helsingin yliopisto, the University of New South Wales, Stanford University, and the University of Victoria. He was the Arch W. Shaw National Fellow at the Hoover Institution as well as a visiting scholar at the Institut d'Économie Industrielle, the Instituto de Análisis Económico (CSIS), the Center for Economic Institutions in the Institute of Economic Research at Hitotsubashi University, the Collegio Carlo Alberto, and the Gary Becker Milton Friedman Institute for Research in Economics at the University of Chicago.

Paarsch earned a B.A. (Honours), First Class, in economics from Queen's University in 1980 as well as an M.S. degree in statistics in 1983 and a Ph.D. degree in economics with a minor in statistics in 1987, both from Stanford University. His primary research interests are in applied econometrics, particularly forestry economics, specifically auctions. He has published journal articles in both applied and theoretical econometrics as well as computational economics, industrial organization, labor economics, and personnel economics.

This is his third book. His first (with Han Hong) is entitled *An Introduction to the Structural Econometrics of Auction Data*, and his second (with Timothy P. Hubbard) is entitled *Auctions*. Both were published by the MIT Press.

Konstantin Golyaev is an applied economist and data scientist who lives and works in Seattle. Golyaev earned a B.S. degree in economics in 2004 from the State University— The Higher School of Economics in Moscow as well as an M.A. degree in economics in 2005 from the New Economic School, also in Moscow. Subsequently, he earned an M.A. degree in 2008 and a Ph.D. degree in 2011, both in economics and both from the University of Minnesota. His primary research interests are in applied econometrics, particularly industrial organization.

Name Index

Subject Index